# Don't Give Up the Ship!

## MYTHS OF THE WAR OF 1812

DONALD R. HICKEY

*Foreword by*
DONALD E. GRAVES

UNIVERSITY OF ILLINOIS PRESS
*Urbana and Chicago*

First published in Canada by Robin Brass Studio Inc.
www.rbstudiobooks.com

Published and distributed in the United States of America by
University of Illinois Press
1325 South Oak Street
Champaign, IL 61820-6903
www.press.uillinois.edu

Printed and bound in Canada

**Library of Congress Cataloging-in-Publication Data**
Hickey, Donald R., 1944–
Don't give up the ship : myths of the War of 1812 / Donald R. Hickey ;
    foreword by Donald E. Graves.
p. cm.
Includes bibliographical references and index.
ISBN-13: 978-0-252-03179-3 (cloth : alk. paper)
ISBN-10: 0-252-03179-2 (cloth : alk. paper)
1. United States—History—War of 1812—Miscellanea. 2. United
    States—History—Errors, inventions, etc. I. Title.
E364.9.H53        2006
973.5'2—DC22    2006006463

For Connie, my best friend

## MEMORY

*Jan Paderewski (1860–1941) was a renowned composer and pianist who attended the Paris Peace Conference in 1919 to promote the re-establishment of Poland, which had been partitioned and annexed by its more powerful neighbors in the eighteenth century. Paderewski then served briefly as the new nation's first prime minister. Although he had made a great deal of money performing, Paderewski had given most of it to charity. Hence, in 1923 he had to tour again, and he continued to give recitals even though his talents declined sharply. Two musicians who heard him in later years were distressed by the sad fate that had befallen their colleague. "I am dismayed by what Jan has forgotten," said one. "I am more dismayed," said the other, "by what he has remembered."*

# Contents

## 2   Battles and Campaigns     48

## 5  The Mechanics of Waging War                               225

# Foreword

*by Donald E. Graves*

I am pleased to contribute a foreword to *Don't Give Up the Ship!*, Professor Donald Hickey's study of the myths and misconceptions of the War of 1812. We are approaching the bicentennial of that conflict and this will inevitably spawn a flood of new titles on a most confusing and misunderstood event in the history of both Canada and the United States. Fortunately, Donald Hickey has entered the game early and produced a book that not only sheds much-needed light on its subject but which will serve as a guide for those who wish to write, study, or read about the war. For this reason alone, the publication of Hickey's work is a matter of celebration, but this book also possesses other attributes.

In the past fifteen years there has been a steady output of writing by historians on both sides of the international border that has not only challenged perceived wisdom about the War of 1812 but considerably expanded our knowledge of it. Donald Hickey has taken full advantage of this recent and exciting scholarship and has incorporated much of it in the pages below. This is a second attribute or strength of *Don't Give Up the Ship!*, which can aptly be described as (for want of a better term) "leading edge" in terms of War of 1812 studies, and which reflects a growing interest in the conflict.

This interest is a relatively new phenomenon. When I began professional study of the War of 1812, more decades ago than I like to remember, there were remarkably few reliable sources available and many of those were tarred with the brush of national chauvinism, which limited their utility. American historians wrote from their point of view, Canadian historians from theirs, and those few and brave British historians who dared venture into the area only too often displayed a hapless confusion resulting from limited access to primary sources and an appalling ignorance of North American geography. The earlier scholarship of the war exhibited longstanding national attitudes toward the conflict. Donald Hickey is fully aware of these national beliefs and the effect they have had on the historiography of the war.

The third attribute of his book is that, as an American historian, he has made a commendable effort to explore and explain the British and Canadian side of the conflict. The happy result is that not only will the Canadian reader learn a great deal about the American experience of the war—particularly its diplomatic, commercial and political origins, which are well delineated in this book—but the American reader will learn much about how his northern neighbors view the conflict.

As a Canadian (and a proud descendant of Loyalists who fought for the Crown in 1776–83), I wish to make it perfectly clear that I do not agree with everything in the pages that follow. In debates with the author, however, that have been played out at a number of academic conferences, we have agreed to disagree on certain things, both respecting, but not entirely admitting, the other's standpoint. But perhaps that is as it should be and the fact is that we tend to agree more than we disagree.

The one thing about which we are of like mind is the negative influence of the great number of historical myths about the war, most of which were born in the nineteenth century. This book is primarily a critical examination of those myths and Hickey has taken aim squarely at them, utterly demolishing many, and revising, amending, or curtailing others. This is a much-needed and long-overdue corrective that forms perhaps the most important attribute of *Don't Give Up the Ship!*, a work that is, fundamentally, a fascinating examination of historical legends: their origins, context, proponents, growth or accretion, interpretation and accuracy.

In sum, this is an important book on the War of 1812 that will appeal and be useful to both professional scholar and interested general reader. It covers a broad cross-section of subject matter from diplomacy to battles on land and sea and includes a large and colorful cast from presidents down to individuals of both sexes and many different races. Its pages will stimulate and educate— and they may also infuriate as the author cuts down some long-cherished and tall-grown misbeliefs. In doing so, Donald Hickey has produced a book destined to become a fixture on the bookshelves of all those interested in the War of 1812 and early nineteenth-century North American history.

DONALD E. GRAVES
Wolf Grove, Upper Canada

# Preface

Studying the War of 1812 can become an obsession. As many students of the conflict have discovered, once you're hooked, it can be difficult to get free. This has certainly been my experience. In 1972 I finished a dissertation on Federalist opposition to the war. After writing a series of articles on the conflict, I published a book, *The War of 1812: A Forgotten Conflict* (1989). This was a broad synthesis designed to integrate political, diplomatic, and military history, and with its publication I thought I was done with the war and moved on to other projects.

However, in the years that followed, the war kept reappearing in my life. After several years, I published an abridgement, *The War of 1812: A Short History* (1995). There were also numerous requests in the 1990s for encyclopedia articles, some of which asked me to treat an aspect or an angle of the war that I had not previously considered. In addition, I regularly lectured on the war in the courses that I taught at my home institution, Wayne State College in Nebraska, and periodically discussed the conflict with other "eighteen-twelvers" via letter or e-mail or at history conferences or historic sites. These recurring encounters with the War of 1812 forced me to rethink old issues and confront new ones.

Then there were visiting teaching assignments at the U.S. Army Command and General Staff College (in 1991–92) and the U.S. Naval War College (in 1995–96), where we talked a great deal about wars and warfare. My experience at the Naval War College was particularly illuminating, for we examined case studies from antiquity to the present. Although not explicit, our real aim (as my colleague Brad Lee put it) was to figure out how to win wars. The War of 1812 was not one of our cases, but that conflict was never far from my thoughts. In the years that followed, I found myself wondering how we could best measure success in those wars that seemed to end without clear-cut victory, and I concluded that we needed to rethink who the winners and losers were in the War of 1812.

In 2000, I decided to catch up on the recent literature on the war by writing a paper on the books and articles that had appeared since the late 1980s. The literature proved to be far more extensive than I had imagined, and I ended up writing a much longer and more comprehensive essay than I had anticipated. The final product appeared in the *Journal of Military History* in 2001.[1] Writing that article stimulated a good deal of thinking about the war and considerable discussion with other scholars. The result was this book.

My focus here is on the mythology of the war. Most of the myths that I deal with are just plain misconceptions, or, in the colorful words of Will Rogers, "what we know that ain't so." Other myths are more complicated. They are notions that are widely accepted but are based on legend, faith, or wishful thinking rather than on hard evidence. Some of these myths may be true and provable; others may be true but unprovable because of insufficient evidence. The vast majority, however, are untrue or highly unlikely.

Why do we embrace and perpetuate so many myths? There are a number of universal reasons. Myths help us make sense out of complicated or frightening events; they provide us with heroes and fulfill our need for inspiring stories; they promote local, regional, and national pride; and they put a human face on history and demonstrate that we can indeed influence the course of events. Myths, in other words, help us construct a history that we are comfortable with and that meets certain deep-seated needs.

Where did the myths of the War of 1812 come from? Many originated with the participants themselves, who misunderstood, misstated, or misremembered what had actually happened. Writers who followed in their wake relied on these sources and sometimes added their own embellishments. Mythmaking flourished in the nineteenth century because legend and lore were widely accepted as a substitute for verifiable history. On the American side, patriotism and chauvinism coupled with the desire to establish a national identity shaped the mythmaking process. On the Canadian side, an interest in fostering imperial connections and a desire to establish a Canadian identity drove the process. By demonstrating that they had faithfully supported Great Britain during the War of 1812, Canadians could show their imperial loyalty and at the same time establish an identity for themselves. Even in Great Britain, where the war was quickly forgotten, there was a widespread willingness

William James (1780?–1827) was a pioneer in writing modern naval history, but as an ardent defender of the Royal Navy, he propagated many myths about the War of 1812. (James, *Naval History of Great Britain*)

to embrace myths to preserve the reputation of the Royal Navy. In all three nations, history was made to serve broader national purposes.

Although the number of people directly responsible for inventing or propagating myths about the War of 1812 runs into the thousands, three nineteenth-century writers played a special role: William James, Benson J. Lossing, and Henry Adams. Between them, these men did more than anyone else to promote, popularize, and legitimatize myths connected to the war.

William James (1780?–1827) was a pioneering British naval historian. An attorney who spent the early part of the War of 1812 in the United States, James was annoyed at "the jeers and boastful taunts" that were directed at him and by the patriotic puffery in American accounts of the naval battles.[2] Taking refuge in Halifax and then returning to Great Britain, James decided to produce his own history of the war. He previewed some of his views in a pamphlet and then published *A Full and Correct Account of the Chief Naval Occurrences of the Late War* in 1817.[3] The following year, he produced a history of the land operations of the war, and this work also included a good deal of naval history that had not made it into his earlier work.[4] In the 1820s, he followed with his monumental multi-volume work on *The Naval History of Great Britain,* in which he developed more fully some of the positions he had earlier staked out.[5]

James's works show a good grasp of naval lore, and his presentation of data (often in tables) gives his scholarship a modern flavor that is unique among early naval histories. He was way ahead of contemporaries in seeking to use primary sources to compare the opposing forces in the naval battles, and his studies are far more analytical than any contemporary work on either side of the Atlantic. Even today, his works are a valuable source of information, especially on the British navy.

James's main problem was that he was trying to serve two masters: the cause of historical truth and the prestige of the Royal Navy. In the end, the latter triumphed. As James himself conceded, "I was the champion of the [British] navy on every occasion."[6] As a result, James's work became an important vehicle for propagating myths on the naval war.[7]

Benson J. Lossing (1813–91) was a prolific and successful popularizer of American history in the nineteenth century. He had considerable success with a travelogue and sketchbook featuring Revolutionary War sites that was first published in 1851–52, and later he produced a similar work on the Civil War.[8] In between, he focused on the War of 1812. After doing some preliminary research in the 1850s, he traveled some 10,000 miles in the United States and Canada, examining archival material, talking to veterans, and sketching people, battlefields, and other sites and scenes. The result, published in 1868, was *The Pictorial Field-Book of the War of 1812.*[9]

Lossing's study of the War of 1812 is by far his best field book. The work has a wealth of information, and despite its anti-

Title page of Benson J. Lossing's popular book on the War of 1812, which spread many misconceptions about the conflict. (Lossing, *Pictorial Field-Book of the War of 1812*)

quarian flavor, it remains useful even today. Lossing sought to be fair to both sides in the war, and he was not afraid to criticize Americans or to question their motives. On the other hand, he uncritically repeated a great many tales that he heard, and as a result his work did much to fix and popularize myths touching on many aspects of the war.[10]

Henry Adams (1838–1918) was a literary blue blood whose ancestry included two presidents. An accomplished writer whose autobiography and other works are still read today, Adams produced a nine-volume *History of the United States of America* covering the years 1801 to 1817 that was long considered the standard work on the period and can still be consulted with profit today.[11] Based on multi-archival work, Adams's *History* is arguably the first modern study of the War of 1812. But because his own ancestors played a role in the period, Adams was not a disinterested observer. With considerable justice, his work has been portrayed as a subtle and yet extended defense of his family.[12]

Adams deeply resented British encroachments on American rights, and he had an unrealistic view of what the United States might do to redress those grievances. He was also sharply critical of just about all the leaders, whether in power or in opposition, on both sides of the Atlantic. There were few heroes in Adams's story. Instead mismanagement and incompetence loomed large, and spite and partisanship often carried the day. Although Adams did not succumb to the sort of unthinking patriotic enthusiasm that tempted so many of his contemporaries, he was nonetheless a strong nationalist whose cynical and skewed view of the period was responsible for initiating and spreading many myths on the political, diplomatic, and military history of the war.

The circumstances may have changed, but many of the myths of the War of 1812 that were propagated in the nineteenth century live on today. Sometimes they survive even after they have been disproved. Writers perpetuate them because they make for good stories, and even accomplished historians may find it easier to repeat a familiar story than to do the work needed to get at the truth. On occasion, I was guilty of this practice in my first book on the war.

What follows is a review of the myths associated with the War of 1812 and its causes. In some cases I have traced the source of the myth, but in others I have been content simply to expose the myth. I have included some myths that were exploded long ago because they have a way of reappearing, especially in popular works.

But this book is not only about the myths of the war. I have also taken the opportunity to treat other topics that I think need to be addressed. These topics deal mainly with the role that various people or groups played in the war and the way the war was waged. Most of this material will be found in the chapters entitled "Soldiers, Sailors, and Civilians" and "The Mechanics of Waging War."

This work may be considered a companion to my first book on the war. It is designed to stand alone so that readers without any background on the War of 1812 can profit from it. But anyone who wants a more basic or comprehensive treatment of the conflict may wish to consult my first book, or perhaps some other general study on the war, such as J. Mackay Hitsman's fine Canadian work.[13]

The Prologue presents an overview of the period and seeks to understand the problems that the United States and Great Britain faced and how they responded to those problems. The Prologue also includes a brief summary and overview of the war. The text proper, Chapters 1 through 6, examines the myths, large and small, associated with the war and explores a range of other issues connected to the war. The Epilogue assesses the legacy of the war and is followed by a detailed chronology. Rounding out the work are four appendices. The first two examine popular songs associated with the war; the third looks at shipwrecks and rebuilt ships from the war; and the fourth explores the origins of the war's name.

Such is the breadth of this project that despite all the help I have received (see Acknowledgments below), I have no doubt made some mistakes and perpetuated some myths. Readers who wish to bring errors to my attention should contact me at the e-mail address below.

DON HICKEY
Wayne, Nebraska
<dohicke1@wsc.edu>

# ACKNOWLEDGMENTS

In writing this work, I have incurred numerous debts. An earlier version of the essay in Appendix D was published in the *Journal of the War of 1812*. I also previewed some of my ideas in a column that I contribute to that journal.[1] I am indebted to Chris George, the editor, for permission to reprint material.

There is a large and growing body of students of the War of 1812 scattered across the United States and Canada, and there are even a few kindred souls in the United Kingdom. I have found members of this group to be unusually congenial and cooperative, willing to share their valuable time and research. Many who belong to this 1812 fraternity helped make this book what it is.

Most helpful were several Canadians who freely shared their knowledge of the war and Canadian history. First and foremost, I am indebted to Donald E. Graves. The pre-eminent student of the war's military history, Graves is a worthy successor to those great Canadian scholars who came before him, Ernest A. Cruikshank, J. Mackay Hitsman, and George Stanley. Graves read the entire manuscript and freely shared his extraordinary command of the history and literature of the war. He also made sure that I did not treat it simply as an American story but paid due attention to the Canadian, British, and native participants as well.

Another accomplished Canadian scholar, Robert Malcomson, also read the manuscript and was exceptionally helpful. Malcomson is the leading naval historian of the war, and he not only saved me from many mistakes but patiently answered a great many questions, particularly on naval terminology and armaments. In addition, he shared his manuscript, *Historical Dictionary of the War of 1812* (which has since been published), and this proved to be an invaluable tool.[2] Another fine Canadian scholar, Carl Benn, also read the entire manuscript. At heart an intellectual historian, Benn willingly shared his extensive knowledge, especially on the role of Indians and Canadian history. Major John Grodzinski, CD, of the Royal Military College of Canada was also very helpful. He read the entire manuscript and posed many questions that forced me to rethink some of my treatments in the work.

I am also indebted to several Americans for reading the manuscript. Most helpful was David Curtis Skaggs, whose detailed commentary led to many corrections and forced me to re-examine some of the issues that I addressed. Also helpful was Bob McColley, my mentor and long-time friend, who knows more about the history of the early American republic than anyone I know and therefore was particularly well qualified to make comments on the larger framework of the war. Chris George and Scott Sheads shared their extensive knowledge of war in the Chesapeake and repeatedly steered me to pertinent materials.

Dave Edmunds read the material on Indians and made a host of suggestions that improved the text. Michael Crawford, Christine Hughes, and Charles Brodine of the Naval Historical Center read those portions of the manuscript devoted to naval history and corrected a number of mistakes. Two other naval historians, Spencer Tucker and Tyrone Martin, Commander, USN (ret.), also read this material and not only saved me from errors but also brought some new material to my attention. Faye Kert, Canada's expert on privateers, read my treatment of this subject, shared her own research, and patiently answered my questions.

Gene Smith made a number of excellent points on the Gulf Coast campaign that forced me to rethink its significance. John McNish Weiss of Great Britain shared his extensive knowledge on the fate of American runaway slaves, and his careful reading of successive drafts greatly improved my treatment of this subject. Marilyn Zoidis, Senior Curator on the Star-Spangled Banner Project at the Smithsonian, read over my treatment of the flag and made a number of useful suggestions.

I would also like to thank Dave Bennett, Mike Harris, and Jeff Patrick, for sharing their knowledge on the little-understood War of 1812 in what might be called the Central West or the St. Louis Theater, that is, in southern Illinois, Missouri, and Iowa. I am indebted to Paul W. Schroeder for providing information on the European context and for sharing the anecdote on Jan Paderewski that appears at the beginning of this work. Peter Rindlisbacher provided essential information on projects to rebuild ships from the period. Two long-time friends helped out as well. Kathryn Roberts Morrow brought her finely honed editorial skills to bear on the manuscript, and Frank Pytko used his keen eye to ferret out errors and ensure clarity.

Still others that I want to thank for sharing knowledge or providing assistance are Catherine Allgor, Randy Bertolas, Vicky Bondy, Scott Butler, Jim Carr, René Chartrand, Clayton Cramer, William C. Davis, Bill Dudley, Nancy Farron, David Fitz-Enz, John Fredriksen, Mark Hayes, Fred Hopkins, Sister Maria Gabriel, John Morris, Dave Nichols, Lawrence H. Officer, John Plotkin,

Walter Rybka, Mariam Touba, Natasha Urlic, Rosemary Vyvyan, Tami Worner, and Matt Warshauer.

In addition, I want to thank the entire staff of the U.S. Conn Library at Wayne State College. I am particularly indebted to June Davidson at the Interlibrary Loan desk, who was invariably pleasant and efficient in fulfilling my requests for material. June's successor in that post, Terri Headley, also has been very helpful. Four other Wayne State librarians—Jan Brumm, Dave Graber, Maria Johnson, and Gayle Poirier—helped out as well. I am also indebted to Linda Teach and Dawn Hirschman, two remarkably efficient Wayne State staff members who sometimes went beyond the call of duty to facilitate my work on this project.

I wish to thank the following institutions for providing information or access to materials: Grinnell College, Mississippi Department of Archives and History, New-York Historical Society, Omaha Public Library, Ontario Historical Society, Stanford University, Toronto Public Library, Troy Public Library, University of Nebraska at Lincoln, and University of Nebraska at Omaha.

For the illustrations that grace this volume, I owe a debt of gratitude to several people. Edmund Elfers, the director of the Wayne State College Office of Teaching and Learning Technologies, and his student assistant, Ben Vrba, did a splendid job of digitizing and cleaning up the images that I gave them. Scott Sheads and Anna von Lunz shared illustrations from the large and growing collection at Fort McHenry National Monument and Historic Shrine. They were assisted by Nancy Bramucci of the Maryland State Archives. Spencer Tucker and Kevin Crisman shared some illustrations that they own. Finally, maritime artist Peter Rindlisbacher not only produced the cover that graces this work but generously shared other artwork from his impressive portfolio.

Last but not least, I owe a debt to my wife, Connie Clark, whose probing questions inspired this book as well as its title and who read the entire manuscript. She not only caught many errors, but her astute suggestions made the work more accessible to all readers.

D.R.H.

# A NOTE ON TERMINOLOGY AND NUMBERS

There were seven British North American colonies in 1812. Six—Upper Canada, Lower Canada, New Brunswick, Nova Scotia, Prince Edward Island, and Cape Breton Island—were linked together, while the seventh—Newfoundland—had a separate status (and did not join the Canadian federation until 1949.) For the period of the War of 1812, these colonies are most accurately referred to as "British North America." However, contemporaries, especially in the United States, often used the term "Canada" even though this designation was not correct before the confederation of Upper and Lower Canada, New Brunswick, and Nova Scotia into the Dominion of Canada in 1867. For the sake of convenience, I have generally referred to the colonies as "Canada," although I have occasionally preferred "British North America" when I wanted to stress their relationship to the mother country.

I have also followed common practice in using the terms "United States" and "America" interchangeably. To refer to aboriginal people, I have used the words "Indian" or "native" since the term "Native American" does not work well for Indians living in Canada, and terms like "aboriginal," "First People," and "First Nation" are not used in the United States. Similarly, the term "African-American" is not appropriate for black people living in Canada or serving in the British armed forces. Hence, I refer to all blacks and mulattos as "blacks."

Some battles are known by more than one name. I have generally referred to them by their most common name. In a small number of cases where two names are common (such as the Battle of the Thames/Moraviantown), I have used them both, and in the Chronology I have listed all names that have had any currency.

Although modern military doctrine recognizes three levels of action and analysis—tactical, operational, and strategic—I have preferred to retain the traditional distinction between tactics (which focuses on individual battles) and strategy (which focuses on a campaign or on the entire war). In addition, while some writers use military terms in a precise manner to indicate the actual size of an armed engagement, I have used these terms in the traditional fashion a little more loosely. In my usage, an "operation" is any military undertaking and may or may not include actual combat; an "engagement" is any armed exchange; a "skirmish" is a minor engagement; a "battle" is a major one; and a "raid" is a sudden surprise attack on enemy-held territory. A "massacre" is any engagement in which almost everyone on one side, combatant and non-combatant alike, is killed, or in which a significant number of non-combatants or unarmed combatants are killed.

Even though it is conventional to label all American warships "USS" (for United States Ship) and all Royal Navy warships "HMS" (for His Majesty's Ship), this is neither accurate nor does it accord with contemporary usage. A ship is technically a three-masted vessel with square sails as well as fore and aft sails. "USS" was rarely used in the American navy, and when it was, it could refer to either a ship or a sloop. The use of "HMS" was more common in the Royal Navy, but it was far from widespread, and it, too, could refer to either a ship or sloop.

In accordance with contemporary usage, I have identified American warships in the following manner: the *Constitution* is referred to as the "U.S. Frigate *Constitution*," the *Hornet* is the "U.S. Sloop *Hornet*," and so on for brigs, schooners, and gunboats. I have identified British warships in a similar fashion. Thus, His Majesty's Ship *Shannon* is identified as "H.M. Ship *Shannon*," His Majesty's Sloop *Cherub* is called "H.M. Sloop *Cherub*," and similarly for other British warships. British warships on the northern lakes were part of the Provincial Marine prior to Sir James Yeo's assumption of command on behalf of the Royal Navy in May of 1813. Hence, they are labeled as "P.M. Sloop *Queen Charlotte*," "P.M. Brig *Caledonia*," and so on.

Occasionally, the Royal Navy authorized an officer to fly a special pendant and assume the title of commodore. Sir James Yeo received this privilege when he was ordered to the Great Lakes in 1813.[1] Hence, I have used this title for him. I have identified all other British naval officers by rank, which (in ascending order) was: lieutenant, commander, captain, rear admiral, vice admiral, and admiral. American naval officers whose command included more than one ship usually assumed the title of commodore, but before 1862 this title had no official standing. As Robert Malcomson has shown, the Navy Department used the title during the war in addressing certain officers, mainly senior captains who sometimes commanded more than one ship, such as Isaac Chauncey, William Bainbridge, John Rodgers, Stephen Decatur, and Thomas Tingey.[2] I have followed Navy Department practice for these men. For all others, even those who commanded a squadron and were occasionally addressed as commodore (such as Hugh G. Campbell, Joshua Barney, and

Oliver H. Perry), I have used their actual rank, which was (again in ascending order) lieutenant, master commandant, and captain.

Warships in the Age of Sail were rated by the number of guns they officially carried. Thus the U.S. Frigate *Constitution*, 44, was designed to carry 44 guns, while H.M. Ship *Shannon*, 38, was designed to carry 38. But most naval commanders liked to increase their firepower by carrying extra guns. Because of this practice, there was usually a discrepancy between the number of guns a ship was rated to carry and the number it actually carried. The *Constitution*, for example, carried 52–55 guns during the war, while the *Shannon* carried 52. I have listed in parentheses after each ship the number of guns that it actually carried. Thus, America's best known frigate might be identified as "U.S. Frigate *Constitution* (52)" and Great Britain's best known frigate as "H.M. Ship *Shannon* (52)."

If the ship was under construction or unarmed, I have simply given its rating. If its armaments changed during the war and I am not referring to a particular moment of service, I have listed the range of guns it carried. Hence, "U.S. Sloop *Argus* (rated 18)" and "H.M. Ship *Wolfe* (21–23)." I have used the same system for privateers. Thus, Nova Scotia's most successful privateer is identified as the "*Liverpool Packet* (5)."

All such numbers, however, must be treated with caution. The number of guns actually carried on a ship depended not simply on the wishes of the commanding officer but also on what was available or what best complemented guns already on board. Sometimes this figure was never recorded, or contemporary sources present conflicting evidence. Hence, the actual armament that I attribute to each ship represents my best guess.

Even if the armaments given are correct, it should be remembered that the number of guns a warship carried was not a definitive guide to its firepower. The size of the guns was critical. A warship carrying 20 32-pounders, for example, had more firepower than one carrying 30 18-pounders. Also important was the range of the guns, the kind of projectiles they fired, the quality of the gunpowder on hand, and the size and training of the crews operating the guns.

I do not believe that it is useful to compare costs during the War of 1812 with costs today by converting the original figures into current dollars or pounds using a consumer price index table. Such a comparison greatly understates the cost of things in 1812. People have so much more wealth today that many can now afford what few could buy 200 years ago. For example, although prices in the U.S. increased almost 14-fold from 1812 to 2003, a much larger proportion of the population could afford a $140 rifle in 2003 than could afford a $10 rifle in 1812. To put it another way, as a per capita share of the U.S. Gross Domestic Product, $10 in 1812 is equivalent to $3,512 in 2003.[3]

Comparing contemporary costs in dollars and pounds, however, is another matter. Prior to 1873, the accepted rate of exchange for certain limited purposes, such as computing tariffs, was known as the "nominal par," which was £1 = $4.44.[4] But merchants conducted their own transactions at the market rate of exchange, which varied considerably over time. Lawrence H. Officer has developed a statistical series showing the annual market rate of exchange from 1791 to the present. Between 1791 and 1810 the value of £1 ranged from a low of $4.13 in 1799 to a high of $4.75 in 1794. In the years around the War of 1812, the range was greater. The rate was $3.82 in 1811; $3.62 in 1812; $3.75 in 1813; $4.24 in 1814; $4.90 in 1815; and $5.22 in 1816. In the decade from 1817 to 1826, the rate fell to between $4.50 and $4.98. Whenever I thought it might be useful, I have used Officer's handy conversion table to present contemporary costs in both currencies. For the war as a whole, I have averaged the exchange rates for 1812, 1813, and 1814, which works out to £1 = $3.87. For the entire period 1793–1815, the average is £1 = $4.37.[5]

D.R.H.

# The United States
# and Great Britain
# in a War-Torn World

T he world was a very dangerous place in 1812, and it had been that way
for two decades. The French Revolution had erupted in 1789, sending
shock waves across Europe and beyond. In the words of Alexander
Hamilton, it was like a series of volcanoes, "the last still more dreadful than
the former, spreading ruin and devastation far and wide."[1] This eruption precipitated a general European war in 1792, when France declared war against
Austria and the First Coalition was formed to resist French aggression. The
following year, France declared war on Great Britain, and for more than 20
years thereafter, these two nations were almost continuously at war. Known as
the French Revolutionary Wars (1793–1801) and the Napoleonic Wars (1803–
15), this worldwide contest rocked the entire transatlantic community and
put Great Britain and the United States on a collision course that ultimately
led to the War of 1812.

The British considered the European conflict a life-or-death struggle, and
given the way that France looted conquered nations and bullied vassal states,
the British view was probably correct. Winning meant not simply defeating
the French but also making sure that France did not dominate the Continent.
"The security of Europe is essential to the security of the British Empire,"
declared Lord Auckland in 1799. "We cannot separate them."[2]

To prevail in the European war, Great Britain had to do three things. First, it had to line up allies on the Continent, for with a population in 1792 of only 9,000,000 (with an additional 5,000,000 in Ireland), it could only defeat a more powerful and more populous France (with 27,000,000 people) with the help of other nations.[3] Secondly, it had to preserve a healthy economy so that it could feed its people, fuel its war machine, and provide subsidies to its allies on the Continent. And finally, it had to preserve its naval supremacy so that it could protect its commerce, destroy the trade of its enemies, prevent an invasion of the home islands, and move troops, money, and supplies to theaters of war around the globe.

The Royal Navy played a particularly vital role in the British war effort, but its very success led to growing tension with the United States. By driving enemy commerce from the seas, the navy opened the door to lucrative commercial opportunities for American merchants sailing under a neutral flag. The British needed to ensure that these merchants did not supply France with goods and commodities that would enable it to win the war. They also needed to ensure that Americans did nothing else that would significantly undermine Britain's war effort.

A rising commercial power, the United States had to find a way to protect its rights and promote its commercial interests in a world at war. This was a daunting task. For a second-rate power with limited military and financial resources, it was no easy matter to face down Great Britain, the world's leading naval power, or France, the world's leading land power, as long as these nations were locked in a titanic struggle. Although the European belligerents might want friendly relations with the United States, they would never sacrifice vital interests nor undermine their war effort to achieve that end. War with the United States, in other words, was always preferable to defeat in Europe. This greatly limited America's foreign policy options.

In the 1790s, the fate of the United States was in the hands of the Federalists, a party headed by George Washington, Alexander Hamilton, and John Adams. Under their leadership, the new nation pursued a policy of financial and military preparedness. Hamilton's financial program in the early 1790s put the nation's finances on a sound footing and provided the means of paying for war preparations and war. In addition, the army was expanded from 840 in 1789 to 5,400 in 1801, and a navy was built that included 13 frigates. The Federalists also began construction of six ships-of-the-line.

The Federalists hoped that by pursuing a policy of neutrality the United States could steer clear of the European war. But such a policy was likely to favor Great Britain, which was America's principal commercial partner, and in any case strict neutrality amounted to repudiating the treaty of alliance that the United States had signed with France in 1778 during the American Revolution, a treaty that was still in force.

In 1793, President Washington issued the Neutrality Proclamation, urging Americans to avoid committing any acts of hostility against the European belligerents. The following year Congress passed the Neutrality Act, which prohibited American citizens from participating in the European war. That same year the United States signed the Jay Treaty with Great Britain, resolving a host of outstanding Anglo-American problems, some of which dated back to the American Revolution. This treaty also defined neutral and belligerent rights and established the terms of trade between the two nations. The Jay Treaty became the sheet anchor of American foreign policy for the rest of the 1790s and remained in force into President Thomas Jefferson's first term. In the benevolent commercial environment that it fostered, the American economy flourished.

French leaders, however, were furious with the Jay Treaty, which they considered a betrayal of the Franco-American alliance. By severing diplomatic relations and launching a war on American trade, the French hoped to bully the U.S. into repudiating the Jay Treaty and at the same time to enrich themselves at the expense of America's far-flung and lucrative commerce. The XYZ affair in 1797 pushed the two nations into an undeclared naval war. An American delegation sent to Paris was approached by three French agents, who were designated "X," "Y," and "Z" in the diplomatic report sent back to the United States. As a price for opening formal negotiations with France, the agents demanded an official apology, a bribe of £50,000 ($222,000), and a loan of $12,000,000 (£2,703,000). The American delegates rejected these demands, and the publication of their report in the U.S. prompted outrage that resulted in the Quasi-War (1798–1801), a limited war fought on the high seas.

The U.S. Navy and armed merchant vessels performed remarkably well in this contest. The French, who had hoped for a bloodless shakedown rather than a bloody war, soon indicated an interest in restoring normal relations. The Convention of 1800 ended the war and also suspended the treaty of alliance with France as well as a commercial treaty that dated back to the same period. In exchange for getting out from under these treaties, the United States had to waive all claims for compensation for the French depredations that had occurred since the adoption of the Jay Treaty.

During the Quasi-War, the U.S. and Great Britain worked together in what was a loose de facto alliance. The two nations shared intelligence on French intrigue, and their navies cooperated in a host of ways. Besides exchanging signals to prevent an armed clash, they shared cruising duties in the West Indies and cooperated to provide convoys to merchantmen. The Royal Navy even covered American waters while American warships were in the West Indies. In this cooperation on the high seas, the United States clearly came out ahead because its navy was so much smaller. The United States also profited from a British decision to give the young republic some war material and to authorize the sale of a lot more. American purchasing agents in Great Britain bought sails, anchors, cartridge paper, saltpeter (for gunpowder), and a huge number of naval guns.[4]

The Federalists had steered the ship of state through the 1790s effectively, but the Republicans won the election of 1800, and Jefferson assumed the presidency the following year. While the Federalists had pursued a policy of preparedness, the Republicans embraced a policy of retrenchment. They reduced taxes, cut back on government spending, and made paying down the national debt a top priority. As part of this policy, the U.S. Army was reduced from 5,400 to 3,300 men, most of the nation's warships were laid up, and the timber acquired for construction of the ships-of-the-line was used for other purposes.

Initially, Republican policies did no harm to the United States because in Europe the Peace of Amiens (1801–03) virtually eliminated any encroachments on American rights. But this peace was fleeting. It settled none of the fundamental issues that divided Britain and France, and most contemporaries recognized that it was little more than an armed truce. With the resumption of hostilities in 1803, the world again became a hazardous place, and the United States once again found its basic rights and vital interests under attack. In late 1805, Vice Admiral Horatio Nelson's great victory at Trafalgar established the Royal Navy as undisputed mistress of the seas, while Napoleon's equally dramatic victory at Austerlitz ensured France's mastery of the Continent. Thereafter the two powers sparred, but, much like a tiger and a shark intent on mortal combat, they found it difficult to get at one another.

Eager to find a way to bring Britain to its knees, France in 1806–07 established the Continental System, which barred any trade from Great Britain to European ports under French control. The British retaliated in 1807–09 with the Orders-in-Council, first prohibiting neutrals from trading between enemy ports, then requiring all trade with French-controlled ports to pass through Britain, and finally blockading all ports under French control. These countervailing regulations made most American ships trading with Europe fair game and thus dramatically increased the risks that American merchants faced as they sought to make a profit in a world at war.

Nor was this all. The renewal of the European war in 1803 re-ignited a host of other maritime issues that had troubled Anglo-American relations in the 1790s. The most important of these was impressment, the British practice of removing seamen from American merchant vessels to man the ships of the Royal Navy. In addition, British and American officials feuded over British violations of American waters, differing definitions of contraband, British enforcement of the Rule of 1756 (which prohibited trade in time of war that was not allowed in time of peace), and British naval blockades (which, to be legal, had to be adequately publicized and strictly enforced).

Still another problem that exacerbated Anglo-American relations was recurring Indian warfare in the Old Northwest. Although the United States never considered this problem a cause for war against Britain, it nonetheless loomed large among westerners, who were convinced that the British were behind the native depredations. Angered over what they saw as a deadly Anglo-Indian alliance, westerners were willing to support U.S. efforts to force the British to show greater respect for the nation's maritime rights on the high seas.

Although the Jay Treaty had addressed some of the maritime issues, the pertinent clauses expired in late 1803, and Jefferson's administration refused British overtures to renew them. As a substitute for the Jay Treaty, American and British agents negotiated the Monroe-Pinkney Treaty in 1806, but Jefferson was so unhappy with this agreement that he refused to submit it to the U.S. Senate for approval. The following year Anglo-American relations took a turn for the worse, first when a Royal Navy ship fired on an American warship in the notorious *Chesapeake* affair; then when Great Britain threatened to step up impressment from neutral merchant ships; and finally when Britain issued the first of its Orders-in-Council threatening American trade with the Continent.

Having rejected the fruits of the Monroe-Pinkney negotiations, Republican leaders were left with little choice but to try coercive measures. The administration already had persuaded Congress in 1806 to adopt a partial non-importation act, barring certain British imports, although the law was suspended until December 1807. That same month Congress adopted an embargo, a non-exportation law that prohibited American ships and goods from leaving port. When these measures failed to win any concessions, Congress in 1809 substituted a non-intercourse act that opened trade with the rest of the world while continuing to prohibit any commerce with Britain and France or their colonies. This law, in turn, was replaced in 1810 by Macon's Bill No. 2, which reopened all trade. Then in 1811 Congress came full circle by adopting a new non-importation act that barred all British imports.

The restrictive system, as these measures were called, was aimed mainly at Great Britain and secondarily at France. As an instrument of foreign policy, it was an abject failure. It undermined American prosperity and government revenue without winning any concessions from Britain or France.

Having concluded that Great Britain was the nation's principal antagonist, President James Madison, who had succeeded Jefferson in 1809, asked Congress in late 1811 to prepare for war. The following June, Madison recommended a declaration of war even though the nation was still ill-prepared for such a contest. Despite stiff opposition from the Federalists and some antiwar Republicans, Congress complied with the president's request, and on June 18, 1812, Madison signed the war bill into law. This marked the beginning of the War of 1812.

The War of 1812 may seem in retrospect like a simple Anglo-American conflict that resulted from a failure of bilateral diplomacy, but the war cannot be divorced from its larger context. The War of 1812 was a direct outgrowth of the Napoleonic Wars. If there had been no war in Europe, there would have been no war in North America. Indeed, for the British the war with the United States was just another dimension of a larger world war. Neither the outbreak of the War of 1812, nor its course once it had begun, can be understood outside that larger context.

By the time the United States had declared war, Great Britain had been at war with France for close to 20 years. Under a succession of mostly Tory ministries, the British government had pursued a policy of resistance to change at home, repression in Ireland, and opposition to the French Revolution and French expansion abroad. Throughout this period, Great Britain was France's most inveterate and persistent foe, and the years of war had taken a heavy toll.

By 1812, Britain, which was now supporting a military establishment of 300,000–400,000 men, had already lost thousands of soldiers, sailors, and marines in battle and tens of thousands to disease.[5] In the West Indies alone, more than 45,000 British soldiers perished between 1793 and 1801. Most, around 95 percent, were victims of disease, principally malaria and a virulent strain of yellow fever that had recently migrated from Africa.[6] Total British military deaths during the French Revolutionary and Napoleonic Wars have been conservatively put at 290,000.[7] Since some civilians lost their lives as a direct result of the war, Britain's war-related deaths must have topped 300,000.

If the human cost to Great Britain of waging the European war was huge, so, too, was the financial toll. Excluding veterans' benefits and postwar interest charges on the war debt, the total cost was over £1 billion ($4.37 billion).[8] Despite a heavy tax load (which included an onerous land tax and the first modern income tax), the British national debt soared from £245,000,000 ($1.1 billion) in 1793 to £834,000,000 ($4.1 billion) in 1815.[9] The British government spent over £31,000,000 ($152,000,000) in 1815 just to service the national debt.[10] This was almost as much as the United States spent on the entire War of 1812.[11]

In sum, the cost to Great Britain, in lives and treasure, of waging the French Revolutionary and Napoleonic Wars was both staggering and unprecedented. Nor was any end in sight in 1812. Great Britain had taken part in five Continental coalitions since 1793, and none had succeeded in defeating France or even in effectively curbing French power. In fact, the Fifth Coalition, forged in the spring of 1809, had lasted only a few months before Napoleon's victory over Austria at Wagram had ended it. The collapse of this coalition left the British without any major allies on the Continent. By this time the Duke of Wellington had launched a major campaign in the Spanish Peninsula, but Britain's only allies were Portugal, Sicily, and a diverse army of Spanish rebels who had refused to accept Napoleon's decision to put his brother on the throne of Spain.

In the summer of 1812, the British campaign in the Spanish Peninsula was going well, and France's invasion of Russia, which was launched just five days after the American declaration of war, brought another potential ally into the field. But the war against France could not be won in the Peninsula alone, and almost everyone assumed that Napoleon would dispose of Russia just as he had disposed of every other Continental foe. It was only at the end of 1812 that the dimensions of Napoleon's defeat in Russia were known in Britain. In the wake of the French disaster, a new coalition gradually took shape. The Sixth Coalition ultimately won the war in Europe, although victory was not in sight until the Allies won the Battle of Leipzig in October of 1813, and the war did not end until the following spring. Few in June of 1812 could foresee this outcome.

Most Britons were understandably miffed, if not angered, by the American declaration of war. They were convinced that their very survival was at stake in the European war and that the future of Western Civilization hung in the balance. Many saw the American decision as a stab in the back by an ungrateful nation that not only had profited from the European war but also failed to appreciate British sacrifices to preserve Western Civilization. Far from punishing the United States, however, the British could do little more than fight a holding action in North America until the European war was over.

Hoping to win the War of 1812 by targeting Canada, the United States launched a three-pronged attack in 1812 that ended in disaster. In the West, an Anglo-Indian force captured an American stronghold on Mackinac Island, compelled the surrender of an entire American army under the command of Brigadier General William Hull at Detroit, and then beat back an American counterattack at Frenchtown on the River Raisin in present-day Michigan. A second American army surrendered after being defeated at Queenston Heights on the Canadian side of the Niagara River, while a third conducted little more than a demonstration on the Lake Champlain front before withdrawing to the United States. Thus the young republic had little to show for its efforts in 1812 except defeat and humiliation.

In 1813, the United States launched another three-pronged assault on Canada, and this time it enjoyed more success, but only in the West. In northwest Ohio, the U.S. withstood two Anglo-Indian sieges at Fort Meigs and beat back a British and Indian attack on Fort Stephenson. Master Commandant Oliver H. Perry then won a decisive American naval victory on Lake Erie, which paved the way for an important victory on land about 65 miles east of Detroit when Major General William Henry Harrison's army defeated a much smaller Anglo-Indian force in the Battle of the Thames or Moraviantown. This gave the United States effective control over most of the Old Northwest as well as an indeterminate portion of western Upper Canada.

On other fronts in 1813, however, initial American success was followed by failure. In the spring, after occupying the Upper Canadian capital of York (present-day Toronto), the U.S. captured Fort George on the Niagara Peninsula and drove the British from the entire west bank of the Niagara River. At

EASTERN NORTH AMERICA
IN 1812

the other end of Lake Ontario, the U.S. successfully defended Sackets Harbor from a British attack. Thereafter, the U.S. suffered a series of reverses. On the Canadian side of the Niagara River, the British regained the initiative with victories at Stoney Creek and Beaver Dams and induced the U.S. to evacuate Fort George. The British then captured Fort Niagara and, in retaliation for the American burning of Newark (present-day Niagara-on-the-Lake), put the torch to the settlements on the American side of the Niagara River. Farther east, the British defeated American armies at Crysler's Farm (near Williamsburg, Ontario) and at Châteauguay (present-day Allan's Corners in Quebec), thus foiling a major campaign that had targeted Montreal. As a result, after two years of warfare, the United States controlled most of the Old Northwest but was no closer to conquering Canada or to winning the war.

In 1813 the United States also found itself at war in the Old Southwest with a powerful Creek faction known as the Red Sticks. Initially co-belligerents and later allies of Great Britain, the Creeks delivered a significant blow to the United States in the summer of 1813 when they overran Fort Mims (near present-day Tensaw, Alabama) in what is commonly called the Fort Mims Massacre. However, the U.S. counterattacked later that year, and in early 1814 Major General Andrew Jackson decisively defeated the Creeks in the bloody Battle of Horseshoe Bend (near present-day New Site, Alabama). This ended the Creek War.

In the final year of the War of 1812, it was mainly the British who were on the offensive. Napoleon's defeat and abdication in the spring of 1814 had brought peace to Europe for the first time in a decade. This enabled Great Britain to shift its military and naval forces to the American war. The U.S. was able to mount only two offensives. The first, a major campaign on the Niagara front, led to fierce fighting on the Canadian side of the river at Chippawa, Lundy's Lane, and Fort Erie. Although the fighting was inconclusive, the American offensive stalled, and Major General Jacob Brown's invading army withdrew to the United States with little to show for its efforts. The second offensive, more limited in scope but also more successful, was a deep raid launched by Brigadier General Duncan McArthur from Detroit into western Upper Canada.

Elsewhere, the U.S. was on the defensive. A large British army under Sir George Prevost invaded upper New York but withdrew after an American naval victory on Lake Champlain engineered by Master Commandant Thomas Macdonough threatened British supply lines. A second British force successfully occupied eastern Maine. A third invaded the Chesapeake, and after defeating an American army at Bladensburg, occupied the nation's capital at Washington, D.C. Before departing, the British burned most of the public buildings and a few private ones as well.

Moving up the Chesapeake, the British next targeted Baltimore. En route to this city, a British army defeated an American force at North Point in Maryland but lost one of its better commanders, Major General Robert Ross, in a preliminary engagement. Moreover, the British were forced to withdraw without subduing Baltimore when the Royal Navy could not silence the guns of Fort McHenry and thus offer naval support to the assault by land. The British launched their final campaign of the war on the Gulf Coast. Although they captured an American flotilla of gunboats on Lake Borgne, the British were defeated decisively in early 1815 by Andrew Jackson's army in the Battle of New Orleans.

If the United States performed worse than Americans had expected in the war on land, the new nation did much better than expected in the war at sea, at least initially. American warships won a series of duels with British warships early in the war. The U.S. Frigate *Constitution* (54–55) defeated H.M. Ship *Guerrière* (49) and H.M. Ship *Java* (49), and the U.S. Frigate *United States* (56) defeated H.M. Ship *Macedonian* (49). The British returned the favor when H.M. Ship *Shannon* (52) bested U.S. Frigate *Chesapeake* (50) in 1813 and when a squadron defeated the U.S. Frigate *President* (52) in 1815. A number of smaller vessels engaged in similar actions. Although much publicized, these naval duels had little impact on the course of the war, and in the end each side could claim about the same number of victories on the high seas.

American privateers harassed British merchant ships around the globe but particularly in the Caribbean, off the coast of Canada, and in Britain's home waters. But the British retaliated with a naval blockade that was gradually expanded to include the entire American coast. The Royal Navy targeted the Delaware and Chesapeake bays in early 1813, the remaining ports in the middle and southern states in late 1813, and then New England in the spring of 1814. In addition, British warships and privateers made American trade almost impossible.

Although the two sides discussed peace almost as soon as the war began, serious negotiations did not get under way until the summer of 1814, when British and American envoys met in Ghent (in modern-day Belgium). On December 24, the opposing envoys signed the Treaty of Ghent (also known as the Peace of Christmas Eve), which provided for ending the war, returning all conquered territory, and restoring the *status quo ante bellum*.

The war had been a far more difficult trial for the United States than for Great Britain. Still, both sides were relieved that it was over. A wary peace followed, and although that peace was often threatened by recurring border violence and other problems, it proved durable. It thus set the stage for the era of Anglo-American friendship and cooperation that followed in the twentieth century and that has endured to this day.

CHAPTER 1

# The Causes
# of the War

Historians often disagree over the causes of war. This is hardly surprising because wars are complex events that usually have multiple causes. Those who control the levers of power may support war for different or even contradictory reasons. Figuring out which reasons deserve primacy can be a daunting task, and honest scholars may disagree. Historians may even disagree on the causes of those wars that seem clearly linked to certain issues, such as the Mexican-American War and territorial expansion, the American Civil War and slavery, and World War II and Axis aggression.

The War of 1812 is no exception. Most of the research on the causes of the war has been done by Americans. Canadians have done little because most, not unreasonably, have seen the conflict as little more than a war of territorial aggression against their homeland. The British have done even less work because they see the conflict as a decidedly minor contest—little more than a footnote to the all-important and all-consuming Napoleonic Wars.

Even among American historians, it has been difficult to reach a consensus. In the nineteenth century, the prevailing view was that the United States went to war to force the British to give up the Orders-in-Council and impressment and to make concessions on other maritime issues (particularly territorial waters, contraband, and naval blockades). In the early twentieth century, the land hunger thesis took center stage. According to this view, the U.S. declared war to seize Canada, either to satisfy a demand for more land or to put an end to British control over Indians in the Old Northwest. After World War II, the maritime interpretation again dominated, although some scholars championed other issues, such as the desire to promote trade and prosperity, the need to uphold national honor or vindicate republican institutions, or the wish to promote the interests of a fragmented Republican party.

Today, it is still difficult to find a consensus on what caused the War of 1812. Although most American scholars continue to emphasize maritime issues, they disagree over whether the Orders-in-Council or impressment was more important and over the role of the other issues. Canadian scholars, on the other hand, may concede the importance of maritime issues but are still likely to champion the land hunger thesis.

There are a fair number of oft-repeated errors, both factual and interpretative, associated with the causes of the war. One might attribute this to the lack of consensus on the causes, but there are two other reasons that may be more compelling. One is the failure to understand the larger international context and to appreciate the problems that Great Britain confronted in waging a seemingly endless war against Revolutionary and Napoleonic France. For Britain, winning this war took precedence over all else and affected almost every decision of state. Under these circumstances, it is hardly surprising that the British were reluctant to concede major American demands and remarkable that they were willing to make any concessions at all. Under similar circumstances, the French refused to bend at all. The other reason that scholars have trouble understanding the causes of the war is that they no longer read the diplomatic correspondence between the two nations. Diplomatic history has been a dying field for at least 20 years. Most scholars today rely heavily on older diplomatic studies, or, worse yet, on newer studies that draw heavily on those earlier studies. This leaves far too much room for error.

## THE COMING OF THE WAR

**Rating Jefferson's Presidency.** One of two presidents associated with the coming of the War of 1812 is Thomas Jefferson, who held office from 1801 to 1809. Jefferson's first term was stellar. After winning a closely contested election that was determined by the House of Representatives, he showed a remarkable talent for keeping his own fractious party together and for winning converts from Federalism. His command over Congress enabled him to get almost everything he wanted, and his policies were so successful that they appeared to put the Federalist party on the road to extinction.

The hated internal or excise taxes adopted by the Federalists in the 1790s were repealed in 1802, and yet the government's income rose because Europe's wartime demand for American exports and re-exports spurred imports and thus the customs revenue. This not only promoted American prosperity but, coupled with the administration's frugal policies, enabled the Treasury to run such large surpluses that as much as 70 percent of the government's annual income could be used to service and extinguish the national debt. Jefferson launched the historic Lewis and Clark Expedition in 1803. In addition, a successful war against Tripoli (1801–05) enhanced the nation's international standing, as did the Louisiana Purchase (1803), which more than doubled the size of the United States at a cost of pennies per acre. This transaction alone assured Jefferson's place in history.

Jefferson's second term, however, was deeply troubled. Jefferson had stumbled at the end of his first term with the failed impeachment trial of Judge Samuel Chase, and he stumbled again two years later with the failed treason trial of Aaron Burr. Moreover, with Britain and France expanding their war on neutral trade, the United States had to contend with ever greater encroachments on its rights. The president never found a successful policy for dealing with this European threat.

Jefferson had a particularly bad year in 1807. At the beginning of the year, he refused to submit to the Senate the recently negotiated Monroe-Pinkney Treaty, which would have resolved many Anglo-American differences. In the summer of 1807, the British attack on the U.S. Frigate *Chesapeake* precipitated a diplomatic crisis that threatened to end in war. Instead of seeking an equitable adjustment, Jefferson overreached by trying to use the affair as a lever to force Great Britain to give up impressment altogether, a decision that gave the British the high moral ground and made any settlement impossible. At the end of 1807, Jefferson blundered again, this time by seeking to extract concessions from Great Britain and France with the embargo, a non-exportation law that kept American ships and goods in port. This measure undermined American prosperity and cut sharply into government revenue.

When the European belligerents still refused to cave in to American demands, Jefferson's administration asked Congress for ever more draconian

Thomas Jefferson (1743–1826) had a distinguished public career, but most of his great achievements came before his presidency. His disastrous second term (1805–09) set the stage for the War of 1812. (Portrait by Gilbert Stuart. Library of Congress)

enforcement acts designed to close loopholes in the embargo and prevent smuggling. These acts raised serious constitutional issues, alienated and emboldened the Federalists, and yet failed to win any concessions from the European belligerents. The embargo was lifted as Jefferson limped out of office, but the Republicans were now saddled with a policy that committed them to use the nation's trade as an instrument of foreign policy to win concessions from Britain and France. The restrictive system, as this program was called, led the nation to the War of 1812.

What are we to make of Jefferson's presidency? In ten presidential surveys or studies conducted since 1980, Jefferson ranks from 4th to 8th, averaging 5th out of 36–41 presidents.[1] Only George Washington, Abraham Lincoln, and Franklin Roosevelt rank consistently ahead of him. How could a president with such a disastrous second term be ranked so highly? Jefferson fares well in part because he was such a strong leader, but he also profits from other considerations. Modern liberals like him because he was an articulate spokesman for democracy and an intellectual with broad and eclectic interests. They also like him because he offered his embargo as an alternative to war. Modern conservatives like Jefferson because he favored limited government, although he did not always live up to his principles.[2]

Jefferson's reputation also benefits from his other achievements. He wrote the Declaration of Independence in 1776, promoted democracy in Virginia in the 1780s, founded the University of Virginia in 1819, and in general showed a remarkable talent for articulating the finest aspirations of the American people. In other words, Americans love Jefferson for what he stood for and for what he did before and after he was president, and this colors their evaluation of his presidency.

As a statesman, Jefferson ranks as of one of America's finest, but as a president he does not. A more steely-eyed assessment of his presidency, one that takes proper account of his failures as well as his successes, would surely place him no higher than 10th and perhaps as low as 15th.[3]

**Has Free Ships–Free Goods Been Overrated?** The issue of free ships–free goods (that is, that neutral ships should be allowed to carry enemy-owned property in time of war) is sometimes portrayed as an important issue in the early nineteenth century and even as a cause of the War of 1812. But this issue did not play a significant role in America's prewar diplomacy.

Devised by the Dutch, the doctrine of free ships had considerable appeal on the continent of Europe. Small naval powers liked it because it enabled them to use neutral ships to carry on their trade whenever they were at war; and neutrals liked it because it offered enhanced commercial opportunities. The British, however, resisted the new doctrine. Intent on using their naval power to destroy enemy trade, they claimed that the older principle that permitted belligerent nations to confiscate any enemy-owned property found on neutral ships was still in force.

The United States enthusiastically embraced free ships–free goods during the American Revolution and thereafter became the world's leading proponent of the doctrine. By 1800, however, the U.S. government had allowed this issue to recede into the background. By then, American merchants had built up sufficient capital that they could purchase enemy property before shipping it. This Americanized the property and thus protected it from seizure even under the British doctrine. Moreover, buying and reselling property earned much larger profits than simply freighting it from one port to another. "The boasted principle of free ships, free goods," said Federalist Fisher Ames in 1802, "would deprive the United States of a great part of the fair profits of their neutrality. Belligerent nations could in that case transact their own affairs, and neutrals would have no gains but freight."[4]

In its diplomacy after 1800, the United States sometimes raised the issue of free ships–free goods, but it did so mainly as a point of principle. The administration did not object to the seizure of enemy property on neutral ships, and in 1814 President Madison himself conceded that "it seems to have been generally understood, that the British doctrine was practically admitted."[5]

**Why Was the Monroe-Pinkney Treaty Important?** In 1794 the United States and Great Britain negotiated the Jay Treaty, which forged an Anglo-American accord that allowed American trade and hence the entire American economy to flourish. The commercial clauses of this treaty expired in 1803, and the United States refused a British offer to renew them. However, after the Royal Navy seized a large number of American merchant vessels in the Caribbean in the winter of 1805–06, Congress pressured President Jefferson into seeking a new agreement with Britain. Jefferson asked Baltimore lawyer William Pinkney and the resident U.S. minister in London, James Monroe, to undertake the negotiations. The result of their mission was the Monroe-Pinkney Treaty, which was signed on the last day of 1806.

In the realm of commerce and neutral rights, the Monroe-Pinkney Treaty offered the United States more than the Jay Treaty, and yet Jefferson refused to submit the agreement to the Senate. It was therefore lost. Why did Jefferson toss away this opportunity to resolve so many differences with Britain? His principal objection was that the treaty failed to provide for an end to impressment. In addition, he thought that France was likely to win the war in Europe and that in the ensuing peace settlement Great Britain would be forced to concede a much broader definition of neutral rights. Why, Jefferson reasoned, should the United States accept modest gains when in due time

James Monroe (1758–1831) and William Pinkney (1764–1822) both served in President Madison's war cabinet, but in 1806 the two men negotiated a treaty with Great Britain that might have averted war if the United States had ratified it. (Lossing, *Pictorial Field-Book of the War of 1812*)

DON'T GIVE UP THE SHIP!

the British would be forced to make much more generous concessions to its enemies in Europe?

Even if the British did not lose the war in Europe, Jefferson was confident that the United States could always play its trump card—American trade restrictions—to force the British to make greater concessions on the issue of neutral rights. Jefferson turned out to be wrong on both issues: France did not win the war in Europe, and the restrictive system did not work. Most scholars dismiss the Monroe-Pinkney Treaty because it was never implemented, but this seems misguided. Although we cannot know for certain what would have happened if the treaty had been ratified, its rejection does appear to have been a major blunder and a fundamental turning point in the period. By rejecting this treaty, the United States missed a chance to reforge the Anglo-American friendship of the 1790s and to take a path that might have led to peace and prosperity instead of one that led to trade restrictions and war.[6]

**Impressment.** The British navy played a central role in the French Revolutionary and Napoleonic Wars, and it grew steadily in strength. The number of vessels that it had in commission rose from 135 in 1793 to 584 in 1812.[7] There was a corresponding increase in the number of seamen authorized by Parliament to man these ships, rising from 36,000 in 1793 to 114,000 in 1812.[8]

Recruiting seamen for the Royal Navy was never easy. Discipline could be harsh, and the pay was poor and purposely kept at least six months in arrears to deter desertion. The work was also dangerous. From 1793 to 1815, close to 100,000 seamen and marines in the Royal Navy perished, mainly from accident or disease.[9] Worst of all in the eyes of many British seamen, there was no end to naval service. While merchant ships discharged and paid off their crews at the end of each cruise, the Royal Navy did not. Instead, the men were shuttled from ship to ship, often even denied an opportunity for shore leave between cruises. Given these conditions, it is hardly surprising that the Royal Navy was invariably shorthanded in time of war.

There were perhaps 118,000 sailors in the British merchant marine in 1792, and some of these men as well as some foreign seamen could be lured into naval service.[10] But voluntary recruitment always fell short of need, and the only way to make up the difference was by impressment, that is, by forcing men into service. Throughout the French Revolutionary and Napoleonic Wars, press gangs were active in British seaports, snaring seamen (and some

Impressment, the forcible removal of seamen from American merchant vessels by the Royal Navy, was a leading cause of the War of 1812. Unlike the sailor in this illustration, which was produced about 1890, most seamen did not resist because they knew they risked a flogging if they did. (Magazine illustration. Library of Congress)

unlucky landlubbers as well). Press gangs also took seamen from British merchant ships, but they could only target incoming ships, and if the removal of seamen left any merchant ship shorthanded, the Royal Navy had to provide temporary substitutes. In all, the Royal Navy probably got 50 percent of its seamen in this period from impressment, and with desertions running about 500 a month during the Napoleonic Wars, there was rarely a lull in the practice.[11] "Without a press," commented the great naval hero Horatio Nelson, "I have no idea how our Fleet can be manned."[12]

The British also claimed the right to remove British seamen from American vessels, but only in certain cases. This aspect of impressment was a leading cause of the War of 1812, but it has been the source of much confusion. The British did not claim the right to impress from neutral warships or in neutral waters (both of which were considered an extension of a nation's territory), although they occasionally did so.[13] They claimed the right to impress only from merchant vessels on the high seas and in their own waters (and the United States did not contest this right in British jurisdiction).[14]

Although the British occasionally conferred citizenship on foreigners and recognized the right of their own people to become American citizens, they insisted that no one could renounce British citizenship. In other words, becoming the citizen of another nation did not release one from the obligations of British citizenship. The British therefore retained the right to impress British citizens who had become naturalized American citizens.

The impressment of naturalized Americans was not a major source of controversy between the two nations for two reasons. First of all, before 1848 the United States did not claim that taking on American citizenship absolved an individual from the obligations of previous citizenship.[15] Secondly and more importantly, few British seamen bothered to go through the naturalization process. The American merchant marine employed around 70,000 men a year in the Age of Jefferson.[16] Of these, perhaps 30 percent were British.[17] And yet between 1796 and 1812 only about 1,500 foreign seamen became American citizens.[18] Thus, contrary to popular belief, few naturalized Americans were actually impressed into British service.

The real problem was that the Royal Navy impressed British subjects and (by accident, negligence, or design) native-born American citizens from American merchant ships. The British practice sometimes left American vessels (which usually sailed with smaller crews than their European counterparts) dangerously shorthanded, forcing an unscheduled and costly detour to the nearest port to find replacements. More importantly, it deprived American citizens of their freedom.

To secure the release of American victims of impressment, the United States usually had to go through diplomatic channels, a process that could take years. In the meantime, American seamen were subjected to the harshness of British naval discipline and to all the dangers of fighting a war that was not their own. Moreover, even in the 1790s, when they were being most cooperative, the British did not release more than about 50 percent of those impressed seamen that the U.S. claimed were American citizens.[19] In some cases, they did not find the evidence presented conclusive or persuasive; in others, they considered the impressed seamen volunteers. Any seaman accepting the naval bounty or pay was considered a volunteer even if he was not British and was originally impressed into service.

How many Americans were forced into British service? Based on State Department figures, contemporary American newspapers often reported that 6,257 Americans had been impressed between 1803 and 1812. This figure included some duplications, but it probably omitted other cases that went unreported. Based on various figures provided by the State Department, one might conservatively estimate that 3,000 Americans were impressed from 1793 to 1802 and 7,000 from 1803 to 1812. Thus, in all, perhaps 10,000 American citizens were impressed into British service during the French Revolutionary and Napoleonic Wars.[20]

Could the British be forced to give up impressment? Probably not, since they believed that surrendering the practice would lead to wholesale desertions from the Royal Navy, the collapse of their naval power, and thus defeat in the European war. Given these circumstances, the United States would have been better advised to treat the issue not as a cause for war but simply as the price (albeit a stiff price and one paid in human suffering) for doing business in a world at war.[21]

**The *Chesapeake* Affair.** On June 22, 1807, H.M. Ship *Leopard* (52) stopped the U.S. Frigate *Chesapeake* (40) off the coast of Virginia and demanded to search for four deserters known to be on board. When the *Chesapeake* refused, the *Leopard* unleashed several broadsides, killing three members of the American ship's crew and wounding 16 others (one of whom later died). The British then removed the four men, three of whom proved to be American citizens who had deserted from the Royal Navy after being impressed into service.[22]

In the ensuing court martial, Commodore James Barron, the senior officer on the *Chesapeake,* was found guilty of not preparing the ship for action and was suspended from the U.S. Navy for five years. In separate trials, Captain Charles Gordon, commander of the *Chesapeake,* and Captain John Hall, commander of the U.S. Marine detachment on board, were both privately

When H.M. Ship *Leopard* fired on the U.S. Frigate *Chesapeake* in 1807, it created a war scare. The *Chesapeake* affair remained a sore spot in Anglo-American relations until it was settled in late 1811. (Sketch by F.S. Cozzens. Naval Historical Center)

reprimanded for negligence, while Gunner William Hook was dismissed from the service for "wilful[l]" negligence.[23]

The *Chesapeake* affair generated outrage in the United States. Nathaniel Macon, a North Carolina Republican, claimed that "the nation had been smitten by one of the great Powers of the earth—its sovereignty had been attacked."[24] Other Republicans insisted that it was "the eve of war," or that the two nations were "about to go to war," or that they were already "in a state of war."[25] Although the United States adopted war preparations, it waited to see if the British would disavow the attack.

Although in the past the British had claimed the right to impress from neutral warships, by 1807 they considered these ships an extension of a nation's territory and thus not subject to search. Hence, in the *Chesapeake* affair they were willing to offer apologies and compensation to the victims or their families. But efforts to reach a settlement were stymied, first by Jefferson's attempt to use the affair as a lever to force the British to give up impressment altogether and then by Britain's insistence that the United States first revoke an order barring British warships from American ports. Because it defied easy settlement, the *Chesapeake* affair festered, serving to remind Americans how arrogant the Royal Navy could be and how lightly the British regarded American sovereignty.[26]

What is not widely known is that the *Chesapeake* affair was actually settled prior to the War of 1812. On November 12, 1811, the British agreed to disavow the attack, pay reparations, and restore the two surviving victims. (The British subject had already been hanged, and one of the three Americans had died in a Halifax hospital.) Although it does not appear that the damages were ever fixed or paid, the two Americans were solemnly restored to the U.S. Frigate *Chesapeake* on July 11, 1812 (about three weeks after the declaration of war), by officers from the hired cartel schooner *Brim,* which had sailed into Boston Harbor under a flag of truce. Since both nations had signed off on the *Chesapeake* settlement more than seven months before the declaration of war, this incident cannot be considered a cause of the war.[27]

What is also little appreciated is how much of a haven for British deserters American national ships had become before the War of 1812 precisely because they were normally off limits to British press gangs. At the time of the incident, about half of the enlisted men in the U.S. Navy were foreigners, and British officials estimated that 150–200 of the 381 seamen on board the *Chesapeake* were British subjects. Although this may have been an exaggeration, Captain Stephen Decatur, who took command of the ship after the incident, acknowledged that he had discharged 150 foreign seamen from the crew.[28]

**The Orders-in-Council.** British restrictions on neutral trade with the Continent of Europe were known as the Orders-in-Council and were one of the leading causes of the War of 1812. It is often said that the Orders-in-Council prohibited American trade with the Continent, but this is incorrect. The Orders were far more complicated than this, and the restrictions they imposed on American trade changed over time.

There were three sets of Orders-in-Council. The first decree, issued in January 1807, prohibited neutrals (that is, Americans) from trading between enemy ports. A second set of Orders, issued in November 1807, forced neutrals wishing to trade with the Continent to ship their cargoes through Great Britain. A third Order, issued in April 1809, scrapped the previous restrictions in favor of a strict blockade that barred all trade with any European ports between the Ems River in northwest Germany and Pesaro and Orbitello in Italy.

The Orders-in-Council never applied to all of Europe. They targeted only those ports that were under French control. At one time or another, ports in Portugal, Spain, the Baltic, the Ottoman Empire, and the Austrian Empire

This contemporary cartoon depicts a smuggler using a British license to try to get high-grade tobacco to a British warship in violation of the embargo. Federalist critics used a snapping turtle to symbolize the embargo because, like America, the turtle responded to threats by withdrawing into its shell. Critics also spelled embargo backwards—"o-grab-me"—because the measure threatened almost everyone's livelihood. (Lossing, *Pictorial Field-Book of the War of 1812*)

were free from French control and thus open to neutral trade under the British rules. Moreover, before 1809 the British allowed the shipment of certain commodities directly from the United States to the Continent. And beginning in 1807 the British issued 10,000 licenses a year that provided an exemption from the Orders-in-Council. Although most of these licenses went to British subjects, they were readily available on the open market to anyone with enough cash.

The Orders-in-Council worked a hardship on American merchants and served as a pretext for the seizure of a large number of American merchant ships and their cargoes. Nevertheless, there were still plenty of ways for canny merchants to get their cargoes to the Continent and make a profit. Moreover, unlike impressment, the British never considered the Orders-in-Council essential to their war effort. In fact, they were little more than an attempt to continue British maritime profits and to appease hard-liners in Britain who resented America's rising prosperity. Ultimately, the British bowed to growing domestic pressure and lifted the Orders, although by then the United States had already gone to war. But the Orders never should have been considered a cause for war. Instead, Americans should have treated their losses under the Orders-in-Council the same way they should have treated impressment: not as a cause for war but as the price of doing business in a world at war.[29]

**The Restrictive System.** The group of laws limiting American trade in the years before the War of 1812 is known as the restrictive system. It included a partial non-importation act in 1806, an embargo in 1807, a non-intercourse act in 1809, and a second non-importation act in 1811. These measures grew out of the Republican belief that American trade could be used to achieve foreign policy objectives. By limiting trade with Great Britain and France, the Republicans thought they could force the European belligerents to make concessions to the United States on the maritime issues in dispute. Aside from contributing to Britain's belated repeal of the Orders-in-Council (which came too late to avert war), the restrictive system was a failure.[30]

The non-importation act adopted in 1811 is often mistakenly called a non-intercourse law. However, unlike the non-intercourse act of 1809, it did not bar the export of American goods to Great Britain or its possessions. Attempts to enforce the 1809 law had shown that, while the United States could effectively bar British ships and goods from American ports, it could not prevent American ships and goods from reaching British ports once they sailed. Acknowledging this limitation, American officials opted to target only the import trade in 1811.[31]

Republicans defended the restrictive system as a peaceful alternative to war, and most historians have followed their lead. This has given the restrictive system a certain cachet in some scholarly circles, and Jefferson and Madison have been praised for a noble attempt to find an alternative to war. However, instead of modifying or even repealing the last non-importation act when the United States went to war, Republicans kept this measure on the books and gradually added others: an enemy trade act in 1812, a ban against using enemy licenses in early 1813, and then a sweeping embargo in late 1813.

Although some of these measures were legitimate war measures, their main purpose was not to impede Britain's war effort but to undermine its prosperity. In other words, they were coercive measures rather than war measures. Moreover, in the first 18 months of the war President Madison pestered Congress with requests for a host of other restrictions (none of which he got) designed to put additional pressure on Great Britain.

For most Republicans, the restrictive system was not an alternative to war but rather a policy that could be used in conjunction with war. As War Hawk Henry Clay put it: Even if the United States were defeated on the battlefield, "if you cling to the restrictive system, it is incessantly working in your favor," and "if persisted in, the restrictive system, aiding the war, would break down the present [British] Ministry, and lead to a consequent honorable peace."[32]

It was only after news arrived at the end of 1813 of Napoleon's defeat at Leipzig, which shattered France's Continental System and opened most of northern Europe to British trade, that the United States repealed the restrictive system and later substituted a more conventional enemy trade act that targeted Britain's war effort rather than its economy. Even then, a hard-core group of Republican restrictionists in Congress and the country denounced the new policy.[33]

**Assessing American Trade and Prosperity, 1789–1807.** American trade soared in the early national period. The French Revolution that erupted in 1789 led to a general European war that by 1793 had thoroughly disrupted normal commercial patterns. As the leading neutral, the United States soon found itself in the enviable position of trading with belligerent nations that could not supply their own needs. The European powers and their colonies developed a voracious appetite for American food, raw materials, and other goods, and as a result American exports rose dramatically, from $20,000,000 in 1790 to $108,000,000 in 1807. American imports followed a similar trajectory, soaring from $23,000,000 in 1790 to $139,000,000 in 1807. Tax revenue from shipping and trade, which provided the main source of income for the U.S. government, also rose dramatically, from less than $3,000,000 in 1790 to $16,000,000 in 1808.[34]

Taken together, American trade and revenue figures from 1790 to 1807 suggest extraordinary economic growth. American exports in this period increased 440 percent and American imports 504 percent. Similarly, the revenue that the federal government derived from trade rose 433 percent.[35] As a result, this era has been called an age of "unparalleled prosperity."[36]

This assessment, however, understates the problems that American merchants faced in a world at war. British and French restrictions took a heavy toll on American trade, and under these conditions some merchants were unable to turn a profit. Between 1803 and 1812, the British and French (and their respective allies) seized about the same number of ships. The total was close to 1,700. The ships alone were worth $18,000,000 and the cargoes they carried probably more.[37] Although some of these vessels were released, their owners still incurred heavy expenses because of their detention.

Moreover, the trade figures overstate the degree of economic activity in the United States for several reasons. First, part of the increase in the value of trade was the result of inflation. The consumer price index in the United States rose 26 percent between 1790 and 1807.[38] In addition, the population in these years increased from 3,900,000 to 6,600,000, an increase of 69 percent.[39] Hence, over the 18-year period, the inflation-adjusted per capita increase in the export trade was only about 154 percent, roughly a third of the unadjusted figure.

Finally, fully half of all exports were actually re-exports, that is, goods imported into the United States and then re-shipped to foreign markets. Most of this indirect trade was undertaken to circumvent the British Rule of 1756, which held that trade closed to a nation in time of peace could not be opened in time of war. American merchants normally were prohibited from carrying goods between France and Spain and their West Indian colonies, but in time of war, when their own merchant vessels were driven from the sea, the European belligerents threw this trade open to neutrals. American merchants, eager to take advantage of this opportunity, found that they could circumvent the British rule if American ships broke their voyage by stopping in the United States. This transformed a direct trade into two separate branches that the British reluctantly sanctioned. Unlike exports generated by the domestic sector, however, re-exports benefited a relatively small number of people.

If re-exports are excluded from the general trade figures for this period, the result is a much more modest increase in American trade. From 1790 to 1807, domestic exports rose from $20,000,000 to $49,000,000. If inflation and population growth are factored in, then the nation's per capita increase in the export of domestic products in this era was just 15 percent. To be sure, this figure would be pushed higher by invisible exports (such as money earned from freight and insurance), which were not officially recorded. Even so, the per capita inflation-adjusted increase was far less dramatic than the raw un-adjusted figures suggest. Domestic exports probably accounted for only 15 percent of the gross domestic product in this era anyway. Similarly, retained imports for this period rose from $22,000,000 to $79,000,000. But if inflation and population growth are factored in, retained imports increased by only 68 percent per capita.[40]

Does this mean that the United States did not prosper in the years from 1790 to 1807? Not at all. It merely suggests that the nation experienced a more modest rate of economic growth than some scholars have suggested, and that other sectors (particularly agriculture) played a more important role. In fact, it appears that the rate of growth for the economy as a whole was roughly 4.4 percent per annum, which was in line with the annual growth rate for the entire period from 1800 to 1860. All of this suggests that the growth rate would have been about the same even without the European war. This was a healthy growth rate, one that could easily boost living standards in a growing population, but it was not a rate of growth that was exceptional. Those who study the run-up to the War of 1812 and the impact that of European wars on the U. S. economy would do well to keep this in mind.[41]

**Who Killed American Prosperity, 1807–15?** Some scholars have blamed the destruction of American prosperity and the attendant loss of government revenue in the years after 1807 on the British and French restrictions on neutral trade. There is no denying that these restrictions took a heavy toll, but to assess their impact two issues need to be addressed: Did the European belligerents seize so many American ships that trade was effectively destroyed, or did the Europeans impose so many constraints on American trade that it was difficult if not impossible to make a profit?

Federalist merchants in New England claimed that they could make a profit if only one ship in three got through, but this was true only in a few cases where foreign markets were particularly starved for imports. For most merchants, the loss of two-thirds of their fleet, together with the cargoes they carried, would have been devastating, but only the unlucky suffered this fate.

From 1803 to 1812, the British and French and their allies seized about 1,700 American merchant vessels, an average of about 200 a year. For the mercantile community as a whole, these losses do not appear to have been devastating. For one thing, the number of ships lost each year did not actually increase during the period of European restrictions. The average yearly loss was about the same for the two periods, 1803–07 and 1807–12.[42] Moreover, an annual loss of 200 ships from 1807 through 1811 represented only about 4.4 percent of the total number of American ships engaged in foreign trade.[43] The figures available from Baltimore also suggest modest losses. From 1789 to 1812, the merchants of Baltimore lost less than 6 percent of their fleet.[44] Since peacetime insurance rates ran about 7 percent, the losses experienced by merchants in Baltimore, as well as those in the rest of the nation, seem to have been within tolerable financial limits.

About 65 percent of American trade went to European markets in the Age of Jefferson.[45] The evidence of the impact of the European restrictions on these markets is ambiguous. Americans could always trade on the periphery of Europe, and while Baltic ports became overstocked with American goods by 1811, the Iberian Peninsula continued to offer profitable markets because of the needs of the large and growing British army there. Markets in the British Isles also remained profitable.

One bit of evidence seems more conclusive. The tonnage of American ships engaged in foreign trade, which steadily increased in the Age of Jefferson, did not reach its peak until 1810. In fact, the increase from 1806 (the last year when trade was unrestrained by European or American restrictions) to 1810 was almost 22 percent.[46] Would American merchants have put more ships into service if they were likely to lose them or if they did not have promising markets? It seems unlikely.

It is true that some American merchants lost too many ships or were unable to find profitable markets and as a result were forced to withdraw from business or were driven into bankruptcy. But for the American mercantile community as a whole, it appears that their losses were manageable and their markets sufficiently profitable. This seems to confirm what Federalists at the time claimed: that the European depredations were costly but not crippling, and that it was still possible for merchants to turn a profit in this dangerous, war-torn world.

If the British and French did not kill American prosperity in this period, then who did? It was none other than the United States government, whose policies of economic coercion and war had a devastating impact on American trade and public revenue. Domestic exports, which had peaked at $49,000,000 in 1807, fell to $9,000,000 the following year, not because of the European depredations, but because the American embargo prohibited American ships and goods from leaving port. After fluctuating between $31,000,000 and $45,000,000 in the ensuing years of less restricted trade, domestic exports plummeted to $7,000,000 during the War of 1812.[47]

Revenue from trade also plummeted as a direct result of American policies. After reaching a peak of $16,000,000 in 1808, government revenue fell to $7,000,000 in 1809 because of the embargo, and to $6,000,000 in 1814 during the War of 1812, and this despite the fact that the customs duties had been doubled at the beginning of the conflict. It was thus the policies of the U.S. government, not those of the European belligerents, that undermined American prosperity and government revenue in the years from 1808 to 1815.[48]

**Did the British Incite the Indians?** Indians living in the fertile territory of the Old Northwest (the present states of Ohio, Indiana, Illinois, Michigan, and Wisconsin) faced relentless pressure from the United States to surrender their lands and move farther west. Tensions mounted after 1809, when Governor (later Major General) William Henry Harrison of Indiana Territory imposed the last of a series of dubious treaties on a few compliant Indian leaders. By this time a pan-Indian movement headed by the influential shaman Tenskwatawa, known as the Prophet, and his brother Tecumseh had gained considerable support in a bid to resist additional encroachments. Indian raids increased, and open warfare became a distinct possibility.

The British had a close relationship with the Indians in the Old Northwest on both sides of the border. They supplied them with trade goods and weapons and sought to keep them in alliance to bolster British chances in any war with the more populous United States. But the British walked a fine line. They wanted to make sure that the Indians sided with them, but they did not want their native allies to provoke a war, nor would they go to war against the United States simply because their Indian allies did. Compounding the problem was the behavior of Britain's Indian agents, who were often married to Indians and had other ties to the natives, and as a result tended to overstate Great Britain's commitment. In fact, the British did not aid the Indians when they fought American troops at Fallen Timbers in 1794 (although a number of Canadian volunteers did) or at Tippecanoe in 1811.

Most Americans, especially in the West, did not understand the finer points of British Indian policy. They were reluctant to admit that native hos-

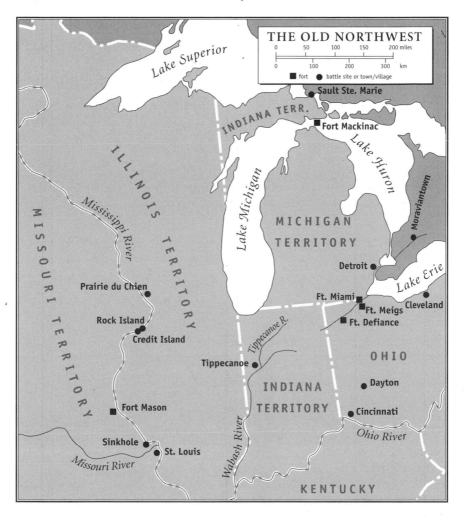

tility usually resulted from American lawlessness on the frontier and America's appetite for Indian lands. Convinced that British officials were inciting Indian violence, they blamed Great Britain for the brutal attacks that occurred on western settlements before the War of 1812. But the British actually tried to restrain their native allies. What few Americans at the time realized was that the British did not actually control the Indians. Although most were willing to follow Great Britain's lead, there were some, such as the militant Potawatomis, Sauks, and Kickapoos, who had their own agenda and their own way of resisting American expansion. These Indians did not consult the British when they decided to go on the warpath.[49]

**The Battle of Tippecanoe.** An important battle has often been linked to the War of 1812 even though it was fought more than seven months before the declaration of war. This is the Battle of Tippecanoe, which took place on November 7, 1811. Governor William Henry Harrison precipitated the battle by marching an army of 1,000 regulars and volunteer militia to Prophet's Town (near present-day Lafayette, Indiana) in the heart of Indian country. His aim was to destroy the village to put an end to native raids on the frontier, although these attacks were probably carried out by Indians who had little connection to Prophet's Town. After making camp near the Indian village, Harrison was attacked in the predawn hours by a coalition of 500 Indians—

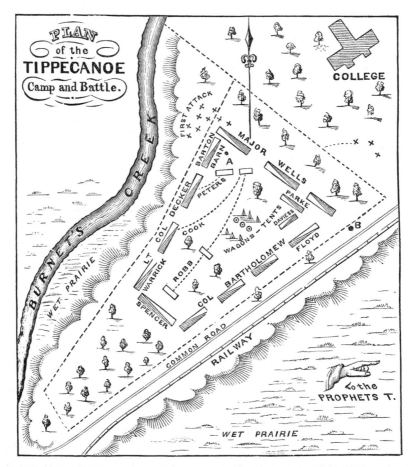

The Battle of Tippecanoe in 1811 touched off an Indian war in the Old Northwest that merged into the War of 1812. (Lossing, *Pictorial Field-Book of the War of 1812*)

This collection of Indian paraphernalia shows a peace pipe as well as a scalp. (Lossing, *Pictorial Field-Book of the War of 1812*)

mostly Kickapoos, Winnebagoes, and Potawatomis—under the leadership of the Prophet.

Despite heavy losses, Harrison's men held their ground and then drove off the Indians with a counterattack on their flanks. After the Indians fled, Harrison marched into Prophet's Town, burned it to the ground, and destroyed the Indians' vital food supplies. American soldiers reportedly also disinterred Indian bodies from their graves.[50]

***Did Harrison Mismanage the Campaign?*** After the Battle of Tippecanoe, Harrison complained that he was "violently" and "illiberally" attacked in the newspapers for the way he managed the campaign.[51] He came under fire from the partisans of Colonel John P. Boyd, a regular army officer who had participated in the battle and thought that Harrison gave too much credit to the militia in his after-action report. Harrison also was criticized by the friends of Major Joseph H. Daviess, a Kentucky militia officer who was killed in the battle. Daviess, who was Chief Justice John Marshall's brother-in-law and had other ties to Federalists, had favored launching a pre-emptive attack against the Indians the previous day.[52] Harrison's management of the campaign was a subject of criticism as late as 1840, when he ran for the presidency. Two of the most persistent charges were that he camped on a site suggested by the Indians and that the night attack had caught him by surprise. Neither charge has any real merit.

Harrison had parleyed with a band of Indians the day before the battle. They appeared eager for peace and urged him to camp that night so that they could continue talking the next day. Since he was under orders to avoid war if at all possible, Harrison felt obliged to comply. The Indians even told him that a nearby elevation with a creek running through it offered a good campground. Harrison dispatched two of his officers to inspect this general area, and from a number of possibilities they picked the best site. "No intima-

Governor (later Major General) William Henry Harrison (1773–1841) won a close victory at Tippecanoe in 1811 and a more decisive one at the Thames two years later. He went on to become president in 1841, although his one-month term, which ended with his death from pneumonia, is the shortest on record. (Portrait by Rembrandt Peale, detail). National Portrait Gallery, Smithsonian Institution)

tion was given by the Indians of their wish that we should encamp there," said one of the officers who picked the site, "nor could they possibly have known where the army would encamp until it took its position."[53]

Although Daviess expected the Indians to launch a night attack, most of the American officers, including Harrison, were skeptical because the Indians had passed up more favorable opportunities earlier in the march. When the Indians did attack shortly before reveille, Harrison was up, but most of the Americans were still sleeping. But Harrison had prepared for this very contingency by ordering his men to sleep with their arms (as they had on the entire march) and to bed down in formation so that they would be properly positioned in the event of an attack. "The order of encampment," Harrison later said, "was the order of Battle for a night attack."[54]

Harrison's mistakes prior to the battle were of a different order. He failed to fortify his camp, and he allowed his men to build large fires that illuminated them in

Brigadier General John P. Boyd (1764–1830) served with the British army in India before returning home to join the U.S. Army. A mediocre officer, Boyd feuded with William Henry Harrison after Tippecanoe in 1811 and was beaten by a much smaller British force at Crysler's Farm in 1813. (Lossing, *Pictorial Field-Book of the War of 1812*)

the night. Harrison later claimed that he did not have enough axes to build breastworks, although his men did have enough to fortify their campsites earlier in the march. He defended the fires because he expected a battle the next day and wanted to ensure that his men got a good night's rest on a particularly cold and rainy night. Once again, however, this was at odds with his practice earlier in the campaign, when large fires had been kindled outside the camp to illuminate any attacking force.[55]

**Was Tippecanoe a Decisive American Victory?** The Battle of Tippecanoe later helped propel Harrison into the presidency, and it is sometimes depicted as an unalloyed American victory. Harrison himself described it as "a complete and decisive victory" and as "a glorious victory."[56] It was indeed an American victory both because it scattered the Indians and because the American army followed up by destroying Prophet's Town and the Indian food supplies there. But the victory was far from overwhelming or decisive.

Two months after the battle, a Kickapoo chief who was present at the battle told British agent Matthew Elliott that his tribe had saved its food by burying it. He also told Elliott that only 25 Indians had been killed. Although he undoubtedly understated Indian losses, Harrison's losses—almost 200 killed and wounded—were probably three times the casualties sustained by the Indians. The heavy American losses were remarkable for a defending army facing a smaller attacking force in this era.[57]

Harrison's Indian allies claimed that the Prophet had been discredited and his confederacy greatly weakened, but Britain's Indian allies told a different story. The Prophet still had some influence in the Old Northwest, and the pan-Indian movement remained potent. "The Prophet and his people do not appear as a vanquished enemy," Elliott concluded; "they re-occupy their former ground."[58]

**What Was the Significance of Tippecanoe?** Although the Battle of Tippecanoe did not involve British soldiers nor make war between the United States and Great Britain inevitable, it cemented the Anglo-Indian alliance. It also inflamed American opinion against the British because the Indians were armed mostly with British weapons, and the British were presumed to be behind their hostility. "We have had but one opinion as the cause of the depredations of the Indians," said *Niles' Register* in early 1812; "they are instigated and supported by the British in Canada, any official declaration to the contrary notwithstanding."[59]

The Battle of Tippecanoe was the opening round of the Indian War in the Old Northwest, which became an integral part of the War of 1812. Although not actually part of the Anglo-American conflict, Tippecanoe was an important prelude, and the Treaty of Ghent acknowledged as much by nominally restoring to the Indians all their possessions, rights, and privileges as of 1811.[60]

## THE DECISION FOR WAR

**The British Offer on the License Trade.** Although the British gave little hint that they might suspend or repeal the Orders-in-Council in early 1812, they did make another proposal that has been largely ignored although it might have averted war. In May of 1812 Britain offered the United States an equal share of its license trade with the Continent. The licenses gave those who held them the right to trade in defiance of the Orders-in-Council. Since Great Britain issued an average of 10,000 licenses a year, this offer was significant. In effect, the British were willing to suspend the Orders-in-Council in practice as long as American merchants conducted their trade with the Continent under British licenses.

The United States dismissed the British offer, and it was quickly forgotten. Admittedly, it came very late, just weeks before the declaration of war, and it raised both a practical problem (how would the licenses be distributed?) and a sovereignty issue (would accepting this offer compromise American independence?). Nevertheless, the offer warranted more serious consideration than the United States gave it, and historians have been remiss in ignoring it.[61]

**The Lure of Canada.** In late 1811, as the debates on war preparations were under way in the U.S. Congress, John Randolph of Roanoke, a dissident Republican from Virginia, delivered a speech that was to reverberate through history. "Agrarian cupidity," he said, "not maritime right, urges the war. Ever since the report of the Committee on Foreign Relations [urging war preparations] came into the House, we have heard but one word—like the whip-poor-will, but one eternal monotonous tone—Canada! Canada! Canada!"[62]

Most scholars have stressed that maritime issues, particularly the Orders-in-Council and impressment, caused the war, and this view has the weight

John Randolph of Roanoke (1773-1833), the acid-tongued antiwar Republican from Virginia, never matured properly and thus retained his boyish looks into manhood. His speech in Congress attributing the conflict to land hunger cast a long shadow over the war's historiography. (Portrait by Gilbert Stuart. Library of Congress)

of evidence behind it. Whether speaking in Congress, in their newspapers, in the diplomatic documents, or in personal letters, Americans in the years before the War of 1812 devoted far more attention to the maritime issues than to the prospect of acquiring Canada. Randolph's argument, however, has never gone away. It enjoyed considerable vogue in the early twentieth century, when its proponents argued that the United States went to war either to get more farmland or to put an end to British influence over American Indians. Even today Randolph's view still has some adherents in the United States and a great many more in Canada.

Why has the annexationist myth been so durable? For one thing, Republican leaders at the time talked openly about how easy it would be to conquer Canada. As early as 1810, Henry Clay claimed that "the militia of Kentucky are alone competent to place Montreal and Upper Canada at our feet," and shortly after the declaration of war Thomas Jefferson boasted that "the acquisition of Canada this year, as far as the neighborhood of Quebec, will be a mere matter of marching."[63] The notion of quick victory, commented the Boston *Yankee* in late 1812, "had taken deep root in Washington . . . and will not be easily exterminated. It is supposed that the show of an army, and a few well directed proclamations would unnerve the arm of resistance, and make conquest and conciliation synonymous."

The idea that the United States could conquer Canada in what John Randolph called "a holiday campaign" was a colossal misconception.[64] This misconception rested on a host of smaller misconceptions: that the U.S. had an effective regular army; that the nation's militia was a reliable force and that citizen soldiers were willing to serve abroad; that logistical problems would not hamper operations; that British regulars and their Indian allies could be swept aside; and that the population of Canada—a combination of old French residents, Tory refugees, and recent American immigrants—would either welcome an invasion or put up very little resistance.

Another reason for the popularity of the annexationist myth is that the U.S. government never clarified its position on Canada during the war. It never said that it would hold any conquered territory as ransom for concessions on the maritime issues, nor did it repudiate the annexationist proclamations issued in 1812 by Brigadier General William Hull on the Detroit frontier and by Brigadier General Alexander Smyth on the Niagara frontier. Doubtless the government wanted to keep all its options open in case the British proved more willing to part with Canada than with their maritime pretensions. Doubtless, too, Republican leaders did not want to forestall the annexation of territory if they later concluded that public opinion or public policy demanded it. Indeed, it is hard to imagine the United States voluntarily surrendering Canada if it had been conquered, but that does not mean that the desire for Canada caused the war.

Still another reason for the appeal of the annexationist myth is that in the West the desire for Canada really did fuel the war movement. Moreover, this sentiment grew everywhere as the war progressed. This was partly because of the growing cost of the war (the more Americans paid in blood and treasure, the more they needed Canada to justify their losses), and partly because the military victories in the West in 1813 appeared to make the conquest of Canada more likely (although in truth these victories were too far west to affect the outcome of the war). A Boston newspaper captured the prevailing sentiment in late 1813: "Too much valuable blood has already been shed, and too much treasure expended, to permit us to indulge for a moment the idea of resigning this country."[65]

The annexationist myth also dovetails nicely with the long-term interest of the United States in Canada. Americans fully realized the many advantages that might accrue from the acquisition of Canada. It would remove Great Britain, a powerful rival, from the nation's northern flank; it would put an end to foreign influence over American Indians and leave Americans in control of the still lucrative fur trade; it would eliminate artificial trade barriers on the northern frontier and secure an invaluable east-west transportation route that included the Great Lakes and the St. Lawrence River; and it would open vast new expanses of farmland to American settlers.

The United Colonies had tried to conquer Canada in 1775, and although this campaign had failed, American interest in Canada remained undiminished. Nor did this sentiment abate after the War of 1812. It remained a force in American politics until the end of the nineteenth century, fueled by assorted Irish nationalists, Anglophobes, and visionaries who expected Manifest Destiny to carry the American flag to the North Pole.

But none of this proves that the United States went to war in 1812 to acquire Canada. The confusion here is over ends and means. Henry Clay, a western War Hawk who spearheaded the war movement and supported expansion, put the matter clearly in late 1812. "Canada was not the end but the means," he said, "the object of the War being the redress of injuries, and Canada being the instrument by which that redress was to be obtained."[66] Republican Thomas Wilson of Pennsylvania made the same point a little differently. The conquest of Canada, he insisted, was neither "a motive to commence the war or a primary object." It was instead "an inevitable consequence."[67]

There is another way of looking at this matter. Without the maritime issues, is it likely that the United States would have declared war on Great Britain in 1812 to get Canada? Probably not. However, if the United States had had no territorial ambitions, is it likely that it still would have gone to war in 1812 over the maritime issues? Probably so. In short, what drove American foreign policy in this period was not the wish to acquire Canada (as desirable as this might be) but a determination to win recognition for what contemporaries called "Free Trade and Sailors' Rights."[68]

**Was National Honor at Stake?** Some scholars have argued that the United States went to war in 1812 to uphold national honor.[69] Is this true? Yes and no. On the one hand, many Americans, especially in the South, took matters of honor very seriously.[70] In fact, members of Congress from the slave states produced 69 percent of the votes for war.[71] Many of these people did indeed talk about the need to vindicate the nation's honor, and a successful war, or even an unsuccessful war that was well prosecuted, might accomplish this end.

But honor is an elusive and abstract entity, and in international relations it rarely stands alone. It is perhaps best seen as a lens through which events in the outside world are interpreted. At most, such a lens can distort events so that they seem more important or more demeaning than they actually are. In

1812, many Americans looking through the lens of national honor saw British maritime practices, particularly the Orders-in-Council and impressment, as intolerable. But these policies were far from trivial, and even historians, far removed from 1812 and little influenced by old-fashioned views of honor, have judged them a legitimate cause for war. It is hard to blame the war on national honor when the issues themselves were so weighty.

**Who Were the Real War Hawks?** Conventional wisdom holds that a group of Republicans in the U.S. House of Representatives propelled a reluctant party and nation into war. Federalists dubbed these men "War Hawks." One scholar has suggested that this term ought to be discarded because all Republicans embraced war only reluctantly.[72] Most scholars, however, have accepted the label although they do not agree on how many Republicans it fits. The number given has been as few as 5 and as many as 82 (and this despite the fact that only 79 members of the House voted for war).

Where does the truth lie? Undeniably, Republicans in the House (as well as the Senate) ran the gamut. At one end of the spectrum in the House, there was a small number of Republicans, perhaps 11 in all, who not only spoke consistently, earnestly, and emphatically for war but also worked to advance the war movement. At the other end were those Republicans who were decidedly against war. In fact, 16 Republicans in the House and seven in the Senate voted against the declaration of war. Most Republicans fell in between these extremes. They voted for war but only with considerable reluctance.

Some scholars have tried to identify the War Hawks by looking at House voting patterns. As a result, those Republicans who voted against certain war preparations—such as raising taxes, authorizing certain kinds of troops, or building new warships—have been excluded from the ranks of the War Hawks. This is wrongheaded because there were a number of Republicans who enthusiastically supported war but differed on how best to fight or finance it. Other Republicans who consistently voted for war preparations are sometimes classified as War Hawks. This too is misguided because many of these men were backbenchers with little influence over their colleagues and thus in no position to advance the war movement except with their votes.

Who, then, were the real War Hawks? The group undoubtedly was headed by Henry Clay of Kentucky. The House of Representatives was a fractious body, and the Twelfth Congress included a large number of new members.

Henry Clay (1777–1852), America's leading War Hawk, promoted war in 1812 and then helped end that war two years later as a member of the American peace delegation. (Detail, portrait by unknown artist. National Portrait Gallery, Smithsonian Institution)

As speaker of the house, Clay (in the words of a Republican senator) "reduc'd the chaos to order."[73] He packed key committees with War Hawks, effectively employed secret sessions, interpreted House rules in a manner favorable to the war movement, moved the debate on war measures along, and in general made sure that the administration and Congress advanced steadily down the path to war. The other War Hawks were Richard M. Johnson of Kentucky; Felix Grundy of Tennessee; Langdon Cheves, William Lowndes, John C. Calhoun, and David R. Williams of South Carolina; George M. Troup of Georgia; John A. Harper of New Hampshire; Ezekiel Bacon of Massachusetts; and (despite later getting cold feet) Peter B. Porter of New York.

These 11 men played an indispensable role in the war movement. Without their leadership, commitment, and speeches, the Twelfth Congress, like its predecessors, probably would have adjourned without a declaration of war.[74]

**When Did the U.S. Declare War?** Some scholars have assumed that the U.S. went to war on June 19, 1812, because on that date President James Madison issued a proclamation announcing that a state of war existed. But war was actually declared when the president signed the war bill into law on June 18.[75] This act, not the announcement made the following day, marked the beginning of the War of 1812. In fact, Madison's proclamation expressly stated that Congress "have declared by their act, bearing [the] date [of] the 18th day of the present month, that war exists between the united Kingdom of Great Britain and Ireland, and the dependencies thereof, and the United States of America and their territories."[76]

*How Close Was the Vote for War?* Compared to other war votes in American history, the vote on the declaration of war in 1812 was very close. In the House of Representatives, the vote was 79–49; in the Senate, 19–13.[77] Only 61 percent of the members voting supported war. Although the nation has had closer votes in recent years on resolutions authorizing the president to use force, this is the closest vote on any formal declaration of war in American history.

*Was the War Vote Sectional?* The vote on the declaration of war is usually treated as a sectional vote, that is, a vote that divided members of Congress along regional lines, but this misses a more fundamental division. It is true that 80 percent of House and Senate members from Pennsylvania, the South, and the West voted for war, while 67 percent of those from New York, New Jersey, and New England voted against it. But the sectional vote was actually a reflection of party sentiment. Republicans, who generally favored war, were dominant in Pennsylvania, the South, and the West, while Federalists, who opposed war, were strongest in the North and East. The vote on the declaration of war was first and foremost a party vote: 81 percent of Republicans (98 out of 121) voted for it, while 100 percent of Federalists (39 out of 39) voted against it. To put this another way, on what was undoubtedly the most controversial issue of the day, almost 86 percent of the members of both houses of Congress voted with their party.[78]

*Was the War Vote Political?* While the United States went to war mainly to force the British to give up the Orders-in-Council and impressment, what is rarely acknowledged is that Republican leaders were also driven by political considerations. A declaration of war, they believed, would enable them to preserve power, unify their party, and silence the Federalists. Republicans identified the interests of their party with those of the country and thus made no attempt to conceal their political motivation.[79] Although this hardly seems a noble reason for going to war, historians have given Republican leaders a pass on this issue. Indeed, the very historian who uncovered this dimension of Republican thinking concluded that the party had "no other option" but to go to war.[80]

*Was the U.S. Bluffing?* Most scholars ignore an important dimension of the declaration of war: that it was a kind of bluff. Many Republican leaders believed that the British did not take American protests or the threat of war seriously and that the mere decision for war might bring them to their senses.

The threat of war, in other words, might win concessions so that no actual fighting would be necessary.

This explains why both President James Madison and Secretary of State James Monroe carefully laid out American terms for peace to the departing British minister, Augustus J. Foster, shortly after war was declared. It also explains why Madison sent out peace feelers after Foster left. "The sword was scarcely out of the scabbard," Madison said, "before the enemy was apprized of the reasonable terms on which it would be resheathed."[81] This puzzled the British, for the practice in Europe was to defeat an enemy on the battlefield before discussing terms. By offering terms first, the United States appeared to be bypassing the most crucial part of the whole war-making process: actually forcing the enemy to submit.[82]

**When Did the British Declare War?** News of the American declaration of war reached London on July 30, 1812.[83] The British were reluctant to respond with war measures of their own because they were confident that news of the repeal of the Orders-in-Council would induce the United States to reverse the decision for war. The British government had already ordered the Royal Navy to ignore any American privateers that might be sent to sea, and even after learning that war had been declared, British officials still hoped for peace.[84] Although an Order-in-Council embargoed all American merchant ships in port, the Treasury ordered those with licenses cleared for sailing.[85] In the end, most Americans ships were permitted to sail, and the vast majority arrived safely in the United States loaded with British goods.

British hopes for peace were soon dashed. The Madison administration was unwilling to call off the war unless Great Britain promised to give up impressment, which the British refused to do. By October it was clear that no common ground could be found. Hence, on October 13 the British government issued an Order-in-Council authorizing "general reprisals . . . against the ships, goods, and citizens of the United States."[86]

Some scholars have said that Great Britain issued its own declaration of war against the United States on January 9, 1813. This is untrue. What the British government promulgated on that date was a declaration defending its position on the issues that had caused the war and arguing that throughout this period it had treated the United States "with a spirit of amity, forbearance, and conciliation."[87] No further action was necessary anyway because the

Order-in-Council issued the previous October authorizing reprisals was tantamount to a declaration of war. As the British *Naval Chronicle* put it, "Ever since the 18th of June have the United States of America been at war against England. But it is only since the 13th of October that we have been placed in a corresponding attitude towards that commonwealth."[88]

**Would an Atlantic Cable Have Averted War?** Because the British announced the repeal of the Orders-in-Council about the same time that the United States declared war, it is sometimes said that an Atlantic cable would have averted war. This is probably true. To understand why, one must look at two factors: the relative importance of the issues and the timing of the British announcement.

In his war message sent to Congress on June 1, 1812, President Madison mentioned impressment and violations of American waters followed by the Orders-in-Council.[89] The two issues he listed first were not the most important but rather those that had been around the longest, posed the most unambiguous threat to American sovereignty, and were likely to elicit the most patriotic response from the American people. But neither issue had ever generated much talk of war. In fact, the violation of American waters was a second-tier issue that did not rank with the Orders-in-Council and impressment.

Even impressment, although causing the loss of the Monroe-Pinkney Treaty in 1806 and precipitating the *Chesapeake* affair in 1807, had never been seen as a cause for war. It was elevated to this status only in 1812. As the diplomatic correspondence and the debates in Congress make clear, the Orders-in-Council loomed much larger. The House report that was issued in response to the president's war message put the issues in their proper order, giving precedence to the British assault on American trade by the Orders-in-Council and related measures and devoting more space to this issue than to all others combined.[90]

Lord Castlereagh, the British foreign secretary, announced on June 16, 1812, that the Orders would be suspended if the United States suspended the non-importation act of 1811.[91] This posed no problem because the American trade restriction had been adopted specifically to force the British to give up the Orders. The war bill had been introduced in the House on June 3, and the House had passed it in a remarkable two days. The Federalists had remained silent because the Republicans were unwilling to permit a public debate. Instead, the House met in secret session.[92]

In the Senate, however, the bill ran into considerably more trouble. On June 11 the Senate voted to amend the war bill so that it merely authorized the navy and privateers to launch reprisals at sea against British ships. The following day, however, the Senate reversed itself when the president pro tem voted against the amendment, producing a tie vote that killed the proposal and thus restored the original bill. On the 16th, the day that Castlereagh made his announcement, the Senate beat back a proposal to postpone the bill for six days by an uncomfortably close margin of 17–15. The Senate did not approve of final passage until June 17, and before taking this vote Republicans had to defeat a new amendment that would have limited the reprisals to the high seas and included France as well as Britain. The vote against this amendment was 18–14.[93]

If the news of Castlereagh's announcement had arrived by June 17, the bill almost surely would have been killed or postponed by the Senate. It is likely that this would have happened regardless of the administration's wishes, although the administration probably would have supported postponement. President Madison later said that the declaration of war "would have been stayed" if he had known about the repeal of the Orders, and several other Republican leaders agreed.[94]

However, any debate over whether an Atlantic cable would have averted war is misguided. The first transatlantic cable was not in place until 1858, and it quickly broke down. A serviceable cable was not available until 1866. Although these cables ran from Newfoundland to Ireland, there were already connecting lines in place that linked Newfoundland to Washington and Ireland to London. Hence it was possible, briefly in 1858 or at any time after 1866, to send messages from London to Washington.[95] But these developments took place a half century after the War of 1812. The Atlantic cable question is interesting today mainly because it forces us to evaluate the relative importance of the issues that caused the war. One can often find later developments that might have prevented a war, but any discussion of such matters is strictly academic because it forces one to posit the existence of things before their time.

**Could War Have Been Averted without an Atlantic Cable?** For those interested in statesmanship, a more pertinent question to ask is whether Great Britain and the United States could have averted war in 1812 without doing anything fundamentally different, that is, without modifying their basic policies. The answer to this question is "yes." While the United States was reluctantly moving toward war, the British were actually moving in the opposite direction, hoping through a series of concessions to avoid hostilities. If the British had coordinated and publicized these concessions better, and if the United States had read British cues correctly, then war probably could have been avoided.

The first step the British took was settling the *Chesapeake* affair in late 1811. Although this issue had festered so long that the settlement was received with little grace in the United States, at least the issue was now off the table. In the spring of 1812, the British navy ordered its officers to avoid clashes with American ships and to treat American citizens with care. The Admiralty also ordered its ships to steer clear of the American coast. The British government followed up in May by offering the United States a share of the lucrative license trade.

Thus, even before the repeal of the Orders-in-Council, the British government was seeking to conciliate the United States, although these efforts were badly coordinated and poorly publicized and thus had no impact on American policy. The United States, for its part, was represented in London by Jonathan Russell, a *chargé d'affaires* who was blind to the changing direction of British policy. What was needed in London was a more astute diplomat, such as Rufus King or William Pinkney or perhaps James Monroe, who could better read the British signals. The United States also needed to realize that the British offer on the license trade was a major concession that not only opened the door to lucrative commercial opportunities but also might presage the collapse of the entire system for regulating trade by the Orders-in-Council. In sum, war could have been averted if the British had better publicized their attempts at conciliation and if the United States had paid closer attention to the nuances of British policy.[96]

**Was the War of 1812 a Second War of Independence?** At the time many Americans justified and explained the War of 1812 by appealing to the imagery and ideology of the American Revolution. Then, as now, the conflict was portrayed as a second war of independence. As John C. Calhoun put it on the eve of the war: "If we submit to the pretensions of England, now openly avowed, the independence of this nation is lost. . . . This is the second struggle for our liberty."[97]

This was an exaggeration. At no time in this period did the British actually threaten American independence. Throughout the French Revolutionary and

Napoleonic Wars, Britain's perspective was preeminently European. Whatever policies Great Britain adopted before 1812 were designed not to subvert American independence but to win the war in Europe, and however much these policies encroached upon American rights, that effect was incidental to their main purpose. Once the war in Europe was over, those policies would end.

By the same token, after the War of 1812 began, Britain was cautious, and its goals always remained largely defensive. Even when the British took the offensive in 1814, they were still thinking in defensive terms. They invaded the United States and demanded territorial concessions not because they sought to recolonize or permanently cripple the United States but because they wanted to secure Canada and its Indian allies against future aggression. For the United States, American independence in this war was never on the line in any real sense.

For people in British North America, by contrast, a lot more was at stake. Although Canada was not yet an independent nation but rather a collection of colonies, its very survival as a political entity was nonetheless at risk. After all, Canadians were resisting American aggression, and if they lost, Canada might be absorbed by the United States and overrun by land-hungry American settlers. If this happened, Canada would never develop a distinctive identity nor become an independent nation. Instead, it would simply be part of a larger American union.

For the Indian nations engaged, even more was at stake. For those living in the United States, this war was part of a larger struggle to maintain their lands and their way of life. For those living in Canada, the stakes were much the same. Defeat in this war could cost any Indian tribe not simply its independence but ultimately its lands and perhaps its identity as well.

In sum, the War of 1812 might be called a war of independence, or perhaps more accurately, a war of survival. But those with the most to lose were not Americans, but rather Canadians and Indians.

CHAPTER 2

# Battles and
# Campaigns

T he War of 1812 was a limited war with the United States and Great
Britain each using limited means to achieve limited objectives. The
aims of each nation, however, were very different, and so, too, were
their plans for achieving those aims.

In time of war, nations need a coherent plan to achieve victory. War plans
are based on strategy, which (unlike battlefield tactics) focuses on the big picture. Each belligerent must figure out how best to deploy its resources to win
the war. Modern war plans are often the product of years of staff work. Such
was the case with the famous Schlieffen Plan developed by Germany prior to
World War I. Before the late nineteenth century, however, staff planning was
in its infancy, and thus war plans were often developed on the fly, either right
before or even after hostilities had erupted.

Tension between Great Britain and the United States often ran high in this
period, and there had been at least two actual war scares (over British ship
seizures in 1794 and the *Chesapeake* affair in 1807). Hence, the British over the
years had put considerable thought into how best to defend Canada. They
planned to rely on militia, quasi-regular local units, and Indian allies backed
by a small garrison of regulars. The defense of Quebec would be their top
priority, and, if necessary, they might abandon Upper Canada altogether. The
Royal Navy would help by ferrying troops and supplies across the Atlantic

and by defending Quebec and the lower St. Lawrence River. The navy would also destroy American trade and fishing and raid American cities on the Atlantic seaboard.[1]

The United States, by contrast, had given little thought to how best to prosecute war against Great Britain. It was nonetheless clear that if America were to prevail in 1812 it needed to pursue an offensive strategy. After all, the United States had declared war on Great Britain to force an end to certain maritime practices. The young republic could not therefore fight a defensive war as it had in the American Revolution. To force the British to change their policies, the U.S. needed to find some way to apply pressure.

The easiest way appeared to be by targeting Canada. Great Britain's North American colonies were thinly populated and lightly defended, and if the United States could seize Canada, it would have a bargaining chip that might be used to force the British to modify their maritime practices. This strategy, however, was not carefully thought out. Conquering Canada proved far more difficult than almost anyone in the United States imagined, and even if the campaign had succeeded, there was no guarantee that the British would make the concessions demanded. This would leave the U.S. with little choice but to annex Canada, something that many Americans, especially in the West, favored anyway.

But if the United States conquered and annexed Canada, what was to stop the British from using their considerable military and naval might to try to retake it? As late as December of 1814, James Monroe, the acting secretary of war, was convinced that if the British lost Canada, they would never be able to recover it. "The reconquest of Canada will become, in the opinion of all enlightened men, and of the whole British nation, a chimerical attempt. It will, therefore, be abandoned."[2] This claim appears to have rested more on wishful thinking than on any solid evidence or reasonable assumption.

By the time that Monroe made his comment, the war in Europe was over, and the British had a sizeable force at their disposal. Hence, even though the British public might be war-weary, it is hard to believe that the British nation would have docilely accepted its second defeat at the hands of the United States in little more than 30 years. It seems more likely that the British would have either made some attempt to retake Canada or launched major campaigns against the Atlantic or Gulf coasts to force the United States to disgorge Canada as a price for peace. All of this suggests that even a successful campaign against Canada might not have won the war for the U.S.

If American officials had any doubts about conquering and holding Canada, they did not voice them. In accordance with their plan, the United States invaded Canada in 1812 and in 1813 but without success. By the time the campaigning season opened in 1814, the war in Europe had ended, which freed so many British military and naval assets that the initiative in the American war would soon shift dramatically. Hoping to exploit their numerical advantage before they lost it, American officials launched a major offensive in 1814 on the Niagara front. Although this was repulsed, U.S. leaders still did not give up. Monroe planned a fresh invasion of Canada in 1815 with a new army raised by conscription. With this force, he insisted, "We can break the power of the enemy on this continent," and "once broken down, it will never rise again."[3]

The end of the War of 1812 forestalled this campaign, although in truth Monroe's plan was wildly optimistic if not delusional. Congress refused to authorize conscription, and it seems highly unlikely that any army that the U.S. put in the field in 1815 would have been able to overcome the military might that the British could then have brought to bear. Even if the flow of British men and material to North America was temporarily halted by the return of Napoleon for his Hundred Days, it still seems unlikely that the U.S. would have made much progress in its bid to conquer Canada.

If American strategy remained hopefully offensive throughout the war, British strategy was consistently defensive. In the first two years of the contest, the British sought to hold on to Canada by defeating the invading armies at the border. The operations conducted outside of Canada—the blockade of the American coast, the predatory raids in the Chesapeake, and even the assault on American trade on the high seas—were all designed to put pressure on the United States and to compel it to divert resources from the war against Canada.

Even in 1814–15, British strategy remained essentially defensive. The offensive campaigns undertaken in northern New York and on the Gulf Coast, the occupation of eastern Maine, the stepped-up raids on the Atlantic coast, and the tightening of the naval blockade were all designed to take the pressure off Canada and to win bargaining chips that could be used in the peace negotiations to win greater security for Canada and its Indian allies. The aim of these operations, in other words, was not to crush or conquer the United States, nor even to alter fundamentally the balance of power in North America, but simply to secure a favorable enough peace settlement to guard against future aggression from the south.[4]

One might criticize both sides in this war for being overly optimistic. Americans did not realize how difficult conquering Canada would be, and when they had their best chance in 1812–13, they were wholly unprepared and failed miserably. The British, for their part, underestimated how much force it would take to impose their will on the United States in 1814–15, and thus they, too, failed. Both sides, in other words, underestimated the military power that was needed to achieve their goals. This is not uncommon in war.

Compared to other conflicts in this period, the War of 1812 was something of an anomaly. A second-rate power that was significantly outclassed militarily was seeking to impose its will on a great power by seizing its territory in a remote part of the globe. With its attention firmly riveted on Europe, Great Britain at first merely sought to defend its territory. Even later, when the initiative in war shifted, the British sought little more than greater security for the future. In the end, they had to settle for a good deal less—a return to the *status quo ante bellum*—not because of a proven inability to secure their aims, but because of a general war weariness brought on by more than two decades of conflict in Europe.

Battles often take on a life—and a mythology—of their own, and those in the War of 1812 are no exception. Each side in this war could take pride in not having surrendered any territory in the peace negotiations, and each could point to certain battles that saved the day. As a result, some battles have become freighted with exaggerated claims of their importance or with other myths that distort their essential character. Even some of the lesser battles in the war have suffered this fate.

## THE CAMPAIGN OF 1812

**What Was the First Land Action?** The first military action on land took place on June 26, 1812, a mere eight days after the declaration of war, when American civilians seized Carleton Island in the St. Lawrence River just east of Lake Ontario. Although occupied by the British before the war, this island was actually part of the United States. The operation was launched by an innkeeper from Millins Bay, New York, named Abner Hubbard. Learning of the declaration of war, Hubbard led three other Americans in a small boat to the island, where they surprised a sergeant and three invalid soldiers. The small irregular American party took possession of the island, and the soldiers they captured became the conflict's first prisoners of war.[5]

**What Was the First Land Battle?** The first campaigning in the War of 1812 took place in the West. The climax of this campaign was Brigadier General William Hull's surrender of Detroit on August 16, after a one-day artillery duel. Prior to this, British forces had seized Hull's unarmed schooner *Cuyahoga* in the Detroit River on July 2, and American forces had bombarded Sandwich (present-day Windsor, Ontario) on July 5 and 8 and fought a series of small engagements in Canada near the Canard River between July 16 and 25. Hull's

attempt to keep his supply lines open to Ohio led to two additional engagements: the Battle of Brownstown on August 5 (near present-day Gibraltar, Michigan) and the Battle of Maguaga on August 9 (near present-day Trenton, Michigan). The Fort Dearborn Massacre (in present-day Chicago) took place on August 15—the day before Hull's surrender.[6]

Since the *Cuyahoga* was taken without resistance and the artillery fire on Sandwich was not returned, the skirmishes at the Canard River were the first engagements on land in the War of 1812. In the first of these, on July 16, a force of Ohio militia under Colonel Lewis Cass surprised John Dean and James Hancock, two British sentries who reportedly fell asleep after a drunken binge and missed an order to retreat from the north side of the river. The two British soldiers unwisely opened fire. As a result of return fire, Hancock was killed and Dean captured. This skirmish was a decidedly small affair, but it was the first military engagement on land, and it produced the first battle casualty and probably the first scalping as well.[7]

**Who Took the First Scalp?** Who took the first scalp in the War of 1812 is a matter of some dispute. Robert Lucas, who served as a private in an Ohio unit of volunteer militia, claimed that on July 16, in the first skirmish at the Canard River, an Indian allied to the British scalped redheaded James Hancock, the British private who had been mortally wounded, and then tried to sell the scalp to British officials. It was "a good trick," concluded Lucas, "for an indian to make the British Gov. pay for their own Soldiers Scalps."[8]

On the other hand, William Hamilton Merritt, a Canadian militia officer, claimed that on July 25, in another skirmish at the Canard River, Captain William McCulloch of the U.S. Army scalped an Indian and "showed it in camp as a matter of exultation." According to Merritt, the Indians allied to the British in the Old Northwest had promised earlier not to take any scalps, but when they learned what McCulloch had done, they called a grand council, denounced McCulloch, and renounced their promise.[9]

Indians and whites alike in the American West took scalps as war trophies. (Lossing, *Pictorial Field-Book of the War of 1812*)

Robert Reynolds, in charge of the British

commissary at Fort Amherstburg, presented a third version of the first scalping. He confirmed the stories told by Lucas and Merritt but reversed their order. He claimed that McCulloch took an Indian scalp on an early reconnaissance expedition shortly after the Americans crossed the river and occupied Sandwich on July 12. Furious over this incident, the Indians allied to the British renounced the promise they had made to Major General Isaac Brock to give up scalping. A day or two later, the Americans returned to the Canard River and killed Hancock. Chancing on the body was Main Poc ("Crippled Hand"), a crude but influential Potawatomi wabeno or sorcerer who had a reputation for powerful medicine and drunken rages. Main Poc scalped the body and took his trophy to Fort Amherstburg. There several of Hancock's comrades recognized the red hair and "gave him [Main Poc] a good thrashing for his pains."[10]

Where does the truth lie? It appears that both scalpings took place. Reynolds's chronology is evidently incorrect because American forces reported no engagements prior to July 16. If Reynolds's chronology is corrected, then all three stories can be reconciled. It thus appears that the first scalp was taken on July 16 by the British Indian ally Main Poc, although he took it from a British soldier. There is no evidence from British sources that he tried to sell the scalp. Since the British discouraged scalping, it is not likely that Main Poc would have offered the scalp for sale. He probably just exhibited it as a trophy of war. The first scalp on the American side was taken by Captain William McCulloch on July 25. McCulloch, who was described by a contemporary as "brave, intrepid and skil[l]ful in the department of spies," was himself killed and scalped by Indians in the Battle of Brownstown on August 5, 1812.[11]

Before the war was over, a great many scalps were taken on both sides. Although most were taken from dead people, in a some cases the victims were still alive. The British sought to discourage scalping altogether, and in the East it had died out. In the West, however, Americans and Indians alike continued to take scalps as war trophies whenever they could.

**Why Did General Hull Surrender Detroit?** The first major campaign of the war ended in disaster for the United States when Brigadier General William Hull surrendered Detroit to an Anglo-Indian force on August 16, 1812. Hull had laboriously cut a road through Ohio to get his army to Detroit. But the British and their Indian allies captured his baggage (including his papers) and threatened his supply lines. When Hull learned that the American out-

Brigadier General William Hull (1753–1825) surrendered his entire army at Detroit in 1812, thus ending the American threat in this theater for the year. (Lossing, *Pictorial Field-Book of the War of 1812*)

post at Mackinac had fallen, he was convinced that he would soon be overrun by "the Northern hive of Indians."[12] Instead of pressing ahead while he still held a military advantage, Hull became defensive and took refuge in Fort Detroit. When Major General Isaac Brock shrewdly played the "Indian card," warning that he would not be able to control his native allies once the assault had begun, Hull surrendered Detroit as well as the American troops in the nearby wilderness.

The British were surprised at how little shame or remorse Hull showed over his surrender. Instead, he was so "loud in his complaints against the government at Washington" that he was paroled so that he might air his views publicly at home.[13] Hull, whose supply lines were threatened by Indians, initially claimed that he surrendered because he lacked powder and provisions and was overmatched by Brock's larger army, but none of this is true. The British found 5,000 pounds of powder in the fort as well as huge quantities of other war material, and contemporary reports indicated 15–25 days of provisions on hand. In addition, Hull's army was roughly the same size as Brock's.[14]

After Hull returned to the United States on parole, he was court-martialed. He now claimed in his defense that Major General Henry Dearborn had not made an adequate demonstration farther east to relieve the pressure on him. The court (which was presided over by Dearborn) was unimpressed by this argument and convicted Hull of cowardice and neglect of duty. The court sentenced Hull to be shot, although it recommended that the sentence be commuted because of Hull's Revolutionary War service. President Madison complied with this request.

Hull and his descendants, as well as some historians, have repeated his claim that he was abandoned to the fates when Dearborn did not campaign more vigorously in the east. This argument is without merit. Dearborn's main area of responsibility in northern New York was simply too distant to affect operations on the Detroit River. Even Dearborn's decision to sign an armistice had no impact on Hull's campaign. The armistice went into effect on August 9, just a week before Hull's surrender, which did not leave either side enough time to send troops farther west. American operations on the Niagara front could have affected the outcome at Detroit by forcing the British to concentrate their resources farther east, but Dearborn had only nominal control over this front, and it is unlikely that the United States could have mounted a diversion here in a timely enough fashion to affect operations at the other end of Lake Erie. Hull, who had earlier suffered a stroke and lost his taste for battle, was responsible for his own fate. His campaign failed mainly because of a lack of nerve.[15]

**The First Major Battle: Queenston Heights.** On October 13, 1812, the United States invaded Canada across the Niagara River. The objective was modest: the establishment of a lodgement on the Canadian side of the river, essentially as a diversion in favor of what was supposed to be the main attack on Montreal. An assault force of U.S. regulars and New York militia that ultimately was commanded by Winfield Scott secured a position on Queenston Heights and waited for additional militia to cross the river to reinforce them. But the militiamen stayed put, citing their constitutional right to refuse to serve on foreign soil. As a result, a combined force of British regulars, Canadian militia, and Indians overwhelmed the American army and compelled it to surrender. Although Major General Isaac Brock was killed in a hastily-organized counterattack, the British victory at Queenston Heights was decisive in this theater, for it effectively ended American operations on the Niagara front in 1812.[16]

Queenston Heights is sometimes portrayed as the first battle of the war, but by this time there had already been significant campaigning in the West. In addition, it was not even the first battle on the Niagara frontier since four days before a fierce musket and artillery duel had erupted on the Niagara River when an American force surprised the British and seized P.M. Brig *Detroit* (6) and P.M. Brig *Caledonia* (3).[17] The Battle of Queenston Heights is better remembered as the first major land battle of the war in which there were significant casualties on both sides, and as the decisive battle on the Niagara front in 1812.

***Why Did American Militia Refuse to Fight?*** Although the New York militia claimed that they could not be forced to serve on foreign soil, this claim should be taken with a grain of salt. In the spring of 1812, Congress had publicly debated whether militia could serve beyond American borders, and no

American troops were able to cross the Niagara River and scale the formidable bluffs at Queenston Heights but could not overcome the refusal of New York militia to reinforce them. The result was a decisive Anglo-Indian victory in the first major battle of the war. (Lossing, *Pictorial Field-Book of the War of 1812*)

doubt some New York militia learned their rights from this debate, which was widely reported in the press. However, these men were mostly Republicans who probably knew what was expected of them when they were marched north in the summer of 1812.

It seems more likely that these "sunshine patriots" were unnerved by the sound of gunfire and the war cries that came from across the river, and by the sight of the dead and wounded who were ferried back into American territory. "The commencement of [this] battle," said an observer, "and a considerable number of dead and mangled bodies which were brought to our shore in the return boats, caused a depression of mind on this side which could not be effaced. . . . None [of the militia] could be got to cross, and many were constantly deserting."[18] The sight of additional British regulars marching up from Fort George to reinforce their comrades at Queenston only served to increase the determination of American militia to stay put.

Had the American attack met with little resistance, most of the militia probably would have crossed the river. A failure of nerve, not constitutional scruples, probably best explains why so many citizen soldiers chose to sit out this battle.[19]

***Did Brock Have a Fiancée?*** Legend has it that Brock said goodbye to his fiancée, Sophie Shaw, on the way to meet his destiny at Queenston Heights. Although he once had an interest in a woman in Britain, there is no evidence that he was ever engaged to be married or that he had any romantic ties in Canada.[20]

***The Legend of Brock's Horse.*** The iconography of Queenston Heights often depicts Brock on a horse named Alfred. There is even a small bronze statue of Alfred encased in a glass box at Queenston. The inscription says that Brock and later his aide, Lieutenant Colonel John Macdonell, rode this horse into battle at Queenston Heights and that Alfred (along with both riders) was killed that day. The horse's role in the battle has even been commemorated in a pamphlet.[21]

Although Brock rode a horse from Fort George to Queenston Heights, the notion that it was Alfred did not appear in print until 1859. There is no contemporary evidence that Brock rode Alfred to the battle or that he even owned a horse by that name. When Governor-General Sir James Craig departed from Quebec for Britain in June 1811, he left Brock a horse named Alfred, but it is unknown if the horse was ever shipped to Brock. Brock never mentioned the horse in any of his correspondence, nor did anyone else who was close to him. The entire story of Alfred's role in the battle is probably a later concoction based on Craig's legacy.[22]

***What Were Brock's Last Words?*** Two contemporary accounts published in Canadian newspapers just after the Battle of Queenston Heights reported that as he lay dying Brock had said, "Push on the York Volunteers" or "Push on, brave York Volunteers."[23] Many years later another contemporary remembered him saying, "*Push on my boys!*"[24] Although he may have uttered words like these earlier in the battle, it is unlikely that he spoke them after he was shot. Captain John B. Glegg, Brock's aide-de-camp, told Brock's brother two days after the battle that his final words were: "My fall must not be noticed or impede my brave companions from advancing to victory."[25] This sounds like something that Glegg invented to ennoble Brock's death.

The account of George S. Jarvis, a 15-year-old volunteer with the 49th Regiment of Foot, rings truer. He was near Brock when he was hit and was probably the first person to reach him. When he asked Brock if he was badly hurt, the latter "placed his hand on his breast and made no reply, and slowly sunk down."[26] Because Brock had sustained a chest wound that quickly filled his lungs with blood, he died almost immediately and probably did not say anything.[27]

***Who Killed Brock?*** Several Americans claimed credit for firing the fatal shot that killed Brock. The only credible claim was made by Robert Walcot, who told his story to a Philadelphia newspaper in 1880. Walcot said he saw Brock leading his men in a counterattack at Queenston. Being a good marksman, he borrowed a musket from an infantryman and rammed home a second ball on top of the first already in the barrel. He then took aim at Brock, fired, and watched the British general fall.[28] Walcot's account includes many details that add to its verisimilitude, and his testimony closely matches the report of George Jarvis, who watched Brock go down. Walcot's account is also consistent with the location of the entrance and exit holes made by the bullet in the coat worn by Brock that day.

Nevertheless, there are several problems with Walcot's story. The veteran was in poor health and close to 100 years old when he told this tale, and although almost 70 years had elapsed since the incident, he had never before mentioned the subject, at least publicly. Moreover, even though Walcot remembered serving extensively in the war (evidently in the militia as well as the regular army), there is no record of his service. Although it is possible that Walcot killed Brock, the evidence is inconclusive. This is not surprising. In the fog of war, it is often difficult to pin down responsibility for any given death.[29]

A contemporary account of the American assault on Fort George in 1813 sheds light on Walcot's claim. When an American sharpshooter was asked by an officer if he had hit every man he aimed at, he replied, "Yes Sir, all that I took aim [at] went down when I fired, but perhaps some of the other boys put them down as they were all shooting as fast as they could load." Moreover, one

Major General Isaac Brock (1769–1812) won a dramatic victory at Detroit before being killed in the Battle of Queenston Heights in 1812. Today, Canadians revere him as a great hero. (Portrait by unknown artist. Library and Archives Canada)

This picture, inaccurate in many details, depicts Major General Isaac Brock's death in the romantic manner of battlefield deaths popularized by artist Benjamin West in the eighteenth century. (Painting by John D. Kelly. Library and Archives Canada)

man he had aimed at actually fell before he had a chance to fire. "If I had shot at that instant I would have thought that I had killed him when in fact it was some other one."[30]

Such is the stress of close combat and the frailty of the human memory that postwar accounts of battlefield experiences—especially those, like Walcot's, rendered long after the fact—have to be treated with considerable skepticism.

***Where Did Brock Fall?*** In 1860 a cenotaph was erected to mark the spot where Brock was killed. The project was probably hurried so that it would be ready for dedication when the Prince of Wales arrived for a visit later that year. The cenotaph is located on level ground at the south end of the town of Queenston. At the time of his death, Brock was leading a charge to retake the redan battery on the hillside, which a detachment of American soldiers under Captain John E. Wool had captured. It seems unlikely that any of the Americans defending the battery would have been far enough down the escarpment to hit someone standing where the cenotaph is located. Moreover,

George Jarvis witnessed the fatal event, and he reported that Brock was shot, not on level ground, but as "he led the way up the mountain at double quick time."[31] Thus it is unlikely that Brock was killed where the cenotaph is located. He probably fell near marker #4 in the Parks Canada tour, which is located about 200 yards southeast of the cenotaph up the escarpment.[32]

**Brock's Well-Traveled Remains.** Despite all the mythology that has grown up around Major General Brock, one story is true: his remains are well traveled. Brock had the rare distinction of being buried four times. Although he was already well regarded in 1812, Brock's success at Detroit, combined with his heroic death at Queenston, transformed him into a genuine Canadian hero.

Initially, the deceased major general and his provincial aide-de-camp, Lieutenant Colonel John Macdonell (who was also killed at Queenston Heights), were buried in a bastion, then known as the York Battery, in the northeast corner of Fort George, some six miles north of where Brock had fallen. A participant called the funeral ceremony "the grandest and most solemn . . . that has ever been seen in Upper Canada."[33] The remains of the fallen heroes were not disturbed during the American occupation of the fort in 1813.

In 1824 a monument was built on Queenston Heights to honor Brock, and the remains of the two men were reinterred in a vault under the base of the structure. The circular memorial was 135 feet high and contained a winding staircase inside and an observation deck on top. At the time, it was the tallest memorial in North America.

In this sketch of Queenston Heights, Major General Brock's cenotaph (erroneously placed in 1860) appears in the foreground and the second monument honoring the fallen hero is in the background. (Lossing, *Pictorial Field-Book of the War of 1812*)

In 1840, an attempt was made—possibly by an Irish-born anti-British terrorist named Benjamin Lett—to blow up the monument. Most of the crown was blown off, the staircase was destroyed, and deep cracks appeared in the main structure. At a public meeting, the monument's builder, an engineer named Francis Hall, claimed that he could repair the structure for £370, but others present thought the damage was too extensive and wanted to build a new monument. The monument was left standing until 1853, when it was demolished. It took three charges of explosives to do the job, which suggests that perhaps Hall was right. Before the demolition, the remains of Brock and Macdonell were temporarily buried for a third time in a private cemetery at Willowbank, an estate in Queenston belonging to the prominent Hamilton family.

A second, more impressive monument was completed on the heights in 1853. Capped by a 16-foot statue of Brock, the structure is 185 feet tall. A staircase inside the column (now closed to the public for safety reasons) provides access to an enclosed observation deck below the statue. It was then the second tallest memorial of its kind in the world after Christopher Wren's 202-foot column commemorating the Great Fire of London in 1666.[34] The remains of Brock and Macdonell were reinterred in the base of the monument in the fall of 1853. This was their fourth and final resting place.

The Brock monument still commands the surrounding countryside. It is an impressive reminder of Brock's sacrifice in the War of 1812 and of Canadian patriotism and independence. It is also one of the most visible links that Canadians have today to the War of 1812.[35]

The second monument honoring Major General Brock was erected on Queenston Heights in the 1850s after the first was destroyed. (Lossing, *Pictorial Field-Book of the War of 1812*)

## THE CAMPAIGN OF 1813

**The American Assault on York.** On April 27, 1813, the United States launched a successful amphibious attack against York (present-day Toronto) in Upper Canada. Although the U.S. won the battle, upon departing, the British ignited their powder magazine, generating such a huge explosion that it rattled windows at Fort Niagara more than 30 miles away. Debris from the blast killed Brigadier General Zebulon Pike and a host of American soldiers. Hence in the entire battle, the United States sustained 320 casualties, while the British suffered only 157.

Enraged by the explosion and poorly disciplined anyway, American soldiers looted the town and burned the provincial parliament and several other public buildings. They were joined in the plunder by British subjects, including some released from the jail and others who came in from the countryside. The Americans seized one British schooner that proved unfit for service, while the British destroyed another warship as well as a large quantity of naval stores and equipment.[36]

*Grenadier Pond.* Legend has it that Grenadier Pond in Toronto is named for the retreating grenadiers from the 8th Regiment of Foot who drowned when they fell through the thin ice that covered the pond. This is a fable. There was no ice on the pond that April, and it was named later in the century for soldiers from Fort York who often fished there.[37]

*Canadian Militia at York.* Some popular accounts have suggested that Canadian militia played a significant role in the defense of York and that 40 militiamen were killed in the explosion, but this is untrue. The militiamen were held back by their commanding officer, and only six died in the engagement.[38]

*The Impact of the Battle.* Almost every account says that the capture of York deprived the British squadron on Lake Erie of essential equipment, but this claim needs to be qualified. Commodore Isaac Chauncey reported that a considerable quantity of weapons and ordnance "was put up in boxes and marked for Niagara and Malden," and that the British burned a store that "was filled with Cables, Cordage, Canvass, Tools and Stores of every kind for use on this Lake and Lake Erie."[39] In an oft-cited letter to the British government, Sir George Prevost appeared to confirm this when he claimed that the loss of war material and naval stores at York hampered British operations on

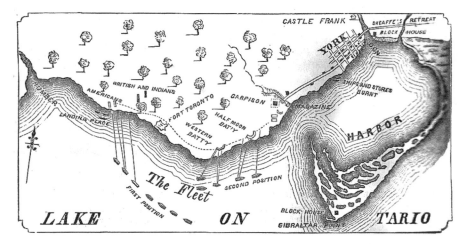

The U.S. launched a successful amphibious attack against the provincial capital of York (now Toronto) in 1813. (Lossing, *Pictorial Field-Book of the War of 1812*)

Lake Erie. "The ordnance, ammunition and other stores for service on Lake Erie," he said, "were either destroyed or fell into the enemy's hands when York was taken."[40]

Although this claim has some merit, it must be taken with a grain of salt. Not only was the York shipyard desperately short of ordnance and naval stores, but each provincial commander along the supply line in Canada was reluctant to send anything farther west that he needed, both because he wished to protect his own turf and because the sites farther east were rightly considered more important. Although senior officials had to obey orders, they had some latitude in setting priorities. Officials at Quebec were slow to send anything west that they deemed essential to the defense of their city. Similarly, officials at the shipyard in Kingston were slow to send materials to the shipyard at York, and officials at York were slow to send materials to the shipyard at Malden. Most of the ordnance headed for Malden bypassed York anyway. It therefore seems unlikely that the fall of York played a critical role in the subsequent British defeat on Lake Erie.[41]

The Battle of York had a more immediate impact on the assault on Fort George, which was the next U.S. target. Because of adverse weather, the American soldiers could not get away from York as planned. Trapped in their vessels for almost a week, they suffered from disease. This, coupled with the heavy casualties sustained at York, forced the American high command to give the men extra time to recuperate once they got to Fort Niagara. Additional troops also had to be brought in from Sackets Harbor and other locations. As a result, the assault on Fort George was delayed, although this had no perceptible effect on the success of the American campaign.[42]

**The Battle of the Thames/Moraviantown.** After the British lost the Battle of Lake Erie, Major General Henry Procter found his position on the Detroit River untenable and marched his Anglo-Indian force east toward Burlington Heights (present-day Hamilton). At the insistence of Tecumseh and his Indian allies, Procter made a stand at Moraviantown (near present-day Thamesville, Ontario). The British were spread along two thin lines north of the Thames River, while the Indians covered their right flank just south of an impassable swamp. Colonel Richard M. Johnson persuaded Major General William Henry Harrison to allow him to make a cavalry charge with his mounted Kentucky volunteer militia. Bursting through the British lines, Johnson's men dismounted and then caught the British in a cross fire. Once it became clear that the battle was lost, Procter fled east with a few members of his staff. The Indians continued their resistance until Tecumseh was killed. They then melted into the forest. In the Battle of the Thames (also known as the Battle of Moraviantown), the American victory was complete, and the United States now controlled most of the Old Northwest.[43]

*How Decisive Was the Battle?* Although the Battle of the Thames shattered Tecumseh's Indian confederacy and re-established American hegemony in the Old Northwest, it was not quite as decisive as usually portrayed. The victory did mean greater security for Americans living in the Old Northwest, mainly because the British were unwilling to divert the resources needed to contest control. But the region remained an active theater of war. Some Indians, particularly the band of Potawatomis led by Main Poc, refused to come to terms with the United States, while others who made peace refused to honor their treaty obligations. Even without much British support, Indians continued to raid American settlements in Illinois and Indiana. Nor was the United States able to dislodge the British from the critical post on Mackinac Island. The British held this fort to the end of the war, using it as a base for controlling those Indians who remained loyal to them.[44]

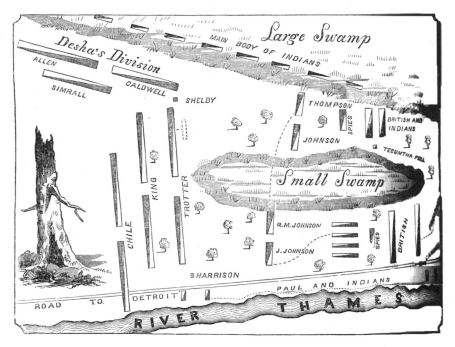

The U.S. defeated a much smaller Anglo-Indian force in the Battle of Moraviantown on the Thames River east of Detroit in 1813. The great Shawnee leader Tecumseh was killed north of the small swamp. (Lossing, *Pictorial Field-Book of the War of 1812*)

If the British had retained control over this region, they might have made a more determined bid in the peace negotiations to secure the Indian barrier state or reservation that they proposed in the Old Northwest. However, it hardly seems likely that the United States would have agreed to this proposition. Nor does it seem likely that the British would have prolonged the war to secure it. In the end, the Treaty of Ghent probably would have been the same even without the American victory at the Thames.

Like the Battle of New Orleans, the Battle of the Thames had its most profound and enduring impact in the realm of western mythology. Those who fought in the battle could lay claim to having played a central role in taming the Old West and in defeating the British there. The battle helped create a president (Harrison), a vice president (Johnson), 3 governors, 3 lieutenant-governors, 4 U.S. senators, and 20 U.S. congressmen. Countless other successful candidates for local office also traded on their service at the Thames.[45]

***Who Killed Tecumseh?*** The shot that killed Tecumseh in the Battle of the Thames has been described as "one of the most controversial shots in frontier history."[46] At the center of this controversy is Colonel Richard M. Johnson, who holds three unique distinctions: he was credited with killing Tecumseh in 1813, he was elected to the vice presidency in 1837 by the U.S. Senate (rather than the electoral college), and Abraham Lincoln described him as the only person he knew "who was in favor of producing a perfect equality, social and political, between negroes and white men."[47] Known as "Tecumseh" Johnson, the Kentucky colonel became a national hero whose role in the Battle of the Thames helped propel him into the vice-presidency.[48]

At the Thames, Johnson rode a gray horse into the right side of the Anglo-Indian line, which was anchored by Tecumseh's followers. Johnson's small detachment of men—a "forlorn hope" whose purpose was to draw enemy fire—ran into a hail of bullets. In a matter of seconds, Johnson was wounded four times and his horse was hit seven times. Both horse and rider were slumping when Tecumseh reportedly rushed at Johnson with a raised tomahawk to deliver the final blow. Johnson, however, managed to .pull his pistol from a holster and deliver a fatal chest wound to the Shawnee leader. Immediately thereafter Johnson left the field, and Tecumseh's followers melted away.

Johnson did not at first positively identify the Indian he killed as Tecumseh. Johnson's wounds had rendered him nearly insensible, and he had never seen the great Indian before. In later years, Johnson was willing to accept the credit, although he remained skeptical. "They say I killed him," he once said; "how could I tell? I was in too much of a hurry, when he was advancing upon me, to ask him his name, or inquire after the health of his family."[49]

Colonel Richard M. Johnson (1780–1850), a congressional War Hawk in 1812, took part in the American invasion of Canada in the Old Northwest the following year. Although wounded four times in the Battle of the Thames, he still managed to kill an Indian who was in all probability Tecumseh. (Portrait by John Neagle. Library of Congress)

However, a number of participants in the battle, Indians as well as whites, credited him with killing Tecumseh, and several of these knew what the Indian leader looked like. It therefore seems likely that Johnson did indeed kill Tecumseh.[50]

***What Happened to Tecumseh's Remains?*** Tecumseh was undoubtedly killed at the Thames, but what became of his body? Some contemporaries claimed that it was carried off by his native comrades and secretly buried. This is almost certainly untrue. Kentucky militia searched the ground after the battle. Although the wounds and swelling made it difficult for those who knew Tecumseh to identify his body positively, several Kentuckians were sure they had found him, and their identification was confirmed by British prisoners of war.

Eager to take home trophies of war, the Kentucky volunteers mutilated Tecumseh's body. He was scalped, his clothing was carried off, and large and small swatches of his skin were taken for razor strops or souvenirs. "I [helped] kill Tecumseh and *[helped] skin him*," recalled a veteran of the battle a half century later, "and brot Two pieces of his yellow hide home with me to my Mother and Sweet Harts."[51] In accordance with common practice, Harrison subsequently ordered the bodies on the battlefield buried in mass graves. Undoubtedly Tecumseh's remains were dumped into one of these graves.[52]

**The Lanterns at St. Michaels.** In August 1813, the British targeted St. Michaels on the Eastern Shore of Maryland. Although the town had a shipyard, the British were unaware of it, and when their operation went awry, they withdrew without destroying it. According to local lore, the inhabitants of St. Michaels put out their ground-level lights and hung lanterns from trees and second-story houses to induce the British to overshoot the mark with their artillery. This legend is untrue. The British attack was actually made after dawn (although fog did inhibit visibility). No contemporary account mentions the lantern story. It did not surface until the 1880s, and it did not gain currency until 1913, when St. Michaels was planning a centennial commemoration of the battle.[53]

**How Many Died in the Fort Mims Massacre?** On August 30, 1813, a group of Creek militants, known as Red Sticks, overwhelmed the defenders of Fort Mims 40 miles north of Mobile. Many of the defenders suffered horrible deaths, perishing in burning buildings or at the hands of their captors after the fighting was over. The Fort Mims Massacre inflamed the Old Southwest

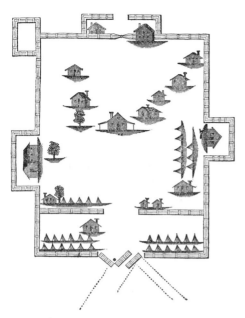

Fort Mims in modern-day Alabama was the site of a fierce battle in 1813 known as the Fort Mims Massacre. American losses, which were exaggerated at the time, inflamed opinion in the Old Southwest much as the River Raisin Massacre did in the Old Northwest. (Lossing, *Pictorial Field-Book of the War of 1812*)

against the Creek militants, and ultimately Andrew Jackson made the Red Sticks pay dearly, wiping out virtually their entire force at the Battle Horseshoe Bend in 1814.

Contemporary accounts put American losses at Fort Mims at 400 or 500, and these inflated figures still occasionally appear in history books. The actual number of Americans killed was probably less than 250, and there were even a few survivors. Moreover, it seems likely that the Indians sustained about as many casualties in the assault as the white defenders.[54]

**The Burning of Newark/Niagara.** In the fall of 1813, the United States began to withdraw troops from the Niagara frontier to support Major General James Wilkinson's campaign on the St. Lawrence River. By the end of the year, Brigadier General George McClure of the New York militia had concluded that his position was now so untenable that he decided to withdraw his dwindling force from Fort George and return to the American side of the river. Before departing, however, he ordered the burning of nearby Newark (whose official name was Niagara and has since become Niagara-on-the-Lake). Ostensibly, McClure sought to deprive the British and their Indian allies of winter lodging, although in his hasty departure he left Fort George, two barracks, and 1,600 tents standing.[55] The inhabitants of Newark were given 12 hours' notice to vacate their homes before the town was torched on December 10.[56] This heartless act was later disavowed by the U.S. government, though not before the British had burned virtually every town on the American side of the Niagara River in retaliation.[57]

How many people were driven from their homes in Newark/Niagara? Sir George Prevost claimed that the burning of "upwards of 150 houses" had "forced 400 helpless women and children to quit their dwellings."[58] However, three American officers issued a statement that few inhabitants were actually in the town when it was ordered evacuated. They also insisted that the homes of a few who refused to leave were left standing and that those who did leave were offered food and lodging on the American side of the river.[59] Prevost, who was not there, was likely to believe the worst, while the American officers, who were there, had an interest in minimizing the tragedy.

Who was right? The Americans were right in that few people were probably actually in the town when the order was given, and a few houses probably were spared. But Prevost was also right in suggesting that this ill-advised act deprived some 400 people of their homes and much of their personal property.

## THE CAMPAIGN OF 1814

**How Innovative Were General Scott's Training Methods?** In the summer of 1814, Brigadier General Winfield Scott took part in heavy campaigning on the Niagara frontier. His brigade spearheaded the American victory at Chippawa, took part in the bloody standoff at Lundy's Lane, and then participated in the successful defense of Fort Erie. In his memoirs, written almost a half century later, Scott attributed his success to the training methods that he had employed at his camp near Buffalo in the spring of 1814. However, many of the details that he provided were inaccurate.

Contrary to his later claim, Scott did not have to create his own rules for camp life or rely on a French drill manual (although he carried one with

Major General Winfield Scott (1786–1866), who represented a new breed of American professional army officer, took part in the campaigns on the Niagara front until knocked out of action in the Battle of Lundy's Lane in 1814. (Portrait by unknown artist. National Portrait Gallery, Smithsonian Institution)

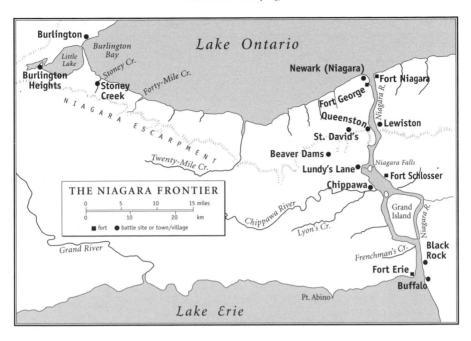

him). Instead, he used standard U.S. government publications that were based on the French manual. While he apparently did form his officers into squads so that they could learn the new drills and then teach them to the men, this was far from innovative but rather a common practice in the British army and some armies on the Continent. Moreover, he trained only about half of the men in the Left Division, and he trained them for slightly less than ten weeks rather than three months. In short, while Scott did a fine job of training his men and this training played a crucial role in the ensuing campaign, his accomplishment was hardly the innovative tour de force that he suggested in his memoirs.[60]

**The Battle of Chippawa.** The United States Army won a major victory in the Battle of Chippawa on July 5, 1814, when Major General Jacob Brown's army carried the day against a British force of about equal size under Major General Phineas Riall. While Indians and militia fought in the forest on his left flank, Scott's well-trained brigade deployed in a line and took on Riall's left flank, maintaining its formation despite heavy artillery fire. A fierce exchange of musket fire followed, and when his left sagged, Riall ordered a withdrawal. The result was a clear American victory against a veteran British army. This was the first time in the war that an American force defeated a veteran British force of equal size on an open field.[61]

In the final phase of fighting in the Battle of Lundy's Lane, an American force captured an important battery of British field guns. (Engraving by William Strickland. *Portfolio*)

**What Inspired Cadet Gray?** Scott later claimed in his memoirs that because his troops were dressed in gray uniforms (rather than the standard American blue) Riall thought be was facing militia from Buffalo. According to Scott, when the Americans did not break under the British artillery barrage, Riall exclaimed, *"Why, these are regulars!"*[62] One of Scott's twentieth century biographers modified Riall's words to read: "Those are regulars, by God!"[63] This is the version that is found in most accounts of the battle as well as in American military lore. Although the story may be true, there is no contemporary evidence to support it. Scott recorded the episode a half century after the battle, and while it is conceivable that he got the story from a British officer that he met after the war, it seems more likely that he invented the entire tale or at least embellished what he had heard.[64]

Scott claimed in his memoirs that in recognition of the American victory at Chippawa the U.S. Military Academy at West Point adopted gray uniforms. He repeated this claim in an interview with Benson J. Lossing several years later.[65] This is not quite true. The cadets at West Point had already been wearing gray coats in 1814 because of a shortage of blue cloth. After the war, the Military Academy officially changed its uniform color to gray on the grounds of economy and appearance. Only later did the Academy embrace the notion that the color honors the American army for its performance on the Niagara frontier in 1814.[66]

**Who Won the Battle of Lundy's Lane?** Major General Jacob Brown followed up his victory at Chippawa three weeks later by engaging Lieutenant General Gordon Drummond's British force a little farther north at Lundy's Lane. This five-hour slugfest, conducted within earshot of the mighty Niagara Falls, was the bloodiest battle of the war. Both sides claimed victory, the Americans because they had overrun a powerful battery in the center of the British line, and the British because they were left in command of the field when the Americans withdrew.

Tactically, the battle was a draw. Neither side had been defeated, and the losses were about equal. The Americans reported 860 killed, wounded, or missing; the British reported 878, although some of their missing later turned up. Strategically, Lundy's Lane was a clear victory for the British because they had blunted the offensive and compelled the Americans to withdraw into Fort Erie. The United States, on the other hand, had lost the initiative in this theater. Although there was additional fighting at Fort Erie, the Americans withdrew from Canada when the campaigning season was over.[67]

**The British Assault on Fort Erie.** After the battles of Chippawa and Lundy's Lane in the summer of 1814, American troops on the Niagara front withdrew to Fort Erie. On August 15 Lieutenant General Gordon Drummond launched a four-pronged night assault on the fort, but the attack ended in disaster. An Indian demonstration on the west side of the fort failed to materialize. At the southern end of the fort, British soldiers under Lieutenant Colonel Victor Fischer were ordered to remove their flints to ensure that they did not lose the element of surprise by firing their muskets prematurely, but their scaling ladders were too short. Hence they could neither get over the fort's wall nor respond to American fire with musket fire of their own. After sustaining heavy losses, they retreated in confusion. At the northern end of the fort, one British assault force under Colonel Hercules Scott was defeated, while a

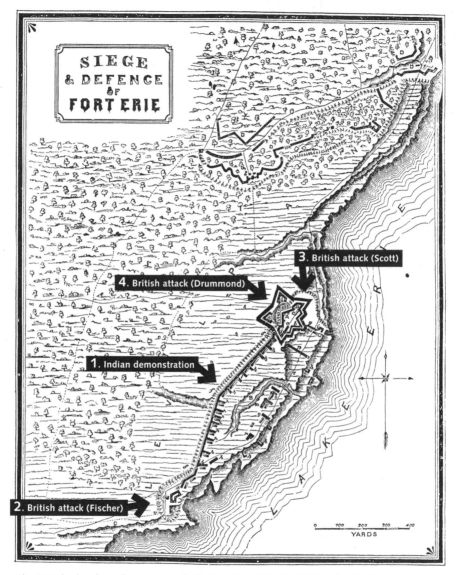

The British plan for a four-pronged attack on Fort Erie in 1814 ended in disaster when a magazine exploded at the fourth point of the attack. (Adapted from Lossing, *Pictorial Field-Book of the War of 1812*)

second under Lieutenant Colonel William Drummond managed to penetrate a bastion that anchored the American position, but then a huge explosion blew Drummond's force to bits. This effectively ended the battle. The British had sustained 905 killed, wounded, and missing (compared to only 130 for the Americans) and had nothing to show for their casualties.[68]

***What Caused the Deadly Explosion?*** At the time British soldiers claimed that the explosion in the bastion of Fort Erie was caused by a mine that had been placed there in advance or that a magazine had been intentionally detonated by an American soldier, an American in a British uniform, or a British deserter. But there is no evidence that a mine was planted or that anyone purposely touched off the explosion. Rather, the explosion was probably an accident, most likely caused when a magazine was detonated by the intense firefight that was taking place around it.

***Did Colonel Drummond Refuse Quarter?*** Brigadier General Edmund P. Gaines, who was in charge of the defense of Fort Erie, claimed in his official report that Lieutenant Colonel William Drummond had repeatedly said, "Give the damn Yankees no quarter." Second Lieutenant John Watmough also thought he heard repeated cries of "no quarter, no quarter."[69] Although some have denied that Drummond uttered these words, the evidence seems strong enough to establish the case. It is not clear whether Drummond spoke without thinking in the heat of battle or meant to give a direct order, although any words uttered by a commanding officer in battle must be taken as the latter, and soldiers in mortal combat probably would not need much encouragement to follow such an order.

Does this mean that there would have been a bloodbath at Fort Erie if the British had prevailed? Hardly. Once American resistance had come to an end, a few soldiers in the front lines might have been killed, but then Drummond or some other officer probably would have ordered an end to the killing. Any other scenario would have been unlikely because killing defenseless soldiers in this situation would have served no end and might have invited retaliation.[70]

**The Battle of Plattsburgh.** In the late summer of 1814, Lieutenant General George Prevost invaded upper New York. He hoped to secure Canada by seizing Plattsburgh, closing off the invasion route that ran into Canada along Lake Champlain and the Richelieu River. The occupation of this territory would also give the British a bargaining chip in the peace negotiations then under way.

While Prevost threatened Brigadier General Alexander Macomb's smaller American army at Plattsburgh, Captain George Downie attacked Master Commandant Thomas Macdonough's American squadron in the adjacent waters of Plattsburgh Bay on Lake Champlain. In the ensuing battle, Downie was defeated. With the loss of control of Lake Champlain, General Prevost's supply line was threatened and he feared being cut off. Hence he ordered the British army to retire to Canada. He was sharply criticized for having denied his experienced British army an opportunity to give the much smaller American army a good thrashing.[71]

**How Large Was the British Army?** Some students of this campaign have claimed that Lieutenant General Prevost's army was 14,000 or 15,000 strong and that it was dominated by veterans of the Peninsular War. Neither claim is true. The invasion began on August 31, 1814. We know that the army's strength five days later (when it reached Plattsburgh) was 10,038. This was the largest army ever to invade the United States. If the sick are deducted, the effective force at this time was 9,903. In addition, 1,831 men had been detached for other duties—guard, escort, rear, and baggage. Hence, the actual force that confronted the American army at Plattsburgh was 8,072 strong. Moreover, only 33 percent of this force had taken part in the Peninsular War. The British army at Plattsburgh was formidable but not as formidable as Americans later made it out to be.[72]

**How Close Did the British Come to Victory?** Although a British victory on Lake Champlain surely would have been followed by a British triumph on land, what is little appreciated is how close the British army came to success anyway. The problem was that the army could not find a ford to cross the Saranac River and thus bring its overwhelming force to bear on the American position. The British knew there was a ford near Pike's Cantonment, but they wasted an hour and a half searching for it. When they finally found it and crossed the river, they scattered the defending militia and were soon in a position to attack the main American army from the rear. But by then it was too late, for at that very moment orders arrived from Lieutenant General Prevost calling for a withdrawal.[73]

In his after-action report, Brigadier General Macomb claimed that he had repeatedly repulsed the British army when it tried to cross the river to make a frontal assault. Some writers, taking Macomb at his word and unaware that the main British attack was coming from a different direction, have credited Macomb with winning the land battle. This is far from the truth. The engagement that Macomb claimed to have won was little more than a series of skirmishes designed to hold his army in place until it could be attacked from the rear.[74]

With a little more luck (or better intelligence), the British might have found the ford earlier and thus defeated the American army before they lost their squadron on the lake. Although it is likely that Prevost would have eventually ordered a withdrawal anyway because of his exposed supply lines, the entire campaign might be remembered differently. Macdonough's reputation might actually be greater because he might be remembered as the naval officer who compelled a British army to withdraw after it had won a major battle. Macomb's reputation surely would have suffered because he would have been defeated. The entire campaign would not be remembered as an unalloyed American victory, but rather as a campaign with mixed results, with both sides able to claim a share of the bragging rights.

***Who Plundered Plattsburgh?*** British troops occupied a number of houses in Plattsburgh but did very little plundering. After their departure, however, American militia poured into the town and stripped many of the houses bare. According to one local resident, "The militia after the enemy retreated broke open stores and houses which the enemy left untouched and plundered them of everything that could be carried away."[75] American predators, in other words, did more harm than the enemy to private property.

***How Many British Soldiers Deserted after the Battle?*** Contemporary accounts reported a large number of desertions when the British withdrew, perhaps as many as 1,000 men. This is an exaggeration. British military records show that the actual number of deserters during the entire campaign was only 239. Moreover, contrary to popular belief, the deserters were not Peninsular veterans disillusioned with Prevost's leadership. Only a handful of these troops deserted. Most actually came from other units.[76]

**The Capture of Washington.** The low point in the War of 1812 for the United States was undoubtedly the British occupation of Washington in August of 1814. Neither Secretary of War John Armstrong nor any other high official in the government thought that the capital was in jeopardy because it had no real strategic value. It was then just a small town in the Potomac wilderness. When the government belatedly was stirred to action, it put Brigadier General William H. Winder in charge of the defense preparations, but he was not up to the job.

The U.S. also had to rely heavily on militia, who were wholly undependable in the face of enemy fire. Secretary of State James Monroe (who had no authority in the matter) compounded the problem by tampering with the initial deployment of the American troops who blocked the road to Washington at Bladensburg, Maryland. A British force overran this position, although it suffered heavy casualties, mainly from artillery fire from Captain Joshua Barney's determined band of seamen and marines. The militia retreat from the battlefield was far from orderly, and it was remembered in parody and poetry as "the Bladensburg races."

With the road to the capital now open, the British marched into the largely empty city, where they burned most of the public buildings. They also destroyed some private property: a home from which they took sniper fire, several ropewalks that manufactured rope for the U.S. Navy under government contract, and virtually everything in the office of the semi-official *National Intelligencer,* which was the administration's mouthpiece. They spared the building itself because it was owned by an antiwar Federalist. The following day the British decamped for their ships in the Chesapeake. This coup de main was the high-water mark of British operations in the war, and London newspapers were reportedly annoyed that British commanders had not used "Washington" as the dateline in their after-action reports.[77]

***Why Did the British Burn Washington?*** The British burning of public buildings in Washington is usually portrayed as retaliation for the American destruction in 1813 of the public buildings in York, which was the capital of Upper Canada. But some scholars believe that the British were actually retaliating for the American destruction of Port Dover and nearby settlements in 1814. After York, both sides had burned private property on the Niagara River in the winter of 1813–14. Governor Sir George Prevost subsequently issued a proclamation ordering his troops to refrain from such acts if American troops followed suit. When the Americans burned Port Dover in May of 1814, Prevost asked Vice Admiral Sir Alexander Cochrane to retaliate on American towns in the Chesapeake. Cochrane issued orders to carry out Prevost's request, and the public buildings in Washington were subsequently burned.[78]

There are two problems with attributing the destruction of Washington to Prevost's request. First, Major General Robert Ross, who oversaw the destruction of Washington, said that it was in retaliation for York. According to Charles J. Ingersoll, "Ross continually deplored the tragedy which he said he had to perform, occasioned, he added, by the American burning of the British

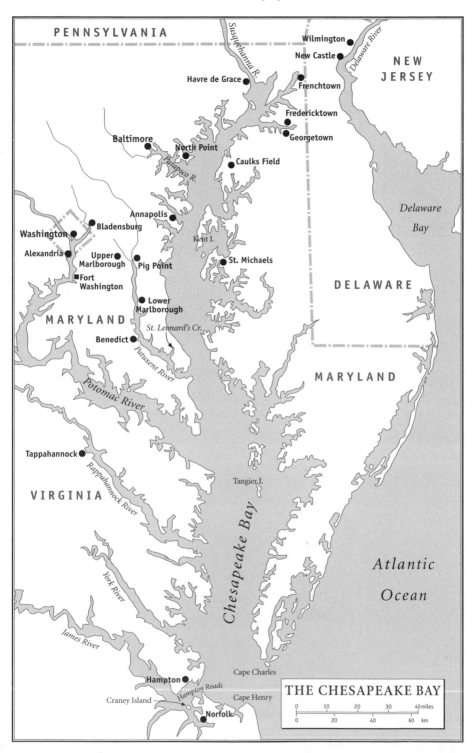

PENNSYLVANIA

Wilmington

New Castle

*Susquehanna R.*

Havre de Grace

Frenchtown

NEW
JERSEY

*Delaware River*

Fredericktown

Georgetown

Baltimore

North Point

*Patapsco R.*

Caulks Field

Delaware
Bay

Annapolis

Bladensburg

Washington

*Kent I.*

Alexandria

Upper
Marlborough

Pig Point

St. Michaels

DELAWARE

Fort
Washington

Lower
Marlborough

MARYLAND

*St. Leonard's Cr.*

Benedict

MARYLAND

*Patuxent River*

*Potomac River*

Tappahannock

*Tangier I.*

VIRGINIA

*Rappahannock River*

*Chesapeake Bay*

Atlantic

Ocean

*York River*

*James River*

Cape Charles

Hampton

*Hampton Roads*

Cape Henry

Craney Island

Norfolk

### THE CHESAPEAKE BAY

| 0 | 10 | 20 | 30 | 40 miles |
|---|----|----|----|----------|
| 0 | 20 | | 40 | 60 km |

capital in Canada."[79] Secondly, true retaliation for the burning of Port Dover would have entailed the destruction of private property in Washington. Rear Admiral George Cockburn, who took his orders from Cochrane and accompanied Ross's army into Washington, was reportedly in favor of torching everything, but it was Ross's call, and he insisted (with few exceptions) that the army leave private property alone.[80] Therefore the original story—that Washington was burned in retaliation for the destruction of York—appears to be correct.[81]

For torching buildings in Washington, the British army was criticized, not only in the United States and Great Britain but even by officers in the British army. Burning the public buildings in an occupied capital was rare in European warfare, but that was because local officials usually asked for terms and formally surrendered the city. The British searched for someone to discuss terms of surrender with in Washington, but they found no takers. Every responsible official had fled. The lack of a formal capitulation clouded the status of the city, although in point of fact the British were pretty lenient in their treatment of the city and its people.

No one denied that enemy military property could be destroyed, and under the circumstances the destruction of other public property was also probably justified. Only if the public property had a higher purpose—such as a library or museum—was it likely to be considered sacrosanct. Even then, however, there were no guarantees. During the first occupation of

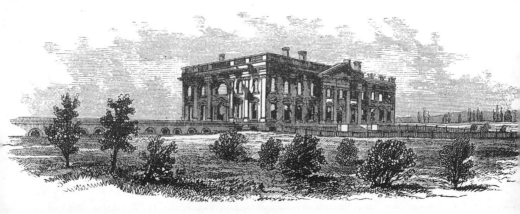

The British burned the White House in 1814. Only a shell survived, and reconstruction was not completed until 1818. (Lossing, *Pictorial Field-Book of the War of 1812*)

York in the spring of 1813, American soldiers and sailors looted the private subscription library. This was such "a great source of mortification" to the U.S. naval officers that Commodore Isaac Chauncey rounded up as many of the stolen books as he could find in his squadron and returned them in a truce ship.[82]

In Washington, House clerks later said that they would have removed the small library in Congress if they had had sufficient transportation, but wagons and carriages were in great demand.[83] Major General Ross apparently regretted the loss of the library. "Had I known it in time," he reportedly said, "the books most certainly should have been saved."[84] The British did not burn the post office building when told that it housed patents and scientific models and that these were in any case private property.[85]

***Who Plundered Washington?*** The nation's capital was plundered during the British occupation but not by British soldiers. There was some British plundering, but British officers dealt harshly with it. "To give the Devil his due," said one resident, the "conduct [of the British] here was as orderly as could have been expected."[86]

There was far more plundering by locals who took advantage of the evacuation of the city and the chaos that ensued. The editor of the *National Intelligencer,* whose printing press was destroyed by the British, credited the army of occupation with remarkable restraint. "No houses were half as much *plundered* by the enemy," the newspaper reported, "as by the knavish wretches about the town who profited of the general distress."[87] Here, as at Plattsburgh, local predators violated private property more than the British.

***When Did the President's House Become the "White House"?*** Conventional wisdom holds that the president's house was not called the "White House" until after the War of 1812, when it was rebuilt and painted white. This is not true. Although commonly called the "President's House," the building had always been whitewashed, and the term "White House" was in use before the war. In the spring of 1811, Francis James Jackson, the former British minister to the United States, wrote that his successor, Augustus J. Foster, would "act as a sort of political conductor to attract the lightening [sic] that may issue from the Clouds round the Capitol and the White House at Washington."[88] Since Jackson had been recalled from the United States the previous year, the name almost certainly was in use in 1810, and probably even earlier.[89]

The term "White House" came into more general use after the building was given a coat of oil-based white paint when it was rebuilt in 1817. Officially, however, it was still referred to as the "President's House" until mid-century, when it became the "Executive Mansion." It was not until 1901 that President Theodore Roosevelt signed an executive order changing the official name to the "White House." That name has been used on presidential stationery and in all official documents ever since.[90]

***Did the British Dine at the White House?*** Most accounts of the burning of Washington report that before torching the White House the British high command ate a meal there that had been prepared for the president. Following Major General Robert Ross's lead, British accounts usually portray the meal as a "victory dinner" that had been prepared for Madison and his generals in anticipation of success over the advancing British army. This entire story has been challenged by some historians, who cite the testimony of Madison's White House steward, "French John" Sioussat, who later claimed that "no preparations for dinner or eating" had been made that afternoon, and that if any meal had been prepared, the British would not have eaten it because of a fear of poisoning.[91]

There is no evidence to suggest that a "victory dinner" had been prepared. The White House often entertained, and this was probably just a typical dinner to which local dignitaries and well-connected visitors were invited. Many years later, Paul Jennings, the president's black valet, remembered that "all the Cabinet and several military gentlemen and strangers were expected."[92]

The British almost surely drank and probably ate in the White House. While it is true that British officers feared poisoning, this fear was confined to the field. From American leaders, the British expected—and usually got— much better treatment. At the time, a resident of Washington reported that the British found a silver cup and some wine and then drank a toast: "Peace with America, & down with Madison." In addition, many British officers reported eating in the White House.[93] Lending further credence to the story is the testimony of Madison's valet. "Mrs. Madison ordered dinner to be ready at 3, as usual," Jennings recalled in 1865. "I set the table myself, and brought up the ale cider, and wine, and placed them in the coolers."[94]

**The British Assault on Baltimore.** After the British burned Washington, they returned to their ships and the following month sailed up the Chesapeake Bay to Baltimore. This city was targeted not only because it was the home port of many American privateers but also because it boasted considerable maritime wealth. In addition, it was known to be the most fiercely Republican and anti-British city in America.

The British landed at North Point and from there marched toward the city, eight miles away. Three miles into their march, the British met with resistance, and in the Battle of North Point suffered heavy casualties before forcing the militia that blocked their path to give way. Worse yet, in a skirmish before the battle, Major General Ross was mortally wounded. The loss of this able and much-beloved officer was a terrific blow. "It is impossible to conceive the effects which this melancholy spectacle produced throughout the army," recalled a junior British officer.[95]

When the British got to the outskirts of Baltimore, they realized that the defenses they faced were formidable. Major General Samuel Smith had persuaded practically the entire city to pitch in on their construction. Behind the earthworks were at least 10,000 armed men, anchored by Commodore John Rodgers's Naval Brigade, which consisted of almost 1,200 sailors and marines.

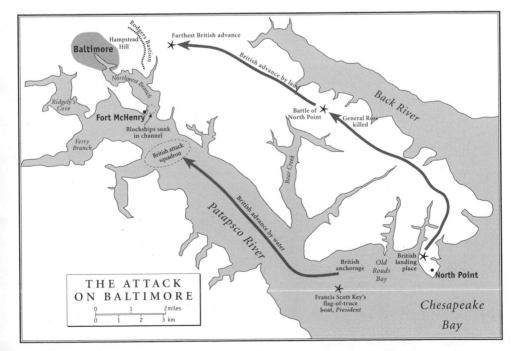

THE ATTACK ON BALTIMORE

Major General Samuel Smith (1752–1839), merchant, soldier, and statesman, long dominated the politics of Maryland. Although no friend of President Madison or his administration, Smith supported the war and did a superb job of preparing the defenses of Baltimore when the British threatened the city in 1814. (Lossing, *Pictorial Field-Book of the War of 1812*)

To soften up the American lines, the British navy moved up the Patapsco River. But to get within range, their ships first had to silence the guns of Fort McHenry, a star-shaped coastal fortification that had been built to protect the city and harbor from waterborne assault and that was now under the command of Major George Armistead. A British squadron that included five bomb ships and the rocket ship *Erebus* (26) bombarded the fort for some 25 hours with round shot, explosive shells, and Congreve rockets but inflicted only minimal damage.[96]

With the main British fleet in Old Roads Bay at the mouth of the Patapsco River was a 35-year-old Federalist attorney, Francis Scott Key, who had come in the truce sloop *President* to try to secure the release of an imprisoned American doctor.[97] The British had already decided to release the doctor but refused to let the Americans leave until the bombardment of Fort McHenry was over. The next morning, when Key realized that the British navy was withdrawing and that an American flag still flew over the fort, he was moved to write a poem which became "The Star-Spangled Banner."

***Did General Ross Disparage the American Militia?*** Like most British regulars, Ross had little but contempt for American militia. British experiences in the Chesapeake only reinforced this view because time and time again militia units were easily swept aside. Told that Baltimore was defended by a large number of militia, Ross reportedly said: "I don't care if it rains militia, I will sup in Baltimore tonight or in hell."[98]

This remark actually combines two quotations attributed to Ross. According to one account, published in 1878, Ross dismissed a report that militia defended Baltimore, saying that he would take the city "if it rains militia." According to another account, published in 1863, he told the owner of the house where he was staying not to prepare dinner that evening, explaining that "I shall sup in Baltimore tonight or in hell." These bombastic remarks would be more credible if they had been attributed to the spirited Rear Admiral George Cockburn, but for the mild-mannered Ross they were out of character. In addition, Ross did not land on North Point until September 12, and he remained constantly on the move until he was killed later that day. Finally, the remarks were reported too many years after the war to be credible.[99]

*Who Killed General Ross?* Local legend credits two teenage boys, 18-year-old Henry McComas and 19-year-old Daniel Wells, with killing Ross in a skirmish before the Battle of North Point on September 12. The boys were

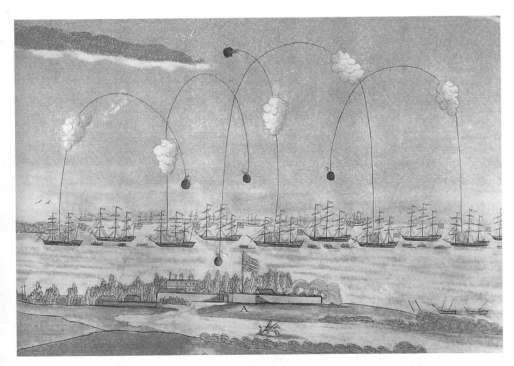

This depiction of the bombardment of Fort McHenry shows (probably erroneously) the large garrison flag flying as British explosive shells rained down on the post. (Painting by unknown artist. Fort McHenry National Monument, National Park Service)

with the 1st Rifle Battalion of the Maryland militia when Ross approached on horseback with his advance. Both boys supposedly took aim and fired simultaneously, killing Ross with a ball that passed through his arm and lodged in his chest. The boys themselves were immediately thereafter killed.

In "The Boy Martyrs of Sept. 12, 1814," a short play published in 1859, Clifton W. Tayleure immortalized the role of McComas and Wells in the death of Ross.[100] More recently, Wheeler Jenkins has claimed that by killing Ross, the boys "completely demoralized the invading forces and as a result they retreated to their ships and left the country." Today, says Jenkins, the boys would be candidates for the Medal of Honor. "The fact that only two men were instrumental in effecting such a monumental change in the course of events in warfare has few parallels in history."[101]

Jenkins's claim is hyperbolic, and the story about the two boys is dubious anyway. No contemporary evidence links McComas and Wells to Ross's death, nor was the assertion widely accepted for many years. In fact, in 1858, when

a monument was erected to honor the boys for their sacrifice, it made no mention of the claim that they had killed Ross because it was too controversial.

Major General Robert Ross (1768–1814) was transferred to North America after distinguishing himself in the Peninsular War. He commanded the British force that occupied Washington but was killed outside of Baltimore three weeks later. This romanticized print depicts his impending death with a Congreve rocket zooming by in the background. (Engraving by G.M. Brighty. Library of Congress)

It is impossible to know who shot Ross. It could have been someone from McComas and Wells's rifle company. Or it could have been someone from one of the other militia units in the field that day. Some men in those units, who were carrying muskets, claimed that they had taken aim at Ross, too. Since Ross was in front of his men, it is even conceivable that he was accidentally shot by one of his own.[102] At the time, British leaders gave conflicting testimony over whether he was hit by a rifle ball or a musket ball. Given the penetration of the shot—through Ross's arm and into his chest—it is perhaps a little more likely that it came from a rifle. But this is conjecture. Even an eyewitness who saw Ross fall probably would not know where the shot came from or whether it was from a rifle or musket.[103]

***The Fort McHenry Flag.*** The flag that normally flew over Fort McHenry, made of wool with cotton stars, was huge, measuring 30 by 42 feet. It cost $406 to make, which is as much as an unskilled laborer earned in two or three years. Since most flags today are a lot smaller, it is often assumed that the Fort McHenry flag was unique in 1814. This view appears to be supported by an oft-cited letter that Major Armistead, Fort McHenry's commander, wrote in 1813, saying that he wanted "to have a flag so large that the British will have no difficulty in seeing it from a distance."[104] Although the Fort McHenry flag is the largest surviving flag from the period, it was not exceptionally large. Contemporary illustrations from the period depict most garrisons (and most large warships, too) with huge flags. The purpose was to show friend and foe alike for miles around who controlled the fort or warship and to project an image of strength and power.

The flag that the British captured at Fort Niagara in 1813, which still survives, measures 24.5 by 27 feet. A decade earlier, Armistead (then a captain at this post) had requested a much larger one, 42 by 48 feet, which would have been 60 percent larger than the Fort McHenry flag. It is not known whether this flag was ever made, but contemporary illustrations show Fort Niagara flying a very large flag indeed.[105] Perhaps to deter such excesses, Secretary of War John C. Calhoun in 1818 fixed the maximum size of garrison flags at 20 by 40 feet.[106]

It is widely assumed that the big flag flew during the British bombardment of Fort McHenry, but this is not so. It flew only during the first part of the attack, if at all. Like most military installations, Fort McHenry had two flags, a large garrison flag and a smaller storm flag (which measured 17 by 25

Major George Armistead (1780–1818) commanded Fort McHenry when it was bombarded by the Royal Navy in 1814. The fort's large flag remained in the family's possession until it was turned over to the Smithsonian in 1907. (Portrait by Rembrandt Peale. Maryland Historical Society)

The famous Fort McHenry flag survives, although it is fragile and shows the effects of age. (National Museum of American History, Smithsonian Institution)

feet).[107] The storm flag (which has since been lost) was undoubtedly flown during most, if not all, of the bombardment because of stormy weather. Several eyewitnesses describe the larger garrison flag being hoisted in the morning after the bombardment was over, and one reported that "Yankee Doodle" accompanied the ceremony.[108]

Neither flag actually represented the state of the Union in 1814. Even though there were 18 states, the flag in use then, which had been fixed by Congress in 1794, had 15 stripes and 15 stars. Not until 1818 did Congress authorize a new flag with 13 stripes and 20 stars and provide for adding a new star each time another state joined the Union.[109]

Francis Scott Key was eight miles from Fort McHenry during the bombardment. Contrary to popular belief, he was not on a British warship that night but rather on the *President,* the truce vessel that had brought him there. Some scholars have suggested that, given the weather and distance, he could not have seen the flag. Key never claimed to have seen the flag during the night. In fact, the original broadside and newspaper accounts of the song indicate that he lost sight of the flag after darkness fell. Moreover, the poem says that "the Rockets' red glare, the Bombs bursting in air, / Gave proof through the night that our Flag was still there." What Key meant by these words was not that he could see the flag but simply that as long as the fort was under fire he knew that it must still be in American hands. The original broadside and newspaper reports confirm that once dawn broke Key did indeed see the flag, and many years later Key remembered nervously pacing until dawn brought the flag into view. He probably used a spyglass, which certainly would have made it possible to see the flag.[110]

After the war the Fort McHenry flag remained in the possession of the Armistead family. Over the years, it was occasionally displayed, and swatches were periodically cut off the ends, in some cases to remove damaged material and in others to patch the interior of the flag. Some swatches were also given away as souvenirs. These cuts shortened the flag by some eight feet. One of the stars is also missing.

What happened to the missing star? Some accounts claim that it was shot away during the bombardment, but this is untrue. The flag shows no evidence of battle damage, and an examination of the fibers near the missing star shows that it was cut out. In 1873 Armistead's granddaughter claimed that the star was "cut out for some official person."[111] In 1917 *National Geographic Magazine*, citing local lore, suggested that the recipient was none other than President Abraham Lincoln.[112] This legend has often been repeated, but it is almost certainly untrue. The Armistead family was sympathetic to the South during the Civil War and thoroughly despised Lincoln. There is nothing in the Armistead or Lincoln papers to support the claim, nor is it supported by any other contemporary evidence.[113] The fate of the missing star remains a mystery.

In 1907 George Armistead's grandson loaned the flag to the Smithsonian. Five years later the loan was converted into a gift. Since then the flag has undergone several efforts to preserve it and extend its life. Although very fragile, it remains on public display. It is a great national treasure that is arguably the most visible link to the War of 1812 in the United States today.[114]

**The Birth of "The Star-Spangled Banner."** Francis Scott Key did not at first call his new song "The Star-Spangled Banner." In the initial broadside and newspaper accounts, it was entitled "Defence of Fort McHenry." In 1805, however, Key had written a song honoring Stephen Decatur for his exploits during the Tripolitan War that included the phrase "the star-spangled flag,"

## DEFENCE OF FORT M'HENRY.

The annexed song was composed under the following circumstances—
A gentleman had left Baltimore, in a flag of truce for the purpose of getting released from the British fleet, a friend of his who had been captured
at Marlborough.—He went as far as the mouth of the Patuxent, and was
not permitted to return lest the intended attack on Baltimore should be
disclosed. He was therefore brought up the Bay to the mouth of the Patapsco, where the flag vessel was kept under the guns of a frigate, and
he was compelled to witness the bombardment of Fort M'Henry, which
the Admiral had boasted that he would carry in a few hours, and
that the city must fall. He watched the flag at the Fort through the
whole day with an anxiety that can be better felt than described, until
the night prevented him from seeing it. In the night he watched the Bomb
Shells, and at early dawn his eye was again greeted by the proudly waving
flag of his country.

### Tune—ANACREON IN HEAVEN.

O ! say can you see by the dawn's early light,
   What so proudly we hailed at the twilight's last gleaming,
Whose broad stripes and bright stars through the perilous fight,
   O'er the ramparts we watch'd, were so gallantly streaming ?
And the Rockets' red glare, the Bomb bursting in air,
Gave proof through the night that our Flag was still there ;
     O ! say does that star-spangled Banner yet wave,
     O'er the Land of the free, and the home of the brave ?

On the shore dimly seen through the mists of the deep,
   Where the foe's haughty host in dread silence reposes,
What is that which the breeze, o'er the towering steep,
   As it fitfully blows, half conceals, half discloses ?
Now it catches the gleam of the morning's first beam,
In full glory reflected new shines in the stream,
     'Tis the star spangled banner, O ! long may it wave
     O'er the lar d of the free and the home of the brave.

And where is that band who so vauntingly swore
   That the havoc of war and the battle's confusion,
A home and a country, shall leave us no more ?
   Their blood has washed out their foul footsteps pollution
No refuge could save the hireling and slave,
From the terror of flight or the gloom of the grave,
     And the star-spangled banner in triumph doth wave,
     O'er the Land of the Free, and the Home of the Brave.

O ! thus be it ever when freemen shall stand,
   Between their lov'd home, and the war's desolation,
Blest with vict'ry and peace, may the Heav'n rescued land,
   Praise the Power that hath made and preserv'd us a nation !
Then conquer we must, when our cause it is just,
And this be our motto—" In God is our Trust ;"
     And the star-spangled Banner in triumph shall wave,
     O'er the Land of the Free, and the Home of the Brave

Francis Scott Key's patriotic song describing the bombardment of Fort McHenry
was first published as a broadside in 1814. The broadside includes important
details on how the song came to be written and shows that it was originally
titled "Defence of Fort McHenry." (Sonneck, *"Star Spangled Banner"*)

and he soon renamed his new song "The Star-Spangled Banner." Key did not write the tune that his new creation was set to. The tune was an old song entitled "Anacreon in Heaven" that was popular in British gentlemen's clubs. But Key's earlier work honoring Decatur had been set to this tune, and he clearly had it in mind for his new song because the first broadside and newspaper accounts list it as the tune.[115]

Key's song quickly became a hit and later received such a huge boost from the Civil War and the Spanish-American War that by 1900 it had pushed aside other patriotic tunes, such as "Yankee Doodle" and "Hail Columbia." "The Star-Spangled Banner" was often sung on patriotic occasions, and the American army and navy both adopted it for certain ceremonies, but not until 1931 did Congress pass a resolution designating it the national anthem.[116]

**Were British Soldiers Poisoned in the Chesapeake?** British officers in the Chesapeake repeatedly warned their men to avoid American food and drink lest they be poisoned. Several British officers complained to their American counterparts that their men had been poisoned by drinking local beverages or water from tainted wells. These charges met with vigorous denials. There is evidence of one attempt to poison the British, but it failed. In June 1814, someone reportedly had left a barrel of whiskey laced with arsenic in Calvert, Maryland, for an advancing British force. Clement Dorsey, a prominent local planter, learned of the plot "with astonishment and indignation." Believing that "the American character [was] deeply implicated in this horrible deed," he raced into town to warn the commanding British officer before anyone could drink the whiskey.[117]

That many British soldiers became sick after eating American food or drinking American liquor or water is undoubtedly true. Though British officers saw a plot here, it is far more likely that their men simply contracted one of the many diseases that flourished in the Chesapeake during the summer, which everyone knew was the "sickly season."[118]

**The British Occupation of Maine.** In the summer of 1814 the British occupied eastern Maine, which was then part of Massachusetts. They controlled everything between Eastport and Castine, about 100 miles of the coastline. Because there was so little resistance and no major battle, the campaign is little remembered today. Most residents welcomed the British occupation because it boosted trade with Canada and led to the flow of British cash into the district.[119] The British later used tax revenue collected during the occupation to establish Dalhousie University in Halifax.[120]

***Did the British Require a Loyalty Oath?*** It is sometimes said that the British required all residents in occupied Maine to take an oath of allegiance to the Crown or to leave the district. This is untrue. The British required such an oath only on Moose Island (which they claimed), and even here they assured local residents that the oath was intended to assure neutrality, not perpetual allegiance. Elsewhere in occupied Maine only those who wished to enjoy the commercial privileges of British subjects had to take this oath. All others could remain by simply taking an oath to keep the peace.[121]

***Why Did Massachusetts Refuse to Retake Maine?*** The U.S. government hatched a plan for retaking Maine by sending an army of regulars and militia overland to attack Castine at the southern end of the British occupation zone. The War Department asked Governor Caleb Strong of Massachusetts to call up militia and provide some of the funding. Strong refused. Strong's decision is usually attributed to partisan obstructionism, and there may be some truth in this charge. But his refusal was also based on a lack of state funds as well as strategic considerations. Massachusetts was in the throes of a war-induced depression, which made it difficult for the state to raise money. In addition, Strong's advisers told him that the campaign would fail without naval control of the adjoining waters in the Bay of Penobscot. This assessment was undoubtedly correct.[122]

Graffiti left by British forces who occupied Castine, Maine, in 1814. The image, which was scratched onto a window pane by an army officer, survived as late as 1860. (Lossing, *Pictorial Field-Book of the War of 1812*)

## CHAPTER 3

# The Maritime War

The War of 1812 on the high seas and the lakes has always attracted attention in part because the opposing forces represented two experienced sea-faring nations who shared a common heritage. Great Britain, a dominant sea power since the 1690s, had become known as Mistress of the Seas by the late eighteenth century, although it was only after Nelson's great victory at Trafalgar in 1805 that its supremacy became nearly unassailable. The United States, by contrast, was a small but rising naval power that had already demonstrated its prowess at sea, especially in the Quasi-War with France (1798–1801) and the War with Tripoli (1801–05).

Ultimately, the British prevailed in the maritime War of 1812, but the American victories at sea and on the lakes stunned nearly everyone, and no one more than the British. Americans rushed into print to celebrate the victories, while the British responded with accounts of their own that sought to explain away this challenge to their vaunted sea power. For decades thereafter, the war of words raged, and even today the debate continues.

The eighteenth-century British philosopher and historian David Hume once commented: "There is a natural confusion attending sea-fights, even beyond other military transactions, derived from the precarious operations of winds and tides, as well as from the smoke and darkness." Accounts of these battles "are apt to contain uncertainties and contradictions; especially when composed by writers of the hostile nations, who take pleasure in exalting their own advantages, and suppressing those of the enemy."[1] One might argue that land battles are no less likely to be shrouded in the fog of war and that those who write about them are no less prone to indulge in distortion and puffery to make their side look better. Even so, it does appear that the maritime war of 1812 has produced a disproportionate number of myths and misconceptions.

## THE WAR AT SEA

**U.S. Naval Construction Strategy.** Scholars have differed over what kind of warships the United States should have built for the War of 1812. Some have emphasized that the nation needed capital ships—frigates and ships-of-the-line—to protect its coast and commerce and to meet Britain's larger warships on an equal footing on the high seas; others have insisted that American money could best be spent on fast-sailing sloops-of-war to cruise against British commerce; still others have argued for the construction of warships on the Great Lakes and Lake Champlain to facilitate the conquest of Canada. What the United States actually did was to build very few ships of any kind in the decade before the war and then try to catch up with a multi-faceted construction program that produced capital ships, commerce raiders, and lakers all at once.

Before the war, the United States should have concentrated on capital ships. Some navalists, like Alfred Thayer Mahan and Howard I. Chapelle, have suggested that even a modest fleet might have forced the British to be more circumspect in their diplomacy with the U.S. and thus prevented the War of 1812.[2] But this is doubtful. Great Britain's foreign policy was driven by the imperatives of the Napoleonic Wars, and it is unlikely that the British would made any concessions to America that might have undermined their war effort in Europe.

The real value of an enlarged American fleet was not that it might have influenced British policy but that it was needed to meet other threats in this war-torn world. American trade in the early national period was threatened at one time or another by French and Spanish privateers and buccaneers in the western Atlantic and Caribbean; by French, Spanish, Neapolitan, and Barbary corsairs in the eastern Atlantic and Mediterranean; by French, Danish, and Norwegian cruisers in the North Sea and Baltic; and by assorted pirates operating in waters remote from Europe, especially in the Indian Ocean.

There was no reason for the United States to put up with these depredations simply because it could not adequately defend its trade against the British threat. As Federalist Josiah Quincy put it in 1812, "Because we must submit to have our rights plundered by one Power, does it follow that we must be tame and submissive to every other? . . . Because there is one leviathan in the ocean, shall every shark satiate his maw on our fatness with impunity?"[3] The Quasi-War and the Tripolitan War had demonstrated how effective even a modest navy could be against those lesser powers that looted American commerce, and an expanded blue-water fleet in the Age of Jefferson would have enabled the republic to combat depredations around the globe.

Once the War of 1812 began, however, the United States should have suspended any blue-water construction program to focus on the northern lakes. There was no point in building additional capital ships for service on the high seas. The lead time was so long they were unlikely to be ready for service before the war ended, and even if they were ready, they most likely would be captured or sunk or bottled up in port, where they would invite attack and might have to be destroyed so that they did not fall into British hands. This was the fate of the U.S. Sloop *Adams* (28), which had to be torched when the British occupied eastern Maine.

What about building ships to cruise against British commerce? This made some sense because commerce raiders could do considerable damage to British trade and thus force the Royal Navy to divert more warships to commerce protection. Unlike privateers, navy raiders did not have to turn a profit. Hence, they could destroy their prizes rather than risk recapture by sending them to a friendly port. However, targeting British commerce was not likely to shorten the war. It made more sense for the U.S. to rely on privateers to harry British commerce because they did not require any capital investment by the government (although they did compete for scarce resources, including experienced seamen).

Since the War of 1812 could be won only by conquering Canada, it was imperative for the United States to build warships on the northern lakes. Control of the lakes would enable the United States to move men and material quickly and easily into Canada. Moreover, the northern lakes were the one place where the United States could outbuild the British because of a huge logistical advantage. While the British had to ship most of their material and equipment and even some of their shipbuilders across the Atlantic, the United States could build squadrons on the Great Lakes and Lake Champlain with materials and manpower available in the United States. Although the conquest of Canada was not likely to be easy even under the best of circumstances, an ambitious inland naval construction program offered the best chance of success.

**U.S. Naval Deployment Strategy.** In 1845 Captain Charles Stewart claimed that the U.S. government planned to use American warships as floating batteries to protect ports and harbors, but that he and fellow naval officer Commodore William Bainbridge persuaded the administration to send the ships to sea. This is not quite true. Secretary of the Navy Paul Hamilton had suggested using the navy strictly for harbor defense, but President James Madison overruled him.[4]

The real debate in the months before the war was whether to concentrate or disperse the navy and whether to order it to patrol American waters or to send it out to sea. Ultimately, Commodore John Rodgers took most of the ships to sea in a concentrated force in search of a rich British convoy, but several ships sailing alone won such spectacular victories that the administration thereafter followed a strategy of dispersal.[5]

**U.S. Naval Operations.** Most accounts of the war at sea emphasize the spectacular duels that American frigates and smaller vessels won, especially early in the war. The British found American success vexing and humiliating. Learned exchanges took place in the *Naval Chronicle* seeking to explain the defeats, and the Admiralty sent out confidential orders to all station commanders that British frigates should not "attempt to engage, single handed, the larger Class of American Ships."[6] The British later gave as good as they got and won several notable victories. Even so, the American victories were unexpected and served notice on the world that the new nation was a rising naval power. And yet, however much they boosted morale, the American frigate victories were without strategic importance. At most they forced the British to be more cautious.

The real strategic success of the American navy came not from its frigate victories but from concentrating its warships early in the war, forcing Britain's Halifax squadron to do the same to avoid being defeated in detail. This meant the British could not blockade the American coast in the early months of the war and thus took few prizes. Alfred Thayer Mahan, who favored a large fleet, made this point in his study of the War of 1812 in the early twentieth century.[7]

Although Mahan's claim is sometimes dismissed as navalist propaganda, it is borne out by contemporary documents, including those of British naval officials. "We have been so completely occupied looking for Commodore Rodgers's squadron," one British officer complained, "that we have taken very few prizes."[8] In fact, a New York newspaper reported that 266 merchant vessels arrived safely in New York's harbor between April 6 and August 22, 1812, and Governor Daniel D. Tompkins claimed that the United States lost no more vessels in the summer of 1812 than it had in the previous years of peace.[9]

The safe return of so many American ships dramatically increased the nation's stock of goods, generated a huge increase in government revenue, and secured the seamen that the United States needed to man its warships and privateers. This remarkable story demonstrates that in the Age of Sail even a small navy achieving a brief semblance of parity in its own waters could significantly affect the operations of a great but distant naval power.[10]

**How Effective Was the British Blockade?** The best use the British could make of their naval power in the war was to drive American trade from the seas and blockade the American coast, and this they did with telling effect. Admiral Sir John Borlase Warren established an unofficial blockade of the American coast from Charleston, South Carolina, to Spanish Florida in the fall of 1812. He gradually extended this blockade in 1813 to the rest of the American coast south of New England, and in April 1814 Vice Admiral Sir Alexander Cochrane added New England.[11]

The effects of the blockade on American trade were immediate. Most merchant vessels were bottled up in port, and for those that sought to get to sea, insurance rates were prohibitive. The shipbuilding and seafaring trades suffered, and so, too, did agriculture because little could be sent to foreign markets (except under British license) or moved by coasting vessels (except to nearby American markets). The interior transportation network was too crude and undeveloped to pick up the slack, and gluts and shortages appeared everywhere on the Atlantic seaboard.

Admiral Sir John Borlase Warren (1753–1822) commanded the Royal Navy in North American waters during the first year and a half of the war. Although a competent officer, he was recalled in late 1813 because the Admiralty favored more energetic prosecution of the war against America's Atlantic seaboard. (*Naval Chronicle*)

Total exports shrank from $61,000,000 in 1811 to $7,000,000 in 1814, and total imports from $53,000,000 to $13,000,000. The number of American ships engaged in foreign trade also plummeted, from 984,000 tons in 1811 to 60,000 tons in 1814. Even the coasting trade became dangerous. In less than three months in late 1813, Captain Robert Barrie's squadron, operating in the Chesapeake, seized or destroyed 72 American merchant vessels, mostly small coasters. Government revenue suffered as well. Despite doubling the customs duties in 1812, the government saw its income from this source plummet from $13,000,000 in 1811 to $6,000,000 in 1814.[12]

Although a modest portion of the decline in trade and revenue might be attributed to the short-lived American embargoes of 1812 and 1813, the real damage was done by the British blockade. Indeed, the effect of this exercise in British sea power on American trade and government revenue was little short of devastating. The economic cost to the United States, which was not difficult to anticipate, was probably more than the cost of all the depredations committed by British warships and pri-

Vice Admiral Sir Alexander Cochrane (1758–1832) replaced Warren as the commander of the Royal Navy in North American Waters. He stepped up raids on the Atlantic coast, particularly in the Chesapeake. (Engraving based on a portrait by William Beechey. Library and Archives Canada)

vateers against American commerce in the entire period from 1793 to 1812.

As effective as the British blockade was in undermining the economic and financial health of the United States, its military impact was more problematic. Some American warships and privateers managed to slip out of port during the war, and they took a heavy toll on British trade and drove up British insurance rates to unprecedented levels. British merchants lost an average of more than 53 ships a month to armed American ships during the War of 1812, and their total losses have been estimated at $45,000,000 (roughly £11,600,000). By contrast, the British lost only 36 ships a month to their European enemies in the French Revolutionary Wars (1793–1802) and only 41 ships a month to them in the Napoleonic Wars (1803–14).[13]

What accounts for the failure of the British blockade as a military measure? Nature certainly played a part. The Royal Navy was charged with sealing off a 2,000-mile coastline that was dotted with inlets and shallows that were nearly impossible to patrol effectively. Storms often blew blockading ships off station, allowing American vessels to slip out to sea. The elements also took a heavy toll on Britain's wooden navy, and the nearest bases, at Halifax and Bermuda, lacked major repair facilities, skilled workmen, and essential materials. For major repairs, the Royal Navy had to dispatch its warships to Great Britain 3,000 miles away.[14]

The Admiralty was also responsible for the military shortcomings of the blockade, refusing to assign the ships needed to do the job. Vice Admiral Cochrane called for 100 ships to enforce the blockade, and the Admiralty thought that it had assigned this many as early as February 1813. But so many of these ships were diverted to other duties—coastal raids, convoy duty, and the pursuit of American warships—or were in transit or undergoing repair, that there were rarely more than about 25 percent of this number actually enforcing the blockade.[15]

This was understandable before Napoleon's defeat in the spring of 1814 because winning the war in Europe was always Britain's top priority. But even after peace was restored in Europe, the Admiralty allowed economy to trump strategic needs in America. Throughout the War of 1812, the Admiralty lacked the vision to see clearly what was needed in the American theater, preferring instead to blame any shortcomings in the blockade on local commanders, most notably Admiral Warren.[16] Thus what should have been the most effective application of naval power in the war never quite lived up to its potential.[17]

**Were American Frigates Actually Ships-of-the-Line in Disguise?** The British found their early frigate losses hard to swallow. In almost 20 years of warfare with France and Spain they had lost only a few duels and occasionally had won even when their ships were overmatched. In fact, they had not lost a single frigate battle since 1803. In the first five months of the War of 1812, by contrast, they lost three frigate engagements: *Guerrière* (49), *Java* (49), and *Macedonian* (49) were all defeated by heavy American frigates.

After being defeated by the *United States* (56), Captain John S. Carden, the *Macedonian's* commanding officer, thought he knew why. "On being taken onboard the Enemys Ship," he told the Admiralty, "I ceased to wonder at the result of the Battle; the *United States* is built with the scantline [scantling timbers] of a seventy four gun Ship, mounting thirty long twenty four pounders (English Ship Guns) on her Main Deck, and twenty two forty two pounders, Carronades, with two long twenty four pounders on her Quarter Deck and Forecastle."[18]

Following Carden's cue, British officials sought to justify their frigate losses by claiming that American frigates were really ships-of-the-line in disguise. "Though they may be called Frigates," said the Admiralty in a secret order to all station commanders, they "are of a size, Complem[e]nt and weight of Metal much beyond that Class, and more resembling Line of Battle Ships."[19]

This became the standard line of defenders of the Royal Navy thereafter. In 1815, "Veritas" (probably Montreal merchant John Richardson) claimed that in the 1790s Federalists had called the new ships "frigates" "as a trick upon the democrats" but had "boasted of their being in effect 74's in disguise" and then later had found it "more convenient for their national vanity, to play off the trick upon us."[20]

Although this was nonsense, British naval historian William James made a more reasoned argument in 1817. The capture of the U.S. Frigate *President* made it possible for the British to examine a heavy frigate, and James claimed that its scantling was the same or even slightly larger than that in a British 74-gun ship-of-the-line and that its masts were thicker than those on the 64-gun British ship. Since the U.S. Frigate *Constitution* had even stouter sides, James claimed that its walls were at least equal to those of a British 80-gun ship. James concluded that overall the big American frigates were comparable to 60- or 64-gun British ships.[21] Admiral Sir John Borlase Warren's assessment was similar. The frigates, he said, were "in reality . . . small Two Decked Ships."[22]

The big American ships fit the technical definition of a frigate, which was a square-rigged warship "mounting [its] principal ordnance on a single covered gundeck."[23] But there is no denying that they were significantly more powerful than the standard British frigate. They were larger and had thicker hulls; they were armed with a more powerful complement of long guns (which included 24-pounders instead of 18-pounders); and they carried bigger crews. Because of their size, they even had an edge over heavy British frigates like the *Endymion* (51). Moreover, their oversized timbers coupled with their complete (albeit exposed) second gun decks made them resemble ships-of-the-line.[24]

Still, in number of guns, weight of broadside, and crew size, the heavy American frigates were actually comparable to the larger British fourth rate ships, which carried 50 to 60 guns. Although the largest of these ships were sometimes classified as line-of-battle ships, they were so undersized compared to the 74-gun battleships that they had all but vanished from the Royal fleet by the War of 1812. Hence the British claim that their frigates had been defeated by ships-of-the-line was misleading because it implied that the American ships were similar to 74-gun ships and thus much more powerful than they actually were.[25]

The problem that the British faced in 1812 was not simply that their frigates were outclassed by larger and more powerful vessels but that their naval commanders had faced no serious challenges since 1805. As a result, training on many Royal warships had slipped, and (with the blessing of an Admiralty eager to save powder) little time was spent on target practice. In addition, Britain's best ships were likely to be assigned to the European war in 1812, which meant that the stations in the West Indies and Halifax got what was left. Finally, British warships were almost always undermanned because of a severe shortage of available seamen. A combination of inferior ships, poor training, and manpower shortages left the Royal Navy ill-equipped to contend with the U.S. Navy early in the war.

The British certainly would have been justified in claiming that their frigates had been beaten by bigger, more powerful ships. In fact, in almost every naval engagement in the War of 1812, the more powerful ship won. This was to be expected and was no disgrace to the loser.

**Did British Seamen Man U.S. Warships?** Nineteenth-century British writers presented another argument to justify their losses in the war at sea. They claimed that the American navy was manned by British subjects. After he was defeated by the U.S. Frigate *Constitution,* James R. Dacres, captain of H.M. Ship *Guerrière,* told a court martial: "I felt much shocked, when on board the *Constitution,* to find a large proportion of that ship's company British seamen."[26] A lieutenant from HMS *Java* made a similar accusation. "Most of the crew of the *Constitution,*" he said, "were known to be English, and many of them our prime sailors."[27]

William James put the British complement on the *Constitution* during its first cruise at about 45 percent (out of a crew of 450 men), and Edward Pelham Brenton claimed that these crew members "were leading men, or captains of the gun crews."[28] Nor did the British think the crew of the *Constitution* was unique. According to James, British subjects made up a third of the crews on American warships. "For many years previous to the war," he wrote, the United States had "been decoying the men from our ships, by every artful stratagem." Hence, the U.S. Navy was able "to pick their complements from a numerous body of seamen."[29]

Before the war, British subjects did indeed work in large numbers on American warships. The average for the U.S. Navy as a whole was probably between 35 and 40 percent, and on some ships, such as the frigates *Philadelphia* and *Chesapeake,* it may have been over 50 percent.[30] British subjects and other foreign nationals were attracted to U.S. service because the pay was steady and the working conditions tolerable. In addition, there was little danger of being impressed into British service because neutral warships were generally considered immune to search. In fact, in 1803 the secretary of the navy predicted that the resumption of the war in Europe would drive foreign merchant seamen into the U.S. Navy because "they dare not trust themselves to the protection of the merchant service officers and they are sure of being safe from impressment in ours."[31]

After the *Chesapeake* affair in 1807, however, the Navy Department ordered its commanders to discharge all foreigners, especially deserters from foreign warships, and to employ only American citizens.[32] Although the ban on foreigners was often ignored, it probably did reduce the proportion of British seamen on American warships. Moreover, once the War of 1812 began, British seamen asked for guardship or shore duty, or more commonly,

Captain James R. Dacres (1788–1853) was the first British naval commander to lose a frigate in the war. He erroneously claimed that the U.S. Frigate *Constitution* had beaten H.M.S. *Guerrière* because the American ship was manned by British seamen. (Lossing, *Pictorial Field-Book of the War of 1812*)

left U.S. service altogether. Driven by patriotic motives, the prospect of getting killed in action, or (what was worse) the fear of being captured and hanged as a deserter or traitor, most British subjects were determined to avoid serving on American warships as long as the War of 1812 lasted.[33]

Probably less than a dozen British subjects were on the *Constitution* during its early wartime cruises, and this number declined as the war progressed. The Royal Navy identified some British subjects on the American ships that it captured, most notably the *Chesapeake* and *Nautilus*, but the numbers found were never large. Nor is there evidence that any other American warship had a large complement of British subjects. Even some of those who were identified as British were actually Americans who had deserted from the Royal Navy after being impressed into service or men who had immigrated to the United States or had been in American service for so long that they were British subjects in name only.[34] Theodore Roosevelt thought that British subjects might have constituted as much as 10 or 15 percent of the total on some American warships but that the average was much lower.[35] There is no contemporary evidence to suggest that this estimate might be wrong.

**Did "Picked" Crews Give the U.S. Navy an Edge?** Equally unfounded was the common British claim, which apparently originated with Captain John S. Carden, commander of H.M. Ship *Macedonian*, that American warships had "picked" crews, that is, that they were manned by the best American seamen.[36] In fact, navy recruiters had to compete for men with privateers, and they frequently came out second best because privateers offered the prospect of more loot, a shorter enlistment period (the duration of the cruise instead of two years of service), and much easier discipline (although miscreants could still be tried by court martial when a privateer reached an American port or made contact with an American warship).

As the war progressed, the navy even lost experienced seamen to the army, which offered ever richer bounties. By the end of the war, the army was offering recruits who enlisted for the duration of the war $124 and 320 acres of land, while the most the navy offered was $48, extra pay for service on the lakes, and a term of service that had been shortened to six months or a year. "The inducements held out for men to enter the Army," said Master Commandant Thomas Macdonough in March of 1814, "is said to be the cause of the recruiting service of the Navy being so dull."[37] In all, 5.1 percent of U.S. Army recruits were seamen.[38]

American warships had good crews, not because they were British or "picked" men, but because the small American navy drew from a large and experienced merchant marine and because most naval commanders drilled their men incessantly.

**What Was the First Naval Battle?** The first naval battle, which was also the first battle of any kind in the War of 1812, was fought a mere five days after the declaration of war. Commodore John Rodgers, who commanded a squadron of warships headed by the U.S. Frigate *President* (54), put to sea from New York on June 21, only an hour after hearing that a state of war existed. He sailed in search of a large British convoy that was known to be headed from Jamaica to the British Isles.

On June 23, Rodgers spotted H.M. Ship *Belvidera* (42). The American squadron tried to run down the British ship, but only the *President*

Captain John D. Rodgers (1773–1838) was the ranking U.S. naval officer in the War of 1812. As commanding officer of the U.S. Frigate *President,* he was injured in the first battle of the war against H.M. Ship *Belvidera.* (Lossing, *Pictorial Field-Book of the War of 1812*) got within range. The two ships exchanged a number of rounds before the *Belvidera* escaped in the night after lightening its load by dumping equipment and water. The *President* sustained 22 killed and wounded, 16 from the explosion of a gun. Rodgers was among the wounded, his leg having been broken by the exploding gun. The *Belvidera* suffered seven killed or wounded. Although the battle was inconclusive, the *Belvidera* came out ahead, not only because it had sustained fewer casualties and managed to escape from a powerful squadron, but also because the engagement might be the reason that a nearby British convoy escaped detection.[39]

**What Were the First Naval Prizes?** On June 5, 1812, the U.S. Brig *Oneida* (18), Lieutenant Melancthon Woolsey commanding, stopped the British merchantman *Lord Nelson* at the mouth of the Genesee River on Lake Ontario. The British vessel was carrying a cargo from Prescott to Newark/Niagara, but because Woolsey did not think it had proper papers, he seized it for violating America's 90-day prewar embargo. The U.S. Navy purchased the ship for $3,000 and converted it into the U.S. Schooner *Scourge* (10). The *Scourge* did good duty on Lake Ontario until August 1813, when it capsized in a storm and took most of its crew to the bottom of the lake.

Although the *Lord Nelson* was treated as a prize of war, it was actually taken before the declaration of war for violating the embargo. Moreover, as a British ship trading between British ports in time of peace, it was not actually in violation of American trade laws. The Canadian owners of the ship protested, but it was not until 1927 that the United States government finally paid out almost $24,000 (£5,000) in compensation to the shipowners' heirs.[40]

The first real naval prizes were taken by Captain Hugh G. Campbell, who was at St. Marys, Georgia, at the end of June 1812 when he learned of the declaration of war. Campbell was in charge of an American flotilla of gunboats that earlier had taken part in the occupation of part of Spanish East Florida. As soon as the news of war arrived, he ordered the seizure of all British vessels in the vicinity. Three British merchant ships loaded with timber, the *Emperor*, *Experiment*, and *Adventurer*, were taken on June 29. These were the first prizes taken by either navy in the war. The vessels were not taken on the high seas, but rather in American waters (which violated U.S. policy of permitting the removal of British property) or in Spanish waters (which violated Spanish sovereignty), but no one apparently challenged the legality of the captures.[41]

**Who Captured the First Warship?** Although the United States won the early naval battles in the war, the British had the honor of capturing the first enemy warship. On July 16, 1812, a large British squadron under Captain Philip Broke of H.M. Ship *Shannon* (52) was making a sweep through American waters when it fell in with the U.S. Brig *Nautilus* (14), Lieutenant William M. Crane commanding. Although Crane ditched some of his guns, shot, and water, the *Nautilus* could not outrun its pursuers and was forced to strike its colors. The *Nautilus* was the first warship that either side lost in the war.[42]

Almost a month after the capture of the *Nautilus,* the British navy sustained its first loss. On August 13, 1812, H.M. Sloop *Alert* (18?) challenged U.S. Frigate *Essex* (46). The British ship was overmatched and had to strike its colors eight minutes into the battle with seven feet of water in its hold. The *Alert* suffered three casualties, the *Essex* none at all.[43]

**The U.S. Frigate *Constitution*.** The most famous ship in American naval history is probably the U.S. Frigate *Constitution,* affectionately known as "Old Ironsides." Commissioned in 1798, the *Constitution* was one of the new oversized frigates designed by Joshua Humphreys of Philadelphia. It was rated at 44 guns, but during the War of 1812 it carried 52–55 guns. While 44-gun ships were nothing new, Humphrey's design managed to blend speed, firepower, and stout construction into an almost unbeatable combination. As a result, the *Constitution* could outfight any other frigate and outrun anything bigger.

The *Constitution* had a particularly illustrious career during the War of 1812. It escaped from a British squadron in a celebrated 57-hour chase in 1812 and in three ensuing battles defeated four British ships: H.M. Ship *Guerrière* (49), H.M. Ship *Java* (49), H.M. Ship *Cyane* (33), and H.M. Ship *Levant* (21). Rebuilt several times after the war, it survives today.[44] (For more on the *Constitution,* see Appendix C.)

Despite its nickname, the U.S. Frigate *Constitution* did not have an iron hull. The first American iron-hulled ship (the U.S.S. *Michigan,* a patrol vessel on the Great Lakes) was not built until 1843 and ironclad ships (the first of which was the U.S.S. *Monitor*) had to wait until the 1860s. To defeat the British, the *Constitution* relied on its superior design (including an oak hull that was two feet thick), a large complement of heavy 24-pounder guns, and a bigger and well-trained crew.

Captain Isaac Hull (1773–1843) served as the commanding officer of the U.S. Frigate *Constitution* early in the war. His successful flight from a British squadron followed by his victory over H.M. Ship *Guerrière* helped redeem family honor and boost national morale that had sunk with the surrender of his uncle, Brigadier General William Hull, at Detroit. (Lossing, *Pictorial Field-Book of the War of 1812*)

According to Moses Smith, a seaman on the *Constitution,* the ship got its nickname in 1812 during its engagement with H.M. Ship *Guerrière.* Writing in 1846, Smith claimed that a large enemy shot hit the hull, "but the plank was so hard it fell out and sank in the waters." As a result, "the cry arose: 'Huzza! Her sides are made of iron!'" From this, Smith concluded, "the name of the Constitution was garnished with the familiar title: 'OLD IRONSIDES.'"[45]

Is this story credible? Yes, it is. In 1813 Midshipman Pardon Mawney Whipple appeared to corroborate it. Unlike Smith, Whipple was not on board the American ship during its engagement with the *Guerrière,* but he joined the crew shortly thereafter. Writing to a friend in 1813, he said that he was serving on a ship "which has already so eminently distinguished herself as *Old Ironsides*; a name which has been given her by the sailors, supposing that her sides are impenetrable from the circumstances of very few shot having as yet penetrated her side."[46]

**H.M. Ship *Shannon* v. U.S. Frigate *Chesapeake*.** After a string of five defeats at sea, Great Britain won a major victory on June 1, 1813, when H.M. Ship *Shannon* (52) defeated the ill-starred U.S. Frigate *Chesapeake* (50). Although British naval officers had once drilled their men extensively in gunnery, that practice had fallen off after Trafalgar. There were no major enemies left on the high seas, and, according to William James, guns were "now seldom used but on salutes."[47] Moreover, because of a powder shortage, the Admiralty discouraged the use of live ammunition in gunnery practice. It was not until March of 1813 that the Admiralty reversed itself on this matter. As a result of

The British had good reason to celebrate when H.M. Ship *Shannon* defeated the U.S. Frigate *Chesapeake* in 1813. Not only had they won their first major naval victory of the war, but they could also claim bragging rights in the only duel of evenly matched frigates. (Engraving by Joseph Jeakes after a painting by John T. Lee. Library and Archives Canada)

this order, Admiral Sir John Borlase Warren ordered ships on the American station to work on their gunnery skills.[48]

Captain Philip Broke, commander of H.M. Ship *Shannon*, had ignored Admiralty policy after Trafalgar. Not only did he drill his men constantly, but he insisted that live ammunition be used in gunnery practice. He also outfitted his ship at his own expense with gun sights and other devices to improve aim, and he developed a sophisticated technique for training his guns on a concentrated area of an enemy ship to maximize the destructiveness of his fire.[49] By contrast, his American counterpart, Captain James Lawrence, was new to the U.S. Frigate *Chesapeake.*

Lawrence sought to inspire his men by flying a white banner that read "Free Trade and Sailors' Rights," but it was in vain. In their engagement, *Shan-*

*non* shot up the *Chesapeake,* boarded, and in bloody hand-to-hand combat took control of the American ship—all within 15 minutes. Lawrence received a fatal wound in the battle. Since 228 men were killed or wounded on the two ships, this was the bloodiest frigate action of the war.[50]

The American people mourned Lawrence's loss, and he became the only American naval figure to achieve hero status in defeat.[51] The British, on the other hand, had neither accepted nor understood their earlier defeats at sea and thus were ecstatic over Broke's victory. The *Naval Chronicle* called the triumph "the most brilliant act of heroism ever performed," and in Parliament the news "was repeatedly cheered with the loudest and most cordial acclamations from every part of the House."[52] Broke, who never fully recovered from a serious cutlass wound to his head sustained in the battle, became the darling of the Realm and was showered with honors and gifts. Ever thereafter he was known as "Broke of the *Shannon.*"

As for the *Shannon,* it instantly became Britain's most celebrated warship after Vice Admiral Horatio Nelson's flagship, H.M. Ship *Victory* (104). William James, who dedicated his naval history of the War of 1812 to Broke, probably summed up the common view in Great Britain when he suggested that this victory alone offset all the American naval triumphs because this was the only battle between evenly matched ships that ended in decisive victory.[53] Twenty years after the battle, when the ship was docked at the mouth of the Thames, an admiral there said, "I show the dear old *Shannon* as a 'lion' here," and as late as 1892 a British historian could still report that *Shannon*'s name was "dear to every Briton."[54]

The clash between the *Chesapeake* and the *Shannon* never would

Captain Philip Broke (1776–1841) turned H.M. Ship *Shannon* into a formidable warship by training his crew constantly and fitting the frigate with advanced aiming devices. This led to his victory over the U.S. Frigate *Chesapeake* in 1813. (Lossing, *Pictorial Field-Book of the War of 1812*)

have occurred if the opposing commanders had followed the spirit of their orders. On February 22, 1813, Secretary of the Navy William Jones had ordered American ships to sail alone so that they could concentrate on destroying British commerce.[55] Although these orders did not explicitly prohibit naval duels, Lawrence's decision to meet the *Shannon* ran counter to their spirit. Likewise, Broke had sent off other British ships in the hope of luring Lawrence into battle. Even though New England was not yet under blockade, this had weakened the British naval presence that the Admiralty wished to maintain near all major ports.[56] In short, this celebrated clash never should have occurred.

***Minor Myths.*** This famous battle generated a large number of minor myths in the nineteenth century. Contrary to popular belief, Lawrence did not accept Broke's written challenge to engage in battle. Although Broke did send a challenge, it arrived after Lawrence had left port. Nor is it likely that fellow officers Isaac Hull and Stephen Decatur tried to talk Lawrence out of the duel. No naval officer was likely to discourage Lawrence from accepting a challenge because all were looking for an opportunity to distinguish themselves.

Lawrence did not bid farewell to his two sons before the battle. His only son was born after Lawrence's death and died in infancy. Nor did Lawrence wear a medal that had been awarded to him after an earlier victory in the U.S. Sloop *Hornet* (20). The medal had not yet been authorized or struck. Nor did people in Boston watch the engagement from their rooftops. The battle was thirty miles out to sea and thus too far away.[57]

A report of the engagement was sent to Great Britain in Broke's name, and it is sometimes used as a source for understanding the battle. But Broke was so seriously wounded that he could not write the report. It was written by the senior port officer at Halifax, Captain Thomas Bladen Capel, who interviewed the *Shannon's* officers and then secured Broke's approval to send it home in his name. But Capel was not an eyewitness, and the report is filled with errors.[58]

The *Chesapeake's* defeat has sometimes been attributed to a crew that was foreign-born, inexperienced, drunk, or sullen (because of a failure to receive prize money from a previous cruise). But most of the men were experienced American seamen, only a few were actually intoxicated, and almost all apparently had received their prize money before sailing. In addition, almost three-quarters had served together on the *Chesapeake* under the previous commander, and Lawrence himself was impressed with their discipline and training. The problem was that Lawrence was saddled with inexperienced officers and he had had little opportunity to train with his men. Despite these liabilities, Lawrence's men performed remarkably well during the battle, doing more damage to the *Shannon* than that vessel did to the *Chesapeake*. Even the mutiny in the middle of the battle of a Portuguese tar who was unhappy over prize money had so little effect on the outcome of the battle that his actions were not even mentioned in the court martial of a junior officer that grew out of the defeat.[59]

Why then did the *Chesapeake* lose the battle? First of all, the American ship was plagued by bad powder, which was a problem for several American warships during the conflict. Next, Lawrence passed up a chance to rake the *Shannon,* which could have changed the outcome of the battle. But last and most importantly, the *Shannon's* first fire was so well directed and took such a heavy toll on the officers, men, and ship that the *Chesapeake* never recovered. Broke's rigorous gunnery practice was decisive in shaping the outcome of the battle.[60]

**Captain Lawrence's Last Words.** During the engagement, Captain James Lawrence sustained a mortal wound, and as he was carried below, his last words reportedly were "Don't give up the ship!" This became a national slogan and the motto of the U.S. Navy, and the expression is still sometimes used to encourage persistence in faltering enterprises.

Did Lawrence utter these words? Apparently so. One contemporary who saw the *Chesapeake* and its crew shortly after the battle said that Lawrence had several times said, "Don't give up the ship!" Other contemporaries quoted Lawrence as saying, "Don't surrender the ship!" or "Never give up the ship."[61] James Fenimore Cooper, who based his early history of the American navy on interviews with eyewitnesses and other contemporaries, quoted Lawrence as saying, "Never strike the flag of my ship."[62]

Each of these accounts may well be true, since Lawrence probably expressed his wishes in several different ways. The pithiest version—"Don't give up the ship"—made the rounds, and Master Commandant Oliver H. Perry helped fix this version in the public mind by putting it on a banner flown over his flagship, U.S. Brig *Lawrence* (20), during the Battle of Lake Erie.[63] However, even though we can ascribe the famous expression to Lawrence,

Captain James Lawrence (1781–1813) was killed when his ship, the U.S. Frigate *Chesapeake,* was defeated by the British frigate *Shannon.* Lawrence's words—"Don't give up the ship!"— were not his last, and his ship was lost. Nevertheless, this phrase became the motto of the U.S. Navy. (Lossing, *Pictorial Field-Book of the War of 1812*)

these words were not his last. He remained conscious after being carried below on June 1 and survived for three days (until June 4). Although in great agony, he criticized his officers for surrendering the ship and probably spoke of other things as well.[64]

Many people who have heard or even repeated Lawrence's famous words probably do not know that the *Chesapeake* was taken shortly thereafter. Although no American actually surrendered the ship, the British gained control of the vessel, pulled down the American flag, and ran up their own. The *Chesapeake* was then taken into Halifax as a prize of war. It was later sent to Great Britain and in 1816 taken out of service. Four years later it was broken up and its timbers used in the construction of houses in Portsmouth and a flour mill in Wickham.[65]

***The Longest-Serving Officer in the Royal Navy.*** It is not well known that one of the British officers on board the *Shannon* became the longest-serving officer in the British navy. This was Provo Wallis (1791–1892). Born in Halifax, Wallis was put on the rolls of the Royal Navy when he was four years old, although he actually joined the service as a midshipman when he was 13. By 1813 he was a 22-year-old second lieutenant, serving on the *Shannon.*

Because Broke was wounded in the battle and his first lieutenant killed, Wallis commanded the *Shannon* on its voyage to Halifax after the battle, while the ship's third lieutenant guided the *Chesapeake.* The voyage took five days, during which young Wallis never removed his clothes and slept very little. The victors enjoyed a huge reception in Halifax, and Wallis was soon rewarded with a promotion to commander.

Wallis remained in the navy and did his last sea duty in 1858. By this time he was a 67-year-old admiral and had been going to sea for half a century. But the aging officer was far from done with the Royal Navy. A quirk in Royal Navy rules allowed any officer who had commanded a ship during the French Revolutionary or Napoleonic Wars to remain on active duty and draw full pay until death. Wallis became Admiral of the Fleet, the senior rank in the navy, when he was 85. Refusing to retire, he survived until 1892, having celebrated his 100th birthday. By this time he had been on the navy's rolls for 96 years and in the service for 88 years. Neither record is ever likely to be broken.[66]

**Who Captured the U.S. Frigate *President*?** One of the British naval victories in the war was the capture of the heavy frigate *President* (52) on January 15, 1815. Some British accounts assign the capture to H.M. Ship *Endymion* (51), implying that an overmatched British frigate defeated a much larger American ship.[67] The *President*, which had lost its fine sailing qualities when it had run aground the night before, actually knocked the *Endymion* out of action but suffered such crippling damage that Decatur chose not to resist an assault from two other British ships, *Pomone* (40) and *Tenedos* (46), even though neither ship was yet within range. Decatur has been rightly criticized for giving up too easily, but the big American frigate lost to a British squadron, not a single ship.[68]

**The Cruise and Capture of the U.S. Frigate *Essex*.** One of the most exotic and romantic cruises of the naval war was that of the U.S. Frigate *Essex* in the Pacific. In 1800, during the Quasi-War with France, Captain Edward Preble had taken the *Essex* (32) around the Cape of Good Hope, making it the first American warship to cruise in the Indian Ocean.[69] In 1813, under the command of Captain David Porter, the *Essex* (now loaded with 46 guns) became the first U.S. warship to round Cape Horn and cruise in the Pacific.

In the Pacific, Porter visited tropical islands and seized British whaling ships while at the same time protecting American whalers. At the end of 1813, the British sent a squadron of three ships, including H.M. Ship *Phoebe* (46 or 53), Captain James Hillyar, and H.M. Sloop *Cherub* (26), Captain Thomas Tucker, to track down the *Essex*. The *Phoebe* and the *Cherub* showed up in Valparaiso when Porter was there. When Porter later tried to make a run out of the harbor, he lost his topmast. Although he was still in Chilean waters, the two British warships closed in for the kill. After a bloody engagement, Porter struck his colors.[70]

Porter claimed that he did $5,000,000 (£1,333,000) worth of damage to the British while in the Pacific, $2,500,000 by taking British prizes and another $2,500,000 by saving American ships. These figures were grossly inflated. Porter took 12 British whalers, but five—including three of the most valuable—were recaptured. The remaining seven had a combined value of probably no more than $300,000 (£80,000). There were no armed British ships cruising in the Pacific until Porter drew them there. The only thing that Porter did to protect American whalers was to disarm a piratical Peruvian cruiser that was looting American vessels. This probably saved no more than $200,000 (£53,000). Thus the net damage that Porter did to the British combined with the net amount that he saved Americans was probably only 10 percent of the $5,000,000 that he claimed.[71]

Porter was furious over the British violation of Chile's territorial waters, but the British dismissed the matter as of little importance. Chile was still nominally a colony of Spain, which was allied to Great Britain. It was then in the throes of a civil war, and agents of both the United States and Great Britain were seeking to influence the outcome. Given Chile's uncertain status, it is easy to argue that its waters deserved no special protection, and the United States conceded as much by never protesting the British violation. Moreover, although he never mentioned it in his reports to the Navy Department, Porter himself had violated Chile's waters on several earlier occasions.

He burned a prize, fired on one British warship, and launched a stillborn gunboat attack against another, all in Chile's territorial waters.[72]

Porter accused Hillyar of continuing to fire on the *Essex* after he knew it had

Captain David Porter (1780–1843) took the U.S. Frigate *Essex* on a remarkable cruise in the Pacific, raiding British ships with impunity until a small Royal Navy squadron tracked him down and defeated him. (Lossing, *Pictorial Field-Book of the War of 1812*)

surrendered, and Hillyar accused Porter of conniving at the escape of his crew after the ship had struck its colors. Both commanders were probably wrong. The British doubtless did not realize that the American ship had surrendered, and the Americans appear to have fled the ship before it surrendered. This was simply a case of the fog of war leading to unwarranted accusations on both sides after the action was over.[73]

**How Effective Were Jefferson's Gunboats?** If the principal innovation in the U.S. Navy in the 1790s was the heavy frigate, the main development in the Age of Jefferson was the introduction of the gunboat. These vessels, built to a number of designs, were 40–60 feet long, measured 50–100 tons burden, carried a crew of 20–60 men, mounted one or two 18-, 24-, or 32-pounder guns, and could be propelled by either sail or oar. Gunboats appealed to President Jefferson for several reasons: They were cheap (typically $5,000–$10,000 each); they were designed for coastal defense (not deep-sea operations); they did not require a large naval establishment (militia could man them, and they could be laid up easily); and they could be built and deployed across many different jurisdictions, thereby spreading their political and economic benefits. The United States spent $1,500,000 building 174 gunboats during Jefferson's presidency.

Defenders of the gunboat, who have been mainly scholars interested in burnishing Jefferson's reputation, have argued that some European naval powers had gunboats in their fleets, that the vessels had proven particularly valuable in the shallow coastal waters of the Mediterranean, and that they had the endorsement of knowledgeable American army and naval officers. Supporters have also suggested that building the gunboat fleet provided junior officers with valuable naval construction experience and an early opportunity for an independent command. In addition, gunboats were useful for enforcing the nation's trade laws and suppressing the slave trade. As an inexpensive, versatile, and strictly defensive instrument of war, gunboats seemed ideally suited for an economy-minded administration that had little interest in projecting the nation's power beyond American waters.[74]

Enemies of the gunboat, who have been mainly writers interested in promoting a big-ship navy, have argued that the vessels offered no protection to American commerce and only limited protection to the nation's exposed coast. Critics have pointed out that the vessels were hard to maneuver, handled poorly in rough waters, and drew so much water—four to eight feet—that they could not operate in very shallow waters. Critics also have argued that they suffered from recoil problems when their guns were fired, offered little protection to their crews, and were too slow to catch speedy interlopers in American waters. "They are too heavy to Row," said Joshua Barney, "and too clumsy to sail, and are only fit to lay *moor'd*, to protect a pass, or Assist a Fort."[75] It was also difficult to recruit for gunboat duty. This meant that the government had to rely heavily on free blacks or draft seamen who had enlisted for service on conventional warships.[76]

Most of Jefferson's gunboats were laid up in Madison's presidency after the secretary of the navy reported that gun for gun they cost more to build and operate than frigates, required more crewmen, and rotted in a year if left unrepaired.[77] Some 62 gunboats were still in service in 1812, and during the war many of those that had been laid up were brought back into service.

Jefferson's gunboats were useful during the War of 1812, but their contribution was modest. Gunboats at New Orleans that were loaded with extra guns slowed down the British advance across Lake Borgne, thus giving Major General Andrew Jackson extra time to prepare his

Captain Joshua Barney (1759–1818), already a naval hero from the American Revolution, continued his remarkable career during the War of 1812, first as a successful privateer captain, then as commander of the Chesapeake flotilla, and finally commanding sailors and marines in the Battle of Bladensburg. (Lossing, *Pictorial Field-Book of the War of 1812*)

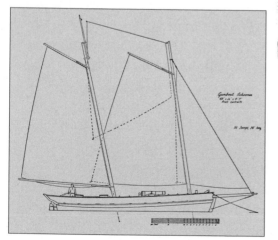

This sketch shows a schooner-rigged gunboat equipped with a single large naval gun. (Chapelle, *American Sailing Navy*)

defenses. Gunboats also played a role in the defense of Craney Island, served as transports for the navy, captured a number of small British vessels that ventured into American waters, helped defeat the Baratarian pirates and seize West Florida (including Mobile), and provided protection for local trade, especially in the shallow waters along the South Atlantic coast. Despite these accomplishments, Jefferson's gunboats never lived up to expectation. They proved unable to protect the nation's coast, and they never fully justified the money spent on them.

A better argument can be made for other shallow-draft vessels that were built for a variety of special purposes during the war. Both sides built or acquired a substantial number of these vessels. Variously called "gunboats," "galleys," "row galleys," or "barges," they were built to many different specifications and thus varied considerably in size, appearance, sailing qualities, and firepower. Some even lacked masts and sails or decks, while others were simply converted merchantmen.

What all these vessels had in common was the ability to maneuver in shallow waters with oars or sweeps. This meant that they were not dependent on the wind and could fire on any target that they could bring within range. Their main liability was their limited firepower—usually one or two big guns—and their large manpower needs. "The Galleys are liable to the Serious objection," said Secretary of the Navy William Jones, "of requiring a great number of men, in proportion to their efficient force, but then they have the advantage of attacking the enemy in calms and light winds, and in narrow waters . . . and of retreating into creeks, rivers and shoal waters from a superior foe."[78] These shallow-draft vessels were particularly useful on those inland waters that were inaccessible to large oceangoing warships.

American gunboats played a supporting role in the victories on Lake Erie and Lake Champlain, and before Captain Joshua Barney was forced to scuttle them, his barges interfered with British operations in the Chesapeake. The barges performed much better than the Jeffersonian gunboats that were part of Barney's flotilla because they were much easier to maneuver and drew far less water. "They row fast," said Secretary of the Navy William Jones, and even when fully loaded, they "draw but 22 Inches water."[79] This made it easier for them to escape from British warships by rowing into shallow rivers or creeks. They had the additional advantage of being relatively cheap. At $2,500 each, they cost about half the price of the cheapest gunboats.[80]

The British also made good use of shallow-draft vessels. Gunboats played a critical role in keeping the St. Lawrence open to British supply boats and harassing Major General James Wilkinson's invading force as it sailed down the river before the Battle of Crysler's Farm in late 1813. They also forced the surrender of the U.S. Sloop *Growler* (11) and U.S. Sloop *Eagle* (11) when these two schooners ventured too far down the Richelieu River in 1813, and they opened up Lake Borgne by defeating the smaller American flotilla there in 1814. Both sides also used gunboats on Lake Ontario for scouting duty and for close-in support of larger warships.

None of the warships built on the inland seas during the war were intended to last, and the shallow-draft vessels were no exception. Both sides sold off or junked these vessels after the conflict was over. The United States also gradually disposed of the original Jeffersonian gunboats. Thereafter the United States, like Great Britain, devoted its resources to a more conventional blue-water navy.[81]

**Did the French Navy Help the U.S.?** The role of the French navy in the War of 1812 is usually ignored, although it actually played a small part and could have played a much larger one. It is true that the British had established undisputed command of the seas with their great naval victory at Trafalgar in 1805, but the French fleet was by no means destroyed. Thereafter, most French warships remained in port, where the Royal Navy could not get at them. Instead, the British had to devote considerable naval resources to blockading French ports, both to keep French squadrons divided and to attack them if they ventured forth.[82]

Although the British eventually captured all of France's overseas naval bases, Napoleon never gave up his dream of building a fleet that could challenge Great Britain's, and after his great victory at Austerlitz in 1805, he had most of the resources of Europe at his command. Drawing on these resources, he began in 1807 to rebuild France's fleet at more than a dozen ports, mostly in the Mediterranean. A fleet of 150 ships-of-the-line, he reasoned, could overpower Britain's fleet, which averaged just over 100 ships-of-the-line in this period. Keeping even this number of ships in commission taxed Britain's resources and manpower, and matching a French building program would have been difficult.

By 1814 Napoleon had 80 battleships at his disposal and another 35 under construction, which seemed to put him within striking distance of challenging Britain at sea.[83] But by then the French building program had already run aground, not only because Napoleon was running out of time but also because he lacked enough skilled seamen. Both were a direct outgrowth of the war on the Continent, and particularly Napoleon's ill-advised invasion of Russia in 1812.

As early as 1808 Napoleon started conscripting French seamen into his army for service in the Peninsular War. This practice accelerated after he lost an army in Russia in 1812. Roughly 20,000 French seamen served in the French infantry in Germany in 1813, and another 5,000 were transferred to the French artillery in early 1814. Still more seamen were conscripted into the land forces for the final defense of France that spring.[84]

How did the French building program affect the War of 1812? At the outset, the British had to concentrate their ships in European waters to deal with the growing French menace. This left too few ships in the American theater to blockade the coast when it would have done the most good: in the summer of 1812, when millions of dollars of American ships and cargoes and thousands of American seamen were at sea, trying to get home. Had the French been able to mount a credible naval threat later in the war, the British navy would have been hard-pressed to wage war effectively in both theaters simultaneously. If a serious French naval threat had materialized, doubtless the British would have done what they always did and put the European war first. This would have further weakened an already weak British blockade in America and thus aided the United States still more.

**Privateers—"The Militia of the Sea."** The War of 1812 was the last major war in which private armed vessels played a significant role. Although the terminology was not always consistent, there were two kinds of private armed vessels: (1) privateers, which were armed and had a large crew (75–150 men, depending on the size of the ship) but carried no cargo; and (2) letters-of-marque, which were armed and had a smaller crew (20–40 men) but carried a cargo. Privateers were fitted out to cruise against enemy commerce, while letters-of-marque were armed for defensive purposes and carried on trade, although they might take a prize if an opportunity presented itself. In practice, governments made little distinction between the two kinds of vessels in time of war. Each carried the same commission, and each had to give bond to use its weapons legally.[85]

Although privateers might be built expressly for cruising, in most cases they were simply speedy merchant vessels that were pierced to carry naval guns. Privateers needed speed to run down enemy merchant vessels and to escape enemy warships, but privateer captains had to think about more than just speed. A privateer that carried little ballast in its hold so that it could pick up speed by riding high in the water ran the risk of being top-heavy, especially if it carried too many guns on its main deck. A top-heavy vessel could capsize in rough seas. In the interest of safety, privateering captains had to strike a balance between speed and stability.

Known as "the militia of the sea," privateers offered small naval powers a way of annoying an enemy's commerce and provided a source of income to merchants and sailors as well as to governments (which either taxed the prizes or shared in the proceeds from their sale). But privateers were no substitute for a navy. They were not under the control of the national government, they could not protect a nation's coast or commerce, and they were unlikely to have a decisive effect on the outcome of a war. The most they could do was to drive up the cost of doing business (including insurance rates) for enemy merchants and thus increase the political and economic pressure to end a war.

Unlike naval vessels, which were under orders to destroy an enemy's shipping and were not afraid to fight, privateers were looking for easy prizes. Profit, not patriotism, was their motivation. Hence they invariably fled from enemy warships and were unlikely to risk an encounter with a merchant vessel that was armed unless it was thought to carry a particularly valuable cargo.

Although it is usually assumed that privateers forced unarmed or lightly-armed merchant vessels to surrender because of their superior armament, this was not always the case. Sometimes manpower was the deciding factor. The typical merchant vessel of less than 100 tons carried only 3 or 4 crewmen, and even large merchantmen of 250–300 tons carried only 12–15. Privateers, by contrast, usually carried at least 50 men and more commonly 100 or even 150 men.[86] This gave privateers a huge advantage in boarding and also enabled them to put a prize crew on board any captured vessel and continue to cruise for other prizes. Lightly-armed and thinly-manned merchant vessels often surrendered to privateers because they feared more being overwhelmed by armed and angry boarders than being cut up by naval guns.[87]

***The Role of American Privateers.*** The United States had a significant advantage in 1812 because its merchants knew about the declaration of war first and thus could fit out privateers before the British could react. The act declaring war that was passed on June 18, 1812, authorized privateering, but no commissions were issued until after June 29, three days after Congress passed a law laying down the rules and regulations for private armed ships.[88]

The first privateers to get to sea were mostly small pilot boats equipped with one large center gun, often called "Long Tom." These vessels carried 50 or 60 men armed with muskets, sabers, boarding pikes, and the like. According to one privateer captain, this "was quite enough to capture almost any British merchantman, at this stage of the war."[89] Later, when British merchants began to arm their ships, Americans had to increase the manpower and firepower of their privateers. Some, like the *America* (20–22) of Salem, the *Chasseur* (15–16) out of Baltimore, or the *True-Blooded Yankee* (18), which sailed from Brest, France, carried 15–25 naval guns and a crew of 150 and were every bit as formidable as small warships.

The privateer *America* (20), a schooner sailing out of Salem, Massachusetts, was one of the fastest vessels afloat in the War of 1812 and reportedly took 26 prizes in three successful cruises. (Maclay, *American Privateers*)

Normally, the western Atlantic would have teemed with potential targets for American privateers, but this was not the case in 1812. The non-importation act of 1811 barred British ships and goods from American ports, and this greatly reduced the number of British vessels that might be found nearby. Moreover, Congress authorized the president to grant passports to British merchants to ship property in the United States home. This was accepted practice under international law, and one of the clauses of the Jay Treaty, though now expired, had expressly guaranteed merchants 12 months to remove their property in the event of war.[90] Congress also exempted from seizure any packet boats that had left Great Britain with dispatches for the United States prior to September 1, 1812. The administration even ordered the release of two such boats that were seized by privateers in early July, before this measure became law.[91]

The United States relied more heavily on privateers to prosecute the war at sea after 1812 because fewer American warships could escape from port once the British blockaded the coast. Known for their speed, American privateers were coveted even by the Royal Navy. In October of 1813, Admiral Sir John Borlase Warren described nine captured privateers and letters-of-marque that he purchased for tender, harbor, and river service as "particularly fine Vessels of their Class and extremely fast Sailers."[92]

Although they normally sought to avoid British warships, occasionally American privateers fought rather than fled. In one of the fiercest engagements, the American privateer *Decatur* (7), sailing out of Charleston, South Carolina, not only captured H.M. Sloop *Dominica* (16) but in deadly hand-to-hand combat inflicted 75 percent casualties on the crew of the British warship.[93]

In the course of the war, the United States issued more than 1,100 commissions. Many ships received more than one commission because they were refitted for additional cruises. A majority of the commissions went to the three biggest maritime states: Massachusetts, Maryland, and New York. American privateers captured at least 1,410 British merchant ships. A third of these probably made it to an American port; a sixth were destroyed, ransomed, or used as cartels; while the remaining half were recaptured by the British.[94] The large number of merchant vessels taken in waters around the British Isles was particularly galling to Britain's mercantile community. Insurance rates in the Irish Channel reached a record high of 13 percent.[95] Angry British merchants responded by sending spirited memorials to Whitehall protesting the lack of protection.

The success of American privateers, however, should not be overemphasized. Even if privateers took an average of 500 prizes a year, that was still only about 2.5 percent of the British merchant fleet, and if half of the ships taken were recaptured, Britain's annual loss was only 1.25 percent. Admittedly, British merchants were more likely to lose their larger oceangoing vessels to American privateers, and for any recaptured ship they had to pay a salvage fee of one-sixth or one-eighth of their value. But far from being deterred by the threat from American privateers, British merchants actually increased the size of their commercial fleet slightly during the War of 1812.[96] In the end, British commercial losses at sea were far from devastating, and American privateers played only a minor role in inducing the British government to end the conflict.[97]

***The Role of British Privateers.*** Although privateering is usually associated with the United States in the War of 1812, British privateers also cruised for American prizes. How many British privateers were active and how many prizes they took is unknown. During the whole period of the French Revolutionary and Napoleonic Wars (1793–1815), the British government issued 4,000 commissions to privateers.[98] The London *Gazette* thought that the Royal Navy and British privateers took around 1,400 American prizes between them, and at least one British naval historian has suggested that this figure understated the total.[99] Even though the Royal Navy probably accounted for at least 75 percent of these prizes, British privateers still must have done considerable damage to American trade.

With so many lucrative targets nearby, Canadians were particularly active in privateering. Preferring to rely on small and lightly armed vessels, Canadian privateers usually cruised close to home. Privateering provided a huge boost to the economy of the Maritime provinces. Halifax teemed with ships preparing for cruises and with prizes brought in for adjudication, and the naval base there provided a ready market for captured food, naval stores, and ships.

More than 40 privately armed vessels sailed from ports in Nova Scotia and New Brunswick, and they brought in a total of 204 American prizes. Much of the damage was done by just three vessels—the *Liverpool Packet* (5), *Sir John Sherbrooke* (18), and *Retaliation* (5)—which brought in 80 prizes. According to one scholar, privateering produced a "commercial bonanza" that contributed to the "unprecedented prosperity" that the Maritime provinces enjoyed during the war.[100]

In sum, American merchant ships dared not leave port during the War of 1812 unless they were unusually fast. They had to be able to outrun not only the Royal Navy but also British privateers. Privateering, in short, was a weapon that both sides in the War of 1812 used to good advantage.

## THE WAR ON THE LAKES

**Who Took the First Prize on Inland Waters?** The first prize of the war taken on inland waters was the unarmed sloop *Commencement,* a small American merchantman carrying a cargo of salt and a crew of four that was captured about six miles from Buffalo on Lake Erie on June 27, 1812. Word of war had just reached the British side of the Niagara River (but not the American side), and the sloop had innocently set sail into Lake Erie from Buffalo when it was captured by two privately armed British boats and taken to Fort Erie as a prize of war.[101]

**The Battle of Lake Erie.** The Battle of Lake Erie was the most important battle in the Old Northwest. Master Commandant Oliver H. Perry's squadron sailed from its base at Put-in-Bay, South Bass Island, to challenge the British squadron under Commander Robert H. Barclay. The British were overmatched but lost only when Perry changed ships in the middle of the battle. After the guns on his flagship, U.S. Brig *Lawrence* (20), were knocked out of commission, Perry was rowed to the U.S. Brig *Niagara* (20), and this enabled him to bring fresh batteries to bear on the enemy, which turned the tide in the battle. Perry's victory gave the U.S. control of Lake Erie and enabled Major General William Henry Harrison to defeat an Anglo-Indian force in the Battle of the Thames/Moraviantown. This battle gave the U.S. control over most of the region.

Perry's celebrated victory had all the necessary ingredients to become a great American legend: a decisive battle on water that led to a significant victory on land, one of the highest casualty rates in the history of naval warfare, a great American hero with a reputation for luck, a dramatic moment (Perry's changing of ships), a stirring battle flag motto ("DON'T GIVE UP THE SHIP"), an inspired ship name (the U.S. Brig *Lawrence* was named after fallen naval hero James Lawrence), a celebrated after-action report ("We have met the enemy and they are ours"), and a long and bitter postwar feud between the two American principals in the battle (Perry and Jesse Elliott).

The Battle of Lake Erie guaranteed Perry's place in American history, and the mystique attached to the battle has been fed by the survival of a very powerful symbol of the battle: Perry's battle flag. It has long been on display at the U.S. Naval Academy in Annapolis, Maryland, where it has inspired generations of midshipmen.[102]

The Battle of Lake Erie itself was certainly decisive. It was the first time that the United States had ever defeated an entire enemy squadron and one of the few times that Great Britain had ever lost a squadron. Not only did it secure American naval superiority on Lake Erie, but it also paved the way for the American victory on land. The land battle, in turn, produced additional American heroes (most notably William Henry Harrison and Richard M.

The turning point of the Battle of Lake Erie came when Master Commandant Oliver H. Perry took command of the U.S. Brig *Niagara* and unleashed fresh broadsides into the British squadron. (Painting by Peter Rindlisbacher. Courtesy of the artist)

THE NORTHERN THEATER

0    50    100 miles
0   50  100  150 km

■ fort    ● battle site or town/village

Lake Superior

St. Joseph I.

■ Fort Mackinac

Lake Michigan

Lake Huron

Georgian Bay

Nottawasaga Bay

● Penetanguishene

Nottawasaga R.

L. Simcoe

Bay of Quinte

CANADA

UPPER

York ●

Lake Ontario

Stoney Creek ●

Burlington Bay

Ft. George ●■ Fort Niagara

Charlotte ●

Queenston ●

Niagara R.

Genesee R.

Malcolm's Mills ●

Grand R.

Ft. Erie ■● Black Rock

● Buffalo

MICHIGAN

TERRITORY

St. Clair R.

Thames R.

Moraviantown ●

Port Dover ●

Long Point

Lake Erie

Detroit ●

Sandwich ■

Detroit R.

Malden (Fort Amherstburg) ■

Erie ●

Raisin R.

Frenchtown ●

Put-in-Bay

Fort Miami ■

Maumee River

Fort Meigs ■

● Cleveland

PENNSYLVANIA

Fort Defiance ■

Sandusky R.

Fort Stephenson ■

Allegheny River

BLACK SWAMP

OHIO

Pittsburgh ●

Urbana ●

Ohio River

Dayton ●

VA.

VA.

This is a facsimile of Perry's battle flag, which flew from his flagship in the Battle of Lake Erie and now is at the U.S. Naval Academy in Annapolis, Maryland. (Lossing, *Pictorial Field-Book of the War of 1812*)

Johnson) and led to the death of Indian great Tecumseh and the disgrace of the British commanding officer, Major General Henry Procter.

Although all this is true, the Battle of Lake Erie lacked any broader significance because it was fought far from the centers of power, population, and commerce in the East. No American victory in this remote wilderness could wrest Canada from the British, nor could any British victory here secure Canada. Although the Battle of Lake Erie was decisive in this theater, it did not affect the outcome of the war and probably did not even affect the peace negotiations at Ghent.[103]

*How Quickly Was Perry's Squadron Built?* The bulk of Perry's squadron was built at Presque Isle on Lake Erie. Some accounts claim that the squadron was completed in 70 or 90 days because master shipbuilder Noah Brown arrived on the scene in early March of 1813 and the ships were launched in late May. But work on the ships was actually begun under Daniel Dobbins in September of 1812, and the vessels were not fully rigged, equipped, and ready for service until July of 1813. Although the squadron was constructed in a remarkably short time, it took ten months, not two or three.[104]

Master Commandant Oliver H. Perry (1785–1819) won immortality in 1813, first with his victory over the British squadron on Lake Erie and then with his after-action report, "We have met the enemy and they are ours." (Portrait by George Delleker. National Portrait Gallery, Smithsonian Institution)

This is a facsimile of Perry's famous report after the Battle of Lake Erie. Written in pencil on the back of an old letter, the after-action report was dispatched to Major General William Henry Harrison. (Lossing, *Pictorial Field-Book of the War of 1812*)

*A Wagonload of Powder.* In 1913, when the centennial of Perry's great victory was commemorated, one of the highlights was the shipment of a wagonload of powder from the factory of E.I. du Pont de Nemours and Company in Wilmington, Delaware, to Erie, Pennsylvania, where it was put aboard the recently rebuilt *Niagara*. The original event was depicted in a painting executed by Howard Pyle in 1912. Du Pont's own records, however, do not support this story. Although the company sold a lot of powder to the U.S. Army during the War of 1812, it sold none to the navy nor did it ship any to Erie.[105]

*Why Did Barclay Lift His Blockade?* When Perry completed the construction of his squadron at Presque Isle in July 1813, he faced the difficult and dangerous task of moving his ships across a sandbar into open water. This task would leave him vulnerable because he would have to strip his larger vessels of their guns and other equipment so that they could be lifted across the bar by floats known as "camels." Barclay had been patrolling these waters with the British squadron, but at this critical moment he sailed for Port Dover. This enabled Perry to get his ships across the bar without being molested.

Why did Barclay lift his blockade? Some contemporary documents mention a storm, which could have forced him into port for minor repairs. Or he might have gone to Port Dover to resupply his squadron. Ships built for service on the lakes were shallow-draft vessels because it was more important for them to be able to cruise in shallow waters than to undertake an extended voyage that would require a large hold capacity. But this meant that they had to resupply frequently.

Why did Barclay remain off station for so long? Locals later blamed him for transporting a pretty widow from Fort Amherstburg to Port Dover and then

Commander Robert H. Barclay (1785–1837) was defeated by a more powerful American squadron in the Battle of Lake Erie in 1813. For the second time in his naval career, he sustained serious battle wounds. (Portrait by unknown artist. Toronto Reference Library)

lingering there to attend a public dinner in his honor. But this story surfaced long after the fact and is probably untrue. It is more likely that Barclay remained in Port Dover to await the arrival of badly needed seamen that he hoped were en route.[106]

*Perry's Luck.* Oliver H. Perry's luck before and during the Battle of Lake Erie was remarkable. Infuriated by an apparent lack of respect and support from his superior, Commodore Isaac Chauncey, Perry sought a transfer a month before the battle, but fortunately for him the secretary of the navy denied his request. A fog prevented the British from attacking that portion of Perry's squadron that was built at Black Rock when it was moved from the Niagara River into Lake Erie, and the British never mounted an attack on his squadron when it was under construction at Presque Isle or when it was moved unarmed over the sandbar into Lake Erie. The wind changed in Perry's favor right before the main battle. Perry's squadron clearly outclassed Barclay's, but the latter put up a good fight, which made Perry's victory seem all the more impressive. Moreover, even though almost every officer and most of the enlisted men on board the U.S. Brig *Lawrence* were killed or wounded, Perry himself escaped injury. He also escaped injury when he transferred his command to the U.S. Brig *Niagara* (and this despite the hail of fire raining down on him) and when he sailed the *Niagara* back into the heart of the battle.

Like so many lucky people, however, the "Wilderness Commodore" made his own luck. He was courageous, aggressive, resolute, and decisive, and these traits served him well in battle. He sought a command on the lakes that many other naval officers avoided because they saw no prospect for either glory or prize money. He did a remarkable job of overseeing the construction of his squadron. He was careful to wear a plain seaman's jacket during most of the battle, which made him a less conspicuous target for snipers. He was smart enough to realize that changing vessels could determine the outcome of the battle and cool enough to execute the maneuver. And he came up with an after-action report that guaranteed his place in history. But his luck eventually ran out. He died from yellow fever on his 34th birthday in 1819 while en route to Trinidad after completing a diplomatic assignment in Venezuela.[107]

**The "Burlington Races."** On September 28, 1813, Commodore Sir James Yeo's British squadron engaged Commodore Isaac Chauncey's squadron on Lake Ontario about 12 miles south of York. Yeo's flagship, H.M. Ship *Wolfe* (21), was seriously damaged, and hence the British squadron fled toward Burlington Heights with Chauncey in pursuit. For 90 minutes the two squadrons sailed west, driven by gale force winds in what is usually called the "Burlington Races."

Local lore holds that Yeo escaped by riding the surging surf over a sandbar into what was then called Little Lake or Burlington Lake but has often

H.M. Ship *Wolfe* sailed across Lake Ontario in the "Burlington Races" but, contrary to popular opinion, never surged over a sand bar into Hamilton Harbour. (Painting by Peter Rindlisbacher. Courtesy of the artist)

been mistakenly called Burlington Bay (and is now Hamilton Harbour). This story is untrue. Burlington Bay is actually east of Hamilton Harbour in Lake Ontario near the town of Burlington. Moreover, no contemporary source mentions Yeo's navigational feat. The British ships drew far too much water to pass over the sandbar, there was no convenient opening through it, and a wooden bridge over what opening there was made passage impossible anyway. Yeo actually anchored his squadron outside the bar in Burlington Bay. Chauncey, fearing that the winds might drive his ships on to the shore, gave up the pursuit, thus ending the engagement.[108]

**The Battle of Lake Champlain.** If the Battle of Lake Erie was the great inland naval battle of 1813, the Battle of Lake Champlain was the great inland naval battle of 1814. It was more significant because it helped shape the outcome of the war in a more populous and thus more important theater. The campaign began when Lieutenant General George Prevost marched a large army into upper New York in the late summer of 1814. Shortly thereafter, Captain George Downie brought a British squadron down Lake Champlain to attack Master Commandant Thomas Macdonough's American squadron, which was at anchor in Plattsburgh Bay. In the ensuing battle, the two squadrons hammered away at one another with heavy artillery fire. For the United States, the bulk of the fire was delivered by the U.S. Corvette *Saratoga* (26), the U.S. Brig *Eagle* (20), and the U.S. Schooner *Ticonderoga* (17); for Great Britain, it was delivered by H.M. Ship *Confiance* (37) and H.M. Sloop *Linnet* (16). Downie was

Master Commandant Thomas Macdonough (1783–1825) won the most significant American naval victory of the war on Lake Champlain in 1814 by winding his flagship around in the middle of the battle. (Portrait by Thomas Gimbrede. National Portrait Gallery, Smithsonian Institution)

quickly killed, and eventually both the *Saratoga* and *Confiance* were knocked out of action.

At this point, Macdonough performed the masterstroke that decided the battle. Having set his kedge anchors some distance away from his flagship, he was able to "wind" the *Saratoga* around and thus bring a fresh battery to bear on *Confiance*. Downie's anchors had been shot away when he approached the American squadron, and thus Lieutenant James Robertson, who had assumed command after Downie's death, could not match Macdonough's maneuver by rotating the *Confiance*. With his fresh battery, Macdonough pummeled the British ship into submission, and most of the British squadron surrendered. With the loss of control of Lake Champlain, Prevost ordered his army to return to Canada, and the campaign ended.[109]

***Construction of the U.S. Brig* Eagle.** In the shipbuilder's war that preceded the battle, speed was at a premium. Both sides raced ships to completion, using green timber and taking shortcuts in design and construction. The U.S. Brig *Eagle* (20) was launched 19 days after construction began and was completely outfitted and ready for service 14 days later. In 33 days, an astonishingly short time, standing timber had been transformed into a warship ready for action. Adding this brig to the American squadron tipped the balance on Lake Champlain in Macdonough's favor and made victory possible.[110]

***Macdonough's Masterstroke.*** Macdonough's maneuver in the battle is sometimes depicted as a stroke of genius, but it was hardly unusual. Winding was commonplace in harbors because it made it possible to move ships without putting up their sails. In addition, ships fighting at anchor often prepared for this maneuver so that they could change fronts or bring a fresh battery to bear on the enemy. In the Second Battle of St. Leonard's Creek in the Chesapeake, the British warships blockading the river used their cables to turn their ships so that they could respond to American batteries that had opened up on them from the nearby heights. Macdonough's success was not a result of uncommon genius but rather of good planning and sound execution.[111]

***Who Used Hot Shot?*** In his after-action report, Master Commandant Macdonough claimed that "the *Saratoga* was twice set on fire by hot Shot from the Enemy's Ship."[112] Years later, James Fenimore Cooper, who probably got his information from naval officers, said: "The Americans found a furnace on board the Confiance, with eight or ten heated shot in it."[113] Still later,

Theodore Roosevelt reported that after the battle "every American officer who went aboard the *Confiance* saw the furnace and the hot shot."[114] The Royal Navy, however, prohibited such furnaces, and in their court martial, the surviving British naval officers denied that they had had a furnace on board. They suggested that the *Saratoga* must have been hit by hot shot from an American battery on shore that was aiming for the British ships but missed its mark.[115]

Where does the truth lie? The evidence suggests that there was no furnace on the British ship. The *Confiance* was still unfinished when it sailed, and putting a heavy furnace on board when so much basic work still needed to be done seems unlikely. In addition, it was tricky and dangerous to move hot shot from a furnace to a gun. The operation was much safer on land, which was why the Royal Navy prohibited hot shot on its ships. Whatever the American officers who boarded the British ship saw, it seems unlikely that it was a hot shot furnace.[116]

Could the *Saratoga* have been hit by hot shot from an American shore battery? Again, this seems unlikely. Although it appears that Brigadier General Alexander Macomb had a furnace for hot shot available for use on shore, there is no evidence that he used it against the warships on the lake.[117] Macdonough did not mention any such artillery support, and Macomb said that he considered providing support, but no gun was fired because everyone on shore was "convinced that the vessels were beyond their reach."[118] Both squadrons were apparently beyond the range of any shore batteries.[119]

But if the hot shot came from neither the British ship nor the American shore, where did it come from? This is a mystery that defies easy explanation. The only other possibility, and it is sheer speculation, is that perhaps something else caused the fire on the *Saratoga*.

**Where Was the Greatest Naval Arms Race of the War?** The most remarkable naval arms race of the War of 1812, and one of the most remarkable of this period, took place not in the great dockyards facing the sea, but rather on the shores of Lake Ontario, which was inaccessible to oceangoing vessels. In this shipbuilder's war, each side sought to outbuild the other to gain command of the lake.[120] The climax of this construction program came in September of 1814, when the British launched H.M. Ship *St. Lawrence* (104 guns) from the shipyard at Point Frederick in Kingston. The ship was outfitted and

H.M. Ship *St. Lawrence,* one of the most powerful ships in the world, was put into service on Lake Ontario on October 16, 1814. Four days into its maiden voyage, the British ship was struck by lightening, damaging the main mast and killing or wounding several crew members. (Painting by Peter Rindlisbacher. Courtesy of the artist)

put into service the following month. This gave the British command of Lake Ontario for the rest of the war.

Compared to oceangoing warships, the shallow-draft *St. Lawrence* was flimsy and unstable. About a third of its guns were carronades, so it needed to be close to an enemy to take full advantage of its firepower. But that firepower was impressive. Measured by the

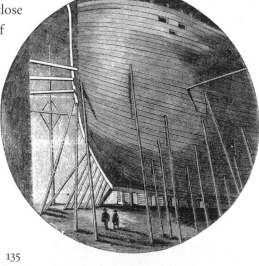

The American answer to the powerful British ship *St. Lawrence* on Lake Ontario was the *New Orleans,* named after the battle fought near the end of the war. Never completed, the ship is shown here under construction. (Lossing, *Pictorial Field-Book of the War of 1812*)

weight of its broadside, the *St. Lawrence* was the most powerful ship in the British navy and one of the most powerful in the world. Its broadside was twice that of the heavy American frigate *Constitution* (52–55); 36 percent larger than H.M. Ship *Victory* (104), Vice Admiral Horatio Nelson's flagship at Trafalgar; and more than 5 percent larger than even the super first-rate, H.M. Ship *Caledonia* (120), which was considered the finest ship in the British navy.

The British had two other first rates, *Canada* and *Wolfe*, on the stocks at Point Frederick when the war ended. Nor was the United States idle. At the shipyard at Sackets Harbor, Americans had two huge ships under construction, *Chippewa* and *New Orleans*, that were supposed to be more powerful than the British ships. Thus, if the War of 1812 had continued for another year, five of the most powerful ships in the world might well have been battling for supremacy on Lake Ontario.[121]

The U.S. built its warships for service on Lake Ontario at Sackets Harbor. Shown leaving port is the ill-fated U.S. Schooner *Hamilton*, which sank in a storm in 1813. (Painting by Peter Rindlisbacher. Courtesy of the artist)

## CHAPTER 4

# Soldiers, Sailors, and Civilians

T he interaction of soldiers, sailors, and civilians has always shaped the character and outcome of wars. Technology and equipment also play a role, but in the War of 1812 neither side could claim a significant advantage in these areas. Hence, there was a greater premium on the talent, training, and experience of individuals.

The United States had a much larger population than Canada, but it was never able to fully capitalize on this advantage. At the beginning of the war, it could overcome neither the stupendous logistical problems that it faced nor the advantages that the British enjoyed in military experience. By the time the U.S. had gained some experience and developed a better logistical system, the British had an army in North America that was too large to overcome. Hence, the United States was never able to impose its will on the British or to conquer Canada.

The War of 1812 produced its share of heroes and scapegoats. Because the conflict was only a footnote in their history, the British never knew their heroes or quickly forgot them. In the United States and Canada, however, the story was different. The war played such an important role in forging the identity of these two nations that their wartime heroes took on a special meaning, their place in history forever secure. For the same reason, those heroes gradually became inescapably enshrouded in myth.

## WARTIME LEADERSHIP

**Rating Madison's Presidency.** James Madison, who served as president from 1809 to 1817, was intimately connected to the War of 1812. Unlike Jefferson, Madison did not have the luxury of a honeymoon term. Instead, he inherited Jefferson's European crisis, and, as the chief architect of the restrictive system, he showed no interest in jettisoning the futile and costly policy of using American trade as an instrument of foreign policy. Thus, after the embargo was lifted at the end of Jefferson's presidency in early 1809, the nation suffered through a period of non-intercourse and non-importation before going to war against Great Britain in 1812.

Madison did not prepare the nation adequately for war. The trade restrictions that he endorsed after 1809 deprived the government of much-needed revenue to finance a major war, and his failure to throw his weight behind the renewal of the National Bank in 1810–11 deprived the nation of a valuable, and perhaps essential, financial institution. In addition, Madison did not insist that war be delayed until the nation's military preparations had matured or that a sound policy for financing the war be adopted. Perhaps not all of this was feasible, but surely Madison could have done more. Instead, he put his faith in the vain hope that Britain would quickly cave in to American demands or that Canada would quickly succumb to American arms.

Madison lacked Jefferson's talent for managing other Republicans or for winning converts. Partly because of his temperament and partly because of constitutional scruples about the proper role of the president, he was never as strong a leader as Jefferson. Although willing to support a declaration of war, he never appeared to be out in front of the war movement.

James Madison (1751–1836) was a gifted statesman but a weak president. Cautious and retiring, he failed to give energetic direction to the war effort. (Portrait by Gilbert Stuart. Library of Congress)

Federalists might call it "Mr. Madison's War," but the conflict never really bore his stamp. It would probably be more accurate to say that Madison happened to be president when the War of 1812 occurred.

As a wartime president, Madison showed commendable restraint in resisting cries to limit the civil liberties of his domestic opponents, but in other ways his penchant for inaction undermined the war effort. He tolerated dissension and disloyalty in his cabinet, he was often unable or unwilling to impose his will on Congress, and he was slow to get good commanders into the field. His refusal to dismiss the bungling, self-serving, and disloyal James Wilkinson from the army in 1812 was particularly unfortunate. As a result, this one-time Spanish spy made considerable mischief, first in New Orleans and then in the critical St. Lawrence River theater.

In the summer of 1813 Madison became ill for five weeks, most likely a victim of dysentery. His very life was despaired of. Although Congress that summer probably drifted more than was customary, Madison's influence over that body was so weak that his poor health did not make much difference. Nor did it have much effect on the course of the war in the field.

Madison's shortcomings as a wartime president were clear to those who knew him. "His spirit and capacity for a crisis of war," declared Congressman Charles J. Ingersoll of Pennsylvania, "are very generally called in question." "Our President," added John C. Calhoun, "has not . . . those commanding talents which are necessary to controul those around him."[1] Even his fellow Virginians questioned Madison's leadership. His "amiable temper and delicate sensibility," said one, "are the real sources of our embarrassments."[2] Many Americans shared these reservations. As a result, Madison barely won reelection in 1812, coming closer to defeat than any other wartime president.[3]

Presidential surveys and studies take into account Madison's weakness as a leader, but they are still far too generous in their assessment. In nine surveys and assessments conducted since 1980, Madison ranks from 9th to 20th, averaging 15th out of 36–41 presidents.[4] Although this is more accurate than the assessments of Jefferson, Madison, like Jefferson, benefits from other factors. He had a wonderful cast of mind and a penetrating intellect; he collaborated with Jefferson in a commendable lifelong career of public service; and he had a number of exceptional accomplishments to his credit. Not only was he the father of the Constitution and the author of the Bill of Rights, but as Jefferson's secretary of state he showed a remarkable talent for marshaling legal precedents and logical arguments in the state papers that he crafted.

In spite of Madison's many gifts and accomplishments, it is hard to imagine how he can be ranked in the top half of American presidents. It is not simply that he was a weak wartime president, but the restrictive system and the War of 1812, after all, were at the heart of a failed foreign policy. Under these circumstances, Madison probably deserves to rank no higher than 25th.[5]

**Sir George Prevost's Leadership.** If American historians have overrated Madison's wartime leadership, British and Canadian historians have underrated that of Sir George Prevost. This is mainly because Prevost, unlike Madison, actually took the field during the war, and he became the scapegoat for the failure of Britain's campaign in New York in 1814.

Prevost had had a distinguished military and civilian career in the West Indies before being appointed lieutenant governor of Nova Scotia in 1808 and then governor of all of Canada and commander-in-chief of British North America in 1811. As a civilian administrator, Prevost did a fine job of managing hostile factions in Canada. In sharp contrast to his predecessor, Sir James Craig, who was accused by the French-speaking population in Lower Canada of unleashing a "reign of terror" against them, Prevost (who spoke French and had experience governing a captured French colony in the West Indies) worked at conciliation. He did an equally good job of orchestrating the defense of British North America during the War of 1812.[6] In the first two years of the contest,

he pursued a cautious and conservative policy, which was in accordance with his orders and entirely appropriate given the defensive nature of the war and his limited resources.

Lieutenant General Sir George Prevost (1767–1816) should be remembered as the savior of British North America, but his weak battlefield performance damaged his reputation, and he became the scapegoat for the failure of Britain's New York offensive in 1814. (Engraving by Samuel W. Reynolds after a portrait by unknown artist. Library and Archives Canada)

Prevost realized that because of slow communication with the mother country and Canada's limited shipping season (typically May to November), he could not replace any battlefield losses sustained in the summer until the following spring. This may explain why he was overly cautious as a battlefield commander. In 1813 he oversaw an assault on Sackets Harbor, which ended in failure, and a reconnaissance in force against Fort George, which was hardly necessary to get the information that he sought on enemy strength and readiness. Moreover, he had a penchant for making enemies, and this as much as anything explains why he fared so badly in postwar assessments. Even so, had the War of 1812 ended in mid-1814, he might well be remembered today as the savior of Canada. But the war did not end then, and Prevost's final campaign undid his reputation.

The British government shipped some 10,000 troops to Prevost in the summer of 1814, and shortly thereafter he marched this army into upper New York. His aim was to provide for the security of Canada by seizing a large chunk of American territory on the traditional invasion route that ran along the Richelieu River and Lake Champlain. Any occupied territory also would give the British a bargaining chip in the peace negotiations. However, the British government expressly warned Sir George to take care "not to expose His Majesty's Forces to being cut off by too extended a line of advance."[7]

When Captain George Downie's British squadron was defeated on Lake Champlain, Prevost, fearing that he might be cut off, ordered his army to withdraw to Canada. His troops, some of whom were Wellington's veterans, were already angry over having to comply with a rigorous dress code, and the withdrawal infuriated them. These ill-disposed soldiers, working with civilian political allies in Lower Canada and Britain and supported by a British naval establishment determined to hang Downie's defeat on Prevost, launched an attack on the governor. Recalled to Great Britain, Prevost demanded a court martial to clear his name but died in early 1816 before the court could convene.[8]

Although Prevost's decision to withdraw from Plattsburgh can be criticized, it was in line with his orders—to avoid being cut off in American territory—and it is not inconceivable that even his fine veteran army might have become isolated and suffered a disaster similar to the one that befell Major General John Burgoyne after the Battle of Saratoga in 1777.

Prevost's reputation might have survived his final campaign had he lived long enough to defend himself in Britain or to answer one of his sharpest critics. In early 1815 ten letters appeared under the name of "Veritas" in the Montreal *Herald* attacking Prevost's wartime leadership. The following summer the letters were reprinted as a pamphlet that was more widely circulated. These letters were probably written by John Richardson, an influential Montreal merchant, not to be confused with the Canadian soldier, novelist, and historian of the same name.[9]

"Veritas" condemned Prevost for inadequate war preparations in 1812, for failing to destroy the American squadron at Sackets Harbor and losing control of Lake Erie in 1813, for refusing to reinforce British forces on the Niagara front and retreating from Plattsburgh in 1814, and in general for being indecisive and too defense-minded. "Sir George had the extraordinary facility," said "Veritas," "of either never attempting an active operation, or of thinking of it only when the time for practical execution was past." "The merit of preserving [Canada] from conquest," "Veritas" concluded, "belongs not to him."[10]

Richardson's screed was neither accurate nor fair. It showed no understanding of Prevost's strategy, nor of the manpower and supply problems that he faced. Nevertheless, the indictment helped fix the standard view of Prevost. After Prevost's death, however, no less a figure than the Duke of Wellington called his defense of Canada "one of the brightest pages in the Military annals of Great Britain."[11] Surely given Prevost's distinguished record of service and his role both in administering and preserving Canada, he deserved a better fate then and is entitled to a better reputation today.[12]

**Army Leadership.** Leadership in the opposing armies played a central role in shaping the outcome of the War of 1812. The British depended on a corps of professional officers, who on the whole were a capable lot. The United States, on the other hand, relied on a combination of professional officers, militia officers, and political appointees, most of whom lacked command and combat experience.

Through most of the eighteenth century, the British army had been the Royal Navy's weak sister, and prior to the French Revolutionary Wars, the practice of purchasing commissions had saddled the army with far too many young and inexperienced officers. The service was also greatly weakened by widespread absenteeism of its gentlemen officers. However, the Duke of York transformed the army during his first tour as commander-in-chief (1795–1809). He reduced the proportion of purchased commissions to about 20 percent, and he cut back significantly on absenteeism. His reforms, coupled with years of experience gained by hard fighting in the West Indies, Egypt, the Mediterranean, Portugal, and Spain, had transformed the British army by 1812 into a formidable force.[13]

The United States, by contrast, lacked a professional and experienced officer corps. The Military Academy at West Point, founded in 1802, had produced some officers, but not enough by 1812 to make much of a difference. Moreover, except for an occasional Indian war, there had been little opportunity for battlefield experience since the American Revolution. The lack of professionalism and experience put the new nation at a huge disadvantage in 1812. It was not until the last year of the war that the United States finally fielded a group of officers who could meet the British on equal terms.

Although one might call the War of 1812 a "colonel's war" because there were so many small-scale engagements, the mortality rate of the general officers says something about the leadership style and courage in each army. The British lost four senior major generals in the War of 1812: Isaac Brock at Queenston Heights in 1812, Robert Ross at North Point near Baltimore in 1814, and Edward Pakenham and Samuel Gibbs at New Orleans in 1815. The United States, on the other hand, lost four junior brigadier generals: two regular army officers, Zebulon Pike at York and Leonard Covington at Crysler's Farm in 1813, and two New York militia officers, John Swift on a patrol near Fort George in 1814 and Daniel Davis in the sortie from Fort Erie shortly thereafter.

British generals, professional to the core, were always willing to put themselves in harm's way. As Major General John Lambert said of Pakenham, he "never in his life could refrain from being at the post of honour, and sharing the danger to which the troops were exposed."[14] Some American generals were willing to risk all, too. Besides the four brigadier generals who were killed in action, Andrew Jackson, Jacob Brown, and Winfield Scott showed considerable courage in the heat of battle. In fact, Scott was so reckless that it is a wonder that he survived the war.

The U.S. also had a number of "political generals" who preferred to manage their campaigns from the safety of the rear. This group included men who were commissioned because of their political connections (such as Henry Dearborn, William Hull, Stephen Van Rensselaer, Wade Hampton, and William Winder) as well as those who were professional soldiers but put politics or personal advancement first (most notably James Wilkinson). Although many factors shaped the outcome of the war, the lack of experience and heavy reliance on political generals help explain America's poor showing in 1812 and 1813.

*Who Were the Best British Generals?* The British were reasonably well served by their generals in this war. Most were experienced professional officers who had been in combat and were accustomed to command. Although the best British officers were in Europe, those sent to North America were nonetheless more experienced and combat-tested than their American counterparts, at least early in the war. Moreover, Sir George Prevost, the architect of Canada's successful defensive strategy in 1812–13, did a good job of managing these men and the assets they had at their disposal.

Conventional wisdom rates Major General Isaac Brock as the best British general, and this assessment is undoubtedly correct even though Brock was killed early in the war. Brock was a shrewd and energetic officer who inspired confidence, understood how to use military intelligence and wage psychological warfare, handled his Indian allies well, and efficiently managed his men and logistics although responsible for two fronts at opposite ends of Lake Erie. Initially he shared the British high command's skepticism about the feasibility of defending Upper Canada, but Brock ultimately concluded that the province could be saved. If not for him, Upper Canada probably would have been abandoned in 1812.

Brock has been faulted for placing himself in too much jeopardy at Queenston Heights (and thus getting killed), but this was the way that military leaders often inspired their men. When someone asked Brock shortly before his death to be more careful, he reportedly said: "How can I expect my men to go where I am afraid to lead them?"[15] Nor was his leadership style unusual. Most generals in this era led from the front.

If Brock had a weakness, it was not that he was reckless but that he was evidently uninterested in details. "Poor General Brock's high spirit," commented one British officer, "would never descend to particulars."[16] Like many men of vision and action, Brock was apparently bored with the drone work that was necessary to carry out his plans.[17]

Lieutenant General Gordon Drummond ranks second to Brock. He managed his assets efficiently on the Niagara frontier. After the United States had evacuated Fort George on the Canadian side in late 1813, he launched a successful counterattack, seizing Fort Niagara on the American side. His ruthless

Lieutenant General Gordon Drummond (1772–1854) showed excellent command skills when he took charge of British operations on the Niagara frontier at the end of 1813. (Painting by Malcolm Drummond, 1885. M400. McCord Museum, Montreal)

retaliation for the burning of Newark/ Niagara, which left the American side of the Niagara in flames, was both appropriate and effective in that it further intimidated and demoralized the American militia. In 1814, when General Jacob Brown returned to Canada with a large and well-trained force, Drummond achieved a tactical draw at Lundy's Lane, which induced the American army to take refuge in Fort Erie. Drummond might be criticized for not pursuing the American army after Lundy's Lane, but both armies were utterly exhausted. Less justified was his assault on Fort Erie, which was ill advised and led to a costly British defeat. Even so, he effectively blunted the American offensive, ensuring that this part of Upper Canada remained in British hands, and before the year was out Brown's army had returned to the United States.[18]

Two army officers serving in other theaters—Major General Robert Ross and Major General Edward Pakenham—were also accomplished leaders. Both had earned superb reputations in the Peninsular War, and yet both were killed in America. Ross spearheaded the successful assault on Washington before losing his life outside Baltimore. Pakenham's only American campaign ended in disaster at New Orleans. He can be criticized for his frontal assault against the American line, although the outcome might have been different had he faced any American commander other than the redoubtable Andrew Jackson.[19]

***Who Were the Best American Generals?*** On the American side, the generals early in the war were far worse than their British counterparts. By the end of the war, however, several fine leaders had emerged, and the best American generals were every bit as good as their British counterparts.

Andrew Jackson is often rated the best American general, and this is probably justified. He showed a remarkable talent for overcoming obstacles, and

Major General Jacob Brown (1775–1828) was an exceptionally able regular army officer who came up through the New York militia. He never hesitated to fight, and he knew how to manage men and material to achieve results. (Engraving by unknown artist after a portrait by Alonzo Chappel. Library and Archives Canada)

by sheer force of personality, he got more than any other American general out of untrained militia and volunteers as well as unseasoned regulars. Jackson had a good understanding of logistics and of the problems of waging warfare in the wilderness, and because he had come up through the militia, he knew how to manage citizen soldiers. The series of victories he won over the Creeks in the Old Southwest and over the British at New Orleans, feats that were accomplished mainly with militia, established his military reputation and ultimately catapulted him into the White House. He sometimes ignored orders from Washington and imposed too draconian a regimen upon his men, but he might not have succeeded had he done otherwise.[20]

Ranking just behind Jackson is Major General Jacob Brown, a first-class officer who is little remembered today even though he played a central role in the War of 1812. Like Jackson, Brown came up through the ranks of the militia and always worked well with citizen soldiers. Like Jackson, he understood logistics and wilderness warfare and never shied away from battle, although he was more of a slugger and lacked Jackson's grasp of tactics. Unlike Jackson, Brown engaged large numbers of British troops on open ground, beating them at Sackets Harbor and Chippawa as well as in the American sortie from Fort Erie. After the war, he served as commanding general and played a crucial role in shaping the postwar army.[21]

Winfield Scott was another American general officer who distinguished himself during the war. Sometimes called "the hero of three wars" because he played a significant role in the War of 1812, the Mexican War, and the Civil War, Scott did a fine job of leading men at Queenston Heights in 1812, Fort George in 1813, and Chippawa in 1814. He also did a superb job of training his brigade in 1814. Like Jackson and Brown, Scott had a taste for battle, but sometimes he was reckless if not foolhardy. At Lundy's Lane in 1814, he refused to withdraw despite holding an untenable position and suffering dreadful losses. Hence his performance must rank below that of Jackson or Brown.[22]

Also in the second tier but ranking behind Scott was Major General William Henry Harrison. Like Jackson and Brown, Harrison was a frontier general who understood wilderness logistics and could manage regulars as well as militia. He deserves credit for building up the western army in 1812, working effectively with Master Commandant Oliver H. Perry in 1813, and engineering the close American victory at Tippecanoe in 1811 and the more decisive victory at the Thames in 1813. The following spring, however, he became so angry over Secretary of War John Armstrong's meddling that he abruptly resigned his commission.[23]

Major General Peter B. Porter of the New York militia also deserves high praise. He did an exceptional job of leading militia in the defense of Buffalo in 1813 and militia and Indians at Chippawa, Lundy's Lane, and Fort Erie in 1814. Even before Porter's finest hour in the sortie from Fort Erie in 1814, Major General Jacob Brown called him a man of "rare qualifications" and "a brave and efficient officer" who possessed a "mind cool and collected" under fire.[24] Porter was the only militia officer that Congress honored with a gold medal and doubtless would have followed Jackson and Brown into the high command of the regular army if the war had lasted much longer.[25]

Major General Peter B. Porter (1773–1844) of the New York militia was, like Andrew Jackson and Jacob Brown, a gifted militia officer. He showed his command skills in the bloody fighting on the Niagara frontier in 1814. (Lossing, *Pictorial Field-Book of the War of 1812*)

***Who Were the Worst Generals?*** If the War of 1812 produced first-class generals, it also exposed some bad generals. Who was the worst? On the British side, there are several candidates for this distinction, although it is difficult to pick a winner because all had some redeeming characteristics.

Major General Henry Procter (who was a colonel at the beginning of the war) was a good regimental officer who had contributed to British success in the Old Northwest early in the war. Promoted to general in 1813, Procter soon showed that he was not up to his new command responsibilities. He was defeated in the Battle of the Thames after Perry's victory forced the British to withdraw from Detroit. Although Procter blamed the defeat on his men, he was badly outnumbered, and a military court rightly convicted him of mismanaging the campaign.[26]

In contrast to Procter, Major General Sir Roger Sheaffe was a poor regimental officer who was so harsh with his men that they once had mutinied against him. As a general officer, he was cautious and unimaginative and did not inspire confidence. Although Sheaffe must be credited with a modest share of the British victory at Queenston Heights in 1812, he so mismanaged the deployment of his troops that his non-commissioned officers were barely able to unscramble them in time to prevail.[27] Moreover, Sheaffe was roundly criticized in 1813 for abandoning York without putting up much resistence to an invading American force. Since he was badly outnumbered, this criticism was not entirely justified, but by then he was so unpopular that Sir George Prevost removed him from command.[28] Another general officer, Major General Francis de Rottenburg, was a veteran who did not perform as well as expected during the War of 1812. De Rottenburg had arrived in Canada in at the age of 53 in 1810 with an impressive résumé and a reputation for the innovative use of light infantry. But like so many of his American counterparts, he was now past his prime and had become much too cautious. He did little during the war to enhance his reputation and much to alienate the local population.[29]

On the American side, there are more candidates for the distinction of being the worst general: Brigadier General William Hull (who was called "the Old Lady" and lost his nerve at Detroit); Major General Henry Dearborn (who was known as "Granny" and showed no stomach for command or battle); Brigadier General Alexander Smyth (who refused to take part in a planned invasion across the Niagara River in 1812 and was called "Van

Bladder" because of his pompous proclamations); Brigadier General William Winder (who mismanaged the defense of Washington in 1814); and Major General James Wilkinson (an inveterate intriguer who never won a battle or lost a court martial).

Wilkinson is the winner in this dubious category because he combined bad military decisions with a talent for unsavory and self-serving actions that ignored the needs of the nation and the welfare of his men. Although he had little combat experience, Wilkinson managed to work his way up the command ladder in the American army, and when "Mad" Anthony Wayne died in 1796, he became the army's ranking officer.

Wilkinson was known to have an appetite for booty and a penchant for intrigue, and it was widely and correctly suspected that he was a Spanish spy and agent. John Randolph of Roanoke described him as the only man he knew "who was from the bark to the very core a villain," and others shared this view.[30] But as much as they despised Wilkinson, his enemies were never able to topple him from power. Although repeatedly examined by army boards and military courts, he always managed to land on his feet, partly because he had a talent for cultivating his superiors and partly because he was good at covering his tracks.

In 1806 Wilkinson was a central player in Aaron Burr's conspiracy to detach the West from the United States, but by turning against Burr, he managed to escape punishment. Three years later, Wilkinson ordered his army

of 2,000 men to make camp in the swamps of Terre aux Boeufs near New Orleans so that he could line his pockets (legally and illegally) and pursue the pleasures of the Crescent

Major General James Wilkinson (1757–1826) was the worst general on either side in the war and probably the worst general in American history. A corrupt intriguer, he usually put his own interests over those of his men and the nation. (Detail, portrait by unknown artist. National Portrait Gallery, Smithsonian Institution)

City. In a year, he lost half of his command, some to desertion but most to disease. This was the worst peacetime disaster to befall the U.S. Army in the early national period.[31]

Because of his shady reputation, the War Department was reluctant to send Wilkinson to the Canadian frontier even after war had been declared. By 1813, however, he had made so many enemies in New Orleans that the militia would not serve under him and Louisiana's U.S. senators, both of whom were Republicans, threatened to go into opposition if he were not removed. To quell this incipient rebellion, the administration ordered Wilkinson to the St. Lawrence frontier in March of 1813.[32]

Wilkinson took his time traveling north, leaving New Orleans in June and reaching Sackets Harbor in August with orders from the War Department to attack Montreal from the west in conjunction with Major General Wade Hampton, who was to approach from the south. Wilkinson had so little confidence in the mission that he asked for permission to surrender if things went badly, and during the campaign he dosed himself with so much laudanum to cope with dysentery that he could hardly manage his command. Dogged by Colonel Joseph Morrison's British force, he dispatched Brigadier General John P. Boyd to do battle with Morrison at Crysler's Farm, only to see the American army routed by a much smaller British force. Giving up the campaign, Wilkinson went into winter quarters at French Mills in New York, where his men suffered egregiously from exposure and want. Wilkinson mounted his final campaign in March of 1814 against the village of Lacolle Mill (modern Cantic, Quebec), only to fail again.

Wilkinson was soon relieved of command and subsequently dropped from the ranks of the army. Never in its history was the U.S. Army so ill-served by a senior officer. Wilkinson was not simply the worst general officer on either side in the War of 1812 but probably the worst general in American history.[33]

**Did Wellington Refuse the American Command?** It is often said that the Duke of Wellington refused the American command when it was offered to him in the fall of 1814. This is untrue. In a pair of letters to the prime minister (Lord Liverpool), the Iron Duke did not reject the offer but rather said that the government should not consider sending him to America before the following spring (because of the critical state of affairs in Europe) nor

The Duke of Wellington (1769–1852), Britain's greatest general in the Napoleonic Wars, was offered the North American command in 1814. Contrary to popular belief, he did not refuse the offer. (Engraving by Henry H. Meyer after a portrait by William Beechey. Library and Archives Canada)

should it expect much success from him. "I feel no objection to going to America," he said, "though [without control of the lakes] I don't promise to myself much success there."[34] In a letter written about the same time to Lord Bathurst, the secretary of state for war and the colonies, Wellington repeated that he had "no objection whatever" to going to America in the spring. "It will be for you to consider whether I can be most useful to you there, here, or elsewhere."[35]

**Naval Leadership.** Although the outcome of the War of 1812 was determined by what happened on land, both belligerents had a rich maritime tradition and first-class naval commanders. Within the limits of their service, each nation used its naval power to good effect. The British established a blockade of the United States which was somewhat porous but nonetheless had a crushing effect on American trade and government revenue. The United States, for its part, responded with some stirring naval victories at sea, but where American naval power was most telling was on the inland seas: Lake Erie, where Master Commandant Oliver H. Perry cut Britain's supply line to the West; Lake Champlain, where Master Commandant Thomas Macdonough forced a British army to withdraw; and Lake Borgne, where Lieutenant Thomas ap Catesby Jones slowed the British advance on New Orleans.[36]

*Who Were the Best British Naval Commanders?* Picking the best British naval commander in the war is no easy task. All were accomplished professionals with impressive resumes. Admiral Sir John Borlase Warren and Vice Admiral Sir Alexander Cochrane did a good job of managing Britain's naval assets in the Atlantic theater, providing transportation and support for the

Rear Admiral George Cockburn (1772–1853) was the pre-eminent naval figure on the British side in the war. Although hated in the U.S. for his predatory warfare in the Chesapeake, he showed excellent command skills and always obeyed the rules of war as he understood them. (Portrait by W. Greatbatch. Library and Archives Canada)

British raids along the coast and sealing off the United States with a blockade. Similarly, although largely ignoring Lake Erie and Lake Champlain, Commodore Sir James Yeo did a fine job of building up and preserving his naval force on Lake Ontario, thus denying the United States command of this more important lake.

The Royal Navy also had a number of excellent ship commanders. Captain Philip Broke of H.M. Ship *Shannon* (52) had trained his crew so well that he captured the U.S. Frigate *Chesapeake* (50) in 15 minutes. Similarly, Captain James Hillyar managed his assets intelligently in the Pacific, shutting down the depredations of the U.S. Frigate *Essex* (46) and ultimately defeating the American ship. Perhaps even more impressive was the service of Commander (later Captain) William H. Mulcaster, who was not only an excellent ship commander on Lake Ontario but also did a fine job with a detachment of Yeo's squadron in the warfare waged on the St. Lawrence River in 1813.

But the outstanding British naval figure in this war was Rear Admiral George Cockburn. If the British wanted to wage predatory warfare in the Chesapeake, Cockburn was the best man for the job. Demonstrating a remarkable flair for amphibious warfare, he led marines and seamen in one successful raid after another, sometimes using rockets to panic opposing militia. Despite waging this kind of unconventional warfare, Cockburn maintained excellent discipline among his men and scrupulously adhered to the laws of war as he understood them. It was a tribute to his talents that an American surgeon referred to him as "Admiral—or General Cockburn, for he appeared to be called [by his men] one or the other indif[f]erently."[37]

Cockburn might be criticized for endorsing the failed attacks on Craney Island and Fort McHenry and for having too keen an interest in plunder. But he was largely responsible for two of Britain's greatest successes in the Chesapeake: the destruction of Captain Joshua Barney's flotilla of gunboats on the Patuxent River and the capture and occupation of Washington. Cockburn not only proposed the attack on the capital but later persuaded Major General Robert Ross to persist even after a message had arrived from Vice Admiral Cochrane urging withdrawal.

In his report after the capture of Washington, Ross said: "To Rear Admiral Cockburn who suggested the attack upon Washington and who accompanied the Army I confess the greatest obligation for his Cordial co-operation and advice." Colonel Arthur Brooke made a similar comment in his report after the failed attack on Baltimore. "I feel every obligation," he said, "to Rear Admiral Cockburn for the council & assistance which he afforded me, and from which I derived the most signal benefit."[38] Although comments like this in after-action reports were commonplace and might be dismissed as pro forma, here they suggest that the army commanders genuinely held Cockburn in high esteem.[39]

***Who Were the Best American Naval Commanders?*** The American navy also had a number of deserving candidates for the top officer. Captain Joshua Barney did a fine job of harassing the British fleet as the commanding officer of the Chesapeake flotilla and then distinguished himself in the defense of the nation's capital in the Battle of Bladensburg. The frigate commanders also showed excellent fighting skills. Captain Isaac Hull did a fine job of outrunning a determined British squadron in 1812, and Captain David Porter made an impressive cruise in the Pacific in 1813. Even more noteworthy was the record of Captain Charles Stewart in 1815. He showed uncommon tactical skill when he led the *Constitution* (52) to victory over H.M. Ship *Cyane* (33) and H.M. Ship *Levant* (21) and then did a good job of evading capture and getting back into port with one of the prizes. Some of the junior officers who commanded smaller ships also showed considerable talent. Master Commandant Johnston Blakeley had a fine run with the U.S. Sloop *Wasp* (22) in 1814 until his ship was lost at sea.

Also impressive were the command talents shown on the northern lakes. Both Master Commandant Oliver H. Perry and Master Commandant Thomas Macdonough did a good job of overseeing the construction of their squadrons, and both worked well with the army in joint operations. Both also won important naval victories that had a significant impact on the course of the war in their respective theaters. In the West, Perry's victory on Lake Erie forced the British to withdraw from the Detroit River and ultimately led to the destruction of Tecumseh's Indian confederacy, thus depriving the natives of any real chance of securing a protected homeland in the Old Northwest. Macdonough's victory on Lake Champlain was no less significant. It forced the British to withdraw from New York, thus depriving them of a valuable bargaining chip in the peace negotiations.

Perry's performance in the Battle of Lake Erie is the stuff of legends. His decision to switch to the U.S. Brig *Niagara* after his flagship, U.S. Brig *Lawrence*, had been knocked out of action showed remarkable presence of mind. It is not often that a naval officer has an opportunity to command two warships in the same battle, and given the extraordinary lethality of this particular battle, it took exceptional coolness and courage under fire for Perry to execute the switch and then return to the deadly action from which he had just escaped. Perry showed what Theodore Roosevelt called "the most determined courage," "great fertility in resource," and an "indomitable determination not to be beaten."[40] Perry added to his reputation with his memorable note to Major General William Henry Harrison, "We have met the enemy and they are ours."[41]

Macdonough's performance on Lake Champlain, however, was more impressive, and he deserves to be remembered as the best American naval officer. He showed the same coolness and presence of mind on Lake Champlain that Perry had shown on Lake Erie, and his tactical masterstroke, winding his flagship to bring a fresh battery to bear on the enemy, was every bit as important to victory as Perry's decision to change ships. Moreover, Macdonough faced a more formidable foe, and he showed better strategic and tactical sense.

Since the British needed to open their supply route across Lake Erie, Perry did not have to rush into battle, nor was there any reason to allow his slower ships to lag behind his van. He could have waited for the British to attack, and when he chose instead to attack, he could have kept his ships in tighter formation so that they could better support one another. Perry's impatience to fight overcame his strategic and tactical good sense, and as a result the outcome of the Battle of Lake Erie was closer than it should have been.[42]

By contrast, Macdonough took full advantage of his defensive position on Lake Champlain. By judiciously lining up his ships, he exploited the prevailing winds so that the British squadron could not attack from the best direction. And by anchoring his flagship, he not only ensured a stable fighting platform but also set the stage for the masterstroke that won the battle. In addition, Macdonough demonstrated a trait that good commanders often exhibit but was sometimes lacking in Perry: an ability to get along with other people.

Perry's career was marred by rancorous personal relations, particularly with fellow officers in the naval establishment. He clashed with Commodore Isaac Chauncey during the war and with Lieutenant Jesse Elliott afterwards. In 1816 he struck a U.S. Marine officer. For this, he was reprimanded and later fought a bloodless duel.[43] Macdonough, by contrast, seemed to get along well with just about everyone: not only army officers, but also fellow naval and marine officers as well as government officials and other civilians. His commands were never marred by the sort of interpersonal strife that dogged Perry's career, and this contributed to his effectiveness as a leader.[44]

**Who Were the Worst Naval Commanders?** It says something about the high quality of the opposing navies that there were not many bad commanding officers on either side. Much of the criticism might be directed at good officers who made bad decisions. On the American side, Commodore Isaac Chauncey was certainly competent but was probably too cautious on Lake Ontario and was unwilling to cooperate with the U.S. Army in 1814. Likewise, Captain James Lawrence, another good officer, was probably too quick to put America's limited naval assets at risk by courting a duel with H.M. Ship *Shannon* (52). More criticism might be directed at Captain Arthur Sinclair, whose performance on Lake Erie was lackluster, and still more at Lieutenant Jesse Elliott, who apparently held the U.S. Brig *Niagara* (20) back in the Battle of Lake Erie and periodically succumbed to fits of petty jealousy. But even Elliott's record was not uniformly bad or undistinguished, for earlier he had made a successful attack on P.M. Brig *Caledonia* (3) and P.M. Brig *Detroit* (6) in the Niagara River.

On the British side, Admiral Herbert Sawyer, commander of the British naval force at Halifax in 1812, was indecisive and slow to respond to the outbreak of war. That same summer, Captain Thomas Laugharne of H.M. Sloop *Alert* (18?) mistook the far more powerful U.S. Frigate *Essex* (46) for a merchantman and was forced to strike his colors a mere eight minutes into the ensuing battle. But the Royal Navy was so impressed with his pluck that after he was acquitted in a court martial, he was given another command. More worthy of blame was Commander John Taylor of H.M. Sloop *Espiegle* (18?). He stood by in 1813 when the U.S. Sloop *Hornet* (20) defeated H.M. Sloop *Peacock* (20), and for this he was dismissed from the Royal Navy.

## REGULARS AND VOLUNTEERS

**Wellington's Troops in America.** After the Battle of New Orleans, Americans bragged about how they had defeated Wellington's finest, who had been sent to America after they defeated Napoleon. In other words, American forces had defeated "the conquerors of the conquerors of Europe." In later years, many Americans thought that the entire last year of the war had been waged against Wellington's regulars, but this is untrue.

Great Britain started sending regulars from the European theater after the Battle of Leipzig in October of 1813, but these deployments did not become significant until after Napoleon had abdicated and had been forced into exile the following April. Even then, Wellington's troops did not constitute a majority of the reinforcements, for they were drawn not just from the Peninsula but from other commands in Great Britain, Europe, the West Indies, and South Africa. At no time did Wellington's troops make up a majority of British regulars in the War of 1812.

Wellington's troops did not arrive in America until mid-1814. They served on the Niagara front, in upstate New York, and in the Chesapeake. They also served on the Gulf Coast, which was the only place where they constituted a majority of British troops. Wellington's troops played a role in the British victory at Washington and in the successful British skirmishing on the march to Plattsburgh (although the loss of naval power on Lake Champlain led to their withdrawal from New York). At Fort Erie and New Orleans, on the other hand, American forces prevailed. The U.S. record against Wellington's veterans was commendable, although not as impressive as Americans later remembered.[45]

**The Role of Canadian Regulars.** The role that Canadians played in regular or quasi-regular units during the War of 1812 has not been fully understood or appreciated. There were two special classes of units that were raised in Canada: (1) fencible units, which were regular units raised locally by the

Crown that were not liable for service outside North America; and (2) provincial units, which were raised (and paid for) by the provincial governments and were not part of the regular army but in many ways were like regulars.

Six fencible units were recruited in Canada during the war, five of which saw combat.[46] The best known is probably the Glengarry Light Infantry. Initially, the plan was to recruit this unit mainly from a disbanded Scottish regiment that had settled in Glengarry County, Upper Canada. By 1812, however, the lack of success in this county combined with the growing threat of war had forced recruiters to cast their net wider. In the end, the men were drawn from across Upper and Lower Canada, particularly Kingston and Quebec, and had little if any military experience. The Glengarry Lights saw combat in almost every theater on the Canadian-American border during the War of 1812, and their casualties were extensive.[47]

About 20 provincial units were raised in Canada.[48] The units were typically small, but most saw at least some action during the War of 1812. Among the best known was the Canadian Voltigeurs, a unit raised from the French-speaking population in Lower Canada and commanded by Lieutenant Colonel Charles de Salaberry. This unit saw considerable combat and played a key role in the British victory at Châteauguay. Another provincial unit, the Incorporated Militia Battalion, was raised in Upper Canada and saw extensive combat on the Niagara frontier in 1814. No less important were two transportation units, the Corps of Canadian Voyageurs and its successor, the Provincial Commissariat Voya-

The Glengarry Light Infantry was a fencible unit raised locally but trained and used like regulars. The Glengarry Lights saw action in almost every theater on the Canadian-American border and suffered extensive casualties. (Drawing by G.A. Embleton. Parks Canada)

geurs, which were responsible for moving men and material along the St. Lawrence River and for protecting this vital waterway from interdiction.

Canadian writers have sometimes treated these units as if they were militia, which has contributed to the myth that militia won the war. American writers, on the other hand, have largely ignored these units because they had no clear counterpart in the United States. The nearest equivalent to fencible troops were U.S. Volunteers, the one-year men raised in 1812 who saw little combat and proved so unruly and undisciplined that they were disbanded. The closest analogy to the provincial units was the long-term troops that were raised by seven states near the end of the war to ease the burden on militia.[49]

**The Companies of Independent Foreigners.** Some of the worst atrocities of the War of 1812 occurred when some 2,000 British soldiers attacked Hampton, Virginia, on June 25, 1813. Taking part in the attack were two companies of unruly Frenchmen, mostly deserters from the French army and former prisoners of war, who had been enlisted in the British army to meet persistent manpower shortages. Although they were supposed to perform garrison duty in the West Indies in order to release British regulars for more important service, they were instead shipped to America. The Frenchmen were impossible to control, in part, it seems, because one of their officers (most of whom were French) was stealing their pay.

At Hampton, the British swept aside the defending militia, and the French companies then went on a rampage of killing, raping, stealing, and burning. According to Charles Napier, a young British officer who later gained fame in India, "Every horror was committed with impunity, rape, murder, and pillage: and not a man was punished!"[50] Since the men were under Napier's command, he must bear responsibility for losing control. After the incident, the French companies were exiled to Halifax, where they continued to cause trouble until they were finally shipped back to Europe and disbanded.[51]

In his after-action report, Colonel Sidney Beckwith called these troops "Canadian Chasseurs," and nineteenth-century historian Benson J. Lossing referred to them as "Chasseurs Britanniques."[52] Because of these labels, historians have sometimes assumed that the troops were French Canadians or had some other tie to Canada. Although some militia in Lower Canada were known as "Canadian Chasseurs," the Independent Companies had no connection to them. The only correct label for these units is Independent Companies of Foreigners.[53]

**The Canadian Volunteers.** One of the most remarkable units that served in the war was a band of renegades from Canada under the leadership of Joseph Willcocks. This group consisted mainly of American-born men who had migrated to Upper Canada before the war, probably to take advantage of 200-acre land grants or other economic opportunities. Most had never given up their attachment to the United States or American culture. Certainly, they did not consider themselves British, nor did they feel any great attachment to their adopted land.

In July of 1813, after the fall of Fort George, Joseph Willcocks led some 75 of these men into the American camp. With a military commission from Major General Henry Dearborn, Willcocks organized the men into the Canadian Volunteers. The men wrapped a green ribbon around their hats and affixed a white cockade—a salute, perhaps, to the Stuarts (whose color was white) and United Irishmen (who favored green), a combination surely calculated to irritate, if not infuriate, the British.

At one time or another, 164 men served in the unit, but the Volunteers proved far more effective than their numbers would suggest. They provided excellent intelligence to the American command on the Niagara frontier, and they were very good in combat as well. When the British captured Fort Niagara in late 1813, the American position on the entire front collapsed, and the Canadian Volunteers were the only unit to offer effective resistance. The Volunteers continued to distinguish themselves in 1814. They took part in every major engagement on the Niagara—Chippawa, Lundy's Lane, and the defense of Fort Erie—and they performed as well as, if not better than, any other American unit.

But the Canadian Volunteers also had a dark side. They used their intimate knowledge of the Canadian population to arrest and punish those loyal to the Crown and to burn and plunder their property. No doubt they were also settling some old scores. Willcocks oversaw the burning of Newark/Niagara in late 1813, while other Canadian Volunteers oversaw the destruction of Port Dover and probably St. Davids as well.

The Canadian Volunteers were extremely useful to the United States, but American leaders were reluctant to embrace them fully. Willcocks claimed that with enough money for bounties he could raise 600–800 additional recruits from the disaffected in Upper Canada, but the U.S. government never provided the funds. As a result, the unit remained small. Because their pay was almost always in arrears (as it was for most American units), the Volunteers also had an unusually high desertion rate. After Willcocks was killed in September of 1814, the unit melted away. The Canadian Volunteers were officially disbanded in June of 1815, three months after the war ended.

The Volunteers were branded as traitors by British officials in Canada, their property was confiscated, and they were barred from ever returning. To compensate them for their losses and reward them for their service, the United States government gave them land. This compensation was certainly justified. Man for man, they were one of the most effective units fighting on the American side in the war. They also engaged in far more vicious warfare than any other unit (Indians excepted), and the legacy of destruction they left in Upper Canada was not soon forgotten.[54]

**Who Was the Canadian Paul Revere?** In 1813 a 28-year-old lieutenant in the Incorporated Militia named Duncan Clark was sent west of Elizabethtown (now Brockville) on the St. Lawrence River to report on American troop movements. On November 5, when he saw Major General James Wilkinson's huge armada moving down the river, Clark commandeered a plough horse and spread the word to Canadian communities downriver that the Yankees were coming. This timely warning from the Canadian Paul Revere enabled local inhabitants to steer clear of Wilkinson's advancing army.[55]

## MARINES

**The Role of the Royal and Colonial Marines.** British marines played a conspicuous role in the War of 1812. The British government had raised marines as early as 1664, but the force was part of the British army and was disbanded 25 years later. Not until 1747 were marines placed under the Admiralty, and not until 1755 did the force become permanent. That year the British government raised a marine force that was continued after the Seven Years' War was over. In 1802 all such troops were designated Royal Marines. Lord St. Vincent, who was instrumental in securing the royal designation, believed that: "If ever the hour of real danger should come to England, they [Royal Marines] will be found [to be] the country's sheet anchor."[56]

On rare occasions, Great Britain supplemented its regular marine force with special levies. Vice Admiral Sir Alexander Cochrane raised Colonial

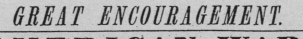

# GREAT ENCOURAGEMENT.

## AMERICAN WAR.

What a Brilliant Prospect does this Event hold out to every Lad of Spirit, who is inclined to try his Fortune in that highly renowned Corps,

# The Royal Marines,

### When every Thing that swims the Seas must be a

# PRIZE!

Thousands are at this moment endeavouring to get on Board Privateers, where they serve without Pay or Reward of any kind whatsoever; so certain does their Chance appear of enriching themselves by PRIZE MONEY! What an enviable Station then must the ROYAL MARINE hold,—who with far superior Advantages to these, has the additional benefit of liberal Pay, and plenty of the best provisions, with a good and well appointed Ship under him, the pride and Glory of Old England; surely every Man of Spirit must blush to remain at Home in Inactivity and Indolence, when his Country and the best of Kings needs his Assistance.

Where then can he have such a fair opportunity of Reaping Glory and Riches, as in the Royal Marines, a Corps daily acquiring new Honours, and there, when once embarked in the BRITISH FLEET, he finds himself in the midst of Honour and Glory, surrounded by a set of fine Fellows, Strangers to Fear, and who strike Terror through the Hearts of their Enemies wherever they go!

He has likewise the inspiring Idea to know, that while he scours the Ocean to protect the Liberty of OLD ENGLAND, that the Hearts and good Wishes of the whole BRITISH NATION, attend him; pray for his Success, and participate in his Glory!! Lose no Time then, my Fine Fellows, in embracing the glorious Opportunity that awaits you; YOU WILL RECEIVE

# Sixteen Guineas Bounty,

And on your Arrival at *Head Quarters*, be comfortably and genteelly CLOTHED.—And spirited Young BOYS of a promising Appearance, who are Five Feet high, WILL RECEIVE TWELVE POUNDS ONE SHILLING AND SIXPENCE BOUNTY and equal Advantages of *PROVISIONS* and *CLOATHING* with the Men. And those who wish only to enlist for a limited Service, shall receive a Bounty of ELEVEN GUINEAS, and Boys EIGHT. In Fact, the Advantages which the *ROYAL MARINE* possesses, are too numerous to mention here, but among the many, it may not be amiss to state,—*That if he has a WIFE, or aged PARENT, he can make them an Allotment of half his PAY: which will be regularly paid without any Trouble to them, or to whomsoever he may direct: that being well Clothed and Fed on Board Ship, the Remainder of his PAY and PRIZE MONEY will be clear in Reserve for the Relief of his Family or his own private Purposes. The Single Young Man on his return to Port, finds himself enabled to cut a Dash on Shore with his GIRL and his GLASS, that might be envied by a Nobleman.—Take Courage then, seize the Fortune that awaits you, repair to the ROYAL MARINE RENDEZVOUS, where in a FLOWING BOWL of PUNCH, in Three Times Three, you shall drink*

## Long live the King, and Success to his Royal Marines

The Daily Allowance of a Marine when embarked, is—One Pound of BEEF or PORK.—One Pound of BREAD —Flour, Raisins, Butter, Cheese, Oatmeal, Molasses, Tea, Sugar, &c. &c. And a Pint of the best WINE, or Half a Pint of the best RUM or BRANDY; together with a Pint of LEMONADE. They have likewise in warm Countries, a plentiful Allowance of the choicest FRUIT. And what can be more handsome than the Royal Marine's Proportion of PRIZE MONEY, when a Sergeant shares equal with the First Class of Petty Officers, such as Midshipmen, Assistant Surgeons, &c. which is Five Shares each; a Corporal with the Second Class, which is Three Shares each; and the Private, with the Able Seamen, One Share and a Half each.

☞ *For further Particulars, and a more full Account of the many advantages of this invaluable Corps, apply to Sergeant Fulcher, at the Eight Bells, where the Bringer of a Recruit will receive* THREE GUINEAS.

S. AND I. RIDGE, PRINTERS, MARKEDPLACE, NEWARK.

The Royal Marines promised new recruits food, clothing, and a generous enlistment bounty as well as the prospect of glory and prize money. (Field, *Britain's Sea-Soldiers*)

Marines in the West Indies in 1808 and in North America in 1814–15. Unlike Royal Marines, who were raised by Royal warrant and paid by the Treasury, Cochrane's Colonial Marines were raised under his authority, paid out of public funds at his disposal, and disbanded at the end of hostilities. But while they were in service, these troops were uniformed and armed like Royal Marines; they were trained and commanded by Royal Marine officers; and they often fought in mixed units with the Royal Marines.

British marines performed the usual duties of marines on warships. As the Royal Navy's police force, they maintained order and suppressed mutinies (although some marines took part in the great mutinies at Spithead and the Nore in 1797). They also guarded prisoners, manned coastal fortifications, and protected navy yards and approaches to harbors. Marines boarded enemy ships and defended their own ships from enemy boarders, and they helped man the ship's guns when needed. In addition, they took part in amphibious operations, which became ever more important in the worldwide contest for dominion that Britain waged against France in the Second Hundred Years' War (1689–1815).

In time of battle, marines in the Age of Sail are best remembered for sharpshooting from the "tops" on ships, but most actually provided small-arms fire from the quarterdeck. Rather than being armed with rifles, they usually carried a short-barreled weapon known as a ship's musket or a sea service musket. This was a modified Brown Bess with a 37-inch barrel, two inches shorter than the infantry musket.

Since marines were considered landsmen, the Admiralty could not secure men for this service by impressment. During the French Revolutionary and Napoleonic Wars, it offered bounties, as high as £30 ($139) in 1808, and recruited foreigners, who formed an ever-growing portion of the whole. The Admiralty also offered soldiers a bounty to transfer to the marines.

Because of a shortage of seamen in this period, the Admiralty occasionally used the Royal Artillery on warships. The expertise of this branch was also valuable for managing the tricky charges of the powerful mortars used on bomb ships. But the use of soldiers on warships created disputes between the services over lines of authority. The Admiralty responded in 1804 by creating the Royal Marine Artillery. This specially-trained force, which was clearly under naval jurisdiction, managed not only the mortars but also other naval artillery and Congreve rockets on ship and shore.

Parliament had authorized 31,000 Royal Marines at the time of the War of 1812, although the actual number in service was undoubtedly smaller. Only a small portion saw service in the American war. An unknown number served in the British ships blockading the U.S. coast or in Royal ships that engaged American warships or privateers or captured American merchant ships on the high seas.

An additional number of Royal Marines, perhaps 4,000 in all, actually served ashore in the American theater. Initially, the Royal Navy relied on shipboard marines for its amphibious operations in the Chesapeake, but the number of these operations increased so dramatically in 1813 that the British government decided to send marine battalions to America. The 1st and 2nd Battalions (including two companies of Royal Marine Artillery and a Rocket Corps) were shipped from the Spanish Peninsula to the Chesapeake in 1813. After seeing action, the 2nd Battalion was broken up, and its men were used to bring the 1st Battalion up to full strength. The 3rd Battalion was shipped to the Chesapeake in 1814 and was later reformed into a new 2nd Battalion. A new 3rd Battalion was then created from existing units as well from as six companies of Colonial Marines that were raised locally from runaway slaves. In addition to these three battalions, an oversized company of Colonial Marines was raised from communities of maroons (run-away slaves and their descendants) in the backcountry of Florida and Georgia.

British marines in the War of 1812 fought in almost every battle at sea and took part in almost every amphibious operation ashore. Although they served in every theater that had ready access to the sea, their most conspicuous role was in the Chesapeake, where they took part in the raiding operations in 1813–14, including the assaults on Craney Island, Washington, and Baltimore. They also participated in the raid on Hampton, Virginia, in 1813 but refused to follow the Independent Companies of Foreigners in the orgy of violence that ensued. Elsewhere on the Atlantic coast, British marines took part in the occupation of Maine in 1814 and of Cumberland Island, Georgia, in 1815.

On the northern frontier, British marines in 1814 participated in the defense of Lacolle Mill, the attack on Oswego, the Battle of Lundy's Lane, the assault on Fort Erie, and the Battle of Lake Champlain. They also played a role in the major engagements on the Gulf Coast, including the two attacks on Fort Bowyer and the Battle of Lake Borgne. In addition, they fought in every battle in the New Orleans campaign, including the main battle (when they took part in Britain's successful operation on the west bank of the Mississippi River) and the bombardment of Fort St. Philip.[57]

**The Role of the U.S. Marines.** Unlike Royal Marines, U.S. Marines are the forgotten service in the War of 1812. Founded in 1775 and disbanded after the Revolutionary War, the marines were re-established in 1798 during the Quasi-War with France and have been in existence ever since. Not yet known as "Leathernecks" (although they wore the leather neckpiece that was responsible for this nickname), the marines were the least desirable of the services, attracting more black sheep, ne'er-do-wells, and adventurers than the other services.

Marine privates in the War of 1812 were paid less than the navy's ordinary seamen and received a far smaller bounty than army privates. Recruitment was therefore difficult, and the service remained chronically short of the men needed to carry out its wartime duties. Desertion was also common. Marines were subject to the army regulations on land but navy regulations at sea. Because the army prohibited flogging in 1812 but the navy did not follow suit, this meant that during the war marines guilty of infractions could be whipped afloat but not ashore.

As the navy's police force, U.S. Marines performed the usual duties during the War of 1812. They maintained order on warships, guarded prisoners, served in coastal fortifications, and protected navy property. Like their British counterparts, they used short-barreled ship's muskets, mainly to provide small-arms fire from the quarterdeck. Besides boarding enemy ships and defending their own ships from enemy boarders and manning guns when needed, U.S. Marines also operated special guns, such as the multi-shot Chambers Gun that was sometimes mounted on a ship's capstan. Occasionally, they also took part in amphibious operations.

The marines had an authorized level of 1,800 men in 1812 and 2,700 in 1814, although the Corps's actual level during the War of 1812 probably never exceeded 1,000 men. Marines contributed to some of the American naval victories, but their finest hour at sea was probably in the *Chesapeake-Shannon* duel, when they sustained more than 75 percent casualties.

Small detachments of marines served on the Great Lakes, in the Chesapeake, and on the Gulf Coast. They played a particularly conspicuous role in the Chesapeake, where they joined Captain Joshua Barney's command in mid-1814. Under Captain Samuel Miller, they took part in the Second Battle of St. Leonard's Creek on June 26 and then in the Battle of Bladensburg two months later. U.S. Marines also distinguished themselves at New Orleans, first in the Battle of Villeré's Plantation on December 23, 1814, then as part of Jackson's line in the main battle of January 8, 1815. The marines emerged from the war with newfound respect from their rivals in the navy but remained largely a forgotten service.[58]

## MILITIA

**The Role of Canadian Militia.** One of the oldest and most venerable Canadian myths associated with the War of 1812 is that the militia saved Canada. This myth originated after the first campaign on the Detroit frontier. In late 1812, a song appeared, apparently written by Private Cornelius Flummerfelt of the York militia, that credited the victory at Detroit to Canadian volunteers. (For more on this song, see Appendix B.)

About the same time, the Reverend John Strachan delivered a sermon at York predicting that one day historians would record that with the aid of only "a handful of regular troops," the Loyalist population of Upper Canada "repelled its invaders, slew or took them all prisoners, and captured from its enemies the greater part of the arms by which it was defended." No country could boast of men who had shown "greater valour, cooler resolution, and more approved conduct." These hardy souls, Strachan concluded, "have emulated the choicest veterans, and they have twice saved the country."[59] Returning to this theme in 1814, Strachan claimed that Upper Canada had been preserved in 1812 by "the astonishing exertions of the Militia" and that thereafter "their services [had] continued . . . to a much greater degree than could have been anticipated."[60]

Forty years later, Gilbert Auchinleck, one of Canada's early students of the war, went further. Writing in 1855, he said that not only had Canadian militiamen "achieved the expulsion of the invading foe" with the help "of a mere handful of British troops," but so thoroughly was their spirit aroused that Canadians "would, unaided, have won the day" even if the mother country had been able to send nothing more than "regular officers only, to discipline and lead them."[61]

A quarter of a century after this, the Rev. Egerton Ryerson, a prominent Methodist clergyman who served for many years as Upper Canada's superintendent of education, weighed in on the issue. Although Ryerson was too young to serve in the War of 1812, he was old enough to remember it, and his father as well as three older brothers had served.[62] In a history of Canadian Loyalists published in 1880, Ryerson pasted together material from other works to tell the story of the war. Even though this material demonstrated that British regulars and Indians had played a central role in the contest, Ryerson chose to ignore the evidence before his eyes and instead gave the lion's share of credit to Canadians. "The Canadas," he said in his introductory remarks on the war, "with a frontier of more than 1,000 miles, and aided by a few regiments of regular soldiers, sent as a mere guard for the principal cities, from Halifax to Amherstburg, resisted the whole military power of

An Upper Canadian militia officer in 1814 is shown here. Although Canadian militia provided essential support services, their combat role in the war was much exaggerated in later years. (Drawing by G.A. Embleton. Parks Canada)

the United States." Returning to this theme later in his work, he concluded that "for more than two years, the colonies had been thrown almost entirely upon their own prowess and resources, with the assistance of a few British soldiers, for their own defence against an invading enemy fifty times more populous than themselves."[63]

The myth that Flummerfelt and Strachan invented and that Auchinleck and Ryerson expanded upon proved to be remarkably durable because it served the larger cause of Canadian patriotism and nationalism. The Canadian people wanted to believe that local men had saved their country, and

Canadian boosters and historians were happy to oblige by perpetuating the myth. In addition, there was some truth in the myth because local men did contribute to the defense of Canada, both in a combat and supporting role, not only as short-term militia but also in the long-term fencible and provincial units that were raised in Canada. Later generations had a tendency to blur the lines between the militia and other local troops. As a result, the militia got credit for the accomplishments of fencible and provincial units. The militia myth was appealing for another reason: it justified the policy, which nearly every generation of Canadians supported after the War of 1812, of keeping defense spending in peacetime at a minimum.

The myth did not come under fire until 1928. "That the Militia sprang to arms," said Colonel C. F. Hamilton, "marched to the frontier in their peacetime organizations and under their amateur officers, and beat off the invaders, is grotesquely untrue." Hamilton gave some credit to the militia, but he gave much more to the British regulars serving in Canada and to the quasi-regular units that were raised locally.[64]

The myth came under more sustained fire in the 1950s, when two respected military historians, George Stanley and C.P. Stacey, challenged it. Stanley suggested in 1954 that the notion that militia had saved Canada "was only a legend." He attributed British success early in the war to the superior leadership, training, and discipline of regulars and concluded that "the regular soldier bore the brunt of defending British North America in 1812–14."[65] Four years later Stacey made the same point. "The regulars," he said, "did more than supply the leadership. They usually did the lion's share of the actual fighting."[66]

In the years that followed, some scholars went further, stressing that the Canadian population was largely disaffected and at best remained neutral in the war. But this goes too far. It is true that militiamen sometimes deserted or sought paroles from the occupying American army in order to avoid further service. But this did not necessarily mean that these men were disaffected. More likely, they simply wished to return home because they could earn more money there, their crops needed tending, or they wished to protect their families and property from marauders. Even where militiamen were manifestly unreliable, such as on the Detroit frontier in 1812, victory was a remarkable tonic. "The militia have been inspired . . . with confidence," reported Major General Isaac Brock after the fall of Detroit. "The disaffected are silenced."[67]

Out of a population of 500,000 in 1812, Canada had about 90,000 citizen soldiers available for service.[68] Canadian militia units served extensively in the conflict, but their combat role waned as the war progressed, and throughout the contest they were used primarily as auxiliary troops. Canadian militia officers were subordinate to British regular officers regardless of rank. As a result, British regulars always remained in charge of operations, and the messy command disputes that plagued American operations, especially early in the war, never arose.

Canadian militia played a significant role in the engagements at Detroit, Queenston Heights, and Frenchman's Creek in 1812; at Ogdensburg, Fort Meigs, and Châteauguay in 1813; and at Lundy's Lane in 1814. However, except on a few occasions, such as the raid on McCrae's house in 1813 and the Battle of Malcolm's Mills in 1814, militia usually served with regulars, who did the bulk of the fighting. Besides playing second fiddle to regulars in battle, militiamen were more likely to perform non-combat duties. They garrisoned forts, cleared surrounding lands, built fortifications and ships, protected transportation routes, delivered messages, and managed the commissariat. They also served as a kind of police force in disaffected areas.

Four groups of land forces contributed to the defense of British North America—regulars, Indians, long-term local troops, and militia—and the contribution of each group was essential. Nevertheless, it should be emphasized that Canada was saved mainly because Great Britain had an experienced professional army on hand, and on the battlefield these troops received crucial assistance from their Indian allies. The role of local troops, whether in the militia or in long-term fencible or provincial units, was less important. Their contribution was less central than the nineteenth-century mythmakers claimed, but it was also more important than twentieth-century debunkers maintained.[69]

**The Role of American Militia.** There is an equally durable myth that militia saved the United States in the War of 1812, or at least played a central role in the defense of the nation. The successes of militia in this contest, on top of similar success stories from the Revolution, strengthened the notion that citizen soldiers were the palladium of liberty and the nation's first line of defense. And here, as in Canada, assorted boosters, patriots, and historians in the nineteenth century were happy to propagate the myth.

There is no denying that the United States had to rely heavily on militia, both because it took time to build up its regular forces and because there were never enough regulars to conduct all the planned offensive operations on the Canadian border or to meet every British threat, especially along the Atlantic seaboard. Out of a population of 7,700,000 in 1812, the nation had 703,000 citizen soldiers available for duty in the 17 states and perhaps another 20,000 in the 5 territories.[70] In the course of the war some 458,000 men were called into service.[71] Citizen soldiers either played a role or were expected to play a role in almost every campaign.

The militia system produced five accomplished generals during the war. Three (Andrew Jackson, Jacob Brown, and William Henry Harrison) were rewarded with regular army commissions; the other two (Peter B. Porter and Samuel Smith) remained in the militia. Although sometimes militia units performed well, more often than not they were badly led, badly equipped, badly trained, and wholly undependable under enemy fire. Compounding the problem was the way that militia companies were formed. Men from a number of different militia units were sometimes thrown together into freshly minted companies. The men did not know each other, nor did they know their officers. Hence, they lacked unit cohesion and esprit de corps and were reluctant to follow orders, especially in life-threatening situations.[72]

A lieutenant in the 1st Regiment, Maryland Volunteer Artillery, is shown here. American militia, including some volunteer units like this one, played an important role in the war, but this role, like that of their Canadian counterparts, was exaggerated in later years. (Painting by Keith Rocco. Fort McHenry National Monument, National Park Service)

Citizen soldiers were especially unsuited for offensive operations because their tour of duty was so short, typically three months. In addition, many refused to serve outside the country. This was true not only of militiamen in the New England and middle states, but even of some in the West.[73]

The use of militia with regulars sometimes created a command problem because under U.S. law regular officers outranked militia officers only if they were of equal or greater rank. This meant that sometimes a high-ranking but inexperienced militia officer was in charge of an operation. In 1812, for example, Major General Stephen Van Rensselaer of the New York militia was in charge of the American invasion across the Niagara River. Miffed that he was outranked by such an inexperienced militia officer, Brigadier General Alexander Smyth of the regular army refused to cooperate. The federal government subsequently tried to avoid this problem by calling out detached companies of militia or by making sure that a high-ranking regular officer was present to take command. This created hard feelings among militia officers, and on occasion Federalist state leaders in New England refused to allow their militia units to serve under regular officers.[74]

American militiamen served in two different ways during the war: as volunteers on campaign or in emergencies when the enemy threatened. Volunteer militiamen usually performed better, especially if they were campaigning with regulars under competent leadership. This was particularly true in the Old Northwest, where they played a significant role in the defense of Fort Meigs and the Battle of the Thames, and in the Old Southwest, where they performed well in the Creek War and the New Orleans campaign. Volunteer militia also played an important role in the Battle of Lundy's Lane and in the defense of Fort Erie.

When responding to emergencies, however, men from militia units were far less reliable. Disorganized and without competent leadership, they easily panicked and fled from the field. This explains why the British were able to move freely about the Chesapeake in 1813 and 1814 and why they were able to occupy the nation's capital. Referring to one British raid in 1814, Captain Joshua Barney commented: "The Militia, according to custom, appeared *after* all was over."[75]

On balance, the record of American militia in the War of 1812 was far from impressive. Even in the West they were hardly a substitute for regulars, and elsewhere they were not even a reliable first line of defense. Whether taking part in offensive operations at the beginning of the war or defensive operations near the end, citizen soldiers rarely lived up to expectation. It was only when viewed through the fuzzy lens of history that the militia appeared to play a starring role in the War of 1812.[76]

**Why Was the Militia so Poorly Armed?** One thing that is not widely known is how badly armed the American militia was in the War of 1812. This is puzzling because Americans in this era are usually depicted as both well armed and well versed in the use of arms. In addition, a 1792 militia law (which was still in force during the War of 1812) required all members of the militia to provide their own shoulder arms, ammunition, and powder (as well as other accouterments), although there was no penalty for non-compliance.[77] Even though state and federal arsenals in 1807 had about 350,000 shoulder arms, these weapons were manufactured to a host of different standards and many were out of repair.[78]

The lack of militia weapons appeared to be so acute in some parts of the country, particularly in the South and West, that the government took remedial action. Congress authorized the sale of 30,000 arms to the states during the Quasi-War with France in 1798 and appropriated $200,000 a year for state arms beginning in 1808, when there was a war scare with Great Britain. But only a fraction of the authorized money was spent, and less than 30,000 arms were transferred to the states under these programs prior to 1812.[79]

How could the militia be so poorly armed in a nation in which arms supposedly abounded? Although it has been argued that arms were not widely held in early America, this is surely untrue.[80] The United States undoubtedly had more arms per capita than any other nation in the world (although they were probably just about as numerous in Canada). Recent scholarship has suggested that about half of all men in the state militias owned arms.[81] Of those called into service, however, the figure was much lower, and officials repeatedly complained of how badly armed the militia was. In 1794, for example, the secretary of war said that the government had to issue 10,000 arms to the 15,000 (actually 13,000) citizen soldiers called out to deal with the Whiskey Rebellion.[82]

What explains this discrepancy? For one thing, the proportion of militia that was armed varied considerably from state to state. It was as low as 3 percent in Maryland and as high as 92 percent in Connecticut. For New England as a whole, the figure was 83 percent, while for the South it was only 34 percent.[83] Those who complained about the lack of militia arms were more likely to have experience in states in which gun ownership was less common. The four states that provided militia for suppressing the Whiskey Rebellion, for example, averaged less than 31 percent in gun ownership.[84]

In addition, some men refused to bring their weapons when called into service, either because they feared losing or damaging them or because their guns (which might be fowling pieces or pistols) were unsuitable for military service. For those with a proper weapon, the temptation to bring "Old Betsy" must have been very strong, but many resisted the urge. Every weapon was unique, and no doubt some men considered their guns too precious to risk in actual campaigning. Apparently recognizing this, most states fined men for failing to bring arms to a muster but not for showing up unarmed when called into actual service.[85]

Moreover, most men who showed up for militia service were young, and then, as today, wealth was related to age. Men in their teens and twenties were less able to afford guns than men in their forties and fifties. The older and more affluent, on the other hand, were more likely to escape service. Some were professionals, such as physicians, bankers, educators, and officeholders, who were exempt from militia service. Others evaded service by offering bounties to secure volunteers to fill local militia quotas or by hiring substitutes to serve in their place if they were drafted. In 1790 Secretary of War Henry Knox had warned that such substitutes would be drawn from "the most idle and worthless part of the community."[86] Heavy reliance on the poor helps explain why citizen soldiers called into service (including those who served against the Whiskey Rebels) were so poorly armed.

The Canadian militia also appeared to be badly armed in the War of 1812, and for many of the same reasons. Lord Dorchester complained in 1790 that the people were so "enervated" that few brought their arms to militia parades even though "it is imagined, every house has at least one gun, and some two or three."[87] For actual service, Canadian militia was selected in much the same way as American militia. Local companies were expected to supply quotas, which meant that the rich could offer bounties to ensure that the quotas were met. If a quota was not filled, men were chosen by lot, and the more affluent who were selected could hire substitutes.[88] Colonel Edward Baynes reported in 1814 that some substitutes in Canada received as much as £50 ($212) for a year's service.[89]

Thus in Canada, as in the United States, the youngest and poorest dominated the service, and many did not own guns. Yet this did not mean that people living in Canada were unfamiliar with arms. As Major General Isaac Brock put it, "the generality of the Inhabitants" in Canada was "acquainted with the use of the Musket."[90]

## INDIANS

**Native Allies and Adversaries.** In some ways the War of 1812 was the last of the North American colonial wars. In the first series of wars (1689–1763), Great Britain had wrested control of North America from France. In the last series (1775–1815), Americans fought the British over the same prize. Indians played a significant role in every one of these wars. They were coveted as allies because they excelled as scouts and skirmishers, and in the sparsely settled New World their numbers could easily tip the balance in either direction. In addition, they could force an enemy to keep its militia at home for fear of an attack. Such was the fear that Indians inspired that their mere presence on the battlefield could shape the outcome.

But Indian allies could also be a liability. The warriors and their dependents had to be fed. They also had to be feted with gifts because sharing was an essential part of native culture. But supplying food and presents in the remoter parts of the New World was no easy task, and the cost could be enormous. "No one," said a Canadian observer in 1813, "can have any idea of the expense in taking out [on campaign] a lot of Indians. . . . There is no end to their wants."[91] Indians often took what they wanted from friend and foe alike, and to their white allies this could be exasperating. "Upon the subject of the Indians," complained a junior officer in the British quartermaster department, "I cannot help observing that their conduct becomes outrageous in proportion to the impunity with which they offend."[92]

The allegiance of the Indians could evaporate for the slightest of reasons, and large numbers could desert even before a battle began. Moreover, if they had any ties to the enemy, they might warn of an impending attack. Nor was it easy to predict when Indians might turn hostile. As one American Indian agent put in it 1813: "Indians allways profess the greatest friendship untill the moment arrives that the[y] mean to make an attack."[93]

Essentially light infantry, Indians preferred to rely on stealth and hit-and-run tactics, hoping to strike terror in their enemy while minimizing their own casualties. Unlike their white counterparts, they were rarely willing to take calculated losses because the members of a given war party were often related through an extended kinship system. Their aim, said the great Sauk leader Black Hawk, was "to *kill the enemy* and *save their own people.*"[94]

Indians were puzzled by European tactics, which were far more deadly to both sides. Black Hawk explained these tactics to fellow Sauk and Fox Indians after witnessing several battles in the War of 1812. "They march out," he said, "in open daylight, and *fight,* regardless of the number of warriors they may lose! After the battle is over, they retire to feast, and drink wine, as if nothing had happened; after which, they make a *statement in writing,* of what they have done—*each party claiming the victory!* and neither giving an account of half the number that have been killed on their own side."[95]

On occasion, natives adapted well to European military operations. Indians took part in Great Britain's loose siege of Fort George in 1813 and closer siege of Fort Erie in 1814, and some Indians appreciated the value of artillery and fortifications. Most Indians, however, did not adapt well to conventional European warfare. They showed little interest in artillery and usually could not be counted on to support linear movements, sieges, cavalry charges, or the defense of fortifications. In the eyes of Europeans, this significantly reduced their military value.

Worse still, Indians tended to be invisible in defeat and implacable in victory. To minimize casualties, they often fled at the first sign that a battle was going badly. Their white allies found this exasperating. As Major General Henry Procter put it, "The Indian Force is seldom a disposable one, never to be relied on, in the Hour of Need."[96] On the other hand, when victorious, Indians sometimes took scalps, drank excessively, plundered indiscriminately, and treated prisoners of war with cruelty.

Indian atrocities had some military value since they could enhance a tribe's reputation for prowess and keep potential enemies from the battlefield. Although a growing number of Indians exposed to white contact—including important leaders like Tecumseh, Black Hawk, and John Norton—had begun to question scalping and other such practices, they remained all too common during the War of 1812, especially in the remoter parts of the West.

British and American officers sometimes tried to ransom enemy prisoners from their Indian allies, but often there was little they could do to protect captives. Thomas Verchères de Boucherville, a French Canadian in British service during the War of 1812, reported that his Potawatomi allies killed a young American soldier even though they had agreed to sell him to the British. Verchères complained that "if we were to rebuke them in this crisis and compel them to observe our manner of warfare . . . , they would withdraw from the conflict."[97] Whites realized that they could not do without the unique talents that Indians brought to the battlefield, nor could they risk the possibility that their enemies might woo the Indians if they did not. As Governor-General James Craig bluntly put it in 1807, "If we do not employ them, there cannot exist a moment's doubt that they will be employed against us."[98]

Some Americans were every bit as brutal as the Indians. William Henry Harrison commented that "a great many of the Inhabitants of the Fronteers consider the murdering of Indians in the highest degree meritorious."[99] In the West, Americans often fought a vicious war of extermination, killing, carving up, or scalping any hapless native—friend or foe, combatant or non-combatant, man or woman—who happened to cross their path.

In early 1813 scouts from Captain Nathan Boone's Mounted Rangers, who were stationed at Fort Mason (in present-day Saverton, Missouri), seized Black Hawk's adopted son, who was hunting legally on the Illinois side of the Mississippi River, dragged him across the river (where the U.S. had prohibited hunting), and then, on the grounds that his presence was illegal, unmercifully killed him.[100] "He had been most cruelly murdered!" Black Hawk reported. "His face was shot to pieces—his body stabbed in several places—and his head *scalped!* His arms were tied behind him!"[101] Sometimes Americans even extended their vindictiveness beyond the

Mohawk warriors of the Grand River Iroquois decorated themselves with paint, jewelry, medals, and crosses to prepare for battle. The Grand River natives, led by John Norton, made a significant contribution to the defense of Upper Canada. (Drawing by Sempronius Stretton. Library and Archives Canada)

grave, mutilating corpses after a battle or digging up and scattering the remains of those who had been buried.

The British referred to the Indians as "Nitchies," which was a corruption of the Ojibway/Chippewa word "Niigii," which meant "friend" or "comrade."[102] Most Indians in the War of 1812 lined up with the British because they shared the common goal of resisting American expansion. Some 11,000 northern warriors, 80 percent of whom lived in the United States, sided with Great Britain, but almost half of this number were Sioux, who lived too far away to play much of a role in the war. Much more useful were the Grand River Iroquois, who had left New York after the American Revolution to live on a tract (now known as the Six Nations Reserve) that the British had created for them about 50 miles west of the Niagara River in Upper Canada. Another 4,000 warriors in the South lined up against the United States in the Creek War. For its part, the U.S. initially could count on about 1,800 native warriors in the North, although this number increased significantly after the American victory at the Thames in 1813. The U.S. had an additional 2,000 native allies in the South.[103]

Most of the great Indian leaders sided with the British. Among them were the legendary Shawnee brothers, Tecumseh and Tenskwatawa (the Prophet), who headed the last great pan-Indian movement in the Old Northwest; John Norton, the Scottish-Cherokee who became a leader of the Grand River Mohawk and played a significant role in British victories on the Niagara front; Main Poc, the powerful Potawatomi medicine man and warrior whose influence among some of the western tribes rivaled that of Tecumseh and the Prophet; Black Hawk, the Sauk leader who fought Americans in the remote Mississippi Valley and later spearheaded the last resistance to American expansion in the Old Northwest; and William Weatherford, the Anglo-Creek leader who headed Red Stick resistance in the Old Southwest.

Even though most of the Indians sided with Great Britain, the United States could count on the support of several influential leaders. The most notable was the Seneca chief Red Jacket, who had sided with the British in the American Revolution but convinced his fellow tribesmen in New York to line up with the U.S. in the War of 1812. The aging leader led a band of Senecas in the fighting that took place in the woods in the Battle of Chippawa in 1814.[104] No less important was the Shawnee leader Black Hoof, who had fought Americans in the early 1790s but thereafter encouraged accommodation and acculturation. He remained loyal to the United States during the War of 1812 and took part in the Battle of the Thames/Moraviantown, although earlier he had sustained a nasty mouth wound.[105]

Because they were far less successful in recruiting native allies, American leaders generally sought to minimize their role in the War of 1812, but without much success. On the Detroit frontier, Brigadier General William Hull threatened "a war of extermination" if "the savages are let loose to murder our Citizens and butcher our women and children." "*No white man,*" he said, "*found fighting by the Side of an Indian will be taken prisoner. Instant destruction will be his Lot.*"[106] On the Niagara frontier, Brigadier General Alexander Smyth accused the British of hiring Indians "to murder women and children and kill and scalp the wounded." Although this was untrue, Smyth himself offered a reward of $40 (£11) "for the arms and spoils [that is, scalps] of each savage warrior who shall be killed."[107]

There were full-scale Indian wars in both the Old Northwest and Old Southwest, and Indians had a surprisingly high profile in the War of 1812. They played a particularly important role in the defense of Upper Canada. Their presence often gave the British numerical parity or superiority on the battlefield, and without their assistance Upper Canada might have fallen to the United States. In addition, the mere fact that there were so many Indians in the Old Northwest that were hostile to the United States had a direct impact on American strategy. Instead of focusing on more important targets in the East, the U.S. repeatedly sent troops and supplies to counter Indians in the West. Since Canada could never be conquered in the West, this greatly diminished American chances of winning the war.

Indians played a crucial role in helping the British win control of the Old Northwest in 1812 and hold it through early 1813. Without Indians, the American forts at Mackinac, Detroit, and Chicago would not have fallen in 1812, and the first American invasion might have succeeded. Without Indians, the first phase of the second American invasion in 1813 would not have been stopped at Frenchtown, nor would the British have been able to mount offensives against Fort Meigs (in present-day Perrysburg, Ohio) and Fort Stephenson (in Fremont, Ohio).

But if Indians played a crucial role in British victories in the West, they also contributed to the British defeat there because of the intractable supply problems they created. Major General Henry Procter's quartermaster at Fort

Amherstburg in 1813 had to find 14 head of cattle and 7,000 pounds of flour a day to feed more than 14,000 Indians as well as the British troops there.[108] This drained his supplies at such an alarming rate that Commander Robert H. Barclay was forced to challenge Master Commandant Oliver H. Perry on Lake Erie to keep British supply lines open even though the British squadron was overmatched. Barclay's defeat compelled Procter to withdraw his army from the Detroit River, but Indians slowed him down and forced him to make a stand. The result was the Anglo-Indian defeat at the Thames/Moraviantown.

Procter's defeat established American dominance in the Old Northwest, but contrary to popular belief, it did not end the war there. Although many tribes made their peace with the United States, others did not. In 1814, British war parties, consisting mainly of Indians, captured the American fort at Prairie du Chien and defeated American forces at Rock Island and Credit Island. That same year Indians also helped ward off an assault on Fort Mackinac and block Brigadier General Duncan McArthur from advancing across the Grand River when he carried out his deep raid into Upper Canada from Detroit. In May of 1815, in one of the last engagements of the war, Indians skirmished with American forces in the Battle of the Sinkhole near St. Louis.

Indians also played a role on both sides in almost every campaign on the Niagara frontier. Their part in the British victory at Queenston Heights in 1812 was particularly important. The following year, they won the Battle of Beaver Dams (at present-day Thorold, Ontario), played a role in bottling up American forces in Fort George, and fought in the various engagements at nearby Ball's Farm. They also took part in the devastating British counterattack on the other side of the Niagara River, destroying the American and Tuscarora settlements there. In 1814, they scouted and harassed the American army that crossed into Canada, and they fought on both sides in the Battle of Chippawa. Although less conspicuous farther east, Indians played a role in the British victory at Lacolle Mill in 1812 and in the American victory at Sandy Creek in 1814. In addition, Indians served on both sides in the fighting on the St. Lawrence front.[109]

Indians also played an important role in the war in the Old Southwest and on the Gulf Coast. The United States had to devote considerable resources to the Creek War, and Andrew Jackson prevailed in the climactic Battle of Horseshoe Bend at least in part because he had a sizeable number of Indian allies on his side. Native sharpshooters also contributed to the American success in the New Orleans campaign.[110]

The war in the West was especially bloody. Potawatomis were furious when Captain Nathan Heald, ordered to abandon Fort Dearborn in 1812, promised to give his public property to the Indians but withheld arms and whiskey. The Potawatomis responded with the Fort Dearborn Massacre. One American soldier who had been saved by a friendly Indian claimed that he saw Potawatomis cut off Captain William Wells's head and then carve out his heart and eat it.[111]

For the Indians, Wells's grisly end was probably both a mark of respect and a matter of justice. As a "white Indian" who had been captured by the Miamis and raised by Little Turtle, Wells had shown great prowess on the battlefield. However, after forsaking his Miami friends to rejoin the white population on the Kentucky frontier, he had served as an interpreter and Indian agent. As an interpreter, he had played a role in the hard treaties that were imposed on the Indians prior to Tippecanoe, and as an Indian agent, he had cheated the natives out of part of their annuities and blocked Quaker attempts to teach them farming.[112]

In 1813, during the first siege of Fort Meigs, two British officers who walked through an Indian camp were stunned at what they saw: "the scalps of the slain drying in the sun, stained on the fleshy side with vermillion dyes" and "hoops of various sizes, on which were stretched portions of human skin." Worse yet, in one tent, they found Indians preparing a meal in a kettle suspended over a large fire. "Each warrior had a piece of string hanging over the edge of the vessel, and to this was suspended a food, which ... consisted of part of an American."[113]

In 1814 Captain Arthur Sinclair reported an equally gruesome scene after the failed attack on Mackinac. Some of the Americans who fell into Indian hands were butchered and then "had their *hearts* and *livers* taken out, which were actually cooked and feasted on ... by the Savages." "This cannibal act," concluded Sinclair, "must ever be viewed with indignant horror by the cristian world," and yet the British made no attempt to stop it.[114] The British were equally powerless to stop the Creek Red Sticks in the Old Southwest from eating their American prisoners.[115]

Americans reciprocated in kind, rarely taking warriors as prisoners, sometimes slaying women and children, and often appropriating human trophies to celebrate success on the battlefield. In 1814, for example, the Creek warriors in the Battle of Horseshoe Bend did not seek quarter, nor did Jackson offer any. Instead, the Indians were hunted down and killed. Although most of the Indians escaped after the Battle of the Thames in 1813, volunteer militia from Kentucky carved up Tecumseh's body, taking home swatches of his skin for souvenirs.[116] That same year an American army officer who had fought in every Indian war since the 1790s reportedly boasted that he had accumulated 30 scalps and expected to have 50 before he died.[117]

The crucial role that Indians played in this war is not widely understood. Without Indians, the whole character of the war might have been different, and Upper Canada might have fallen into American hands. Nor is the devastating impact that this war had on the natives fully appreciated. Many tribes saw their numbers thinned, their relations with other tribes disrupted, and their ability to control their future significantly impaired. For Indians living east of the Mississippi River, the War of 1812 was a watershed event from which they never fully recovered.

**Tecumseh and the Pan-Indian Movement.** The best-known Indian in the War of 1812 is undoubtedly the Shawnee leader Tecumseh, who came closer than any other Indian leader to forging a grand native alliance. Tecumseh argued that lands were held in common by all Indians and thus could not be sold without unanimous consent. In principle, this made it impossible for American officials to buy lands from individual tribes, let alone from a few compliant Indians who might not even represent their tribes. Although Tecumseh followed the teachings of his brother the Prophet in giving up liquor, he was more flexible in embracing other trappings of white civilization.

Tecumseh was an exceptional leader, and whites on both sides of the border appreciated his greatness. Major General Isaac Brock claimed that "a more sagacious or a more gallant warrior does not . . . exist." Tecumseh was "the Wellington of the Indians."[118] Similarly, William Henry Harrison considered the respect and obedience that Tecumseh's followers paid him "really astonishing" and concluded that he was "one of those uncommon geniuses, which spring up occasionally to produce revolutions and overturn the established order of things."[119] Today, Canadians remember Tecumseh as a national hero who helped save Canada in the War of 1812, while Americans have elevated him to the rank of Pontiac and Crazy Horse as one of those great noble souls who resisted American expansion.

Tecumseh (1768?–1813) was the great
Shawnee leader who sought to mold North
American Indians into a confederation. His
pan-Indian movement did not survive his
death at the Battle of the Thames in 1813.
There is no surviving portrait of Tecumseh, but
this sketch, by Benson J. Lossing, was drawn
from a pencil sketch, now lost, made by Pierre
le Dru around 1808. (Lossing, *Pictorial Field-
Book of the War of 1812*)

There are some aspects of Tecumseh's character and career, however, that
are not widely understood. He was not
the only leader of the pan-Indian movement but simply one in a long line
that stretched back to Powhatan in the seventeenth century and forward to
Wovoka (the Ghost Dance leader) in the late nineteenth. Moreover, his influence was restricted largely to the Old Northwest, and even there he missed
out on many of the battles in the War of 1812. Finally, he may not have been
the most significant Indian to side with the British in the war.

It was Tecumseh's brother, the Prophet, who revived the pan-Indian
movement and instilled a religious component that gave the movement staying power. As late as 1811, Harrison invariably referred to this group of Indians
as "the Prophet and his friends," or "the
Prophet and his party," or "the Prophets
party."[120] Tecumseh, on the other hand,
was simply "the Prophet's brother."[121]
British Indian agent Matthew Elliott

Tenskwatawa, better known as the Prophet
(1768–1837), was Tecumseh's brother
and the founder of a pan-Indian religious
movement that Tecumseh transformed into
a political and military alliance. The Prophet
suffered a blow from the Indian defeat at
Tippecanoe but still retained significant
influence. (Lossing, *Pictorial Field-Book of
the War of 1812*)

used this same phrase in early 1812.[122] Not until 1810 did Tecumseh emerge as a leader in his own right, and not until the Prophet's defeat at Tippecanoe in November 1811, or perhaps even later, did he eclipse his brother in the pan-Indian movement.

Moreover, Tecumseh was not always in the British camp. Before the Treaty of Fort Wayne in 1809, which was the climax of a series of dubious land cession treaties imposed on the Indians by Harrison, both Tecumseh and his brother were a force for peace. They rejected the much more militant posture of the western tribes, and they resisted British blandishments for an alliance. The 1809 treaty, however, put Tecumseh and the Prophet on a collision course with the United States and forced them into a British alliance. In the only surviving likeness of Tecumseh, which is based on an earlier drawing that is now lost, Benson J. Lossing depicted the Shawnee leader in a British uniform because Lossing thought that he was a brigadier general in the British army.[123] Although the British sometimes gave their native allies a uniform or "chief's coat" that resembled a uniform, Tecumseh had no military commission.

Tecumseh enhanced his reputation among Indians by supposedly predicting the New Madrid earthquakes in 1811. According to this story, Tecumseh had said that he would stamp his foot on the ground and shake the earth. The earthquakes had followed soon after. But this story did not surface until 1827. What is more likely is that Tecumseh simply said that the Great Spirit would show his displeasure with Indians for alienating their lands and adopting white ways and that the earthquakes had ensued.

Tecumseh's reputation for nobility rests in part upon his opposition to torturing and killing prisoners taken in battle. This reputation was enhanced when he intervened to protect American prisoners taken in the first Battle of Fort Meigs in 1813. What is rarely mentioned is that Tecumseh was by no means unique among Indians in opposing torture, and that he had no prisoners of his own because in battle he apparently offered no quarter.

Because of the native tradition of personal independence, Tecumseh's command over his followers was never as absolute as whites imagined. Even among his own tribe, there was a sizeable faction that opposed him. Only about 40 Shawnees fought with Tecumseh at the Battle of the Thames. In fact, more Shawnees fought on the American side in this battle.[124]

Tecumseh played a major role in the British triumph in the West in 1812, but he also played a significant role in their defeat in 1813. He refused to concede the need for a strategic retreat from the Detroit River after the British lost control of Lake Erie, insisting instead that the British make a stand. The result was the Anglo-Indian disaster at the Thames, which not only resulted in Tecumseh's death but also drove large numbers of his Indian allies into the American camp.

Nor did Tecumseh's star burn brightly for very long. Less than 21 months after Tippecanoe, Indians were defecting from his cause because of the lack of Anglo-Indian success in 1813, and in another two months he was dead. If one takes the longer view, it appears that Tecumseh's reputation has been inflated at the expense of his brother's, and that both men played a critical role in forging the pan-Indian movement. The Prophet and his religious teachings formed the basis for the coalition of warriors opposed to American expansion before the War of 1812, and Tecumseh imposed his political and military vision upon his brother's religious movement.[125]

**John Norton: Mohawk Chief.** If Tecumseh's significance has been overrated, that of another Indian, John Norton, has been underrated. Born and raised in Scotland, John Norton was a Scottish-Cherokee mixed-blood who moved to Canada, where he embraced aboriginal life among the Grand River Iroquois in Upper Canada. A protégé and adopted nephew of the great Mohawk leader Joseph Brant, Norton was adopted into the Mohawk tribe and became a chief. Although he shared some of Tecumseh's pan-Indian views, like his mentor Joseph Brant, he believed that the survival of native culture depended on adopting certain European practices and beliefs: private property, improved agriculture, and Christianity. He had close ties with the Clapham set, a group of wealthy and influential evangelical reformers in Great Britain, and he served as their agent among the Iroquois in Canada, distributing the *Gospel of Saint John,* which he had translated into Mohawk.

Sir Walter Scott's brother claimed that Norton knew four European and 12 Indian languages. Like Tecumseh, Norton had contacts with a number of tribes, although he lacked the broad influence and following of the Shawnee leader. Norton had to contend with divisions among the Grand River Indians, who were torn between siding with the British and following the advice of their allies on the American side of the border, who favored neutrality.

Norton also had to contend with hostility from the British government, since both Francis Gore, the lieutenant governor of Upper Canada, and

John Norton (1770–1830?) was a Scottish-Cherokee mixed-blood who became a Mohawk leader. Not only did he help keep the Grand River Iroquois loyal to Great Britain, but he fought in almost every engagement on the Niagara frontier. (Portrait by Mary Ann Knight. Library and Archives Canada)

William Claus, the corrupt deputy superintendent of Indian affairs, worked tirelessly to discredit him, not only with British officials but also with the Grand River tribes.[126] Norton eventually prevailed against his enemies by persuading Sir George Prevost to recognize him as leader of the Grand River tribes with the exclusive power to distribute presents to the Indians. This enhanced Norton's power among the Iroquois and extended his influence to some tribes farther west. Young men from those tribes followed him, said Neywash, a western chief, because "he speaks loud, and has Strong Milk, and Big Breasts, which yield plentifully."[127]

Although the number of Indians that Norton brought to the battlefield varied considerably and was never large, he nonetheless played a significant role in the fighting on the Niagara front. Norton's finest hour came during the Battle of Queenston Heights in 1812, when he was wounded but his outnumbered Indian force held the American invaders at bay until British reinforcements could overpower them. Norton also took part in a host of subsequent engagements on the Niagara front: at Stoney Creek, Beaver Dams, Ball's Farm, and Fort Niagara in 1813; and at Chippawa, Lundy's Lane, and Fort Erie in 1814. In addition he took part in some of the lesser skirmishes on the Niagara frontier.

Queenston Heights established Norton's reputation, and shortly thereafter Major General Roger Sheaffe appointed him to the "Rank of Captain of the confederate Indians."[128] After the war, he was brevetted a major in the British army in recognition of his services. Even Major General Francis de Rottenburg, who considered Norton "a great intriguer," showed considerable respect for him as a warrior, calling him "a fighting man."[129]

Norton sometimes put the interests of the Iroquois on both sides of the border above those of the British. For this he can hardly be faulted, but his British allies found it exasperating. Major General Phineas Riall was furious when Norton in July of 1814 allowed Indians from the American side of the border to hold a council with the Grand River Iroquois in Burlington. Riall was convinced that this council dampened the war spirit of Britain's native allies.[130]

Even so, Norton's contribution to the British war effort was significant because success on the Niagara front was crucial to the preservation of Upper Canada. More than anyone else, he ensured that at least some of the Grand River Indians fought alongside British regulars in the defense of Canada. Without his influence, the entire Grand River confederation might have remained neutral, and that could have turned the tide against the British on the Niagara front. American success on this front probably would have had a greater impact on the peace negotiations than American success farther west had.

After the war, Lieutenant General Gordon Drummond wrote an appreciation of Norton's contribution. "This man," he said in 1815, "is of the coolest and most undaunted courage and has led the Indians with the greatest gallantry and much effect on many occasions against the enemy."[131] Norton deserves to be ranked with Tecumseh and the Prophet for the crucial role that he played in aiding the British cause during the War of 1812.[132]

## BLACKS

**Blacks in the Armed Services.** Blacks played a significant role on both sides in the War of 1812. Although most blacks in the United States were slaves, there were about 200,000 free blacks, which was 2.6 percent of the population, and many were eager to serve their country.[133] Initially the U.S. Army and Marine Corps did not accept black recruits, although the army soon relented to meet manpower needs. In the end, a fair number of blacks served in the army, although none are known to have served in the marines. Blacks also served in state military forces, especially later in the war when most states became desperate to find men who would perform volunteer militia duty or serve in the newly-authorized state armies.[134]

A disproportionate number of free blacks (as well as some slaves) found employment in the U.S. Navy, privateers, and the merchant fleet. Of the 14,739 American maritime prisoners of war held in four depots in Britain during the

A black soldier in Joshua Barney's Chesapeake flotilla is shown here. Black men were an important part of the crews of gunboats and barges because it was difficult to recruit for this service. (Painting by Keith Rocco. Fort McHenry National Monument, National Park Service)

War of 1812, 2,664 or 18 percent were blacks.[135] They probably made up 10 percent of the crews on U.S. warships and perhaps 20 percent on privateers. They constituted an even larger proportion of the crews on gunboats because it was so difficult to recruit for this service.[136]

Of the blacks who served on oceangoing vessels, over 1,200 ended up at the notorious British prison at Dartmoor. There they lived in a barracks that was ruled with an iron hand by "King Dick," who was between six-foot-three and six-foot-five inches tall and later became a leader of the black community in Boston.[137]

Blacks fought for the United States in almost every battle and helped prepare defensive works in almost every major city on the eastern seaboard and the Gulf Coast.[138] Their white commanding officers generally praised their performance. After the U.S. Frigate *Constitution* defeated H.M. Ship *Guerrière*, Captain Isaac Hull commented that he "had never had any better fighters." "They stripped to the waist and fought like devils . . . utterly insensible to danger and . . . possessed with a determination to outfight the white sailors."[139]

The British also employed blacks in the war. The British army frequently recruited blacks as musicians, and blacks served in the Royal Navy and on privateers as well. In fact, Lieutenant Charles F. Grandison of the U.S. Navy reported that a British privateer with eight guns that was operating off the South Atlantic coast in late 1812 was "man[ne]d Chiefly with blacks about 70 in Number."[140] Britain's 2nd West India regiment (which included some recruits from the Chesapeake) served in the Atlantic theater, and about 700 troops from the 1st and 5th West India regiments took part in the Gulf Coast campaign.[141] Blacks could also be found in the Canadian militia and in fencible and provincial units (local units raised for long-term service). There were blacks, for example, in the Glengarry Light Infantry.[142]

There was even a black independent militia unit in Canada. Organized by Captain Robert Runchy, this small unit was known as Runchy's Company of Colored Men and was used mainly as a labor corps.[143] Blacks in all the British uniformed services were more likely than their American counterparts to be treated like whites.

**Blacks and the Indians.** Occasionally blacks were spotted fighting alongside natives in the Indian wars that raged in the Old Northwest and Old Southwest during the War of 1812. Almost nothing is known about these men. Some may have been free blacks or runaway slaves adopted into a tribe. Others may have been mixed-bloods (the offspring of a black-native union) who had been part of the tribe since birth.[144]

A black U.S. infantry soldier is shown here. The U.S. Army at first barred black recruits, but manpower needs forced a change in policy. (Painting by Keith Rocco. Fort McHenry National Monument, National Park Service)

**Runaway American Slaves.** Fearful of causing unrest among their own slaves in the Caribbean, British officials ordered their military leaders not to encourage an uprising in America. "You will on no account," Lord Bathurst wrote to an army officer, "give encouragement to any disposition which may be manifested by the Negroes to rise against their masters."[145] But to keep Americans guessing, these orders were not made public.

Runaway slaves in the Chesapeake started seeking sanctuary with the British as early as March 1813. Then in the spring of 1814, Vice Admiral Sir Alexander Cochrane issued a proclamation offering all interested Americans a "choice of either entering into His Majesty's Sea or Land Forces, or of being sent as FREE Settlers, to the British Possessions in North America or the West Indies."[146] This appeal clearly targeted the Chesapeake's large slave population. Cochrane gave his subordinate, Rear Admiral George Cockburn, a thousand copies of the proclamation to circulate, and its purpose was understood by all classes of people.[147] The proclamation generated fears of a slave insurrection throughout the Chesapeake and affected the deployment of militia in the region for the remainder of the war.[148]

Cochrane's proclamation was not without precedent. Lord Dunmore had anticipated it by almost 40 years when he issued a more explicit appeal in 1775 for able-bodied male slaves in Virginia to desert their Rebel masters and join the British army.[149] Although the peace treaty signed in 1783 prohibited Great Britain from "carrying away Negroes or other private property of the American inhabitants," many runaways left with the British.[150] In the ensuing years, the United States repeatedly demanded compensation, but the British steadfastly refused.[151]

Shortly after Cochrane issued his proclamation in 1814, the British established a base on Tangier Island, and it served as a magnet for runaways from around the Chesapeake. "The *Negroes*," Captain Joshua Barney commented in August 1814, "flock to them from all quarters."[152] The British employed the runaways as scouts, guides, messengers, and pilots. Although some preferred to continue this kind of work, many were interested in actual military service.

Cochrane had earlier raised a Corps of Colonial Marines in the West Indies, and on his instructions, Rear Admiral George Cockburn enlisted volunteers from the Chesapeake into three companies of a new Corps of Colonial Marines. Cockburn recruited an additional three companies from runaways in Georgia in early 1815 after he moved his operations south and established a base on Cumberland Island. These six companies were undersized and probably included a total of around 550 men. Another large company of Colonial Marines, about 325 strong, was enlisted in early 1815 from maroon communities located in the backcountry of Florida and Georgia.[153]

By all accounts, the Colonial Marines made excellent soldiers. In 1814, they fought with distinction in the Battle of Bladensburg outside Washington and in the Battle of North Point en route to Baltimore. They also took part in the assault on Point Petre on Cumberland Island, Georgia, in 1815. Not only did they perform well in battle, but, with no safe place to run to, they never deserted. In fact, when two Colonial Marine prisoners of war were reportedly hanged by their American captors, it served as a warning to the rest that their only safe haven was with the British.[154]

British officers had nothing but praise for the Colonial Marines. Captain Charles B.H. Ross of the Royal Navy praised them for their "great spirit and vivacity," their "perfect obedience," and their "worth as skirmishers."[155] Cochrane was also impressed, commenting that the Colonial Marines showed "extraordinary steadiness and good conduct when in action with the Enemy."[156] Even Cockburn, who was initially skeptical about their potential military value, was won over. He called them "excellent Men" who "make the best skirmishers possible for the thick Woods of this Country."[157] Cockburn even wanted some of the Colonial Marines on his flagship because he considered them "stronger" and "more trustworthy" than his regular marines.[158]

How many slaves escaped to freedom during the War of 1812? Based on evidence submitted, an Anglo-American commission in 1825 put the figure at 3,601.[159] This did not include some claims that were unproven and others that were never submitted or were submitted too late. Nor did it include the claims of slaves who fled from Spanish Florida. The total was probably around 4,000. This was the largest emancipation of slaves between 1807, when the Mutiny Act freed some 10,000 slaves in British military service, and 1833, when the Abolition Act mandated the liberation of all slaves in the British colonies, including some 665,000 in the West Indies.[160]

What became of the American runaways? It was widely believed in the United States that they were sold back into slavery in the British colonies. Two eyewitnesses even reported that they had seen evidence of this in the Bahamas and Halifax. But the U.S. and the British governments conducted separate investigations into these claims and thoroughly discredited them.[161]

Most of the runaways settled in the Maritime provinces. Known as the "Refugee Negroes," they did not fare well. Dogged by poverty, many, particularly in Nova Scotia, died from smallpox or malnutrition. Despite neglect, suffering, and discrimination, descendants of the original refugees can still be found in the Maritimes today.[162]

The British sought to persuade the Colonial Marines to continue their service after the war in army units, first offering to transfer them to West Indian regiments and then offering them a separate regiment of their own. But the black soldiers rejected both offers and were re-settled in Trinidad. Their descendants today still call themselves "Merikens."[163]

Some of the runaways from the Gulf Coast settled around the Negro Fort in Florida and either perished when the fort's magazine exploded during an American assault in 1816 or were enslaved when the fort surrendered.[164] Others escaped to join another group from the Gulf Coast that had settled with the Seminoles in Florida and later moved to the Bahamas.[165]

The United States claimed that the removal of any slaves who were still on American territory or in American waters when ratifications of the Treaty of Ghent were exchanged at 11:00 p.m. on February 17, 1815, violated Article 1, which prohibited "carrying away . . . any Slaves or other private property."[166] Although some blacks had already been shipped to Bermuda and Nova Scotia, the American interpretation would have forced the return of all the rest.

The British, however, took a different view. On the Atlantic coast, Rear Admiral Cockburn insisted that the British were bound to return only those runaways who had sought sanctuary after the exchange of ratifications. Major General John Lambert took the same view on the Gulf Coast.[167] Even the return of some runaways from the Atlantic coast who had arrived in British camps after this date was surreptitiously blocked by British naval officers. Among those who were returned, however, were several who had enlisted in the Colonial Marines. A nineteenth-century historian of the Royal Marines called this "so disgraceful a transaction" that it "cast a stigma upon the character of the british nation."[168] Ultimately, the British conceded that they were responsible for providing compensation for those they carried off who were still on American territory when the war ended, but not for those who were aboard British ships even if those ships were in American waters.

This matter remained a bone of contention between the two nations for a decade after the war. It was finally put to the Czar of Russia for arbitration, and he ruled that the British were bound to provide compensation for all slaves removed at the end of the war. To settle these claims, the British in 1826 agreed to pay $1,200,000 (£244,000). The commission established by the United States to pay out the money evidently allowed all provable claims because it was impossible to tell which slaves were still in American jurisdiction when the war ended and which had already been carried away in British ships.[169]

**Runaway Canadian Slaves.** Although the role of runaway slaves in the Chesapeake during the War of 1812 is well known, what is never mentioned is that runaway slaves from Canada probably fought for the United States during the conflict. Upper Canada prohibited the importation of slaves in 1793 and provided for the gradual emancipation of the children of slaves. But the institution lingered on until it was finally abolished in all British colonies in 1833.[170]

A number of Canadian slaves, some of whom belonged to British Indian agent Matthew Elliott, slipped across the Detroit River in 1806 and settled in Michigan. Although the Northwest Ordinance of 1787 prohibited slavery in Michigan, a confusing welter of French, British, and American laws and treaties permitted those who already owned slaves to keep them, and the census of 1810 showed that there were still 24 slaves living in the territory. Nevertheless, Governor William Hull refused Canadian pleas to return the runaways, and territorial judge Augustus B. Woodward ruled against Canadian suits to force their return. The former slaves therefore remained in the United States as free men.[171]

Hull treated all runaways as U.S. citizens and even included them in a black militia company that he organized in 1806. Although Hull disbanded this company before the war, some of the runaways probably served in the volunteer militia units that fought on the Detroit frontier in 1812–13.[172] In addition, Hull in 1812 gave three blacks commissions in the U.S. Army.[173] One or more of these men may have been former Canadian slaves who had served in the disbanded Michigan militia unit.

## WOMEN

**The Role of Women.** Women played a significant supporting role in the War of 1812, as they have in most wars. In the United States and Canada, women fed and nursed soldiers and civilians who participated in the war, managed businesses and farms when their men were gone, provided counsel to their husbands, and in general performed a number of support services that were vital to the war effort. In the United States, women also helped produce ammunition since it was difficult to hire men for this kind of work at the prevailing wage. Native women contributed to the war effort as well, most notably by feeding and nursing warriors who participated in the campaigns.

This is an idealized portrayal of Fanny Doyle, who serviced artillery firing hot shot from Fort Niagara. The hot shot was actually fired from the roof of the old French castle inside the fort. (Drawing by T. Walker. Library and Archives Canada)

On occasion, American, Canadian, and Indian women also took part in the battles of the War of 1812.

The supporting role that women played in this era is not fully appreciated today because most nation states now have an established bureaucracy to provide essential support services to their troops. This kind of bureaucratic support was in its infancy in the early nineteenth century. Hence, the duties performed by women were essential to maintaining any nation's war-making capacity.

**Women and the Armed Services.** It is well known that women almost always traveled with armies. These women were part of a larger community of civilians who marched in the train of campaigning soldiers. This community was often a sizeable group that included merchants, peddlers, and sutlers who sold food and other goods to the army; wagoners, artisans, and laborers who worked for the army; servants and slaves who waited on the officers; and occasionally refugees fleeing from the enemy or seeking protection.

The women in this community can be divided into two classes: army women, who were the wives of the soldiers and were officially recognized by being granted rations, and camp followers, who had no legal status. Army women and camp followers provided comfort and companionship to the soldiers and performed a number of essential tasks, such as cooking, sewing, washing, cleaning, nursing, and hauling food and water to the front lines. Sometimes women joined men on the battlefield, and occasionally they took part in the fighting. Some of the women might have been prostitutes, but this was probably less common than lore has suggested because most armies required each woman to be attached to a man. Although an army could be overrun with women if it camped near a big city, in most cases their presence was carefully controlled to minimize any fighting over them and to maintain order.

Most women attached to an army subsisted by charging a small fee for the various domestic services they provided. However, European armies recognized the contributions of women by putting some of them on the rolls and granting them rations. These were the army women. In the British army, such women, who had to be married to soldiers they marched with, received one half of the daily ration. Their children received a third of a ration, although this ended when boys reached the age of 9 and girls the age of 12. Normally, the British army allowed up to six women and their children on the rolls for every 100 enlisted men and non-commissioned officers when they were on active duty overseas. When the men were on "foreign service," that is, assigned to a garrison overseas, they were expected to be there for some time, and thus the allotment of women was increased to 12 together with their children. Most of the units assigned to Canada before the War of 1812 were considered on foreign service and thus were entitled to the more generous allotment.

Some British commanding officers did not allow any women on the rolls, while others allowed their men to bring more women than the number sanctioned, although the extra ones could not draw rations. Officers themselves were entitled to bring their families on campaign, and even though most received additional rations because of their rank, in some cases they also drew rations for their dependents. In Canada, however, only the most junior officers were supposed to be accorded this privilege. On occasion, British officers had mistresses with them, although they could not draw extra rations for them.[174]

British army women were sometimes considered a liability and could be ordered out of a theater if circumstances warranted. In June 1813, for example, all the women and children attached to the British army in Upper Canada were ordered to Montreal to preserve rations for the men serving in the theater. The evidence, however, suggests that this order was not fully complied with, probably because the army could not do without the duties that some women performed.[175]

Women were also attached to the U.S. Army during the War of 1812 and performed the usual camp duties. They were also employed in the medical corps, hauled food and water to men in the front lines, and occasionally took part in battles. Fanny Doyle was the wife of an American artillery private who was captured in the Battle of Queenston Heights. Five weeks later, on November 21, 1812, Fanny Doyle took part in a fierce artillery duel between Fort George and Fort Niagara. According to Lieutenant Colonel George McFeeley, she showed "extraordinary bravery" in the engagement. "During the most tremendous cannonading I have ever seen, she attended the six-pounder on the [Fort Niagara] mess-house [roof] with red hot shot, and showed fortitude equal to the Maid of Orleans [Joan of Arc]."[176]

Imitating the British, the U.S. Army allowed rations for some army women during the Revolutionary War. Near the end of the conflict, the allowance was fixed at one extra ration for every 15 soldiers. For the War of 1812, this allowance was reduced to one extra ration for every 17 soldiers. In addition, the U.S. Army customarily provided rations for women serving as matrons and nurses in army hospitals.[177]

Women were also attached to the British navy. Any time a Royal warship showed up in port, either at home or abroad, it was invariably overrun by wives, girlfriends, and prostitutes, although to maintain order, each woman was supposed to be attached to a man. These women were expected to debark before the ship left port, but this was not always the case.

Some women were permitted to sail on warships. The Admiralty left the matter up to the individual ship commanders. Although most commanders considered the presence of women unchristian or disruptive, and some seamen considered it unlucky, there were others, especially on the navy's larger ships, who took a different view.

Some officers—commissioned, warrant, and petty—brought their wives or girlfriends with them, and so, too, on occasion did common seamen. The

Royal Navy's civilian employees—pursers, schoolmasters, and chaplains— occasionally brought their wives as well. Some women brought their children aboard, and there were even a few babies born at sea. Unlike army women, navy women were neither officially acknowledged nor entitled to rations. They usually provided for themselves by doing little chores for the officers and men. As Admiral Philip Charles Durham put it in 1813, "We are compelled in a fleet to have a few women, to wash and mend,"[178]

Did women sail on American warships? Occasionally they did, although the practice was far less common than in the Royal Navy. There were five wives on board the U.S. Frigate *Chesapeake* in 1803 when it served in the Mediterranean during the Tripolitan War, and a child was born while the ship was at sea.[179] Commodore Stephen Decatur signed up two women to serve as nurses on the U.S. Frigate *United States* in 1813, although the British blockade prevented the ship from getting to sea.[180] It is possible that women served on other American warships during the War of 1812, but the record is silent.

Unlike army women, females on warships could not be left behind out of harm's way before a battle. Instead, they were usually sent below, where they tended to the needs of the wounded or served as powder monkeys, delivering powder from the magazine to the guns. In a few cases, they even helped operate the guns. Though less likely to be wounded than men, such women were never out of danger, and occasionally they were injured or killed in battle. Although it has been said that a British woman perished on board H.M. Ship *Confiance* in the Battle of Lake Champlain, this claim does not appear to be supported by any contemporary evidence.[181]

Indian women also occasionally took part in battles. In the Battle of Campbell's Island, an Indian force consisting of Sauks, Foxes, and Kickapoos attacked Captain John Campbell's flotilla of boats in the Rock River in July 1814. After the battle, a British eyewitness, Colonel William McKay, reported that "the [Indian] women even jumped on board [a gunboat] with their hoes, etc., some breaking heads, others breaking casks, some trying to cut holes in her bottom to sink her, and others setting fire to her decks."[182]

**Laura Secord's Heroic Trek.** The best known Canadian heroine of the War of 1812 is Laura Secord. Born Laura Ingersoll in Massachusetts in 1775, she came from a family that supported the American Revolution but moved to Canada in the mid-1790s to take advantage of greater opportunities to acquire land.

Two years later she married merchant James Secord and settled in Queenston. When her husband was called up for militia duty and wounded at Queenston Heights in 1812, Secord rescued him from the battlefield. The following year, she learned (probably from American officers dining at her house) that the United States planned to launch a surprise attack against Lieutenant James FitzGibbon's small force at Beaver Dams. Since her husband was still incapacitated by his battle wounds, Secord decided that she would have to warn FitzGibbon herself.

Setting out in the early morning on June 22, 1813, Secord traveled all day through difficult terrain. By the time darkness set in, she had covered almost 20 miles. Shortly thereafter she stumbled onto some Indians, one of whom cried out, "Woman! What does woman want here?"[183] With some difficulty, Secord persuaded one of the Indians to take her to FitzGibbon's camp. FitzGibbon responded by organizing an attack against the approaching American force, but the night passed without incident.

The Americans did not actually leave Fort George until the evening of June 23. When the Indians realized an American force was headed their way, they sprang a trap at Beaver Dams. FitzGibbon arrived with a small body of regulars just as the Americans were preparing to surrender. Greatly exaggerating the size of his force, FitzGibbon persuaded Colonel Charles Boerstler to surrender his entire American army, close to 500 men. The news of Boerstler's capitulation caused so much consternation in Washington that Republican leaders insisted that President Madison replace the lackluster theater commander, Major General Henry Dearborn.

Laura Secord (1775–1868) played a role in setting up the Battle of Beaver Dams in 1813 by walking more than 20 miles to warn of a pending American attack. She lived long enough to receive belated recognition for her contribution and today is Canada's best known woman associated with the war. (Lossing, *Pictorial Field-Book of the War of 1812*)

Laura Secord's role in setting up the victory at Beaver Dams was largely forgotten until 1860, when the Prince of Wales, who was visiting Canada, took notice of her contribution. She was then 85 years old but survived for another eight years. From 1860 on she was part of the pantheon of Canadian heroes.

Once Laura Secord had achieved fame in 1860, her story grew in the telling.[184] Tales that she took certain props with her on her trek as cover, such as a cow, milk stool, or milk pail, are false. It is also untrue that she had to slip by American scouts, that she made the trip barefoot, and that she traveled in the dead of night. Finally, it is certainly an exaggeration to suggest that she saved Canada, Upper Canada, or even the Niagara District. The Battle of Beaver Dams, however, is significant for other reasons: (1) It was the largest victory achieved by Indians in the war; and (2) it induced American troops to stay penned up in Fort George, largely nullifying their influence on the Canadian side of the Niagara River.

Some twentieth-century scholars have moved in the opposite direction, questioning whether Secord actually arrived in time to affect the outcome of the battle and suggesting that Indians preceded her with the vital intelligence.[185] Contemporary sources indicate that an Indian messenger brought news of the American advance on June 24, 1813.[186] No contemporary account mentions Secord's warning. In his brief after-action report, FitzGibbon merely says that "I received information that about 1,000 of the enemy, with two field guns, were advancing towards me from St. Davids."[187]

However, a statement that FitzGibbon penned in 1827 surfaced in 1959 testifying to the vital role that Secord played. "In consequence of this information," FitzGibbon wrote of Secord's warning, "I placed the Indians under [John] Norton together with my own Detachment in a Situation to intercept the American Detachment, and we occupied it during the night of the 22d—but the Enemy did not come until the morning of the 24th when his Detachment was captured."[188]

So what are we to make of Laura Secord? She did indeed make her heroic trek, she was the first to warn of an impending attack, and even though the attack was delayed, her warning may have put the British and Indians on heightened alert. Laura Secord thus deserves a share of the credit for the victory at Beaver Dams, although the significance of her contribution to the war effort has been exaggerated over the years.[189]

**Dolley Madison's Heroism.** The most famous woman on the American side of the war is probably Dolley Payne Madison. The widow who married James Madison created a glittering social life for her shy and retiring husband and on occasion offered him advice on politics and matters of state. Dolley Madison served as the de facto First Lady for widowed Thomas Jefferson during his presidency (1801–09). After her husband succeeded Jefferson, she furnished the White House and made it even more of a social center in Washington. Indeed, such was her visibility and such was the demand for invitations to her parties that in many ways she helped define the modern role of the First Lady and make the White House the center of Washington's social scene.

Dolley Madison (1768–1849) was the leading American woman in the war. Not only did she develop the role of First Lady, but she also saved many White House treasures (while sacrificing her own property) when the British threatened the nation's capital in 1814. (Based on a portrait by Gilbert Stuart. Library of Congress)

Dolley Madison's most important service came during the War of 1812. In the summer of 1813, when her husband was deathly ill, she nursed him back to health and also served as his secretary. The following summer, when the British threatened Washington, her husband spent most of his time in the field, and she was largely responsible for overseeing the evacuation of the White House.

On August 23, 1814, with the British marching toward the capital city, Dolley packed some cabinet papers in trunks so that they could be loaded into her carriage if it became necessary to leave Washington. She might have prepared more items for removal, but no wagons were available because everyone was scrambling to move property out of the city. "Our private property must be sacrificed," she told her sister, "as it is impossible to procure wagons for its transportation."[190] The president returned that evening, and this was the last night that the Madisons spent in the White House.

The following day the British won the Battle of Bladensburg, and the road to the capital city lay open. With the president again in the field, it was up to the First Lady to supervise the removal of property. Having secured a wagon, Dolley loaded it with "the plate and most valuable portable articles belonging to the house" and sent it to the Bank of Maryland.[191] Although pressed to leave, she insisted on securing the full-length portrait of George Washington usually attributed to Gilbert Stuart. Unable to unscrew the picture from the wall, she ordered the frame broken and gave the canvas for safekeeping to two New Yorkers, Robert DePeyster and Jacob Barker.

Dolley then hastened out of the city. Her husband returned to the White House just after she left, and then he fled, only a little ahead of the British. The Madisons spent the next several days in the Virginia countryside, linking up on August 25 at Wiley's Tavern, some 15 miles from the capital. The president returned to Washington on August 27, and Dolley followed the next day. With the White House in ruins, the first family moved into the Octagon House, which had been the French minister's residence. In the ensuing years, Dolley Madison furnished this home with second-hand furniture and helped transform it into a temporary White House.

The challenges that Dolley Madison faced as First Lady were unique and suggest that she was a genuine hero. She not only helped define the role of First Lady in peacetime, but during the War of 1812 she played an important role in preserving White House treasures and ensuring continuity in the Executive Mansion.[192]

**Who Was Louisa Baker/Lucy Brewer?** Shortly after the War of 1812, a 24-page pamphlet was published in Boston entitled *An Affecting Narrative of Louisa Baker, A Native of Massachusetts*. This was the first of a series of pamphlets that appeared under several titles, most commonly *The Female Marine*.[193] These pamphlets described the remarkable life and adventures of Louisa Baker (also known as Lucy Brewer). Born in Plymouth County in rural Massachusetts, Baker was seduced as a young woman. Fleeing in shame to Boston, she worked for three years in a brothel. In 1812 or 1813 she disguised herself as a man and enlisted in the U.S. Marines, serving for the rest of the war as a musketeer in the tops on the U.S. Frigate *Constitution*. After collecting her prize money at the end of the war, she had several further adventures before settling down and marrying a wealthy and respectable gentleman named Charles West.

This story fits into the literary tradition of the female warrior. This tradition is not entirely fictional since female warriors have been documented throughout history. After the American Revolution, for example, the U.S. government awarded a pension to Deborah Sampson Gannett for her service (under the name of Robert Shurtleff) in the Continental army. The Louisa Baker/Lucy Brewer story, however, is pure fiction, the invention of printer Nathaniel Coverly, Jr., and/or a hack writer that he employed named Nathaniel Hill Wright.

There is no record of the birth or life of Baker/Brewer in Plymouth County, nor does anyone using her male pseudonym, "George," appear on the roster of the U.S. Frigate *Constitution* during the War of 1812. It would have been difficult anyway for a woman to evade the physical examination administered at the time of enlistment or to survive undetected in the close quarters of a warship in the Age of Sail. Though this story is sometimes accepted as truth and presented as an example of what a determined and resourceful woman could achieve in the early nineteenth century, the tale is unadulterated fiction and represents hope and aspiration rather than reality.[194]

## HATRED, RESENTMENT, AND INTOLERANCE

**Wartime Hatreds.** By its very nature, war always generates hatred. In retrospect, the War of 1812 may seem like a gentlemanly contest between two English-speaking nations, each committed to a righteous cause, fair play, generous and humane behavior, and the rule of law. But contemporaries saw things differently. To Americans, Great Britain was an overbearing bully seeking to recolonize the United States by forcing the young republic to accede to maritime practices that were at once costly, illegal, and inhumane. To the British, the United States was an upstart bastard nation of mercenary French sympathizers who had stabbed Britain in the back at the height of its war to uphold Western Civilization against French tyranny.

Although each side tried to follow the accepted international rules governing warfare, these rules did not always provide clear guidance, and combatants on both sides sometimes violated the law or acted in ways that were not clearly sanctioned. Moreover, even when obeying international law, both sides committed acts, such as confiscating private property or destroying public buildings, that generated an enormous amount of resentment.

Americans, often assisted by Canadian traitors, plundered Upper Canada; burned public buildings at York; torched private buildings at Newark/Niagara, Port Dover, and St. Davids; and destroyed almost every grist mill in the District of London. American soldiers, particularly militiamen, frequently looted Canadian homes and committed atrocities against Indians and occasionally against Canadian non-combatants. In fact, Brigadier General George McClure openly conceded that he could not control the New York militia stationed at Fort George in 1813, and Dr. Cyrenius Chapin's band of mounted New York riflemen did so much looting on the Canadian side that U.S. regulars called them "Dr. Chapin and the Forty Thieves."[195]

The British, for their part, burned private buildings on the American side of the Niagara River and in the Chesapeake and incinerated public buildings in Washington, D.C. French deserters and prisoners of war who had enlisted in the British army committed atrocities at Hampton, Virginia, and Britain's Indian allies killed prisoners of war and non-combatants at Fort Mims, on the River Raisin, and at Fort Meigs. In addition, British soldiers, like their American counterparts, sometimes looted private homes or robbed and assaulted civilians. British militia also killed or wounded close to 70 unruly American prisoners of war in the notorious Dartmoor Massacre in 1815.[196]

Although some of the buildings—the mills in the London district and the public buildings in Washington—were legitimate targets of war, many that were destroyed were not. The plunder, burning, and atrocities committed by both sides left a legacy of bitterness and hatred that persisted long after the war was over. This was especially true on the Niagara River frontier. Such was the devastation on both sides of the river that Canadians and Americans living there probably suffered more from this war than people living anywhere else.

**The Most Hated Man in the U.S.** Who was the most hated man in the United States during the War of 1812? It was probably Rear Admiral George Cockburn. After serving with distinction and rising up the command ladder in the Royal Navy during the French Revolutionary and Napoleonic Wars, Cockburn was sent to America in 1812. In 1813, he spearheaded British operations in the Chesapeake, burning and plundering a good deal of private property.

The British claimed the right to seize or destroy maritime property, which usually meant ships and cargoes in port as well as any goods in nearby warehouses. They also treated tobacco found in any warehouse as fair game. They considered other private property fair game when they met with resistance. Sometimes they burned vacant homes, claiming that the buildings had been used for military purposes, that their owners must be serving in the militia, or that the owners had fled because they were hostile to the British. Private property also was plundered or burned to bring the war home to Americans, and sometimes British soldiers plundered on their own.

To his victims, Cockburn's entire war effort in the Chesapeake seemed an unjustified abomination. "Cockburn's name was on every tongue," reported a congressman who traveled from Philadelphia to Washington in 1814, "with various particulars of his incredibly coarse and blackguard misconduct." "The wantonness of his barbarities" added *Niles' Register*, "have gibbetted him on infamy."[197] Although the real admiral pronounced his name "*Co*-burn" (with the emphasis on the first syllable), Americans preferred to call him "Cock-*burn*," emphasizing the second syllable.

The attack on Washington in 1814 was largely Cockburn's idea. When Major General Robert Ross got his army near Washington, Cockburn persuaded him to continue to the capital city despite Vice Admiral Sir Alexander Cochrane's call for withdrawal. Once in Washington, Cockburn oversaw the destruction of some of the public buildings as well as the contents of the office of the semi-official *National Intelligencer*. In fact, he apparently favored torching the entire city, public and private buildings alike.[198]

Cockburn continued his predatory raids in the Chesapeake until the onset of cold weather in late 1814, when he shifted his operations to the St. Marys River on the Georgia-Florida border as a diversion for the attack on New Orleans. Americans denounced Cockburn as "the Great *Bandit*," "the notorious incendiary and infamous scoundrel," and "the *savage* Cockburn."[199] His brand of warfare was not soon forgotten.[200]

The popular view of Cockburn, however, is overdrawn. It is true that he was infuriated by some American wartime practices, particularly guerrilla warfare, sniping, and the use of mines, and in response he could inflict severe punishment on any guilty community. On the other hand, Cockburn claimed that he adhered to "the principles of humanity" and that he was driven by "a sincere desire to lessen to individuals the hardships inseparable from war."[201] Americans in the Chesapeake, he concluded, "suffered perhaps less real loss and inconvenience than was ever experienced by people inhabiting a country made the theater of hostile operations."[202] This assessment is close to the truth. The Patuxent was probably the hardest hit region in the Chesapeake, and yet people living there suffered less than those living on the Niagara front and far less than just about anyone who had ever lived in a war zone in Europe.

In a host of ways, Cockburn sought to uphold the eighteenth-century ideal of minimizing the impact of the war on non-combatants. Although sometimes accused of undervaluing the supplies that he took from the local population, he paid for them in cash or in bills drawn on the British government. He insisted that an American who had fed a number of shipwrecked British naval personnel be reimbursed even though the wreck had not occurred on his watch and he considered the bill inflated. He apparently turned loose some captured American merchant vessels whose loss would be a particular hardship on their owners, and he allowed civilians to travel freely across the Chesapeake and to fish in its waters. He also refused to interfere with mail delivery.

Cockburn was a known enemy of looting and generally maintained good discipline among his men—although as a navy man he could not control army looting. According to Margaret Bayard Smith, his behavior in Washington was exemplary. "I must praise his moderation," she said; "indeed his conduct was such as to disarm the prejudices that existed. During the stay of their troops in the city, it was so still you might have heard a pin drop on the pavement."[203] Later, when the war ended, he refused to return any runaway slaves who had arrived in his camp before the actual ratification of the peace treaty.[204]

Some British army and naval officers liked Americans; at least they liked those American officers that they met before or during the war. Other British officers genuinely disliked Americans. Vice Admiral Sir Alexander Cochrane, for one, compared them to unruly dogs. "Like Spaniels," he said, "they must be treated with great severity before you ever make them tractable."[205]

Cockburn fell somewhere in between. He did not dislike Americans, nor did he take the war against them personally. He was simply fighting what he considered a just war against a sometimes recalcitrant and stubborn foe. He followed the rules of war as he understood them, and in general his interpretation of those rules was humane and reasonable. "There was certainly little in [his behavior]," concluded Theodore Roosevelt, "to warrant the warmth of the execrations heaped upon him by his foes."[206]

**The Most Hated Man in Canada.** Who was the most hated man in Canada during the War of 1812? As much animosity as Cockburn generated in the Chesapeake, it probably does not match the raw hatred produced in Canada by another man, one who was virtually unknown in Great Britain and the United States. This was the Canadian Joseph Willcocks, who was not only a traitor but waged a particularly brutal form of warfare against his former countrymen.

An immigrant from Ireland, Willcocks was a newspaper editor who held a seat in Upper Canada's provincial assembly before the war. An opponent of the Crown, this "turbulent Irishman," as Lieutenant Governor Francis Gore called him, reveled in his opposition.[207] "I am flattered," he said on the eve of war in 1812, "in being ranked among the enemies of the measures of the Kings Servants in this Colony—I glory in the distinction."[208] Willcocks promised to do everything necessary to uphold the rights of the people. "I pledge myself to . . . detect and expose every attempt made to impose upon the honest credulity of a Loyal, and already too much abused people."[209]

In early 1812 Willcocks helped defeat Major General Isaac Brock's plan to suspend habeas corpus and to require all residents to renounce allegiance to any foreign power. Until mid-1813, however, he remained loyal to the Crown. He helped to secure the allegiance of the Six Nations; he served as a volunteer in the Battle of Queenston Heights; and he recruited men for the Incorporated Militia.

In July 1813, after the loss of Fort George appeared to turn the tide of the war in Upper Canada, Willcocks visited Major General Henry Dearborn's camp and offered his services to the United States. Armed with a commission from Dearborn, Willcocks organized his followers into a unit known as the Canadian Volunteers. Willcocks proved remarkably adept at ingratiating himself to his American masters. In late 1813 Brigadier General George McClure named him "Police Officer" for Fort George and Newark/Niagara, which gave him exceptional authority to control movement into and out of the American camp and to arrest Canadians who remained loyal to the Crown. At the same time, Willcocks's Volunteers made a significant contribution to the American war effort in Upper Canada. (For more on this unit, see above, "The Canadian Volunteers.")

American field commanders gave Willcocks a commission as a major and then as a lieutenant colonel, but he visited Washington, D.C., in the spring of 1814 in search of greater official support. Although the War Department appointed him a "Lieutenant Colonel of Volunteers in the service of the United States," it refused to take his unit into the regular army or to provide him with money to recruit more men. Instead his unit was attached to Peter B. Porter's brigade of New York militia and Indians. When he returned to the Niagara in May, Willcocks took part in the campaigning there and for a time even commanded Porter's brigade. He was killed in a skirmish outside Fort Erie on September 5, 1814.

Willcocks's defenders on both sides of the border have portrayed him as a proponent of liberty who became disillusioned with arbitrary government in Canada in 1813 and concluded that the United States was a more hospitable home to both freedom and the rule of law. But this explanation ignores his opportunism and careerism and does not explain why he pursued such a vicious form of predatory warfare against his former countrymen in Canada. Willcocks did on occasion raise the banner of liberty, but he seems to have been more interested in furthering his own interests and punishing all who would not follow his lead.

In the end, Willcocks's brand of warfare proved counterproductive. Instead of terrifying the people of Upper Canada into submission, Willcocks's arbitrary arrests and depredations increased popular support for the British government. By helping to turn the Niagara district into a wasteland, Willcocks also left a legacy of hatred and fear that contributed to the growth of Canadian nationalism.[210]

**Did Republicans Threaten Freedom of Speech?** Every American history textbook takes note of the notorious Sedition Act of 1798, an ill-advised Federalist attempt to suppress criticism of public policies. These same textbooks, however, fail to mention that Republicans made a similar attempt to suppress opposition in 1812, although instead of using a law they resorted to violence and intimidation.

The Federalists enacted the Sedition Act during the Quasi-War with France. It was designed to curtail public criticism by punishing sedition, that is, the act of exciting discontent against the government. The law is invariably viewed as a gross infringement on the First Amendment, although it was actually an improvement over the common law because it included certain safeguards to protect the rights of the accused. Truth was a defense, the prosecution had to prove malicious intent, and the jury rather than the judge decided if the spoken or written words were actually seditious. Although these safeguards occasionally had been recognized in common law cases, this was the first time that they were enshrined in statutory law. In practice, however, they were ineffective because Federalist juries guided by Federalist judges regularly convicted Republican defendants for simply criticizing the government. In 1798–99, 18 people were indicted under the Sedition Act. Of these, 11 were convicted or pleaded guilty, and only four were acquitted. Against the other three, the charges were dropped or discontinued.[211]

Although enforced in a partisan manner, the Sedition Act did not silence Republican critics, nor did it keep them from winning the election of 1800. The law was undoubtedly an assault on freedom of speech, and the Republicans probably benefited from its unpopularity.[212]

In 1812 several Republicans, most notably Supreme Court Justice Joseph Story and Attorney General William Pinkney, suggested that the Republican government adopt a sedition act to control criticism of the War of 1812, but President Madison demurred.[213] That year, however, Republican mobs took matters into their own hands, destroying Federalist presses in Savannah, Georgia; Norristown, Pennsylvania; and Baltimore, Maryland. The rioting in Baltimore persisted for six weeks and was particularly vicious. The worst night of violence, in July of 1812, left one Federalist, Brigadier General James M. Lingan, dead and two others, Major General Harry Lee (the father of Civil War general Robert E. Lee) and Alexander Contee Hanson (co-publisher and co-editor of the Baltimore *Federal Republican),* with internal injuries from which they never recovered. Federalist editors elsewhere in the middle and southern states received anonymous warnings that summer to tone down their own opposition to the war or risk a similar fate. There was enough violence and threats of violence to suggest a pattern.

Were Republican leaders in any way responsible for this violence? Yes, they were, mainly because during the winter and spring of 1812 they had repeatedly warned that if the nation went to war they would brook no opposition. As Tennessee War Hawk Felix Grundy put it in the House of Representatives in May of 1812, once war is declared, the only question would be "are you for your country or against it."[214] In time of war, echoed the Baltimore *American,* "there are but two parties, *Citizen Soldiers* and *Enemies—Americans* and *Tories.*"[215] "He that is not for us," declared the Washington *National Intelligencer,* the nation's leading Republican newspaper, "must be considered as against us and treated accordingly."[216]

In private, Republican talk of violence was more explicit. John G. Jackson, a former congressman and the president's son-in-law, told Madison that if Federalists opposed the war, *"Tar & Feathers* will cure their penchant for our enemy."[217] Former president Thomas Jefferson expressed similar views. In a letter written to President Madison shortly after the declaration of war, the Apostle of Freedom said: "The Federalists . . . are poor devils here, not worthy of notice. A barrel of tar to each state south of the Patomac will keep all in order, & that will be freely contributed without troubling government. To the North, they will give you more trouble. You may there have to apply the rougher drastics . . . hemp [for hanging] and confiscation [of property]."[218]

If Republican leaders encouraged violence with their comments, they were also reluctant to denounce the lawlessness or to take effective action to suppress it. In Baltimore, rioters had little to fear from those responsible for keeping the peace. Afraid of retaliation in the streets or at the polls, city officials confronting mobs usually chose persuasion and appeasement over coercion. State officials refused to intervene, and federal officials kept their distance, too. When the postmaster in Baltimore sent an express to Washington warning that a mob was threatening the post office, President Madison refused to take any action. While conceding that the Baltimore post office was "under the sanction of the U.S.," Madison doubted that "any defensive measures were within the Executive sphere."[219]

The violence in 1812 undoubtedly had a chilling effect on freedom of speech, not only in Baltimore but elsewhere in the South as well. Like the Sedition Act of 1798, however, it boomeranged on the party in power and contributed to Federalist election gains in the fall of 1812. Most scholars have refused to confront the issue of Republican violence, and as a result the story never gets into textbooks. The message that textbooks ought to drive home is that if Federalist behavior in 1798 was reprehensible, Republican behavior in 1812 was even worse. After all, it is surely better to fine and imprison dissidents than leave them to the mercies of a bloodthirsty mob.[220]

## UNSUNG HEROES

**Forgotten Soldiers and Civilians.** Any war is likely to have a lot of unsung heroes. Before the twentieth century, soldiers and civilians alike from the lower ranks were often forgotten, however heroic their contribution might have been. Few left any written record, and when these heroes and those who knew them passed from the scene, their deeds died with them. We are much more likely to have a record of the deeds of those from the upper ranks in society, such as military officers and civilian officials. But while officers had a formal mechanism for recording their deeds on the battlefield—after-action reports—civilians usually did not. Historians have to tease the records a little more to uncover these unsung heroes. Even when good records are available, scholars may disagree on who qualifies as a hero. The four unsung heroes treated below—two soldiers and two civilians, two Americans and two Canadians—must be taken as merely a representative sample of a much larger number that the War of 1812 produced.

**Lieutenant John M. Gamble.** One of the unsung American military heroes was John M. Gamble, a lieutenant in the U.S. Marine Corps who had a remarkable adventure in the Pacific. Gamble was born into a fighting family in 1790. His father had served as a major in the Continental Army during the American Revolution, and his three brothers would later perish in the naval service. He was only 17 when he received his commission as a marine officer.

Gamble commanded a detachment of 31 marines that sailed into the Pacific on board the U.S. Frigate *Essex* (46) in 1813. The *Essex* took so many prizes that Captain David Porter ran short of personnel to man them. To command his sixth prize, the British whaler *Greenwich*, which was refitted as a 14-gun warship, he chose Lieutenant Gamble. In his journal, Porter wrote: "I had much confidence in the discretion of this gentleman; and, to make up for his want of nautical knowledge, I put two expert seamen with him as mates, one of whom was a good navigator."[221] This is probably the only time in American history that a U.S. Marine has commanded a warship. Cruising in the Pacific, Gamble deftly maneuvered his ship to take the 14-gun British ship *Seringapatam*. He now commanded two ships, and later Porter put him in charge of a third.

In the fall of 1813 Porter sailed his growing squadron of ships to the Marquesas (now part of French Polynesia), where he built a fort and took part in

Lieutenant John M. Gamble (1790–1836), U.S. marine, had a remarkable adventure in the Pacific. Besides commanding a small squadron of ships, he fought in local wars, suffered through a mutiny, sustained a painful ankle wound, traveled 2,000 miles on open waters without adequate navigational equipment, and finally became a prisoner of war. (Portrait by unknown artist. Courtesy of Captain Sherwood Picking, USN, and Naval Historical Center)

a local war. Although he won the war, many of his men became involved with local women and as a result became increasingly mutinous. Porter sailed away in December, leaving Gamble behind with 21 men, some British prisoners of war, and three prizes, the *Greenwich, Seringapatam,* and *Sir Andrew Hammond.* Shortly thereafter, Gamble fought a successful engagement against the natives and then cruised the islands in search of provisions. After returning to his base, however, some of his men mutinied, freed the British prisoners, and seized control of the *Seringapatam.* Gamble was tied up, and later he accidentally received a nasty pistol wound in one of his ankles.

With its new crew, the *Seringapatam* put to sea with Gamble and several men who had remained loyal to him locked below. The prisoners were subsequently put in a boat, which they managed to row back to shore. There they again had to contend with hostile natives. In the ensuing engagement Gamble scared off the natives by manning the guns on the *Sir Andrew Hammond* by himself.

After burning the *Greenwich,* Gamble and his tiny and sickly crew of seven set sail for Hawaii, then known as the Sandwich Islands. Despite lacking a compass, spyglass, charts, and maps, they managed to reach their destination, some 2,000 miles away, on May 31, 1814, after 15 days at sea. Putting to sea again, Gamble's ship was captured by H.M. Sloop *Cherub* (26), one of the British ships that had earlier defeated the *Essex* (46). Gamble now learned for the first time that the *Essex* had been lost.

Gamble was taken to Valparaiso and then around the Horn to Rio de Janeiro, where he remained a prisoner until news arrived that the war was over. He returned to the United States on August 27, 1815, almost three years after his departure.[222]

Gamble remained in the marines in the postwar era. He had been promoted to captain while in the Pacific, and eventually he attained the rank of lieutenant colonel. But his wartime service had broken his health, and he now walked with a limp. He retired from the service in 1834 and died two years later at the age of 46. Few people could claim such a remarkable experience during the War of 1812. "No Marine officer in the service," Captain Porter later said, "ever had such strong claims as Captain Gamble. . . . None have been placed in such conspicuous and critical situations, and . . . none could have extricated themselves from them more to their honor."[223]

**Lieutenant Miller Worsley.** If John Gamble was an unsung military hero on the American side, Miller Worsley holds that distinction on the British side. Born on the Isle of Wight in 1791, he went to sea as a volunteer in the Royal Navy when he was only 11 years old. Two years later he became a midshipman, and in 1813 he was promoted to lieutenant. By then he was a seasoned veteran, having taken part in the Battle of Trafalgar. Shipped to America in 1813, he served as first lieutenant on H.M. Ship *Princess Charlotte* (42) on Lake Ontario and participated in the assault on Oswego in May 1814.

Later that year Worsley was appointed to the naval command on Lake Huron. Although the British still retained Mackinac in 1814, their position on the lake was precarious. Master Commandant Oliver H. Perry's victory on Lake Erie in 1813 had given the U.S. naval superiority on the western lakes, and Perry's successor, Captain Arthur Sinclair, was determined to retake Mackinac and destroy the British post on the Nottawasaga River on Georgian Bay. Although the British beat back an assault on Mackinac on August 4, 1814, their only warship on the lake was a supply ship, H.M. Schooner *Nancy* (3). In the hope of preserving this ship from the powerful squadron that Sinclair had brought into Lake Huron, Worsley moved the *Nancy* as far up the Nottawasaga as possible.

On August 13, 1814, Sinclair arrived at the Nottawasaga. The following day his men spotted the *Nancy,* which was close to the lake because the river ran parallel to the shore. Sinclair started bombarding the ship and a nearby block-

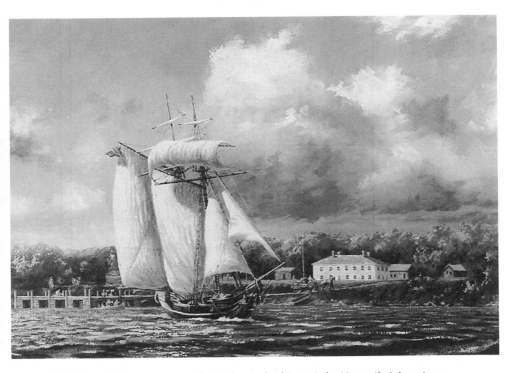

H.M. Schooner *Nancy* was a small British supply ship on Lake Huron that Americans destroyed in 1814 when they attacked the Nottawasaga River. (Painting by Peter Rindlisbacher. Courtesy of the artist)

house. Worsley resisted for seven hours, but, outgunned and outmanned, he was planning to blow up the *Nancy* when an American shell blew up the blockhouse and set fire to the ship. Worsley and his walking wounded fled into the wilderness. Confident that he now fully controlled Lake Huron, Sinclair left only two schooners, the *Tigress* (1) and *Scorpion* (2), to cruise its waters.

Worsley, however, was not yet done. Returning to the Nottawasaga River, he led two bateaux and a canoe back into Lake Huron and then made a heroic 380-mile, six-day voyage in those open vessels to the vicinity of St. Joseph Island. Warned by Indians that the *Tigress* and *Scorpion* were nearby, Worsley hid his boats on an island and made his way to Mackinac by canoe. Hatching a plan to seize the American vessels, Worsley received support from Lieutenant Colonel Robert McDouall, who was in command at Fort Mackinac.

Worsley's expanded force consisted of his own small Royal Navy detachment, a detachment from the Royal Newfoundland Regiment commanded by Lieutenant Andrew H. Bulger, a band of natives headed by Indian Agent

Robert Dickson, and four bateaux armed with two guns from the fort. Although Worsley had overall command, it was a joint operation, and Bulger was given command of one of two armed bateaux.

Leaving his Indians behind, Worsley on the night of September 3, 1814, quietly sailed his flotilla toward the *Tigress*, which was now separated from its sister ship. After a brief but fierce engagement, the British boarded and seized control of the American ship. Worsley sent his prisoners to Mackinac and then, still flying the American flag, waited to make contact with the *Scorpion*. Catching the second American ship by surprise on the morning of September 6, Worsley boarded and seized that vessel as well.

In less than 72 hours, Worsley had completely changed the balance of power on Lake Huron. Although the British hold on the lake remained tenuous, their position was materially improved, for they could now resupply Fort Mackinac, provide food and trade goods to their Indian allies, and protect Canadian fur traders.[224]

"The whole affair," commented Theodore Roosevelt, "reflected great credit on the enterprise and pluck of the British without being discreditable to the Americans."[225] Roosevelt's assessment did justice to Worsley but was probably too generous to Lieutenant Daniel Turner, who was in charge of the American warships and had been warned by Sinclair to beware of a waterborne attack from Fort Mackinac.

Worsley was commended for his daring and was promoted to commander, although not until July 1815. Lieutenant General Gordon Drummond thought the promotion should have come sooner. Not long after the war, Worsley returned to his home on the Isle of Wight and was never again offered a naval command. Dogged by financial problems, he died in 1835.[226]

**The Reverend John Strachan.** Canada's great unsung civilian hero of the War of 1812 is a man who is unknown in Great Britain and the United States and unappreciated in Canada. This is the Rev. John Strachan (1778–1867), the rector of York, whose courage, determination, and civic-mindedness during the War of 1812 not only contributed materially to the war effort but also helped shape the future of Canada.

Born in Scotland, Strachan (pronounced "Strawn") graduated from King's College in Aberdeen in 1797. Two years later he emigrated to Kingston, Upper Canada. There he earned a living as a teacher and was ordained in the Church

of England. Initially he took a pragmatic view of his faith, emphasizing mo-
rality and good works. "Religion is only valuable," he commented in 1805, "as
it makes us better men."[227] In later years, however, he embraced High Angli-
canism with its emphasis on a more transcendent and sacramental faith.

In 1803 Strachan became rector of Cornwall, a position he held until 1812.
Very quickly he developed a reputation for being a first-class teacher and parish priest, and in the ensuing years he educated and ministered to the spiri-
tual needs of many of Upper Canada's future leaders. An appreciation was
penned by former student John Beverley Robinson, the future chief justice
of Upper Canada, when he was appointed attorney general of the province
in 1818. "To you I am indebted," he wrote Strachan, "for whatever success has
attended, or may attend, me throughout life."[228]

Strachan was hard-working and ambitious, sometimes aloof, invariably
passionate about his causes, and always generous to those in need. He married the widow Ann Wood McGill in 1807, and thereafter her ample means,
combined with his own modest income, enabled him to live well and to provide money for those people and causes that he deemed worthy of support.
An accomplished and compulsive writer, Strachan maintained an extensive
correspondence, not only with his former students but also with other prominent figures in Canada and Great Britain. To promote the many causes that
he championed, he published numerous articles, pamphlets, and books. This
body of work established him as Upper Canada's most prolific intellectual in
the first half of the nineteenth century.

In 1812 Strachan was lured to York to become rector there when Major
General Isaac Brock offered to supplement his income by making him chap-
lain to the York garrison as well as to the provincial legislative council. By
this time, Strachan had become a staunch Canadian patriot and an outspo-
ken enemy of the United States and its form of egalitarian democracy. "In
point of real happiness," he said in 1809, "the British are far superior to the
inhabitants of this celebrated republic. . . . The frequency of their elections
keeps them in a continual broil."[229] A visit to a New York City court en route
to Canada in 1799 had convinced him that "the science of cheating seems to
be very well understood in the States," and in 1807 he commented that the
American people were "*vain & rapacious* and without *honor.*"[230] Fearful that
American culture might infect Canada, he complained that "the spirit of lev-
elling seemed to pervade the province."[231]

Strachan gave a hint of the kind of man he was when he was aboard a merchant vessel sailing from Kingston to York on Lake Ontario at the beginning of the War of 1812. Just west of Kingston, what appeared to be a hostile American ship came up from the rear. The captain of Strachan's schooner planned to surrender. Although seasick, Strachan seized the vessel, forced the captain below, and prepared to fight. Fortunately, the approaching ship proved to be British.

Like so many later Canadians, Strachan was convinced that the United States went to war, not to force Britain to modify its maritime practices, but rather to annex Canada. "The conquest of the Canadas particularly Upper Canada," he said in 1813, "is . . . the true cause of the war in order to dissolve our connection with the Indians." The maritime issues, he insisted, were "mere popular baits."[232]

During the war years, Strachan used pen and pulpit to promote the defense of Canada. Although he had purchased two military books from Brock's estate, he had the impatience of the amateur and showed little understanding of the manpower and logistical problems that the British faced in the war. He favored an aggressive strategy in Upper Canada, and he was critical of those British commanders, particularly Sir George Prevost and Sir James Yeo, that he considered too defense-minded.

The Reverend John Strachan (1778–1867), shown here in an 1847 portrait in all his High Anglican glory, performed a host of valuable services during the War of 1812. He protected civilians during the American occupation of York in 1813, ministered to sick and wounded soldiers sent to York, and established the Loyal and Patriotic Society of Upper Canada to assist those who were harmed by the war. (Mezzotint after G.T. Berthon. Toronto Reference Library)

Early in the war, Strachan wrote a letter to influential Montreal merchant John Richardson in which he enumerated 15 reasons for an offensive strategy. "Forbearance will never answer with our present enemy," he commented; "it is founded upon a most fallacious idea of the American character."[233] A month later he made the same point to the Duke of Wellington. Americans, he said, "must suffer all the rigours of war and we must procure that peace from their fear."[234] Still later he told Lieutenant Governor Francis Gore: "All our losses & disasters have arisen from forbearance—whenever we attack we succeed—when we act upon the defensive we are beaten."[235]

Strachan sought to alleviate hardships caused by the war. He regularly visited the many sick and wounded who were sent to York. By the end of the war, this was "upwards of four hundred men, many of them sadly mangled."[236] He also had to bury the dead and console their families. Strachan lent a helping hand to many who were harmed or displaced by the conflict. He also founded and served as president of the Loyal and Patriotic Society of Upper Canada. This organization ultimately raised over £21,000 (approximately $100,000) in the New World and Old to aid militiamen and their families as well as other people in need. Strachan also used the war as a vehicle to boost Canada's sense of identity and patriotism. In fact, in a sermon delivered early in the contest, he developed the myth that the militia had saved Canada during the American Revolution and would do so again during the War of 1812.[237]

Strachan's most courageous service came when the United States captured York in April 1813. The British army had withdrawn, and under dangerous and trying circumstances, Strachan boldly stepped forward to negotiate terms of surrender for the town. In the ensuing days, when violence and looting erupted and civilian officials kept out of sight, Strachan pressed American military authorities, particularly the hapless Major General Henry Dearborn, to adhere to the agreement and put an end to the lawlessness. He personally saved at least one parishioner from a gang of marauding Americans. He also looked after the British wounded in York, a stupendous task given American hostility and little cooperation from his own countrymen. Strachan took charge again when York was occupied a second time later that year. Friend and foe alike long remembered the courage he demonstrated during the American occupation.[238]

Strachan's wartime experience was marred by a dark personal tragedy. Shortly after the first American occupation of York, he had moved his pregnant wife and two children to Cornwall to keep them out of harm's way. Unfortunately, two American brigades passed through the town in November of 1813, and it appears that some American soldiers robbed and sexually assaulted the helpless woman. The experience left her so distraught that friends thought she might not survive. Although she regained her health and lived a long life, she probably never fully recovered emotionally from this brutal experience.

In the years after the war, Strachan had a long and illustrious career as a clergyman and Tory activist in Upper Canada, and he gradually emerged as one of the most influential public figures in the province. He was a member of both the executive and legislative councils, and in 1839 he was consecrated as the first Anglican bishop of Toronto. Throughout this period he fought to uphold the prerogatives of the Church of England. When the Church was deprived of its land reserves in 1854, it lost its semi-official status and any hope of becoming the established church of Canada. Thereafter, Strachan raised the necessary money and created the framework to transform the Church into an independent self-governing denomination. Strachan also fought an unsuccessful rearguard action to block the growing movement for political reform and the union of Upper and Lower Canada. Against his better judgment, the two provinces were combined into the United Province of Canada in 1841.

Education was always dear to Strachan's heart, and he worked tirelessly to promote it in Upper Canada. He was instrumental in establishing the province's public school system, which was based on the Scottish model, and he secured government financial support for the schools long before it became available in Britain. His system of public education survived in Ontario until the 1960s. He had a hand in the founding of McGill University in Montreal and three institutions of higher learning in Toronto: the Diocesan Theological Institution (which has since disappeared) and King's College and Trinity College (both of which are now part of the University of Toronto). Strachan also served as president of King's College.

Strachan, who was born early enough to have seen the end of the American Revolution in 1783, lived long enough to witness the dawn of a new era when (with his blessing) the British North America Act created a united and independent Canada in 1867. As one of the guiding spirits and pillars of what radical William Lyon Mackenzie called the "Family Compact," Strachan was Canada's arch-Tory and leading defender of the old order in the nineteenth century. Generations of Canadian scholars have portrayed him as an opponent of progress and modernization, as a foil for Mackenzie and others who favored fundamental reforms designed to hurry Canada into a new era.

This characterization of Strachan is unfair, not only because it slights the many ways in which he contributed to the emergence of modern Canada, but also because it ignores his heroic and patriotic service during the War of 1812. For his contributions during that war, John Strachan should be remembered as one of the great figures in Canadian history. No less than Sir George Prevost, Major General Isaac Brock, Tecumseh, and John Norton, he helped preserve Canada in what was arguably the most critical period in its history. His longtime foe, Methodist clergyman Egerton Ryerson, freely conceded that during the War of 1812 Strachan "acted the part of a true, a bold and generous patriot."[239] Moreover, unlike the other heroes of the conflict, Strachan continued to contribute to Canada's development for more than a half century after the war was over. "By force of character, dogged perseverance, strength of will, and singleness of purpose," the Toronto *Globe* said upon his death, Strachan "made himself no mean place in the history of Canada."[240]

**Judge Augustus B. Woodward.** America's unsung civilian hero in the War of 1812 was a territorial judge in Michigan who is all but forgotten today. Judge Augustus B. Woodward (1774–1827) performed many of the same functions in occupied Detroit that John Strachan performed in occupied York. Showing both courage and determination, Woodward served as a buffer between the British and the civilian population of Detroit, and more importantly, worked to save those American soldiers who had been taken prisoner by the Indians in the Old Northwest in 1812–13.

Born in New York City, Woodward graduated from Columbia College in 1793. Two years later, while living in Virginia, he became the friend and protégé of Thomas Jefferson. In 1797 he launched a law practice in Washington, D.C., where he helped incorporate the city and then served on its first council. In 1805, when the Michigan Territory was organized, Woodward's life took a new turn when President Jefferson appointed him one of the three federal judges in the new territory, a position he held for almost 20 years.

When Woodward arrived in Detroit in mid-1805, his impact was immediate. The entire city had just burned down, and he played a material role in its reconstruction. His plan for a new city, modeled after Washington, D.C., called for broad, tree-lined streets with numerous small parks. Although much modified in later years, this plan was adopted, and one of the principal streets in Detroit still bears Woodward's name. Woodward dominated the territorial judiciary and compiled its law code, officially entitled *The Laws of Michigan* (1806) but commonly called "The Woodward Code." Woodward also played a central role in the territorial legislature, which consisted of the governor and the three judges. Woodward was fluent in French, which added to his influence because this was the only language spoken by many people in the territory.

Woodward, who never married, was willful, determined, eccentric, and sometimes arbitrary. He was also quick to make enemies, and on at least one occasion he was nearly impeached.[241] After a brief honeymoon, he broke with the territory's first governor, William Hull, and thereafter the two officials constantly feuded.[242] But Woodward also gave tone to the intellectual life of early Michigan. Even Hull called him "a scientific man" who "may suggest many brilliant things, which after being pruned, and qualified, may be useful."[243] Despite his eccentricities, Woodward was particularly useful in a crisis. A later Michigan supreme court judge characterized him as "one of those strange compounds of intellectual power and wisdom in great emergencies, with very frequent caprice and wrongheadedness, that defy description."[244]

Before moving to Michigan, Woodward had written treatises on the sun and on the government of the District of Columbia. The structure of government was a subject that always interested him. In 1809 he published *Considerations on the Executive Government of the United States,* a book calling for a plural executive modeled after the French Directory of 1795, and in 1811 he published a series of articles in the Philadelphia *Aurora* calling for the creation of a cabinet department on domestic affairs.

Michigan was under enemy rule for an extended period during the War of 1812—from the fall of Detroit in August 1812 to the British evacuation after Perry's victory on Lake Erie in September 1813. Woodward was the only major federal official to remain in Michigan after Detroit surrendered. Although he did not exercise any judicial functions nor accept a British offer to serve as secretary (and thus their official liaison), he did what he could to serve the population. "Amidst a scene of general disaster, devastation and ruin," Woodward said, he sought "to sustain . . . the claims of my country, and the rights of my fellow-citizens; and to promote, as much as was practicable, in such arduous circumstances, a spirit of humanity, charity, and mercy."[245]

Woodward tried to assist the sick and wounded, and he saved a number of lives by using his own money, as well as money he raised from others, to ransom American soldiers that Great Britain's Indian allies brought to Detroit. He also facilitated the notification of the relatives of those Kentuckians who were held as prisoners by the British. He intervened with the British military governor, Colonel Henry Procter, to prevent the deportation of a number of residents from Detroit. He also interceded to save the life of Whitmore Knaggs, an American Indian interpreter who had earlier assaulted him but was now threatened with execution for having appeared in arms after the British paroled him.[246]

Woodward worked well with Procter, but the relationship soured abruptly in early 1813 when the American judge collected depositions proving that Britain's Indian allies had killed and scalped a number of American prisoners after the Battle of Frenchtown in the River Raisin Massacre. Since Procter had left the prisoners without an adequate British guard, it was hard to avoid the conclusion that he was responsible. Furious with this insinuation, Procter thereafter was barely willing to talk to Woodward. His effectiveness gone, Woodward decided to leave the territory.

Although many of the residents of Detroit asked Woodward to stay and continue his good works, he departed for American-controlled territory in February of 1813.[247] Passing east through Canada, he traveled to Albany and then Washington, where his knowledge of the River Raisin Massacre and the Old Northwest made him a minor celebrity. The depositions he had collected were included in a major congressional report on Britain's wartime violations of international law.[248]

The U.S. resumed control of Michigan when the British withdrew in the fall of 1813, and territorial government was re-established the following year. Woodward returned to Michigan at the end of 1814, and shortly thereafter peace was restored. The war and the British occupation, however, had left the territory devastated. Food and clothing were in short supply, numerous houses had been stripped of their glass and floorboards, and many fences had been destroyed or burned for fuel. Those people living along the River Raisin were so destitute that they were reduced to eating boiled hay. "The desolation of this Territory," Woodward concluded, "is beyond all conception."[249]

Once again, as he had after the fire of 1805, Woodward devoted his energies to reconstruction. Especially important was the way he used his influence in Washington to secure assistance for the hungry and now poverty-stricken people. The War Department responded by distributing $1,500 in flour to the people on the River Raisin.

With the war now over, Woodward resumed his feuds and other interests. In 1816 he produced a book entitled *A System of Universal Science* that sought to classify all knowledge; the following year he played an instrumental role in founding the University of Michigan; and the year after that he helped establish the Detroit Lyceum. Although President James Monroe did not renew Woodward's appointment in 1824 because of rumors that the judge was a drunkard, when he learned that these rumors were false, Monroe appointed Woodward to a territorial judgeship in Florida, where he spent his last years.

Woodward was one of those outsized figures who left a big footprint on the developing American West. During the War of 1812, he took the initiative to ameliorate conditions and to help those who suffered most, and even his enemies recognized his contributions. Although he was neither as altruistic nor as influential as Canadian John Strachan, he nonetheless deserves to be better remembered for the central part he played in early Michigan as well as for his contributions during the War of 1812.[250]

## BIRTH OF A SYMBOL

**Where Did "Uncle Sam" Come From?** Like most nations, America has often been depicted by symbols. In the eighteenth century, it was the brash and young Yankee Doodle (who originated during the French and Indian War) and then the older and shrewder Brother Jonathan and the more stately Columbia (both of whom surfaced during the American Revolution). The War of 1812 produced another great icon that ultimately superseded all the others and became the universally recognized symbol for the United States and its government. This was Uncle Sam.

Conventional wisdom holds that Uncle Sam originated in Troy, New York. Located on the east bank of the Hudson River seven miles north of Albany, Troy was an important market town. During the War of 1812, it became an entrepôt for food and munitions for the U.S. Army. Troy supplied the huge army camp 15 miles to the south at Greenbush, New York. It was also near the confluence of the Hudson and Mohawk rivers, which put Troy on the supply route for American forces operating on Lake Ontario and Lake Erie as well as in northern New York.

Uncle Sam was first mentioned in a broadside entitled "HIEROGLYPHICS of John Bull's Overthrow: or A View of the Northern Expedition in Miniature." Apparently produced somewhere in eastern New York in the early spring of 1813, the broadside contains two references to Uncle Sam in doggerel that appears under a series of images. The first reference is in a couplet under Napoleon:

> If uncle Sam needs, I'd be glad to assist him,
> For it makes my heart bleed we live at such a distance.

The other reference, which appears under Commodore John Rodgers's image, predicts that John Bull and his Indian allies will suffer the same fate as Major General John Burgoyne in 1777:

> He builds on the Indians that now with him join'd,
> But if Uncle Sam lives, they will all be Burgoyn'd.[251]

Six months later, on September 7, 1813, the Troy *Post* carried a piece supplied by an antiwar Federalist that spoke of the "ill-luck" of the war that "lights upon UNCLE SAM'S shoulders." The contributor then explained: "This cant name for our government has got almost as current as 'John Bull' (for the British). The letters U.S. on the government waggons, etc. are supposed to have given rise to it."[252]

How did the phrase actually originate? In 1830 the New York *Gazette* published an article that offered an explanation. It was contributed by an anonymous reader who was probably moved to write by the recent death of Elbert Anderson, a government contractor during the War of 1812. The article linked Uncle Sam to a Troy beef packer named Samuel Wilson. A genial and warm-hearted person, Wilson was known locally as "Uncle Sam," apparently because he employed so many of his kinsmen. During the War of 1812, Wilson supplied salted beef to Anderson. It was shipped in boxes marked "E.A." (for Elbert Anderson) and "U.S." (for United States).

When one of Wilson's employees asked what the initials "U.S." on the beef boxes stood for, another reportedly replied, apparently in jest, "Uncle Sam," meaning Samuel Wilson. The story made the rounds among Wilson's workers, many of whom later enlisted in the U.S. Army, and before the campaign of 1812 was over, people were referring to the government itself as "Uncle Sam."[253]

This story has been widely credited, and even the U.S. Congress has endorsed it. In a joint resolution adopted on September 15, 1961, Congress saluted "'Uncle Sam' Wilson, of Troy, New York, as the progenitor of America's national symbol of 'Uncle Sam.'"[254]

Is the story true? It is certainly credible. It was contributed by someone who claimed that he heard the original exchange, and when he later saw the nickname in print, he commented that it would be strange indeed if "Uncle Sam" became "a national cognomen." Moreover, Wilson had been supplying meat to the army since at least 1811, so there was plenty of time during the war for the story to develop.

There are, however, certain problems with the story. First, there was no mention of Wilson in the original Troy *Post* article discussing the origins of the term even though the editor of this small-town paper surely knew Wilson and might well have added a note of explanation if he thought Wilson was part of the story. But the editor remained silent, and Wilson was not linked to the story until the publication of the New York *Gazette* article 17 years later.

Moreover, how likely is it that Wilson's employee was unfamiliar with the abbreviation "U.S."? The most common abbreviation for the nation then was probably "U. States" or "UStates," but "US" and even "USA" were sometimes used. Commanding naval officers usually labeled their warships "U.S." or "US," as in "U.S. Frigate *Constitution*" or "US Sloop *Hornet*," and occasionally they referred to navy yards in a similar fashion.[255] The U.S. Frigate *Chesapeake* even carried two stars on its quarters, one marked with a "U" and the other with an "S."[256]

Between 1795 and 1815, the U.S. government acquired some 200,000 Model 1795 muskets and well as several thousand Model 1803 rifles and short-barrelled ship's muskets, and most of these weapons were stamped with the letters "US." It also bought several thousand cutlasses for the navy between 1797 and 1812 that bore this stamp.[257] Other government property was probably marked similarly, and as public purchases soared in 1812, doubtless the amount of property carrying this designation also increased.

American soldiers would have had ample opportunity to become familiar with the abbreviation during the war. It is possible, perhaps even likely, that a soldier in late 1812, speaking to other soldiers, converted the abbreviation into

"Uncle Sam," a symbol representing the U.S. government or nation, originated during the War of 1812. Over time Uncle Sam evolved into the gaunt, bewhiskered, aging man wearing patriotic clothing depicted in this well-known recruiting poster. (Poster art by James Montgomery Flagg. Library of Congress)

"Uncle Sam" and that the use of this avuncular nickname caught on, and, like so much military jargon through the ages, quickly spread through the army. This would be consistent with the contemporary impression that the term was most commonly used in the army.

If "Uncle Sam" was the invention of some anonymous soldier, what then was Sam Wilson's role in the story? It is entirely possible that the term was already in use when it was turned into a local joke at Wilson's meat packing warehouse. If this is the case, then Sam Wilson was not the inspiration for the term, but rather someone whose association with it in an important army supply town helped spread the use of the phrase among soldiers and civilians alike.

After its first appearance, Uncle Sam showed up in a number of other newspapers during the war. The term was often used derisively in the Federalist press. It was also closely linked to the army. In early 1814, the New York *Herald* described a group of half-starved and neglected war wounded as "'*Uncle Sam's*' hard bargains." Later that year a correspondent writing to the Boston *Gazette* referred to army musicians as "a band of *Uncle Sam's* Music."[258] Although most people in the North were now familiar with the term, shortly after the war Hezekiah Niles felt the need to define "Uncle Sam" for his broader audience as "a cant term in the army for the United States."[259]

After the war, the term lost its negative connotation and came into wider use, eventually replacing Yankee Doodle and Brother Jonathan in the public prints. Uncle Sam was first depicted in a cartoon in 1832, but it was not until the 1870s that *Harper's Weekly* cartoonist Thomas Nast crystalized the modern image: a gaunt and bewhiskered aging man decked out in striped pants and a top hat. James Montgomery Flagg gave this image still wider currency in 1917 with his "I Want You" recruiting poster, which was used in both world wars and may be the best known poster ever produced in the United States. Between them, Nast and Flagg established Uncle Sam as a figure who is recognized around the world.[260]

## CHAPTER 5

# The Mechanics of Waging War

The War of 1812 differed from the Napoleonic Wars in Europe. For one thing, the armies were much smaller. The opposing forces in the principal battles were typically 2,000–5,000 strong, and the largest army, which Sir George Prevost marched into upper New York in 1814, was only 10,000 strong. The armies of the Napoleonic Wars, by contrast, ranged from 50,000 to 100,000 between 1803 and 1807 and from 100,000 to 200,000 thereafter. The largest army, which Napoleon marched into Russia in 1812, was 500,000 to 600,000 strong. By European standards, the armies operating in America were tiny and the battles they fought small affairs indeed.

Although the weapons used on both sides of the Atlantic were generally the same, the mix on the battlefield was often different. Field artillery played less of a role in the American war because it was difficult to move these heavy pieces through the wilderness. Six-pounders played a role in some of the battles, but larger field pieces were uncommon. Rifles, on the other hand, played a somewhat greater role because they were widely held in the West, and volunteer militia sometimes brought these weapons into the field. Their role, however, has often been overrated.

Battles sometimes unfolded differently in America. British and American tactical doctrine was similar, and the War of 1812 lacked the widespread irregular warfare that was so common in the American Revolution. Nevertheless, many battles in the War of 1812 did not follow doctrine. Skirmishing and ambushes were more common, both sides used Indian auxiliaries (who fought by their own rules), and volunteer militia on both sides were more likely to make use of the cover offered by the forest and to take careful aim with their shoulder arms.

The terrain in America was also far different from that of Europe. North America was not densely populated, which made it more difficult for armies to live off the land. Even the eastern part of the continent was still one vast wilderness that was heavily wooded and without good roads. Transportation and communication were primitive, and logistical problems often had a significant impact on campaigns.

All this is not to suggest that soldiers moving between Europe and America in the early nineteenth century would find themselves in a completely unfamiliar environment. Depending on where they served, they might find similarities. In Spain, guerilla warfare was widespread, and in some parts of Germany rifles were in common use. Dense forests still survived in some parts of Europe, and logistical problems could be as daunting there as in North America. Even some local auxiliaries in Europe might resemble Indian allies more than professional soldiers. Similarly, in America conventional battles might take place in open fields without Indian allies and with the musket and artillery determining the outcome. In addition, waging war in this era made the same demands on soldiers everywhere. There was no escaping the pain and death, the marching and hauling, the hunger and thirst, the excitement and danger, and the interruption of sleep and exposure to the elements. Despite these similarities, however, warfare in the New World could be strikingly different from warfare in the Old.

A great deal has been written about the battles and leaders of the War of 1812. There has been far less on what might be termed the mechanics of waging war, that is, tactics, weapons, logistics, intelligence, and the like. As a result, this dimension of the war is less encrusted with mythology, but it also deserves a fuller and more systematic treatment than it gets in the standard histories.

## MILITARY TACTICS

**Tactics and Conventional Warfare.** If strategy deals with the big picture, tactics focus on the little picture: how to deploy assets on the battlefield to achieve victory. Tactically, the War of 1812 was preeminently conventional in character. While there were a few ambushes, some irregular warfare, and the use of Indian auxiliaries (mostly in the West), both sides nonetheless strove to wage conventional campaigns whenever they could.

Great Britain was accustomed to relying on trained regulars and conventional tactics to achieve its military objectives. If the United States was to conquer Canada, it had to find some way to match the British in training, discipline, and tactics; it needed to devise an effective command and control system; and it had to develop an efficient system of logistics that would enable it to wage war on distant frontiers. In this respect, the War of 1812 was very different from the American Revolution. Although the Continental Congress had launched a campaign against Canada in 1775, that campaign had ended in disaster, and thereafter the American people were content to wage a defensive war that did not require the conquest of any enemy beyond the original 13 colonies.

Unlike guerrilla warfare, conventional warfare in the eighteenth and nineteenth centuries required considerable training. The rule of thumb in Europe was that it took two years to turn a raw recruit into a disciplined and reliable soldier, although this period could be shortened considerably by a hardworking and determined drill master. In time of war, few nations could afford the luxury of adequate training. In the 1790s, French conscripts were trained as they marched to the theater of war, and other nations had to send their troops into battle with far less training than was desirable.

Soldiers needed considerable practice so that they could use their muskets most efficiently on the battlefield. This meant mastering a manual of arms, the step-by-step process for loading and firing a musket. Once this was mastered, soldiers on the battlefield could respond efficiently to the two basic commands, "load" and "fire." Soldiers also needed to learn the marching evolutions or movements so that they could maneuver with precision as part of a larger force both to prepare for battle and to change positions or fronts once a battle was joined. Finally, they needed training to develop the discipline to hold their positions in the face of heavy enemy fire in what was invariably a dangerous, chaotic, and smoke-filled environment.

Prior to most battles, opposing armies performed a series of maneuvers that brought them together. They usually lined up facing one another with one or both armies advancing to close the gap. Soldiers on each side started the battle with their muskets loaded and fired a volley on command. Most unit commanders insisted on continued volley fire, but the chaos of the battlefield usually precluded this. After several volleys, soldiers usually fired at their own pace. The armies did not normally get close enough to use the bayonet or to engage in hand-to-hand combat. Before that happened, one side usually beat an orderly retreat or broke and ran.

Once the battle had been decided, a short, informal truce might be called to regroup and bury the dead. This practice was more common in North America than in Europe. The bodies of high-ranking officers (such as Major General Edward Pakenham and Brigadier General Zebulon Pike) might be shipped home in a barrel of spirits, but most officers were buried in individual graves on the battlefield. Enlisted men, on the other hand, were buried in mass graves, typically in one or more long trenches.

Even with the most disciplined troops, a battle plan often did not survive first contact with the enemy. Hence, battles frequently unfolded in ways that defied accepted tactical doctrine or even coherent analysis. The weapons of the day emitted prodigious amounts of white smoke, and this could so obscure everyone's vision that no one, from the commander on down, might know what was actually happening. As one student of weaponry has put it, a "fire fight was, in fact, a groping half-blind affair."[1] In addition, orders could miscarry or be misunderstood, unanticipated changes in the terrain could completely stymie a tactical movement, and columns or lines could simply collapse into chaos for no apparent reason. Indeed, such was the confusion on the battlefield that what actually happened was sometimes in doubt. Hence, after-action reports and even historical accounts can present very different descriptions of how a battle unfolded or what the turning point was.

**British Tactical Doctrine.** British tactical doctrine was well fixed by 1812 although it allowed for considerable flexibility to meet different battle conditions. British troops were organized into battalions, the strength of which might vary because their size was set by Royal warrant. Like all armies, British troops usually marched to the battlefield in columns of march. The width of these columns depended on the terrain and the roads. When the troops reached the battlefield, they usually remained in columns until action was expected, at which time the men were deployed into two-deep lines, with the light infantry companies serving as skirmishers on the flanks or in advance of the main army.

British troops usually remained in a line while maneuvering on the battlefield. By regulation, the space between individual soldiers was set at two feet, although in practice three feet was more common. The British line offered considerable firepower along an extended front, but if a line was too thin, it might be broken by enemy assault. In the Battle of the Thames, Major General Henry Procter's small force was spread in two lines that were so thin—the men in each line were probably six feet apart—that Colonel Richard M. Johnson's mounted Kentucky volunteers blew right through them, dismounted, and caught the British in a cross fire.

In battle, the British emphasized fire discipline and rate of fire. Soldiers were expected to hold their fire until the enemy was well within range and then pour it on. It was also essential for advancing soldiers to hold their positions in the line and to stand tall. Only if they stopped was one line likely to be ordered to kneel in front of another. "Crouching, ducking, or laying down when advancing under fire are bad habits," said Lieutenant General Gordon Drummond in a general order issued in the summer of 1814, "and must be corrected."[2]

**American Tactical Doctrine.** The United States, by contrast, did not have a fixed tactical doctrine in 1812. Some army commanders still used Frederick von Steuben's *Blue Book* from 1778, and a few even followed the British doctrine developed by David Dundas in 1792. Most, however, embraced the tactical doctrine developed by the French in 1791. This doctrine envisioned using a column of march to get to the battlefield but left up to the commander whether to prepare for battle by deploying in two-deep lines or forming into columns of maneuver or attack (which were much wider than columns of march). In either case, skirmishers were not used.

Like the British, Americans emphasized fire discipline and rate of fire, but their ratio of hits when firing volleys was often less than that of the British army because they lacked experience and aimed too high. When firing at their own rate, however, they were more likely to take aim, although this was not easy with a heavy musket equipped with only a rear sight in the smoke-filled battlefields of the day. Some contemporaries observed that the Americans were better shots than the British. "The Americans," said the Sauk leader Black Hawk, "shoot better than the British, but their soldiers are not so well clothed, or provided for."[3]

William Henry Harrison and Andrew Jackson created effective volunteer militia fighting forces in the Old Northwest and Old Southwest in 1813, but no American commander managed to train an effective regular force until Brigadier General Winfield Scott put his mind to the task at Buffalo in the spring of 1814. Using a manual developed by Alexander Smyth based on 1791 French doctrine, Scott trained his entire brigade to the same standard. In the ensuing summer, Scott's force met the British in two set-piece battles at Chippawa and Lundy's Lane. Although the British won the campaign by blunting the American offensive, American troops for the first time showed that they could meet the British on equal terms on an open field.

Other battles (such as the Thames and New Orleans) might be more celebrated by the American people, but it was at Chippawa and Lundy's Lane that the U.S. Army achieved its tactical goals in the war, and these battles became the gold standard by which the army measured other battles. In recognition of his achievement, Scott was appointed chair of a board of officers charged with setting American tactical doctrine. Upon Scott's recommendation, the board promptly adopted the 1791 French doctrine in its entirety for the U.S. infantry manual. In the years that followed, Scott contented himself with merely translating the latest French manuals (but affixing his own name to them), and, although weak on light infantry, these became the standard texts for the U.S. Army until the Civil War.[4]

## THE WEAPONS OF WAR

**Artillery.** Smooth-bore muzzle-loading artillery played an increasingly important role in the wars of the eighteenth and nineteenth centuries. Artillery could be found in the field (field guns), in forts (garrison guns), and on warships (naval guns). Most American guns were made out of iron because the nation was blessed with an abundance of high-grade iron ore suitable for casting. British field guns, on the other hand, were cast in bronze although they were usually called "brass" guns. Brass guns were easier to cast, lighter and more mobile, and less likely to blow up than iron guns, but they cost a lot more, heated up more quickly, and wore out sooner.

British 9-pounder iron field gun on display at Fort George. (Photograph by Robert Malcomson)

There were three basic kinds of artillery: (1) guns or cannons, which had long barrels and usually fired on a relatively flat trajectory parallel to the ground or at a slight elevation ranging up to 14 degrees; (2) howitzers, which had shorter barrels and fired at a variable but greater angle of elevation (15 degrees or more); and (3) mortars, which had the shortest barrels and fired at a more exaggerated angle (typically fixed at 45 degrees). Although the range of artillery depended on the size of the gun and projectile and the quality of the powder, normally gun or cannon fire had greater range and impact. Howitzers and mortars, on the other hand, could fire over friendly troops or obstructions and target enemy troops within fortifications. British bomb ships were armed mainly with mortars, some of which were so large they could outdistance any other artillery.

Guns were rated by the weight of their shot. The smallest in common use were 3-pounders, the largest 42-pounders. Typically, field artillery consisted of 6-, 9-, and 12-pounders, while guns in garrisons and on warships were larger. Howitzers and mortars, on the other hand, were rated by the diameter of their bore, most commonly 5.5–10 inches for howitzers and 8–13 inches for mortars.

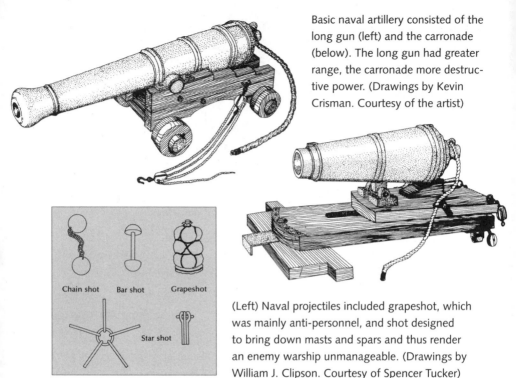

Basic naval artillery consisted of the long gun (left) and the carronade (below). The long gun had greater range, the carronade more destructive power. (Drawings by Kevin Crisman. Courtesy of the artist)

Chain shot    Bar shot    Grapeshot

Star shot

(Left) Naval projectiles included grapeshot, which was mainly anti-personnel, and shot designed to bring down masts and spars and thus render an enemy warship unmanageable. (Drawings by William J. Clipson. Courtesy of Spencer Tucker)

Carronades were a special kind of lightweight, short-range weapon used on warships, privateers, and armed merchant ships. They were popular because they took up less space than conventional guns, required a much smaller gun crew, and used a smaller powder charge (and thus were not prone to bursting). Carronades fired conventional projectiles, but they ranged in caliber from 6-pounders to 68-pounders. The latter were known as "smashers" because the massive and slow-moving projectiles they fired often did great damage to the hull of a wooden ship. High-velocity projectiles, by contrast, usually created a cleaner hole and could simply blow right through a ship's hull.

Vice Admiral Horatio Nelson's flagship, H.M. Ship *Victory* (104), mounted two 68-pounder carronades on the forecastle that did good duty at Trafalgar in 1805, and it looked like these light, compact guns might be the wave of the future. However, the War of 1812 demonstrated their liabilities. A ship armed with long guns could lay off at a distance and pound a carronade-armed vessel to pieces. In the Battle of Lake Erie, the British and American squadrons were armed mainly with carronades and fearful of the enemy's long guns. Commander Robert H. Barclay claimed that Master Commandant Perry's long guns "did great execution" against two of his ships, although Perry actually closed as quickly as possible to take advantage of his own carronades.[5] The U.S. Frigate *United States* (56) took advantage of its long guns to defeat H.M. Ship *Macedonian* (49) in 1812. This is also how H.M. Ship *Phoebe* (46 or 53) and H.M. Sloop *Cherub* (26) in 1814 defeated U.S. Frigate *Essex* (46), which was armed mainly with carronades. Taking this lesson to heart, the United States never again sent a frigate to sea without a substantial complement of long guns.[6]

There were several basic kinds of artillery projectiles. Most common was round or solid shot, today commonly called "cannon balls." Round shot could be heated red-hot in the hope of torching an enemy target. In 1812, both sides used hot shot in an artillery duel between Fort George and Fort Niagara. In 1813, hot shot was used by the British army in the first siege of Fort Meigs and by the American army firing on Fort George from Fort Niagara and defending Fort Ontario from a British attack. It was also used effectively by Brigadier General Jacob Brown against Captain William Mulcaster's gunboats in the St. Lawrence in November of 1813. In 1814, hot shot was used by American troops who attacked a British squadron that sailed up the Potomac River and by the British in the destruction of the U.S. Schooner *Carolina* (13) on the lower Mississippi River. In addition, a British fencible unit compelled the surrender of Fort Shelby at Prairie du Chien in 1814 merely by threatening to use hot shot. Finally, the U.S. Frigate *Constitution* (52) was fitted out with a furnace for hot shot during its last wartime cruise. Captain Charles Stewart claimed that it could heat 21 24-pounder shot "in 22 minutes with a pine wood fire."[7]

A second form of projectile was the explosive shell, which consisted of a hollow iron sphere that was filled with powder and a timed fuse. Closely related was shrapnel, which was used exclusively by the British and consisted of shells filled with powder and small iron balls. "The Star-Spangled Banner" describes exploding shells and shrapnel as "the Bombs bursting in air" over Fort McHenry in 1814.[8] Still another kind of shell was the carcass, an incendiary projectile packed with some combination of pitch, saltpeter, sulfur, and powder that was designed to ignite enemy buildings or ships.

For close action (up to 300 yards), the preferred form of projectile was case shot or canister, which consisted of a tin can that disintegrated upon firing, releasing a deadly spray of small iron balls or scrap iron. Also used in close action in naval battles was grape shot, which typically consisted of nine iron balls, weighing (depending on the size of the gun) from 6 to 64 ounces each, that were bound together prior to firing in a canvas bag that was secured to a base and spindle. When fired, the bag, base, and spindle disintegrated while the balls headed toward their target.

Field guns fired round shot and case shot. British field guns also fired shrapnel. Howitzers and mortars, on the other hand, usually fired exploding shells or shrapnel. Although they could also fire case shot, they rarely did so because these projectiles were more effective when fired at close range in a flat trajectory. Naval and garrison guns fired round, case, or grape shot. Navies also employed several other kinds of projectiles. To destroy masts, spars, sails, and rigging, warships sometimes fired bar shot (two half iron balls connected by an iron bar), double-headed shot (two iron balls connected by an iron bar), chain shot (two iron balls connected by a chain), and star shot (five iron rods connected to a ring that opened up when fired). The U.S. Frigate *President* (52) disabled H.M. Ship *Endymion* (51) with star shot in early 1815 before surrendering to other British ships.

The artillery of this age was not easy to master. Both armies in the War of 1812 required better educated officers in this service than in the infantry or cavalry. British artillery officers could not buy a commission but had to attend the Royal Artillery School at Woolwich. In the United States, the Military Academy at West Point was established in 1802 to train artillery and engineering officers.

For the rank and file, the artillery was a physically demanding service. The British required artillerymen to weigh at least 182 pounds so that they could muscle the heavy weapons, which weighed up to four tons and had to be repositioned after each shot. The United States also preferred large men for this service. Loading and firing the weapons was a team effort that required a sizeable crew. A crew of 15 worked a 32-pounder American naval gun (although the British got by with 12), while 9 men worked an American 6-pounder field gun. Artillery services in the field also required a large number of horses to haul their weapons and shot.

The normal rate of fire in battle was one or two rounds a minute. Aiming or "laying" the weapons was more art than science. Fuses for shell and shrapnel had to be properly cut, and the wind, humidity, and age of the gun all had to be taken into account. The range of the largest field guns was around 1,200 yards, although a ricochet could carry round shot farther. The range of big naval guns firing at an elevation was about 3,000 yards, although some large mortars with huge charges could reach 4,000 yards. At even 500 yards, however, hitting a target was no easy task and required considerable experience. At sea, it was even harder because of the pitch, roll, and yaw of the ship. When the U.S. Frigate *United States* (56) fought H.M. Ship *Macedonian* (49) in 1812, the two ships exchanged some 2,500 shots, but only 100 found their mark (with 95 hitting the British ship and only 5 hitting the American).[9]

Artillery work was dangerous because the weapons could blow up, killing or maiming an entire gun crew and anyone else in the vicinity. In addition, artillery could attract counterbattery fire (although the British army officially discouraged this practice because infantry units were considered more lucrative targets). The weapons also could be overrun by enemy troops eager to put the guns out of action or to turn them around. Guns in danger of being overrun were usually spiked, which meant that a metal rod was jammed down the vent hole to render the gun inoperable.

Artillery performed its best service in the War of 1812 in water-related campaigns. Navy guns were the primary weapon in every naval engagement on the high seas as well as in the American victories on Lake Erie and Lake Champlain and the British victory on Lake Borgne. Navy artillery also played an important supporting role in the American assaults on York and Fort George; the British attacks at Sackets Harbor, Forty Mile Creek, Craney Island, and Fort Ontario; and the American defense of New Orleans.

In the land war, artillery played a decisive role in the American defense of Fort Stephenson, where a British assault force was cut down by a 6-pounder named "Old Betsy"; and in most of the battles fought in the New Orleans campaign in 1814–15, including the main battle on January 8, when Andrew Jackson's eight batteries of guns shredded the advancing British line with canister and grape shot. The best guns in Jackson's line were actually naval guns. Artillery also played a significant role in the battles at Sackets Harbor, Crysler's Farm, Chippawa, Lundy's Lane, Fort Erie, and Bladensburg.

There were a few occasions when artillery conspicuously failed to do the job. At Lacolle Mill in 1814, Major General James Wilkinson's field guns hardly dented the British blockhouse before the American general ordered a withdrawal. That same year the Royal Navy's heavy guns were unable to make much of an impression on Fort McHenry, thus forcing the British to give up their attack on Baltimore. Nor did a heavy Royal Navy bombardment have much effect on Fort St. Philip on the lower Mississippi River in 1815.[10]

**Congreve Rockets.** Congreve rockets were probably the most terrifying weapon used in the War of 1812. Rockets originated in China and were brought to Europe by Marco Polo. Although initially used on the battlefield, by the late seventeenth century they had been relegated to signaling devices. However, they continued to be used in combat on the Indian subcontinent, and British soldiers who served there saw their potential. In the early nineteenth century, William Congreve, Jr. (1772–1828), whose father was an officer in the Royal Artillery, developed a British version that could be employed in combat.

Resembling skyrockets, Congreve rockets had three components: a head, which contained solid shot, case shot, exploding shell, or shrapnel of various weights (typically 12 to 42 pounds); an attached cylinder, which contained the propellant; and a long stick, which was supposed to provide stability. Congreve rockets were cheaper, lighter, faster, and easier to fire than conventional artillery; they had a range of up to two miles and could serve as incendiary weapons; and their noisy effects sometimes unnerved even hardened veterans. They were successfully tested

The Congreve rocket was part of a new weapons system designed for use in the field and on warships. Although rockets could panic inexperienced troops, they never lived up to expectation because they were too hard to aim. (Congreve, *Details of the Rocket System*)

in several offshore bombardments in the Napoleonic Wars and were used effectively in the Battle of Leipzig in 1813.

In the War of 1812, the British sent one of their two rocket ships, H.M. Sloop *Erebus* (26), to American waters. This ship had been fitted out and equipped under Congreve's personal supervision in early 1814. Congreve rockets did considerable duty in several theaters. In 1814, they were used at Lundy's Lane on the Niagara front and at Lacolle Mill and Plattsburgh on the Lake Champlain–Richelieu River front. On Lake Ontario, the British used them against Oswego in the spring of 1814 and planned to use them against Sackets Harbor that summer. They fitted out several rocket boats for an attack on the American squadron at Sackets Harbor, but after they lost gunboats deemed essential to the enterprise in the Battle of Sandy Creek, they called off the attack.[11]

The British made especially good use of Congreve rockets in the Chesapeake. Rockets panicked the militia at Bladensburg, thus opening the road to Washington. They were also used against militia in the Battle of North Point, though here they were less effective. H.M. Sloop *Erebus* fired rockets on Fort McHenry as part of the British assault on Baltimore, and when the bombardment failed, Francis Scott Key immortalized "the Rockets' red glare" in "The Star-Spangled Banner."[12] The British also used Congreve rockets in their campaign against New Orleans in 1814–15. Rocket units were present at each battle, including the main one on January 8, and they covered the British army's retreat after its defeat.

Casualties from rockets were rare. Major General Jacob Brown was apparently injured by a rocket at Lundy's Lane, and a militiaman at Havre de Grace, Maryland, was killed, the only known rocket fatality in the war. In truth, the rockets were too inaccurate to be very effective. A young British officer conceded that they were "very destructive," but only "when accurately fired, which is rarely the case." This officer reported that a Congreve rocket fired from the shore in 1814 came within 100 yards of a ship that had been targeted on Lake Erie. However, a second rocket "went off hissingly and whizzeningly, but just as it should have cleared the wood, its tail touched a bough and it came flying back towards us, putting us all to the rout."[13] Nor was it necessary for Congreve rockets to ricochet to threaten those who had fired it. Their trajectory was so unpredictable that sometimes they reversed course for no apparent reason.

An American officer who faced rockets at Lacolle Mill in 1814 said: "They might answer a good purpose for burning a town or frightening raw troops, but in the field they are a poor contrivance for killing men, when compared to the rifle and the musket."[14] Although several other nations, including the United States, subsequently adopted them, rockets never lived up to their promise as a light, mobile weapons system that would fit between field artillery and muskets.[15]

**Muskets.** The standard shoulder arm in the War of 1812 was the smoothbore muzzle-loading musket. Soldiers armed with muskets generally used prepared cartridges that consisted of a paper tube (often waxed or greased) containing gunpowder and a ball. Loading the weapon was complicated because it required tearing the cartridge open with one's teeth, pouring some of the powder into the pan, and then forcing the rest of the cartridge down the barrel with a ramrod.

The normal rate of fire was two or three rounds per minute, although this rate could not be sustained for long because the weapon heated up and the men tired. Under ideal conditions, the musket was accurate up to 100 yards, and a lucky shot could be lethal at 200 or even 300 yards. A British observer in Canada wondered "how it was possible that so many men escaped in a regular action while exposed to thousands of balls."[16] But since the weapons were inaccurate and not commonly aimed, the vast majority of shots missed their mark. As a result, it took a great deal of fire on the average to bring down an enemy soldier. This explains why armies usually emphasized the fire discipline of the unit rather than that of the individual soldier.

Muskets misfired about 20 percent of the time for any number of reasons. Sometimes the flint failed or the touch hole became too clogged with spent powder. The U.S. War Department signed a contract for pistols with interchangeable parts in 1813, but the age of interchangeable parts for shoulder arms lay in the future.[17] Hence any musket that broke down had to be repaired in the field, sent to a gunsmith, or discarded.

*The Brown Bess.* The British version of the musket was the Land Pattern musket. It was often called the Tower musket because it bore an inspection stamp from the Tower of London, but more commonly it was known as the "Brown Bess," probably because the barrel often took on a brown color as a result of service. The most common version in use during the War of 1812 was

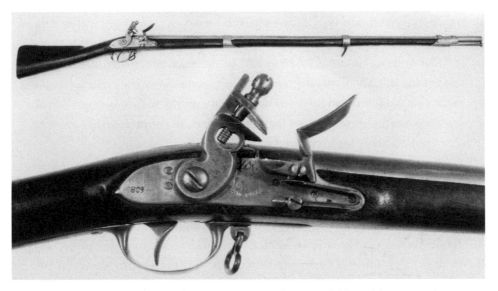

The standard weapon of issue for U.S. troops was the Springfield Model 1795 musket (and later variants). (Parks Canada)

the India Pattern, which the British government had adopted in 1797. This weapon was a little over 55 inches long, had a 39-inch barrel, and weighed just under 10 pounds. It had a .75-inch bore and fired a .71 caliber soft lead ball weighing about an ounce. The British government produced so many of these muskets—more than 1,600,000 between 1804 and 1815 alone—that the India Pattern is probably the most common flintlock that survives today. To load and fire the Brown Bess, the British manual of arms prescribed 16 basic steps and a number of additional special purpose steps.[18]

*The Springfield Model 1795.* In the United States there were still many British muskets (dating from the colonial era or bought during the Quasi-War in the late 1790s) and even more French muskets (tens of thousands of which were imported during the American Revolution), but most muskets used in the War of 1812 were American made. The most common was the Springfield Model 1795, which was gradually improved over time. This model and its later variants were manufactured at the U.S. armories at Springfield, Massachusetts, and Harpers Ferry, Virginia, as well as by private arms makers. Between 1795 and 1815, more than 200,000 muskets of this pattern were produced for the U.S. government, and an additional number was produced for use of the militia under state contract. Patterned after France's light 1768 model, the 1795 model typically weighed about 9 pounds, was 59.5 inches long, and had a 44.5 inch barrel. It had a .69 inch bore and fired a .65 caliber ball.

The American manual of arms had compressed the 16-step British process for loading and firing the musket into 12 steps. Since the process was the same, this did not speed up the American rate of fire. In fact, because British soldiers were more experienced than their American counterparts, they probably fired a little faster in the heat of battle.[19]

***How Effective Was "Buck and Ball"?*** Americans sometimes loaded their muskets with two or three buckshot (each typically about a quarter of an inch in diameter) as well as the standard round ball. This combination, known as "buck and ball," increased the chance of randomly hitting something but greatly reduced the accuracy of aimed fire and the lethality of the projectiles. In the assault on Fort George in 1813, a British officer who was hit by five buckshot, including one that went through his nose, survived.[20] Most British soldiers dismissed buckshot as a mere annoyance, and when they captured cartridges containing buckshot, they sometimes issued them to their Indian allies. Hence, there were some Americans who fell prey to "buck and ball."[21]

**Rifles.** Whenever the British encountered heavy small-arms fire in the War of 1812, they were inclined to think that they faced Kentucky (that is, Pennsylvania) rifles and perhaps even Kentucky riflemen. In fact, there were far fewer American rifles—shoulder arms with a rifled (grooved) bore—in the War of 1812 than the British imagined.

Although rifles were popular in the West, they did not figure very prominently in the fighting elsewhere. Even in the West, regular troops were armed mainly with muskets. This was the standard weapon that was found in federal and state arsenals. It was also the weapon of choice for most people who owned personal shoulder arms in the East.[22]

While muskets were rarely accurate at more than 100 yards, a skilled American rifleman could hit a target at 200–300 yards and occasionally even beyond. But the rifle was harder to use and maintain in the field. Unlike the musket, which used a pre-made cartridge, rifles often used a finer grade of powder (and sometimes two grades—one for the pan and one for the barrel chamber) and an individually cast ball. Not only did the rifle take longer to load, but it was also less reliable because its grooved barrel was more likely to foul. In addition, although the rifle was considered a good weapon for

Although the Pennsylvania rifle was more widely available, U.S. troops were issued the Harpers Ferry Model 1803 or a model made by private manufacturers under an 1807 contract. Shown here is the 1807 model. (West Point Museum Collections, U.S. Military Academy)

ambushing, sniping, and skirmishing, it was not considered suitable for conventional infantry assaults.[23]

*The Harpers Ferry Model 1803.* Before the War of 1812, the U.S. government produced 4,000 rifles at the armory at Harpers Ferry, Virginia. These were not the Kentucky or Pennsylvania rifles of lore, but rather the Harpers Ferry Model 1803, which was a sturdy, short-barreled, heavy caliber weapon that packed a punch but lacked the range of rifles manufactured for private use. These rifles weighed 9 pounds, were 49 inches in length, had a 33-inch barrel, and fired a .54 caliber lead ball. The government also contracted with Pennsylvania gunsmiths for an additional 1,800 rifles in 1807. Most of these weapons weighed 9 pounds, were 52–54 inches long, and fired a .54 caliber ball. The 5,600 rifles that the U.S. government made or contracted for before the War of 1812 made up only a small portion of the rifles used on the American side during the conflict.[24]

*The Pennsylvania Rifle.* Rifles produced for private use, usually referred to as the Kentucky or Pennsylvania rifle, made up a majority of American rifles in the war. These weapons were manufactured to many different specifications. A typical one might weigh 11 pounds, have an overall length of 60 inches, be fitted with a 44-inch barrel, and fire a .45 caliber lead ball.[25]

No rifles were manufactured in Kentucky before the War of 1812. The weapon known as the Kentucky rifle was actually designed and manufactured in Pennsylvania and thus is more accurately known as the Pennsylvania rifle. However, a popular song after the War of 1812 celebrated the role of Kentucky riflemen in the Battle of New Orleans, and this irrevocably linked the weapon to Kentucky. (See Appendix A for more on the song.)

Most American riflemen who served in the war were volunteer militia who brought their own arms into the field. Hence, the Pennsylvania rifle dominated. Those volunteer riflemen who did not have rifles were sometimes issued muskets.[26] Volunteer militiamen using the Pennsylvania rifle distinguished themselves in a number of battles in the West, most notably at the Thames, in the Creek War, and at New Orleans.

*U.S. Rifle Units.* When the war began, the U.S. Army had only one regiment of riflemen, the 1st U.S. Rifles, which was created in 1808. Several companies from this regiment fought at Tippecanoe in 1811, but some of the men were actually armed with muskets. In early 1814, Congress created three more rifle regiments (the 2nd, 3rd, and 4th), but riflemen never amounted to more than 10 percent of the regular army, and some rifle units were still armed with muskets.[27]

U.S. rifle units using government-issued rifles played an important role in establishing beachheads in the assaults on York and Fort George in 1813, and their contribution to the American victories at Sandy Creek and Conjocta in 1814 was decisive. On most other occasions, however, their role was less conspicuous, especially after their best leader, Major Benjamin Forsyth, was killed in a skirmish at Odelltown in June 1814.[28]

Man for man, U.S. riflemen may have been the most effective American soldiers in the field, but their contribution to the American war effort has been exaggerated. Although the myth of American riflemen persisted in the popular mind after the War of 1812, the U.S. Army brass and its allies in Congress did not buy into it. Three of the U.S. rifle regiments were eliminated in the postwar reduction of the army, and the last was dropped in 1821.[29]

*The Baker Rifle.* The British answer to the American rifle was the Baker rifle. Developed by gun maker Ezekiel Baker for a British Board of Ordnance trial in 1800, it was a justly celebrated weapon. It was comparable to the rifle produced at Harpers Ferry rather than the privately-manufactured Pennsylvania weapon. It weighed about 9 pounds, had a 30-inch barrel with a .615 to .70 inch bore, and an overall length of just under 46 inches. Unlike American rifles, the Baker was more likely to be loaded with a prepared cartridge, especially when used by British regulars, and thus it could be loaded and fired more rapidly. Although the Baker did not have the same range as the Pennsylvania rifle (only 150–200 yards as opposed to 300 yards), it was (like the Harpers Ferry rifle) a sturdy weapon, less likely to break down under field conditions.

The British manufactured some 30,000 Bakers from 1800 to 1815. The Baker was distributed not only to the British rifle units but also to some militia and volunteers and to some foreign units. Unlike the United States, the

British often issued sword-bayonets with their rifles. These were longer than conventional bayonets to make up for the shorter barrel of the rifle. Riflemen were thus ordered to "fix swords" (rather than bayonets), although in fact this edged weapon was rarely used in combat.[30]

People living in Upper Canada, particularly in the western part, were well armed with rifles, though not the Baker. The most commonly owned rifles were of private British manufacture. There were some American and French rifles in the mix, and as more Americans emigrated to Canada in the years before the War of 1812, they brought more American rifles with them. Canadians generally favored heavier shot for their rifles, which cut down on their range but increased the lethality of their fire. Those living on the frontier could shoot every bit as well as their American counterparts. Isaac Weld, who visited Upper Canada in 1796, reported that "they shoot almost universally with the rifle gun, and are as dexterous at the use of it as any man can be."[31]

***British Rifle Units.*** The British shared a common view among Europeans that riflemen were vulnerable to musket volleys and bayonet charges because it took them longer to load their weapons. Hence they generally preferred to attach their rifle units to larger musket forces that could protect them. The British also faced a problem in recruiting riflemen: they did not have a large body of trained civilians to draw upon. In Canada, however, this problem did not exist.[32]

The British created a rifle corps in the 1790s that consisted of two regiments, the 60th and the 95th. The 60th had originated in 1755 as a regiment of foreigners recruited for service in America. Although some of its men were armed with rifles, most carried muskets. It was not until 1797, when the 5th Battalion was added, that the 60th Regiment had an all-rifle battalion. The new battalion was commanded by Lieutenant Colonel Francis de Rottenburg, who wrote an influential treatise on light infantry and rifle tactics. De Rottenburg later had a major command in Upper Canada during the War of 1812. The other seven battalions that made up the 60th continued the older tradition of attaching rifle companies to larger units armed with muskets.

The 95th was organized by taking men from other units in 1800 and was known as the Rifle Corps until 1802, when it was given a numerical designation. Like the 5/60th, it consisted only of riflemen. The 95th, which ultimately consisted of three battalions, gained lasting fame because so many of its men wrote memoirs recording the unit's prowess on the battlefields of Europe. Sir

Sidney Beckwith, one of the most accomplished commanders of the 95th, also saw action in the Chesapeake campaign during the War of 1812 although, like de Rottenburg, he was no longer attached to a rifle unit.[33]

The British Rifle Corps fought with distinction in the Peninsular War, its men often serving as light infantry and firing the first and last shots of the battle. The only units from the Rifle Corps to serve in the War of 1812 were five companies of the 3/95th, which were sent to the Gulf Coast, where they played a conspicuous role in the New Orleans campaign. They took part in the Battle of Villeré's Plantation on December 23, 1814; the British reconnaissance in force on December 28, 1814; and the main battle on January 8, 1815, when they reached Jackson's line before being driven back. They sustained surprisingly few casualties in this bloody engagement, probably because they were deployed in skirmishing order.[34]

Great Britain reduced its rifle corps to three battalions in 1815. In later years, the 95th became the King's Royal Rifle Brigade and the 60th the King's Royal Rifle Corps. These units went through additional organizational changes in the nineteenth century and today are part of a single regiment, the Royal Green Jackets.[35]

**The Bayonet.** Both armies in this war were issued socket bayonets 15–17 inches long that fit over the barrel of the musket, and both embraced tactical doctrines that emphasized the importance of the bayonet in combat.[36] But on the battlefields of Europe and America, bayonets rarely played a significant role because one side or the other commonly broke and fled before cold steel could come into play. As one student of the subject has put it, "The fear of the bayonet, rather than the bayonet itself, was the deciding factor."[37]

A contest of bayonets was rarely welcomed. Not only was it a particularly gruesome and bloody form of close combat, but in such a melee commanding officers lost control over their men. In the wilderness of North America, bayonets could actually be a liability. Recognizing this, Sir George Prevost in 1814 ordered all troops serving "on outpost duties" to keep their bayonets sheathed. Fixed bayonets, he said, "form a Conspicuous object visible at a great distance [because they reflected light], are an inconvenient incumbrance in the Woods, and from the nature of the duties of Light Troops can be rarely required, and never so suddenly but that the Soldier will have ample time to fix his Bayonet."[38]

Bayonets were sometimes used in the War of 1812 to silence sentries or pickets who had been taken by surprise. They also figured prominently in several engagements. Captain "Big Sam" Dale of the Mississippi militia achieved legendary status when he used a bayonet to dispatch several Creeks in early November 1813 in the so-called Canoe Fight in the Alabama River. American troops used a bayonet charge effectively against the Creeks in the Battle of Autosee in late November 1813 and again at the Battle of Calabee Creek the following January.

In December 1813, in the night assault on Fort Niagara, British troops relied exclusively upon their bayonets to subdue the surprised American garrison. In the summer of 1814 bayonets played a role in the close-in fighting at Fort Erie and in the ensuing American sortie from that fort against British artillery batteries. Bayonets also played a significant role in the confused night fighting on December 23, 1814, at Villeré's Plantation south of New Orleans.[39]

## LOGISTICS

**Supplying a Wilderness War.** The movement of men and material—that is logistics—always plays an important role in war. The lack of supplies or equipment can directly affect the outcome of a battle. In addition, armies march on their stomachs, and if they are not adequately fed or supplied with clothing, equipment, or other necessities, morale is likely to plummet, impairing fighting effectiveness. The logistical problems that both sides faced in the War of 1812 were prodigious because so much of the contest was waged over difficult terrain in remote wilderness areas and in weather that could be unusually harsh by European standards. As one scholar has put it, "Nature, not yet subdued by man, interposed stupendous obstacles."[40]

Transportation drove up the cost of supplying the opposing forces to dizzying heights. Many of the roads were so bad that they were impassable much of the year. In winter heavy or wet snow could close them; in warmer weather rain could wash them out. Haulers needed either dry roads or the right kind of snow cover. In the winter, said one Canadian, snow "is just the thing that we pray for, and which makes our roads so good."[41] Even under ideal conditions, however, heavy wagons could cut such deep ruts that traffic in any season could slow to a crawl.

Waterways offered a much better option, but violent storms or heavy rain could render them dangerous and a lack of sufficient water to carry traffic could make them unusable. Unless they froze enough to bear significant weight, they could be unusable in the winter. They were also more likely to be exposed to enemy disruption.

Sparse settlement in many contested areas made it impossible for armies to live off the land as they advanced. The nearest sources of supply, even for food and forage, might be days or even weeks from the front. Moreover, since both sides were struggling for naval superiority on the northern lakes, navies competed with armies for the scarce supplies.

It was an enormous challenge to move the vast supplies needed to support troops on the frontier, and the challenge was compounded by the need to include adequate forage for any pack and draft animals that were used to haul the supplies. Even simple communication could be problematic. The vast distances made it difficult for officials in the East to get their orders to the front in a timely fashion, or for those on the front to make their needs known to their superiors back East.

Throughout the War of 1812, moving armies had a tendency to outrun their supplies, and sometimes it was difficult to maintain even stationary troops. American forces in winter quarters at Greenbush, New York, in 1812–13 and at French Mills, New York, in 1813–14 suffered huge losses from lack of food, clothing, and housing.

Although such losses in British camps were less common, the British faced other problems. Upper Canada, although a net exporter of food before the war, was far less able than the more populous American states to support the influx of military personnel during the contest, especially when so many men were taken from their farms for militia duty or other war-related tasks. In addition, the British had to find a way to feed their numerous Indian allies. The warriors and their dependents consumed huge quantities of provisions on the Detroit frontier in 1813 and on the Niagara frontier in 1814. Indeed, by the spring of 1814, Britain's native allies in Upper Canada were consuming 1,200 barrels of flour a month, which was 50 percent more than the British army in the area.[42]

**American Supply Routes.** For the United States, there were two main supply routes. One ran from Philadelphia to Pittsburgh, and from there due north to Lake Erie; or down the Ohio River and then northwest to the forts that guarded the frontier; or farther down the Ohio and Mississippi rivers to posts in the Old Southwest (including New Orleans).

Pittsburgh played a particularly crucial role on this supply route. No other city of comparable size on either side was so close to the contested wilderness areas. Known as the "Gateway to the West," this bustling city of 6,000 in 1812 had an extensive manufacturing base that included an anchor and anvil factory, three large ropewalks, and three foundries. Pittsburgh was thus in a unique position to supply the needs of American armies and squadrons operating on the northern and western frontier.

The other American supply route ran from New York up the Hudson River to Albany. From there, supplies could be carried to three destinations: (1) northeast across a land and river route to Lake Champlain; (2) west along the Mohawk River and connecting waterways to Lake Ontario; or (3) southwest from the Mohawk River and connecting waterways to Seneca Falls, and from there via a tough overland route to the Niagara frontier 115 miles away.

Oswego was the entrepôt for supplies flowing across the Mohawk River route to American forces stationed at Sackets Harbor or operating elsewhere on Lake Ontario. Buffalo, which was supplied by the Mohawk River–Seneca Falls route as well as by other routes across New York state, was the entrepôt for American forces operating on the Niagara frontier. Some supplies from Buffalo also flowed across Lake Erie to American depots (including Detroit) farther west.

The United States had the advantage of interior and protected supply lines and of a much larger frontier population to support its operations. The combined population of Kentucky (407,000), Ohio (231,000), and New York (959,000) was more than 20 times that of Upper Canada (77,000).[43] The direction of the currents in several major river systems also favored the United States. While the British had to work against the current to move supplies up the St. Lawrence River, the U.S. was moving with the current when it used the Lake Champlain–Richelieu River route to move supplies north, the Ohio River to move supplies to the West, or the Mississippi River to move them to the Gulf Coast.

In spite of these advantages, the logistical problems that the United States faced defied easy solution. Even with several manufacturing centers in the West, the nation still had to move vast quantities of war material across the Appalachian Mountains. Prior to the advent of the canal or railroad, this was a difficult and costly task. Faulty planning, a flawed administrative structure, crude roads, unimproved river channels, and a shortage of hard cash all combined to slow the flow of goods to the front. This often meant that supplies reached the front long after they were needed.[44]

**British Supply Routes.** For Great Britain, the logistical problems were even more daunting. The British had to ship their troops, war material, navy equipment, and even some of their food to Canada from the mother country 3,000 miles away. British officials could not count on local sources for food because Canada was still comparatively undeveloped, and a combination of militia duty and the needs of the transport service drew large numbers of men away from their farms. The best place for the British to buy food was actually in the United States, and this traffic steadily grew during the war.

The main supply route within Canada ran up the St. Lawrence River and into the Great Lakes. The water route from the mouth of the St. Lawrence to the British post at St. Joseph in the upper reaches of Lake Huron was 1,500 miles long. War material and provisions moved along this supply route slowly, and the cost was considerable. It took six weeks to get goods from Montreal to the British squadron on Lake Ontario. The cost of moving six 32-pounder guns between these points in 1813 was £2,000 ($7,500). To move the frame of the British frigate *Psyche* (rated 56) from Montreal to Kingston in 1814 cost a staggering £12,000 ($51,000). Although the contractor charged a fair price, this was nonetheless the cost of a small warship.[45]

In the summer, the British had to fight a strong current on the St. Lawrence and usually had to portage their goods around the various rapids west of Montreal. Moving a boat against the current required a bigger crew (usually twice as large) and took twice as long. It also doubled the cost. In the winter, the river iced up, and the British had to use sleighs. Although they were easier to move than wagons, they lacked the carrying capacity of boats. Worst of all, the St. Lawrence ran along a battle front, which meant that supply boats and sleighs needed an armed escort.

From Kingston at the mouth of the St. Lawrence, supplies moved by land or water to York, and from there across Lake Ontario to British forces on the Niagara front or in Burlington. From Burlington, supplies could be portaged overland to Port Dover and then moved by ship across Lake Erie to Fort Amherstburg. Other supplies reached Fort Amherstburg that were sent up the

Grand River, portaged to the Thames River, and then moved down that river to Lake St. Clair and the Detroit River.

The British also used another route to move supplies from Lake Ontario to the West. Goods were portaged 30 miles overland from York to the Holland River, then via Lake Simcoe and a land and water route into Georgian Bay and Lake Huron proper. Once on the lake, supplies could be ferried to either Fort Amherstburg or Fort Mackinac. After losing control of Lake Erie in 1813, this route played an indispensable role in keeping Mackinac supplied.

Although the British had the advantage of a mostly water route, it was a long route and much of it was exposed to enemy interference. The United States, however, did very little to disrupt the British supply route. Ogdensburg, New York, was left ungarrisoned during most of the war even though it offered the best spot for intercepting supplies that were headed up the St. Lawrence River. In a single week in 1814, 200 British boats passed by Ogdensburg.[46] The failure of the United States to threaten this supply route was a reflection of a larger failure of its strategic vision. For the United States, the focus throughout this war was always too far west.

The British were surprised that the United States did not do more to interfere with the flow of goods up the St. Lawrence River, and they worked tirelessly to make this route more reliable and secure. They built a series of defensive works to protect the route, and they developed a transportation corps from voyageurs of the North West Company to operate supply boats and garrison towns on the river. Commanded by Lieutenant Colonel William MacGillivray, an experienced merchant, this unit was known as the Corps of Canadian Voyageurs in 1812 but was reorganized into the Provincial Commissariat Voyageurs in 1813. Thanks to British diligence, by the end of the war the St. Lawrence supply route was both more efficient and less vulnerable to enemy disruption than it had been at the beginning of the conflict.[47]

**What Was the Impact of Logistics?** Logistics determined the outcome of a number of campaigns in the War of 1812. Brigadier General William Hull surrendered Detroit in 1812 in part because he could not maintain his supply lines to Ohio. Commander Robert Barclay did not have the logistical support to compete with the American building program on Lake Erie in 1813, and he felt obliged to challenge the more powerful American squadron to try to keep his supply route open. When Barclay was defeated, the British could no longer supply their soldiers and Indian allies on the Detroit River frontier, and thus even if a large U.S. force had not threatened them, they had no choice but to withdraw to the east. Similarly, when the British defeat on Lake Champlain in 1814 threatened their supply lines, Sir George Prevost thought it prudent to return to Canada even though he enjoyed overwhelming superiority on land. On the other hand, the British capture of the *Tigress* (1) and the *Scorpion* (2) on Lake Huron in 1814 dramatically improved their position, for they could now better supply Fort Mackinac and their Indian allies on the upper lakes.

Such were the logistical problems of this war that it is little wonder that offensive operations so often bogged down. The advantage almost always lay with the army that was already in place rather than the army that was on the move. This gave the British a huge strategic advantage in the conflict because they would win if they simply maintained the status quo. The United States, by contrast, could not win without conquering Canada, a task that may have been beyond the young republic's logistical capability.

**What Were the Most Impressive Marches?** Before the advent of the railroad, marching played a particularly important role in warfare. Whenever possible, nations sought to move their men by water. The British took advantage of their command of the sea during the War of 1812 to launch numerous amphibious operations along the Atlantic and the Gulf Coast, and both nations moved men across the Great Lakes when they could. But this was the exception rather than the rule. Even when an army followed a waterway, such as the St. Lawrence or Richelieu rivers or Lake Champlain, there were rarely enough boats available to transport both men and supplies. Hence, the men marched alongside the waterway. Marching men usually covered only 15 or 20 miles a day, and they often arrived at the front tired, hungry, and foot-sore.

Several British units had to make the grueling march from New Brunswick to Kingston, a distance of 750 miles. Two such marches stand out. In the late winter and early spring of 1813, the 104th Foot marched from Fredericton, New Brunswick, to Kingston, Upper Canada. The weather that year in eastern Canada was particularly bad, with the temperatures often hovering below zero and with more snowfall than the country had seen in years.

Departing from Fredericton over a six-day period between February 16 and 21, the men trudged through deep snow and fought dangerously low temperatures. Each night they built crude huts to escape the cold. They laid over in Quebec for ten days and then proceeded on to Kingston, most arriving there on April 12. They had covered 700 miles in less than two months, averaging almost 17 miles a day despite taxing conditions. It was a difficult, even a heroic, march, and yet there were surprisingly few cases of serious frostbite. Even so, the men of the 104th, who had been recruited locally from the Maritime provinces and Lower Canada, never quite recovered from the ordeal. Illness and desertion plagued the unit, and although some of the men saw combat, most were assigned to garrison duty at Kingston for the rest of the war.[48]

No less impressive was the march made the following year by 210 seamen under the leadership of Commander Edward Collier. Departing from Saint John, New Brunswick, on January 29–30, the men traveled by sleigh to Fredericton and thence to Presque Isle in present-day Maine. From there they marched to Kingston, arriving on March 22. Although the weather was not as bad as the previous year, it was still a Canadian winter, and the seamen were unaccustomed to marching or to such harsh winter weather. Although they left a trail of looting in their wake, they arrived at Lake Ontario in good shape and joined the Royal Navy squadron there.[49]

**The Great Rope Walk.** One of the great logistical feats of the war was the transportation of a huge naval cable in New York from Sandy Creek to Sackets Harbor 20 miles away. Although the deed went unnoticed at the time, many years later several eyewitnesses set down their recollections. Despite some variations in the details, the basic story they told is certainly true.

An American flotilla of boats moving war material and naval stores from Oswego to Sackets Harbor in May 1814 took refuge in Sandy Creek to evade a British squadron patrolling Lake Ontario. In the Battle of Sandy Creek, American troops on June 1 defeated a British force that ventured up the creek, but the American boats could not return safely to the lake. Most of the cargo was transported to Sackets Harbor overland in wagons, but no wagon was large enough to carry a huge cable of raw hemp that was to be spun into the rigging for the *Superior,* a heavy frigate then under construction. The cable was 300 feet long, 19–22 inches in circumference, and weighed 9,600 pounds.

After some delay, Colonel Allen Clark's 55th Regiment of New York Militia offered to carry the rope on their shoulders. Part of the rope was lifted into a wagon, and the remainder was carried by the detachment. Perhaps 100 men, including officers, took part in what might be styled the "Great Rope Walk." The men traveled a mile at a time and then rested. Their shoulders got so raw that they had to make pads of straw and grass for protection. Although many deserted along the way, others appeared to take their places.

The cable reached Sackets Harbor on the evening of June 10, about 30 hours after leaving Sandy Creek. The men were greeted with cheers and military music when they arrived and were also rewarded with a barrel of whiskey and $2 a day in bonus pay.[50]

## MILITARY POSTS

**Forts.** It was not easy to maintain forts in the early nineteenth century. Many forts were built on the Atlantic or Gulf coasts, where they were subject to the corrosive effects of snow and rain, salt and sea, and heat and wind. Even those built inland were usually built on a waterway and thus were subject to similar if less damaging effects from nature. Forts were sometimes built out of stone or brick, but more commonly they were constructed of wood that was subject to decay and earth that was subject to erosion. If not kept up, which was often the case, forts often had to be rebuilt every 20 years or so. Rebuilt forts were sometimes moved or renamed. Contemporaries, however, did not always embrace the new name, and documents do not always fix the fort's location. Three forts from the War of 1812—Amherstburg, Mackinac, and Ontario—have generated confusion among historians.

**Fort Malden or Fort Amherstburg?** The British occupied seven forts on American soil (including one at Detroit) at the end of the American Revolution. When they evacuated these forts in 1796 in accordance with the Jay Treaty, they planned a new series of forts on Canadian soil. To replace the post they had abandoned at Detroit, the British built one across the Detroit River. Occasionally contemporaries referred to this post as Fort Malden and the nearby town as Amherstburg.[51] Almost all historians have followed this practice, but it is incorrect.

The original town plan, which was prepared in 1796 by A. Iredell, the deputy surveyor of the Western District, refers to the township as Malden, and a gazetteer prepared three years later by David William Smith, the surveyor general of Upper Canada, refers to the "Township of Malden." The town is listed as Malden on a surviving map as well. Similarly, the military documents from the late 1790s refer to Fort Amherstburg or the "garrison at Amherstburg." A map from the same period also refers to the post as Fort Amherstburg, as does a report prepared by the head of the Royal Engineers in Canada in 1811.[52]

The same usage continued during the War of 1812. In the summer of 1812, Major John B. Glegg, Major General Isaac Brock's aide-de-camp, issued two sets of general orders that were dated "Headquarters, Fort Amherstburg," and Brock himself referred to "the Garrison at Amherstburg."[53] Captain Matthew C. Dixon of the Royal Engineers dated one of his letters "Fort Amherstburgh," and in his correspondence Sir George Prevost, the governor-general of Canada, repeatedly used the terms Fort Amherstburg or "the Garrison at Amherstburg."[54] The great Mohawk chief John Norton, who visited Amherstburg, also referred to it as "that post" or as one of the "Forts" on the Detroit River.[55]

How did the names of the fort and the town get reversed? The British destroyed Fort Amherstburg when they retreated east in the wake of Master Commandant Oliver H. Perry's victory on Lake Erie in 1813, but the Americans rebuilt the post during their occupation and evidently called it Fort Malden. This fort was restored to the British at the end of the war, and before it fell into decay in the 1820s, the British appear to have referred to it indifferently as Fort Amherstburg or Fort Malden. When the British rebuilt the fort in the 1830s, it officially became Fort Malden, but the little town that had grown up next to it continued to be called Amherstburg.[56] Historians who use these designations for the War of 1812 are following common practice but are nonetheless guilty of an anachronism.

**Fort Michilimackinac or Fort Mackinac?** Contemporaries and historians alike have referred to the fort on Mackinac Island in Michigan as Fort Michilimackinac or Fort Mackinac. Although the two terms are closely related, only the latter designation is correct. Fort Michilimackinac was a post built by the French in 1715 south of the straits of Mackinac on the Michigan mainland where Mackinac City is located today. The British took possession of this post at the end of the French and Indian War in 1761 and occupied it until 1780, when they abandoned it in favor of a new and more secure post which they built on Mackinac Island. They designated the new post Fort Mackinac.

Situated high upon Mackinac Island, Fort Mackinac was the key to control of the upper lakes. (Lossing, *Pictorial Field-Book of the War of 1812*)

The Peace of Paris in 1783 called for Fort Mackinac to be turned over to the United States, but the British retained possession until 1796, when they finally relinquished it under the terms of the Jay Treaty. The British captured Fort Mackinac in 1812 and retained control despite an American attempt to retake it in 1814. The fort was not restored to the United States until after peace was proclaimed in 1815. During their wartime occupation, the British commonly referred to the post as Fort Michilimackinac, thus contributing to the confusion that persists today.[57]

**Fort Oswego or Fort Ontario?** The United States in 1812 had two important sites at the eastern end of Lake Ontario: Sackets Harbor, which was equipped with a dockyard for the construction of American warships for service on the lake; and Oswego, which was a major supply depot because it was located at the mouth of the Oswego River, which was at the end of a supply route that stretched back to New York City.

To protect Oswego, the British had built a fort on the western bank of the river at its mouth in 1727. Although officially designated Fort Oswego, this post was also called Fort Chouaguen and Fort Pepperell. In 1755, a second fort was built on the eastern bank of the river, apparently to replace the first fort. The second fort officially was called Fort of the Six Nations, although it was often referred to as Fort Oswego or East Fort. Shortly thereafter, a third fort, variously known as Fort George, New Fort Oswego, Fort Rascal, or West Fort, was started but never completed a half mile southwest of the original fort.

The French destroyed all three forts in 1756 during the French and Indian War. Three years later, the British rebuilt the second fort, that is, the one on the east bank. This fort was officially designated Fort Ontario, although like its two predecessors it often was referred to as Fort Oswego.

The British evacuated Fort Ontario during the American Revolution, and American forces destroyed it. But the British re-occupied the ground in 1782 and rebuilt the fort yet again. The British retained control of this post until 1796, when it was turned over to the United States in accordance with the Jay Treaty.

Oswego was such an important way station in the supply route to Sackets Harbor during the War of 1812 that the British twice targeted it. An amphibious assault in June of 1813 was called off when the British concluded that the site was too well defended. Returning with a larger force in May of 1814, the British captured the fort. Although they seized some supplies, they missed a much larger cache some 12 miles upriver above Oswego Falls. As a result, the naval construction program at Sackets Harbor was largely unaffected.

Although the official name of the fort remained unchanged during this period, as late as the War of 1812 some contemporaries referred to the post as Fort Oswego. Many historians have followed this practice, but it is technically incorrect. Throughout its history, the official name of the post was always Fort Ontario.[58]

## DESERTERS

**Why Did Soldiers and Sailors Desert?** Desertion from the army or navy was commonplace in the eighteenth and nineteenth centuries. In time of war, when military forces had to expand quickly, recruiters often inveigled, conscripted, or dragooned men into service, and the incidence of desertion rose accordingly. Deserters might flee behind their own lines or cross over to the enemy. In most cases, enemy-controlled territory offered the nearest and safest refuge. Army deserters were rarely forced to fight against their countrymen and thus were unlikely to be captured in battle, and unless they were in

> ## Notice
>
> All American Soldiers who may wish to quit the unnatural war in which they are at present engaged will receive the arrears due to them by the American Government to the extent of five months pay, on their arrival at the British out Posts. No man shall be required to serve against his own country —

This informal British notice invited American soldiers to desert, promising a reward and exemption from military service against their former comrades. (Lossing, *Pictorial Field-Book of the War of 1812*)

an enemy fort that surrendered or behind enemy lines that were completely overrun, they were probably safe from punishment. Navy deserters, on the other hand, were likely to be in greater danger because they were accustomed to making their living at sea, where they were always vulnerable to capture.

Militiamen in the War of 1812 were the biggest offenders. Whole units sometimes decamped because they had grown weary of military service or wanted to go home to look after their crops. Even among regulars, however, desertion was common. In every theater there was a steady stream of army and navy deserters moving in both directions across the front or moving away from the front toward the rear.

Why did solders and sailors desert? In some cases, it was because of appalling conditions in camp brought on by bad weather, food or housing shortages, the presence of disease, or the absence of proper medical care. In others, it was because they had become homesick or wished to avoid punishment for some infraction of the rules. Some men deserted because they had developed a hearty dislike for their officers or for the regimen of military life. The desertion rate in the U.S. Rifle Corps, for example, rose after Benjamin Forsyth was killed. Forsyth's men were accustomed to his lax discipline and resented his successor, Lieutenant Colonel Daniel Appling, who was a stickler for the rules.[59]

Some men deserted because they did not have enough liquor to drink, while others deserted because they had too much. Some deserted because they had not been paid, while others left because they had. Even in the British army pay was sometimes in arrears, but the problem was especially common in the cash-strapped American forces. Hoping to exploit this, the British on one occasion promised five months' pay to any American soldier "who may wish to quit the unnatural war in which they are engaged." Such deserters were promised that they would not have to fight against their countrymen.[60]

Some men ran away because they were bored with inactivity or tired of the manual labor that they had to perform on fortifications. According to Major General Phineas Riall, despite extra rations of food and spirits, soldiers in the King's Regiment occupying Fort Niagara in 1814 "have got sulky and dissatisfied" and as a result the desertion rate had soared. "The men are sick of the place," he concluded, "tired and disgusted with the labor to which they see no end."[61] The desertions occurred partly because the fort was in American territory, and it was easy for the disaffected to slip away and find refuge behind American lines. But as soon as Lieutenant General Gordon Drummond announced that the men at the fort would be relieved, the desertions ended.[62]

If some men deserted because they were bored or tired of manual labor or the monotonous routine of camp life, others deserted for the opposite reason. In one case, which was far from unique, an American soldier told the British that he had deserted because "he was afraid of hard fighting."[63] Similarly, after news arrived in 1813 of the heavy losses sustained by the U.S. Frigate *Chesapeake* when it was taken by H.M. Ship *Shannon*, there was a rash of desertions from the U.S. Frigate *Constitution*, which was then in Boston fitting out for another cruise.[64]

**What Was the Desertion Rate?** How common was desertion in the War of 1812? Among land forces, it was undoubtedly less common than in the American Revolution, when the desertion rate for American troops was probably over 30 percent and for British troops at least 20 percent.[65] One scholar has put the desertion rate in the U.S. Army during the War of 1812 at 12.7 percent and has concluded that only one in five of these men was actually returned to service.[66] If all classes of American land forces are included (regulars, militia, and the short-term U.S. Volunteers raised in 1812), the desertion rate was probably around 20 percent.

For the British, the desertion rate on the frontier, especially among locally raised fencible and provincial units, was a matter of some concern. "I regret to say," Colonel Edward Baynes told Sir George Prevost in 1814, "that Desertion has proved a great drain to all the corps employed on the Frontier duties." Baynes attributed the problem to "the ideal blandishments of the United States." These were so "insidiously inculcated into the minds of our Soldiers" that "corps of the highest established reputation & discipline have not escaped the mortifying disgrace of frequent Desertions."[67]

Fencible and provincial troops were more likely to desert for several reasons. Despite their training, many never developed the discipline of the long-term regulars. In addition, they were better able to survive alone in the wilderness, and they could call upon local connections for help. Lord Bathurst, the secretary of state for war and the colonies, hoped that the regiments the government was sending from Europe, which were "composed of a very different description of men," would be more reliable, and this proved to be the case.[68]

The desertion rate for British fencible and provincial troops and militia was probably comparable to that of similar units in the United States. About 25 percent of the Glengarry Light Infantry, a fencible unit, deserted during the war.[69] Similarly, 25 percent of the 2nd Leeds militia from the Johnston District deserted to the enemy between July 1812 and late 1814, and 21 percent of the 2nd Norfolk militia from the London District went over to the enemy between June 1812 and June 1814.[70] The British, however, relied less heavily on local units than the United States. Hence their overall desertion among their land forces was undoubtedly lower, perhaps around 15 percent. More definitive figures must await a full analysis of all the returns on both sides.

What was the desertion rate in the opposing navies? It was undoubtedly much higher for the British, who relied on impressment to keep their fleet manned. In the Chesapeake Bay, the Royal Navy fought a constant battle during the war to prevent sailors and marines from seeking refuge ashore. Some made it, others died in the attempt, while still others were caught and punished.[71] Since the U.S. Navy relied on volunteer seamen who served only for a year or two, the desertion rate was lower. Even so, Americans who had soured on their service, especially in gunboats or barges, did not hesitate to desert.[72] Definitive figures for both navies must await further study.

Although flogging was banned in the American army, the British army continued to use the cat-o'-nine-tails to maintain discipline. (Painting by Eugene Leliepvre. Parks Canada)

**How Were Deserters Punished?** What happened to deserters who were caught? Although desertion was a capital crime in all armies and navies, lesser penalties were the norm in the War of 1812. In the United States, Congress banned flogging in the army in 1812.[73] Some regulars who deserted from the army were branded, had their ears cropped, or were subjected to some other form of corporal punishment. Others were sentenced to hard labor, imprisoned, fined, forfeited their pay, or were drummed out of camp.[74] Sailors and marines who deserted from the U.S. Navy were commonly flogged, although they were occasionally executed.[75]

Some deserters who were sentenced to death, particularly if they were young or there were other mitigating circumstances, received a last-minute reprieve. Execution became more common later in the war, although it was usually reserved for the worst cases: those who were found in an enemy camp or were guilty of bounty jumping, that is, enlisting and taking the bounty in one area and then deserting and re-enlisting elsewhere. Although the usual method of execution was by firing squad, some deserters, including several who were found on British ships after the Battle of Lake Erie, were hanged.[76]

Great Britain was more likely to execute regulars (including fencibles) who deserted, even if they were first offenders, although some received a flogging or escaped punishment altogether. Sir George Prevost remitted the sentences of some deserters, and Lieutenant General Gordon Drummond pardoned others who returned to service even though they had served in the U.S. Rifle Corps.[77] Deserters from the Royal Navy were likely to be executed, especially if captured on board enemy warships or privateers.[78] Sometimes, however, they escaped with a flogging.[79]

The British were usually willing to go further than the United States to capture regular (including fencible) deserters. Upper Canada passed a law in early 1812 that offered a reward of £5 provincial money (£4.5 pounds sterling or about $17) to anyone who brought in a regular army deserter.[80] Bounty hunters were authorized to call upon the inhabitants of the province for assistance.[81]

Sometimes the British used Indians to deter desertion or to bring in deserters. In 1813, desertion from Kingston became so common that, according to one observer, "the Indians were employed to intercept the deserters in the woods, and were allowed a reward for every soldier, dead or alive, they brought into town." Some of the mutilated bodies that the Indians delivered were put on public display as a warning to other soldiers.[82] Similarly, in early 1815 Captain Andrew Bulger sought to deter desertion from a Canadian unit of mutinous Michigan fencibles that he commanded at Prairie du Chien by directing the Indians "to bring in the head of any man who may attempt it."[83]

Both sides held local troops—such as the provincial units raised in Canada and the federal Volunteers raised in the United States—to a lesser standard than regulars. Militia were held to a lesser standard still, especially if they acted as a group. When whole units deserted (which was common), they were rarely punished.

Flogging militia was outlawed in Upper and Lower Canada as well as in the United States.[84] The British usually sentenced militia deserters to be imprisoned or transported overseas for a period of three to seven years. A few who sought to entice others to desert were sentenced to be shot, but this sentence was usually commuted to transportation overseas for life.[85] In the United States, the punishment of militia deserters was more lenient. In some cases, they were simply humiliated by being paraded in front of their regiments to the tune of "Rogue's March." More typically, they were sentenced to a short period of hard labor or extra duty and forfeiture of some pay and of their whiskey ration. Those who returned voluntarily were likely to be treated even more leniently, and many deserters were simply pardoned.[86] Execution of militia was so uncommon—and considered so unduly harsh—that when a Vermont citizen soldier shot and killed a fleeing deserter that he had been sent to apprehend, the shooter was indicted for murder and escaped conviction only because the jury could not reach a decision.[87]

In the course of the war, the U.S. Army executed 205 men, almost all of whom were deserters. Additional deserters from the U.S. Navy also suffered the ultimate punishment. The total number of American military executions for desertion during the war was probably around 250.[88] The British figures for all services were probably a little smaller because they relied more heavily on flogging and other punishments and because British regulars were better disciplined.

**Andrew Jackson and Deserters.** The only commander on either side who held the militia to a high standard was Major General Andrew Jackson. The frontier general kept the military courts in his camp busy. In early 1814, he approved the death penalty for John Woods after the 18-year-old private in the 28th Regiment of the West Tennessee Militia obstinately disobeyed orders. Woods became the first citizen soldier executed in the United States after the Revolution.[89]

Jackson was equally unforgiving of deserters, and there was not much safety in numbers. On more than one occasion, he ordered regulars to fire on militia units if they tried to leave camp. In addition, he went after some 200 members of the 1st Regiment of the West Tennessee Militia who left camp in defiance of orders. Although ordered into service for six months, the men believed that they could not be forced to serve more than three months, and the law at the time was probably on their side. Jackson, however, was convinced that the men had been legally ordered out for six months. Hence, he ordered them arrested and tried by a military court in Mobile. All were found guilty. Most were sentenced to forfeit a portion of their pay and were drummed out of camp with their heads shaved. Although this sentence was reasonable, the court went much further with the six ringleaders, a sergeant and five privates.

Andrew Jackson (1767–1845) was the pre-eminent American general in the war. His victory over the British at New Orleans influenced the way Americans remembered the war and catapulted Jackson into the presidency. (Engraving by James B. Longacre after a portrait by Thomas Sully. Library of Congress)

In early December 1814, they were convicted of mutiny as well as desertion and were sentenced to be shot by a firing squad. Showing no mercy, Jackson approved the findings and the sentences on January 22, 1815. A month later the executions were carried out.

Was this sentence reasonable? Probably not. It is true that these men were leaders and that those convicted of encouraging others to desert were often treated harshly, but there were several mitigating circumstances. The militia-men had acted as a group, there was a genuine difference of opinion over their term of service, and all were apparently first-time offenders. There was another consideration as well. Having received such a bloody rebuff at New Orleans on January 8, the British were unlikely to attack again. With the city now secure, Jackson could afford to be magnanimous and to wait before ap-proving the sentences. As it happened, news of peace soon arrived, and this would surely have justified setting the sentences aside. Instead, Jackson's fin-est hour was ever thereafter tainted by the largest mass execution of militia in American history.[90]

## MILITARY INTELLIGENCE

**Gathering Intelligence.** Information plays a vital role in warfare. It must be studied to produce intelligence, which can be used to shape the outcome of a battle. History is littered with battles won or lost because of good or bad intelligence. Securing reliable information, however, is rarely easy, and if the enemy has a different language and culture, which is usually the case, the task is that much harder. In the War of 1812, however, gathering intelligence was much easier because the two sides shared a common language and a similar culture as well as a porous border. Hence both sides could develop their intelligence by drawing from a variety of sources.

**Newspaper Sources.** The newspapers of the day were surprisingly free with military information. This was especially true of American papers, which contained a great deal of information on the movement of troops and supplies. The British, however, made only limited use of this source because they did not have enough spies in the United States, and by the time American newspapers made their way into Canada or to a British warship, the information was usually outdated.

Canadian newspapers also were a source of intelligence for Americans. A British naval officer later commented that "everything done and intended to be done in Halifax was known in America through the Halifax newspapers."[91] Like their British counterparts, however, American leaders did not do much to exploit this source of information.

**Civilian Sources.** People proved to be a much better source of information. The borders were completely unregulated, and civilians, though technically enemy aliens, moved freely back and forth for business or personal reasons. There was considerable trade on the northern frontier, and this led to the exchange of information that sometimes found its way into military camps as rumor or report. Lieutenant Colonel Thomas Pearson of the British army complained that American traders crossing the St. Lawrence into Canada afforded "constant intelligence . . . to the enemy of all our Movements and Military dispositions."[92] On the other hand, Americans who sold provisions to British troops in Canada or to British ships in American waters sometimes supplied information as well.[93]

Sometimes civilians provided information that was both timely and valuable. When Major General Gordon Drummond planned to seize Fort Niagara at the end of 1813, he secured valuable information from Canadian civilians who had been repatriated from the American side. Similarly, Brigadier General George McClure learned that Drummond was planning such an operation from a resident of Canada (probably an American) who fled across the river to the American side.[94]

In the Old Northwest, some of the French residents had the trust of all parties (including the Indians) and thus could move freely from camp to camp. Sometimes they shared information.[95] In addition, many residents on both sides of the Detroit River considered loyalty a matter of convenience and willingly provided information to any soldiers present, whatever army they belonged to. This was especially true in the western part of Upper Canada, which was virtually a no-man's land after the U.S. victory at the Thames in 1813.[96] Even in the more settled parts of the East, an army occupying enemy territory could usually pick up information simply by asking the civilian inhabitants. British ships in the Chesapeake and off the coast of Georgia also got considerable information from runaway slaves.[97]

**Military Sources.** Both sides relied heavily on military personnel for information. The slightest pretext was used to send a flag of truce into the enemy's camp in the hope of securing intelligence. "It was the scandal of the times," said an American staff officer, "that the enemy frequently made use of flags of truce in a way that perverted their true and honorable design; sending them in, when he had little other reason than a wish to pry into his neighbor's business."[98]

Both sides also got information from prisoners of war, who might be willing to talk to the enemy or who brought useful information home when they were exchanged or paroled (that is, permitted to return home by promising not to fight again until exchanged). A Canadian militia officer, for example, who was paroled from Fort George after its capture reported on American strength on the Niagara front.[99] Sometimes escaped prisoners of war brought valuable information home with them. After making his escape, an American schoolmaster taken under guard from Niagara Falls to York and Kingston told American naval officials what he had seen in the British dockyards and what he had heard from British officers.[100]

Deserters were an even better source of information. They often had access to useful military information, and they had a strong interest in ingratiating themselves to the enemy. Lieutenant General Gordon Drummond called deserters "my best source of information" in 1814 and lamented that this source dried up in September of that year, perhaps because the campaigning season in 1814 was winding down.[101] Both sides on the northern frontier relied heavily on deserters for information on the enemy's strength and intentions. Deserters told American officials at Fort Meigs in 1813 that the British were packing up and were about to lift their siege.[102] The opposing commodores on Lake Ontario, Isaac Chauncey and Sir James Yeo, each got detailed information on enemy ship construction programs from deserters.[103]

After the Battle of Queenston Heights in 1812, Mohawk chief John Norton reported that "every few days, we gained intelligence through the means of Deserters that were constantly coming to us."[104] The following year, Lieutenant Colonel John Harvey got such detailed information from three Americans who deserted from Fort George that he sent not only their depositions but also the deserters themselves to Yeo to be interviewed.[105]

**Spies.** Both sides sent spies into enemy territory. Indians were useful because they could move through the wilderness unseen, while local turncoats were valuable because they knew their way around and their movements were unlikely to arouse suspicion. For most intelligence, however, each side had to rely on spies who lacked these advantages.

On the American side, Commodore Isaac Chauncey got detailed information on British military and naval preparations from agents that he sent to Kingston in 1814.[106] Captain Arthur Sinclair and Colonel John B. Campbell relied heavily on Canadian turncoats, particularly Abraham Markle, for information on the Port Dover area before they raided it in 1814.[107] Major General James Wilkinson reported that he got military and naval intelligence on British preparations across the border in 1814 from "secret agents."[108]

British spies were no less active in the United States. In mid-1813 Commodore Stephen Decatur complained that in the waters around New London, Connecticut, there was "a constant communication kept up with the enemy." Later that year, when Decatur tried unsuccessfully to slip out to sea, he was convinced that someone had betrayed him to the British with blue signal lights. The "blue light affair" became a national scandal that touched off a debate in Congress.[109] The British also had agents who were active at Sackets Harbor, New York, and in Norfolk, Virginia.[110]

An agent that the British sent to Sackets Harbor in early 1815 was particularly successful. Not only was he able to pace off the length of the keels of American warships under construction there, but, even more remarkable, "at Utica, he dined two days successively with Generals Dearborne, Izard, Lewis & Porter," who had gathered for the last court martial of Major General James Wilkinson. According to the British spy, "They all seemed to think that if the conscription [bill] failed [which it did] that their Campaign would be defensive."[111]

On other occasions the information acquired by spies was more dubious. Augustus de Diemer, a British spy who visited New York, picked up some useful information on American forces serving on the Niagara River in 1812, but he also claimed that half of New York and a third of Vermont belonged to a secret organization called the Benevolent Society and had taken an oath "never to take up arms except in case of Invasion."[112] Although the Federalist-controlled Washington Benevolent Society was indeed active in these states, de Diemer's numbers were inflated, and the oath that he mentioned was most likely fictitious.

Fortunately for spies, it was very difficult to prosecute them. The Navy Department urged that suspected spies be tried by military courts if they were enemy aliens and by civilian courts if they were U.S. citizens, but making a case was never easy.[113] A spy who was caught in New York in 1813 unwisely admitted that he was a sergeant in the British army and was hanged.[114] But he was a rare exception. Most suspected spies were never convicted.

De Diemer was arrested in New York because he was a known Loyalist, but he was released "upon declaring himself to be a French Man."[115] Similarly, British spy Joel Ackley was jailed for almost ten months in Albany but was finally released for lack of evidence. The British later rewarded him for his services.[116] Another British subject, budding naval historian William James, took advantage of his residence in the United States during the first year of the war to study warships that were under construction in Philadelphia or had sailed into the Connecticut River. James also examined the defenses of Stonington. American officials became suspicious of him but could do no more than order him to join other enemy aliens in the interior. James later took refuge with the British fleet off the Connecticut coast, shared the information he had collected, and even offered to lead an attack on Stonington.[117]

In another case, a "Violent Fed[eralist]," probably John Parren of Maryland, was confined for several days by Captain Joshua Barney for hanging around an American camp in between visits to the British fleet.[118] Another American citizen, Samuel Stacy, was arrested for gathering information on the American squadron at Sackets Harbor, but Secretary of War John Armstrong ordered his release on the dubious grounds that "a citizen cannot be considered as a spy."[119] In yet another case, Lieutenant Colonel Benjamin Forsyth's famed rifle unit captured a known British spy in a raid on Odelltown and brought him to the United States. When the British retaliated by seizing an American and holding him as a hostage, the United States had to release the British spy.[120]

**Intelligence at Sea.** Both sides also sought intelligence on enemy forces at sea. This came from a variety of sources: newspapers that reported the arrival or departure of warships, neutral vessels willing to share information they picked up in enemy ports or in chance encounters on the high seas, and friendly privateers and merchant ships that evaded capture. Although this kind of information was often dated, it sometimes suggested where enemy warships might be found or where they were headed.[121]

**Intelligence Coups and Disasters.** The business of gathering information was usually mundane and the results unspectacular. Occasionally, however, there was an intelligence coup or failure of such significance that it determined the outcome of a battle or even a campaign.

At the beginning of the war, the British seized the *Cuyahoga* in the Detroit River. This had all of Brigadier General William Hull's papers on board, thus alerting them that a large American army was headed their way.[122] Later, the British captured a mail bag from Detroit that supplied vital information on the American army and its declining morale. Major General Isaac Brock made good use of this information and persuaded Hull to surrender by threatening an Indian massacre.[123]

If successful British intelligence contributed to Hull's defeat, so, too, did an American intelligence failure. When Hull learned that the British had captured Fort Mackinac, he assumed that this had "opened the Northern hive of Indians, and they were swarming down in every direction."[124] Hence, he called off his invasion of Upper Canada and withdrew to Fort Detroit. With his supply line threatened and a large-scale attack imminent, he surrendered his entire army.

Hull greatly overestimated the size of the force he faced. Tecumseh had cleverly paraded the same Indians in view of the fort three times to make it appear that his force was much larger than it was; and Brock had clothed some of his militia in discarded scarlet army tunics to magnify the size of his regular force.[125] In addition, most of the Indians who stoked Hull's fears were still neutral. Only after his surrender showed which way the wind was blowing did they embrace the British cause.[126] Moreover, even though Brock was playing on the well-known western fear of an Indian massacre, as the commanding officer he would have been under a very strong obligation to try to prevent any atrocities during or after any battle that took place.

The United States suffered a much greater intelligence disaster in August 1813 at Fort Mims in modern-day Alabama. Major Daniel Beasley, who was in charge of Fort Mims, ignored warnings of a possible Creek attack and even ordered two slaves whipped who had reported seeing Indians in the neighborhood. As a result, the Creeks caught the Americans by surprise, and the fort's main gate could not be closed because blowing sand had lodged it open. The Battle of Fort Mims (which took a heavy toll on both sides) is known as the "Fort Mims Massacre" because so few Americans survived the disaster.[127]

## MARTIAL LAW

**Martial Law in the United States.** The Battle of New Orleans propelled Andrew Jackson into the presidency, but it also revealed his darker side, for in the pursuit of victory Old Hickory could be harsh, tyrannical, and vindictive. No doubt this contributed to Jackson's success on the battlefield for his men feared him more than they feared the enemy, and thus (unlike many sunshine soldiers in this age of rugged individualism) they usually did as they were told. Even so, Jackson's tyranny was not soon forgotten, and his actions in New Orleans dogged him for the rest of his life.

When Jackson arrived in New Orleans on December 1, 1814, he found the Crescent City vulnerable to attack and the people apathetic, disaffected, and demoralized. Two weeks later, on December 16, he issued a proclamation that called upon everyone to rally to the defense of the city and that imposed martial law.[128] "Those who are not for us are against us," he said, "and will be dealt with accordingly."[129]

Jackson's aim in proclaiming martial law was threefold: (1) To ensure control over the resources in the city; (2) to prevent spies from moving freely into and out of New Orleans; and (3) to end the panic that had gripped the city. Even though this was the first time that martial law had ever been proclaimed in the United States, New Orleans was the largest and richest city west of the Appalachian Mountains and offered an irresistible target for the large British force that was known to be on the Gulf Coast. Thus, as a practical matter, Jackson's decision was probably justified.

Where Jackson left himself open to criticism was in the actions he took after the Battle of New Orleans was fought on January 8, 1815. Although the British remained on the Gulf Coast, by February any threat they posed to New Orleans had faded, and unofficial news of peace had arrived. By March 6, Jackson had received news from a variety of official sources that peace had been restored. This prompted him to propose an armistice to the British and dismiss the militia who had been called out *en masse.*[130] But martial law remained in effect. Only after Jackson had received definitive news of peace on March 13 was martial law lifted.[131] By then, however, the Hero of New Orleans was openly feuding with the local elite.

On March 3, state senator Louis Louaillier wrote a newspaper article suggesting that martial law be lifted. Jackson ordered him arrested, and when U.S. District Court Judge Dominick A. Hall issued a writ of habeas corpus ordering Louaillier released, Jackson refused to honor the writ and instead jailed Hall. A military court found Louaillier innocent of any wrongdoing. By this time, it was clear that the war was over anyway. Nevertheless, Jackson overruled the court and kept the senator in jail. At the same time, he released Hall but banished him from the city.

Once martial law had been lifted, Judge Hall hauled Jackson into court, charging him with contempt. Jackson sought to defend himself by seeking to read a paper justifying the imposition of martial law, but Judge Hall refused to let Jackson proceed. The issue was not whether martial law was justified but whether Jackson's treatment of the court was contemptuous. Rebuffed, Jackson refused to answer the court's questions (which in truth were designed to establish that he had treated the court disrespectfully) or to offer any other defense. Judge Hall found Jackson guilty and fined him $1,000.

Legally, this case probably played out as it should have since at the time the prevailing view was that it was unconstitutional to subject civilians to military rule under any circumstances.[132] Hence, even though Jackson might justify martial law by appealing to necessity, he still could be held accountable afterwards, especially for any excesses.

In 1866 the U.S. Supreme Court ruled in *Ex parte Milligan* that martial law could not be substituted for civilian law unless the civilian courts had stopped functioning. "Martial rule can never exist," the court ruled, "where the courts are open, and in the proper and unobstructed exercise of their jurisdiction."[133] This could only occur when there was an actual invasion; the mere threat of invasion was not enough. The court was sharply divided (5–4), and some legal scholars have challenged this view. But the case has never been overturned, and it is still the law of the land. Although the *Milligan* case applied to the Civil War, it suggests that Jackson's proclamation of martial law in New Orleans was illegal.

To his credit, Jackson publicly upheld the supremacy of civilian rule and paid his fine. But the matter did not end there, for the general and the judge then engaged in an unseemly war of words over the merits of the case. The administration found the whole matter embarrassing. Although President Madison was probably as committed to civilian rule as any American, he refused to do anything more than issue a private reprimand to his now immensely popular general. Many years later, in the early 1840s, the issue surfaced again when congressional Democrats sponsored a controversial bill to refund Jackson's fine (with interest), now that the elderly hero was broke. The bill became law in 1844, and Jackson got $2,732.

Although it might be argued that Jackson had set an unfortunate precedent for the imposition of martial law, this precedent has rarely been invoked. It is true that state officials have frequently imposed martial law, occasionally over an entire state (such as in Rhode Island during the Dorr Rebellion in 1842), but more commonly over just one or more fractious counties. It is also true that U.S. officials have periodically imposed martial law overseas in American territories. But federal officials have imposed martial law in the United States in only two other crises: During the Civil War (mostly in the occupied South and in unruly or threatened parts of border states), and during Reconstruction (when Congress authorized martial law in all the states of the former Confederacy except Tennessee).[134]

**Martial Law in Canada and British-Occupied Territory.** British officials also imposed martial law during the War of 1812, but the practice did not generate the kind of high-level legal confrontation that it did in the United States. Sir Guy Carleton had proclaimed martial law in 1775 when American troops invaded Canada, but this did not provide a good precedent because during the War of 1812 a shortage of provisions, not an enemy invasion, was usually the triggering mechanism.

Shortly after the British captured Detroit in August 1812, Colonel Henry Procter became the civilian governor of the Michigan Territory. Procter got along well enough with the American population until early 1813, when the River Raisin Massacre produced anger and unruliness. In response, Procter on February 4, 1813, proclaimed martial law. Procter's proclamation expressly suspended "the Civil & Criminal Laws now in Force, in the said Territory."[135] Although Americans in the territory protested, it is unclear how much effect the proclamation actually had. The only U.S. judge who remained in Michigan during the British occupation had not performed any judicial functions since the fall of Detroit, and under martial law the British probably employed routine measures to maintain public order.[136] Although Procter never lifted martial law in the territory, it effectively ended when the British withdrew their last forces from Michigan on September 27, 1813.

Two weeks earlier, on September 13, Procter, who had been promoted to major general and was now in Upper Canada, sought to facilitate his withdrawal by again declaring martial law. He took this action to ensure control over the food supply, wagons, and horses and to deal with "traitorous or disaffected persons."[137] Although Procter did not limit the geographical scope of his measure, as a practical matter it applied only to the Western and London districts. Since this was a sparsely-settled war zone and the effects of the measure were not felt after the British army withdrew, there was little protest from the British population.

In 1814, Captain Andrew H. Bulger declared martial law in what is now Wisconsin. In July 1814, the British captured Fort Shelby at Prairie du Chien and renamed it Fort McKay. When Bulger took command on November 30, he faced a host of problems. He was deep in American territory, far from any British support and without adequate provisions. The lines of authority between Bulger and Indian Agent Robert Dickson were unclear and the loyalty of the Indians in the area was suspect. Worst of all, the Michigan Fencibles, who constituted the bulk of Bulger's military force, were disorderly and defiant.[138]

Matters came to a head on December 31, when the defiance of the fencibles (most of whom were French and Indian mixed-bloods) turned to mutiny. When the sergeant major tried to arrest one of the fencibles, the others came to his aid. The entire unit then took refuge in the barracks, posted guards at the door, and "with drawn bayonets and knives," threatened to kill anyone who tried to make an arrest.[139] Bulger quickly restored order, but to strengthen his hand in this volatile situation, he proclaimed martial law.[140] This had no effect on the fencibles, who were already under military law, but it gave Bulger effective control over everyone else in the area.

Bulger ordered the most defiant mutineers court-martialed. They were found guilty of mutiny and received 150 lashes. This had a salutary effect on the other men, although Bulger continued to distrust them and took "every precaution against treachery or Desertion."[141]

The establishment of martial law probably had little practical effect on civilians living in this sparely-settled territory, and there were few if any protests. In fact, two weeks after martial law was proclaimed, 44 Prairie du Chien residents (who were virtually all French or French-Indian) formally praised Bulger for his effective leadership.[142]

Elsewhere martial law proclaimed by British officials generated more controversy. After the War of 1812 began, Sir George Prevost authorized Isaac Brock and Roger Sheaffe, who served successively as president and administrator of Upper Canada, to declare martial law. Brock was tempted because so many people in Upper Canada early in the war were either openly pro-American or at least reluctant to alienate the American army that was expected to occupy the province. But in the end, neither Brock nor Sheaffe was willing to risk a public backlash by resorting to martial law.[143]

Major General Francis de Rottenburg succeeded Sheaffe as the chief civilian official in Upper Canada, and on November 22, 1813, he declared limited martial law in the Johnstown and Eastern districts, north of the St. Lawrence River. Even though provisions and forage were abundant, de Rottenburg could not secure what he needed for the garrison at Prescott because the people showed "great reluctance" in furnishing them.[144] De Rottenburg's proclamation put the Crown's legal authorities in the province in an "unpleasant predicament" because it appeared to violate English law, which by an Act of Parliament had been in force in Upper Canada since 1791. Lord Bathurst subsequently approved de Rottenburg's proclamation, but only because he thought that the general had issued it in his capacity as president of Upper Canada. In fact, de Rottenburg had proclaimed martial law in his capacity as commander of the British forces in the province.[145]

Lieutenant General Gordon Drummond replaced de Rottenburg in December 1813, and on January 25, 1814, he suspended martial law because "the measure had created much discontent" and because he believed it was no longer necessary. Seeing the food shortage as a logistical problem, Drummond said that the onset of winter had frozen the roads, thus facilitating the movement of food and other supplies.[146] The following month, the House of Assembly in the province adopted a resolution denouncing de Rottenburg's proclamation as "arbitrary and unconstitutional and contrary to and subversive of the established laws of the land."[147]

This appeared to end the matter, but Drummond soon regretted his action, for an acute food shortage developed at Kingston, where the British army needed 5,000 rations a day. Although the provincial legislature was willing to give Drummond a number of tools to control disaffection, it refused to authorize martial law. Hence on April 12, 1814, Drummond acted on his own authority and issued a proclamation imposing limited martial law over the entire province to ensure that he had full access to its food supplies.[148] This, however, led to considerable dissatisfaction and a flood of legal suits against the commissary agents who forcibly purchased provisions and forage for army use. Fortunately for the agents, sympathetic Crown judges later dismissed most of these suits.[149]

Except in the West, British officials who proclaimed martial law had carefully limited its operation. They did not suspend or defy the civilian courts, nor did they set up the sort of overarching kind of military rule that Jackson did in New Orleans. Rather, their aim was simply to secure provisions for their men and forage for their horses. Hence, even though their actions caused some discontent and litigation, the entire experience left no lasting legacy and was quickly forgotten after the war was over.[150]

## CHAPTER 6

# The End
# of the War

Wars occasionally end with a decisive battle. The Battle of New Orleans appeared to be the decisive battle that ended the War of 1812, but this was not actually the case. The Battle of New Orleans neither ended the war nor did it influence the peace negotiations. Still, it was such a huge triumph for the United States that it overshadowed nearly everything else in the last months of the war. It also generated some of the most powerful and lasting myths associated with the conflict. Generations of Americans have used the Battle of New Orleans as a vehicle for imposing their vision on the entire war. Almost immediately, there developed a huge gap between what actually happened at the end of the war, and what Americans chose to remember had happened, and this gap has not diminished with time.

## FINAL BATTLES

**The Battle of Malcolm's Mills.** The last battle of the War of 1812 in Canada was fought at Malcolm's Mills on November 6, 1814. This battle resulted from Brigadier General Duncan McArthur's deep raid into western Upper Canada from Detroit. Although nominally under British control, this territory had been essentially a no man's land ever since the British defeat at the Thames in the fall of 1813. The Battle of Malcolm's Mills is rarely mentioned in the military histories of the war and thus is all but forgotten today.

In the late summer of 1814, McArthur raised 720 mounted soldiers, ostensibly to deal with Potawatomi Indians in the Old Northwest but actually to conduct an extended raid deep into enemy territory to destroy economic resources. Most of the recruits were Kentucky and Ohio volunteer militia, but some 50 U.S. Rangers and 70 Indians were also part of the force.

Departing from Detroit on October 22, 1814, McArthur's force followed the Thames River into Upper Canada. Traveling lightly and moving quickly, the mounted men lived off the year's bountiful harvest, burning mills and other buildings along the way. On November 5, the troops arrived at Brant's Ford on the Grand River. Instead of fording the swollen river and perhaps chancing a raid on Burlington Heights 20 miles away, McArthur kept his men on the western shore of the Grand, from which they exchanged fire with a small British and Indian force on the other side. The Americans then turned south toward Malcolm's Mills (near present-day Oakland), 20 miles northwest of Port Dover.

McArthur's force ran into 400 inexperienced but entrenched militia at Malcolm's Mills. In the ensuing battle, the Americans first tried to encircle the defenders and then routed them with a frontal assault on foot. Casualties on both sides were very light. After the battle, the Americans torched the mills and other local buildings and headed for home, continuing to plunder and burn along the way. McArthur blamed some of the excesses on his Indian allies, "whose customs in war impel them to plunder after victory."[1] On November 17, McArthur and his men reached Detroit, having covered close to 500 miles in just 27 days.

Duncan McArthur (1772–1839) led an American raid deep into Upper Canada in late 1814. His campaign produced the Battle of Malcolm's Mills, the last military engagement of the war in Canada. (Lossing, *Pictorial Field-Book of the War of 1812*)

Although targeting the mills worked a real hardship on the Canadians who owned or used them, there was a military justification for their destruction. Lieutenant General Gordon Drummond earlier had reported "the most alarming deficiency" of provisions for his troops in Upper Canada, "even in the grand essential of flour."[2] Although he had been counting on securing the bulk of his food that winter from local sources, now he had to look elsewhere.[3] Already fed up with Sir James Yeo for refusing to use his ships to supply the needs of the army, Drummond now told the commodore that "nothing less than the aid of the whole Squadron [on Lake Ontario] will be sufficient to relieve the urgent wants of the Right Division of the Army."[4] Yeo, however, was rarely very helpful to the army, and because of the lateness of the season, there was little that he could do on this occasion anyway.

Despite this military justification, British officials were livid over the destruction of so much private property, and Sir George Prevost ordered Drummond to seek out mills in American territory for retaliation. The war ended, however, before Drummond could carry out this order.

The Battle of Malcolm's Mills proved to be the last battle in Canada because the other armies on the Canadian–American frontier were already in winter quarters, and the war ended before another campaigning season opened. Although the battle itself had little significance, McArthur's entire operation illustrated a form of predatory warfare that targeted enemy resources and foreshadowed the deep mounted raids of the American Civil War.[5]

**The Battle of New Orleans.** The last great campaign of the War of 1812 culminated in the Battle of New Orleans. With a population of 25,000, the Crescent City was a rich prize. Not only was it the largest city in the West, but it was the principal entrepôt for the export of western grain, and its warehouses were filled with valuable commodities. But attacking New Orleans was no easy task. Far from the Gulf Coast, the only easy access was up the Mississippi River, but a powerful current at the English Turn made it difficult to get by Fort St. Philip. There were many overland approaches, but the movement of men and material was hobbled by a treacherous terrain that was covered with endless swamps, impenetrable cypress groves, and dense undergrowth. Cold winter rains added to the logistical problems.

The lack of boats hampered the British from the beginning. Because they did not have enough boats, they were not free to choose their approach, and

NEW ORLEANS
AND THE
SOUTHERN
THEATER

Lake Pontchartrain

Les Rigolets

Pass Christiana

CAT I.

Pass Maria

PEA I.

Fort Petites Coquilles

Chef Menteur Pass

Fort St. John

Gentilly

Bayou Bienvenu

New Orleans

Lake Borgne

JACKSON'S LINE

Fort St. Leon

Terre aux Boeufs

Lake of the Ouatchas

Mississippi R.

Bay of R. aux Chênes

Baratarian Bay

Fort St. Philip

Old Fort Bourbon

Bayou La Fourche

Balize

0  10  20  30  miles
0  10  20  30  40  50 km

KENTUCKY

Nashville

TENNESSEE

Huntsville

Fort Deposit

GEORGIA

Tallasahatchee

Fort Strother

Talladega

Coosa River

Enotachopco Creek

Tallapoosa R.

Horseshoe Bend

Fort Jackson

Calabee Cr.

MISSISSIPPI

TERRITORY

Pearl River

Alabama River

Tombigbee River

Burnt Corn

Chattahoochee River

Flint R.

Mississippi River

Natchez

Fort Mims

Fort Stoddert

Perdido R.

SPANISH
FLORIDA

Apalachicola R.

LOUISIANA

Baton Rouge

Lake Pontchartrain

Lake Borgne

Biloxi

Mobile

Pensacola

Negro Fort

New Orleans

Fort Bowyer

CHANDELEUR ISLANDS

Gulf of Mexico

Fort St. Philip

DETAIL ABOVE

0  50  100 miles
0  50  100  150  km

they had to settle for one south of the city on the river. Because of a lack of boats, they could not supply their army with enough artillery and projectiles. And because of a lack of boats, they could not move a force across the river quickly enough to mount an attack on both sides at the same time.

By the time Major General Edward Pakenham arrived on the scene on December 25, 1814, the opposing armies had already clashed in the confused night fighting at Villeré's Plantation, which had ended in a close American victory. Now Jackson was busy building the first of three defensive lines that would stand between the British and the Crescent City. The opposing armies clashed three more times before the main battle on January 8. For this battle, Pakenham's plan of attack was simple. Dividing his army into four brigades, he planned to send three brigades against Jackson's main line on the east bank while dispatching a fourth brigade, under the command of Colonel William Thornton, across the river to seize the American guns there and turn them against Jackson's line. Because the Royal Navy could not get enough boats to Thornton in a timely fashion, he fell behind schedule. Although he ultimately accomplished his mission, by then the main British force had been defeated on the east bank.

In the engagement on the east bank of the Mississippi River, the carnage was dreadful and one-sided. The British lost close to 2,000 men, while Jackson's force sustained only 13 casualties. This was one of the most stunning battlefield triumphs in American history and one of the most lopsided defeats in British military history. Given the cast of characters and results, it is hardly surprising that this battle should play such a large role in shaping the memory of the war in the United States. Nor is it surprising that in Great Britain the army did not soon forget the Royal Navy's failure to provide adequate support. Little wonder as well that so many misconceptions should be associated with this spectacular battle.[6]

***Was the Battle Fought after the War Was Over?*** Since the Treaty of Ghent was signed on December 24, 1814, and the Battle of New Orleans was fought on January 8, 1815, it is often said that the American victory came after the war was over. This is untrue. At the insistence of the British, the Treaty of Ghent provided for an end to hostilities only when both sides had ratified the agreement.[7] This did not occur until February 16, 1815—more than a month after the Battle of New Orleans.

The most accurate contemporary representation of the Battle of New Orleans was produced in 1815. It shows how exposed the entire British army was to artillery and small arms fire from Jackson's main line. (Painting by Jean Hyacinthe de Laclotte. New Orleans Museum of Art. Gift of Edgar William and Bernice Chrysler Garbisch, 1965.7)

***Did the British Seek "Beauty and Booty"?*** One of the most enduring myths associated with the Battle of New Orleans is that the British planned to sack the city if they won. Shortly after the battle, George Poindexter, a district judge in the Mississippi Territory, talked to some British prisoners of war. Based on these conversations, he publicly claimed that the British sign and countersign on the day of the battle had been "BEAUTY, & BOOTY." "Had victory declared on their side," he said, "the scenes of Havre de Grace [Maryland], of Hampton [Virginia], of Alexandria [Virginia], and of St. Sabastians [Spain], would without doubt have been re[en]acted at New Orleans, with all the unfeeling and brutal inhumanity of the savage foe with whom we are contending."[8] The implication was that the British planned to rape and plunder New Orleans if they captured the city. Shortly after the war, American soldiers in the front line at

Major General Edward Pakenham (1778–1815), the Duke of Wellington's brother-in-law, had served with distinction in the Peninsular War. Given command of the Gulf Coast theater, he was killed in the Battle of New Orleans. (Portrait by T. Heaphy. Fortier, *History of Louisiana*)

New Orleans appeared to support this claim when they reported that they "distinctly heard" British officers who were near their line "huzza their men on" with: "Mount the works! Take the city! *And you shall have money and women in plenty.*"[9]

Arsène Lacarrière Latour repeated the "beauty and booty" charge in 1816 because, he said, the British had never denied it.[10] The charge was made again by John Reid and John Eaton in a biography of Andrew Jackson in 1817 and then was amplified by Eaton in a revised edition that he put out in 1824.[11] By the 1820s, the idea had gained wide currency, not only from the Reid-Eaton biography but also from "The Hunters of Kentucky," a popular song of the day. (For more on this song, see Appendix A.) This view is still widely accepted today.

In fact, some modern writers, following the lead of Sir John Fortescue, Britain's pioneer military historian, have even suggested that New Orleans was targeted precisely because it offered such rich plunder. Although he never served in the British army, Fortescue had developed an infantryman's distrust of the Royal Navy, and he claimed that "prize-money had for nearly two centuries been the motive for all amphibious operations recommended by the Navy" and that "New Orleans was no exception." This was not a serious military operation, he concluded, but "a mere buccaneering adventure."[12]

Almost two decades after the battle, the surviving British senior officers who had taken part in the campaign issued a ringing denial. We "most unequivocally deny," they said, "that any such promise [to sack the city] was ever held out to the army, or that the watch word asserted to have been give[n] out, was ever issued."[13]

No city in North America had ever been sacked, and although some atrocities were committed during the War of 1812, no city was sacked. In 1812, Major General Isaac Brock did not threaten to sack Detroit if it did not surrender but merely warned that he might not be able to control his Indian allies once the battle had been joined. Similarly, the British did not sack Washington in 1814 even though they had to fight the Battle of Bladensburg to get to the city, and when they got there, they found no one to surrender the city and sustained sniper fire. Although they burned some of the public buildings, their behavior otherwise was restrained and commendable.

There is no credible evidence that the British planned to sack New Orleans if they had overrun American defenses in 1815. It is true that some Royal Navy officers had a keen eye for booty. And it is possible that some British troops may have joked about the sign and countersign and may even have established an informal recognition system based on these terms. However, the main purpose of the campaign was not to acquire plunder but to provide a diversion for Canada and to capture territory that might be used as a bargaining chip in the peace negotiations.[14]

British leaders had no objection to seizing public property and maritime goods, and they hoped that some inhabitants in New Orleans and the adjacent territory would cooperate with their occupation force. But Lord Bathurst specifically ordered Major General Pakenham "to observe the strictest Discipline" and "to respect the Lives and the Property of all those inclined to a peaceable deportment." In addition, Bathurst, eager to avoid interservice disputes, urged Pakenham to make sure that all prize goods were properly condemned, preferably in the High Court of Admiralty in Great Britain.[15]

British army officers were intolerant of just two things in a fellow officer: (1) showing cowardice in the face of the enemy, or (2) losing control over subordinates.[16] They were no more likely to tolerate widespread pillage or the abuse of private citizens in New Orleans than they had in Washington. In fact, in the Peninsular War, Pakenham had served as the commander of the military police and was charged with enforcing the Duke of Wellington's orders against pillage. By the time he arrived at New Orleans, Pakenham had developed a reputation as a fierce enemy of plunder. At New Orleans, he was undoubtedly prepared to use Redcoats against Redcoats to ensure an orderly occupation and to prevent widespread looting.[17]

***What Was Jean Laffite's Contribution?*** One of the most colorful figures associated with the War of 1812 is Jean Laffite, who would be little known today had he not joined forces with the United States in the Battle of New Orleans. Laffite (sometimes spelled Lafitte) has been variously portrayed as a gentle-

man and bon vivant; a statesman and patriot; a merchant and entrepreneur; a privateersman and filibusterer; an outlaw and pirate; and a smuggler and spy. It might be argued that he was all these things, but his reasons for joining the American cause have often been misunderstood and his contribution to the American victory has been exaggerated.

Laffite's early years are a mystery. He was apparently born in France around 1782 and came to New Orleans with his brother Pierre sometime after 1803. Prior to the War of 1812, the Laffites smuggled goods and slaves into New Orleans from the islands in Barataria Bay some 40 miles south of the Crescent City. The goods were brought to Barataria by privateers using dubious French and Spanish commissions to prey on ships in the Caribbean. Their captures were sometimes so indiscriminate that they amounted to little more than piracy. As the middlemen in this traffic, the Laffites developed close ties with merchants and local officials in New Orleans. "In the streets of New Orleans," said Arsène Lacarrière Latour, "it was usual for traders to give and receive orders for purchasing goods at Barataria, with as little secrecy as similar orders are given for Philadelphia or New-York."[18]

Jean Laffite (1782?–1823?) played a modest role in the American victory at New Orleans but the colorful pirate has enjoyed a larger-than-life reputation ever since. No contemporary portrait of Laffite is known to exist. This sketch was drawn some years after Laffite's death by a man who claimed to have worked for him in 1819. (Sketch by Lacassinier. Galveston *Daily News,* September 19, 1926)

By the fall of 1814, the Laffites' smuggling had become so notorious that U.S. officials threatened to break up their operation. At this point, the British tried to entice Jean Laffite into service. What did they offer? Not $30,000, as Laffite later claimed, but rather a captain's commission (probably in the Colonial Marines) and land grants for Laffite and his men after the war was over.[19] Laffite, however, decided to throw his lot in with the United States, and he remained firm even though an American military force destroyed his Baratarian base in mid-September.

Why did Laffite prefer the United States over Great Britain? Although his decision has sometimes been portrayed as statesmanlike and patriotic, it probably reflected his disdain for the British (he was, after all, French) and, even more, a shrewd and pragmatic assessment of how best to serve his own interests. Betting that the Americans would win the battle or at least control the region after the war was over, Laffite realized that cooperating with the U.S. offered the best chance of escaping prosecution and recovering property that had been seized in the raid on his base.[20]

Although Andrew Jackson considered the Baratarians "hellish banditti," influential locals persuaded him to accept Laffite's help.[21] Laffite fully cooperated with the Americans, although he did not, as is often claimed, give Jackson a huge cache of artillery and shot. The Baratarians had lost their naval guns in the American raid, they were mostly small-caliber weapons, and none was used against the British.[22] Laffite did turn over 7,500 flints to Jackson, and he shared his intimate knowledge of the geography of the lower Delta, which was useful for gathering intelligence.

How important was the contribution of Jean Laffite and the Baratarians to the American victory at New Orleans? It was modest and probably not decisive. Jackson used the Laffite brothers as guides and messengers, and those Baratarians who volunteered for service were put to work on the warships in the river. They also manned two of the eight batteries in Jackson's line during the main battle and helped defend Fort St. Philip when it was later bombarded by the British. But no more than 100 Baratarians served, and they constituted only about 2 percent of Jackson's force. Although Pierre Laffite performed some useful staff duties for Jackson during the main battle, there is no evidence that his more famous brother was anywhere near the action that day or that he took part in, or contributed materially to, any of the other battles in the campaign.[23]

Jean Laffite's contribution in the campaign has been exaggerated and that of his brother largely ignored. In his general orders recognizing those who had contributed to his victory, Jackson praised the Laffite brothers equally and did not mention any fighting they might have done. He simply said: "The brothers Laffite have exhibited the same courage and fidelity."[24]

What accounts for Jean Laffite's inflated reputation? Laffite knew how to toot his own horn, and he was not above embellishment. His reputation also has benefited from a memoir attributed to him that greatly exaggerates the contribution of Laffite and the Baratarians to the victory at New Orleans.[25] This work, which surfaced in the 1950s, is almost surely spurious and certainly inaccurate, and yet some historians have treated it as both authentic and reliable.[26] Another reason for Laffite's reputation is the simple appeal of his story. The notion that a gentleman pirate and smuggler might have contributed to the spectacular American victory at New Orleans has been too much for filmmakers, novelists, and historians to resist. Even the National Park Service has succumbed. In 1978 the Park Service named the New Orleans battleground and the other sites that it manages in Louisiana (20,000 acres in all) the Jean Lafitte National Historical Park and Preserve.[27]

**What Role Did Bales of Cotton Play in Jackson's Lines?** It is sometimes said that Jackson built his defensive lines out of mud and cotton bales. This is an exaggeration. Cotton bales were indeed used underneath the gun platforms to prevent them from sinking into the mud. They were also used in the main line around the embrasures through which the guns fired, but when some of these ignited in an artillery exchange several days before the main battle, they were removed. Cotton bales played only a small role in Jackson's line.[28]

**Did Riflemen Win the Battle?** Another widely repeated myth is that American riflemen played a major role in the U.S. victory at New Orleans. This view was propagated after the war by a popular song, "The Hunters of Kentucky." (For details, see Appendix A.) Although snipers did annoy the British throughout the campaign, the role they played in the main battle was decidedly subordinate.

Riflemen opened up when the British got within range, roughly 300 yards, but most were unable to take aim at any target because the smoke was too thick. In fact, many did not actually look over the defensive works but simply held their weapons above them and fired. The men with rifles probably did less damage than those with muskets, who were far more numerous. Moreover, the eight batteries of heavy guns that anchored Jackson's line probably did more damage than all the small arms combined, and they were joined by another battery of naval guns on the opposite shore that fired on the British flank. An examination of the location of the various British units on the battlefield done by Donald E. Graves shows that those with the heaviest casualties were in front of the American guns, not American riflemen. The British sustained many of their casualties long before they got within small arms range.[29]

*What Uniform Did the 93rd Regiment Wear?* Contrary to some depictions, the 93rd Regiment of Foot, the Scottish Highlander unit at New Orleans that was cut to pieces as it marched diagonally across the battlefield, did not wear kilts. Rather the men in this unit wore trousers.[30]

*How Close Did the British Come to Victory?* Despite the one-sided outcome of the Battle of New Orleans, some contemporaries, as well as some scholars, have suggested that the British were close to victory and could have won. The most credible argument is that Pakenham should have delayed his main attack until Thornton had secured the west bank and turned the American guns on Jackson's main line. But this would have forced Pakenham to withdraw his men, many of whom had advanced to vulnerable forward positions, and might have given Jackson time to launch a counterstrike on the west bank. It also would have meant that Pakenham's main attack would be conducted across an open field in broad daylight with the enemy on alert.

Although Thornton might have annoyed Jackson's line and perhaps degraded his firepower, the main British force still would have faced the same long odds: defeating an army of equal strength that was behind fortifications, supported by superior artillery, and under the firm control of an able commander. Even if Thornton's support had enabled the main British force to achieve a breakthrough, it probably would not have changed the outcome of the battle. The exposed British army lost so many officers that the command structure was effectively shattered. Hence it would have been difficult, if not impossible, to exploit any breach in Jackson's line. Moreover, unlike the British, who had committed their reserves, Jackson still had his own reserves available for service.[31]

The point is not that the British army was irrevocably doomed on that fateful day. Rather it is merely to suggest that to win the British needed more than the sort of help that Thornton's force could offer from the west bank. For its officer corps to remain functional, the British army needed a lot more luck than it got. The British were never close to victory, and it would have taken better planning and execution as well as exceptional luck to change the outcome of the battle.

***What Would a British Victory Have Meant?*** It is sometimes said that if the British had won at New Orleans, they would have refused to give up the city and instead would have abandoned the peace treaty. However, the British sent their instrument of ratification to the United States on the same ship that carried the American copy of the treaty. Far from contemplating any changes in the agreement, the British actually feared that the United States might seek revisions. Anthony St. John Baker, the minor British functionary who carried the treaty to the United States, was instructed to agree to suspend hostilities only if the United States ratified the agreement unconditionally. It seems inconceivable that Baker would have continued the war on his own authority even if the British had won a major victory at New Orleans.

Some historians have made much of the fact that the British government questioned the legality of the Louisiana Purchase and authorized Major General Pakenham to establish temporary government if he captured the territory. According to this argument, the British could retain Louisiana without violating the peace treaty because they were bound by the terms of the agreement to restore only American territory, and in their view Louisiana was still Spanish.

This argument is not credible. In the peace negotiations at Ghent, the British did indeed challenge the legality of the Louisiana Purchase. They also criticized the U.S. for its designs on Florida and Canada and for dispossessing the Indians. They did this to prove that the U.S. had long evinced "a spirit of territorial aggrandizement."[32] Their aim was not to force the U.S. to give up ill-gotten territorial gains in the South, but to build a case for concessions in the North that would enable them to better protect their Canadian provinces and Indian allies.

By late 1814 British leaders were almost as eager for peace as American leaders, and there is no evidence that they would permit the fate of Louisiana to get in the way. The prime minister, Lord Liverpool, told George Canning how relieved he was to end the American war. "You know how anxious I was," he said, "that we should get out of this war as soon as we could do so with honour." Liverpool claimed that Wellington agreed. The Iron Duke "was particularly solicitous for peace" once he became convinced that the British could "take and hold" no important territory except New Orleans, "and this settlement is one of the most unhealthy in any part of America."[33]

The British had already launched their policy of accommodating the young republic in the interest of promoting trade and friendship, and there is no hint in any British government document of any plans to hold on to Louisiana after the decision for peace was made. Like Fort Mackinac, Fort Niagara, Fort Bowyer, and the Maine coast, any captured territory in Louisiana, including New Orleans, would have been restored at the end of the war. To have done otherwise would have killed any prospect for an accord and probably led to a renewal of war, something the war-weary British government was eager to avoid.[34]

***How Decisive Was the Battle?*** The Battle of New Orleans is often portrayed as the most decisive battle of the war, and over the years exaggerated claims have been made on its behalf. It has been credited with reinforcing plantation slavery, dooming Indian resistance, solidifying American control over the region, and paving the way for further expansion to the south and west. But these claims rest mainly on the assumption that the British would have retained control of at least part of Louisiana if they had won the battle, and this was hardly likely.

The Battle of New Orleans was decisive but only in this theater and only because it put an end to a major British threat to New Orleans and the region. The battle occurred too late to have any broader effect on the outcome of the war. If it was a defining moment in American history, it was not because it changed the course of the war or fundamentally shaped the future of the region, but because it boosted American self-confidence and enabled Republicans to forge the myth of American victory. In the wake of this battle, the war could hardly be mentioned in public in the United States without evoking proud memories of how a motley American army had decisively defeated the very troops who had ended the great Napoleon's reign in Europe.

**What Was the Last Battle of the War?** The Battle of New Orleans is sometimes presented as the last battle of the war, but there were several engagements after this. More than a month later, on February 11 (the day the peace treaty reached the United States), the same British force that had been defeated at New Orleans compelled the surrender of Fort Bowyer on Mobile Bay after light skirmishing.[35] This, however, was not the last battle.

On February 20, 1815 (four days after the United States had ratified the peace treaty), the U.S. Frigate *Constitution* (52), cruising near the Madeira

The U.S. Sloop *Peacock*, commanded by Master Commandant Lewis Warrington, took part in the last hostile action of the war in June, 1815, in the Indian Ocean. Refusing to believe word from the East India cruiser *Nautilus* that the war was over, Warrington fired on the British ship, killing and wounding a number of its crew. (Chapelle, *American Sailing Navy*)

Islands in the eastern Atlantic, defeated H.M. Ship *Cyane* (33) and H.M. Ship *Levant* (21) in one of the finer tactical triumphs of the Age of Sail.[36] Four days after this engagement, six barges dispatched by Rear Admiral George Cockburn up St. Marys River in southern Georgia sustained about 30 casualties from Americans firing on them from both sides of the river.[37]

On March 16, 1815, the British rocket ship H.M. Sloop *Erebus* (26) fired on U.S. Gunboat #168 off the coast of Georgia.[38] A week later, on March 23, the U.S. Sloop *Hornet* (20), cruising in the South Atlantic before news of peace had spread to those waters, defeated H.M. Sloop *Penguin* (19), causing extensive casualties.[39] Two months later, on May 24, a group of Sauk and Fox Indians led by Black Hawk (who was seeking vengeance for the murder of his adopted son) skirmished with a detachment of U.S. Army Rangers and Missouri militia northwest of St. Louis near present-day Old Monroe, Missouri, in an engagement known as the Battle of the Sinkhole.[40] But even this was not the last battle.

On June 30, almost four and a half months after the peace treaty was ratified, in the Indian Ocean near Sumatra, the U.S. Sloop *Peacock* (22), under Master Commandant Lewis Warrington, encountered the East India cruiser *Nautilus* (14), Lieutenant Charles Boyce commanding. Refusing to believe Boyce's hail that the war was over, Warrington demanded that the *Nautilus* haul down its colors. When Boyce refused, *Peacock* opened fire, which the *Nautilus* returned. After suffering 15 casualties without doing any material damage to the *Peacock,* the *Nautilus* surrendered. The battle was one-sided, and Warrington showed bad judgment in initiating the action. Boyce was seriously injured in the exchange, and two weeks later his right leg had to be amputated.[41] Although a British writer in the nineteenth century claimed that Congress gave Boyce a life pension, this appears to be untrue.[42]

The *Peacock–Nautilus* engagement was the last battle of the War of 1812, although some Indian tribes that were either Great Britain's allies or co-belligerents remained at war and continued to conduct predatory raids in the West. The last of these tribes, the Otoes and the Poncas, did not make peace with the United States until June 24–25, 1817.[43]

## THE TREATY OF GHENT

**The Peace Negotiations.** The three men who shaped British policy in Europe and North America in 1814—Prime Minister Liverpool, Foreign Secretary Castlereagh, and the Duke of Wellington—showed remarkable vision and foresight. In Europe, despite the fact that Revolutionary and Napoleonic France had been responsible for enormous death and destruction, it was not in Britain's interest to crush or dismantle its ancient foe. Hence at the Congress of Vienna, as long as they could preserve Britain's vital interests and maintain a balance of power on the Continent, British leaders favored a peace that everyone, even the French, could live with.[44]

British leaders showed the same judicious restraint in their negotiations with the United States. Although anxious to provide better security for Canada and their Indian allies, they had no wish to prolong the War of 1812, nor did they seek a vindictive peace. Still, achieving their aims in negotiations with the unbending peace envoys who represented the United States was no easy task. As a result, the peace negotiations dragged on longer than anyone had anticipated, and the British came away empty-handed.[45]

Once the Orders-in-Council were repealed in 1812, impressment was the only obstacle to peace. Since the British were unwilling to make concessions on this issue, the war continued for another two and a half years. Although the British rejected a Russian mediation offer made in early 1813, they subsequently offered to negotiate directly with the United States. But they were in no hurry because Napoleon's capitulation in the spring of 1814 had ended the European war and put them in the driver's seat in the American war. Time was now unmistakably on their side. As they continued to shift ever more men and material from the Old World to the New, the military balance was tipping decisively in their favor.

By the time the peace negotiations finally got under way in August 1814 in Ghent (in present-day Belgium), the United States had dropped its demands on impressment and was willing to restore peace on the basis of the *status quo ante bellum* (returning to conditions as they were before the war). As their price for peace, however, the British now demanded territorial concessions in present-day Minnesota and Maine, the establishment of an Indian barrier state or reservation in the Old Northwest, the American demilitarization of the Great Lakes, and an end to American fishing privileges in Canadian waters.

The American envoys were astonished at these demands. They naively believed that the United States had the right to declare war on Great Britain, try to conquer Canada, and in the event of failure, to call off the war without paying a price. When President Madison received the British terms in the fall of 1814, he shrewdly published them. This shored up support for the war, although most Federalists not unreasonably insisted that the British terms offered a fair basis for negotiation.

The American envoys were so stunned by the British terms that they considered peace unlikely and assumed that the negotiations would soon break up. Although the mood of the American delegation was gloomy, conventional wisdom holds that Henry Clay, an inveterate gambler, thought that the British might be bluffing. Clay was pessimistic about the prospects for peace, but he realized that a rupture over the British terms was likely to unite American opinion and increase opposition to the war in Great Britain. Perhaps, he suggested, the British were "attempting an experiment on us"—dragging out

The Treaty of Ghent was signed on December 24, 1814. At the center of this picture, the two delegation heads, William Gambier on the left and John Quincy Adams on the right, are shaking hands. On the far left is Anthony St. John Baker, secretary to the British commission, who brought the ratified British copy of the treaty to the U.S. (Lithograph of painting by A. Forestier. Library and Archives Canada)

the negotiations in the hope of striking a decisive blow against the United States that would significantly improve their bargaining position. If this were the case, Clay suggested, then there was still hope that the British "would ultimately abandon their pretensions."[46]

Clay's hunch was correct. The British were indeed hoping that military gains would improve their bargaining power, and they were buoyed by the news that Washington had been taken. However, this was quickly followed by news that they had been rebuffed at Baltimore and Plattsburgh.

As a result, the British gave up their initial demands and suggested that peace be restored on the basis of *uti possidetis,* which meant that each side would keep whatever territory it held. If this were acceded to, the British would retain Fort Niagara, Fort Mackinac, and much of Maine, while the United States would keep Fort Erie and Fort Amherstburg. The British hoped to retain Fort Niagara (which would give them control over the mouth of the Niagara River), Fort Mackinac (which commanded the upper lakes), and northern Maine (to facilitate communication between Quebec and Halifax) but to exchange eastern Maine for forts Erie and Amherstburg.[47] But the Americans still refused to budge.

At this point, the British government asked the Duke of Wellington to accept the American command. Although the Iron Duke agreed, he suggested that what the British needed was "not a General, or General officers and troops, but a naval superiority on the Lakes." Without this, he claimed, there was little hope of success and little justification for making territorial demands on the United States.[48] The great man's opinion gave the British government the cover it needed to jettison its last territorial demands. As a result, the British caved in and agreed to peace on the basis of the *status quo ante bellum.*

British leaders showed good judgment in retreating from their successive demands. Failure on the battlefield made them more vulnerable to criticism. Domestic foes attacked the ministry not only for the way it was managing the war but also for the heavy tax burden that the conflict entailed. Another year of warfare was sure to be costly. Developments on the Continent also played a role. Although Napoleon's return for the Hundred Days was still several months off, there were already rumblings of discontent in France that worried British officials. In addition, negotiations for a general peace at the Congress of Vienna had been rocky, and the American war had become a burden and an embarrassment to the British. "The negotiations at Vienna are not proceeding in the way we could wish," said Lord Liverpool, "and this consideration itself was deserving of some weight in deciding the question of peace with America."[49] Writing from Vienna, Lord Castlereagh congratulated Liverpool on "being released from the millstone of an American war," and added: "It has produced the greatest possible sensation here, and will, I have no doubt, enter into the calculations of our opponents."[50]

**Did the War Annul the Paris Peace Treaty of 1783?** Some scholars have suggested that the outbreak of war in 1812 abrogated the terms of the peace treaty signed by Great Britain and the United States at the end of the American Revolution. Had the War of 1812 been a typical European war, all previous treaties between the belligerents would have been suspended pending the outcome of the latest conflict.[51] Only those treaty clauses that were expressly exempt would have remained in force. But since it was rare for any belligerent to wish to upset long established settlements, it was commonplace for each new peace treaty to explicitly reaffirm the older ones.[52]

At the beginning of the negotiations at Ghent, the British government took the position that the recent hostilities annulled all previous Anglo-American treaties.[53] The American envoys objected, claiming that the War of 1812 had no effect on the Paris Peace Treaty. Because of its unique nature establishing American independence, the Americans argued that this treaty was a "permanent compact, not liable, like ordinary treaties, to be abrogated by a subsequent war between the parties."[54]

At issue was whether the United States would continue to enjoy a lucrative fishing concession in British waters off Canada that the 1783 treaty guaranteed. This concession was paired with another far less valuable one, the British liberty to use the Mississippi River. The British hoped to cancel the fishing concession, which they called a "privilege," unless they gained something of comparable value in return. The Americans, on the other hand, hoped to retain the fishing concession, which they called a "right" or "liberty," without offering an equivalent.

In the end, the British gave in, and neither the 1783 treaty nor the two concessions it guaranteed were mentioned in the Treaty of Ghent. Although in principle the British could still maintain that the War of 1812 had cancelled both concessions, in private they conceded that having raised the issue without securing any clause in the new treaty meant that in practice the concessions continued.[55] And this proved to be the case.

After the war British use of the Mississippi gradually lapsed because the fur trade was already receding, and canals and later railroads would change transportation patterns in Canada. Those British subjects in central or western Canada who wanted to export furs or any other goods found it cheaper to use Canadian transportation routes than to send their cargo overland to the headwaters of the Mississippi and thence downriver to the Gulf of Mexico. The fishing concession, by contrast, remained valuable. Although the United States and Great Britain negotiated a new deal on the issue in 1818, it remained a source of recurring controversy until the two powers agreed to binding arbitration in 1909 and then established the Permanent Mixed Fishery Commission in 1912.[56]

**Why Did the U.S. Drop Impressment?** The semi-official Washington *National Intelligencer* maintained that the United States dropped its demands on impressment because the end of the war in Europe had rendered the issue moot. This is nonsense. Secretary of State James Monroe conceded to the American envoys that the administration had to drop impressment because the chances of winning concessions on this issue (which in truth were never very strong) had vanished altogether with Napoleon's defeat.[57]

Although willing to give up on impressment to secure peace, the United States did not completely abandon its claims. For more than a quarter of a century after the war, the U.S. government periodically pressed the British to give up the practice. The British were willing, even eager, to make some concessions to foster accord, but they were unwilling to give up the practice altogether or to make the kind of concessions that would satisfy the United States. Fortunately, they had little need to resort to impressment after 1815, and by the 1850s they had instituted a five-year enlistment period and other reforms that ensured a sufficient number of volunteers for the Royal Navy. Nevertheless, they never formally gave up the right to impress British seamen into service, even when they were found on neutral vessels.[58]

**The Indian Barrier State.** The most significant British demand in the peace negotiations called for the creation of an Indian reservation in the Old Northwest. This reservation would embrace a third of Ohio, half of Minnesota, and almost all of Indiana, Illinois, Michigan, and Wisconsin. The American envoys claimed that this would deprive the United States of a third of its territory. Although this claim has often been repeated, the land in question comprised only about 250,000 square miles or roughly 15 percent of the landmass of the United States in 1814. Living in the territory were roughly 100,000 whites and perhaps 40,000 Indians (about twice the figure usually given).[59]

It is important to keep in mind that the British peace envoys clearly indicated that the size of the reservation was subject to negotiation. But they nonetheless misrepresented their government's position on the issue in two ways. First, they mistakenly presented the demand for a reservation as a *sine qua non,* when in fact the British government was willing to consider other ways of protecting its Indian allies. Secondly, although the British government wished only to prevent Americans from purchasing land in the Indian barrier state (thus tacitly acceding to the acquisition of land in "defensive" wars), the British envoys insisted that the United States refrain from acquiring territory "by purchase or otherwise."[60] In short, Great Britain's interest in protecting its Indian allies was far less determined than the British envoys imagined.[61]

**When Did the War End?** In Europe the normal practice was to provide for an end to hostilities whenever a peace treaty was signed. As soon as official word reached the front or fronts, the fighting actually ended. If the battlefields were nearby or if the opposing armies were not actually engaged, there might not be any fighting after the treaty was signed.

Contrary to popular belief, the signing of the Treaty of Ghent on December 24, 1814, did not end the War of 1812. Why not? Because the British refused to agree to the usual provision in European peace treaties. On three different occasions—in 1794, 1803, and 1806—either the president or the Senate had insisted on changes in a treaty that American agents had renegotiated in Europe. The British feared that this might happen again. If it did, they might find themselves in the awkward position of having ended hostilities after signing a treaty that the United States refused to ratify without changes. The British would then have no choice but to agree to the changes or to restart the war.

At first the British proposed that hostilities end when the two sides had exchanged ratifications of the treaty. When the American delegation pointed out that this could needlessly prolong the war if the British instrument of ratification were lost at sea (as was the case with the Jay Treaty), the British agreed to halt hostilities when each side had ratified the agreement. Hence, Article 1 stipulated: "All hostilities both by sea and land shall cease as soon as this Treaty shall have been ratified by both parties."[62] When the two sides exchanged instruments of ratification, the treaty would become binding.[63]

Anthony St. John Baker, the secretary to the British peace delegation, hurried the treaty from Ghent to London, arriving on December 26. The following day the Prince Regent ratified the agreement, and Baker headed for Portsmouth to carry the instrument of ratification to America.[64] Baker sailed on H.M. Sloop *Favourite* (or *Favorite*), which also carried the American copy of the treaty. The ship arrived in New York on February 11, 1815, and the American copy of the treaty reached Washington three days later. On February 15, Madison submitted the treaty to the Senate, and the following day the Senate voted its unanimous approval.[65]

Contrary to popular belief, the Senate does not ratify treaties. Rather it is the president who does so, although he must have the consent of two-thirds of the Senate. Thus the treaty was actually ratified later on February 16, when Madison signed the agreement in the Octagon House, which had become his temporary residence after the White House was burned. Baker arrived in Washington at 8:00 p.m. on February 17, and three hours later he and Secretary of State James Monroe exchanged instruments of ratification.[66] This completed the diplomatic process for restoring peace.

Did American ratification on February 16, 1815, end the war? Yes and no. Although formally and officially both sides agreed that the war was now over, hostilities still continued because it took time to disseminate the news to the various fronts, some of which were quite remote. Recognizing this, the delegates at Ghent had provided in the treaty for restoring captures at sea only if they were made a certain number of days after ratification, ranging from 12 days in the western Atlantic to 120 days in distant parts of the world.[67] Because of slow communications, there were some minor battles and skirmishes fought after February 16, the last of which was the clash between the U.S. Sloop *Peacock* and the East India cruiser *Nautilus* on June 30, 1815. This was the last hostile action of the War of 1812.

## WINNERS AND LOSERS

**Estimating Casualties.** By European standards, the War of 1812 never amounted to much. The armies and battles were a lot smaller, and so, too, were the battlefield losses. Casualties in the principal battles usually measured in the hundreds. In the Napoleonic Wars, by contrast, they measured in the thousands or even the tens of thousands. But these raw figures are deceptive. Measured as a proportion of the North American population, or of the armies engaged, the casualties in the War of 1812 were much more severe. At Lundy's Lane, the bloodiest battle of the war, the losses were comparable to those of the worst battles of the Napoleonic Wars.

It is not easy to determine the casualties in wars before the twentieth century. Those reported killed might have deserted or might have been captured, while some reported as wounded later died from their wounds. There was little attempt to keep records of those who were disabled or killed by accident or disease, and camp diseases took a particularly heavy toll before the advent of modern medicine.

The problem of coming up with reliable numbers for the War of 1812 is further compounded by the participation of Indians (who usually did not record their casualties) and militia (who might serve for a short tour and then return home with a debilitating or fatal camp disease). All of these problems not only cast considerable doubt on official figures, which grossly understate actual losses, but also make it difficult to arrive at a reasonable estimate of those losses. Thus, the figures presented below must be taken as nothing more than very rough estimates.

***American Losses.*** Official documents suggest that 528,000 men served in the land forces of the United States during the war: 57,000 regulars, 10,000 volunteers, 3,000 rangers, and 458,000 militia.[68] Since the number of regulars was probably undercounted, the total is probably closer to 540,000.[69] Another 20,000 served in the navy or marines.[70] A much larger number, perhaps 40,000, served on the 515 privateers that the United States commissioned during the war.[71] This would put the total number who served for the United States in the war at around 600,000.

The number killed in battle is usually given as 2,260.[72] To this figure, we must add the 5,240 enlisted men, non-commissioned officers, and musicians in the U.S. Army that John Stagg's analysis suggests died from accident or disease.[73] This would put the total at 7,500. We must also add those civilians who perished in Indian raids in the West, privateersmen who were killed in action or died from accident or disease, and naval personnel and militia who died from accident or disease. The number of militia who died is especially important in this tally because citizen soldiers accounted for more than 75 percent of all those who served, and undoubtedly a sizeable number contracted a camp disease from which they died after being discharged from service. In all, one might reasonably guess that 15,000 Americans died from all causes as a direct result of the war.[74]

This figure may seem high, especially with official battle deaths making up only 15 percent of the total. But it must be remembered that before the twentieth century medical knowledge was primitive and the weapons of war inefficient. As a result, the United States suffered more deaths from disease than from enemy fire in every war prior to World War II. Penicillin and improved weapons irrevocably reversed the balance in that war.

**British and Canadian Losses.** Unfortunately, we do not know how many men served in the land and naval forces of Great Britain in the War of 1812, nor do we know how many British or Canadians served in privateers. We do know that British regular troop strength in North America peaked at 48,000 in late 1814 and that there were an additional 4,000 provincials in service, although the total number of regular and provincial troops who served in the war was somewhat higher.[75] It is impossible to distinguish naval personnel serving in this war from those serving elsewhere in the world because even in remote waters they probably spent a portion of their time chasing or engaging American privateers or warships. Still, it seems reasonable to assume that the British had fewer men engaged on land than the United States and more engaged at sea. Because the British called far fewer militia into the field, the total number of men engaged by the British was undoubtedly significantly smaller than the total engaged by the United States.

Donald E. Graves has calculated that in Upper and Lower Canada 2,733 British soldiers in regular and provincial units died in combat or perished from accident or disease between June 1812 and December 1814.[76] A few more undoubtedly perished from accident or disease before peace was restored in February 1815. We must also add any British soldiers who perished in combat or from accident or disease elsewhere in British North America, such as the Chesapeake Bay (which was particularly unhealthy during the summer campaigning season) and the Gulf Coast, and any militiamen who perished in combat or from accident or disease (including any who contracted a camp disease and later died at home). Naval and marine personnel who perished in combat or from accident or disease must also be added to the total. The Royal Navy lost about 5,000 men a year during its peak levels in the last stages of the Napoleonic Wars. If we reckon that 15 percent of the total was in the American war, then another 2,250 must be added to the number of British deaths in the War of 1812. And to this total must be added any privateersman who perished in combat or from accident or disease as well as a few civilians who were killed in combat. A reasonable guess of all those who perished on the British side as a direct result of the war might be 10,000.

**Indian Losses.** Although figures on native casualties are elusive, the information that we have suggests that the Indians fared badly in the war. We know that in their war with Andrew Jackson in the Old Southwest, the Creeks (who started as co-belligerents before becoming British allies) suffered comparatively large losses—at least 1,500 killed.[77] In the North, total Indian losses were probably no more than 1,000.[78]

Although Indians did not normally stay in the field long enough to suffer from the usual camp diseases, they had less immunity to those diseases that they did contract from whites or blacks. Donald E. Graves has suggested that starvation was the biggest killer of Indians, followed by disease. Exposure also probably took a toll. Out of a population of 76,000 Indians (warriors and non-warriors alike) who participated in the war, Graves estimates that around 10,000 men, women, and children died from all war-related causes. Even if this estimate is too high, and the Indians suffered only 7,500 deaths, their losses were still little short of catastrophic.[79]

**Who Won the War?** Many wars produce a clear result, but not the War of 1812. Reflecting this ambiguity, scholars assessing the outcome have reached very different conclusions. In the nineteenth century, the acerbic Henry Adams appeared to argue that by signing a disgraceful treaty both Great Britain and the United States had lost the war, while more recently Canadian Wesley Turner has suggested that both Canada and the United States won.[80] Some American scholars have argued that the U.S. won.[81] Some British and Canadians have insisted that the U.S. lost.[82] In between, one finds the most widely-held view that neither side won and that the war ended in a draw.[83] In the colorful language of John R. Elting, the contest ended in "what westerners later would call a 'Mexican standoff.'"[84] While this may be true in a strictly military sense, it understates British and Canadian success, overstates American success, and ignores the fate of the Indians.[85]

Who really won? There are actually five groups of participants that must be considered: (1) The United States, (2) Great Britain, (3) Britain's North American colonies (that is, Canada), (4) Indians living in the United States, and (5) Indians living in Canada. The United States initiated the war, while Great Britain and its colonies fought a defensive war. Most of the Indians on both sides of the border sided with the British and were also fighting a defensive war.

Battles and campaigns frequently offer a reliable guide to the outcome of a war but only if they are significant and decisive enough. The British surrender at Yorktown (1781), the Allied triumph at Leipzig (1813), and the American capture of Mexico City (1848) all either ended a war or clearly foreshadowed its outcome.

The War of 1812, however, did not produce any battles of this character. It produced only battles that turned the tide in a particular theater, and even then the result was often not lasting. Moreover, the only theaters that truly mattered were those on the Canadian-American frontier, and both sides recognized this. Fully two-thirds of all the regular troops who served in the war were deployed along the Canadian-American border.[86] However spectacular operations elsewhere might be, contemporaries understood that they were subordinate to the campaigns in the North.

In the Old Northwest, the fall of Mackinac and Detroit in the summer of 1812 gave the British and their Indian allies command of the region, but only until the autumn of 1813, when the American victories on Lake Erie and at the Thames reversed the outcome. On the Niagara front, the British victory at Queenston Heights effectively ended the American campaign in 1812, but with the seizure of Fort George in early 1813 the Americans recovered their momentum, only to lose it again in late 1813 when they withdrew from Fort George. The British not only re-occupied Fort George; they captured Fort Niagara and devastated settlements on the American side of the river. On the St. Lawrence and Lake Champlain fronts, the British victories at Crysler's Farm and Châteauguay ended the American threat in 1813, but Britain's own threat to upper New York ended with the defeat of Captain George Downey's squadron on Lake Champlain in 1814.

In the Chesapeake, the British capture and burning of Washington was little more than a raid, and the failed attack on Baltimore was similar in nature. Even if this attack had succeeded, the British planned to do nothing more than seize government property and military stores and confiscate or destroy maritime property. On the Gulf Coast, even the stunning American triumph at New Orleans was of only limited strategic significance. Although decisive in this theater, the battle occurred too late in the war to carry any broader significance.

Although no key battles determined the outcome of the war, there were two crucial battles that shaped the future for Indians. The Battle of the Thames in 1813 broke the back of Tecumseh's confederacy, not only because the great Indian leader perished in the engagement but also because the British were driven from the region. This made most of the tribes in the Old Northwest amenable to peace with the United States. Similarly, the Battle of Horseshoe Bend in 1814 shattered the power of the Red Sticks in the Old Southwest and very nearly destroyed the Creek nation. Although these battles suggest how badly the Indians fared in the war, they obscure the different fate suffered by Indians living on the opposite sides of the border.

Is it fair to conclude that because the War of 1812 ended in a draw on the battlefield the conflict itself ended in a draw? Not necessarily. After all, using this same logic, one could argue that the Korean War and the War in Vietnam both ended in a draw, and yet the United States won the former (because it prevented the advance of communism) and lost the latter (because it failed to achieve the same end).

To determine who won the War of 1812, one must look beyond battles and campaigns. The best way to gauge success or failure in this war (as in most wars) is to look at the aims or objectives of the belligerents. In war, it matters less how armies and navies perform in battle than whether the participants achieve the aims for which they are contending.

The British and the Canadians are usually lumped together and simply referred to as "the British," but this is misleading. While this accurately reflects both their legal relationship and their common bond in the British Empire, their aims in the War of 1812, though similar, were not identical.

The overriding aim of the British in this period was to win their war against Napoleonic France on the Continent. Every other foreign policy objective took a back seat to this aim. As an island nation, Britain's lifeblood was its maritime trade and its bulwark was the Royal Navy. The British knew full well that their maritime policies in the Napoleonic Wars risked trouble with the United States, but they were unwilling to give up these policies because they considered them essential not just to their war effort in Europe but to their very survival as an independent nation. The stakes for Great Britain in the War of 1812, by contrast, were more modest. The British wanted to hold on to their North American colonies, but this was subordinate to defeating France.

For Canadians, on the other hand, what happened in America mattered more than what happened in Europe. Most Canadians considered the war in Europe important, but not as important as the war in America. Defeating the United States was the only way that people living in British North America could preserve their identity and remain part of the British Empire. Hence, for most Canadians this war had a higher priority.

Although there was obvious tension between British and Canadian aims during the war, it was the British government that decided where to deploy its military and naval assets. As colonists, people living in Canada had little voice in the matter. As it happened, the British never had to choose between victory in Europe and victory in America. They were able to achieve their aims in both wars. But even if they had lost Canada to the United States, the British probably would have bided their time until the war in Europe was over and then launched a major campaign to retake it.

Canada was the big winner in the War of 1812 because it resisted the American embrace, retained its British connection, and thus laid the foundation for its future independence and nationhood. Great Britain was also a winner because it achieved its aim of preserving Canada, although the British had somewhat less at stake in this matter than Canadians.

What about the United States? The young republic had won its first three wars—the American Revolution (1775–83), the Quasi-War (1798–1801), and the Tripolitan War (1801–05)—but the War of 1812 did not follow this pattern. The United States had declared war in 1812 mainly to force the British to make concessions on a broad range of maritime issues. The two principal ones were the Orders-in-Council and impressment. There were several lesser maritime issues as well: violations of territorial waters, breaches of the rules governing naval blockades, and definition of contraband.

Although the Orders-in-Council were rescinded about the same time that the United States declared war, the British never made any concessions on the other issues. In fact, the Treaty of Ghent did not mention any of the maritime issues that had caused the war. Since the United States had declared war to win concessions on these issues, it seems undeniable that the war represented a failure for American policymakers. In this sense, the United States lost the war.

Some writers have argued that the end of the war in Europe made the maritime issues irrelevant or that by simply fighting for these issues the United States guaranteed against future infringements. There is some merit to these arguments inasmuch as the issues did recede into the background during the ensuing period of European peace, and the British were careful not to impress any Americans during Napoleon's Hundred Days.[87] But the issues did not entirely disappear, and at least partly because of the ambiguity of the Ghent settlement, both sides after 1815 thought that a renewal of war was possible, perhaps even likely. It was not until the Treaty of Washington in 1871 that the war clouds finally dissipated.[88] Moreover, maritime issues very similar to those that caused the War of 1812—definition of contraband, right of search, and naval blockades—bedeviled Anglo-American relations as late as World War I.[89]

What about claims that the United States went to war to uphold national honor or to put an end to an economic depression in parts of the South or West? These issues did not stand on their own but were directly tied to the maritime issues. British practices on the high seas threatened American honor and American prosperity. The only way the United States could uphold its honor and promote its prosperity in the affected regions was to challenge British maritime practices. One might argue that even a failed attempt to confront British maritime practices could (and actually did) enhance American honor, but this seems a pretty thin argument for justifying the war.

What about the argument that the United States sought war to put an end to British influence over American Indians? In his war message, President Madison suggested that British influence might be responsible for Indian depredations in the Old Northwest, but this was the last issue he mentioned, almost an afterthought, and the language he used was tentative. He simply said that it was "difficult to account" for the Indian depredations "without connecting their hostility with that [British] influence."[90] Although this issue loomed large in the West, for most Americans it was a minor cause of the war.

How did the conquest of Canada figure into American war aims? Initially, attacking Canada was simply the easiest way to strike at Britain. There were some Republicans, especially in the West, who favored annexation, and this sentiment grew as the war progressed. But even if some Americans considered Canada an end rather than a means, this does not change the outcome of the war, for the United States was no more successful in conquering Canada that it was in winning concessions on the maritime issues.

It is true that the United States reaped a host of benefits from the war, and that some of these—promoting self-confidence and consensus, subduing the Indians, and winning greater respect abroad—might even be considered war aims. But they were decidedly minor and often ill-defined aims, hardly worth a major war. Moreover, most of these benefits did not depend upon the war but would have been realized in the fullness of time anyway. As a rising power, the United States clearly had time on its side, and just about every American knew it.

If the United States lost the War of 1812, so, too, did the Indians living in the United States. Their aim was to halt the westward movement and thus preserve their lands as well as their way of life (however much it might already be compromised by contact with government agents, missionaries, and traders). They failed to achieve these aims. Although the British initially demanded an Indian barrier state in the Old Northwest, in the end they abandoned their native allies just as they had in the Treaty of Paris in 1783 and the Jay Treaty of 1794.

The Treaty of Ghent called upon the United States to restore to the Indians "all the possessions, rights, and privileges which they may have enjoyed or been entitled to in one thousand eight hundred and eleven," before the eruption of hostilities at Tippecanoe.[91] This phrase was ambiguous and unenforceable. It bound the United States in no meaningful way, nor did it impede the relentless drive west nor the equally relentless dispossession of the Indians. It mattered not which side the Indians living in the United States had fought on, for the result was the same. Andrew Jackson set the pattern in 1814 in the Treaty of Fort Jackson, when he forced the Creeks, friend and foe alike, to cede more than 20,000,000 acres, which was over half their territory. Other tribes that had sided with the United States in the war, such as the Iroquois in New York and the Sandusky Seneca in Ohio, were also dispossessed of their lands. But this policy was not new. Pushing Indians westward dated back to the beginning of the colonial era and had been official policy as long as there had been a nation. The war simply gave this policy added momentum.

The Indians in Canada fared somewhat better. Their aim was also to halt American expansion and thus preserve their lands and way of life, and in achieving these objectives they had more success than their counterparts south of the border. Though most later came under pressure from the advance of white people, this pressure was never as intense as it was in the United States. As a result, Indians in Canada (despite heavy losses in the war) were better able to preserve their land and culture, although they, too, began a retreat to reservations and witnessed the steady loss of their traditional way of life.

So who won the War of 1812? The biggest winner was Canada; then came Great Britain; and then the Indians living in Canada. The biggest losers were the Indians living in the United States; after them came the United States itself, which (the glorious triumphs at sea, on the northern lakes, and at New Orleans notwithstanding) for the first time in its history lost a war.

**Who Won the Peace?** Because the United States had had to jettison all of its maritime demands, Henry Clay called the agreement reached at Ghent "a damned bad treaty" and predicted that the American envoys would "be subject to much reproach."[92] But he was wrong. Clay and his associates had served the United States well. Given the military balance in America, they had secured the best deal possible—certainly far better than Great Britain had anticipated and better than the United States had any right to expect when the negotiations began. Far from being an American failure, the peace negotiations must be rated an American success. The United States lost the war but won the peace.

**Could the U.S. Have Conquered Canada?** Many contemporaries in 1812 assumed that the United States could easily conquer Canada, and this view has never been challenged. Why, then, did the United States fail? Armchair generals have faulted the United States for pursuing a flawed strategy, for frittering away its resources in a pair of three-pronged campaigns in 1812 and 1813 that shifted the focus of operations too far west. All the British outposts in the west were supplied via the St. Lawrence River, and this waterway was commanded by Montreal and Quebec. Control of these two cities meant control of the St. Lawrence River, and this in turn meant control of most of British North America. According to this argument, then, the United States should have concentrated its forces against these cities.

This criticism is sound, but it ignores two realities: first, the pressure that the administration was under to take advantage of support and enthusiasm for the war in the West in order to end the Anglo-Indian menace there; second and more importantly, the state of the American military establishment and the difficulties inherent in waging a war of conquest in the dense and under-developed wilderness of North America.

Several considerations suggest that a even a large concentration of resources in the eastern theater would not have changed the outcome of the war. For one thing, after a decade of neglect the American military establishment was in a deplorable state. The army was undersized, inexperienced, badly led, and

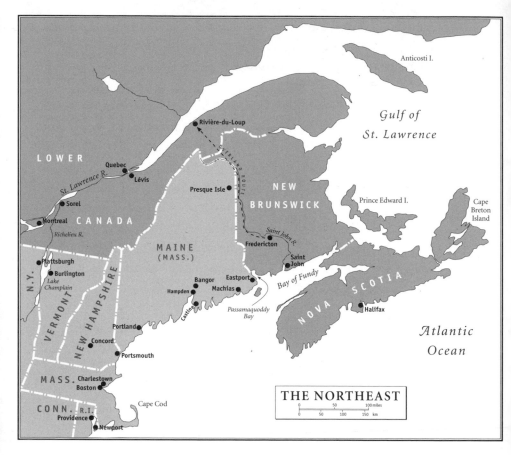

poorly trained. Nor could the militia provide much assistance. Most militiamen were sunshine soldiers, easily terrified at the prospect of bloodshed and unwilling to serve even a few miles across the border let alone deep in enemy territory. Moreover, the logistical problems of supporting operations across several hundred miles of wilderness were formidable if not insurmountable.

Montreal might have been taken. It had never been equipped with adequate defenses, and the Royal Navy could provide support with only its smaller warships because the St. Lawrence River was too shallow there for larger ships. But the conquest of Canada would never be complete without the fall of Quebec, and taking this city was another matter. There is no evidence that U.S. leaders gave much thought to why the British had succeeded in taking Quebec in 1759, or why Americans had failed in 1775.

The British had captured Quebec in 1759 only because of a favorable combination of circumstances. They had a larger and better army than the French, and they controlled the St. Lawrence River with a powerful fleet. Once the British got to the Plains of Abraham, the French decided to sally forth from their fortress and attack, both because they were short of food and needed to protect their supply line to the west and because Quebec's defenses in the rear were weak.[93]

Could the United States in 1812 have duplicated the British feat? Probably not. Given British naval power, Quebec could not be approached up the St. Lawrence from the Atlantic. Nor, given the impenetrable forests of Maine and New Brunswick, could it be easily approached overland from the south. The only feasible approach was via the traditional invasion route along Lake Champlain and the Richelieu River.

An invasion force following this route might take Montreal and then follow the St. Lawrence River to Quebec. But even if an American army got this far and even if it was adequately supplied, Quebec was unlikely to fall. It was perched on a cliff that made it difficult to assault. Various British governors groused about its defenses, but the incremental improvements made over the years had rendered them formidable. Although a citadel or inner stronghold was not constructed until after the war, the walls facing the Plains of Abraham had been rebuilt, and a powerful battery had been erected that commanded the south side of the St. Lawrence.[94]

In defending Quebec, the British had other advantages. The Royal Navy could dispatch its largest ships up the St. Lawrence to provide naval support in the summer and fall, and an American campaign launched later in the season would be fighting the clock, first to avoid a long winter siege and then to secure the city before a British relief force arrived when the St. Lawrence opened in the spring. In addition, the British made it clear that they were willing to sacrifice everything else in Canada to preserve Quebec. As Sir George Prevost put it shortly before the war, "I have considered the preservation of Quebec as the first object, and to which all others must be subordinate."[95]

Even if Upper and Lower Canada fell, the Atlantic provinces, particularly Nova Scotia and Newfoundland, would almost certainly have remained in British hands. Newfoundland was an island that could be defended by the Royal Navy, and Nova Scotia, which included the powerful and important port of Halifax, would have been almost impossible to conquer. By land, a small force could take advantage of the flat and narrow isthmus joining New Brunswick and Nova Scotia to hold off an invading army as long as the British navy protected its flanks. An assault by sea would be even more problematical. Even if an enemy force were landed on the coast, the Royal Navy could prevent it from being supplied, reinforced, or withdrawn. Sir George Prevost, who was not likely to overestimate his ability to defend any part of his domain, was confident that Halifax would survive any attempt to take it.[96]

And what if a substantial part of Canada fell to the United States? Would the British have to choose between caving in to American demands on the maritime issues or acceding to the loss of territory? Or would they instead bide their time until the war in Europe was over and then retake what they considered rightfully theirs? The only hope for the United States was that Great Britain would be defeated in Europe and, thus humbled, would accede to new territorial arrangements in America. If, however, the British won the war in Europe, then even a war-weary public, riding high on the victory over Napoleon, might well support a campaign to reclaim the lost territory in America.

These considerations suggest how problematic America's prospects were in the War of 1812. Given the state of its army, the logistical problems, and the enemy it faced, the War of 1812 was probably unwinnable for the United States. This suggests that the decision to go to war in 1812 was even more reckless and ill-advised than the harshest critics of the Republican administration have suggested.

# The Legacy
# of the War

For the United States, the War of 1812 surely does not rank as one of the
nation's most significant wars. It does not rank with the Revolution,
which established American independence and unleashed the forces
of democracy and constitutionalism. Nor does it rank with the Civil War,
which preserved the nation, ended slavery, and helped usher in the Industrial
Revolution. The two world wars of the twentieth century were also more
significant. World War I marked the emergence of the United States as an economic juggernaut and a first-class military power and fostered the nation's
first real attempt (with the Fourteen Points) to spread its ideals abroad. World
War II confirmed and enhanced these trends. By playing a leading role in
crushing Nazi Germany, Imperial Japan, and Fascist Italy, the United States
emerged as the world's dominant power, a position that was confirmed when
the Soviet Union collapsed at the end of the Cold War. Liberty, democracy,
and free markets flourish today largely because the Allies won World War II.

Measured against these four great wars, all with worldwide consequences,
the War of 1812 seems small indeed. And even some of the nation's other
wars might seem more significant than the War of 1812. The Mexican War,
after all, led to the acquisition of California and the Southwest and ensured
that American culture would have a pronounced Hispanic component. The
Spanish–American War marked the emergence of the United States as a great

power with overseas possessions that stretched from the Caribbean to the western Pacific.

But the War of 1812 should not be dismissed too lightly, for the legacy it left was considerable. If the American Revolution established the nation, the War of 1812 confirmed that nationhood. Convinced that they had won the war, the American people emerged from the contest with a buoyant self-confidence, a clearer idea of their identity, and a newfound sense of purpose.

The war produced a host of symbols that helped define the new nation. The battles of Chippawa, Lundy's Lane, and New Orleans became symbols of American prowess on the battlefield, proof that American troops could hold their own and even defeat "the conquerors of the conquerors of Europe." The Battle of the Thames was long remembered as a defining moment in the Old Northwest, and for almost a half century after the war, January 8, the date of the great victory at New Orleans, was celebrated in cities across the nation. The naval triumphs on Lake Erie and Lake Champlain and the single-ship victories on the high seas also were remembered fondly, for they seemed to demonstrate that the U.S. Navy matched up well against the Mistress of the Seas.

The war left some more visible and tangible symbols that are still venerated today. The U.S. Frigate *Constitution* defeated all comers in the war and is still a commissioned ship in the U.S. Navy, impressive evidence of the nation's prowess in the Age of Sail and of the birth of American naval power. The navy also kept its biggest prize of the war, H.M. Ship *Macedonian*, on the rolls until 1875. This trophy ship served as a reminder that a much weaker United States had once humbled the pre-eminent naval power in the world by bringing one of its frigates into an American port as a prize of war.[1]

The Battle of Baltimore produced both the national anthem and a new reverence and respect for the flag. Although the Fort McHenry flag remained in private hands until the Smithsonian acquired it in 1907 and the "The Star-Spangled Banner" did not become the national anthem until 1931, these symbols nonetheless captured the imagination of the American people at the end of the war and thereafter gradually took on iconic significance. Uncle Sam, now universally recognized as a symbol for the United States or its government, was yet another great symbol that originated in the War of 1812. The war also cemented the reputation of the Pennsylvania rifle, which had done good (if overrated) duty, especially in the West.

The War of 1812 produced several sayings that outlived the conflict. Captain James Lawrence's words, "Don't Give up the Ship," became the motto of the U.S. Navy and appeared on the banner of Master Commandant Oliver H. Perry's flagship during the Battle of Lake Erie. That banner is now held by the U.S. Naval Academy, where it has inspired generations of midshipmen. Perry himself contributed to the language of American nationalism with his pithy after-action report, "We have met the enemy and they are ours," and his words are still remembered today.

Some of those who fought in the war became symbols themselves and were able to trade on their service in public life. Andrew Jackson, the victor over the Creeks in the Old Southwest and over the British at New Orleans, became the great symbol for the nation's heady nationalism, rugged individualism, and frontier democracy and was swept into the presidency in 1828. The War of 1812 made the careers of a host of other military men: Winfield Scott, Jacob Brown, William Henry Harrison, Stephen Decatur, Charles Stewart, Oliver H. Perry, and William Bainbridge, to name only the most conspicuous examples. Citizen soldiers who took part in the battles, particularly at the Thames or New Orleans, could trumpet that participation in any bid for elected office, local, state, or national.

Those who held high-level civilian positions during the war also profited from their service. James Monroe, who served as both secretary of state and secretary of war, followed Madison into the presidency as the third and last member of the Virginia Dynasty. John Quincy Adams, who defected from the Federalist party before the war and then helped forge the peace settlement at the war's end, was also elected president, although he was defeated for re-election by a more powerful symbol of 1812, Andrew Jackson. Similarly, Henry Clay, who helped take the nation into war as a War Hawk and speaker of the house and then helped make peace as a member of the American peace delegation at Ghent, was a three-time loser in the presidential sweepstakes but nonetheless remained a powerful force in government for almost four decades after the war.

Those on the wrong side of the war, by contrast, had to be quick of feet to avoid being cast into the dustbin of history. The restrictive system and the war had given new life to the Federalist party, but this popularity did not outlive the war. However sensible opposition to the War of 1812 might have seemed during the conflict, it took on an unpatriotic patina afterwards. With the restoration of peace, the Federalist party resumed its downward trajectory. By 1816 it had ceased to be a national party. Although it survived for another two decades in parts of New England, it remained out of tune with the rest of the nation, an archaic reminder of a bygone era.

There were other ways in which the War of 1812 left a legacy in the United States. It led to the acquisition of part of Spanish West Florida, although this came at the expense of a neutral rather than an enemy. It effectively ended any threat from Indians in the Old Northwest and Old Southwest. It also promoted defense spending (especially for the navy) in postwar America. For a time after the war, even Republicans conceded the advantages of military preparedness. The war also promoted anglophobia, which, fueled by Irish immigrants, persisted in the United States well into the twentieth century. In addition, America's performance in the conflict won the respect of Europe, a respect that could only increase with the explosive growth of the young republic in the years that followed. More broadly, the war fostered an expansive patriotism and intense nationalism that helped define the new nation and carry its people across the continent.

If the War of 1812 was significant for the United States, it was no less important for Canada. Canadians have never fought a true war of independence or civil war, nor have they ever waged wars of continental or overseas expansion. Although they took part in both world wars, those conflicts were fought overseas, and their role was as part of the British Empire. Under these circumstances, it is hardly surprising that the War of 1812 has assumed a special place in the Canadian psyche. A poll taken in 2000 showed that Canadians ranked the War of 1812 as the third most important event in their history, behind only the establishment of the Confederation (1867) and the completion of the Canadian Pacific Railway (1885).[2]

But it was not always this way. For a variety of reasons, Canadians were slow to commemorate the war or to appreciate its significance. For one thing, many of those who fought in the war were birds of passage. They were not Canadians but simply British soldiers, sailors, and marines who were responding to their sovereign's call to defend a remote corner of the Empire. Some who fought in the theaters on the Atlantic or Gulf Coast never set foot in Canada, and most of those who did left after the war was over. This left Canada with a much smaller corps of veterans to keep the memory of the war alive.

Moreover, people in Canada had little inclination to celebrate the War of 1812 because it was soon followed by one of the most divisive periods in Canadian history, culminating in the Rebellion of 1837–38. In Upper Canada the war itself contributed to the discontent by raising new issues. One issue was whether to continue to welcome American immigrants into the province. Although immigration from the south prior to the war had stimulated economic growth, many American residents had been indifferent if not hostile to British rule and thus uninterested in defending Canada. In 1815–16 British officials adopted a series of measures in Upper Canada that effectively barred Americans from acquiring land or re-occupying land that they had abandoned during the war. Although these measures initially had widespread support, the end of immigration from the south (coupled with a sharp drop in British military spending) had a paralyzing effect on the economy that even a surge in migration from Great Britain could not offset. Some local officials in Upper Canada were so disgruntled with the restrictive policy that they refused to enforce it. After a decade of bitter controversy, British officials finally reversed the policy, although not before giving opposition factions in the province a powerful issue.[3]

Another issue that generated controversy was the indemnification of Canadians for war-related damages. The war was fought mainly in Upper Canada, and British and American soldiers alike destroyed or stole a great deal of private property. British officials acknowledged that some compensation was in order but were slow to make good on this promise. Their tardiness was compounded by a bitter quarrel in the province over who was entitled to compensation. As often happens in such cases, those without influence felt that they were shortchanged, while provincial leaders, many of whom had seen combat or performed other signal services during the war, appeared to be treated generously. In the end, the British government allowed about half of the £400,000 in claims submitted, but it took more than 20 years to complete the payments, and imperial officials forced the province of Upper Canada to pick up part of the tab.[4]

Canadians were slow to commemorate the war for another reason. Long after the contest, Canada remained part of the British Empire and thus was without the kind of national imperative that drove the United States to commemorate the war. Not until Canada became a nation in 1867 did Canadians develop a need for those symbols and myths that nationhood often demands to help a people understand who they are and how they came to be.

Even after Confederation, Canadians were slow to devote much attention to the War of 1812. Although there were some writers, like novelist John Richardson, whose works helped keep the memory of the conflict alive, Canada was far less populous than the United States and did not have the resources to study the war in all its dimensions. Earnest A. Cruikshank produced a great many works in the late nineteenth and early twentieth centuries, and as a result he deserves to be known as the father of Canadian 1812 studies. But Cruikshank was virtually alone in the field, and his main contribution was to assemble documents rather than to interpret the war. Moreover, the narrative and interpretative work that he produced, while sound, was not as richly textured as the multi-archival studies produced by his American contemporaries, Henry Adams, Theodore Roosevelt, and Alfred Thayer Mahan.

Canadians were slow to develop an interest in the war for still another reason. After Confederation, most Canadians were content to consider themselves as part of the British Empire, and the second American war never loomed very large in British imperial history. It was not until after World War I that Canadians moved to assert their independence, both emotionally and politically, from Great Britain, and not until later in the twentieth century that they began to look closely at the War of 1812. The preservation and restoration of 1812 sites was undertaken mainly as make-work during the Great Depression in the 1930s, and serious scholarly research on the war was only begun in the 1950s. Even today, Canadian scholars devote far more attention to the two world wars than to the War of 1812.

Canadian literary output on the War of 1812 continues to lag. Canada still has a relatively small population (only a ninth of that of the U.S.), and although it has several first-class institutions of higher learning, it lacks the huge and well-financed academic establishment that in the United States has produced so many studies. Canadians have done little work on the causes of the war, both because they see the conflict as a simple war of territorial aggression and because they see it as a problem in British, not Canadian, diplomacy. Moreover, basic research on the war itself has been done mainly by independent scholars, and it has been limited in scope. Although battlefield studies on the war flourish in Canada today—and most are a cut above those produced in the United States—scholars seeking basic biographical studies or works on the political, economic, and financial history of Canada during the war are likely to be disappointed.

Still, it would be difficult to overemphasize the legacy of the War of 1812 in shaping Canadian history. Although the Canadian nation evolved peacefully from a collection of small colonies, the War of 1812 in some ways resembled a war of independence and a civil war. It was like a war of independence because (with the help of the British) Canadians resisted foreign subjugation, laid the foundation for establishing national independence, and began to forge a national identity that was clearly distinct from that of the United States. And it resembled a civil war in that Canadians overcame defeatism and collaboration and in the process promoted unity, patriotism, and nationhood.

Canadians came to believe that British and French-speaking residents had joined hands to resist American conquest. Although most of the fighting had taken place in Upper Canada, the French-speaking population had done its part, particularly in the Battle of Châteauguay, and the people of the Maritime provinces had done theirs, mainly through privateering. Sharing in the successful defense of the country fostered a sense of common purpose and probably guaranteed the survival of Anglo-French dualism, which might have perished with an American victory.

The War of 1812 also helped define Canada by creating a series of heroes that in time would assume mythological proportions and figure prominently in the way Canadians remembered the war. The pantheon includes Major General Isaac Brock, the hero of Detroit whose tragic death at Queenston Heights in 1812 only added to his mystique; Tecumseh, the great native leader who sought to forge a pan-Indian alliance before his death at Moraviantown in 1813; Laura Secord, who made her celebrated trek to supply intelligence that set up the British victory at Beaver Dams in 1813; Lieutenant Colonel Charles de Salaberry, whose French Canadians stopped a much larger American force at Châteauguay in 1813; and the under-appreciated rector of York, John Strachan, who worked tirelessly for the British cause throughout the war but performed particularly heroically when American forces invaded and occupied York in 1813. (It speaks volumes about the difficulty of forging a Canadian identity that the two best known members of this pantheon, Brock and Tecumseh, were not actually Canadians, and that only one of five, the French-speaking de Salaberry, was born in British North America.)

The War of 1812 was an important benchmark for Canadians for another reason. For those who had forgotten the invasion of 1775, 1812 served as a powerful reminder that the territorial ambitions of the United States did not stop at its northern border. The principal thrust of American expansion in the nineteenth century might be toward the west, but the War of 1812 demonstrated to Canadians that most Americans expected one day to incorporate Canada into their Union. The border incursions of the 1830s and 1860s served as additional reminders that the principal threat to Canadian sovereignty came from the south. It was therefore imperative for Canadians to keep an eye on their southern flank if they were to preserve their independence. Long after the War of 1812, British and Canadian forces conducting military exercises faced south, for that was the only direction from which there was any conceivable threat. As late as 1931, the Canadian army had a plan of operations (known as Defence Scheme No. 1) to invade the United States in the event of war.[5]

The American threat had another effect: it helped propel Canada into confederation. Throughout the 1850s and 1860s annexationist sentiment, sometimes emanating from the highest levels of the U.S. government, cast a pall over the future of British North America. This gave momentum to the confederation movement. By 1841 Upper and Lower Canada had merged into the United Province of Canada, and the border raids of the Fenians in 1866 induced Nova Scotia and New Brunswick to seek admission into the union as well. With British approval, the Confederation of Canada came into being on July 1, 1867.

In the years that followed, the new Confederation extended its reach to the Pacific, partly in response to developments from south of the border: the construction of the Northern Pacific Railroad, the purchase of Alaska and the extension of the telegraph there, and a new round of Fenian raids. The Confederation offered not only the prospect of a more coherent defense against the American threat but also the hope (which was not immediately realized) that Americans would not always look to the north for satisfaction whenever they had differences with Great Britain.[6]

Capping this phase in Canadian history was the role that the new Dominion played in the negotiations that culminated in the Anglo-American Treaty of Washington in 1871. For the first time Canada (in the person of Prime Minster Sir John A. Macdonald) had a seat on a British diplomatic commission, and for the first time Canada (through the Dominion Parliament) had a voice in the ratification of a British treaty. Although Macdonald was forced to refer a dispute over the American use of Canadian fisheries to arbitration and failed to secure American compensation for recent Fenian raids or American agreement to renew a reciprocity convention, he won a more important objective. By merely signing the treaty, the United States tacitly acknowledged that Canada was here to stay and had a future apart from the United States. For Canadians, this effectively closed out an era that dated back to 1812 or even 1775.[7]

Although the War of 1812 cast a long shadow over the history of Canada, it never carried the same significance for Great Britain. Even though there were as many British troops in North America in 1814 (48,000) as at any time in the Peninsula, and far more than at Waterloo in 1815, the British never considered "the second American war" much more than a footnote to the Napoleonic Wars.[8] In the words of one British scholar, it was "the always peripheral American conflict," and as a result it was quickly forgotten.[9] "As for England," Theodore Roosevelt lamented in 1900, "she knows little or nothing about the war."[10]

Nevertheless, the War of 1812 did affect Great Britain in several ways. One small effect was to exacerbate interservice rivalries. The British army and navy have often blamed one another for failed joint operations, and the War of 1812 was no exception. The Royal Navy tried to blame the army for its defeat on Lake Champlain, and the army sought to blame the navy for its defeat at New Orleans. The war was quickly forgotten by most people in Great Britain, but not by the two services, which had very long memories.

More importantly, the British realized after the War of 1812 that if they wanted to retain Canada, they needed to find better ways to defend it. Although the British gave up their traditional practice of courting Indian allies, they looked for other ways to secure Canada. Shortly after the war, veterans from all the services were offered lands, mainly in the Perth-Rideau region in eastern Upper Canada, in the hope of increasing security.[11] Although this scheme never quite lived up to expectation, it reflected Britain's ongoing attempt to solve what was probably its most difficult security problem in the nineteenth century.

In the decades that followed the war, the British built citadels in Halifax and Quebec, greatly strengthened the defenses of Kingston, and upgraded their defenses elsewhere along the frontier.[12] They also put up £1,000,000 to finance two expensive canal systems to secure their long and exposed supply route to the West. The 124-mile Rideau Canal System (completed in 1832) coupled with the 105-mile Ottawa River Canal System (completed in 1834) linked the St. Lawrence River to Lake Ontario via the Ottawa and Rideau rivers. Protected by a series of blockhouses built near its main locks, this waterway bypassed the most exposed part of the old St. Lawrence River supply route. In addition, the British made a modest contribution to the 28-mile Welland Canal (opened in 1833), which linked Port Dalhousie on Lake Ontario with Port Colborne on Lake Erie, thus bypassing the exposed Niagara River and the portage necessitated by the great falls there.[13] Unable to find a suitable anchorage on the north shore of Lake Erie, the British also developed Penetanguishene on Georgian Bay off Lake Huron into an inland naval base.[14]

There were several problems with British attempts to provide for the defense of Canada. For one thing, study after study showed that the cost of doing the job right was prohibitive. The British were understandably reluctant to spend the money needed, and Canadians were steadfast in their refusal to share the cost. Moreover, even if the recommended defense measures were undertaken, there was no guarantee that Canada would ever be completely secure. The United States was simply growing too fast, and every year the balance of power in North America was shifting more in its favor.[15]

Under these circumstances, the British wisely sought to respond to the potential threat from the south in another way: through accommodation. Once the Napoleonic Wars were over, the environment for an Anglo-American accord was favorable. American merchants were anxious to recapture British markets, and British capitalists were eager to invest in the United States. In addition, Great Britain was looking for a way out of a severe postwar depression and was beginning to dismantle its navigation system and to embrace free trade. Lord Castlereagh, who continued as Britain's foreign secretary until his suicide in 1822, played a particularly important role in promoting friendship with America.

The two nations took the first tentative step in 1815 when they signed a modest commercial convention that renewed some of the clauses of the Jay Treaty that had expired in 1803. Between 1822 and 1830, the British opened their ports in the West Indies to American ships. Although this fulfilled a traditional American foreign policy aim, the concession was far less important than it would have been during the Napoleonic Wars.

In 1817 the two nations signed the Rush-Bagot Agreement, a landmark convention that sharply limited warships on the Great Lakes and Lake Champlain. Both nations profited from avoiding a costly naval arms race, but the United States undoubtedly benefited more because in any crisis it could build a naval force on the lakes more quickly than the British, who were more than 3,000 miles away. Although each side occasionally violated the terms of the agreement, it ultimately established this boundary as the longest undefended border in the world, and it set the stage for the Canadian-American accord of the twentieth century. By 1818 Great Britain was also willing to make significant concessions on impressment, although by this time the United States had lost interest in any real compromise on the issue.[16] The two nations did, however, sign boundary conventions—in 1818, 1842, and 1846—that defined the Canadian-American border, thus eliminating additional sources of friction.

Increasingly after 1815, the British acted as if cultivating the United States was a major foreign policy aim, one that sometimes took precedence over keeping dominions in the British Empire happy. Throughout the nineteenth century, the British were surprisingly quick to ignore the interests of dominion subjects, particularly in Canada, if they threatened to undermine friendship with America.

Great Britain's relationship with the United States, to be sure, was often rocky. For a half century after the Treaty of Ghent, it was widely believed on both sides of the Atlantic that this agreement was but a truce and that the English-speaking nations would come to blows again. Newspapers, magazines, and books in both countries teemed with verbal attacks.[17] Andrew Jackson's hasty and ill-conceived execution of two British subjects in Spanish Florida in 1818 increased the tension, as did recurring violence on the Canadian-American border between 1830 and 1870.

The American Civil War ushered in a particularly difficult time. Tensions rose when the British recognized that a state of belligerency existed and permitted Confederate agents in Britain to purchase commerce raiders that ultimately destroyed some 250 Yankee ships. The U.S., for its part, provoked Britain by removing two Confederate diplomats from the British mail steamer *Trent* in late 1861. Americans thought that Britain might recognize southern independence, and when this fear subsided, the British suspected that a victorious Union army might march on Canada.

The British responded by dramatically increasing their military presence in Canada. By 1868 they had almost 15,000 men there and were spending more than £1,500,000 annually on Canada's defense.[18] Even with this build-up, however, the British realized that they could never match the number of troops that the United States could put on its northern border. Hence, British strategy for waging war continued to call for targeting the Atlantic coast with its naval power. Fortunately, this strategy was never put to a test. Despite some saber rattling, the United States and Great Britain always found peaceful solutions to their problems.

In 1871 the Treaty of Washington addressed a number of outstanding issues and established a system for arbitrating the claims that grew out of the damage done by Confederate raiders purchased in Great Britain during the Civil War. This treaty was an Anglo-American milestone because it resolved so many vexing problems.[19] Despite differences that would later surface and the persistence of anglophobia and annexationist sentiment in the United States, the two English-speaking nations were determined to remain at peace. Hence, by the end of the nineteenth century, what Bradford Perkins has called "The Great Rapprochement" had begun, and this close relationship, unprecedented in the annals of history, continues to flourish today.[20]

In short, British instincts to seek an accommodation with the United States after the War of 1812 were sound. Whatever their differences prior to 1815, thereafter the two English-speaking nations had far more in common. As the United States emerged as a Great Power willing to play an ever larger role in world affairs, the two nations usually found themselves on the same side of international conflicts because of a common interest in promoting democracy, free markets, and the rule of law. As a result, the Pax Britannia of the nineteenth century evolved seamlessly into the Pax Americana of the twentieth, and the world was a better place for it.[21]

And what was the legacy of the War of 1812 for Indians? For these forgotten participants, the war was a disaster. If the United States eliminated its "Indian problem" in the Old Northwest and the Old Southwest, it was because the natives there no longer could mount a credible threat against the new nation. The death of Tecumseh in 1813 had delivered a body blow to the pan-Indian movement, and it never regained its momentum. After the war the Indians could not effectively challenge the United States nor could they call upon European allies to offset the growing power and territorial ambitions of the American people.

The United States ignored Article 9 of the Treaty of Ghent, which required the nation to restore all Indian tribes to their status as of 1811. Nor did the British make any attempt to hold the U.S. to this provision. Despite the central role that Indians had played in the defense of Canada, Great Britain abandoned its native allies.

Although British officials in the West were eager to continue their traditional friendship with the tribes, they had neither the resources nor the support of their government. Indians living south of the border (who constituted 80 percent of Britain's Indian allies) received no military pensions and were discouraged from seeking British aid, and even those in British territory did not always get the sustenance and other assistance that they needed. In the West, concludes the leading student of the subject, "The Treaty of Ghent sounded the death knell of the British-Indian alliance."[22] Although bitterly disappointed by this turn of events, there was little Britain's native allies could do to redeem the situation.

Britain's Indian allies farther east, particularly the Grand River Iroquois, were treated better, but they, too, had lost their strategic value and thus their bargaining power. They frequently needed assistance from the British government and suffered when it was tardy.[23] Like their counterparts south of the border, the Indians in eastern Canada saw their land holdings shrink and came under growing pressure to assimilate, if only because their traditional way of life was no longer viable.[24]

The Indians living in the United States fared much worse. Since they no longer figured in the military plans of Great Britain or any other European power, they had little choice but to reach an accommodation with the United States, and the terms accorded were almost always so unfavorable that there was little hope of retaining their lands or their traditional way of life. Between July 22, 1814, and June 25, 1817, the United States signed 23 peace treaties with 32 tribes.[25] In the generation that followed, the U.S. compelled most of the eastern tribes to surrender their lands, and as a result their traditional way of life disintegrated. A similar fate awaited western Indians in the late nineteenth century.

The fate of North American Indians would surely have been the same without the War of 1812, for a demographic time clock was ticking against them. The war, however, speeded up that clock, and there is no denying that it was a watershed in their history. This was the last war in which control of the continent was at stake. It was also the last hurrah for Indians. Never again would the threat of Indian militarism shape the future of North America, and never again could the Indians expect to protect their homeland from land-hungry whites and the forces of modernism.

For all the belligerents, then, the War of 1812 had significant and lasting consequences. For the United States and Canada, it shaped their national development for the rest of the nineteenth century and beyond. For the British, it helped define their relationship with Canada and their foreign and defense policies in the New World. For the Indians, the war dramatically weakened their geopolitical position and thus robbed them of the leverage needed to preserve their way of life. In short, this forgotten conflict may have been a small war, but it left an outsized legacy that is still evident today.

# Chronology

M ost chronologies of the War of 1812 are marred by errors, partly because they are compiled hurriedly and partly because they draw on
faulty sources. Secondary sources are not always dependable, and even primary sources are sometimes vague or contradictory. Opposing commanders
might give different dates for a military action, and occasionally the same
commander might even present conflicting data. Reports compiled by commanders at sea or in remote parts of the West seem to be especially prone to
ambiguity and error.

The chronology that follows is not tied to the text of this book but instead
is designed to stand alone and serve as a reference tool for anyone interested
in the War of 1812. Hence, there are many events here that are not mentioned
in the text. Because Great Britain was one of the principals in the War of 1812
and the conflict was a direct outgrowth of the Napoleonic Wars, the chronology includes events on both sides of the Atlantic.

In preparing this chronology, I have profited greatly from two unpublished
lists of 1812 sites: a compilation of 306 actions and engagements prepared by
the National Park Service for the American Battlefield Protection Program and
a list of 395 Maryland sites compiled under the direction of Ralph E. Eshelman
and Christopher T. George for several Maryland government agencies and the
National Park Service.[1] Although neither work is definitive or free from errors,
I found both to be exceptionally useful. In fact, the Maryland study could
serve as a model for other states wishing to inventory their 1812 sites.

In an effort to make this chronology as accurate as possible, I have checked
every item against the most authoritative source available. Whenever possible,
this was a primary source. For this purpose, I relied heavily on the published
documentary collections prepared by William Wood, Ernest A. Cruikshank,
and William S. Dudley and Michael J. Crawford.[2] I excluded a number of mi-

nor engagements in the West, on the northern frontier, and in the Chesapeake because I could not find enough information on them. I also excluded most actions of privateers because the information available on their operations is so often incomplete or unreliable.

I have given every name that an engagement has been known by, even those that are incorrect. Thus, "Battle of Mackinac/Michilimackinac." On the other hand, I have ignored minor name differences or variant spellings. I have given the common name for an engagement even if that name overstates the nature of the action. Thus the skirmish at Sodus Point, New York, in 1814 is listed as the "Battle of Sodus Point." To fix the locations of all events in the chronology, I have given the modern state, province, or country in parentheses. If the engagement occurred on water, I have given the body of water or a nearby landmark. When the primary sources present conflicting dates, I have given what I think is the best one. Occasionally, where I could not reach a decision, I have presented both dates. Thus, the date for the Battle of Campbell's Island in 1814 is given as Jul. 21 or 22.

In spite of the care that I have taken in preparing this chronology, it undoubtedly has some errors. Readers wishing to suggest additions or corrections should write me at <dohicke1@wsc.edu>.

## Abbreviations

| | | | | |
|------|----------------|---|------|------------------------------------|
| AU   | Austria        | | UC   | Upper Canada                       |
| BE   | Belgium        | | US   | United States                      |
| CZ   | Czech Republic | | | |
| FR   | France         | | Cap. | Captain                            |
| GB   | Great Britain  | | BG   | Brigadier general                  |
| GR   | Germany        | | MG   | Major general                      |
| IT   | Italy          | | LG   | Lieutenant general                 |
| LC   | Lower Canada   | | | |
| NE   | Netherlands    | | PM   | Provincial Marine                  |
| PO   | Portugal       | | HM   | His Majesty's                      |
| RU   | Russia         | | (n)  | Number of guns an armed ship carried |
| SP   | Spain          | | | |

### NOTE

US states and Canadian provinces are identified by their two-letter postal abbreviations. The principal military and diplomatic events of the War of 1812 are in **bold** type.

**1789**

| | |
|---|---|
| Apr. 30 | George Washington inaugurated as president of US in New York City |
| Jul. 14 | Mob storms Bastille in Paris (French Revolution begins) |

**1791**

| | |
|---|---|
| Jun. 19 | British Parliament splits Quebec into UC and LC |

**1792**

| | |
|---|---|
| Apr. 20 | FR declares war on Austria (French Revolutionary Wars begin) |
| Sep. 20 | Battle of Valmy (FR) |
| Sep. 22 | French revolutionaries in Paris proclaim a republic |
| Nov. 6 | Battle of Jemappes (BE) |

**1793**

| | |
|---|---|
| Jan. 21 | French revolutionaries execute Louis XVI in Paris |
| Feb. 1 | FR declares war on GB |
| Aug. 23 | FR adopts *levée en masse* |

**1793–94**   Reign of Terror (FR)

**1794**

| | |
|---|---|
| Jun. 26 | Battle of Fleurus (BE) |
| Nov. 19 | US and GB sign Jay Treaty in London |

**1795**

| | |
|---|---|
| Oct. 27 | Directory assumes power (French Revolution ends) |

**1796–97**   Napoleon's Italian campaign

**1797**

| | |
|---|---|
| Mar. 4 | John Adams inaugurated as president of US in Philadelphia (PA) |
| Apr. 16–May 15 | Spithead Mutiny (GB) |
| May 12–Jun. 15 | Nore Mutiny (GB) |
| Oct. 18–Dec. 17 | XYZ Affair in Paris (FR) |

**1798–99**   Napoleon's Egyptian campaign

**1798–1801**   US and FR in Quasi-War

**1799**

| | |
|---|---|
| Nov. 9–10 | Coup of Brumaire ends rule of Directory (FR) |
| Dec. 25 | Napoleon becomes First Consul of FR |

**1800**

| | |
|---|---|
| Jun. 14 | Battle of Marengo (IT) |
| Dec. 3 | Battle of Hohenlinden (GR) |
| Dec. 16 | League of Armed Neutrality established |

**1801**

| | |
|---|---|
| Mar. 4 | Thomas Jefferson inaugurated as president of US in Washington (DC) |
| Mar. 17 | Henry Addington becomes prime minister of GB |
| Oct. 1 | GB and FR sign preliminary Treaty of Amiens (French Revolutionary Wars end) (FR) |

**1802**

| | |
|---|---|
| Mar. 25 | GB and FR sign final Treaty of Amiens (FR) |

**1803**

| | |
|---|---|
| May 17 | GB issues letters of marque and reprisal against FR (Napoleonic Wars begin) |
| Oct. 1 | Commercial clauses in Jay Treaty expire |

**1804**

| | |
|---|---|
| May 10 | William Pitt the Younger becomes prime minister of GB |
| May 18 | Napoleon becomes Emperor of FR |

**1805**

| | |
|---|---|
| May 22 | GB issues *Essex* decision, which threatens US re-export trade |
| Oct. 20 | AU surrenders at Ulm (GR) |
| Oct. 21 | Battle of Trafalgar off coast of Spain in Atlantic |
| Dec. 2 | Battle of Austerlitz/the Three Emperors (CZ) |

**1806**

| | |
|---|---|
| Jan. 22 | Francis Gore appointed lieutenant-governor of UC |
| Feb. 11 | Lord Grenville becomes prime minister of GB |
| Apr. 18 | US adopts (but suspends) partial non-importation law against GB |
| Apr. 25 | *Leander* affair (HM Ship *Leander* [56] accidentally kills American seaman John Pierce off New York harbor in Atlantic) |
| May 16 | GB issues Order-in-Council proclaiming Fox Blockade of northern Europe and tacitly suspending *Essex* decision |
| Oct. 14 | Battle of Jena-Auerstädt (GR) |
| Nov. 21 | FR issues Berlin Decree proclaiming blockade of GB (beginning of Continental System) |
| Dec. 31 | US and GB sign Monroe-Pinkney Treaty in London (GB) |

**1807**

| | |
|---|---|
| Jan. 7 | GB issues Order-in-Council barring neutral trade between enemy ports |
| Feb. 7–8 | Battle of Eylau (RU) |
| Mar. 3 | US repudiates Monroe-Pinkney Treaty |
| Mar. 31 | Duke of Portland becomes prime minister of GB |
| Jun. 14 | Battle of Friedland (RU) |
| Jun. 22 | *Chesapeake* affair/*Chesapeake-Leopard* affair (HM Ship *Leopard* [52] fires on US Frigate *Chesapeake* [40] off coast of Virginia in Atlantic) |
| Oct. 17 | GB issues proclamation renouncing impressment from neutral warships but also recalling all British seamen and ordering Royal Navy to impress any found on neutral merchant vessels |
| Nov. 11 | GB issues Orders-in-Council forcing neutral trade with French-controlled ports to pass through GB |
| Dec. 14 | US activates partial non-importation law of 1806 |
| Dec. 17 | FR issues Milan Decree authorizing seizure of neutral ships complying with Orders-in-Council |
| Dec. 22 | US adopts embargo prohibiting US ships and goods from leaving port |

**1808**

| | |
|---|---|
| Apr. 17 | FR issues Bayonne Decree, seizing all American ships entering ports controlled by FR |
| Aug. 21 | Battle of Vimeiro (PO) |

**1809**

| | |
|---|---|
| Jan. 16 | Battle of Corunna (SP) |
| Mar. 1 | US adopts non-intercourse law against GB and FR |
| Mar. 4 | James Madison inaugurated as president of US in Washington (DC) |
| Apr. 19 | US and GB sign Erskine Agreement in Washington (DC) |
| Apr. 26 | GB issues Order-in-Council blockading ports under French control |
| May 22 | GB repudiates Erskine Agreement |
| Jul. 5–6 | Battle of Wagram (AU) |
| Oct. 4 | Spencer Perceval becomes prime minister of GB |

**1810**

| | |
|---|---|
| Mar. 23 | FR issues Rambouillet Decree, sequestering all US ships and cargoes entering French-controlled ports on or after May 20, 1809 |
| May 1 | US adopts Macon's Bill No. 2, reopening trade with GB and FR |
| Aug. 5 | FR establishes Trianon Tariff, barring most imports |
| | FR issues Trianon Decree, condemning all US ships and cargoes entering French-controlled ports on or after May 20, 1809 |

| | |
|---|---|
| Aug. 5 | FR sends Cadore letter to US, offering to rescind Continental System |
| Sep. 27 | Battle of Busaco (PO) |
| Oct. 18 | FR issues Fontainebleau Decree, imposing harsh penalties for smuggling British goods to Continent |

**1811**

| | |
|---|---|
| Feb. 28 | US minister William Pinkney leaves GB |
| Mar. 2 | US adopts non-importation law against GB |
| May 16 | *Little Belt* affair/*President-Little Belt* affair (clash of US Frigate *President* [54] and HM Sloop *Little Belt* [20] off coast of Virginia in Atlantic) |
| Oct. 9 | Isaac Brock appointed president and administrator of UC |
| Oct. 21 | George Prevost appointed captain-general and governor-in-chief of Canada |
| Nov. 4 | War Congress convenes in Washington (DC) |
| Nov. 7 | Battle of Tippecanoe (IN) |
| Nov. 8 | US burns Prophet's Town (IN) |
| Nov. 12 | US and GB settle *Chesapeake* affair in Washington (DC) |
| Dec. 24–Apr. 10 | US enacts war preparations |

**1812**

| | |
|---|---|
| Jan. 1 | Indians raid Hunt Lead Mine (IA) |
| Jan. 8–19 | Siege of Ciudad Rodrigo (SP) |
| Feb. 9 | Indians raid near Clarksville (MO) |
| Feb. 18 | Indians raid near Salt River (MO) |
| Mar. 3 | Indians raid Fort Madison (IA) |
| Mar. 6 | UC adopts militia law |
| Mar. 9 | Madison exposes John Henry spy mission to New England |
| Mar. 16–Apr. 7 | Siege of Badajoz (SP) |
| Apr. 4 | US adopts 90-day embargo, prohibiting US ships from leaving port |
| Apr. 6 | Indians raid near Fort Dearborn (IL) |
| Apr. 7–9 | GB sacks Badajoz (SP) |
| Apr. 11 | Indians raid near Vincennes (IN) |
| Apr. 14 | US adopts 90-day non-exportation law, prohibiting exports |
| May 5 | Indians raid White River (IN) |
| May 10 | FR gives US spurious decree dated Apr. 28, 1811, exempting Americans from the Berlin and Milan decrees |
| May 11 | Prime Minister Spencer Perceval is assassinated (GB) |
| May 19 | US Sloop *Hornet* (20) arrives in New York Harbor from Europe (NY) LC adopts militia law |

| | |
|---|---|
| May 22 | Dispatches from US Sloop *Hornet* (20) reach Washington (DC) |
| May 27 | GB offers US share of license trade in Washington (DC) |
| Jun. 1 | US army departs from Dayton for Detroit (OH) |
| | Madison sends war message to US Congress |
| Jun. 4 | US House of Representatives adopts war bill |
| Jun. 5 | US seizes British merchantman *Lord Nelson* on Lake Ontario |
| Jun. 8 | Earl of Liverpool becomes prime minister of GB |
| | US signs treaty with Wyandots, Shawnees, and Mingoes at Urbana securing right to build road through Indian country (OH) |
| Jun. 16 | GB announces intention to suspend Orders-in-Council |
| Jun. 17 | US Senate adopts war bill |
| Jun. 18 | **President Madison signs war bill into law (War of 1812 begins)** |
| Jun. 18–26 | US sends out peace feelers |
| Jun. 19 | President Madison issues proclamation announcing that state of war exists and urging all Americans to support war effort |
| Jun. 20 | News of war reaches New York City (NY) |
| Jun. 22 | First Baltimore Riot (MD) |
| Jun. 23 | FR invades RU |
| | News of war reaches Albany (NY) |
| | US Frigate *President* (54) clashes with HM Ship *Belvidera* (42) in North Atlantic |
| | **GB repeals Orders-in-Council** |
| Jun. 24 | News of war reaches Norfolk (VA) |
| | News of war reaches Oswego (NY) |
| Jun. 25 | News of war reaches Quebec (QC) |
| | News of war reaches York (ON) |
| | News of war reaches Fort George (ON) |
| | News of war reaches Sackets Harbor (NY) |
| Jun. 26 | US captures Carleton Island in St. Lawrence River (NY) |
| Jun. 27 | Canadian privateers capture American merchantman *Commencement* on Lake Erie |
| | News of war reaches Plattsburgh (NY) |
| | News of war reaches Black Rock (NY) |
| | News of war reaches Halifax (NS) |
| | News of war reaches St. Johns (NB) |
| Jun. 28 | News of war reaches Montreal (QC) |
| | News of war reaches Fort Amherstburg (ON) |
| Jun. 29 | US captures British merchantmen *Emperor*, *Experiment*, and *Adventurer* off coast of Spanish Florida in Atlantic |

| | |
|---|---|
| Jun. 29 | GB captures American merchantmen *Sophia* and *Island Packet* in St. Lawrence River |
| Jun. 30 | LC prohibits departure of ships and goods until Jul. 16 |
| | News of war reaches Lexington (KY) |
| | News of war reaches Kingston (ON) |
| Jul. 1 | US doubles customs duties |
| | News of war reaches Moraviantown (ON) |
| Jul. 2 | News of war reaches US army at Frenchtown while en route to Detroit (MI) |
| | GB captures *Cuyahoga* in Detroit River |
| | Connecticut refuses US request to call out militia |
| Jul. 5 | US bombards Sandwich (ON) |
| Jul. 6 | US adopts first enemy trade law |
| Jul. 8 | US bombards Sandwich (ON) |
| Jul. 9 | News of war reaches New Orleans (LA) |
| | News of war reaches St. Joseph Island (ON) |
| Jul. 11 | In Boston Harbor GB restores deserters taken in *Chesapeake* affair (MA) |
| Jul. 12 | News of war reaches St. Louis (MO) |
| | US invades Canada across Detroit River (MI/ON) |
| | Skirmish near Fort Dearborn (IL) |
| | BG William Hull issues proclamation at Sandwich promising to liberate Canada (ON) |
| Jul. 16 | News of war reaches Thunder Bay (ON) |
| | British squadron captures US Brig *Nautilus* (14) in North Atlantic |
| Jul. 16–19 | US Frigate *Constitution* (55) outruns British squadron in eastern Atlantic |
| Jul. 16–26 | Skirmishing at Canard River/Aux Canards River (ON) |
| Jul. 17 | News of war reaches Mackinac Island (MI) |
| | **GB captures Fort Mackinac/Michilimackinac (MI)** |
| Jul. 19 | GB attacks Sackets Harbor (NY) |
| Jul. 22 | Battle of Salamanca (SP) |
| Jul. 27–29 | Second Baltimore Riot (MD) |
| Jul. 30 | News of war reaches London (GB) |
| | News of repeal of Orders-in-Council reaches Quebec (QC) |
| Jul. 31 | GB embargoes all American ships in British waters |
| | US Schooner *Julia* (2) and US gunboat (1) engage PM Brig *Earl of Moira* (14) and PM Schooner *Duke of Gloucester* (6) in St. Lawrence River |

| | |
|---|---|
| Aug. 1 | LC adopts law to promote circulation of army bills |
| Aug. 4 | News of repeal of Orders-in-Council reaches Boston (MA) |
| | Third Baltimore Riot (MD) |
| Aug. 5 | Massachusetts refuses US request to call out militia |
| | Battle of Brownstown (MI) |
| Aug. 7 | US withdraws from Canada across Detroit River (ON/MI) |
| Aug. 8 | News of repeal of Orders-in-Council reaches New York (NY) |
| Aug. 9 | Battle of Maguaga (MI) |
| | **Henry Dearborn and George Prevost implement armistice** |
| Aug. 10 | PM Sloop *Queen Charlotte* (17) and PM Brig *General Hunter* (10) capture flotilla of American boats on Lake Erie |
| Aug. 13 | News of repeal of Orders-in-Council reaches Washington (DC) |
| Aug. 13 | US Frigate *Essex* (46) captures HM Sloop *Alert* (18?) in North Atlantic |
| Aug. 15 | Fort Dearborn Massacre/Chicago Massacre (IL) |
| Aug. 16 | **GB captures Detroit (MI)** |
| Aug. 16–18 | Battle of Smolensk (RU) |
| Aug. 19 | US Frigate *Constitution* (55) defeats HM Ship *Guerrière* (49) in North Atlantic |
| Aug. 22 | Rhode Island refuses US request to call out militia |
| Sep.-Nov. | State elections ensure Pres. Madison's re-election |
| Sep. 3 | Pigeon Roost Massacre (IN) |
| Sep. 4–16 | Siege of Fort Harrison (IN) |
| Sep. 5–8 | Siege of Fort Madison (IA) |
| Sep. 5–12 | Siege of Fort Wayne (IN) |
| Sep. 7 | Battle of Borodino (RU) |
| Sep. 8 | **US cancels Dearborn-Prevost armistice** |
| Sep. 13–14 | Skirmish near Miami Rapids (OH) |
| Sep. 14 | FR occupies Moscow (RU) |
| Sep. 15 | GB raids Sturgeon Point (NY) |
| Sep. 16 | Battle of Toussaint's Island/Matilda in St. Lawrence River (ON) |
| | US burns Five Medals Town (IN) |
| Sep. 19 | US burns Little Turtle's Village (IN) |
| Sep. 21 | US raids Gananoque (ON) |
| | GB raids Briton's Point (NY) |
| Sep. 29 | Battle of Marblehead Peninsula/Bull Island (OH) |
| Oct. 1 | GB raids Charlotte (NY) |
| Oct. 2 | GB bombards Ogdensburg (NY) |
| Oct. 4 | Battle of Ogdensburg (NY) |

| | |
|---|---|
| Oct. 6 | LC prohibits export of grains and foodstuffs |
| Oct. 9 | US captures PM Brig *Detroit* (6) and PM Brig *Caledonia* (3) in Niagara River |
| Oct. 13 | **Battle of Queenston Heights;** MG Isaac Brock killed (ON) |
| | Artillery duel between Fort Niagara (NY) and Fort George (ON) |
| | **GB authorizes general reprisals against US** |
| Oct. 18 | US Sloop *Wasp* (18) defeats HM Sloop *Frolic* (22) in North Atlantic |
| | HM Ship *Poictiers* (80) captures US Sloop *Wasp* (18) in North Atlantic |
| Oct. 19–Dec. 14 | FR retreats from RU |
| Oct. 23 | Battle of St. Regis (ON) |
| | GB raids French Mills (NY) |
| Oct. 25 | US Frigate *United States* (56) captures HM Ship *Macedonian* (49) in North Atlantic |
| Nov. 9–10 | Battle of Kingston Harbor (ON) |
| Nov. 17 | BG Alexander Smyth issues proclamation from camp near Buffalo promising to annex Canada (NY) |
| Nov. 19 | US invades LC (NY/QC) |
| Nov. 20–22 | US burns Prophet's Town and nearby Indian villages (IN) |
| Nov. 20 | First Battle of Lacolle Mill (QC) |
| Nov. 21 | Artillery duel between Fort George (ON) and Fort Niagara (NY) |
| | Indians raid Wild Cat Creek (OH) |
| Nov. 22 | Second Battle of Tippecanoe/Spur's Defeat (IN) |
| | Skirmish at Maumee River (OH) |
| | HM Ship *Southampton* (41) captures US Schooner *Vixen* (14) in North Atlantic |
| Nov. 23 | US raids St. Regis (QC) |
| | US withdraws from LC (QC/NY) |
| | GB raids French Mills (NY) |
| Nov. 28 | Battle of Frenchman's Creek/Red House/Black Rock/Outposts at Fort Erie (ON) |
| Dec. 11 | US Frigate *Essex* (46) captures HM Packet Brig *Nocton* (10) in South Atlantic |
| Dec. 17–18 | Battle of the Mississinewa River (IN) |
| Dec. 29 | US Frigate *Constitution* (54) defeats HM Ship *Java* (49) off coast of Brazil in Atlantic |

**1813**

| | |
|---|---|
| Jan. 9 | GB publishes declaration defending its position on maritime issues |
| Jan. 15 | News of war reaches Fort Astoria (OR) |
| Jan. 17 | HM Ship *Narcissus* (38) captures US Brig *Viper* (16) in Caribbean |

| | |
|---|---|
| Jan. 18 | First Battle of Frenchtown/River Raisin (MI) |
| Jan. 22 | **Battle of Frenchtown/River Raisin/Second Battle of Frenchtown (MI)** |
| Jan. 23 | **River Raisin Massacre (MI)** |
| Feb. 4 | Col. Henry Procter proclaims martial law in Michigan Territory |
| Feb. 6 | **GB proclaims blockade of Delaware and Chesapeake bays** |
| Feb. 7 | US raids Elizabethtown/Brockville (ON) |
| Feb. 9 | Duck River Massacre (TN) |
| Feb. 22 | GB raids Ogdensburg (NY) |
| Feb. 24 | US Sloop *Hornet* (20) defeats HM Sloop *Peacock* (20) off coast of Guiana in Atlantic |
| Mar. 8 | RU offers to mediate end to War of 1812 |
| Mar. 10 | First runaway slaves in Chesapeake Bay seek refuge on HM Ship *Victorious* (78) |
| Mar. 11 | US accepts RU's mediation offer |
| Mar. 16 | British squadron captures 4 armed American ships in Rappahannock River (VA) |
| Mar. 17–18 | Artillery duel between Black Rock (NY) and Fort Erie (ON) |
| Mar. 18 | Indians raid near Fort Vallonia (IN) |
| Mar. 19 | Sir James Yeo appointed commander of British naval forces on northern lakes |
| Mar. 30 | Indians raid near Buffalo Fort on Salt River (MO) |
| Apr. 3 | Battle of the Rappahannock River (VA) |
| Apr. 5 | GB captures squadron of merchant vessels in Chesapeake Bay |
| Apr. 6 | GB bombards Lewes (DE) |
| | GB raids Strawberry Island (NY) |
| Apr. 8 | Skirmishing near Fort Meigs (OH) |
| Apr. 15 | US occupies part of West Florida (LA/AL) |
| Apr. 16 | Indians raid near Fort Vallonia (IN) |
| Apr. 18 | Indians attack mail carrier near Kaskaskia (IL) |
| Apr. 19 | Indians raid near Kaskaskia (IL) |
| Apr. 23 | GB raids Spesutie Island (MD) |
| Apr. 27 | **US captures York/Battle of York (ON)** |
| Apr. 27–30 | Skirmishing at Fort Meigs (OH) |
| Apr. 29 | GB raids Frenchtown (MD) |
| | Battle of Fort Defiance/Elkton (MD) |
| May 1–9 | **First Siege of Fort Meigs (OH)** |
| May 2 | Battle of Lützen/Grossgörschen (GR) |
| May 3 | GB burns Havre de Grace (MD) |
| | GB destroys Principio Ironworks (MD) |

| | |
|---|---|
| May 3 | GB raids Bell's Ferry/Smith's Ferry/Lapidum (MD) |
| May 5 | Battle of Fort Meigs (OH) |
| | Massacre of US POWs at Fort Miami (OH) |
| | GB occupies Charlestown (MD) |
| May 6 | GB burns Fredericktown and Georgetown (MD) |
| May 15 | US raids Indian village on Mink River (IL) |
| May 20–21 | Battle of Bautzen (GR) |
| May 26 | **GB proclaims blockade of major ports in middle and southern states** |
| May 27 | **US captures Fort George (ON)** |
| May 28 | GB evacuates all posts along Niagara River (ON) |
| May 29 | **Battle of Sackets Harbor (NY)** |
| Jun. 1 | HM Ship *Shannon* (52) defeats US Frigate *Chesapeake* (50) off coast of Massachusetts in Atlantic |
| Jun. 3 | GB captures US Sloop *Eagle* (11) and US Sloop *Growler* (11) in Richelieu River (QC) |
| Jun. 5 | GB raids Gardiners Island (NY) |
| Jun. 5–6 | **Battle of Stoney Creek (ON)** |
| Jun. 8 | Battle of Forty Mile Creek (ON) |
| Jun. 8? | US evacuates Fort Osage (MO) |
| Jun. 10 | US Frigate *President* (54) captures HM Packet Brig *Duke of Montrose* (?) in North Atlantic |
| Jun. 13 | GB captures American supply ships on Lake Ontario |
| Jun. 15 | GB raids Charlotte (NY) |
| Jun. 19 | Francis de Rottenburg appointed president and administrator of UC |
| | Battle of Sodus Point (NY) |
| Jun. 20 | GB raids Sodus Point (NY) |
| | US gunboat flotilla attacks HM Ship *Junon* (46) in Chesapeake Bay |
| Jun. 21 | Battle of Vitoria (SP) |
| Jun. 22 | **Battle of Craney Island (VA)** |
| Jun. 22–23 | **Laura Secord's trek (ON)** |
| Jun. 24 | **Battle of Beaver Dams/Beachwoods (ON)** |
| Jun. 25 | GB attacks Hampton (VA) |
| | US bombship destroys boats of HM Ship *Ramillies* (74) in Long Island Sound |
| Jun. 28–Aug. 31 | Siege of San Sabastian (SP) |
| Jun. 30 | GB captures 2 American merchantmen near Chazy in Lake Champlain (NY) |
| Jul. 4 | Battle near Fort Mason (MO) |
| Jul. 5 | GB raids Fort Schlosser/Black Rock (NY) |

| | |
|---|---|
| Jul. 5 | GB rejects RU's mediation offer |
| Jul. 8 | Battle of Ball's Farm/Butler's Farm (ON) |
| | Indians raid Fort Madison (IA) |
| Jul. 11 | GB raids Black Rock (NY) |
| | Indians raid near Ball's Farm (ON) |
| Jul. 12 | GB raids Ocracoke and Portsmouth (NC) |
| | GB raids Black Rock (NY) |
| Jul. 14 | British gunboats attack US Schooner *Asp* (3) in Yeocomico Creek (VA) |
| Jul. 16 | Indians raid near Fort Madison (IA) |
| Jul. 17 | Skirmish at Ball's Farm (ON) |
| Jul. 19 | US privateers *Neptune* (1) and *Fox* (1) capture HM Gunboat *Spitfire* (1) and 15 supply boats in St. Lawrence River |
| Jul. 20–27 | Siege of Tuckabatchee (AL) |
| Jul. 21 | US raids Frenchman's Creek (ON) |
| | Battle of Cranberry Creek/Goose Creek (NY) |
| | GB raids Swan Point (MD) |
| Jul. 21–28 | **Second siege of Fort Meigs (OH)** |
| Jul. 22 | Battle of Salamanca (SP) |
| Jul. 24 | US launches torpedo attack against HM Ship *Plantagenet* (76) in Lynnhaven Roads near Norfolk (VA) |
| Jul. 24–Aug. 2 | US adopts internal taxes |
| Jul. 27 | Battle of Burnt Corn (AL) |
| Jul. 29 | Boats from HM Sloop *Martin* (18) and HM Ship *Junon* (46) beat off attack from US gunboats off coast of New Jersey in Atlantic |
| Jul. 31 | Skirmish near Lower Sandusky (OH) |
| | GB lifts blockade of Presque Isle (PA) |
| | US raids York (ON) |
| Jul. 31–Aug. 1 | GB raids Plattsburgh (NY) |
| Aug. 1 | GB raids Cumberland Head (NY) |
| | GB raids Point au Roche (NY) |
| | GB raids Swanton (VT) |
| Aug. 1–2 | **Battle of Fort Stephenson (OH)** |
| Aug. 1–4 | US moves squadron from Presque Isle into Lake Erie |
| Aug. 2 | GB raids Burlington (VT) |
| | US adopts law barring use of enemy licenses |
| Aug. 3 | GB raids Cumberland Head (NY) |
| | GB raids Chazy (NY) |
| | GB raids Champlain (NY) |
| Aug. 4?–23 | GB occupies Kent Island (MD) |

| | |
|---|---|
| Aug. 5 | US privateer *Decatur* (7) captures HM Sloop *Dominica* (16) near Bermuda |
| Aug. 8 | US Schooner *Hamilton* (9) and US Schooner *Scourge* (10) sink in storm on Lake Ontario |
| Aug. 10 | GB raids St. Michaels (MD) |
| | GB captures US Schooner *Julia* (2) and US Schooner *Growler* (5) on Lake Ontario |
| Aug. 13 | Battle of Queenstown/Slippery Hill/Hall's Landing/Blakeford Shore (MD) |
| Aug. 14 | HM Sloop *Pelican* (21) defeats US Brig *Argus* (20) off coast of Wales in Irish Sea |
| Aug. 17 | US ambushes Indians near Ball's Farm (ON) |
| Aug. 24 | GB launches reconnaissance in force against Fort George (ON) |
| Aug. 26 | GB raids St. Michaels/Wade's Point (MD) |
| Aug. 26–27 | Battle of Dresden (GR) |
| Aug. 30 | **Battle of Fort Mims/Fort Mims Massacre (AL)** |
| Sep. 1 | Kimball-James Massacre near Fort Sinquefield (AL) |
| Sep. 2 | Indians attack Fort Sinquefield (AL) |
| Sep. 5 | US Brig *Enterprise* (16) defeats HM Sloop *Boxer* (14) in Atlantic off coast of Maine |
| Sep. 6 | Skirmish at Ball's Farm (ON) |
| Sep. 10 | **Battle of Lake Erie/Put-in-Bay** |
| Sep. 11 | Battle of False Ducks on Lake Ontario |
| Sep. 13 | MG Henry Procter proclaims martial law (effective in Western and London districts) (ON) |
| Sep. 14 | US raids Sugar Loaf (ON) |
| Sep. 20 | Skirmish at Odelltown (QC) |
| Sep. 23 | US Frigate *President* (54) captures HM Schooner *Highflyer* (5) off coast of New England in Atlantic |
| Sep. 27 | Battle at Peoria (IL) |
| Sep. 27 | GB evacuates and burns Fort Detroit (MI) |
| Sep. 27 | US re-occupies Fort Detroit (MI) and occupies Fort Amherstburg (ON) |
| Sep. 28 | "Burlington Races" on Lake Ontario |
| Sep. 29 | US occupies Sandwich (ON) |
| | US reestablishes civil government in Michigan Territory |
| | US raids Indian village on Lake Peoria (IL) |
| Oct. 1 | Skirmish at Four Corners (NY) |
| Oct. 4 | Skirmish at Dolsen's farm (ON) |
| | Battle of McGregor's Creek/McGregor's Mills/Chatham/the Forks of the Thames River (ON) |

| | |
|---|---|
| Oct. 5 | US captures flotilla of supply boats on Thames River (ON) |
| | **Battle of the Thames/Moraviantown/Thamesville;** Tecumseh killed (ON) |
| Oct. 6 | Skirmish near Fort George (ON) |
| | US captures 6 vessels in troop convoy near False Ducks on Lake Ontario |
| Oct. 7 | US burns Moraviantown/Fairfield (ON) |
| Oct. 8–11 | US raids Twelve Mile Creek (ON) |
| Oct. 11–13 | US raids Philipsburg and other settlements on Missisquoi Bay (QC) |
| Oct. 16 | British North West Company purchases Fort Astoria from John Jacob Astor's Pacific Fur Company (OR) |
| Oct. 16–19 | Battle of Leipzig/the Nations (GR) |
| Oct. 26 | **Battle of Châteauguay (QC)** |
| Oct. 27 | US raids Frelighsburg (QC) |
| Nov. 1–2 | Battle of French Creek/Frenchman's Creek (NY) |
| Nov. 2 | GB raids Champlain (NY) |
| | GB raids Blackistone Island/St. Clement's Island and St. George's Island (MD) |
| Nov. 3 | Battle of Tallushatchee (AL) |
| Nov. 4 | GB offers US direct peace negotiations |
| Nov. 6 | GB bombards US flotilla at Prescott in St. Lawrence (ON) |
| Nov. 9 | Battle of Talladega (AL) |
| Nov. 10 | Battle of gunboats in St. Lawrence River |
| | Battle of Hoople's Creek/Uphold's Creek (ON) |
| | Vermont orders militia serving in New York to return home |
| Nov. 11 | **Battle of Crysler's Farm/Williamsburgh (ON)** |
| Nov. 12 | Canoe Fight in Alabama River (AL) |
| Nov. 12–13 | Skirmish at Nanticoke Creek (GB captures traitors at John Dunham's home) (ON) |
| Nov. 16 | GB proclaims blockade of Long Island Sound and remaining ports in middle and southern states |
| Nov. 18 | Hillabee Massacre (AL) |
| Nov. 19 | Cap. David Porter proclaims US annexation of Nuku Hiva in Marquesas |
| | GB raids Madrid (NY) |
| Nov. 22 | MG Francis de Rottenburg proclaims martial law in Johnstown and Eastern districts (ON) |
| Nov. 26 | US raids Twenty Mile Creek and Stoney Creek area (ON) |
| Nov. 29 | Battle of Autosee/Tallassee (AL) |
| Dec. 4 | GB raids Cumberland Head (NY) |

| Dec. 10 | US evacuates Fort George and burns Newark/Niagara (ON) |
|---|---|
| Dec. 12 | GB re-occupies Fort George (ON) |
| Dec. 13 | LG Gordon Drummond appointed president and administrator of UC |
| Dec. 15 | GB raids McCrae's house on Thames River (ON) |
| Dec. 17 | US adopts embargo barring all US ships and goods from leaving port |
| | GB raids Derby (VT) |
| **Dec. 19** | **GB captures Fort Niagara (NY)** |
| Dec. 19–21 | GB burns Lewiston, Youngstown, and Manchester (NY) |
| Dec. 23 | Battle of Econochaca/the Holy Ground (AL) |
| | HM Ship *Belvidera* (42) captures unarmed US Schooner *Vixen II* (rated 14) in North Atlantic |
| Dec. 25 | GB drives two vessels ashore at Black Rock (NY) |
| Dec. 27 | GB raids Derby (VT) |
| Dec. 30 | GB burns Buffalo and Black Rock (NY) |

**1814**

| Jan. 9 | US attacks foraging party near Fort Niagara (NY) |
|---|---|
| Jan. 16 | Battle of Clough's Farm (QC) |
| Jan. 22 | Battle of Emuckfau Creek (AL) |
| | US raids Philipsburg on Missisquoi Bay (QC) |
| Jan. 24 | Battle of Enitachopco Creek (AL) |
| Jan. 25 | LG Gordon Drummond lifts martial law in Johnstown and Eastern districts (ON) |
| Jan. 27 | Battle of Calabee Creek (AL) |
| Jan. 31 | US raids Delaware (ON) |
| Feb. 6–7 | GB raids Madrid area (NY) |
| Feb. 14 | US Frigate *Constitution* (52) captures HM Schooner *Pictou* (14) |
| Feb. 14–24 | GB raids Salmon River (NY) |
| Mar. 1 | Indians attack surveyor at Saline Creek (IL) |
| Mar. 4 | Battle of Longwood/Long Woods/Battle Hill (ON) |
| Mar. 14 | UC confiscates lands of anyone fleeing to US |
| Mar. 26 | US military court in Albany finds BG William Hull guilty of cowardice and neglect of duty (NY) |
| **Mar. 27–28** | **Battle of Horseshoe Bend/Tohopeka (AL)** |
| Mar. 28 | HM Ship *Phoebe* (46 or 53) and HM Sloop *Cherub* (26) defeat US Frigate *Essex* (46) off coast of Chile in Pacific |
| Mar. 30 | Second Battle of Lacolle Mill (QC) |
| Mar. 31 | European allies enter Paris (FR) |
| Apr. 2 | GB issues proclamation urging slaves in Chesapeake to join British forces |

| | |
|---|---|
| Apr. 5 | US raids Oxford (ON) |
| Apr. 6 | GB establishes anchorage at Tangier Island (VA) |
| | Napoleon abdicates throne (FR) |
| Apr. 7 | GB raids Pettipaug Point (CT) |
| Apr. 12 | LG Gordon Drummond proclaims martial law in UC (ON) |
| Apr. 14 | US repeals embargo and non-importation law |
| | Indians raid Cooper's Fort (MO) |
| Apr. 20 | HM Ship *Orpheus* (42?) captures US Sloop *Frolic* (22) in Caribbean |
| Apr. 25 | **GB proclaims blockade of New England** |
| Apr. 25 | US proposes armistice |
| Apr. 28 | Napoleon exiled to Elba in Mediterranean |
| Apr. 29 | US Sloop *Peacock* (22) defeats HM Sloop *Epervier* (18) in Caribbean |
| May 1 | Armistice negotiations fail at Champlain (NY) |
| May 5–6 | GB attacks Fort Ontario/Oswego (NY) |
| May 14 | Battle of Otter Creek/Fort Cassin (VT) |
| | Skirmish at Bouquet River (VT) |
| May 14–15 | US raids Dover/Port Dover/Long Point/Campbell's Raid (ON) |
| May 15 | GB raids Pultneyville (NY) |
| May 20 | US raids Port Talbot (ON) |
| May 23–Jun. 21 | Treason trials at Ancaster (ON) |
| May 29 | GB raids Pungoteague Creek (MD) |
| May 30 | Battle of Sandy Creek/Oswego Falls (NY) |
| | European allies and FR sign First Treaty of Paris (Napoleonic Wars appear to end) (FR) |
| May 31 | GB raids Pungoteague Creek (VA) |
| Jun. 1 | Battle of Cedar Point/St. Jerome's Point (MD) |
| Jun. 2 | US occupies Prairie du Chien (WI) |
| Jun. 8–10 | First Battle of St. Leonard's Creek/Patuxent River/Battle of the Barges (MD) |
| Jun. 12 | GB raids Broomes Island (MD) |
| Jun. 14 | GB raids south of Coles Landing (MD) |
| Jun. 15 | GB raids Benedict (MD) |
| Jun. 15–16 | GB raids Lower Marlboro/Ballard's Landing (MD) |
| Jun. 16 | Skirmish at Hall's Creek (MD) |
| Jun. 16–17 | GB raids Sheridan Point (MD) |
| Jun. 17 | GB raids Magruder's Landing/Magruder's Ferry (MD) |
| Jun. 18 | GB raids Coles Landing (MD) |
| Jun. 19 | US captures gunboat at Tar Island in St. Lawrence River (ON) |

| | |
|---|---|
| Jun. 22 | HM Ship *Leander* (60) captures unarmed US Brig *Rattlesnake* (rated 14) in North Atlantic |
| Jun. 26 | Second Battle of St. Leonard's Creek/the Patuxent River (MD) |
| Jun. 27 | **US drops impressment demand** |
| Jun. 28 | US Sloop *Wasp* (22) defeats HM Sloop *Reindeer* (19) in North Atlantic |
| | Skirmish at Odelltown (QC) |
| Jun. 30 | GB raids Lewiston (NY) |
| Jul. 2 | GB raids St. Leonard's Creek (MD) |
| Jul. 3 | US captures Fort Erie (ON) |
| Jul. 5 | **Battle of Chippawa (ON)** |
| Jul. 9 | Skirmish at Thames River in Aldborough Township (ON) |
| Jul. 10 | Wood River Massacre (IL) |
| Jul. 11 | GB captures Eastport/Fort Sullivan (ME) |
| Jul. 12 | HM Ship *Medway* (80) captures US Brig *Siren* (16) off coast of South Africa |
| | GB raids Elkton (MD) |
| Jul. 16 | GB raids Calverton (MD) |
| Jul. 17 | GB raids Sheridan Point, God's Grace, and Huntington (MD) |
| Jul. 17–20 | Siege of Prairie du Chien (WI) |
| Jul. 18 | US burns St. Davids (ON) |
| | GB raids Champlain (NY) |
| Jul. 19 | GB raids Leonardtown (MD) |
| | GB raids Prince Frederick MD) |
| Jul. 20 | GB raids south of Benedict (MD) |
| | US destroys Fort St. Joseph (ON) |
| | GB executes 8 traitors convicted at Ancaster (ON) |
| Jul. 20–21 | GB raids Nomini Creek (VA) |
| Jul. 20–22 | Skirmishing at Fort George (ON) |
| Jul. 21 | US captures British merchantman *Mink* on Lake Huron |
| | US raids Sault Ste. Marie and captures British merchantman *Perseverance* (ON) |
| | GB raids Hallowing Point (MD) |
| Jul. 21 or 22 | Battle of Campbell's Island/Rock River/Black Rock River (IL) |
| Jul. 22 | GB raids near Sandy Point (MD) |
| | US and Miamis, Potawatomis, Ottawas, Shawnees, Kickapoos sign peace treaty at Greenville (OH) |
| Jul. 23 | GB raids St. Clement's Creek (MD) |
| Jul. 25 | **Battle of Lundy's Lane/Bridgewater/Niagara Falls/Niagara/the Falls/the Cataract (ON)** |

| | |
|---|---|
| Jul. 25 | US raids Charlotteville (ON) |
| Jul. 26 | GB raids Machodoc Creek (VA) |
| Jul. 30 | GB raids Chaptico (MD) |
| Aug. | US public credit collapses |
| Aug. | US banks suspend specie payments |
| Aug. 1 | GB raids north of Cove Point (MD) |
| Aug. 2 | GB raids Slaughter Creek (MD) |
| Aug. 3 | Battle of Conjocta Creek/Scajaquada Creek/Shoguoquady Creek/ Conkuichity/Black Rock (NY) |
| | Battle of Kinsale/Yocomico River (VA) |
| Aug. 4 | US attacks Fort Mackinac (MI) |
| Aug. 5 | US squadron drives HM Schooner *Magnet* (12) aground on Lake Ontario |
| Aug. 6–7 | GB raids Coan River (VA) |
| Aug. 6–14 | Skirmishing at Fort Erie (ON) |
| Aug. 7–14 | GB bombards Fort Erie (ON) |
| Aug. 8 | **Peace negotiations begin in Ghent (BE)** |
| Aug. 8–19 | GB lays down initial peace terms (BE) |
| Aug. 9 | US and Creeks sign peace treaty at Fort Jackson (AL) |
| Aug. 9–11 | Battle of Stonington (CT) |
| Aug. 10 | Skirmish near Odelltown (QC) |
| Aug. 11–12 | GB raids St. Mary's River (MD) |
| Aug. 12 | GB captures US Schooner *Somers* (2) and US Schooner *Ohio* (1) in Niagara River |
| Aug. 14 | GB occupies Pensacola (FL) |
| | Battle of Nottawasaga River (ON) |
| Aug. 15 | **Battle of Fort Erie (ON)** |
| Aug. 16 | US raids Port Talbot (ON) |
| Aug. 19–20 | GB lands at Benedict en route to Washington (MD) |
| Aug. 19–Sep. 17 | GB bombards Fort Erie (ON) |
| Aug. 20 | Indians raid Port Talbot (ON) |
| | GB raids Rock Hall (MD) |
| Aug. 20–Sep. 16 | Skirmishing at Fort Erie (ON) |
| Aug. 21 | Skirmish at Nottingham (MD) |
| Aug. 22 | US blows up its Chesapeake flotilla at Pig Point (MD) |
| Aug. 24 | **Battle of Bladensburg (MD)** |
| | US burns Washington Naval Yard, US Frigate *Columbia* (rated 44), and US Sloop *Argus* (rated 18) (DC) |
| Aug. 24–25 | **GB burns Washington (DC)** |

| | |
|---|---|
| Aug. 27 | US blows up Fort Washington/Fort Warburton (MD) |
| | Cap. Thomas Boyle of US privateer *Chasseur* (16) proclaims mock blockade of GB and Ireland |
| Aug. 28 | US captures British commissary agents in London District (ON) |
| | Nantucket declares neutrality (MA) |
| | GB raids Worton Point/Worton Creek (MD) |
| Aug. 29 | GB captures Alexandria (VA) |
| Aug. 29–30 | US raids Oxford (ON) |
| Aug. 30 | Skirmish at Westminster (ON) |
| | GB raids Fairlee Creek (MD) |
| Aug. 31 | Battle of Caulks Field/Moore's Field/Moorefields (MD) |
| Aug. 31 | GB invades New York |
| Sep. 1–11 | **GB occupies 100 miles of US coast from Eastport to Castine (ME)** |
| Sep. 1 | GB captures Castine (ME) |
| | US Sloop *Wasp* (22) defeats HM Sloop *Avon* (20) in North Atlantic |
| | Skirmish near Delaware (ON) |
| Sep. 3 | Battle of Hampden (ME) |
| | US burns US Sloop *Adams* (28) at Hampden (ME) |
| | GB captures US Schooner *Tigress* (1) on Lake Huron |
| Sep. 4–5 | Battle of the White House/Potomac River (VA) |
| Sep. 5 | Skirmish at Indian Head (MD) |
| | Battle of Credit Island/Rock Island Rapids (IA) |
| Sep. 6 | GB captures US Schooner *Scorpion* (2) on Lake Huron |
| | Battle of Beekmantown/Culver Hill (NY) |
| Sep. 6–11 | Skirmishing near Plattsburgh (NY) |
| Sep. 7? | Skirmish near Cooper's Fort (MO) |
| Sep. 9 | US raids Port Talbot (ON) |
| Sep. 11 | GB captures Machias/Fort O'Brien (ME) |
| | Battle of Plattsburgh (NY) |
| | **Battle of Lake Champlain;** Cap. George Downie killed |
| Sep. 12 | Skirmish at North Point; MG Robert Ross killed (MD) |
| | **Battle of North Point/Long Log Lane/Godley Wood/the Meeting House (MD)** |
| Sep. 12 or 13 | GB raids Bear Creek (MD) |
| Sep. 13–14 | **GB bombards Fort McHenry (MD)** |
| Sep. 14 | Francis Scott Key writes "The Star-Spangled Banner" (MD) |
| | GB withdraws from Baltimore (MD) |
| Sep. 15 | Battle of Fort Bowyer/Mobile Bay (AL) |
| Sep. 15–Jun. 9 | Congress of Vienna (AU) |

| | |
|---|---|
| Sep. 16 | US attacks Baratarian pirate base (LA) |
| Sep. 17 | **US sortie from Fort Erie (ON)** |
| Sep. 20 | US raids settlements in Western District (ON) |
| Sep. 26–27 | British squadron defeats US privateer *General Armstrong* (9) in Azores in Atlantic |
| Oct. 11 | US privateer *Prince-de-Neufchatel* (17) defeats flotilla of boats from HM Ship *Endymion* (51) in Atlantic near Nantucket |
| Oct. 15 | Skirmish near Street's Grove/Chippawa (ON) |
| Oct. 19 | Battle of Cooks Mills/Lyons Creek (ON) |
| | GB raids Castle Haven (MD) |
| Oct. 21 | GB offers peace on basis of *uti possidetis* (BE) |
| Oct. 22 | Renegade Americans murder Cap. William Francis of Norfolk militia (ON) |
| Oct. 22–Nov. 17 | **BG Duncan McArthur's Raid (ON)** |
| Oct. 27 | GB raids Tracey's Landing (MD) |
| Oct. 31 | Battle of the Windmills/Kirby's Wind Mill (MD) |
| Nov. 1 | GB raids St. Inigoes (MD) |
| Nov. 5 | US evacuates Fort Erie (ON) |
| | Skirmish at Grand River (ON) |
| Nov. 6 | Battle of Malcolm's Mills (ON) |
| Nov. 7 | US occupies Pensacola (FL) |
| Nov. 27 | GB drops *uti possidetis* (BE) |
| Dec. 2 | GB raids Tappahannock (VA) |
| Dec. 6 | Battle of Farnham Church (VA) |
| Dec. 14 | Battle of Lake Borgne (LA) |
| Dec. 15–Jan. 5 | Hartford Convention meets (CT) |
| Dec. 15–Feb. 27 | US adopts internal taxes |
| Dec. 16 | MG Andrew Jackson proclaims martial law in New Orleans (LA) |
| Dec. 23 | Battle of Villeré's Plantation/Night Engagement at New Orleans (LA) |
| Dec. 24 | **US and GB sign Treaty of Ghent (BE)** |
| Dec. 27 | British artillery destroys US Schooner *Carolina* (13) (LA) |
| | GB ratifies Treaty of Ghent |
| Dec. 28 | British reconnaissance in force at New Orleans (LA) |
| | US Congress rejects conscription |
| Dec. 31 | Cap. Andrew Bulger proclaims martial law at Prairie du Chien (WI) |

**1815**

| | |
|---|---|
| Jan. 1 | News of Treaty of Ghent reaches Congress of Vienna (AU) |
| | Battle of Rodriguez Canal/Artillery Duel at New Orleans (LA) |

| | |
|---|---|
| Jan. 2 | HM Sloop *Favourite/Favorite* (26?) departs from Portsmouth with Treaty of Ghent (UK) |
| Jan. 8 | **Battle of New Orleans/Chalmette;** MG Edward Pakenham and MG Samuel Gibbs killed (LA) |
| Jan. 9–18 | Battle of Fort St. Philip (LA) |
| Jan. 10 | GB occupies Cumberland Island (GA) |
| Jan. 12 | Battle of Lakes Cove (MD) |
| Jan. 13 | GB attacks Point Petre/Point Peter/St. Marys on Cumberland Island (GA) |
| Jan. 15 | British squadron captures US Frigate *President* (52) |
| Jan. 25 | Skirmish at mouth of Bayou Bienvenu (LA) |
| Jan. 28 | British military court in Montreal finds MG Henry Procter guilty of mismanaging Thames campaign (QC) |
| Feb. 4 | US adopts second enemy trade law |
| Feb. 6 | GB raids Tobacco Stick/Madison (MD) |
| Feb. 7 | Battle of the Ice Mound/the Tobacco Stick/James Island/St. James Island (MD) |
| Feb. 11 | HM Sloop *Favourite/Favorite* (26?) reaches New York City with Treaty of Ghent (NY) |
| Feb. 8–11 | Siege of Fort Bowyer (AL) |
| Feb. 12 | Indians raid Busseron (IN) |
| Feb. 14 | Treaty of Ghent reaches Washington (DC) |
| Feb. 16 | US Senate unanimously approves Treaty of Ghent |
| | **Madison ratifies Treaty of Ghent (War of 1812 officially ends)** |
| Feb. 17 | US Congress rejects national bank |
| | US and GB exchange ratifications of Treaty of Ghent (treaty becomes binding) |
| Feb. 20 | US Frigate *Constitution* (52) defeats HM Ship *Cyane* (33) and HM Ship *Levant* (21) off coast of North Africa in Atlantic |
| Feb. 21 | US executes 6 militiamen in Mobile (AL) |
| Feb. 22 | News of peace reaches Albany (NY) |
| Feb. 23 | News of peace reaches Cumberland Island (GA) |
| Feb. 24 | Battle of St. Marys River (GA) |
| Feb. 24? | News of peace reaches Kingston (ON) |
| Feb. 26 | Napoleon escapes from Elba in Mediterranean |
| | US privateer *Chasseur* (15) defeats HM Schooner *St. Lawrence* (13) near Cuba in Caribbean |
| Mar. 1 | News of peace reaches Quebec (QC) |
| | British officials in Quebec proclaim restoration of peace (QC) |
| Mar. 6 | Unofficial news of peace reaches New Orleans (LA) |

| | |
|---|---|
| Mar. 7 | Skirmish at Prairie Fork on Loutre River (MO) |
| Mar. 9 | Treaty of Ghent proclaimed at Quebec (QC) |
| Mar. 11 | British squadron recaptures HM Ship *Levant* (21) in North Atlantic |
| Mar. 13 | Official news of peace reaches New Orleans (LA) |
| | MG Andrew Jackson lifts martial law in New Orleans (LA) |
| Mar. 14 | News of peace reaches main British camp on Dauphin Island (AL) |
| Mar. 16 | HM Sloop *Erebus* (26) attacks US Gunboat #168 (1?) off coast of Georgia in Atlantic |
| Mar. 20 | Napoleon enters Paris and assumes power (Hundred Days begins; Napoleonic Wars resume) (FR) |
| Mar. 23 | US Sloop *Hornet* (20) defeats HM Sloop *Penguin* (19) near Tristan da Cunha in South Atlantic |
| Mar. 28 | News of peace reaches London (GB) |
| Mar. 31 | MG Andrew Jackson convicted of contempt and fined $1,000 (LA) |
| Apr. 4 | Battle of Cote Sans Dessein/Roi's Fort/Tibeau's Fort (MO) |
| Apr. 6 | Dartmoor Massacre (GB) |
| Apr. 16 | News of peace reaches Prairie du Chien (WI) |
| Apr. 24 | News of peace reaches Mackinac (MI) |
| May 20 | Indians raid Femme Osage Valley (MO) |
| May 24 | Battle of the Sinkhole (MO) |
| Jun. 18 | Battle of Waterloo (BE) |
| Jun. 22 | Napoleon abdicates throne (Hundred Days ends; Napoleonic Wars end) (FR) |
| Jun. 30 | **US Sloop *Peacock* (22) defeats East India cruiser *Nautilus* (14) in Indian Ocean (last battle of War of 1812)** |
| Jul. 18 | US and Potawatomis sign peace treaty at Portage des Sioux (MO) |
| | US and Piankashaws sign peace treaty at Portage des Sioux (MO) |
| Jul. 19 | US and Teton Sioux sign peace treaty at Portage des Sioux (MO) |
| | US and Sioux of the Lakes sign peace treaty at Portage des Sioux (MO) |
| | US and Sioux of St. Peter's River sign peace treaty at Portage des Sioux (MO) |
| | US and Yankton Sioux sign peace treaty at Portage des Sioux (MO) |
| Jul. 20 | US and Omahas sign peace treaty at Portage des Sioux (MO) |
| Aug. 21 | British military court at Portsmouth finds Cap. Daniel Pring innocent of mismanaging naval battle on Lake Champlain (GB) |
| Sep. 2 | US and Kickapoos sign peace treaty at Portage des Sioux (MO) |
| Sep. 8 | US and Chippewas, Ottawas, Potawatomis sign peace treaty at Spring Wells (MI) |
| Sep. 12 | US and Osages sign peace treaty at Portage des Sioux (MO) |
| Sep. 13 | US and Sauks sign peace treaty at Portage des Sioux (MO) |

| | |
|---|---|
| Sep. 14 | US and Foxes sign peace treaty at Portage des Sioux (MO) |
| Sep. 16 | US and Iowas sign peace treaty at Portage des Sioux (MO) |
| Oct. 16 | Napoleon arrives at St. Helena in South Pacific |
| Oct. 28 | US and Kansas sign peace treaty at Portage des Sioux (MO) |
| Nov. 20 | European allies and FR sign Second Treaty of Paris (Napoleonic Wars officially end) (FR) |

**1816**

| | |
|---|---|
| May 13 | US and Sauks sign peace treaty at St. Louis (MO) |
| Jun. 1 | US and Sioux of the Leaf, Sioux of the Broad Leaf, Sioux Who Shoot in the Pine Tops sign peace treaty at St. Louis (MO) |
| Jun. 3 | US and Winnebagoes sign peace treaty at St. Louis (MO) |
| Jun. 4 | US and Weas, Kickapoos sign peace treaty at Fort Harrison (IN) |

**1817**

| | |
|---|---|
| Mar. 30 | US and Menominees sign peace treaty at St. Louis (MO) |
| Jun. 24 | US and Otoes sign peace treaty at St. Louis (MO) |
| Jun. 25 | US and Poncas sign peace treaty at St. Louis (MO) |

# "The Hunters of Kentucky"

**"T**he Hunters of Kentucky; or, the Battle of New Orleans" was written in early 1821 by Samuel Woodworth (1784–1842), a printer, poet, and playwright. During the War of 1812, Woodworth had published a Sweden-borgian religious magazine entitled *The Halcyon Luminary and Theological Repository* (1812–13) and a New York newspaper called *The War* (1812–14). He also wrote a host of wartime patriotic songs, most of which are now lost or forgotten. Shortly after the conflict, he wrote a war novel, *The Champions of Freedom, or The Mysterious Chief* (1816). Panned by contemporaries, it, too, was quickly forgotten.

Although he was dogged by poverty throughout his life, Woodworth's play, *The Forest Rose* (1825), probably had the best run of any American play before the Civil War, mainly because it featured a popular Yankee character, Jonathan Ploughboy. Today, Woodworth is best remembered for two poems that were put to music, "The Old Oaken Bucket" (1818)—originally called simply "The Bucket"—and "The Hunters of Kentucky."[1]

Sung to the traditional tune of "Ally Croker" or "The Unfortunate Miss Bailey," "The Hunters of Kentucky" broadly fits the "come-all-ye" format, a narrative form of storytelling that was especially popular among Irish singers. The song became an instant hit when Noah M. Ludlow introduced it to an audience in New Orleans in 1822. It became Andrew Jackson's campaign song when he ran for the presidency in 1828, and it remained immensely popular throughout his two terms in office (1829–37).[2] There was a certain irony in this because although Jackson was the hero of New Orleans, he lived in Tennessee, while Henry Clay, perhaps his fiercest rival, came from Kentucky.

"The Hunters of Kentucky" may have been sung during the Texas War of Independence in the mid-1830s. In 1837 *Davy Crockett's Almanack of Wild Sports in the West* carried the description "Life in the Backwoods, & Sketches of Texas" and had a reference on the cover to "The Hunters of Kentucky."[3] But there is nothing in the text on the song, and it is unlikely that Crockett (who perished the year before at the Alamo) was responsible for the content of any of the almanacs issued under his name.[4] Nor is there any other evidence that the song was sung by Americans who fought in the Texas war.

By contrast, there is unmistakable evidence that the song played a conspicuous role in the border warfare that plagued the United States and Canada in the late 1830s. Many of the American freebooters who invaded Upper Canada in 1837–38 carried rifles and were good marksmen. Calling themselves "Patriot Hunters," they adopted "The Hunters of Kentucky" as their marching song. Their defeat in the Battle of the Windmill near Prescott in 1838 brought this era of filibustering to an end.[5]

"The Hunters of Kentucky" was responsible for propagating three myths about the War of 1812. First, the reference in the fifth stanza to "our Kentucky rifles" established the common name for this weapon even though the rifle was developed and manufactured in Pennsylvania and thus is properly known as the Pennsylvania rifle. Secondly, the song promoted the idea that riflemen won the Battle of New Orleans although most of the damage on the battlefield that day was done by Jackson's artillery. Finally, the reference to "beauty" and "booty" in the eighth stanza spread the idea that the British planned to sack New Orleans if they succeeded in taking the city—although it is highly unlikely that they would have done do. By implication, "The Hunters of Kentucky" lent support to two additional myths: first, that the United States had won the war; and, secondly, that riflemen, particularly from Kentucky, had played a central role in that victory.

Printed versions of the song vary slightly. The version below has been taken from a contemporary broadside.[6]

### "The Hunters of Kentucky; or, the Battle of New Orleans"

*Samuel Woodworth*

Ye gentlemen and ladies fair
    Who grace this famous city,
Just listen, if you've time to spare,
    While I rehearse a ditty;
And for the opportunity,

conceive yourselves quite lucky,
   For tis not often here you see
     A hunter from Kentucky.

       Oh, Kentucky,
       The Hunters of Kentucky,
       Oh Kentucky,
       The Hunters of Kentucky.

We are a hardy, free-born race,
   Each man to fear a stranger,
Whate'er the game we join in chase,
   Despising toil and danger.
And if a daring foe annoys,
   Whate'er his strength or forces,
We'll show them that Kentucky boys
   Are alligators-horses.

       Oh, Kentucky, etc.

I 'spose you've read it in the prints,
   How Packenham attempted
To make Old Hickory JACKSON wince,
   But soon his scheme repented;
For we with rifles ready cock'd,
   Thought such occasion lucky,
And soon around the general flock'd
   The Hunters of Kentucky.

       Oh, Kentucky, etc.

You've heard, I 'spose, how New-Orleans
   Is famed for wealth and beauty;
There's girls of every hue, it seems,
   From snowy white to sooty.
So Packenham he made his brags,
   If he in fight was lucky,
He'd have their girls and cotton bags,
   In spite of old Kentucky.

       Oh, Kentucky, etc.

But Jackson he was wide awake,
   And was'nt scar'd at trifles,
For well he knew what aim we take
   With our Kentucky rifles.

So he led us up to a Cyprus swamp,
    The ground was low and mucky,
There stood John Bull in martial pomp,
    And here old Kentucky.

        Oh, Kentucky, etc.

A bank was raised to hide our breast,
    Not that we thought of dying,
But that we always take a rest,
    Unless the game is flying.
Behind it stood our little force,
    None wish'd it to be greater,
For every man was half a horse,
    And half an alligator.

        Oh, Kentucky, etc.

They did not let their patience tire,
    Before they show'd their faces,
We did not choose to waste our fire,
    So snugly kept our places.
But when so near we saw them wink,
    We thought it time to stop 'em,
And it would have done you good, I think,
    To see Kentuckians drop 'em.

        Oh, Kentucky, etc.

They found, at last, 'twas vain to fight,
    Where lead was all their *booty*,
And so they wisely took to flight,
    And left us all *beauty*.
And now if danger e'er annoys,
    Remember what our trade is,
Just send for us Kentucky boys,
    And we'll protect ye, ladies.

        Oh, Kentucky, etc.

# "The Bold Canadian"

The Canadian counterpart to "The Hunters of Kentucky" is "The Bold Canadian," a song about the British victory at Detroit in 1812. This song has been attributed to Cornelius Flummerfelt, a private in the 1st Flank Company of the 3rd York Militia, who took part in the Detroit campaign and supposedly wrote the lines after traveling to York in late 1812.[1] It seems likely that the lines were actually composed during the march.

Unlike "The Hunters of Kentucky," the words to "The Bold Canadian" were not published until the twentieth century. Until then, the song was passed down through the generations by being sung on marches, at patriotic celebrations, in work details, or on other occasions. Because the song was part of Canada's oral tradition for so long, the lyrics can be found in many variant forms. All versions are cast in the "come-all-ye" form.

In 1907, the Niagara Historical Society published a pamphlet that contained a brief biography of Major General Isaac Brock by Janet Carnochan. In her sketch, Carnochan included a shortened version of the song that she got from Mrs. Alphaeus Cox, who wrote it down from memory after hearing her mother sing it.[2] Twenty years later, the Ontario Historical Society published two other versions, the full text of the Cox version and another version set down by Dr. Robert I. Warner near the end of his life. Warner learned the song from his grandfather, John Lampman, a captain in the 1st Lincoln Militia, who was wounded in the Battle of Lundy's Lane. Warner remembered his grandfather singing the song whenever he drew his pension check or on the anniversary of great battles, such as Waterloo.[3] A third version appeared along with the music in 1960 in a Canadian songbook.[4] These three versions of the song vary considerably in detail. Each has unique lines and stanzas and a different order for the stanzas.

Unlike "The Hunters of Kentucky" (which was not popular for very long) or "The Star-Spangled Banner" (which does not tell much of a story), "The Bold Canadian" remained popular at least until the end of the nineteenth century and tells a pretty good story. The song helped keep the memory of the War of 1812 alive in Canada and served as a reminder to Canadians that they had successfully beaten back American attempts to conquer their land.

"The Bold Canadian" helped perpetuate the militia myth by suggesting that the victory at Detroit was the work of Canadian volunteers. The song gives credit to only one British regular, Major General Isaac Brock, and does not mention the role of the Indians. Thus, what was actually a Redcoat and Indian victory was transformed into a Canadian militia triumph.

The song also promotes the myth of Canadian unity during the war. It gives no hint that any Canadians might have welcomed the American invasion or opposed resistance, no hint that any Canadians felt anything other than steadfast loyalty to the British Crown and empire.

The version of the song printed below is the one remembered by Mrs. Cox.[5] The last two stanzas in this version explicitly credit Canadian volunteers with the victory and celebrate Canadian unity.

### "The Bold Canadian"

*Attributed to Cornelius Flummerfelt*

Come all you brave Canadians
    I'd have you lend an ear
Unto a simple ditty
    That will your spirits cheer,

Concerning an engagement
    We had at Sandwich town—
The courage of those Yankee boys
    So bravely we pulled down.

Their purpose to invade us
    Was to kill and to destroy
To distress our wives and children
    And cause us much annoy.

Our countrymen were filled
    With sorrow, grief and woe
To think that they would fall
    By an unnatural foe.

At length our bold commander
    Sir Isaac Brock by name
Took shipping at Niagara[6]
    And unto York he came.

He said: "My valiant heroes,
    Will you go along with me
To fight those Yankee boys
    In the west of Canady."

"O yes," we all replied,
    "We'll go along with you
Our knapsacks on our back
    And make no more ado."

Our fire-locks[7] then we shouldered
    And straight we marched away
With firm determination
    To shew them British play.

Yes our fire-locks we shouldered
    Forward our course to steer
To meet and fight the invader
    With neither dread nor fear.

At Sandwich we arrived
    Each man with his supply
With bold determination
    To conquer or to die.

Our general sent a flag
    And thus to them did say:
"Surrender now your garrison
    Or I'll fire on you this day."

Our troops then marched over
    Our artillery we did land
And marched straight upon their town
    Like an undaunted band.

They refused to surrender
    They chose to stand their ground
We opened then our guns
    And gave them fire all round.

The Yankee boys began to fear
   And their blood to run cold
To see us marching forward
   So courageous and bold.

Their general sent a flag of truce
   For quarter then they call:
"Hold your hand, brave British boys,
   I fear you'll slay us all."

"Our town is at your command
   Our garrison likewise."
They brought their arms and grounded them
   Right down before our eyes.

And they were all made prisoners
   On board of ship they went
And from the town of Sandwich
   To Quebec they were sent.

We guarded them from Sandwich
   Safe down unto Fort George
And them within the town of York
   So safely we did lodge.

And we're arrived at home
   Each man without a wound
And the fame of this great conquest
   Will through the province sound.

Success unto the volunteers
   Who thus their rights maintain
Likewise their bold commander
   Sir Isaac Brock by name.

And being all united
   This is the song we'll sing
Success unto Great Britain
   And may God Save the King.

# Shipwrecks and Rebuilt Ships

Some warships that were put into service on the Great Lakes, Lake Champlain, and the Chesapeake Bay during the War of 1812 were built so hastily that few records survive of their design or construction. Fortunately, scholars in the United States, Canada, and Great Britain have carried out archaeological investigations of the remains that have produced a better understanding of these ships. The work has been particularly fruitful on the northern lakes, where the cold freshwater environment has helped preserve the wood and iron artifacts. To date, the remains of more than 15 ships have been found.

Master Commandant Oliver H. Perry went into battle on Lake Erie with two nearly identical brigs, the U.S. Brig *Lawrence* (20), which was his flagship, and the U.S. Brig *Niagara* (20), which he later brought up to turn the tide in the battle. Both ships went to rot and in 1820 were scuttled in Misery Bay near Erie, Pennsylvania, the *Niagara* in shallow water and the *Lawrence* in deeper water. In 1875 the hull of a ship thought to be the *Lawrence* was recovered from a shallow water grave and the following year shipped to Philadelphia by rail to be exhibited at the nation's centennial celebration. The ship drew little interest and shortly thereafter was consumed in a warehouse fire. In 1913 another ship, presumed to be the *Niagara,* was raised from somewhat deeper water in Misery Bay.

Since reports from the early nineteenth century indicate that the *Niagara* was in 4 feet of water and the *Lawrence* was in 13 feet, the ships somehow must have been misidentified. It has been suggested that the ship thought to be the *Niagara* was actually P.M./H.M. Sloop *Queen Charlotte* (17), a captured British ship that was sunk in the same waters. But Walter Rybka, senior captain of the rebuilt *Niagara,* has shown that the keel of the British ship was too short to fit the profile of the raised ship. What seems more likely is that the ship raised in 1875 (and destroyed the following year) was the *Niagara*, and the ship raised in 1913 (and rebuilt as the *Niagara*) was actually the *Lawrence*.[1]

The most spectacular discovery of ships from the War of 1812 occurred in 1973, when the schooners *Hamilton* (9) and *Scourge* (10) were found in 300 feet of water on the floor of Lake Ontario. Both vessels were originally merchantmen. American officials seized the British merchantman *Lord Nelson* shortly before the war and converted it to the *Scourge*. Later in 1812 U.S. officials bought the *Diana* from its American owner and then armed it and renamed it the *Hamilton*.

Unfortunately, the naval guns weighed so much that both schooners became dangerously top-heavy and were poor sailers. According to Ned Myers, one of the *Scourge's* crewmen, his ship was "unfit for her duty," and it was often said that "she would prove our coffin."[2] Both vessels sank after capsizing in a storm in the early morning hours of August 8, 1813. All but 16 of the 100 men aboard perished. Ned Myers was one of the lucky survivors.

The vessels landed upright on the floor of the lake. Although their ropes have rotted away and some of their metal fixtures and equipment have corroded, the vessels otherwise appear to be exceptionally well preserved. The United States has transferred title to the two "ghost ships" to the Canadian city of Hamilton. If they are ever refloated, the remains of their crews will be returned to the United States for military burial, and the ships will be displayed on the lakefront in Hamilton.[3]

At least some remains of a dozen other warships from the War of 1812 have been found. These are H.M. Schooner *Tecumseth* (4), which was raised in Georgian Bay; H.M. Schooner *Nancy* (3), a British supply ship on Lake Huron that American forces sank in the Nottawasaga River off Georgian Bay in 1814; H.M. Brig *General Hunter* (10), which was captured in the Battle of Lake Erie in 1813; H.M. Ship *St. Lawrence* (104), H.M. Ship *Prince Regent* (58), H.M. Ship *Wolfe* (21–23), and U.S. Sloop *Jefferson* (20), all of which served on Lake Ontario; U.S. Brig *Eagle* (20), U.S. Schooner *Ticonderoga* (17), H.M. Sloop *Linnet* (16), and an American gunboat (most likely the *Allen*), all of which took part in the Battle of Lake Champlain in 1814; a British gunboat on the Upper St. Lawrence River; and part of Captain Joshua Barney's flotilla of barges and gunboats that served in the Chesapeake Bay.[4]

If studying these remains gives us a better understanding of ships from the Age of Sail, so, too, does restoring or reconstructing them. This enables

The U.S. Frigate *Constitution* had a stellar career in the War of 1812 and is still in commission today. Shown here is "Old Ironsides" in 1860. (Lossing, *Pictorial Field-Book of the War of 1812*)

us to see how these wooden vessels were built and operated. Building and equipping these ships requires a special vocabulary and specialized tools, and sailing the ships requires special skills.

The most famous example of a rebuilt ship from this era is the U.S. Frigate *Constitution* (52–55). Launched in 1797, the *Constitution* began cruising the following year and by 1812 was a seasoned ship. At the beginning of the war, in a superb display of American seamanship, the *Constitution* outran a British squadron. Shortly thereafter it defeated H.M. Ship *Guerrière* (49) and H.M. Ship *Java* (49). Then, in an excellent display of American tactics, the ship defeated H.M. Ship *Cyane* (33) and H.M. Ship *Levant* (21).

Emerging from the war a great national symbol, the *Constitution* was immortalized in a poem written by Oliver Wendell Holmes in 1830 when it was mistakenly thought that the ship was about to be broken up. The *Constitution* continued to play a vital role for the U.S. Navy until withdrawn from active service in 1855. Thereafter, it served as a school ship, a training ship, and a receiving ship.

Tobias Lear had called the *Constitution* "a most fortunate ship" in 1804, and this characterization proved to be apt.[5] In its long career, the ship survived not only the rigors of war, but also fire, mutiny, a hurricane, a couple of groundings, a collision with a steel destroyer (in which "Old Ironsides" might have come off the better), a temporary name change (to *Old Constitution*), and the usual decay that afflicts wooden ships.

In 1940 President Franklin D. Roosevelt ordered the ship recommissioned. It has been refitted and rebuilt numerous times, and although it now has a number of modern features, it is gradually being restored to its appearance in 1812. Still part of the U.S. Navy, the *Constitution* is the oldest commissioned ship afloat in the world, and it takes several cruises a year, including an annual "turnaround cruise" that includes members of the general public chosen by lottery. A million people tour the ship every year at the Charlestown Navy Yard in Boston.[6]

Another fine example of a rebuilt ship is the U.S. Brig *Niagara*, which was originally part of Perry's victorious squadron on Lake Erie. In 1913, to commemorate the centennial of Perry's great victory, the people of Erie salvaged and partly restored a ship they thought was the *Niagara* (although it was probably the *Lawrence*). In 1931 the state took possession of the ship and undertook a new restoration, but progress was slow, and the ship began to deteriorate before the work was completed. For the 150th anniversary of Perry's victory in 1963, the ship was given a cosmetic refurbishment, but thereafter it again began to decay badly.

The U.S. Brig *Niagara*, which turned the tide in the Battle of Lake Erie in 1813, has been rebuilt and now sails the Great Lakes from its home port in Erie, Pennsylvania. (Erie Maritime Museum)

In the 1980s the ship was completely rebuilt. The new two-masted *Niagara*, which has only a few of the original timbers in it, was launched in 1988 in time to commemorate the 175th anniversary of Perry's victory. Two years later work on the ship was completed, and the *Niagara* was officially designated the flagship of Pennsylvania. From its home port in Erie, Pennsylvania, the *Niagara* cruises the Great Lakes in the summer.[7]

Still another example of a ship from the war is the sloop *Friends Good Will*, whose construction was recently sponsored by the Michigan Maritime Museum in South Haven, Michigan. The original merchant vessel of this name was built in 1810 and chartered by the U.S. government to carry military supplies to Fort Dearborn in 1812. Shortly thereafter, the sloop was captured when it sailed into Mackinac Island Harbor after the British had seized the island. The British then armed the vessel and renamed it the *Little Belt*. It was recaptured by the U.S. in the Battle of Lake Erie and taken back into American service. After being driven ashore by a storm near Buffalo, the ship was burned by the British during a raid in January of 1814. The reproduction of this single-masted sloop boasts modern construction materials and safety devices but looks and sails much like its original namesake.[8]

In 1996, to commemorate the tricentennial of Prince George's County in Maryland, a replica was constructed of one of the barges that made up Captain Joshua Barney's flotilla of 18 vessels in the Chesapeake. Known as "No. 19," the 9-ton barge was built to about 80 percent of scale, 10 by 40 feet instead of 12 by 50 feet and mounting 16 oars instead of 20. The vessel was built to this scale so that it could be transported on a trailer. The barge also carries two sails and mounts a naval gun in the bow although the stern is fitted out with a diesel engine. The barge's home port is the Historic Bladensburg Waterfront on the Anacostia River.[9]

There is also an excellent example of a large American privateer from this era. The *Chasseur* (15–16), out of Baltimore, was one of the most famous American privateers in the War of 1812. This early Baltimore Clipper, which was affectionately referred to as "The Pride of Baltimore," not only took a host of prizes but in 1814 sailed into a British port, where its plucky captain, Thomas Boyle, proclaimed a blockade of the British Isles. The following year, the *Chasseur* (15) defeated a British warship, H.M. Schooner *St. Lawrence* (13).

A replica of the *Chasseur* named the *Pride of Baltimore* was built in 1976–77. With rotating crews, this 121-ton ship sailed more than 150,000 miles around the world on goodwill missions on behalf of Baltimore and Maryland. Although the *Pride* had an engine, it lacked other modern safety equipment. En route to its home port from the West Indies in the spring of 1986, the ship rolled over and sank in a squall, taking 4 of its 12 crew members with it. The survivors made it into a rubber life raft but were not picked up for four days and only then because a Norwegian tanker spotted the SOS signal they made with a flashlight.

With a huge outpouring of public support, city and state collaborated on a successor, the *Pride of Baltimore II*, which is a much larger and safer vessel. Launched and commissioned in 1987, the *Pride II* successfully completed its maiden voyage to the West Indies. Since then, as Maryland's goodwill ambassador, it has logged over 200,000 miles and visited some 40 countries.[10]

There is a full-scale replica of a smaller privateer, the 30-ton *Fame*, which sails out of Salem, Massachusetts. The original *Fame*, a fast Chebacco fishing schooner from Salem, was turned into a privateer in 1812. Carrying only one gun and cruising mainly in the nearby waters of British North America, the schooner took 21 prizes before being wrecked in the Bay of Fundy in 1814. The new *Fame*, which was launched in 2003, offers the paying public cruises of Salem Sound.[11]

Canadians have also been busy rebuilding ships from the War of 1812 era. H.M. Schooner *Tecumseth* was a schooner named after the great Shawnee leader, although with a variant spelling of his name. Built at Chippawa in 1814, it was not ready for service until the war was over. In 1817, after being transferred to the Royal Naval Establishment at Penetanguishene on Georgian Bay, it was taken out of service in accordance with the naval limitations of the Rush-Bagot Agreement. By 1827 it was suffering from rot and was scuttled in the waters off Penetanguishene. The remains of the ship were raised in 1953.

A replica based on the original plans (but with modern navigation and safety equipment) was built in 1992. Two years later H.M. Schooner *Tecumseth* became an honorary ship in the British navy. Its home is Discovery Harbour, and although the provincial government has confined the schooner to port for now, it has sailed the waters of Georgian Bay and the Great Lakes.[12]

Canadians have rebuilt another ship that dates from after the War of 1812 but is typical of vessels of its class that served in the conflict. This is H.M. Schooner *Bee*, an unarmed vessel that was originally built at the mouth of the Nottawasaga River on Lake Huron in 1817. Serving as a transport for the

Royal Navy until 1831, it was sold off as surplus property the following year. Its home port was the British naval base at Penetanguishene. In 1984 a replica of this vessel was built with a lead keel, a fiberglass hull, and modern safety and navigation equipment. Although the *Bee* (like the *Tecumseth*) is now confined to port, it, too, has sailed Georgian Bay and the Great Lakes from Discovery Harbour.[13]

Canadians also started to rebuild H.M. Sloop *Detroit*, Commander Robert H. Barclay's flagship on Lake Erie. The original *Detroit* (19) was named in honor of Major General Isaac Brock's victory over the American city in 1812 and was the largest ship built at the Malden shipyard during the War of 1812. Captured by Perry's squadron in the Battle of Lake Erie, it was taken first to Put-in-Bay and then to Erie, Pennsylvania. Although scuttled after the war, it was raised and refitted as a merchant vessel in 1837. In 1841, the ship, now a derelict, was purchased by a group of Americans in Niagara Falls, New York, who wished to use it to make a political statement. They painted the word "Veto" on the ship's sides as a warning to President John Tyler that he was vetoing too many popular bills from Congress. They intended to send the vessel over the falls, but it grounded well above the brink and did not break up until later.

Plans for a full-scale replica of the three-masted *Detroit* were made in the 1980s with the expectation that it would cruise the Great Lakes from Amherstburg. The keel was laid in 2000 and construction begun the following year. However, the project was too ambitious for the limited public financing available, and it has been plagued by bitter disputes over design, construction, and financing. It is now unlikely that the ship will ever be completed.[14]

The British have also restored some period ships. Britain's most famous ship, H.M. Ship *Victory* (104), Vice Admiral Horatio Nelson's flagship in the Battle of Trafalgar in 1805, had no role in the War of 1812 but is a good example of a first rate ship-of-the-line from the period. Launched in 1765 and commissioned in 1778, it remained active almost continuously until 1812, when it was withdrawn from frontline service and moored at the Royal Navy Dockyard at Portsmouth. The ship remained there for more than a century. Badly decayed, it was slated for demolition in 1922, but instead it was moved into dry dock and became the object of the most ambitious naval restoration project ever undertaken. Now fully restored to its 1805 appearance, it is the oldest commissioned ship in the world and is open to the public for touring.[15]

Britain's best known ship from the War of 1812, H.M. Ship *Shannon* (52), was broken up in 1859, but a sister ship, H.M. Ship *Trincomalee* (47), has survived. Launched in 1817 by the East India Company at its dockyard in Bombay, the ship was built of teak, the finest and most durable ship timber in the world. The *Trincomalee* never saw battle and was taken out of service in 1857, but three years later it was fitted out as a training ship for the Royal Navy Reserve, which extended its naval life for another 35 years. Sold into private hands, it continued to serve as a training ship for almost a century thereafter. In 1987 it was transported to Hartlepool on a barge, where a massive public restoration project, costing £5,000,000 and lasting more than a decade, was begun. Major restoration was completed in 2001, and *Trincomalee* is now available for public inspection and ready for sea.[16]

# The Name of the War

When did the War of 1812 become the War of 1812? In other words, when did people start using this phrase to refer to the war? Although this kind of question might be asked about any war, it seems especially appropriate for the War of 1812 because it is the only American war whose name refers to nothing more than the year that the conflict began.[1]

In the hope of answering this question, I decided to look at the titles of books and pamphlets published on the war in the nineteenth century. My assumption was that whenever the name of the war came into general use, it would soon enough show up in book titles. Titles might lag a little behind popular usage, or they might actually be a little ahead of it. Either way, the time lag was unlikely to be very significant. Hence I felt I could rely on the titles as a rough guide to general usage.

To develop a list of titles, I enlisted the aid of Jan Brumm, Head of Circulation and Interlibrary Loan at the U.S. Conn Library at Wayne State College. Using the search engine FirstSearch and the WorldCat data base, she entered as her subject "United States—History—War of 1812" to secure a list of all pertinent titles published between 1812 and 1899. The result was 4,736 titles, about 40 percent of which were published during the war. Most of the titles did not actually refer to the war; and of those that did many were either duplicate copies or later printings or editions of earlier works. Even so, enough titles remained to provide a pretty good sample.

Colin McCoy, a graduate student at the University of Illinois at Urbana-Champaign, also provided assistance. Writing a dissertation on the literature of persuasion in Jacksonian America, McCoy had developed an extensive knowledge of printed sources for the postwar period. He pulled from his own bibliography those titles that bore on the war and helpfully arranged them in chronological order, highlighting the phrases used to refer to the war.

I also drew on Ralph Shaw and Richard Shoemaker's *American Bibliography* and Richard Shoemaker's *Checklist of American Imprints,* which between them list every known book or pamphlet published in the United States between 1801 and 1846.[2] In addition, I mined the two principal bibliographies on the war: John Fredriksen's work, which lists over 6,000 titles, and Dwight Smith's annotated study, which describes close to 1,400.[3]

During the War of 1812, Americans usually referred to the conflict as "the war," or "the present war," or "the war with Great Britain."[4] In one way or another, the contest affected almost everyone, and thus it was rarely far from people's minds. Hence, even a vague reference to "the war" was unlikely to be misunderstood.

There was one significant exception to this pattern. In 1812 John Lowell, Jr., a Boston Federalist, published a 63-page pamphlet entitled *Mr. Madison's War,* which condemned the declaration of war as ruinous and tried to pin responsibility for the decision on President James Madison.[5] Although this pamphlet was reprinted a half dozen times in 1812 and was widely read in the North, Federalist opponents of the war did not embrace Lowell's label for the conflict.[6]

After the war ended, Americans slipped into the habit of referring to the contest as "the late war" or "the late war with Great Britain."[7] Thus when Secretary of the Treasury Alexander J. Dallas wrote a defense of the war, it was originally published under the title *An Exposition of the Causes and Character of the War.*[8] When the pamphlet was reprinted after the war, the title was changed to read *An Exposition of the Causes and Character of the Late War* or *An Exposition of the Causes and Character of the Late War with Great Britain.*[9]

Although this remained the most common way to refer to the war for many years, as early as 1816 William McCarty of Philadelphia published an anonymous history of the conflict (which doubtless he wrote) entitled *History of the American War, of Eighteen Hundred and Twelve.*[10] This popular work went through several editions, some of which appeared under the title *History of the American War of 1812.*[11] There was even a German edition, *Geschichte des Americanischen Kriegs, von 1812.*[12]

McCarty may not have been the first person to use the phrase "War of 1812," but he was the first to use it in the title of a book. And yet despite the popularity of his work, the phrase did not immediately catch on. It did not appear again until 1827, when Richard Emmons published *The Fredoniad, or, Independence Preserved: An Epick Poem on the Late War of 1812*.[13] Like McCarty's work, Emmons's poem was popular, and his work was reprinted in 1830 and 1832. Doubtless Emmons helped bring the phrase "War of 1812" into broader usage.

In the 1830s, several additional works used the phrase. In 1833 Federalist Theodore Dwight published *History of the Hartford Convention: With a Review of the Policy of the United States Government Which Led to the War of 1812*.[14] Three years later former secretary of war John Armstrong published the first volume of his memoir and personal defense, *Notices of the War of 1812*.[15] This was quickly followed by a work by Solomon Van Rensselaer, who had been wounded five times in the Battle of Queenston Heights. In *A Narrative of the Affair of Queenston: In the War of 1812*, Van Rensselaer not only told his own tale but also sought to rebut Armstrong's claims.[16]

Also appearing in 1836 was Isaac Jackson's 32-page pamphlet, *Sketch of the Life and Public Services of William Henry Harrison, Com-*

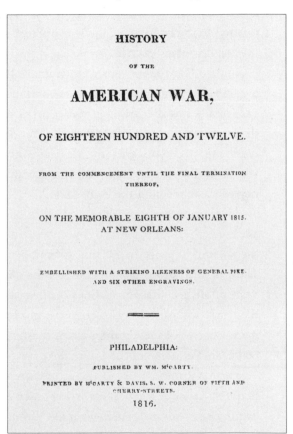

HISTORY

OF THE

AMERICAN WAR,

OF EIGHTEEN HUNDRED AND TWELVE.

FROM THE COMMENCEMENT UNTIL THE FINAL TERMINATION THEREOF,

ON THE MEMORABLE EIGHTH OF JANUARY 1815. AT NEW ORLEANS:

EMBELLISHED WITH A STRIKING LIKENESS OF GENERAL PIKE. AND SIX OTHER ENGRAVINGS.

PHILADELPHIA:

PUBLISHED BY WM. M'CARTY.

PRINTED BY M'CARTY & DAVIS, S. W. CORNER OF FIFTH AND CHERRY-STREETS.

1816.

In 1816 William McCarty published the first book to call the conflict the "War of 1812." Unlike later editions, the title page of the first edition spelled out the year.

*mander in Chief of the North Western Army, during the War of 1812*.[17] Three years later Martin Van Buren sought to boost his presidential campaign with a 24-page pamphlet entitled *Mr. Van Buren on the War of 1812, '15, and Other Important Subjects*.[18]

Thus by the 1830s the phrase "War of 1812" was apparently in wide usage in the United States, although "the late war with Great Britain" still remained the most popular label for the contest. This changed with the Mexican War (1846–48). By this time the War of 1812 was more than 30 years in the past, and with a new war under way, a growing number of Americans were ready to embrace a more concise and precise label for the older conflict. Hence by a slim margin, works on the War of 1812 published during the Mexican War referred to the conflict as "the War of 1812," and this pattern continued after the Mexican War was over.[19]

In the 1850s the movement to embrace the phrase "War of 1812" became a stampede. Although a few writers continued to prefer older labels, this decade finally saw the triumph of McCarty's phrase. The 1850s also witnessed the production of more works on the War of 1812 than any other decade between 1830 and 1900. With the Mexican War now behind them and the Civil War lurking on the horizon, many Americans, including some novelists, were moved to write about the War of 1812.[20]

In addition, veterans in several states, some of whom had held reunions as early as the 1840s, attended conventions in the 1850s both to commemorate the war and to press their claims for compensation for their military service. These organizations usually took on the name Soldiers of the War of 1812. They published the proceedings of their state and national meetings, and these publications always carried the phrase "War of 1812" in the title.[21] In the 1860s, two of these groups also published their constitutions.[22] All of this helped fix the name of the war in the public mind.

Further contributing to the acceptance of the name were the works of Benson J. Lossing, the popular writer and sketch artist. In 1868, Lossing published *The Pictorial Field-Book of the War of 1812,* and six years later he followed with *The American Revolution and the War of 1812.*[23] Both works sold well and were reprinted several times, thus further establishing the name of the war.

In 1893 the General Society of the War of 1812 was organized to bring together the various state groups of veterans (or the descendants of veterans).[24] The General Society published its charter, constitution, and roster in 1893 and again in 1899.[25] The work of this organization further publicized the War of 1812, although by this time there was very little doubt about what the war ought to be called.[26]

Such was the story in the United States. What about Canada and Great Britain? Here the story was different. While the war was in progress, British subjects in Canada and the home islands usually referred to the contest as "the American war" or "the war with America."[27] Although Canadians sometimes referred to the conflict as simply "the war," this was ambiguous because Great Britain was then engaged in a war with France, and, as a part of the British Empire, people living in British North America were involved in that war, too.

Once the War of 1812 ended, people in Canada and Great Britain generally referred to the conflict as "the late American war," "the late war with the United States," or "the late war between Great Britain and the United States."[28] This usage remained the norm for many years.

In Canada, John Richardson in 1842 published a history of the part of the British army that he was attached to in Upper Canada.[29] He called his work *War of 1812.*[30] Although a few other Canadians subsequently used this phrase, it did not catch on until the 1890s, when Ernest A. Cruikshank, the dean of Canadian scholars of the war, helped establish usage with his early publications.[31] Thus by the twentieth century, Canadian scholars were accustomed to referring to the conflict as "the War of 1812," although occasionally they still used the phrase "the War of 1812–14" or "the War of 1812–15."[32]

The British, on the other hand, were slow to follow suit. In Great Britain, the War of 1812 has always been a forgotten conflict—lost in the grand sweep of the far more significant and majestic Napoleonic Wars. Some modern British writers, it is true, have called the contest "the War of 1812," but this phrase is not always capitalized, suggesting that it may be more of a descriptive label than a proper name.[33] Moreover, the same label is sometimes applied to France's invasion of Russia in 1812, a campaign that destroyed a huge French army and thus paved the way for Britain's victory in the Napoleonic Wars.[34]

With no consensus, British writers during most of the twentieth century used a number of other phrases for the War of 1812, such as "the Second American War," "the War of 1812–14/15," "the American War, 1812–1814/15," "the War with the United States, 1813–1815," "the American War of 1812," "the Anglo-American War of 1812," or "the Anglo-American War of 1812–15."[35]

Several works published in the late 1990s and after, however, suggest that the British finally have embraced North American usage.[36] Especially significant in this regard is the publication in 2002 of Carl Benn's *War of 1812* in

Osprey's Essential Histories series.[37] Although Benn is a Canadian, Osprey is a British firm, and as the largest publisher of military titles in the world, its practice should help fix British usage.

To sum up, then, when did the War of 1812 become the War of 1812? For Americans it was the late 1840s, for Canadians it was the 1890s, and for the British, it was the late 1990s. Although there may still be some exceptions, it now appears that after almost two centuries people on both sides of the Atlantic have finally agreed to call this conflict the "War of 1812."

# Notes

## Abbreviations of Officials

*American*

SN: secretary of the navy (Paul Hamilton, William Jones, Benjamin W. Crowninshield)

SS: secretary of state (James Monroe)

SW: secretary of war (William Eustis, John Armstrong, James Monroe)

*British*

CG: captain-general and governor-in-chief of Canada (Sir George Prevost)

FSA: first secretary of the Admiralty (John W. Croker)

SSWC: secretary of state for war and the colonies (Lord Bathurst)

## Abbreviations of Sources

*AC:* U.S. Congress, *Annals of Congress: Debates and Proceedings in the Congress of the United States, 1789–1824,* 42 vols. (Washington, DC, 1834–56) (12–1 refers to 12th Congress, 1st session, and similarly for other sessions).

Antal, *Wampum Denied:* Sandy Antal, *A Wampum Denied: Procter's War of 1812* (Ottawa, 1997).

*ASP: C & N:* U.S. Congress, *American State Papers: Commerce and Navigation,* 2 vols. (Washington, DC, 1832–34).

*ASP: FR:* U.S. Congress, *American State Papers: Foreign Relations,* 6 vols. (Washington, DC, 1833–59).

*ASP: MA:* U.S. Congress, *American State Papers: Military Affairs,* 7 vols. (Washington, DC, 1832–61).

Burt, *United States, Great Britain, and British North America:* A.L. Burt, *The United States, Great Britain, and British North America from the Revolution to the Establishment*

*of Peace after the War of 1812* (New Haven, 1940).

Carter, *Territorial Papers of the United States:* Clarence E. Carter, ed., *The Territorial Papers of the United States,* 26 vols. (Washington, DC, 1934–62).

Cruikshank, *Niagara Frontier:* Ernest A. Cruikshank, ed., *The Documentary History of the Campaign on the Niagara Frontier,* 9 vols. (Welland, ON, nd–1908).

Cruikshank, *Surrender of Detroit:* Ernest A. Cruikshank, ed., *Documents Relating to the Invasion of Canada and the Surrender of Detroit, 1812* (Ottawa, 1912).

*DAB:* Allen Johnson *et al.,* eds., *Dictionary of American Biography,* 22 vols. (New York, 1928–58).

*DCB:* George W. Brown *et al.,* eds., *Dictionary of Canadian Biography,* 14 vols. to date (Toronto, 1966– ).

*DNB* (new): H.C.G. Matthew and Brian Harrison, eds., *Oxford Dictionary of National Biography,* 60 vols. (New York, 2004).

Dudley, *Splintering the Wooden Wall:* Wade C. Dudley, *Splintering the Wooden Wall: The British Blockade of the United States, 1812–1815* (Annapolis, MD, 2003).

Dudley and Crawford, *Naval War of 1812:* William S. Dudley, Michael J. Crawford, *et al.,* eds., *The Naval War of 1812: A Documentary History,* 4 vols. (Washington, DC, 1985– ).

Esarey, *Messages of William Henry Harrison:* Logan Esarey, ed., *Messages and Letters of William Henry Harrison,* 2 vols. (Indianapolis, 1922).

Everest, *War of 1812 in the Champlain Valley:* Allan Everest, *The War of 1812 in the Champlain Valley* (Syracuse, 1981).

Fitz-Enz, *Final Invasion:* David G. Fitz-Enz, *The Final Invasion: Plattsburgh, the War of 1812's Most Decisive Battle* (New York, 2001).

Graves, *War of 1812 Journal of John Le Couteur:* Donald E. Graves, ed., *Merry Hearts Make Light Days: The War of 1812 Journal of Lieutenant John Le Couteur, 104th Foot* (Ottawa, 1993).

Heidler and Heidler, *Encyclopedia of the War of 1812:* David S. Heidler and Jeanne T. Heidler, eds., *Encyclopedia of the War of 1812* (Santa Barbara, 1997).

Hickey, *War of 1812:* Donald R. Hickey, *The War of 1812: A Forgotten Conflict* (Urbana, IL, 1989).

Hitsman, *Incredible War* (updated ed.): J. Mackay Hitsman, *The Incredible War of 1812: A Military History* (1965; updated by Donald E. Graves, Toronto, 1999).

Ingersoll, *Historical Sketch of the Second War:* Charles J. Ingersoll, *Historical Sketch of the Second War between the United States of America, and Great Britain,* 2 vols. (Philadelphia, 1845–49).

Jackson, "Impressment and Anglo-American Discord,": Scott Thomas Jackson, "Impressment and Anglo-American Discord, 1787–1818," Ph.D. dissertation (University of Michigan, 1976).

James, *Naval History of Great Britain:* William James, *The Naval History of Great Britain, From the Declaration of War by France in 1793 to the Accession of George IV,* rev. ed., 6 vols. (London, 1878).

James, *Naval Occurrences:* William James, *A Full and Correct Account of the Chief Naval Occurrences of the Late War between Great Britain and the United States of America* (London, 1817).

Latour, *Historical Memoir:* Arsène Lacarrière Latour, *Historical Memoir of the War in West Florida and Louisiana in 1814–15* (1816; edited and expanded by Gene A. Smith, Gainsville, Fl, 1999).

Lossing, *Pictorial Field-Book of the War of 1812:* Benson J. Lossing, Jr., *The Pictorial Field-Book of the War of 1812* (New York, 1868).

Maclay, *American Privateers:* Edgar S. Maclay, *A History of American Privateers* (New York, 1899).

Mahan, *Sea Power:* Alfred Thayer Mahan, *Sea Power and Its Relations to the War of 1812,* 2 vols. (Boston, 1905).

Owsley, *Struggle for the Gulf Borderlands:* Frank L. Owsley, Jr., *Struggle for the Gulf Borderlands: The Creek War and the Battle of New Orleans, 1812–1815* (Gainsville, 1981).

Perkins, *Castlereagh and Adams:* Bradford Perkins, *Castlereagh and Adams: England and the United States, 1812–1823* (Berkeley, CA, 1964).

Quimby, *U.S. Army in the War of 1812:* Robert S. Quimby, *The U.S. Army in the War of 1812: An Operational and Command Study,* 2 vols. (East Lansing, MI, 1997).

Reilly, *British at the Gates:* Robin Reilly, *The British at the Gates: The New Orleans Campaign in the War of 1812,* rev. ed (Toronto, 2002).

Roosevelt, *Naval War of 1812:* Theodore Roosevelt, *The Naval War of 1812,* 3rd ed. (1883; reprint, with an introduction by H.W. Brands, New York, 1999).

Roosevelt, "War with the United States": Theodore Roosevelt, "The War with the United States," in William Laird Clowes, *The Royal Navy: A History,* 7 vols. (London, 1897–1903), 6: 1–180.

Sonneck, *"Star Spangled Banner":* Oscar Sonneck, *"The Star Spangled Banner,"* (Washington, DC, 1914).

Stanley, *War of 1812:* George F.G. Stanley, *The War of 1812: Land Operations* ([Toronto], 1983).

Wood, *Select British Documents:* William Wood, ed., *Select British Documents of the Canadian War of 1812,* 3 vols. (Toronto, 1920–28).

**Preface**

1. "The War of 1812: Still a Forgotten Conflict?" *Journal of Military History* 65 (July 2001), 741–69.

2. James to Viscount Melville, January 4, 1819, in Holden Furber, ed., "How William James Came to Be a Naval Historian," *American Historical Review* 38 (October 1932), 76.

3. James's pamphlet was *An Inquiry into the Merits of the Principal Naval Actions between Great Britain and the United States* (London, 1816).

4. William James, *A Full and Correct Account of the Military Occurrences of the Late War between Great Britain and the United States of America,* 2 vols. (London, 1818).

5. I have used the revised edition of the *Naval History,* published in 1878, throughout this work.

6. James to Viscount Melville, January 4, 1819, in Furber, "How William James Came to be a Naval Historian," 79.

7. James left few papers, and little has been written about him. See Furber, "How William James Came to Be a Naval Historian," 74–85; J.K. Laughton and Andrew Lambert, "James, William," in *DNB* (new), 29: 747–48; and Lambert's introduction to W. James, *Naval Occurrences of the War of 1812* (1817; reprint, London, 2004), i-vii.

8. Benson J. Lossing, *The Pictorial Field-Book of the Revolution*, 2 vols. (New York, 1851–52) and *The Pictorial Field Book on the Civil War*, 3 vols. (New York, 1868–69). Both works went through several editions.

9. This work has been reprinted seven times: 1896, 1968, 1970, 1976, 1993, 2001, and 2004.

10. For details on Losing's work, see Harold E. Mahan, *Benson J. Losing and Historical Writing in the United States, 1830–1890* (Westport, CT, 1996), and John T. Cunningham's Foreword, in Losing, *Pictorial Field-Book of the War of 1812* (1868; reprint, New York, 1976).

11. Henry Adams, *History of the United States of America [during the Administrations of Jefferson and Madison]*, 9 vols. (New York, 1889–91).

12. Peter Shaw, "The War of 1812 Could Not Take Place: Henry Adams's *History*," *Yale Review* 62 (June 1973), 544–556, and "Blood Is Thicker than Irony: Henry Adams' *History*," *New England Quarterly*, 40 (June 1967), 163–87. In *Henry Adams and the Making of America* (Boston, 2005), Garry Wills rejects the family defense thesis, but he ignores Shaw's work and fails to make his case. Wills's study is principally a gloss on Adams's *History*, but because he is no expert on the Age of Jefferson, he is at Adams's mercy and repeats many of Adams's myths.

13. Hitsman, *Incredible War* (updated ed.)

## Acknowledgments

1. "When Did the War of 1812 Become the War of 1812?" *Journal of the War of 1812* 6 (Summer 2001), 5–11. The column, "Myths and Misconceptions," first appeared ibid., 7 (Winter 2002), 27–29.

2. Robert Malcomson, *Historical Dictionary of the War of 1812* (Lanham, MD, 2006).

## A Note on Terminology and Numbers

1. See Lords Commissioners of Admiralty to Yeo, March 19, 1813, in Dudley and Crawford, *Naval War of 1812*, 2: 436.

2. Robert Malcomson, "'Stars and Garters of an Admiral': American Commodores in the War of 1812," unpublished paper.

3. Figures are based on conversion tables found at: <http://eh.net/hmit/compare/>.

4. For the an explanation of the nominal rate, see Lawrence H. Officer, *Between the Dollar-Sterling Gold Points: Exchange Rates, Parity, and Market Behavior* (Cambridge, UK, 1996), 50–51, 59.

5. See Lawrence H. Officer, "Exchange Rate between the United States Dollar and the British Pound," Economic History Services, EH.Net, 2001, at: <http://eh.net/hmit/exchangerates/pound.php>.

## Prologue: The United States and Great Britain in a War-Torn World

1. Alexander Hamilton, "The French Revolution," [1794], in Harold C. Syrett *et al.*, *The Papers of Alexander Hamilton*, 27 vols. (New York, 1961–87), 17: 586.

2. Quoted in Piers Mackesy, "Strategic Problems of the British War Effort," in H.T. Dickinson, *Britain and the French Revolution, 1789–1815* (New York, 1989), 148.

3. Population figures taken from Stephen Pope, *Dictionary of the Napoleonic Wars* (London, 1999), 197, 240.

4. All of this is detailed in Bradford Perkins's under-appreciated study, *The First Rapprochement: England and the United States, 1795–1805* (Philadelphia, 1955), ch. 8.

5. The authorized level of the Royal Navy peaked in 1810–12 at 145,000 (114,000 seamen and 31,000 marines). Britain's land forces peaked in 1814 at 264,000. This total included 187,000 regulars, 51,000 foreign and colonial troops, and 26,000 British and foreign artillery. See Nicholas Blake and Richard Lawrence, *The Illustrated Companion to Nelson's Navy* (Mechanicsburg, PA, 2000), 67; and Mackesy, "Strategic Problems of the British War Effort," 156.

6. Michael Duffy, "The Caribbean Campaigns of the British Army, 1793–1801," in Alan J. Guy, ed., *The Road to Waterloo: The British*

*Army and the Struggle against Revolutionary and Napoleonic France, 1793–1815* (London, 1990), 29.

7. Major Greenwood, "British Loss of Life in the Wars of 1794–1815 and in 1914–1918," *Journal of the Royal Statistical Society* 105 (1942), 2–5.

8. Norman J. Silberling, "Financial and Monetary Policy of Great Britain during the Napoleonic Wars," *Quarterly Journal of Economics* 38 (February 1924), 221.

9. Rory Muir, *Britain and the Defeat of Napoleon, 1807–1815* (New Haven, CT, 1996), 376.

10. Silberling, "Financial and Monetary Policy of Great Britain," 215.

11. For the U.S., the cost of the war, including interest on war loans and veterans' benefits, was $158,000,000. U.S. Bureau of the Census, *Historical Statistics of the United States, Colonial Times to 1970*, 2 vols. (Washington, DC, 1975), 2: 1140.

## Chapter 1: The Causes of the War

1. The following surveys and studies were used: Chicago *Tribune* (1982), Murray-Blessing (1982), Sienna College (1994), Schlesinger (1996), Ridings-McIver (1997), Intercollegiate Studies (1997), C.D. Strand (1999), C-Span (2000), Faber and Faber (2000), and *Wall Street Journal*/Federalist Society (2001). Except Faber and Faber, these can be found at various sites on the Internet. For the Faber assessment, see Charles F. Faber and Richard B. Faber, *The American Presidents Ranked by Performance* (Jefferson, NC, 2000).

2. Jefferson is often credited with saying, "the best government is that which governs least," but this phrase does not appear in any of his writings. The epigram was the motto of the *United States Magazine and Democratic Review* from 1837 to 1845 and was popularized for modern audiences by Henry David Thoreau. See the title page of any volume of the *United States Magazine and Democratic Review* for these years and also the premier issue: 1 (October 1837), 6. See also Henry David Thoreau, *On Civil Disobedience* (1849), in Brooks Atkinson, ed., *Walden and Other Writings of Henry David Thoreau* (New York, 1950), 635.

3. The literature on Jefferson, most of it fa-

vorable, is vast. For a particularly balanced if somewhat dated treatment of his presidency, see Nathan Schachner, *Thomas Jefferson: A Biography* 2 vols. (New York, 1951), 2: 659–887. See also Forrest McDonald, *The Presidency of Thomas Jefferson* (Lawrence, KS, 1976).

4. Fisher Ames, "Political Review III," reprinted in W.B. Allen, ed., *Works of Fisher Ames*, 2 vols. (Indianapolis, 1984), 1: 472–73. See also Boston *Repertory*, cited in Richmond *Enquirer*, October 11, 1805.

5. Madison to Charles J. Ingersoll, July 28, 1814, in Gaillard Hunt, ed., *The Writings of James Madison*, 9 vols. (New York, 1900–10), 8: 283. For more on this subject, see Donald R. Hickey, "The Monroe-Pinkney Treaty of 1806: A Reappraisal," *William and Mary Quarterly*, 3rd series, 44 (January 1987), 82–83.

6. For a fuller treatment of this lost treaty, see Hickey, "Monroe-Pinkney Treaty," 65–88; and Jackson, "Impressment and Anglo-American Discord," ch. 6, which is particularly good on the British side of the story.

7. James, *Naval History of Great Britain*, 1: Appendix 1, and 5: Appendix 20.

8. Nicholas Blake and Richard Lawrence, *The Illustrated Companion to Nelson's Navy* (Mechanicsburg, PA, 2000), 67.

9. Brian Lavery, *Nelson's Navy: The Ships, Men and Organization, 1793–1815*, rev. ed. (Annapolis, MD, 1994), 187.

10. Ibid., 118.

11. Michael Lewis, *A Social History of the Navy, 1793–1815* (London, 1960), 95–116, 135–39; Dudley, *Splintering the Wooden Wall*, 92.

12. Quoted in G.J. Marcus, *The Age of Nelson: The Royal Navy, 1793–1815* (New York, 1971), 23.

13. The British had effectively abandoned the right to impress from neutral warships more than 100 years earlier in the reign of Queen Anne. See Jackson, "Impressment and Anglo-American Discord," 281–93.

14. Only once, when John Marshall was secretary of state in 1800, did the U.S. explicitly deny Great Britain's right to impress British subjects from American merchant vessels in British ports. See Jackson, "Impressment and Anglo-American Discord," 147–48.

15. James F. Zimmerman, *Impressment of Amer-*

*ican Seamen* (New York, 1925), 250.

16. Adam Seybert estimated that 6 crewmen were required for every 100 tons of merchant shipping and 8 crewmen for every 100 tons of fishing vessels. The average tonnage employed in foreign and domestic trade from 1803 to 1812 was 1,164,000; the average tonnage employed in the fisheries was 49,000 tons. This means that about 70,000 men were employed annually in the merchant marine and about 4,000 in the fisheries. See Seybert, *Statistical Annals . . . of the United States of America* (Philadelphia, 1818), 315, 317.

17. The Admiralty put the figure at 20,000, which would have been around 28.5 percent of the American merchant marine. See Zimmerman, *Impressment of American Seamen*, 275.

18. For the number of foreign seamen who became American citizens, see SS to U.S. Senate, January 6, 1813, in *ASP: C & N*, 1: 955. The figure given, 1,530, is actually the number of naturalized seamen who applied for a certificate of citizenship (a kind of American identification card known generally as a "protection"). The total was actually a little higher because the returns from 1811 and 1812 were incomplete.

19. Zimmerman, *Impressment of American Seamen*, 106.

20. This estimate follows Zimmerman, *Impressment of American Seamen*, Appendix, which has the best discussion of the subject. See also Lewis, *Social History of the Navy*, 436–39.

21. There is a good discussion of the Royal Navy's recruiting problems and the practice of impressment in Lavery, *Nelson's Navy*, Part V. The best account of the entire impressment controversy by far is in Jackson, "Impressment and Anglo-American Discord." See also Zimmerman, *Impressment of American Seamen*.

22. The best account of the attack can be found in Spencer C. Tucker and Frank T. Reuter, *Injured Honor: The "Chesapeake"-"Leopard" Affair, June 27, 1807* (Annapolis, MD, 1996), ch. 1.

23. For an excellent account of the trials, see ibid., ch. 8.

24. Speech of Nathaniel Macon, December 3, 1807, in *AC*, 10–1, 1035.

25. Speeches of John Smilie, Orchard Cook, and Thomas Newton, December 3, 1807, in *AC*, 10–1, 1027, 1029, 1036. For similar sentiments, see speeches of Nathaniel Macon and Matthew Lyon, December 3, 1807, ibid., 1028, 1036.

26. The diplomatic history of this episode can be followed in Burt, *United States, Great Britain, and British North America*, 244–45, 269–70, 280; Bradford Perkins, *Prologue to War: England and the United States, 1805–1812* (Berkeley, CA, 1961), 145–47, 190–97, 211–12; and Jackson, "Impressment and Anglo-American Discord," ch. 7.

27. See Burt, *United States, Great Britain, and British North America*, 244–45, 296–97. The two men were actually restored after the beginning of the war.

28. Perkins, *Prologue to War*, 190; Tucker and Reuter, *Injured Honor*, 121–22.

29. For a good description of the Orders-in-Council, see Reginald Horsman, *The Causes of the War of 1812* (Philadelphia, 1962), 95, 121, 149–50; and Perkins, *Prologue to War*, 147, 200–02, 205–07.

30. The best overview of the restrictive system is Herbert Heaton, "Non-Importation, 1806–1812," *Journal of Economic History* 1 (November 1941), 178–98.

31. The non-importation act of 1811 is printed in *AC*, 11–3, 1338–39. The legislative history of this measure is significant because the House of Representatives passed the bill only after the first successful use of the previous question to shut down debate. See ibid., 1091–95.

32. Speech of Henry Clay, December 7, 1812, in *AC*, 12–2, 299–300.

33. Donald R. Hickey, "American Trade Restrictions during the War of 1812," *Journal of American History* 68 (December 1981), 517–38.

34. Curtis P. Nettels, *The Emergence of a National Economy, 1775–1815* (New York, 1962), 385, 396.

35. Percentages are computed from figures rounded to the nearest million. The increase in government revenue cannot be computed with any precision because the first set of available figures covers almost two years.

36. Douglass C. North, *The Economic Growth of the United States, 1790–1860* (Englewood Cliffs, NJ, 1961), 53.
37. For ship seizures, see George Ewing to SS, June 23, 1811, and Report of SS, July 6, 1812, in *ASP: FR*, 3: 521, 584. Many of these were small ships engaged in the Caribbean trade. I have estimated that the average size of a ship was 175 tons and that it was worth $60 per ton. Thus the average ship was worth $10,500.
38. John J. McCusker, *How Much Is That in Real Money? A Historical Commodity Price Index for Use as a Deflator of Money Values in the Economy of the United States*, rev ed. (Worcester, MA, 2001), 53.
39. U.S. Bureau of the Census, *Historical Statistics of the United States, Colonial Times to 1970*, 2 vols. (Washington, DC, 1975), 1: 8.
40. Percentages are again computed from figures rounded to the nearest million.
41. A good discussion of this subject can be found in Donald R. Adams, Jr., "American Neutrality and Prosperity, 1793–1808, A Reconsideration," *Journal of Economic History* 40 (December 1980), 713–35.
42. See figures provided in George Ewing to SS, June 23, 1811, and Report of SS, July 6, 1812, in *ASP: FR*, 3: 521, 584.
43. The tonnage in this period (1807–11) averaged 856,000 per year. I have reckoned each ship at 175 tons, which would mean there were just under 4,900 ships in service. A loss of 200 would be 4.4 percent of the total. For tonnage figures, see Tonnage from 1789 to 1810 and Tonnage for the Year 1811, in *ASP: C & N*, 1: 897, 958.
44. Jerome R. Garitee, *The Republic's Private Navy: The American Privateering Business as Practiced by Baltimore during the War of 1812* (Middletown, CT, 1977), 25.
45. U.S. Bureau of the Census, *Historical Statistics*, 1: 905.
46. American tonnage engaged in foreign trade rose from 848,000 in 1806 to 984,000 in 1810. See Tonnage from 1789 to 1810, in *ASP: C & N*, 1: 897.
47. Nettels, *National Economy*, 396. Figures for total exports and for domestic and total imports followed a similar pattern.
48. Ibid., 385.
49. Burt, *United States, Great Britain, and British North America*, 101–04, 115–16, 249–53, 302–04, 309; Robert S. Allen, *His Majesty's Indian Allies: British Indian Policy in the Defence of Canada, 1774–1815* (Toronto, 1992), 111–22; R. David Edmunds, "Main Poc: Potawatomi Wabenjo," *American Indian Quarterly* 9 (Summer 1985), 265.
50. Harrison's own description of the battle can be found in letters to SW, November 8 and 18, 1811, and to Charles Scott, December 13, 1811, in Esarey, *Messages of William Henry Harrison*, 1: 614–15, 618–30, 666–72. See also John Sugden, *Tecumseh: A Life* (New York, 1997), 226–36, 258; and Alfred A. Cave, "The Shawnee Prophet, Tecumseh, and Tippecanoe: A Case Study of Historical Myth-Making," *Journal of the Early Republic* 22 (Winter 2002), 637–73.
51. Harrison to SW, January 14, 1812, in Carter, *Territorial Papers of the United States*, 8: 159. See also Harrison to SW, November 8 and December 28, 1811, and to Charles Scott, December 13, 1811, in Esarey, *Messages of William Henry Harrison*, 1: 666–69, 687.
52. Samuel G. Hopkins to Harrison, January 15, 1812, in Carter, *Territorial Papers of the United States*, 8: 161–62; Harrison to Charles Scott, December 13, 1811, and to SW, December 24, 1811, and Resolutions of the Knox County Militia, December 7, 1811, in Esarey, *Messages of William Henry Harrison*, 1: 667–68, 678–80, 683–85.
53. Statement of Waller Taylor, February 22, 1817, in Esarey, *Messages of William Henry Harrison*, 2: 11. See also Waller Taylor to Moses Dawson, July 15, 1823, and William Polk to Washington *National Intelligencer*, February 10, 1840, ibid., 1: 710–11, 716–17.
54. Harrison to Charles Scott, December 13, 1811, in Esarey, *Messages of William Henry Harrison*, 1: 666–72. Quotation from p. 670.
55. [Robert B. McAfee], *History of the Late War in the Western Country* (Lexington, KY, 1816), 38; Alec R. Gilpin, *The War of 1812 in the Old Northwest* (East Lansing, MI, 1958), 12.
56. Harrison to SW, November 8 and December 28, 1811, in Esarey, *Messages of William Henry Harrison*, 1: 614, 687.
57. Elliott to Isaac Brock, January 12, 1812, in Wood, *Select British Documents*, 1: 280–83.
58. Ibid., 1: 282.

59. *Niles' Register* 2 (March 7, 1812), 5.
60. Article 9, Treaty of Ghent, December 24, 1814, in Heidler and Heidler, *Encyclopedia of the War of 1812*, 586.
61. Hickey, *War of 1812*, 42.
62. Speech of John Randolph, December 16, 1811, in *AC*, 12–1, 533.
63. Speech of Henry Clay, February 22, 1810, in *AC*, 11–2, 580; Jefferson to William Duane, August 4, 1812, in Jefferson Papers, Library of Congress, Washington, DC, microfilm edition, reel 46.
64. Speech of John Randolph, December 10, 1811, in *AC*, 12–1, 447.
65. Boston *Independent Chronicle*, November 22, 1813.
66. Henry Clay to Thomas Bodley, December 18, 1812, in James F. Hopkins and Mary W.M. Hargreaves, eds., *The Papers of Henry Clay*, 11 vols. (Lexington, KY, 1959–92), 1:842.
67. Speech of Thomas Wilson, January 17, 1814, in *AC*, 13–2, 1040.
68. For a superb discussion of this entire issue, see Reginald Horsman, "On to Canada: Manifest Destiny and United States Strategy in the War of 1812," *Michigan Historical Review* 13 (Fall 1987), 1–24.
69. Most notably, Norman K. Risjord in "1812: Conservatives, War Hawks, and the Nation's Honor," *William and Mary Quarterly*, 3rd series, 18 (April 1961), 196–210.
70. For a penetrating analysis of the meaning of honor in the South, see Bertram Wyatt-Brown, *Southern Honor: Ethics and Behavior in the Old South* (New York, 1982).
71. The slave states produced 56 of the 79 votes for war in the House and 12 of the 19 votes in the Senate.
72. Roger H. Brown, "The War Hawks of 1812: An Historical Myth," *Indiana Magazine of History* 60 (June 1964), 137–51.
73. Philip S. Klein, ed., "Memoirs of a Senator from Pennsylvania: Jonathan Roberts, 1771–1854," *Pennsylvania Magazine of History and Biography* 62 (April 1938), 231.
74. The best treatment of this subject is Harry W. Fritz, "The War Hawks of 1812," *Capitol Studies* 5 (Spring 1977), 25–42.
75. The act declaring war, which is dated June 18, is printed in *AC*, 12–1, 2322–23.
76. Proclamation of James Madison, June 19,

1812, in *AC*, 12–1, 2223–24. Quotation from p. 2223.
77. *AC*, 12–1, 1636; U.S. Congress, *Journal of the Senate of the United States of America* (Washington, DC, 1921), 12–1, 162.
78. Percentages computed from final vote on war bill in House and Senate cited in previous note.
79. See Hickey, *War of 1812*, 27–28.
80. See Roger H. Brown, *The Republic in Peril: 1812* (New York, 1964), ch. 2, "No Other Option," esp. pp. 39 and 43; also p. 73. This work is otherwise an important study that has stood the test of time.
81. Madison to Congress, March 4, 1813, in *AC*, 12–2, 123.
82. For more on this subject, see Bradford Perkins, *Castlereagh and Adams*, 3–4; Hickey, *War of 1812*, 47–48, 281–82.
83. See London *Times*, July 31, 1812, and London *Morning Chronicle*, July 31, 1812.
84. Perkins, *Castlereagh and Adams*, 11.
85. Order-in-Council, July 31, 1812, in *Naval Chronicle* 28 (July-December 1812), 138–39; London *Morning Chronicle*, August 4, 1812.
86. Order-in-Council, October 13, 1812, reprinted from London *Gazette*, in London *Times*, October 14, 1812.
87. Declaration of Prince Regent, January 9, 1813, in *Naval Chronicle* 29 (January-June 1813), 140–50. Quotation from p. 141. The British government had issued a similar justification after declaring war against France in 1803. See Declaration of His Majesty, [May 18, 1803], in London *Times*, May 19, 1803.
88. *Naval Chronicle* 28 (July-December 1812), 343.
89. Madison to Congress, June 1, 1812, in *AC*, 12–1, 1624–29.
90. Report of House Foreign Relations Committee, June 3, 1812, in *AC*, 12–1, 1546–54.
91. London *Times*, June 17, 1812.
92. *AC*, 12–1, 1630–37.
93. *AC*, 12–1, 265–97.
94. Madison to Henry Wheaton, February 26–27, [1827], in Madison Papers, Library of Congress, Washington, DC, microfilm edition, reel 21; Jefferson to Robert Wright, August 8, 1812, in Jefferson Papers, Library of Congress, Washington, DC, microfilm edition, reel 46; speech of William King, Febru-

ary 5, 1813, in *AC*, 12–2, 1001; Brown, *Republic in Peril*, 37–38.

95. Charles Bright, *Submarine Telegraphs: Their History, Construction, and Working* (London, 1898), 23–50, 78–105; John Steele Gordon, *A Thread across the Ocean: The Heroic Story of the Transatlantic Cable* (New York, 2002), chs. 8–11.

96. Hickey, *War of 1812*, 42–43.

97. Speech of John C. Calhoun, May 6, 1812, in *AC*, 12–1, 1399.

**Chapter 2: Battles and Campaigns**

1. J. Mackay Hitsman, *Safeguarding Canada, 1763–1871* (Toronto, 1968), ch. 4; and Hitsman, *Incredible War* (updated ed.), ch. 2.

2. SW to Chairman of [House and Senate] Military Committee, December 23, 1814, in *ASP: MA*, 1: 610.

3. SW to Daniel D. Tompkins, February 4, 1815, in U.S. Department of War, *Confidential and Unofficial Letters, Sent by the Secretary of War, 1814–1847*, microfilm series M7, National Archives, Washington, DC, reel 1; and SW to Chairman of [House and Senate] Military Committee, December 23, 1814, in *ASP: MA*, 1: 610.

4. See SSWC to CG, June 3, 1814, in Hitsman, *Incredible War* (updated ed.), 289; John K. Mahon, "British Command Decisions Relative to the Battle of New Orleans," *Louisiana History* 6 (Winter 1965), 53–76; Frank L. Owsley, Jr., "The Role of the South in the British Grand Strategy in the War of 1812," *Tennessee Historical Quarterly* 31 (Spring 1972), 22–38.

5. John R. Grodzinski, "The Vigilant Superintendence of the Whole District: The War of 1812 on the Upper St. Lawrence," Master's thesis (Royal Military College of Canada, 2002), 70–71.

6. This campaign is described in Antal, *Wampum Denied*, chs. 3–5.

7. Ibid., 47–48.

8. John C. Parish, ed., *The Robert Lucas Journal of the War of 1812 during the Campaign under General William Hull* (Iowa City, 1906), 31, 36.

9. W.H. Merritt, "Journal of Events Principally on the Detroit and Niagara Frontiers," in Wood, *Select British Documents*, 3: 550.

10. William F. Coffin, *1812: The War, and Its*

*Moral, A Canadian Chronicle* (Montreal, 1864), 198–200. Quotation from p. 200. See also R. David Edmunds, "Main Poc: Potawatomi Wabeno," *American Indian Quarterly* 9 (Summer 1985), 266.

11. [Robert B. McAfee], *History of the Late War in the Western Country* (Lexington, KY, 1816), 73.

12. Hull to SW, August 26, 1812, in U.S. Department of War, *Letters Received by the Secretary of War, Registered Series, 1801–1870*, microfilm series M221, National Archives, Washington, DC, reel 45.

13. Edward Baynes to Isaac Brock, September 10, 1812, printed in James V. Campbell, *Outlines of the Political History of Michigan* (Detroit, 1876), 315n1.

14. Ibid.; Return of Ordnance and Ordnance Stores Taken at Detroit, and Cass to SW, September 10, 1812, in Cruikshank, *Surrender of Detroit*, 154, 218–23; Erna Risch, *Quartermaster Support of the Army: A History of the Corps, 1775–1939* (Washington, DC, 1962), 159.

15. Antal, *Wampum Denied*, chs. 2–5; Quimby, *U.S. Army in the War of 1812*, 1: ch. 2; Hickey, *War of 1812*, 80–84.

16. Robert Malcomson, *A Very Brilliant Affair: The Battle of Queenston Heights, 1812* (Toronto, 2003).

17. Roosevelt, *Naval War of 1812*, 158–60.

18. Quoted in Theodore J. Crackel, "The Battle of Queenston Heights, 13 October 1812," in Charles E. Heller and William A. Stofft, eds., *America's First Battles, 1776–1965* (Lawrence, KS, 1986), 47.

19. For additional evidence, see ibid., and Hickey, *War of 1812*, 87.

20. Malcomson, *Brilliant Affair*, 144.

21. Carl Alfred Friesen, *Alfred the War Horse: The Story of Isaac Brock and His Horse* (St. Catharines, ON, 2000).

22. Malcomson, *Brilliant Affair*, 144 and 293n10.

23. See Hitsman, *Incredible War* (updated ed.), 328n25.

24. Merritt, "Journal of Events," in Wood, *Select British Documents*, 3: 559.

25. Glegg to William Brock, October 14, 1812, in Cruikshank, *Niagara Frontier*, 4: 83.

26. Narrative of G.C. Jarvis, ibid., 4: 116.

27. For a good discussion of this problem, see

Malcomson, *Brilliant Affair*, Appendix A.

28. "General Brock's Death," Philadelphia *Times*, November 22, 1880, reprinted in Ludwig Kosche, "Relics of Brock: An Investigation," *Archivaria* 9 (Winter 1979–80), 100–01.

29. There is a good discussion of Brock's death in Kosche, "Relics of Brock," 47–52, 102–03.

30. Entry of May 27, 1813, in John C. Fredriksen, ed., "Chronicle of Valor: The Journal of a Pennsylvania Officer [George McFeely] in the War of 1812," *Western Pennsylvania History Magazine* 67 (July 1984), 263.

31. Narrative of G.C. Jarvis, in Cruikshank, *Niagara Frontier*, 4: 116. See also letter of John Beverley Robinson, October 14, 1812, in Wood, *Select British Documents*, 1: 613.

32. Malcomson, *Burying General Brock: A History of Brock's Monuments* ([Niagara-on-the-Lake, ON], 1996), 45–47.

33. George Ridout to brother, October 21, 1812, in Cruikshank, *Niagara Frontier*, 4: 147.

34. Today the Washington Memorial (555 feet) and the Bunker Hill Memorial (221 feet) are taller.

35. For a fine account of Brock's burials and monuments, see Malcomson, *Burying General Brock*.

36. The best account of this operation is in Carl Benn, *Historic York, 1793–1993* (Toronto, 1993), 48–64.

37. Ibid., 53n.

38. Ibid., 53–54, 56n; William Chewett *et al.* to John Strachan *et al.*, May 8, 1813, in Cruikshank, *Niagara Frontier*, 5: 193–95.

39. Chauncey to SN, May 7, 1813, in Dudley and Crawford, *Naval War of 1812*, 2: 453.

40. CG to SSWC, July 20, 1813, in Cruikshank, *Niagara Frontier*, 6: 256.

41. See Robert Malcomson, *Lords of the Lake: The Naval War on Lake Ontario, 1812–1814* (Annapolis, MD, 1998), 69, 94.

42. Dearborn to SW, May 13, 1813, in *ASP: MA*, 1: 444: Malcomson, *Lords of the Lake*, 110–11.

43. For details on this battle, see Alec R. Gilpin, *The War of 1812 in the Old Northwest* (East Lansing, MI, 1958), ch. 11, and Antal, *Wampum Denied*, chs. 14–15.

44. William Woodbridge to SW, January 26, 1814, in Carter, *Territorial Papers of the United States*, 10: 500–02; John Sugden, *Tecumseh's Last Stand* (Norman, OK, 1985), 186–93; R.

David Edmunds, *The Potawatomis: Keepers of the Fire* (Norman, OK, 1978), 198–204, and "'A Watchful Safeguard to Our Habitations': Black Hoof and the Loyal Shawnees," in Frederck E. Hoxie *et al*, eds, *Native Americans in the Early Republic* (Charlottesville, VA, 1999), 194–95.

45. J.C.A. Stagg, *Mr. Madison's War: Politics, Diplomacy, and Warfare in the Early American Republic, 1783–1830* (Princeton, 1983), 330n100.

46. Thomas D. Clark, *Frontier America: The Story of the Westward Movement* (New York, 1959), 277.

47. Speech of Abraham Lincoln, September 18, 1858, in Roy P. Basler, ed., *The Collected Works of Abraham Lincoln*, 9 vols. (New Brunswick, NJ, 1953–55), 3: 146. Johnson never married but lived with a light-skinned female slave, Julia Chinn, who bore him two daughters that he raised as his own and tried to introduce into society. See Edgar J. McManus, "Johnson, Richard Mentor," in John A. Garraty and Mark C. Carnes, eds., *American National Biography*, 24 vols. (New York, 1999), 12: 119.

48. Robert Bolt, "Vice President Richard M. Johnson of Kentucky: Hero of the Thames—Or the Great Amalgamator?" *Register of the Kentucky Historical Society* 75 (July 1977), 191–203.

49. Quoted in Louisville *Journal*, reprinted in *Third Annual Report and Collections of the State Historical Society of Wisconsin for the Year 1856* (Madison, 1857), 315.

50. For a fascinating review of all the evidence, see Sugden, *Tecumseh's Last Stand*, ch. 6.

51. Quoted in Thomas D. Clark, "Kentucky in the Northwest Campaign," in Philip P. Mason, ed., *After Tippecanoe: Some Aspects of the War of 1812* (East Lansing, MI, 1963), 94.

52. See examination of the evidence on this question in Sugden, *Tecumseh's Last Stand*, 168–81, 215–20; and Guy St-Denis, *Tecumseh's Bones* (Montreal, 2005), esp. 138–42.

53. See Norman H. Plummer, "Another Look at the Battle of St. Michaels," *Weather Gauge* 31 (Spring 1995), 10–15; and Christopher T. George, *Terror on the Chesapeake: The War of 1812 on the Bay* (Shippensburg, PA, 2000), 62–64, 183n54–184n54.

54. Owsley, *Struggle for the Gulf Borderlands,* 35–39.

55. Ernest Cruikshank, *Drummond's Winter Campaign, 1813,* rev. ed. ([Lundy's Lane, ON], [1900?]), 15–16.

56. George McClure to public, [January 1814], in Cruikshank, *Niagara Frontier,* 9: 48–50.

57. For the U.S. disavowal, see SW to Daniel Tompkins, December 26, 1813, and James Wilkinson to CG, January 28, 1814, ibid., 9: 54, 153.

58. Proclamation of CG, January 12, 1814, ibid., 9: 115.

59. John Rogers, John Wilson, and Donald Fraser to Buffalo *Gazette,* December 21, 1814, ibid., 9: 10.

60. See Winfield Scott, *Memoirs of Lieut.-General Scott,* 2 vols. (New York, 1864), 1: 119–21, for his claims. For a fine analysis of Scott's mythmaking, see Donald E. Graves, "'I have a handsome little army . . .': A Re-examination of Winfield Scott's Camp at Buffalo in 1814," in R. Arthur Bowler, ed., *War along the Niagara: Essays on the War of 1812 and Its Legacy* (Youngstown, NY, 1991), 43–52.

61. The standard work on this battle is Donald E. Graves, *Red Coats and Grey Jackets: The Battle of Chippawa, 5 July 1814* (Toronto, 1994).

62. Scott, *Memoirs,* 1: 129.

63. Charles Winslow Elliott, *Winfield Scott: The Soldier and the Man* (New York, 1937), 162.

64. See Graves, *Red Coats and Grey Jackets,* 186–87.

65. Scott, *Memoirs,* 1: 129; Lossing, *Pictorial Field-Book of the War of 1812,* 806n3.

66. See René Chartrand, "The US Army's Uniform Supply 'Crisis' during the War of 1812," *Military Collector and Historian* 40 (Summer 1988), 64; and Graves, *Red Coats and Grey Jackets,* 181.

67. The standard work on Lundy's Lane is Donald E. Graves, *Where Right and Glory Lead! The Battle of Lundy's Lane, 1814,* rev. ed. (Toronto, 1997).

68. For details of this battle, see Joseph Whitehorne, *While Washington Burned: The Battle for Fort Erie, 1814* (Baltimore, 1992), ch. 5; and Richard V. Barbuto, *Niagara 1814: America Invades Canada* (Lawrence, KS, 2000), ch. 9.

69. Both men are quoted in Donald E. Graves, "William Drummond and the Battle of Fort Erie," *Canadian Military History* 1 (Autumn 1992), 35, 39.

70. For a good discussion of the European background of Drummond's comment, see ibid., 39–41. Graves concludes that Drummond had every right to put soldiers to death in a garrison that resisted assault.

71. For a description of this campaign, see Everest, *War of 1812 in the Champlain Valley,* chs. 10–11; Fitz-Enz, *Final Invasion,* chs. 4–5; and David Curtis Skaggs, *Thomas Macdonough: Master of Command in the Early U.S. Navy* (Annapolis, MD, 2003), chs. 4–6.

72. Donald E. Graves, "'The Finest Army Ever to Campaign on American Soil?': The Organization, Strength, Composition, and Losses of British Land Forces during the Plattsburgh Campaign, September 1814," *Journal of the War of 1812* 7 (Fall/Winter 2003), 6–13.

73. Everest, *War of 1812 in the Champlain Valley,* 185–86; Fitz-Enz, *Final Invasion,* 165–68.

74. Hitsman, *Incredible War* (updated ed.), 255–62. Macomb's report, which was dated September 15, 1814, can be found in Fitz-Enz, *Final Invasion,* 219–24.

75. Quoted in Fitz-Enz, *Final Invasion,* 173.

76. See Graves, "'The Finest Army Ever to Campaign on American Soil?'"

77. There are several good accounts of the Washington campaign. See Walter Lord, *The Dawn's Early Light* (New York, 1972), chs. 5–7; Joseph A. Whitehorne, *The Battle of Baltimore, 1814* (Baltimore, 1997), 113–44; Anthony S. Pitch, *The Burning of Washington: The British Invasion of 1814* (Annapolis, MD, 1998), chs. 4–10; and George, *Terror on the Chesapeake,* chs. 8–9.

78. Cochrane to FSA, July 18, 1814 (with enclosures), in Cruikshank, *Niagara Frontier,* 2: 414–15

79. Ingersoll, *Historical Sketch of the Second War,* 2: 190. Ingersoll was not in Washington at the time, but he was a member of Congress who knew people who were there.

80. For Cockburn's wishes, see G.C. Moore Smith, ed., *The Autobiography of Lieutenant-General Sir Harry Smith,* 2 vols. (London, 1902), 1: 200; and Roger Morriss, *Cockburn and the British Navy in Transition: Admiral Sir George Cockburn, 1772–1853* (Columbia, SC, 1997), 109.

81. For other details of this episode, see Henry Adams, *History of the United States of America [during the Administrations of Jefferson and Madison]*, 9 vols. (New York, 1889–91), 8: 125–27; and Hickey, *War of 1812*, 184–85, 195.

82. Chauncey to Thomas Scott or William Powell, November 14, 1813, in Edith G. Firth, ed., *The Town of York*, 2 vols. (Toronto, 1962–66), 1: 322–23. Quotation from p. 323.

83. See S. Burch and J.T. Frost to Patrick Magruder, September 15, 1814, in *AC*, 13–3, 306–07.

84. Quoted in Ingersoll, *Historical Sketch of the Second War*, 2: 190.

85. Ibid., 2: 184.

86. Letter from Washington, August 27, [1814], in Philadelphia *Aurora*, August 30, 1814.

87. Washington *National Intelligencer*, August 31, 1814.

88. Francis James Jackson to Timothy Pickering, April 24, 1811, in Pickering Papers, Massachusetts Historical Society, Boston, MA, microfilm edition, reel 29. This letter can also be found, slightly edited, in Henry Adams, ed., *Documents Relating to New-England Federalism, 1801–1815* (Boston, 1877), 382–87. The quotation is on p. 385.

89. For another prewar use of this name, see Abijah Bigelow to Hannah Bigelow, March 18, 1812, in Clarence S. Brigham, ed., "Letters of Abijah Bigelow, Member of Congress, to His Wife, 1810–1815," *Proceedings of the American Antiquarian Society* 40 (October 1930), 331.

90. William Seale, *The President's House: A History*, 2 vols. (Washington, DC, 1986), 1: 23, 131, 147, 163, and 2: 654, 1088n3; John Whitcomb and Claire Whitcomb, *Real Life at the White House: Two Hundred Years of Daily Life at America's Most Famous Residence* (New York, 2000), 229.

91. Ingersoll, *Historical Sketch of the Second War*, 2: 187.

92. Paul Jennings, *A Colored Man's Reminiscences of James Madison* (Brooklyn, NY, 1865), 10.

93. Moore Smith, *Autobiography of Harry Smith*, 1: 200; letter from a midshipman on H.M. Sloop *Espoir*, in *Niles' Register* 7 (Supplement), 150; Diary of Col. Arthur Brooke, August 15, 1814, in Christopher T. George, ed., "The Family Papers of Maj. Gen. Robert Ross, the Diary of Col. Arthur Brooke, and the British Attacks on Washington and Baltimore in 1814," *Maryland Historical Magazine* 88 (Fall 1993), 303; James Scott, *Recollections of a Naval Life*, 3 vols. (London, 1834), 3: 303–04; [George R. Gleig], *A Narrative of the Campaigns of the British Army at Washington, Baltimore, and New Orleans* (Philadelphia, 1821), 134–35. See also Seale, *President's House*, 1: 33–36; and Pitch, *Burning of Washington*, 117–18.

94. Jennings, *A Colored Man's Reminiscences*, 10.

95. [Gleig], *Narrative of the Campaigns*, 178.

96. For the Battle of Baltimore, see Scott S. Sheads, *The Rockets' Red Glare: The Maritime Defense of Baltimore in 1814* (Centreville, MD, 1986), chs. 6–8; Lord, *Dawn's Early Light*, chs. 9–11; Pitch, *Burning of Washington*, chs, 14–17; Whitehorne, *Battle of Baltimore*, 159–94.

97. The name of this truce vessel was lost to history until Ralph J. Robinson did some shrewd detective work in the 1950s to uncover it. See Robinson, "New Facts in the National Anthem Story," *Baltimore* 49 (September 1956), 33, 35, 37, 58.

98. Quoted in Scott Sheads, *Fort McHenry* (Baltimore, 1995), 37.

99. William M. Marine, *The British Invasion of Maryland, 1812–1815*, ed. Louis H. Dielman (Baltimore, 1913), 150n, 191.

100. Clifton W. Tayleure, *The Boy Martyrs of Sept. 12, 1814: A Local Historical Drama, in 3 Acts* (Boston, 1859).

101. B. Wheeler Jenkins, "The Shots That Saved Baltimore," *Maryland Historical Magazine* 77 (Winter 1982), 364.

102. The case for Ross's death by friendly fire was laid out for me by Chris George, who considered it "an outside possibility." George to author, October 10, 2005.

103. Communications from "A Sharpshooter" and "One of the Infantry," in Baltimore *American*, November 4 and 6, 1815; George Cockburn to Alexander Cochrane, September 15, 1814, and Cochrane to Viscount Melville, September 17, 1814, in Dudley and Crawford, *Naval War of 1812*, 3: 280, 289; Ma-

rine, *British Invasion of Maryland,* 190–93; Christopher T. George, "Harford County in the War of 1812," *Harford Historical Bulletin,* #76 (Spring 1998), 46–51; George Burden, "Who Killed General Robert Ross?" *Medical Post* 39 (June 24, 2003), 32–33. The conflicting views on Ross's death have been conveniently compiled by Scott S. Sheads in an unpublished manuscript entitled "Major General Robert Ross: A Death Biography" (updated March 12, 2005).

104. Armistead to Samuel Smith, summer 1813, quoted in Lord, *Dawn's Early Light,* 274. Although the letter undoubtedly exists, it cannot be found. See Scott S. Sheads, *Guardian of the Star-Spangled Banner: Lt. Colonel George Armistead and the Fort McHenry Flag* (Linthicum, MD, 1999), 78n17.

105. Armistead to Peter Gansevoort, October 12, 1802, in Fort Niagara Garrison Papers, Buffalo and Erie County Historical Society, Buffalo, NY; Brian Leigh Dunnigan, "Fort Niagara's Star-Spangled Banner: A Garrison Color of the War of 1812," *Military Collector and Historian* 50 (Summer 1998), 76–77; Dunnigan to author, March 2, 2005.

106. John C. Calhoun, Flag Directive, [April?], 1818, in U.S. Department of War, *General Orders and Circulars of the War Department and Headquarters of the Army, 1809–1860,* microfilm series M1094, National Archives, Washington, DC, reel 1.

107. See James Calhoun, bill for American ensigns, August 19, 1813, in Sheads, *Guardian of the Star-Spangled Banner,* 10.

108. Sheads, *Guardian of the Star-Spangled Banner,* 34.

109. Ibid., ch. 3.

110. See Baltimore *Patriot,* September 20, 1814, Baltimore *American,* September 21, 1814, and "Defence of Fort McHenry" (broadside), [September 1814], all reprinted in Sonneck, *"Star Spangled Banner,"* plates 13–15. See also ibid., 68.

111. Quoted in Lonn Taylor, *The Star-Spangled Banner: The Flag that Inspired the National Anthem* (New York, 2000), 53.

112. "The Flags of Our Army, Navy, and Government Departments," *National Geographic Magazine,* 32 (October 1917), 306.

113. Taylor, *Star-Spangled Banner,* 53.

114. Ibid., chs. 3–5.

115. Ibid., 34; "Defence of Fort McHenry" (broadside), [September 1814], reprinted in Sonneck, *"Star Spangled Banner,"* plate 15.

116. See Sonneck, *"Star Spangled Banner,"* 65–95; and Taylor, *Star-Spangled Banner,* ch. 2.

117. Clement Dorsey to Philip Stuart, June 17, 1814, and William H. Dent and Clement Dorsey, Dialogue No. 2, June 17, 1814, in Washington *National Intelligencer,* June 20, 1814. Quotations from Stuart letter.

118. George, *Terror on the Chesapeake,* 173–74.

119. For an overview of this campaign, see William D. Williamson, *The History of the State of Maine,* 2 vols. (Hallowell, ME, 1832), 2: 640–54; and Barry J. Lohnes, "A New Look at the Invasion of Eastern Maine, 1814," *Maine Historical Quarterly* 15 (Summer 1975), 5–25.

120. P.B. Waite, *The Lives of Dalhousie University,* 2 vols. (Montreal, 1994), 1: 8–15.

121. Proclamation of John Sherbrooke and Edward Griffith, September 21, 1814, in *Niles' Register* 7 (October 29, 1814), 117–18; Lewis Clinton Hatch, "Federalists and Democrats—War of 1812," in Lewis Clinton Hatch, ed., *Maine: A History,* 3 vols. (New York, 1919), 1: 74.

122. SW to Henry Dearborn, November 14, 1814, and to Caleb Strong, December 1, 1814, in U.S. Department of War, *Letters Sent by the Secretary of War Relating to Miliary Affairs, 1800–1889,* microfilm series M6, National Archives, Washington, DC, reel 7; Strong to SW, December 9, 1814, in U.S. Department of War, *Letters Received by the Secretary of War, Registered Series, 1801–1870,* microfilm series M221, National Archives, Washington, DC, reel 66.

## Chapter 3: The Maritime War

1. David Hume, *The History of England, From the Invasion of Julius Caesar to the Revolution of 1688,* corrected ed., 8 vols. (London, 1763), 7: 518.

2. Mahan, *Sea Power,* 1: 74; Howard I. Chapelle, *The History of the American Sailing Navy: The Ships and Their Development* (New York, 1949), 173.

3. Speech of Josiah Quincy, January 25, 1812, in *AC,* 12–1, 963.

4. Irving Brant, "Timid President? Futile War?"

*American Heritage*, 10 (October 1959), 85–86; Linda Maloney, "The War of 1812: What Role for Sea Power?" in Kenneth J. Hagan, ed., *In Peace and War: Interpretations of American Naval History, 1775–1978* (Westport, CT, 1978), 46–47.

5. Maloney, "War of 1812," 47–48.
6. FSA to station commanders-in-chief, July 10, 1813, in Dudley and Crawford, *Naval War of 1812*, 2: 183.
7. Mahan, *Sea Power*, 1: 298–99, 319, 326–27, 401–03.
8. Letter from British naval officer at Halifax, October 15, 1812, in *Naval Chronicle* 28 (July-December 1812), 426.
9. George Coggeshall, *History of the American Privateers, and Letters-of-Marque, during Our War with England in the Years 1812, '13 and '14* (New York, 1856), 81; Daniel D. Tompkins to New York legislature, November 3, 1812, in Hugh Hastings, ed., *Public Papers of Daniel D. Tompkins, Governor of New York, 1807–1817*, 3 vols. (New York, 1898–1902), 3: 180.
10. For additional details on this matter, see Hickey, *War of 1812*, 92–93.
11. Dudley and Crawford, *Naval War of 1812*, 1: 561; Dudley, *Splintering the Wooden Wall*, 85; Notice of Foreign Office, December 26, 1812, in *Naval Chronicle* 28 (July-December 1812), 507; Proclamation of John Borlase Warren, November 16, 1813, in *Niles' Register* 5 (December 18, 1813), 264–65; Proclamation of Alexander Cochrane, April 25, 1814, ibid., 6 (May 14, 1814), 182–83.
12. Curtis P. Nettels, *The Emergence of a National Economy, 1775–1815* (New York, 1962), 385, 396, 399; Dudley and Crawford, *Naval War of 1812*, 3: 15.
13. Dudley, *Splintering the Wooden Wall*, 142, 177.
14. For the problems at Halifax, see Barry J. Lohnes, "British Naval Problems at Halifax during the War of 1812," *Mariner's Mirror*, 59 (August 1973), 317–33.
15. FSA to John Borlase Warren, February 10, 1813, in Dudley and Crawford, *Naval War of 1812*, 2: 17; Dudley, *Splintering the Wooden Wall*, 115, 156.
16. See telling letters from FSA to Warren, January 9, February 10, and March 20, 1813, in

Dudley and Crawford, *Naval War of 1812*, 2: 14–15, 16–19, 75–78.

17. Although he overstates the case a bit, Wade C. Dudley presents a good analysis of the shortcomings of the British blockade in *Splintering the Wooden Wall*.
18. Carden to FSA, October 28, 1812, in Dudley and Crawford, *Naval War of 1812*, 1: 551.
19. FSA to station commanders-in-chief, July 10, 1813, ibid., 2: 183.
20. [John Richardson?], *The Letters of Veritas, Republished from the Montreal "Herald," Containing a Succinct Narrative of the Military Administration of Sir George Prevost* (Montreal, 1815), 144.
21. James, *Naval Occurrences*, 17, 20, 135, and James, *Naval History of Great Britain*, 5: 381. Quotation from p. 381.
22. Warren to FSA, January 25, 1813, in Dudley and Crawford, *Naval War of 1812*, 2: 16. For similar sentiments, see *Naval Chronicle* 28 (July-December 1812), 344.
23. Spencer C. Tucker, *Handbook of 19th Century Naval Warfare* (Annapolis, MD, 2000), 3.
24. For the design and construction of the U.S. Frigate *Constitution*, see Tyrone G. Martin, *Creating a Legend* (Chapel Hill, NC, 1997).
25. See Roosevelt, *Naval War of 1812*, 84–86, 437–41; Nicholas Blake and Richard Lawrence, *The Illustrated Companion to Nelson's Navy* (Mechanicsburg, PA, 2000), 23, 32–33; and Brian Lavery, *Nelson's Navy: The Ships, Men and Organization, 1793–1815*, rev. ed. (Annapolis, MD, 1994), 48.
26. James Dacres, address to court, n.d., in James, *Naval Occurrences*, appendix, xx.
27. Lieutenant of HMS *Java* to friend, January 26, 1813, in *Naval Chronicle* 29 (January-June 1813), 453.
28. James, *Naval History of Great Britain*, 5: 386; Edward Pelham Brenton, *The Naval History of Great Britain, from [1783] to [1836]*, rev. ed., 2 vols. (London, 1837), 2: 456.
29. James, *Naval Occurrences*, 95–96, and James, *Naval History of Great Britain*, 5: 387, 401. Quotations from pp. 95–96.
30. For a fine analysis of the composition of American crews, see Christopher McKee, "Foreign Seamen in the United States Navy: A Census of 1808," *William and Mary Quarterly*, 3rd series, 42 (July 1985), 383–93. See

also Bradford Perkins, *Prologue to War: England and the United States, 1805–1812* (Berkeley, CA, 1961), 190.

31. Robert Smith, quoted in Mckee, "Foreign Seamen in the United States Navy," 388.

32. Spencer C. Tucker and Frank T. Reuter, *Injured Honor: The "Chesapeake"-"Leopard" Affair, June 27, 1807* (Annapolis, MD, 1996), 117–22.

33. See editorial note, and Jacob Jones to SN, July 21, 1812, in Dudley and Crawford, *Naval War of 1812*, 1: 170n1–71n1, 198.

34. There is a good discussion of this issue in Roosevelt, *Naval War of 1812*, 59–63.

35. Roosevelt, "War with the United States," 29.

36. Carden to FSA, October 28, 1812, in Dudley and Crawford, *Naval War of 1812*, 1: 551. See also James, *Naval Occurrences*, 75, 312; James, *Naval History of Great Britain*, 5: 373; and Brenton, *Naval History of Great Britain*, 2: 460.

37. Macdonough to SN, March 7, 1814, and Charles Gordon to SN, July 19, 1814, in Dudley and Crawford, *Naval war of 1812*, 3: 94, 397. See also Hickey, *War of 1812*, 91–92.

38. J.C.A. Stagg, "Enlisted Men in the United States Army, 1812–1815: A Preliminary Survey," *William and Mary Quarterly*, 3rd series, 43 (October 1986), 633.

39. Journal of John Rodgers, June 23, 1812, and Richard Byron to Herbert Sawyer, June 27, 1812, in Dudley and Crawford, *Naval War of 1812*, 1: 154–60. See also Roosevelt, *Naval War of 1812*, 87–90.

40. Melancthon T. Woolsey to SN, June 9, 1812, in Dudley and Crawford, *Naval War of 1812*, 1: 274; Emily Cain, *Ghost Ships: "Hamilton" and "Scourge," Historical Treasures from the War of 1812* (New York, 1983), 36, 54–57, 63, 125–26.

41. Hugh D. Campbell to SN, July 18, 1812, in Dudley and Crawford, *Naval War of 1812*, 1: 195–96.

42. William M. Crane to SN, July 29, 1812, ibid., 1: 209–11.

43. David Porter to SN, August 15 and September 3, 1812, ibid., 1: 218–19, 443–46.

44. See Tyrone G. Martin, *A Most Fortunate Ship: A Narrative History of Old Ironsides*, rev. ed. (Annapolis, MD, 1997) and *Undefeated: "Old Ironsides" in the War of 1812* (Chapel Hill, 1996).

45. Moses Smith, *Naval Scenes in the Last War* (Boston, 1846), 33.

46. Whipple to friend, [mid?]-1813, in Norma Adams Price, ed., *Letters from Old Ironsides, 1813–1815, Written by Pardon Mawney Whipple* (Tempe, AZ, 1984), 6.

47. James, *Naval Occurrences*, 93.

48. Standing Orders of John Borlase Warren, March 6, 1813, in Dudley and Crawford, *Naval War of 1812*, 2: 59–60.

49. See Peter Padfield, *Broke and the Shannon* (London, 1968), chs. 1–2; Spencer Tucker, *Arming the Fleet: U.S. Navy Ordnance in the Muzzle-Loading Era* (Annapolis, MD, 1989), 48.

50. For details of the engagement, see Albert Greaves, *James Lawrence: Captain, United States Navy, Commander of the "Chesapeake"* (New York, 1904), chs. 12–13; H.F. Pullen, *The "Shannon" and the "Chesapeake"* (Toronto, 1970), ch. 6; Roosevelt, *Naval War of 1812*, 176–91; and Lossing, *Pictorial Field-Book of the War of 1812*, 701–13.

51. Greaves, *James Lawrence*, 3, 235–36, 258–69.

52. *Naval Chronicle* 30 (July-December 1813), 41; J.G. Brighton, *Admiral Sir P.B.V. Broke, Bart., K.C.B., Etc.: A Memoir* (London, 1866), 296.

53. James, *Naval Occurrences*, [iii], 523.

54. John Beresford, quoted in J.G. Brighton, *Admiral of the Fleet Sir Provo W.P. Wallis, G.C.B., Etc.* (London, 1892), 148. See also Brighton, *P.B.V. Broke*, 296–335; Greaves, *James Lawrence*, 238–45.

55. Circular of SN, February 22, 1813, in Dudley and Crawford, *Naval War of 1812*, 2: 48. Later that year, the administration explicitly ordered some commanders to avoid naval duels. SN to John O. Creighton, December 22, 1813, ibid., 2: 297.

56. Dudley, *Splintering the Wooden Wall*, 94–95.

57. Greaves, *James Lawrence*, 70, 218–19.

58. Brighton, *Provo Wallis*, 119–26.

59. Greaves, *James Lawrence*, 167–71, 174–75, 216–17, 219–20, 223–24, 285–89; D.L. Dennis, "The Action between the Shannon and the Chesapeake," *Mariner's Mirror* 45 (February 1959), 36–45; Padfield, *Broke and the "Shannon,"* 150–51; Tucker and Reuter, *Injured Honor*, 194–95.

60. Greaves, *James Lawrence*, 181–82, 214–15; Tucker, *Arming the Fleet*, 25–26. The *Chesa-*

*peake* lost 38 percent of its crew (145 killed and wounded out of 382), while the *Shannon* lost 25 percent (82 out of 330). Greaves, *James Lawrence,* 209–10.

61. Extract from a letter (from Halifax), June 19, 1813, in Brighton, *P.B.V. Broke,* 213; *An Account of the Funeral Honours Bestowed on the Remains of Capt. Lawrence and Lieut. Ludlow* (Boston, 1813), 26, 50; Greaves, *James Lawrence,* 195–96, 235.

62. James Fenimore Cooper, *History of the Navy of the United States of America,* 2nd ed., 2 vols. (Philadelphia, 1840), 2: 166n.

63. See Lossing, *Pictorial Field-Book of the War of 1812,* 519, 706.

64. Hugh D. Purcell, "Don't Give Up the Ship!" *United States Naval Institute Proceedings* 91 (May 1965), 90–94.

65. Brighton, *P.V.B. Broke,* 442–44.

66. Brighton, *Provo Wallis;* William C. Heine, *96 Years in the Royal Navy* (Hantsport, NS, 1987).

67. See *Naval Chronicle* 33 (January-June 1815), 156–58; and John Hayes to Henry Hotham, January 17, 1815, ibid., 259–62.

68. See Roosevelt, *Naval War of 1812,* 358–62; and Spencer Tucker, *Stephen Decatur: A Life Most Bold and Daring* (Annapolis, MD, 2005), 140–47.

69. Michael A. Palmer, *Stoddart's War: Naval Operations during the Quasi-War with France, 1798–1801* (Columbia, SC, 1987), 203–08.

70. David Porter, *Journal of a Cruise Made to the Pacific Ocean,* 2nd ed., 2 vols. (New York, 1822), *passim;* Roosevelt, *Naval War of 1812,* 267–84.

71. See Porter to SN, July 3, 1814, in Dudley and Crawford, *Naval War of 1812,* 3: 732; Frances Robotti and James Vescovi, *The USS "Essex" and the Birth of the American Navy* (Holbrook, MA, 1999), 177–78, 245–47.

72. James Hillyar to FSA, June 26, 1814, in Dudley and Crawford, *Naval War of 1812,* 3: 719; Robotti and Vescovi, *USS "Essex,"* 219–24, 237–38, 241.

73. Robotti and Vescovi, *USS "Essex,"* 231, 234–35.

74. See, for example, Dumas Malone, *Jefferson and His Time,* 6 vols. (Boston, 1948–81), 5: 498–503. After laying out the case for these vessels, Malone conceded that "most of the

money spent on gunboats now appears to have been wasted." Ibid., 503.

75. Joshua Barney's Defense Proposal, July 4, 1813, in Dudley and Crawford, *Naval War of 1812,* 2: 373.

76. See, for example, Roosevelt, "War with the United States," 95; and Mahan, *Sea Power,* 1: 296, and 2: 154–55, 159.

77. Report of SN, June 9, 1809, in U.S. Congress, *American State Papers: Naval Affairs,* 4 vols. (Washington, DC, 1834–61), 1: 200; Madison to Congress, May 23, 1809, in *AC,* 11–1, 12.

78. SN to Thomas Macdonough, January 28, 1814, in Dudley and Crawford, *Naval War of 1812,* 3: 393–95.

79. SN to Isaac Chauncey, June 7, 1814, ibid., 3: 525–26.

80. SN to Samuel Smith, June 17, 1813, ibid., 2: 150.

81. Spencer C. Tucker, *The Jeffersonian Gunboat Navy* (Columbia, SC, 1993), "The Jeffersonian Gunboats in Service, 1804–1825," *American Neptune,* 55 (Spring 1995), 97–110, and "Gunboats," in Heidler and Heidler, *Encyclopedia of the War of 1812,* 218–19; Gene A. Smith, *"For the Purposes of Defense": The Politics of the Jeffersonian Gunboat Program* (Newark, DE, 1995); Donald G. Shomette, *Flotilla: Battle for the Patuxent* (Solomons, MD, 1981); Dean R. Mayhew, "Jeffersonian Gunboats in the War of 1812," *American Neptune* 42 (April 1982), 101–17; Robert Malcomson, "Gunboats on Lake Ontario in the War of 1812," *Seaways: Ships in Scale,* 7 (January/February 1996), 31–37, (March/April 1996), 27–31, and (May/June 1996), 40–44; Hitsman, *Incredible War* (updated ed.), 152–53.

82. Christopher D. Hall, *British Strategy in the Napoleonic Wars, 1803–15* (Manchester, UK, 1992), 81.

83. Richard Glover, "The French Fleet, 1807–1814: Britain's Problem and Madison's Opportunity," *Journal of Modern History,* 39 (September 1967), 233–52. Glover suggests that Madison may have been counting on a French naval resurgence, but there is no evidence for this claim.

84. Dudley, *Splintering the Wooden Wall,* 177–78.

85. For the general rules governing privateering, see Donald A. Petrie, *The Prize Game:*

*Lawful Looting on the High Seas in the Days of Fighting Sail* (Annapolis, MD, 1999); and Faye Margaret Kert, *Prize and Prejudice: Privateering and Naval Prize in Atlantic Canada in the War of 1812* (St. Johns, NF, 1997), chs. 2–3.

86. Crew size based on figures provided by Faye Kert in letters to the author, Novemeber 8 and 15, 2005.

87. A month after the declaration of war, Hezekiah Niles estimated that in the first 60 days of the war, 150 American privateers averaging 6 guns and 75 men would be at sea. *Niles' Register* 2 (July 18, 1812), 334.

88. Acts of June 18 and June 26, 1812, in *AC*, 12–1, 2323, 2327–32.

89. Coggeshall, *History of the American Privateers*, 3.

90. Article 26, Jay Treaty, November 19, 1794, in Samuel Flagg Bemis, *Jay's Treaty: A Study in Commerce and Diplomacy*, rev. ed. (New Haven, CT, 1962), 481.

91. Act of July 6, 1812, in *AC*, 12–1, 2356; Maclay, *American Privateers*, 227.

92. Warren to FSA, October 25, 1813, in Dudley and Crawford, *Naval War of 1812*, 2: 270.

93. See John Drayton to SS, August 24, 1813, and Charles R. Simpson to Thomas Barclay, August 24, 1813, ibid., 2: 213–17; Maclay, *American Privateers*, 311–17.

94. Jerome R. Garitee, *The Republic's Private Navy: The American Privateering Business as Practiced by Baltimore during the War of 1812* (Middletown, CT, 1977), 32, 243; Dudley *Splintering the Wooden Wall*, 138–39; Maclay, *American Privateers*, 506–07.

95. Roosevelt, "War with the United States," 154.

96. Robert Gardiner, ed., *The Naval War of 1812* (Annapolis, MD, 1999), 28.

97. The best accounts of American privateering during the war are Maclay, *American Privateers*; Coggeshall, *History of the American Privateers*; and Garitee, *Republic's Private Navy*.

98. Michael Lewis, *A Social History of the Navy, 1793–1815* (London, 1960), 329.

99. Brenton, *Naval History of Great Britain*, 2: 539.

100. Kert, *Prize and Prejudice*, 157. Kert's monograph is the best study on Canadian privateering. See also Kert, "Private War, Public Service: Maritime Canada's Private War of 1812," in Directorate of History and Heritage, *Canadian Military History since the Seventeenth Century: Proceedings of the Canadian Military History Conference, Ottawa, 5–9 May 2000* (Ottawa, [2001]), 95–102; Roger Marsters, *Bold Privateers: Terror, Plunder and Profit on Canada's Atlantic Coast* (Halifax, NS, 2004), chs. 10–11; and W.S. MacNutt, *The Atlantic Provinces: The Emergence of Colonial Society, 1712–1857* (Toronto, 1965), 150–52.

101. Amos Hall to Daniel D. Tompkins, June 28, 1812, and New York *Evening Post*, July 8, 1812, in Cruikshank, *Niagara Frontier*, 3: 78, 86.

102. David S. Heidler and Jeanne T. Heidler, *The War of 1812* (Westport, CT, 2002), 85n5.

103. The most recent account of this battle is David Curtis Skaggs and Gerard T. Altoff, *A Signal Victory: The Lake Erie Campaign, 1812–1813* (Annapolis, MD, 1997).

104. Max Rosenberg, *The Building of Perry's Fleet on Lake Erie, 1812–1813* (Harrisburg, PA, 1950), ch. 5.

105. Rosenberg, *Building Perry's Fleet*, Appendix 2.

106. W.A.B. Douglas, "The Honor of the Flag Had Not Suffered: Robert Hariot Barclay and the Battle of Lake Erie," in William Jeffrey Welsh and David Curtis Skaggs, eds., *War on the Great Lakes: Essays Commemorating the 175th Anniversary of the Battle of Lake Erie* (Kent, OH, 1991), 34–36; Skaggs and Altoff, *Signal Victory*, 84–86; Robert Malcomson and Thomas Malcomson, *HMS "Detroit": The Battle for Lake Erie* (Annapolis, MD, 1990), 73–76.

107. Chris J. Magoc, *Erie Maritime Museum and U.S. Brig "Niagara"* (Mechanicsburg, PA, 2001), 17.

108. See Robert Malcomson, "What Really Happened: De-Bunking the Burlington Bay Sandbar Legend," at: <http://www.militaryheritage.com/burlingn.htm>; James Elliott, "Mulcaster's Bravery in 1813 Burlington Races," Hamilton *Spectator*, August 31, 1999.

109. The campaign is described in David Curtis Skaggs, *Thomas Macdonough: Master of Command in the Early U.S. Navy* (Annapolis, MD, 2003), chs. 4–6, and Fitz-Enz, *Final Invasion*, chs. 4–5.

110. Kevin J. Crisman, *The "Eagle": An American Brig on Lake Champlain during the War of 1812* (Shelburne, VT, 1987), 40–53, 217.
111. For an excellent illustrated description of winding, see Michael J. Crawford, "The Battle of Lake Champlain," in Charles E. Brodine, Jr., *et al., Against All Odds: U.S. Sailors in the War of 1812* (Washington, DC, 2004), 66–67. See also Fitz-Enz, *Final Invasion,* 118–19, 160–61; and Shomette, *Flotilla,* 89.
112. Macdonough to SN, September 13, 1814, in Dudley and Crawford, *Naval War of 1812,* 3: 615.
113. Cooper, *History of the Navy,* 2: 356.
114. Roosevelt, *Naval War of 1812,* 341.
115. Testimony of William Drew and Robert Anderson, Court Martial, August 18, 1815, in Wood, *Select British Documents,* 3: 408, 413.
116. For an alternative view, see Fitz-Enz, *Final Invasion,* 239–41.
117. Allan Everest says that Macomb used hot shot to destroy several buildings occupied by the British in Plattsburgh, but he cites the Plattsburgh *Republican,* April 4, 1935, and this newspaper ceased publication in 1916. See Everest, *War of 1812 in the Champlain Valley,* 176 and 218n25.
118. Quoted in Mahan, *Sea Power,* 2: 369.
119. See the excellent map in Crawford, "Battle of Lake Champlain," 63. See also Fitz-Enz, *Final Invasion,* 240–41.
120. C. Winton-Clare [R.C. Anderson], "A Shipbuilder's War," *Mariner's Mirror* 29 (July 1943), 139–48.
121. Robert Malcomson, "HMS *St. Lawrence:* The Freshwater First-Rate," *Mariner's Mirror* 83 (November 1997), 419–33; Blake and Lawrence, *Companion to Nelson's Navy,* 25; Malcomson to author, July 29, 2006. Malcomson is the source for all the figures. The French had some 130-gun ships that might have had more firepower than these lakers.

## Chapter 4: Soldiers, Sailors, and Civilians

1. Charles J. Ingersoll to James Monroe, June 8, 1814, in Monroe Papers, Library of Congress, Washington, DC, microfilm edition, reel 5; Calhoun to James Macbride, April 18, 1812, in Robert L. Meriwether *et al.,* eds., *The Papers of John C. Calhoun,* 28 vols. (Columbia, SC, 1959–2003), 1: 99–100.

2. William A. Burwell to [Wilson Cary Nicholas], February 1, 1813, in Nicholas Papers, University of Virginia, Charlottesville, VA. See also Richard *Enquirer,* December 24, 1812.
3. John Adams was actually defeated for re-election during the Quasi-War in 1800, but by then peace negotiations were under way, and this very limited war was winding down. Had the election been held in the first stages of the war, Adams surely would have won.
4. See ch. 1, note 1, for the surveys and studies used.
5. For a sympathetic and yet balanced assessment of Madison's presidency, see Robert A. Rutland, *The Presidency of James Madison* (Lawrence, KS, 1990).
6. For Craig's problems, see Mason Wade, *The French Canadians, 1760–1967,* rev. ed., 2 vols. (Toronto, 1968), 1: 104–15.
7. SSWC to CG, June 3, 1814, printed in Hitsman, *Incredible War* (updated ed.), 290.
8. For details on the land battle, see Everest, *War of 1812 in the Champlain Valley,* ch. 10, and Fitz-Enz, *Final Invasion,* ch. 5.
9. For a brief discussion on the authorship, see F. Murray Greenwood, "Richardson, John," in *DCB,* 6: 643–44.
10. [John Richardson?], *The Letters of Veritas, Republished from the Montreal "Herald," Containing a Succinct Narrative of the Military Administration of Sir George Prevost* (Montreal, 1815). Quotations from pp. 4 and 108.
11. Quoted in Fitz-Enz, *Final Invasion,* 186.
12. See J. Mackay Hitsman, "Sir George Prevost's Conduct of the Canadian War of 1812," *Annual Report of the Canadian Historical Association* (1962), 34–43; Peter Burroughs, "Sir George Prevost," in *DCB,* 5: 693–98; Everest, *War of 1812 in the Champlain Valley,* 32–39; and Wesley B. Turner, *British Generals during the War of 1812: High Command in the Canadas* (Montreal, 1999), esp. ch. 2. Prevost's military career during the war also can be followed in Hitsman, *Incredible War* (updated ed.), and Stanley, *War of 1812.*
13. Richard Glover, *Peninsular Preparation: The Reform of the British Army, 1795–1809* (London, 1963), ch. 6; Stuart Sutherland, *His Majesty's Gentlemen: A Directory of Brit-*

*ish Regular Army Officers of the War of 1812* ([Toronto], 2000), 4.

14. Lambert to SSWC, January 10, 1815, in Latour, *Historical Memoir*, 313.

15. Quoted in G. Auchinleck, *A History of the War between Great Britain and the United States of America, during the Years 1812, 1813, and 1814* (Toronto, 1855), 114n.

16. Quoted in George Sheppard, *Plunder, Profits, and Paroles: A Social History of the War of 1812 in Upper Canada* (Montreal, 1994), 70.

17. See Frederick B. Tupper, *The Life and Correspondence of Major-General Sir Isaac Brock, K.B.*, 2nd ed. (London, 1847); Turner, *British Generals during the War of 1812*, ch. 3; and C.P. Stacey, "The Defence of Upper Canada, 1812," in Morris Zaslow, ed., *The Defended Border: Upper Canada and the War of 1812* (Toronto, 1964), 11–20, and "Brock, Sir Isaac," in *DCB*, 5: 109–15.

18. Kenneth Stickney, "Drummond, Sir Gordon," in *DCB*, 8: 236–39; Turner, *British Generals during the War of 1812*, ch. 6.

19. E.M. Lloyd and John Sweetman, "Ross, Robert," in *DNB* (new), 47: 838–40; H.M. Chichester and James Falkner, "Pakenham, Sir Edward Michael," in *DNB* (new), 42: 422–23.

20. There are many fine biographies of Jackson. The classic nineteenth-century work is James Parton, *Life of Andrew Jackson*, 3 vols. (New York, 1860). The best modern work is probably Robert V. Remini, *Andrew Jackson*, 3 vols. (New York, 1977–84).

21. See John D. Morris, *Sword of the Border: Major General Jacob Jennings Brown, 1775–1828* (Kent, OH, 2000).

22. The best biographies of Scott are Timothy D. Johnson, *Winfield Scott: The Quest for Military Glory* (Lawrence, KS, 1998), and Allan Peskin, *Winfield Scott and the Profession of Arms* (Kent, OH, 2003).

23. For Harrison's long and varied public career, see Freeman Cleaves, *Old Tippecanoe: William Henry Harrison and His Time* (New York, 1939).

24. Brown to Daniel Tompkins, August 1, 1814, in Cruikshank, *Niagara Frontier*, 1: 103.

25. There is no good published biography of Porter. For a brief summary of his life, see Julius W. Pratt, "Porter, Peter Buell," in *DAB*, 15: 99–100; and John C. Fredriksen, "Porter,

Peter Buell," in John A. Garraty and Mark C. Carnes, eds., *American National Biography*, 24 vols. (New York, 1999), 17: 707–09.

26. For details on Procter's career, see Victor Lauriston, "The Case for General Procter," *Kent Historical Society Papers and Addresses* 7 (1951), 7–17, and Sandy Antal, "Myths and Facts Concerning General Procter," *Ontario History* 79 (September 1987), 251–62.

27. See Robert Malcomson, "'Clubbed': Marching to Victory at Queenston, in Reverse!" *MHQ: The Quarterly Journal of Military History*, forthcoming.

28. For more on Sheaffe's wartime experiences, see Turner, *British Generals during the War of 1812*, ch. 4.

29. For more on de Rottenburg, see Turner, *British Generals during the War of 1812*, ch. 5, and "De Rottenburg, Francis, in *DCB*, 6: 660–62.

30. Randolph to Joseph H. Nicholson, June 25, 1807, in Nicholson Papers, Library of Congress, Washington, DC.

31. For details on this wholly avoidable tragedy, see James R. Jacobs, *Tarnished Warrior: Major-General James Wilkinson* (New York, 1938); 251–60, and *The Beginnings of the U.S. Army, 1783–1812* (Princeton, 1947), 345–52.

32. Hickey, *War of 1812*, 144.

33. The best biography is still Jacobs, *Tarnished Warrior*.

34. Wellington to Lord Liverpool, November 7 and 9, 1814, in Duke of Wellington [son of Iron Duke], ed., *Supplementary Dispatches and Memoranda of Field Marshall Arthur, Duke of Wellington, K.G.*, 15 vols. (London, 1858–72), 9: 422, 425. Quotation from p. 425.

35. Wellington to SSWC, November 4, 1814, in Bathurst Papers, Library and Archives Canada, Ottawa, ON, MG24, A8.

36. The naval war can be most conveniently followed in Roosevelt, *Naval War of 1812*.

37. James H. McCulloh to Samuel Smith, September 14, 1814, typed transcript in William Winder Papers, Maryland Historical Society, Baltimore, MD.

38. Ross to SSWC, August 30, 1814, and Brooke to SSWC, September 17, 1814, in Dudley and Crawford, *Naval War of 1812*, 3: 225, 285.

39. For Cockburn's role in the war, see James Pack, *The Man Who Burned the White House:*

*Admiral Sir George Cockburn, 1772–1853* (Annapolis, MD, 1987), chs. 1, 11–14; and Roger Morriss *Cockburn and the British Navy in Transition: Admiral Sir George Cockburn, 1772–1853* (Columbia, SC, 1997), ch. 3.

40. Roosevelt, "War with the United States," 127.

41. Perry to Harrison, September 10, 1813, in Lossing, *Pictorial Field-Book of the War of 1812*, 530. For Perry's victory, see David Curtis Skaggs and Gerard T. Altoff, *A Signal Victory: The Lake Erie Campaign, 1812–1813* (Annapolis, MD, 1997), ch. 5.

42. See Roosevelt, *Naval War of 1812*, 250–55; and Skaggs and Altoff, *Signal Victory*, 127.

43. For a good account of this episode, see David Curtis Skaggs, "Perry Strikes U.S. Marine," *Naval History* 19 (June 2005), 52–57.

44. David Curtis Skaggs has a fine assessment of Macdonough in *Thomas Macdonough: Master of Command in the Early U.S. Navy* (Annapolis, MD, 2003), 135–39. See also James Fenimore Cooper, *History of the Navy of the United States of America,* 2nd ed., 2 vols. (Philadelphia, 1840), 2: 356–57.

45. See Donald E. Graves, "The Redcoats are Coming! British Troop Movements to North America in 1814," *Journal of the War of 1812* 6 (Summer 2001), 12–18.

46. The fencible units are listed in Hitsman, *Incredible War* (updated ed.), 292, 299.

47. For details on this unit, see Winston Johnson, *The Glengarry Light Infantry, 1812–1816: Who Were They and What Did They Do in the War?* (Charlottetown, PEI, 1998).

48. The provincial units are listed in Hitsman, *Incredible War* (updated ed.), 297–99.

49. For details on the more prominent fencible and provincial units, see entries in Robert Malcomson, *Historical Dictionary of the War of 1812* (Lanham, MD, 2006).

50. William F.P. Napier, *The Life and Opinions of General Sir Charles James Napier, G.C.B.,* 4 vols. (London, 1857), 1: 221.

51. See J. Mackay Hitsman and Alice Sorby, "Independent Foreigners or Canadian Chasseurs," *Military Affairs* 25 (Spring 1961), 11–17; and Donald E. Graves, "'Worthless is the laurel steeped in female tears': An Investigation into the Outrages Committed by British Troops at Hampton, Virginia, in 1813," *Journal of the War of 1812* 7 (Winter 2002), 4–20.

52. Hitsman and Sorby, "Independent Foreigners or Canadian Chasseurs," 11; Lossing, *Pictorial Field-Book of the War of 1812,* 684.

53. Hitsman and Sorby, "Independent Foreigners or Canadian Chasseurs," 12, 17; Graves, "'Worthless is the laurel,'" 9, 17–18.

54. The best discussion of the Volunteers is in Donald E. Graves, "Joseph Willcocks and the Canadian Volunteers: An Account of Political Disaffection in Upper Canada during the War of 1812," Master's thesis (Carleton University, 1982).

55. See Donald E. Graves, *Field of Glory: The Battle of Crysler's Farm, 1813* (Toronto, 1999), 129–30.

56. Quoted in Brian Lavery, *Nelson's Navy: The Ships, Men and Organization, 1793–1815,* rev. ed. (Annapolis, MD, 1994), 146.

57. The clearest and most concise account of the organization and operations of the Royal Marines in the war can be found under the headings of "Royal Marines (RN)," "Royal Marine Artillery (RN)," and "Corps of Colonial Marines (RN)" in Robert Malcomson, *Historical Dictionary of the War of 1812* (Lanham, MD, 2006), 120–21, 484–86. See also Lavery, *Nelson's Navy,* ch. 7; Cyril Field, *Britain's Sea-Soldiers,* 2 vols. (Liverpool, UK, 1924), 1: chs. 17 and 19; Paul Harris Nicolas, *Historical Record of the Royal Marine Forces,* 2 vols. (London, 1845), 2: chs. 4–7; Edward Fraser and L.G. Carr-Laughton, *The Royal Marine Artillery, 1804–1923,* 2 vols. (London, 1930), 1: chs. 1–2, 16–20.

58. Clyde H. Metcalf, *A History of the United States Marine Corps* (New York, 1939), 53–80; Robert D. Heinl, *Soldiers of the Sea: The United States Marine Corps, 1775–1962* (Annapolis, MD, 1962), 17–30, 610; Allan R. Millett, *Semper Fidelis: The History of the United States Marine Corps,* rev. ed. (New York, 1991), 45–51; René Chartrand, *Uniforms and Equipment of the United States Forces in the War of 1812* (Youngstown, NY, 1992), 119–20; Mark V. Hilliard, "Clothing for Five Years: Regulations for Clothing and Notes on Equipment Issued to Enlisted U.S. Marines during the War of 1812," *Journal of the War of 1812* 6 (Fall 2001), 5–14; Gary L. Ohls, "*Semper Fi*—Bladensburg: A Birth of Tradition in the United States Marine Corps, *Journal*

*of the War of 1812* 8 (Fall 2003/Winter 2004), 20–36.

59. Sermon of John Strachan, November 22, 1812, printed in Loyal and Patriotic Society of Upper Canada, *The Report of the Loyal and Patriotic Society of Upper Canada* (Montreal, 1817), 365–66.

60. Strachan to the Great Dugald Stewart, winter 1814, in George W. Spragge, ed., *The John Strachan Letter Book: 1812–1814* (Toronto, 1946), 58.

61. Auchinleck, *History of the War,* 4.

62. Ryerson (1803–82) was nine when the war began. For the role of his family, see Egerton Ryerson, *The Loyalists of America and Their Times: From 1620 to 1816,* 2 vols. (Toronto, 1880), 2: 258.

63. Ibid., 2: 317, 430.

64. C.F. Hamilton, "The Canadian Militia: Universal Service," *Canadian Defence Quarterly* 5 (April 1928), 288–300. Quotation from p. 299.

65. George F.G. Stanley, *Canada's Soldiers, 1604–1954: The Military History of an Unmilitary People* (Toronto, 1954), 178–79.

66. C.P. Stacey, "The War of 1812 in Canadian History," *Ontario History* 50 (Summer 1958), 154–56.

67. Brock to brothers, September 3, 1812, in Tupper, *Isaac Brock,* 285.

68. Estimate based on Hitsman, *Incredible War* (updated ed.), 36, and letter from Carl Benn to author, September 2, 2005.

69. For the role of Canadian militia, see Graves, "Introduction: 'Mac' Hitsman, Sir George Prevost and the Incredible War of 1812," in Hitsman, *Incredible War* (updated ed.), xvii–xix; Sheppard, *Plunder, Profits, and Paroles,* 3–5; William Gray, *Soldiers of the King: The Upper Canadian Militia, 1812–1815* (Erin, ON, 1995), 7–46; and George F.G. Stanley, "The Contribution of the Canadian Militia during the War," in Philip P. Mason, ed., *After Tippecanoe: Some Aspects of the War of 1812* (East Lansing, MI, 1963), 28–48.

70. SW to state governors, April 15, 1812, in U.S. Department of War, *Letters Sent by the Secretary of War Relating to Military Affairs, 1800–1889,* microfilm series M6, National Archives, Washington, DC, reel 5. The returns were only for the states. I have provided the estimate for the territories.

71. U.S Congress, *Report of the Third Auditor Relative to the Officers, Non-Commissioned Officers, and Solders of the Militia, Volunteers, and Rangers of the Late War* [U.S. Serial Set, #302] (Washington, DC, 1836), 78–79. Doubtless many men were counted several times because of multiple tours.

72. John K. Mahon, "The Principal Causes for the Failure of the United States Militia System during the War of 1812," *Indiana Military History Journal* 4 (May 1979), 18–19.

73. See Hickey, *War of 1812,* 81, 87, 88, 137, 145.

74. For details, see Donald R. Hickey, "New England's Defense Problem and the Genesis of the Hartford Convention," *New England Quarterly* 50 (December 1977), 589–598.

75. Barney to SN, August 4, 1814 in Dudley and Crawford, *Naval War of 1812,* 3: 184.

76. For the role of American militia, see especially C. Edward Skeen, *Citizen Soldiers in the War of 1812* (Lexington, KY, 1999).

77. This law is printed in *AC,* 2–1, 1392–95. See also Henry Knox to Speaker of the House, December 10, 1794, in *ASP: MA,* 1: 69.

78. These figures are drawn from a debate on the subject in Congress in late 1807. See speeches of John W. Eppes, John Chandler (a War of 1812 brigadier general captured at Stoney Creek), and Roger Nelson, Dec. 3, 1807, in *AC,* 10–1, 1022–25.

79. The federal government loaned an additional 8,000 arms to uniformed militia corps. For the two laws, see *AC,* 5–2, 3752–53, and *AC,* 10–1, 2860. For the implementation of the laws, see Robert L. Kerby, "The Militia System and the State Militias in the War of 1812," *Indiana Magazine of History* 73 (June 1977), 118.

80. In a pair of award-winning works, "The Origins of Gun Culture in the United States, 1760–1865," *Journal of American History* 83 (September 1996), 425–55, and *Arming America: The Origins of a National Gun Culture* (New York, 2000), Michael A. Bellesiles argued that arms were not widely held in early America. Critics, however, have demolished his work, showing that he misread, misused, and fabricated some of his evidence. Columbia University revoked the prestigious Bancroft Prize that it had awarded Bellesiles

for the book, and Alfred A. Knopf decided against putting out a revised edition, probably because it did not think the book could be salvaged. Clayton E. Cramer did the pioneering work of exposing Bellesiles in "The Truth about Bellesiles' *Arming America*," *America's 1st Freedom* (November/December 2000), 55–57, 68; and "Bellesiles's *Arming America*: Worse than Wrong," *Shotgun News* (November 20, 2000), 24–26, (December 18, 2000), 22–23, and (January 15, 2000), 16–17. For an excellent summary and analysis of the criticism of Bellesiles, see James Lindgren, "Fall from Grace: *Arming America* and the Bellesiles Scandal," *Yale Law Journal* 111 (June 2002), 2195–2249.

81. Robert H. Churchill, "Gun Ownership in Early America: A Survey of Manuscript Militia Returns," *William and Mary Quarterly*, 3rd series, 60 (July 2003), 636. See also Randolph Roth, "Guns, Gun Culture, and Homicide: The Relationship between Firearms, the Uses of Firearms, and Interpersonal Violence," *William and Mary Quarterly*, 3rd series, 59 (January 2002), 224.

82. Henry Knox to Speaker of the House, December 10, 1794, in *ASP: MA*, 1: 70.

83. Churchill, "Gun Ownership in Early America," 636.

84. Thomas P. Slaughter, *The Whiskey Rebellion: Frontier Epilogue to the American Revolution* (New York, 1986), 212; Churchill, "Gun Ownership in Early America," 636.

85. Churchill, "Gun Ownership in Early America," 641.

86. Knox to president, January 18, 1790, in *ASP: MA*, 1: 7.

87. Quoted in J. Mackay Hitsman, *Safeguarding Canada, 1763–1871* (Toronto, 1968), 53.

88. Hitsman, *Incredible War* (updated ed.), 6–7.

89. Baynes to CG, June 18, 1814, in *Collections of the Michigan Pioneer and Historical Society* 15 (1890), 597.

90. Quoted in Hitsman, *Incredible War* (updated ed.), 40.

91. Madelaine Askin to mother, June 23, 1813, in Milo M. Quaife, ed., *The John Askin Papers*, 2 vols. (Detroit, 1828–31), 2: 762.

92. Edward Dewar to Henry Procter, August 28, 1812, in Wood, *Select British Documents*, 1: 512.

93. Thomas Forsyth to SW, April 10, 1813, in Carter, *Territorial Papers of the United States*, 16: 310.

94. Donald Jackson, ed., *Black Hawk: An Autobiography* (Urbana, IL, 1964), 71.

95. Ibid.

96. Procter to CG, August 9, 1813, in Wood, *Select British Documents*, 2: 46.

97. Journal of Thomas Verchères de Boucherville, in Milo Milton Quaife, ed., *War on the Detroit: The Chronicles of Thomas Vershères de Boucherville and The Capitulation, By an Ohio Volunteer* (Chicago, 1940), 92–93.

98. Quoted in Burt, *United States, Great Britain, and British North America*, 249. For an excellent analysis of the Iroquois way of war, see Carl Benn, *The Iroquois in the War of 1812* (Toronto, 1998), ch. 3.

99. Harrison to SW, July 15, 1801, in Esarey, *Messages of William Henry Harrison*, 1: 25.

100. Frederick Bates to Benjamin Howard, January 28, 1813, and Maurice Blondeau to Benjamin Howard, January 23, 1813, in Carter, *Territorial Papers of the United States*, 14: 640, 642.

101. Jackson, *Black Hawk: An Autobiography*, 70.

102. Graves, *War of 1812 Journal of Lieutenant John Le Couteur*, 139n16.

103. Figures are based on estimates supplied by Carl Benn in Hitsman, *Incredible War* (updated ed.), Appendix 5; Gregory Evans Dowd, *A Spirited Resistance: The North American Indian Struggle for Unity, 1745–1815* (Baltimore, 1992), 50; David Nichols to author, August 13, 2003; and Donald E. Graves to author, January 17, 2005. For a good discussion of U.S. Indian allies, see Nichols, "'To Set Them at Deadly Variance': The United States Government and Intertribal Warfare among the Woodland Indians, 1775–1815," paper presented at annual meeting of the Organization of American Historians, Los Angeles, CA, April 26, 2001.

104. Christopher Densmore, *Red Jacket: Iroquois Diplomat and Orator* (Syracuse, 1999).

105. See R. David Edmunds, "'A Watchful Safeguard to Our Habitations': Black Hoof and the Loyal Shawnees," in Frederck E. Hoxie *et al*, eds, *Native Americans in the Early Republic* (Charlottesville, VA, 1999), 162–99, and "Forgotten Allies: The Loyal Shawnees and

the War of 1812," in David Curtis Skaggs and Larry L. Nelson, eds., *The Sixty Years' War for the Great Lakes, 1754–1814* (East Lansing, MI, 2001), 337–51.

106. Proclamation of William Hull, July 13, 1812, in Cruikshank, *Surrender of Detroit*, 59.

107. Smith to Companions in Arms, November 17, 1812, in Cruikshank, *Niagara Frontier*, 4: 216.

108. Robert Gillmor to Edward Couche, September 5, 1813, and Robert H. Barclay, Narrative presented at court martial, [September 1814], in Wood, *Select British Documents*, 2: 291, 303.

109. For the role of Indians on the northern frontier, see Benn, *Iroquois in the War of 1812*; Robert S. Allen, *His Majesty's Indian Allies: British Indian Policy in the Defence of Canada, 1774–1815* (Toronto, 1992), chs. 6–7; and George F.G. Stanley, "The Indians in the War of 1812," *Canadian Historical Review* 31 (June 1950), 145–65.

110. For the role of Indians in the South, see Owsley, *Struggle for the Gulf Borderlands*; Dowd, *A Spirited Resistance*, chs. 8–9; Claudio Saunt, *A New Order of Things: Property, Power, and the Transformation of the Creek Indians, 1733–1816* (Cambridge, UK, 1999), chs. 10–11; and David S. Heidler and Jeanne T. Heidler, *Old Hickory's War: Andrew Jackson and the Quest for Empire* (Mechanicsburg, PA, 1996), chs. 1–2.

111. W.K. Jordan to wife, October 12, 1812, in Esarey, *Messages of William Henry Harrison*, 2: 165.

112. See R. David Edmunds, "Redefining Red Patriotism: Five Medals of the Potawatomis," *Red River Historical Review* 5 (Spring 1980), 18–19.

113. [Major John Richardson], "A Canadian Campaign, by a British Officer," *New Monthly Magazine and Literary Journal* 19 (January 1, 1827), 169. The cannibalism episode has been discretely omitted from Alexander C. Casselman, ed., *Richardson's War of 1812* (Toronto, 1902), 159.

114. Sinclair to SN, November 11, 1814, in Dudley and Crawford, *Naval War of 1812*, 3: 649.

115. John K. Mahon, "British Strategy and Southern Indians: War of 1812," *Florida Historical Quarterly* 54 (April 1966), 295.

116. John Sugden, *Tecumseh's Last Stand* (Norman, OK, 1985), 168–81.

117. Entry of February 15, 1813, in John C. Fredriksen, ed., "Chronicle of Valor: The Journal of a Pennsylvania Officer [George McFeely] in the War of 1812," *Western Pennsylvania History Magazine* 67 (July 1984), 256. McFeely calls the American officer with the scalp collection "a Captain Ballard." None of the seven men named Ballard in Francis Heitman register of U.S. Army officers fits the profile, but the story seems credible. McFeely may simply have had the name wrong. See Francis B. Heitman, *Historical Register and Dictionary of the United States Army*, 2 vols. (Washington, DC, 1903), 1: 187–88.

118. Quoted in Tupper, *Isaac Brock*, 253, 262.

119. Harrison to SW, August 7, 1811, in Esarey, *Messages of William Henry Harrison*, 1: 549.

120. Harrison to John Johnson, [late 1811], Harrison to SW, September 25 and October 13, 1811, ibid., 1: 583, 584, 591, 600.

121. Harrison, quoted in Katherine Elizabeth Crane, "Tecumseh," in *DAB*, 18: 359

122. Elliott to Isaac Brock, January 12, 1812, in Wood, *Select British Documents*, 1: 282.

123. Lossing, *Pictorial Field-Book of the War of 1812*, 283.

124. Edmunds, "'A Watchful Safeguard to Our Habitations,'" 163–64, and "Forgotten Allies," 338.

125. R. David Edmunds, "Tecumseh, the Shawnee Prophet, and American History: A Reassessment," *Western Historical Quarterly* 14 (July 1983), 261–76; Alfred A. Cave, "The Shawnee Prophet, Tecumseh, and Tippecanoe: A Case Study of Historical Myth-Making," *Journal of the Early Republic* 22 (Winter 2002), 637–73. See also Edmunds's two biographical studies, *The Shawnee Prophet* (Lincoln, NE, 1983), and *Tecumseh and the Pursuit of Indian Leadership* (Boston, 1983), and John Sugden, *Tecumseh: A Life* (New York, 1997).

126. Gordon Drummond to CG, April 19, 1814, and military secretary to Drummond, April 26, 1814, in Cruikshank, *Niagara Frontier*, 9: 300, 310; ; C.M. Johnston, "William Claus and John Norton: A Struggle for Power in Old Ontario," *Ontario History* 57 (June 1965), 101–08.

127. Speech of Neywash, June 14, 1814, in Wood,

*Select British Documents,* 3: 726–27.

128. Carl F. Klinck and James J. Talman, eds., *The Journal of John Norton, 1816* (Toronto, 1970), lxxvi.

129. Quoted ibid., cxxi.

130. Riall to Gordon Drummond, July 17, 1814, in Cruikshank, *Niagara Frontier,* 1: 70–71.

131. Quoted in Klinck and Talman, *Journal of John Norton,* lxxx.

132. The best sources of information on Norton are the two introductions and the text in Klinck and Talman, *Journal of John Norton.* See also Klinck's article, "Norton, John," in *DCB,* 6: 550–53. Carl Benn is working on a biography of Norton that promises to shed new light on this important figure.

133. Figures computed from U.S. Bureau of the Census, *Historical Statistics of the United States, Colonial Times to 1970,* 2 vols. (Washington, DC, 1975), 1: 8, 14n1.

134. Gerard T. Altoff, *Amongst My Best Men: African-Americans and the War of 1812* (Put-in-Bay, OH, 1996), 69–73.

135. Ira Dye, "Physical and Social Profiles of Early American Seafarers, 1812–1815," in Colin Howell and Richard J. Twomey, ed., *Jack Tar in History: Essays in the History of Maritime Life and Labour* (Fredericton, NB, 1991), 235.

136. See, for example, Charles Gordon to SN, September 20, 1814, in Dudley and Crawford, *Naval War of 1812,* 3: 308.

137. W. Jeffrey Bolster, *Black Jacks: African American Seamen in the Age of Sail* (Cambridge, MA, 1997), ch. 4. King Dick was also known as Richard Crafus or Richard Seaver.

138. Altoff, *Amongst My Best Men,* chs. 8–12.

139. Quoted ibid., 23.

140. Grandison to SN, November 7, 1812, in Dudley and Crawford, *Naval War of 1812,* 1: 597.

141. Mary R. Bullard, *Black Liberation on Cumberland Island in 1815* ([South Dartmouth, MA], 1983), 47–48; Reilly, *British at the Gates,* 230.

142. Johnston, *Glengarry Light Infantry,* 33, 120.

143. Captain George Fowler to Edward Baynes, May 29, 1813, in Cruikshank, *Niagara Frontier,* 5: 258; Altoff, *Amongst My Best Men,* 90–91; Robin W. Winks, *The Blacks in Canada: A History* (New Haven, 1971), 150.

144. Altoff, *Amongst My Best Men,* 81.

145. SSWC to Thomas Sidney Beckwith, March 20, 1813, in Dudley and Crawford, *Naval War of 1812,* 2: 325. See also SSWC to Edward Barnes, May 20, 1814, ibid., 3: 73.

146. Proclamation of Alexander Cochrane, April 2, 1814, ibid., 3: 60.

147. Cochrane to Cockburn, April 8, 1814, ibid., 3: 61.

148. Christopher T. George, "Mirage of Freedom: African Americans in the War of 1812," *Maryland Historical Magazine* 91 (Winter 1996), 437–40.

149. See Francis Berkeley, *Dunmore's Proclamation of Emancipation* (Charlottesville, VA, 1941).

150. Article 7, Treaty of Paris, November 30, 1782, in Samuel Flagg Bemis, *The Diplomacy of the American Revolution,* rev. ed. (Bloomington, IN, 1957), 262–63.

151. Arnett G. Lindsay, "Diplomatic Relations between the United States and Great Britain Bearing on the Return of Negro Slaves, 1783–1828," *Journal of Negro History* 5 (October 1920), 391–409.

152. Barney to SN, August 4, 1814, in Dudley and Crawford, *Naval War of 1812,* 3: 184.

153. John McNish Weiss, "The Corps of Colonial Marines, 1814–1816: A Summary," *Immigrants and Minorities* 15 (March 1996), 80–84; Bullard, *Black Liberation on Cumberland Island,* chs. 6–7.

154. John McNish Weiss, "The Merikens," paper presented at National Archives Seminar, Kew, Surrey, UK, October 18, 2003.

155. Quoted in Pack, *George Cockburn,* 168.

156. Quoted in Frank A. Cassell, "Slaves of the Chesapeake Bay Area and the War of 1812," *Journal of Negro History* 57 (April 1972), 151.

157. Cockburn to Cochrane, July 17, 1814, in Dudley and Crawford, *Naval War of 1812,* 3: 156.

158. Quoted in Weiss, "Merikens," 9.

159. Henry Clay to Rufus King, May 10, 1825, in *ASP: FR,* 6: 342.

160. John McNish Weiss, "The Corps of Colonial Marines: Black Freedom Fighters of the War of 1812," unpublished paper; Roger Norman Buckley, *Slaves in Red Coats: The British West India Regiments, 1795–1815* (New Haven, 1979), 78–79, 176n63; William A. Green, *British Slave Emancipation: The Sugar Colonies and the Great Experiment, 1830–1865* (London, 1976), ch. 4; Seymour Drescher, *The Mighty Experiment: Free Labor versus Slavery*

in *British Emancipation* (Oxford, UK, 2002) ch. 8; B.W. Higman, *Slave Populations of the British Caribbean, 1807–1834* (Baltimore, 1984), 72.

161. John McNish Weiss, who has investigated this matter, shared his findings in a letter to the author, February 17, 2003.

162. Winks, *Blacks in Canada*, ch. 5.

163. See three works by John Weiss: "Merikens"; "Corps of Colonial Marines," 84–86; and *The Merikens: Free Black American Setters in Trinidad, 1815–16* (London, 2002), chs. 2–3.

164. John W. Covington, "The Negro Fort," *Gulf Coast Historical Review* 5 (Spring 1990), 79–91.

165. Rosalyn Howard, *Black Seminoles in the Bahamas* (Gainsville, 2002), chs. 2–3.

166. Article 1, Treaty of Ghent, December 24, 1814, in Heidler and Heidler, *Encyclopedia of the War of 1812*, 584.

167. Cockburn to John Clavell, March 10, 1815, in Dudley and Crawford, *Naval War of 1812*, 3: 350; Lambert to Andrew Jackson, March 18, 1815, and to Joseph Woodruff, March 20, 1815, in Latour, *Historical Memoir*, 272, 290.

168. Nicolas, *Historical Record of the Royal Marine Forces*, 2: 288.

169. The best discussion of these claims is in John Bassett Moore, *History and Digest of the International Arbitrations to Which the United States has Been a Party*, 6 vols. (Washington, DC, 1898), 1: 350–90.

170. W.R. Riddell, "The Slave in Upper Canada," *Journal of Negro History* 4 (October 1919), 372–85.

171. I. Grant to James Green, August 17, 1807, in *Collections of the Michigan Pioneer and Historical Society* 15 (1890), 42; "Decision of the Supreme Court respecting the Slaves of Matthew Elliott," November 4, 1807, in *Historical Collections of the Michigan Pioneer and Historical Society* 36 (1908), 201; Reginald Horsman, *Matthew Elliott, British Indian Agent* (Detroit, 1964), 158–59; Frank B. Woodford, *Mr. Jefferson's Disciple: A Life of Justice Woodward* (East Lansing, MI, 1953), 84–91; James V. Campbell, *Outlines of the Political History of Michigan* (Detroit, 1876), 234.

172. Petition to the president, [1809], and Augustus B. Woodward to William Hull, July 23, 1810, in Carter, *Territorial Papers of the*

United States, 10: 297, 323; Altoff, *Amongst My Best Men*, 76–77.

173. Augustus B. Woodward to SW, July 28, 1812, in Carter, *Territorial Papers of the United States*, 10: 390.

174. Circular of November 5, 1811, and July 15, 1812, in Wood, *Select British Documents*, 3: 762–64; George Sheppard, "'Wants and Privations': Women in the War of 1812 in Upper Canada," *Social History* 28 (May 1995), 162–63, 175–76; Graves, *Field of Glory*, 399n22–400n22.

175. General Orders of CG, June 10, 1813, in Cruikshank, *Niagara Frontier*, 6: 65; John R. Grodzinski, "The Vigilant Superintendence of the Whole District: The War of 1812 on the Upper St. Lawrence," Master's thesis (Royal Military College of Canada, 2002), 153–54; Graves, *Field of Glory*, 400n22.

176. McFeeley to Alexander Smyth, [November 1812], in Cruikshank, *Niagara Frontier*, 4: 234. See also entry of November 14 [13], 1812, in Fredriksen, "Journal of a Pennsylvania Officer [George McFeely]," 252; Brian Leigh Dunnigan, *A History and Guide to Old Fort Niagara* (Youngstown, NY, 1985), 20. McFeeley called her "Betsy" Doyle.

177. "Rules and Regulations of the Army of the United States," May 1, 1813, in *ASP: MA*, 1: 436.

178. Quoted in Mordecai M. Noah, *Travels in England, France, Spain, and the Barbary States in the Years 1813–14 and 15* (New York, 1819), 12. The best account of women in the Royal Navy is Suzanne J. Stark, *Female Tars: Women aboard Ship in the Age of Sail* (Annapolis, MD, 1996). See also N.A.M. Rodger, *The Wooden World: An Anatomy of the Georgian Navy* (London, 1986), 55, 67, 76–77; Michael Lewis, *A Social History of the Navy, 1793–1815* (London, 1960), 280–87; and Nicholas Blake and Richard Lawrence, *The Illustrated Companion to Nelson's Navy* (Mechanicsburg, PA, 2000), 120–21.

179. Journal of Henry Wadsworth, April 2, 1803, in Dudley W. Knox, ed., *Naval Documents Related to the United States Wars with the Barbary Powers*, 6 vols. (Washington, DC, 1939–44), 2: 387.

180. Harold D. Langley, "Women in a Warship, 1813," *Proceedings of the U.S. Naval Institute* 110 (January 1984), 124–25.

181. The claim appears in C.H.J. Snider, *In the Wake of the Eighteen-Twelvers: Fights and Flights of Frigates and Fore-'n'-Afters in the War of 1812–1815 on the Great Lakes* (London, 1913), 223. Snider invents dialogue and concedes that "the dry bones of record have been clothed with the flesh and blood of fancy" (p. x). His work cannot be considered a reliable source.

182. William McKay to Robert McDouall, July 29, 1814, in British Military Records, Library and Archives Canada, Ottawa, ON, RG8, 695: 15–16.

183. Quoted in Lossing, *Pictorial Field-Book of the War of 1812*, 621n.

184. For the evolution of the Laura Secord myth, see George Ingram, "The Story of Laura Secord Revisited," *Ontario History* 57 (June 1965), 85–96; and Cecilia Morgan, "'Of Slender Frame and Delicate Appearance': The Placing of Laura Secord in the Narratives of Canadian Loyalist History," *Journal of the Canadian Historical Association* 5 (1994), 195–212.

185. The case against Secord is summarized in W.S. Wallace's 26-page pamphlet, *The Story of Laura Secord: A Study in Historical Evidence* (Toronto, 1932).

186. Entry of June 24, 1813, in Graves, *War of 1812 Journal of John Le Couteur*, 126; Klinck and Talman, *Journal of John Norton*, 330–32.

187. FitzGibbon to Peter W. De Haren, June 24, 1813, in Cruikshank, *Niagara Frontier*, 6: 111.

188. Quoted in Ruth McKenzie, *Laura Secord: The Legend and the Lady* (Toronto, 1971), 129.

189. The best case for Secord is laid out by McKenzie in *Laura Secord*, esp. chs. 5 and 10 and Epilogue, and by Ingram, "Story of Laura Secord Revisited," 95–96.

190. Dolley Madison to Lucy Todd, August 23, 1814, in David B. Mattern and Holly C. Shulman, eds., *The Selected Letters of Dolley Payne Madison* (Charlottesville, VA, 2003), 193.

191. Dolley Madison to Lucy Todd, August 24, 1814, ibid., 193.

192. Virginia Moore, *The Madisons: A Biography* (New York, 1979), esp. chs. 10–14; Ethel Stephens Arnett, *Mrs. Madison: The Incomparable Dolley* (Greensboro, NC, 1972), ch. 6; Irving Brant, *James Madison*, 6 vols. (Indianapolis and New York, 1941–61), 6: chs. 21–23.

193. For three variations of this pamphlet, see *An Affecting Narrative of Louisa Baker, A Native of Massachusetts* (Boston, [1815]); *The Adventures of Lucy Brewer, Alias Louisa Baker* (Boston, 1816); and *The Female Marine, or, Adventures of Lucy Brewer* ([Boston?], 1816).

194. See Alexander Medlicott, Jr., "The Legend of Lucy Brewer: An Early American Novel," *New England Quarterly* 39 (December 1966), 461–73; and Daniel A. Cohen, "'The Female Marine' in an Era of Good Feelings: Cross-Dressing and the 'Genius' of Nathaniel Coverly, Jr.," *Proceedings of the American Antiquarian Society* 103 (1994), 359–93.

195. Graves, "Joseph Willcocks and the Canadian Volunteers," 49–51.

196. For the official report on this incident, see Report of Charles King and Francis S. Larpent, April 26, 1815, in *Niles' Register* 8 (July 22, 1815), 354–57. For a recent account of the massacre, see Christopher D. Leonowicz, "The Dartmoor Prison Massacre, April 6, 1815," *Journal of the War of 1812* (Fall 2001), 17–28.

197. Ingersoll, *Historical Sketch of the Second War*, 1: 198; *Niles' Register* 6 (June 25, 1814), 279.

198. G.C. Moore Smith, ed., *The Autobiography of Lieutenant-General Sir Harry Smith*, 2 vols. (London, 1902), 1: 200; Morriss, *Cockburn and the British Navy*, 109.

199. *Niles' Register* 4 (August 21, 1813), 402, and 7 (October 27, 1814), 110; Richmond *Enquirer*, March 29, 1815.

200. For a good summary of Cockburn's predatory operations, see George, *Terror on the Chesapeake*.

201. Quoted in Morriss, *Cockburn and the British Navy*, 95.

202. Quoted in George, *Terror on the Chesapeake*, 165.

203. Smith to Jane Kirkpatrick, August [1814], in Gaillard Hunt, ed., *The First Forty Years of Washington Society, Portrayed by the Family Letters of Mrs. Samuel Harrison Smith (Margaret Bayard)* (New York, 1906), 113.

204. For the incidents recounted in this paragraph, see Pack, *George Cockburn*, 165, 170, 188, 212; Morriss, *Cockburn and the British Navy*, 95–96; and Bullard, *Black Liberation on Cumberland Island*, ch. 8.

205. Cochrane to Viscount Melville, September 3, 1814, in Dudley and Crawford, *Naval War of*

*1812*, 3: 270. For more on Cochrane's hostility to the United States, see C.J. Bartlett and Gene A. Smith, "A 'Species of Milito-Nautico-Guerilla-Plundering Warfare': Admiral Alexander Cochrane's Naval Campaign against the United States, 1814–1815," in Julie Flavell and Stephen Conway, eds., *Britain and America Go to War: The Impact of War and Warfare in Anglo-America, 1754–1815* (Gainsville, FL, 2004), 173–204.

206. Roosevelt, "War with the United States," 70. For more on Cockburn, see Pack, *George Cockburn;* and Morriss, *Cockburn and the British Navy.*

207. Quoted in A.H.U. Colquhoun, "The Career of Joseph Willcocks," *Canadian Historical Review* 7 (December 1926), 290.

208. Niagara *Guardian,* June 9, 1812, reprinted in Wood, *Select British Documents,* 1: 193.

209. Ibid.

210. Willcocks deserves a full-length biography. The best study is Graves, "Joseph Willcocks and the Canadian Volunteers." See also William R. Riddell, "Joseph Willcocks: Sheriff, Member of Parliament and Traitor," *Papers and Records of the Ontario Historical Society* 24 (1927), 475–99; and Colquhoun, "The Career of Joseph Willcocks," 287–93.

211. The assault on free speech in 1798–99 was actually broader than these figures suggest because there were an additional 7 indictments under the common law. Of the seven defendants, two were convicted, two died before they could be tried, one went into hiding, one recanted, and one case was apparently discontinued. All figures have been compiled from James Morton Smith, *Freedom's Fetters: The Alien and Sedition Laws and American Civil Liberties* (Ithaca, NY, 1956).

212. For more on the Sedition Act, see Smith, *Freedom's Fetters,* and Leonard W. Levy, "Liberty and the First Amendment: 1790–1800," *American Historical Review* 68 (October 1962), 22–37.

213. Story to Pinkney, June 26, 1812, and Pinkney to president, July 5, 1812, in Madison Papers, Library of Congress, Washington, DC, microfilm edition, reel 26.

214. Speech of Felix Grundy, May 6, 1812, in *AC,* 12–1, 1410.

215. Baltimore *American,* July 16, 1812.

216. Washington *National Intelligencer,* May 14, 1812.

217. Jackson to president, June 26, 1812, in Madison Papers, Library of Congress, Washington, DC, microfilm edition, reel 14.

218. Jefferson to president, June 29, 1812, in Madison Papers, Library of Congress, Washington, DC, microfilm edition, reel 26. The letter can also be found in Jefferson Papers, Library of Congress, Washington, DC, microfilm edition, reel 46. Despite being readily available, this document has been ignored by scholars working on Jefferson or Madison.

219. Madison to J. Montgomery, August 13, 1812, in John W. Garrett Papers, Johns Hopkins University, Baltimore, MD.

220. For more on the Baltimore riots, see Donald R. Hickey, "The Darker Side of Democracy: The Baltimore Riots of 1812," *Maryland Historian* 7 (Fall 1976): 1–19; and Hickey, *War of 1812,* ch. 3.

221. David Porter, *Journal of a Cruise Made to the Pacific Ocean,* 2nd ed., 2 vols. (New York, 1822), 1: 174–75.

222. Gamble to SN, August 28, 1815, in Dudley and Crawford, *Naval War of 1812,* 3: 774–80; Porter, *Journal of a Cruise,* 2: chs. 19–20; J. Robert Moskin, *The U.S. Marine Corps Story,* rev. ed. (New York, 1987), 48–51; Metcalf, *United States Marine Corps,* 63–69.

223. Quoted in Moskin, *U.S. Marine Corps Story,* 51. I could find no biographical sketch of Gamble. I gleaned what few details I have from the Marine Corps histories cited above.

224. Andrew Bulger to Robert McDouall, September 7, 1814, McDouall to Gordon Drummond, September 9, 1814, Arthur Sinclair to SN, October 24 and 28, 1814, and Daniel Turner to Sinclair, November 1, 1814, all in Dudley and Crawford, *Naval War of 1812,* 3: 604–07, 645–49; Barry Gough, *Fighting Sail on Lake Huron and Georgian Bay: The War of 1812 and Its Aftermath* (Annapolis, MD, 2002), ch. 6.

225. Roosevelt, *Naval War of 1812,* 336.

226. W.A.B. Douglas, "Worsley, Miller," in *DCB,* 6: 817–18. There is no sketch of Worsley in the the in the old or new *DNB,* but there should be.

227. Quoted in Alison Smith, "John Strachan and

Early Upper Canada, 1799–1814," *Ontario History* 52 (September 1960), 166.

228. Quoted in Julia Jarvis, *Three Centuries of Robinsons: The Story of a Family* (Don Mills, ON, 1967), 143.

229. Strachan to James Brown, October 21, 1809, in J.L.H. Henderson, ed., *John Strachan: Documents and Opinions, A Selection* (Toronto, 1969), 26.

230. John Strachan, Autobiography, November 14, 1799, ibid., 14; Strachan to James Brown, October 20, 1807, in Spragge, *John Strachan Letter Book*, viii.

231. Quoted in Smith, "John Strachan and Early Upper Canada," 170.

232. Strachan to Francis de Rottenburg, September, 1813, in Spragge, *John Strachan Letter Book*, 46.

233. Strachan to John Richardson, September 30, 1812, ibid., 15–17. Quotation from p. 15.

234. Strachan to Wellington, November 1, 1812, ibid., 30.

235. Strachan to Gore, January 1, 1814, ibid., 54.

236. Strachan to John Owen, February 24, 1815, in Henderson, *John Strachan: Documents and Opinions*, 53.

237. For more on this, see The Role of Canadian Militia in ch. 4, "Soldiers, Sailors, and Civilians."

238. Strachan modestly describes his contributions in letters to James Brown, April 25, 1813 and Noah Freer, August 2, 1813, in Henderson, *John Strachan: Documents and Opinions*, 40–45, and to [CG], August 2, 1813, in Spragge, *John Strachan Letter Book*, 41–42.

239. Ryerson, *Loyalists of America*, 2: 468.

240. Quoted in David Flint, *John Strachan: Pastor and Politician* (Toronto, 1971), 7. This is the standard biography of Strachan, but it is short and undocumented. For a brief but astute and balanced treatment, see G.M. Craig, "Strachan, John," in *DCB*, 9: 751–66. For a fine account of Strachan's service during the war years, see Carl Benn, "A Georgian Parish, 1797–1839," in William Cooke, ed., *The Parish and Cathedral of St James', Toronto, 1797–1997* (Toronto, 1998), 12–18. Another useful work is Smith, "John Strachan and Early Upper Canada," 159–73. We need a full-scale biography of this important and complex figure.

241. Detroit City Council to president (with en-

closure), July 25, 1807, in Carter, *Territorial Papers of the United States,* 10: 114–22; Campbell, *Outlines of the Political History of Michigan,* 244, 248–52.

242. See, for example, Hull to SW, November 24, 1809, and Woodward to SW, July 28, 1812, in Carter, *Territorial Papers of the United States,* 10: 294–96, 390–91.

243. Hull to president, March 12, 1808, ibid., 10: 207–08.

244. Campbell, *Outlines of the Political History of Michigan,* 238.

245. Woodward to SS, March 22, 1813, in Carter, *Territorial Papers of the United States,* 10: 433.

246. Woodward to Procter, January 29 and February 2, 1813, in *Historical Collections of the Michigan Pioneer and Historical Society* 36 (1908), 277–78, 290–93. See also Whitmore Knaggs to ?, May 24, 1813, ibid., 15 (1890), 302–04.

247. Citizens of Detroit to Woodward, January 6, 1813, ibid., 36 (1908), 271–72.

248. See Report on Spirit and Manner in which the War is Waged by the Enemy, July 31, 1813, in *ASP: MA,* 1: 367–70.

249. Woodward to SW, March 5, 1815, in Carter, *Territorial Papers of the United States,* 10: 513.

250. For a good but very brief account of Woodward, see William L. Jenks, "Woodward, Augustus Brevoort," in *DAB,* 20: 506–07. For a more extended treatment, particularly of the war years, see Woodford, *Mr. Jefferson's Disciple.* There are additional details on Woodward's life scattered through Silas Farmer, *History of Detroit and Wayne County and Early Michigan,* 3rd ed. (Detroit, 1890). The definitive account of this fascinating character has yet to be written.

251. This broadside has been reprinted in Alton Ketchum, *Uncle Sam: The Man and the Legend* (New York, 1959), 40–41.

252. Troy *Post,* September 7, 1813 (transcript supplied by Troy Public Library).

253. New York *Gazette and Daily Advertiser,* May 12, 1830 (transcript supplied by New-York Historical Society). This article has been conveniently reprinted in Ketchum, *Uncle Sam,* 39–41.

254. U.S. Congress, *Congressional Record* (Washington, DC, 1873—), 87–1, 15711, 18230–31,

19298–300, 19628–30. The resolution is printed in *United States Statutes at Large* (Washington, DC, 1874—), 75: 966.

255. For the way that commanders designated their warships, see their letters to SN in Dudley and Crawford, *Naval War of 1812.* For a reference to the "U S Navy Yard New York," see Charles Ludlow to SN, September 29, 1812, ibid., 1: 502.

256. The star with the "U" was destroyed when the *Chesapeake* was taken by H.M. Ship *Shannon,* but the other star was later mounted above the figurehead of the *Shannon* in Broke Hall, home of the captain of the victorious British ship. J.G. Brighton, *Admiral of the Fleet Sir Provo W.P. Wallis, G.C.B., Etc.* (London, 1892), 148–51.

257. Robert M. Reilly, *United States Martial Flintlocks: A Comprehensive Illustrated History of the Flintlock in America from the Revolution to the Demise of the System* (Lincoln, RI, 1986), 51–97, 125; William Gilkerson, *Boarders Away,* 2 vols. (Lincoln, RI, 1991–93), 1: 91–100; 2: 202–09.

258. New York *Herald,* February 5, 1814; Extract of a letter from Hartford, December 16, 1814, in Boston *Gazette,* December 19, 1814.

259. *Niles' Register* 7 (Supplement), 187.

260. Ketchum, *Uncle Sam,* chs. 2–11; Albert Matthews, "Uncle Sam," *Proceedings of the American Antiquarian Society,* new series, 19 (April 1908), 21–65; Jessie F. Wheeler, "Wilson, Samuel," in *DAB,* 20: 343.

**Chapter 5: The Mechanics of Waging War**

1. B.P. Hughes, *Firepower: Weapons Effectiveness on the Battlefield, 1630–1850* (New York, 1974), 109.

2. General Order of Gordon Drummond, August 5, 1814, in Cruikshank, *Niagara Frontier,* 2: 427.

3. Donald Jackson, ed., *Black Hawk: An Autobiography* (Urbana, IL, 1964), 71.

4. Jeffrey Kimball, "The Battle of Chippawa: Infantry Tactics in the War of 1812," *Military Affairs* 31 (Winter 1967–68), 169–86; Donald E. Graves, "'Dry Books of Tactics': US Infantry Manuals of the War of 1812 and After," *Military Collector and Historian* 38 (Summer 1986), 50–61, and (Winter 1986), 173–76; Graves and John C. Fredriksen, "'Dry Books

of Tactics' Re-Read: An Additional Note on U.S. Infantry Manuals of the War of 1812," *Military Collector and Historian* 39 (Summer 1987), 64–65; and Graves, "'I have a handsome little army . . .': A Re-Examination of Winfield Scott's Camp at Buffalo in 1814," in R. Arthur Bowler, ed., *War along the Niagara: Essays on the War of 1812 and Its Legacy* (Youngstown, NY, 1991), 43–52.

5. Barclay to James Yeo, September 12, 1813, in Dudley and Crawford, *Naval War of 1812,* 2: 556–57.

6. Spencer C. Tucker, "The Carronade," *Naval Institute Proceedings* 99 (August 1973), 65–70; James E. Valle, "The Navy's Battle Doctrine in the War of 1812," *American Neptune* 44 (Summer 1984), 174.

7. Quoted in Tyrone G. Martin, *A Most Fortunate Ship: A Narrative History of Old Ironsides,* rev. ed. (Annapolis, MD, 1997), 184.

8. See "Defence of Fort McHenry" (broadside), [September 1814], reprinted in Sonneck, *"Star Spangled Banner,"* plate 15.

9. Spencer Tucker *Arming the Fleet: U.S. Navy Ordnance in the Muzzle-Loading Era* (Annapolis, MD, 1989), 41.

10. Philip J. Haythornthwaite, *Weapons and Artillery of the Napoleonic Wars,* rev. ed. (London, 1996), ch. 4; Robert Wilkinson-Latham, *British Artillery on Land and Sea, 1790–1820* (Newton Abbot, UK, 1973); David T. Zabecki, "Artillery," in Heidler and Heidler, *Encyclopedia of the War of 1812,* 17–24; Donald E. Graves, "Field Artillery of the War of 1812: Equipment, Organization, Tactics and Effectiveness," *Arms Collecting* 30 (May 1992), 39–48, and "American Ordnance of the War of 1812: A Preliminary Investigation," *Arms Collecting* 31 (November 1993), 111–20; Tucker, *Arming the Fleet;* and Richard Glover, *Peninsular Preparation: The Reform of the British Army, 1795–1809* (London, 1963), ch. 4.

11. Gordon Drummond to CG, June 4, 1814, in Wood, *Select British Documents,* 3: 77–78.

12. See "Defence of Fort McHenry" (broadside), [September 1814], reprinted in Sonneck, *"Star Spangled Banner,"* plate 15.

13. Entries of April 23 and July 11, 1814, in Graves, *War of 1812 Journal of John Le Couteur,* 160, 172.

14. Entry of March 30, 1814, in John C. Fredriksen, ed., "Chronicle of Valor: The Journal of a Pennsylvania Officer [George McFeely] in the War of 1812," *Western Pennsylvania History Magazine* 67 (July 1984), 275.

15. Colonel [William] Congreve, *The Details of the Rocket System, Shewing the Various Applications of This Weapon, Both for Sea and Land Service, and Its Different Uses in the Field and in Sieges* (1814; reprint, Ottawa, 1970); Donald E. Graves, *Sir William Congreve and the Rocket's Red Glare* (Bloomfield, ON, 1989); Frank H. Winter, *The First Golden Age of Rocketry: Congreve and Hale Rockets of the Nineteenth Century* (Washington, DC, 1990); David T. Zabecki, "Congreve Rockets," in Heidler and Heidler, *Encyclopedia of the War of 1812*, 120–21; Glover, *Peninsular Preparation*, 69–73.

16. Memoir of P. Finan, in John Gellner, ed., *Recollections of the War of 1812: Three Eyewitnesses' Accounts* (Toronto, 1964), 60.

17. James A. Huston, *The Sinews of War: Army Logistics, 1775–1953* (Washington, DC, 1966), 107.

18. De Witt Bailey and David Harding, "From India to Waterloo: The 'India Pattern' Musket," in Alan J. Guy, ed., *The Road to Waterloo: The British Army and the Struggle against Revolutionary and Napoleonic France, 1793–1815* (London, 1990), 48–57; Anthony D. Darling, *Red Coat and Brown Bess* (Alexandria Bay, NY, 1971), ch. 4; Upper Canada Historical Arms Society, *The Military Arms of Canada* (Alexandria Bay, NY, 1963), ch. 2; Howard L. Blackmore, *British Military Firearms, 1650–1850* (London, 1961), ch. 7.

19. Robert M. Reilly, *United States Martial Flintlocks: A Comprehensive Illustrated History of the Flintlock in America from the Revolution to the Demise of the System* (Lincoln, RI, 1986), 51–97; René Chartrand, *Uniforms and Equipment of the United States Forces in the War of 1812* (Youngstown, NY, 1992), 83–90; James E. Hicks, "United States Military Shoulder Arms, 1795–1935," *American Military History* 1 (Spring 1937), 22–33; James R. Jacobs and Glenn Tucker, *The War of 1812: A Compact History* (New York, 1969), 193–95.

20. [William Jenkins Worth?], "First Campaign of an A.D.C.," *Military and Naval Magazine of the United States*, 2 (1833–34), 202.

21. Carl Benn, *The Iroquois in the War of 1812* (Toronto, 1998), 218n23.

22. See Jefferson's comment on the distribution of shoulder arms in Virginia in Thomas Jefferson, *Notes on the State of Virginia*, ed. William Peden (Chapel Hill, NC, 1955), 88.

23. Neil L. York, "Pennsylvania Rifle: Revolutionary Weapon in a Conventional War?" *Pennsylvania Magazine of History and Biography* 103 (July 1979), 302–24; Charles E. Brodine, Jr., "Henry Bouquet and British Infantry Tactics on the Ohio Frontier, 1758–1764," in David Curtis Skaggs and Larry L. Nelson, eds., *The Sixty Years' War for the Great Lakes, 1754–1814* (East Lansing, MI, 2001), 50.

24. Reilly, *United States Martial Flintlocks*, 123–30.

25. Merrill Lindsay gives the specifications for a large number of rifles in *The Kentucky Rifle* (New York, 1972). For other information on this weapon, see John G.W. Dillin, *The Kentucky Rifle*, 4th ed. (York, PA, 1959); and Henry J. Kauffman, *The Kentucky-Pennsylvania Rifle* (New York, 1960).

26. C. Edward Skeen, *Citizen Soldiers in the War of 1812* (Lexington, KY, 1999), 133.

27. John C. Fredriksen, *Green Coats and Glory: The United States Regiment of Riflemen, 1808–1821* (Youngstown, NY, 2000), 11–13, 43–45.

28. Ibid., 13–43, 45–67.

29. Ibid., 67–71.

30. Blackmore, *British Military Firearms*, ch. 6; Philip Haythornthwaite, *British Rifleman, 1797–1815* (Oxford, UK, 2002), 12–15; Philipp Elliot-Wright, *Rifleman: Elite of the Wars against Napoleon* (London, 2000), 54–55, 73–81.

31. Isaac Weld, Jr., *Travels through the States of North America, and the Provinces of Upper and Lower Canada, during the years 1795, 1796, and 1797*, 4th ed., 2 vols., (London, 1807), 2: 150.

32. Haythornthwaite, *British Rifleman*, 15–16, 22.

33. Ibid., 11–12, 43–44; Elliot-Wright, *Rifleman*, 37–53.

34. Haythornthwaite, *British Rifleman*, 44–52; Elliot-Wright, *Rifleman*, 82–125; William Surtees, *Twenty-Five Years in the Rifle Brigade* (1833; reprint, London, 1973), chs. 16–19;

John R. Grodzinski, "The 3rd Battalion, 95th Regiment at New Orleans: A Much Confused Story," *Journal of the War of 1812* 8 (Fall 2003/Winter 2004), 41.

35. Haythornthwaite, *British Rifleman*, 52–55; Elliot-Wright, *Rifleman*, 126–28.
36. The riflemen of the 95th Regiment were issued bayonets that were 23 inches long.
37. Haythornthwaite, *Weapons and Equipment of the Napoleonic Wars*, 27.
38. [General Order of CG], July 4, 1814, in Wood, *Select British Documents*, 3: 23–24.
39. Quimby, *U.S. Army in the War of 1812*, 1: 357, 401–02, 428, and 2: 457, 846–49.
40. Leonard D. White, *The Jeffersonians: A Study in Administrative History, 1801–1829* (New York, 1951), 216.
41. Alicia Cockburn to Charles Sandys, June 28, 1814, in Wood, *Select British Documents*, 3: 336.
42. Drummond to CG, April 25, 1814, in Cruikshank, *Niagara Frontier*, 1: 11.
43. U.S. Bureau of the Census, *Historical Statistics of the United States, Colonial Times to 1970*, 2 vols. (Washington, DC, 1975), 1: 28, 32, 33; Stanley, *War of 1812*, 49.
44. Samuel T. Anderson to SN, October 8, 1812, in Dudley and Crawford, *Naval War of 1812*, 1: 323; Jeffrey Kimball, "The Fog and Friction of Frontier War: The Role of Logistics in American Offensive Failure during the War of 1812," *Old Northwest* 5 (Winter 1979), 323–43; Erna Risch, *Quartermaster Support of the Army: A History of the Corps, 1775–1939* (Washington, DC, 1962), ch. 5; Marguerite M. McKee, "Service of Supply in the War of 1812," *Quartermaster Review* 6 (March-April 1927), 45–55; Max Rosenberg, *The Building of Perry's Fleet on Lake Erie, 1812–1813* (Harrisburg, PA, 1950), ch. 2; Philip Lord, Jr., "The Mohawk/Oneida Corridor: The Geography of Inland Navigation across New York," in Skaggs and Nelson, *Sixty Years' War for the Great Lakes*, 275–90.
45. Stanley, *War of 1812*, 70. Stanley gives the cost for moving the ship frame from Quebec to Kingston, but it was actually the cost for moving it from Montreal to Kingston. See Robert Malcomson, *Lords of the Lake: The Naval War on Lake Ontario, 1812–1814*, (Toronto, 1998), 295.

46. Hitsman, *Incredible War* (updated ed.), 216.
47. Gordon Drummond to SSWC, January 28, 1814, and George Crookshank to Colley L.L. Foster, December 16, 1814, in Dudley and Crawford, *Naval War of 1812*, 3: 382–83, 662–63; John R. Grodzinski, "The Vigilant Superintendence of the Whole District: The War of 1812 on the Upper St. Lawrence," Master's thesis (Royal Military College of Canada, 2002); Glenn A. Steppler, "Logistics on the Canadian Frontier, 1812–1814," *Military Collector and Historian* 31 (Spring 1979), 8–10; C.P. Stacey, "Another Look at the Battle of Lake Erie," *Canadian Historical Review* 39 (March 1958), 41–51.
48. See Graves, *War of 1812 Journal of John Le Couteur*, 93–111.
49. See "Introduction: Naval Service on Lake Ontario, 1812–1815," and "The Narrative of Lieutenant Henry Kent, Royal Navy, 1814," in Robert Malcomson, ed., *Sailors of 1812: Memoirs and Letters of Naval Officers on Lake Ontario* (Youngstown, NY, 1997), 15–17, 73–80.
50. N.W. Hibbard to A. Hunt, Feb. 10, 1859, and Nat Frame, "The Battle of Sandy Creek, and the Carrying of the Cables for the Superior," in *Transactions of the Jefferson County Historical Society* 3 (1895), 29–31, 38–40; Lossing, *Pictorial Field-Book of the War of 1812*, 800–01; Patrick Wilder, *Seaway Trail Guidebook to the War of 1812* (Oswego, 1987), 57–59.
51. Diary of William McCay, August 14, 1812, in Wood, *Select British Documents*, 1: 548–49; and Charles Gratiot to Andrew Sinclair, January 28, 1815, in Dudley and Crawford, *Naval War of 1812*, 3: 695.
52. Francis Cleary, "Fort Malden or Amherstburg," *Papers and Records of the Ontario Historical Society* 9 (1910), 8–12, 18; Report of Ralph H. Bruyers, August 24, 1811, in *Collections of the Michigan Pioneer and Historical Society* 15 (1890), 54.
53. General Orders of Isaac Brock, August 14 and 15, 1812, and Brock to CG, August 17, 1812, in Wood, *Select British Documents*, 1: 459, 462, 466.
54. Dixon to Ralph H. Bruyeres, July 8, 1812, and CG to SSWC, August 17, 24, and 26, 1812, ibid., 1: 350, 475, 489, 502, 505; CG to Liverpool, May 18, 1812, in Hitsman, *Incredible War* (updated ed.), 284.

55. Carl F. Klinck and James J. Talman, eds., *The Journal of John Norton, 1816* (Toronto, 1970), 341–42.

56. Cleary, "Fort Malden or Amherstburg," 6, 13; Dennis Carter-Edwards to Don Graves, April 25, 2003 (copy in possession of the author).

57. See documents in Wood, *Select British Documents*, 1: 432–55. For additional details on the forts, see George S. May, *The Forts of Mackinac* (Mackinac Island, MI, 1962).

58. Dudley and Crawford, *Naval War of 1812*, 3: 464n1; Charles M. Snyder, *Oswego: From Buckskin to Bustles* (Port Washington, NY, 1968), chs. 1, 2, and 5; Gilbert Collins, *Guidebook to the Historic Sites of the War of 1812* (Toronto 1998), 168–69; Robert B. Roberts, *Encyclopedia of Historic Forts: The Military, Pioneer, and Trading Posts of the United States* (New York, 1987), 570–72; Quimby, *U.S. Army in the War of 1812*, 2: 507–10.

59. Everest, *War of 1812 in the Champlain Valley*, 155.

60. See facsimile of hand-written notice in Lossing, *Pictorial Field-Book of the War of 1812*, 658. The notice is unsigned and undated but appears to be authentic.

61. Riall to Gordon Drummond, March 15, 1814, in Cruikshank, *Niagara Frontier*, 9: 238.

62. Drummond to CG, March 31, 1814, in *Collections of the Michigan Pioneer and Historical Society* 15 (1890), 527.

63. Phineas Riall to Gordon Drummond, July 22, 1814, in Cruikshank, *Niagara Frontier*, 1: 80. For a sampling of the many reasons given for desertion, see Statement of Bill Sherman, December 3, 1812, Statement of David Harvey, December 5 1812, Statement of Joseph Van Horne, [December 1812], and Robert Young to Phineas Riall, March 14, 1814, ibid., 2: 247–49, and 9: 237; "The Memoir of Drummer Jarvis Frary Hanks, 11th Infantry, 1813–1815," in Donald E. Graves, ed., *Soldiers of 1814: American Enlisted Men's Memoirs of the Niagara Campaign* (Youngstown, 1995), 25; General Orders of Daniel D. Tompkins, November 17 and 26, 1814, in Hugh Hastings, ed., *Public Papers of Daniel D. Tompkins, Governor of New York, 1807–1817*, 3 vols. (New York, 1898–1902), 1: 737, 743.

64. Martin, *Most Fortunate Ship*, 183.

65. The desertion rate for the Continental Army was 20–25 percent; for American militia units it was much higher. The British army claimed that only 3,701 of its men engaged in North America and the West Indies deserted in this period, which was only 4 percent of the army's peak level of 92,000. But this excludes German and Tory units, which had a far higher rate of desertion, and it excludes those British soldiers who voluntarily returned to service because they were promised a pardon. See Charles Royster, *A Revolutionary People at War: The Continental Army and American Character* (Chapel Hill, NC, 1979), 71; and Sylvia R. Frey, *The British Soldier in America: A Social History of Military Life in the Revolutionary Period* (Austin, TX, 1981), 72.

66. J.C.A. Stagg, "Enlisted Men in the United States Army, 1812–1815: A Preliminary Survey," *William and Mary Quarterly*, 3rd series, 43 (October 1986), 624.

67. Baynes to CG, June 18, 1814, in *Collections of the Michigan Pioneer and Historical Society* 15 (1890), 697–98.

68. SSWC to CG, June 3, 1814, ibid., 579.

69. Winston Johnston, the leading authority on the Glengarry Lights, has identified about 360 deserters out of a total of 1,457 who served in the unit. Letter to the author, November 30, 2003.

70. William Gray, *Soldiers of the King: The Upper Canadian Militia, 1812–1815* (Erin, ON, 1995), 41–42.

71. Melancthon T. Woolsey to SN, August 8, 1812, Isaac Chauncey to SN, June 11 and July 3, 1813, Manley Dixon to FSA, June 21, 1813, SN to Isaac Chauncey, July 3, 1813, James Yeo to FSA, July 16, 1813, Isaac Chauncey to SN, March 7 and 26 and May 23, 1814, Thomas Macdonough to SN, June 11, 1814, Joshua Barney to SN, June 20 and 24, 1814, George Cockburn to Alexander Cochrane, June 25, 1814, Robert Barrie to Dolly Gardner Clayton, November 11, 1814, and John H. Cocke to James Barbour, December 4, [1814], in Dudley and Crawford, *Naval War of 1812*, 1: 289, 2: 493, 499, 502, 509, 711, and 3: 104, 116, 148, 339, 341, 404, 410–11, 494, 505.

72. Isaac Chauncey to SN, December 1, 1812, Charles F. Grandison to SN, November 7

and December 2, 1812, Edward Cutbush to Charles W. Goldsborough, January 4, [1813], Court Martial of John Perry, February 2, 1813, Jacob Lewis to SN, May 23, 1813, John H. Dent to SN, September 11, 1813, SN to Arthur Sinclair, May 19, 1814, and John M. Gamble to SN, August 28, 1815, in Dudley and Crawford, *Naval War of 1812*, 1: 393, 596, 607–08, 2: 9, 110, 242, 635, and 3: 463, 774.

73. See Act of May 16, 1812, in *AC*, 12–1, 2300.

74. General Orders of Daniel D. Tompkins, November ? and 18, 1814, in Hastings, *Papers of Daniel D. Tompkins*, 1: 734–35, 739; "Memoir of Jarvis Hanks," in Graves, *Soldiers of 1814*, 24, 31; John S. Hare, "Military Punishments in the War of 1812," *Journal of the American Military Institute*, 4 (Winter 1940), 230–38.

75. Franklin Wharton to Daniel Carmick, June 21, 1812, and Court Martial of John Perry, February 2, 1813, in Dudley and Crawford, *Naval War of 1812*, 1: 409, and 2: 535–36;

76. "Memoir of Jarvis Hanks," in Graves, *Soldiers of 1814*, 31; Hare, "Military Punishments in the 1812," 238–39.

77. See Court Martial of Cornelius Gorman, October 27, 1812, and General Order of CG, July 14 and 18, 1813, in Cruikshank, *Niagara Frontier*, 4: 179, and 6: 235, 251–52; and Gordon Drummond to CG, August 8, 1814, in Dudley and Crawford, *Naval War of 1812*, 3: 583. See also Winston Johnston, *The Glengarry Light Infantry, 1812–1816: Who Were They and What Did They Do in the War?* (Charlottetown, PEI, 1998), 78–79; and Everest, *War of 1812 in the Champlain Valley*, 114.

78. See John B. Warren to FSA, October 27, 1813, in Dudley and Crawford, *Naval War of 1812*, 2: 274.

79. David Porter, *Journal of a Cruise Made to the Pacific Ocean*, 2nd ed., 2 vols. (New York, 1822), 2: 220.

80. According to George Sheppard, during the war years provincial money in Canada was worth 90 percent of an equal sum of British money. See Sheppard, *Plunder, Profits, and Paroles: A Social History of the War of 1812 in Upper Canada* (Montreal, 1994), 253.

81. Provincial Statute of Upper Canada, March 6, 1812, in Wood, *Select British Documents*, 1: 171–74.

82. Memoir of P. Finan, in Gellner, *Recollections*

*of the War of 1812*, 106–07. Quotation from p. 106. See also Johnston, *Glengarry Light Infantry*, 182.

83. Andrew Bulger to Robert McDouall, January 15, 1815, in Reuben Gold Thwaites, ed., "The Bulger Papers," *Collections of the State Historical Society of Wisconsin* 13 (1895), 56.

84. The American law expired in the spring of 1814, but since the flogging of regulars was permanently banned, the practice was not reintroduced among militia. See Act of April 10, 1812, in *AC*, 12–1, 2268.

85. See, for example, the militia cases outlined in General Orders of Roger Sheaffe, April 3, 1813, in Cruikshank, *Niagara Frontier*, 5: 145–46.

86. See General Orders of Daniel D. Tompkins, November 4–December 5, 1814, in Hastings, *Papers of Daniel D. Tompkins*, 1: 705–09, 713, 733–48; "The Narrative of Alexander McMullen, a Private Soldier in Colonel Fenton's Regiment of Pennsylvania Volunteers," in Graves, *Soldiers of 1814*, 63; Everest, *War of 1812 in the Champlain Valley*, 56.

87. Everest, *War of 1812 in the Champlain Valley*, 127.

88. Hare, "Military Punishments," 238; Benjamin Homans to Isaac Chauncey, December 19, 1814, in U.S. Department of the Navy, *Letters Sent by the Secretary of the Navy to Officers, 1798–1868*, microfilm series M149, National Archives, Washington, DC, reel 11.

89. General Orders of Andrew Jackson, [March 14, 1814], in Jackson Papers, Library of Congress, Washington, DC, microfilm edition, reel 62; James Parton, *Life of Andrew Jackson*, 3 vols. (New York, 1860), 1: 504–12.

90. Proceedings of General Court Martial Held at Mobile, December 5, 1814, in Jackson Papers, Library of Congress, Washington, DC, microfilm edition, reel 64; Parton, *Andrew Jackson*, 2: 277–300; William C. Cook, "The Coffin Handbills—America's First Smear Campaign," *Imprint* 27 (Spring 2002), 23–37.

91. Admiral Edward Durnford King, quoted in J.G. Brighton, *Admiral of the Fleet Sir Provo W.P. Wallis, G.C.B., Etc.* (London, 1892), 142.

92. Quoted in Grodzinski, "War of 1812 on the Upper St. Lawrence," 203.

93. General Order of SN, July 29, 1813, in Dudley and Crawford, *Naval War of 1812*, 2: 205.

94. Ernest Cruikshank, *Drummond's Winter Campaign, 1813,* rev. ed. ([Lundy's Lane, ON], [1900?]), 17.
95. See, for example, Clay Green to William Henry Harrison, June 20, 1813, and Harrison to SW, August 29, 1813, in Esarey, *Messages of William Henry Harrison,* 2: 474, 532.
96. See Glenn Stott, *Great Evils: The War of 1812 in Southwestern Ontario* (Arkona, ON, 2001), esp. 78.
97. Robert Barrie to John Borlase Warren, November 14, 1813, in Dudley and Crawford, *Naval War of 1812,* 2: 396.
98. [Worth?], "First Campaign of an A.D.C.," 200. For examples, see Ralph H. Bruyeres to CG, January 19, 1813, Charles Stewart to SN, March 22, 1813, and Chauncey to SN, December 9, 1812, May 15 and June 18, 1813, in Dudley and Crawford, *Naval War of 1812,* 1: 365–67, and 2: 316, 416, 462, 495; entries of September 10–11, 1813, in Graves, *War of 1812 Journal of John Le Couteur,* 133–35.
99. John Harvey to Edward Baynes, May 29, 1813, in Wood, *Select British Documents,* 2: 107–08. See also Gordon Drummond to CG, January 25, 1814, ibid., 3: 37–38.
100. William M. Crane to Isaac Chauncey, February 1, 1814, in Dudley and Crawford, *Naval War of 1812,* 3: 392. For other cases, see William Henry Harrison to Oliver H. Perry, August 4, 1813, Chauncey to SN, October 8, 1813, and John S. Skinner to SN, December 6, 1813, ibid., 2: 396, 531, 590.
101. Drummond to CG, September 11, 1814, in Cruikshank, *Niagara Frontier,* 1: 198.
102. Larry L. Nelson, *Men of Patriotism, Courage, and Enterprise! Fort Meigs in the War of 1812* (Canton, OH, 1985), 83.
103. Yeo to John Borlase Warren (enclosure), March 5, 1814, Chauncey to SN, January 20, June 11, and July 3, 1813 and March 26, 1814, and Melancthon T. Woolsey to Chauncey (enclosure), May 7, 1814, in Dudley and Crawford, *Naval War of 1812,* 2: 417–18, 493, 499, and 3: 404, 411, 472–73.
104. Klinck and Talman, *Journal of John Norton,* 311. For similar comments, see ibid., 340, 355. See also Phineas Riall to Gordon Drummond, July [21], 1814, in Wood, *Select British Documents,* 3: 140–41.
105. Harvey to Yeo (with enclosures), September

4, [1813], in Cruikshank, *Niagara Frontier,* 7: 97–98.
106. Chauncey to SN, March 30, 1814 (2 letters) and April 14, 1814, in Dudley and Crawford, *Naval War of 1812,* 3: 411–13, 441.
107. Sinclair to SN, May 27, 1814, ibid., 3: 503.
108. Wilkinson to Thomas Macdonough, April 11, 1814, ibid., 3: 427.
109. Decatur to SN, June 18, 1813, ibid., 2: 139; Hickey, *War of 1812,* 257–59.
110. James Yeo to CG, October 17, 1813, and George Cockburn to John Borlase Warren, March 13, 1813, in Dudley and Crawford, *Naval War of 1812,* 2: 322, 594; Thomas Pearson to Edward Baynes, October 12, 1813, and Report of ?, May 14, 1814, in Wood, *Select British Documents,* 2: 434–35, and 3: 69–70.
111. George MacDonell to Thomas S. Beckwith, February 4, 1815, in Dudley and Crawford, *Naval War of 1812,* 3: 688–90. Quotation from p. 689.
112. Information from Baron De Diemer, 1812, in Wood, *Select British Documents,* 3: 850–52. Quotation from p. 852.
113. SN to Edmund P. Kennedy, July 13, 1814, in Dudley and Crawford, *Naval War of 1812,* 3: 545.
114. Everest, *War of 1812 in the Champlain Valley,* 75.
115. Information from Baron De Diemer, 1812, in Wood, *Select British Documents,* 3: 851.
116. See documents ibid., 3: 855–60; and Everest, *War of 1812 in the Champlain Valley,* 117.
117. William James to Viscount Melville, January 4, 1819, in Holden Furber, ed., "How William James Came to be a Naval Historian," *American Historical Review* 38 (October 1932), 76–78.
118. Barney to SN, June 13 and 16, 1814, in Dudley and Crawford, *Naval War of 1812,* 3: 99, 101.
119. Chauncey to SN, July 4, 1813, ibid., 2: 521; SW to Joseph Anderson, July 26, 1813, in *ASP: MA,* 1: 384.
120. Everest, *War of 1812 in the Champlain Valley,* 154.
121. See, for example, Oliver H. Perry to John Rodgers, September 3, 1812, Rodgers to SN, September 17, 1812, and David Porter to SN, October 2, 1812, in Dudley and Crawford, *Naval War of 1812,* 1: 451–52, 494–96, 505.
122. Thomas B. St. George to Isaac Brock, July 8,

1813, in Cruikshank, *Surrender of Detroit*, 44; Mahan, *Sea Power*, 1: 341.

123. Brock to brother, September 3, 1812, in Frederick B. Tupper, *The Life and Correspondence of Major-General Sir Isaac Brock, K.B.*, 2nd ed. (London, 1847), 284.

124. Hull to SW, August 26, 1812, in U.S. Department of War, *Letters Received by the Secretary of War, Registered Series, 1801–1870*, microfilm series M221, National Archives, Washington, DC, reel 45.

125. W.H. Merritt, "Journal of Events Principally on the Detroit and Niagara Frontiers," in Wood, *Select British Documents*, 3: 554; Hitsman, *Incredible War* (updated ed.), 81.

126. Letter of Charles Roberts, August 16, 1812, in Wood, *Select British Documents*, 1: 444–45; Antal, *Wampum Denied*, 103.

127. Quimby, *U.S. Army in the War of 1812*, 1: 387–92.

128. General Orders of December 16, 1814, in *Niles' Register* 7 (January 14, 1815), 316–17.

129. Ibid., 316.

130. Jackson to John Lambert, March 6, 1815, and General Orders of Jackson, March 8, 1815, in Latour, *Historical Memoir*, 270, 273–74.

131. Jackson to John Lambert, March 13, 1815, and General Orders of Jackson, March 13, 1815, ibid., 274–76.

132. George M. Dennison, "Martial Law: The Development of a Theory of Emergency Powers, 1776–1861," *American Journal of Legal History* 18 (January 1974), 52–79.

133. *Ex parte Milligan* (1866), in Stephen K. Williams, ed., *Cases Argued and Decided in the Supreme Court of the United States*, Book 18, Law. ed. (Rochester, NY), 298.

134. Parton, *Andrew Jackson*, 2: 57–61, 305–21; John Spencer Bassett, *The Life of Andrew Jackson*, rev. ed. (New York, 1928), 745; Matthew Warshauer, "The Battle of New Orleans Reconsidered: Andrew Jackson and Martial Law," *Louisiana History* 39 (Summer 1998), 261–91; William Winthrop, *Military Law and Precedents*, rev. ed. (Washington, DC, 1920), 817–61; James G. Randall, *Constitutional Problems under Lincoln*, rev. ed. (Urbana, IL, 1951), ch. 8.

135. Proclamation of Henry Procter, February 4, 1813, in Carter, *Territorial Papers of the United States*, 10: 428. See also Procter to Roger

Sheaffe, February 4, 1813, in *Collections of the Michigan Pioneer and Historical Society* 15 (1890), 242–43.

136. Augustus B. Woodward to SS, March 22, 1813, in Carter, *Territorial Papers of the United States*, 10: 437; Antal, *Wampum Denied*, 194.

137. Proclamation of Henry Procter, September 13, 1813, in Cruikshank, *Niagara Frontier*, 7: 124.

138. Andrew Bulger to Robert McDouall, December 30, 1814, in Thwaites, "The Bulger Papers," 25–34.

139. Bulger to McDouall, January 15, 1815, ibid., 54–60. Quotation from p. 55.

140. Proclamation of Andrew Bulger, December 31, 1814, ibid., 38.

141. Bulger to McDouall, January 15, 1815, ibid., 56.

142. Inhabitants of Prairie du Chien to Bulger, January 15, 1815, ibid., 52–53.

143. Isaac Brock to CG, July 28, 1812, in *Collections of the Michigan Pioneer and Historical Society* 15 (1890), 122; William M. Weekes, "The War of 1812: Civil Authority and Martial Law in Upper Canada," *Ontario History* (Autumn 1956), 147–54.

144. Proclamation of Francis de Rottenburg, November 22, 1813, in Cruikshank, *Niagara Frontier*, 8: 226.

145. [William D. Powell] to Francis Gore, [late 1813/early 1814], ibid., 8: 227–28.

146. Proclamation of Gordon Drummond, January 25, 1814, and Drummond to SSWC, April 5, 1814, ibid., 8: 226, and 9: 279.

147. Resolution of House of Assembly of Upper Canada, February 19, 1814, ibid., 8: 226–27.

148. Proclamation of Gordon Drummond, April 12, 1814, ibid., 9: 292–93.

149. Drummond to SSWC, April 5, 1814, ibid., 9: 279; Weekes, "Civil Authority and Martial Law," 158–61; Sheppard, *Plunder, Profits, and Paroles*, 160–61.

150. Although there is no comprehensive study of this problem, for a good introduction, see Weekes, "Civil Authority and Martial Law," 147–61, and Donald E. Graves, "'The best means of Suppressing the growing Evil': British Military Commanders and the Use of Martial Law in Upper Canada, 1812–1814," unpublished paper.

## Chapter 6: The End of the War

1. Duncan McArthur to SW, November 18, 1814, in Cruikshank, *Niagara Frontier,* 1: 311.

2. Drummond to CG, August 21, 1814, ibid., 1: 185.

3. Drummond to James Yeo, November 13, 1814, in Dudley and Crawford, *Naval War of 1812,* 3: 659.

4. Drummond to Yeo, November 13, 1814, and Yeo to Drummond, November 14, 1814, in *Collections of the Michigan Pioneer and Historical Society* 15 (1890), 668–59, 675. Quotation from p. 668.

5. Duncan McArthur to SW, November 18, 1814, in Cruikshank, *Niagara Frontier,* 1: 308–12; Stuart A. Rammage, *The Militia Stood Alone: Malcolm's Mills, 6 November 1814* (Summerland, BC, 2000); [Robert B. McAfee], *History of the Late War in the Western Country* (Lexington, KY, 1816), 482–89.

6. The best account of this campaign is Reilly, *British at the Gates.*

7. Article 1, Treaty of Ghent, December 24, 1814, in Heidler and Heidler, *Encyclopedia of the War of 1812,* 583.

8. Poindexter to Natchez *Mississippi Republican,* January 20, 1815, reprinted in Washington *National Intelligencer,* February 13, 1815.

9. Letter from New Orleans, reprinted from Fredericktown *Gazette* in *Niles' Register* 8 (Supplement), 190.

10. Latour, *Historical Memoir,* 168.

11. John Reid and John Henry Eaton, *The Life of Andrew Jackson* (Philadelphia, 1817), 352; John Henry Eaton, *The Life of Andrew Jackson,* [rev. ed] (Philadelphia, 1824), 380–81.

12. Sir John Fortescue, *A History of the British Army,* 13 vols. (London, 1910–30), 10: 151, 155.

13. Declaration of John Lambert, John Kean, William Thornton, Edward Blakeney, and Alexander Dickson, [August 1833], in *Niles' Register* 45 (October 19, 1833), 121.

14. John K. Mahon, "British Command Decisions Relative to the Battle of New Orleans," *Louisiana History* 6 (Winter 1965), 53, 56, 62, 75; and Frank L. Owsley, Jr., "The Role of the South in the British Grand Strategy in the War of 1812," *Tennessee Historical Quarterly,* 31 (Spring 1972), 25, 28.

15. Bathurst to Pakenham, October 24 and 26, 1814, in War Office, 6/2, Public Record Office, London (transcripts provided by John R. Grodzinski). Quotation from October 24 letter.

16. I am indebted to Donald E. Graves for this astute observation about the culture of the British officer corps.

17. Reilly, *British at the Gates,* 314–16; Mahon, "British Command Decisions," 64–66.

18. Latour, *Historical Memoir,* 24.

19. The best analysis of the British offer is in William C. Davis, *The Pirates Laffite: The Treacherous World of the Corsairs of the Gulf* (New York, 2005), 165–72 and 553n66. See also John Sugden, "Jean Laffite and the British Offer of 1814," *Louisiana History,* 20 (Spring 1979), 159–67.

20. Laffite was pardoned after the battle but never regained most of his property.

21. Proclamation of Andrew Jackson, September 21, 1814, in Jackson Papers, Library of Congress, Washington, DC, microfilm edition, reel 62.

22. Robert C. Vogel, "Jean Laffite, the Baratarians, and the Battle of New Orleans: A Reappraisal," *Louisiana History,* 41 (Summer 2000), 271–72.

23. Davis, *Pirates Laffite,* 568n14 and 569n38.

24. General Orders of Andrew Jackson, January 21, 1815, in Latour, *Historical Memoir,* 339.

25. *The Journal of Jean Laffite: The Privateer-Patriot's Own Story* (New York, 1958) has been re-translated and repackaged as *The Memoirs of Jean Laffite: From Le Journal de Jean Laffite,* trans. Gene Marshall (Philadelphia, 1999). For a discussion of its provenance, see Robert L. Schaadt, "The Journal of Jean Laffite: Its History and Controversy," ibid., 11–35.

26. Most notably, Jane Lucas de Grummond in her widely cited book, *The Baratarians and the Battle of New Orleans* (Baton Rouge, LA, 1961).

27. The best assessment of Laffite and the Baratarians is in Vogel, "Jean Laffite, the Baratarians, and the Battle of New Orleans," 261–76, and in Davis, *Pirates Laffite.* Davis's work is a first-class study that supersedes all previous biographies.

28. See Reilly, *British at the Gates,* 296n; and Owsley, *Struggle for the Gulf Borderlands,* 148.

29. James Greathouse, "The Debate over the British Campaign against New Orleans,"

*Journal of the War of 1812* 7 (Summer 2002), 9–10; Reilly, *British at the Gates,* 329; Owsley, *Struggle for the Gulf Borderlands,* 159–60, 163–64. For the artillery battery on the west bank, see John Lambert to SSWC, January 10, 1815, and Daniel T. Paterson to SN, January 13, 1815, in Latour, *Historical Memoir,* 245, 313. Graves presented his conclusions in a letter to the author, November 4, 2005.

30. Reilly, *British at the Gates,* 318n.

31. For an illuminating discussion of the problems that the British faced and an assessment of their chances, see Alexander Campbell Wylly (Pakenham's aide-de-camp) to Duke of Wellington, March 4, 1815, in [Thomas Pakenham], ed., *Pakenham Letters, 1800–1815* ([London], 1914), 253–61.

32. British commissioners to American commissioners, October 8, 1814, in *ASP: FR,* 3: 713, 718, 721. Quotation from p. 721.

33. Liverpool to George Canning, December 28, 1814, in Duke of Wellington, [son of Iron Duke], ed., *Supplementary Dispatches, Correspondence, and Memoranda of Field Marshall Arthur, Duke of Wellington, K.G.,* 15 vols. (London, 1858–72), 9: 513.

34. For a good discussion of British intentions, see James A. Carr, "The Battle of New Orleans and the Treaty of Ghent," *Diplomatic History* 3 (Summer 1979), 273–82.

35. Reilly, *British at the Gates,* 341–42; Owsley, *Struggle for the Gulf Borderlands,* 171–72.

36. Roosevelt, *Naval War of 1812,* 372–77; Tyrone G. Martin, *A Most Fortunate Ship: A Narrative History of Old Ironsides,* rev. ed. (Annapolis, MD, 1997), 195–200.

37. Rembert W. Patrick, *Florida Fiasco: Rampant Rebels on the Georgia-Florida Border, 1810–1815* (Athens, GA, 1954), 289–91. Cockburn to Cochrane, February 27, 1815, in Cockburn Papers, Library of Congress, Washington, DC, microfilm edition, reel 7.

38. Roosevelt, *Naval War of 1812,* 391–92.

39. Ibid., 381–86.

40. Michael D. Harris, "The Battle of the Sinkhole, May 24, 1815," *Journal of the War of 1812* 2 (Winter 1996/97), 8–12; Benjamin Drake, *The Life and Adventures of Black Hawk* (Cincinnati, 1849), 85–90.

41. Roosevelt, *Naval War of 1812,* 389–91; Charles Rathbone Low, *History of the Indian Navy* (1613–1863), 2 vols. (London, 1877), 1: 284–94; Frederick Drake, "Warrington, Lewis, 1752–1851: U.S. Naval Officer," in Heidler and Heidler, *Encyclopedia of the War of 1812,* 543–44.

42. Low, *History of the Indian Navy,* 1: 294. Although Low said that he heard about the pension from Boyce himself, maritime historian Christine F. Hughes could find no evidence of any such pension. Hughes to author, October 11, 2005. For details on the diplomatic fallout of the naval engagement, see Hughes, "Lewis Warrington and the USS *Peacock* in the Sunda Strait, June 1815," in William S. Dudley and Michael J. Crawford, eds., *The Early Republic and the Sea: Essays on the Naval and Maritime History of the Early United States* (Washington, DC, 2001), 115–36.

43. See Charles J. Kappler, ed., *Indian Affairs: Laws and Treaties,* 5 vols. (Washington, DC, 1904–41), 2: 139–40.

44. For a fine assessment of the Congress of Vienna, see Paul W. Schroeder, *The Transformation of European Politics, 1763–1848* (Oxford, UK, 1994), ch. 12.

45. The standard works on the peace negotiations are Frank A. Updyke, *The Diplomacy of the War of 1812* (Baltimore, 1915); Fred L. Engelman, *The Peace of Christmas Eve* (New York, 1962); Bradford Perkins, *Castlereagh and Adams*; and Patrick C.T. White, *A Nation on Trial: America and the War of 1812* (New York, 1965).

46. Clay to SS, August 18, 1814, in Monroe Papers, Library of Congress, Washington, DC, microfilm edition, reel 5; Clay to William H. Crawford, August 22, 1814, in James F. Hopkins and Mary W.M. Hargreaves, eds., *The Papers of Henry Clay,* 11 vols. (Lexington, KY, 1959–92), 1: 972.

47. See SSWC to British commissioners, October 17, 18, and 20, in Henry Goulburn Papers, University of Michigan, Ann Arbor, MI, microfilm edition, reel 1.

48. Wellington to Liverpool, November 9, 1814, in Wellington, *Supplementary Dispatches and Memoranda,* 9: 425–26.

49. Liverpool to Canning, December 28, 1814, in Charles D. Yonge, *The Life and Administration of the Robert Banks, Second Earl of Liverpool,* 3 vols. (London, 1868), 2:76.

50. Castlereagh to Liverpool, January 2, 1815, in Wellington, *Supplementary Dispatches and Memoranda*, 9: 523.

51. For a clear statement of this principle, see Arnold Toynbee, "Anarchy by Treaty, 1648–1967: A Commentary on the Documentary Record," in Fred Israel, ed., *Major Peace Treaties of Modern History, 1648–1967*, 4 vols. (New York, 1967), 1: xxviii.

52. This practice peaked with the Anglo-French-Spanish treaty of 1763, which "renewed and confirmed" 17 treaties dating back to the Treaty of Westphalia in 1648, and the Anglo-French and Anglo-Spanish treaties of 1783, which between them "renewed and confirmed" 16 treaties dating back to Westphalia. The practice was discontinued with the treaties ending the French Revolutionary and Napoleonic Wars because widespread disruption and upheaval had rendered the old treaties irrelevant. See Article 2, Peace of Paris, February 10, 1763, in Israel, *Major Peace Treaties*, 1: 307–08; Article 2, Treaty of Versailles, September 3, 1783, in *The Definitive Treaty of Peace and Friendship, between His Britannick Majesty, and the Most Christian King, Signed at Versailles, the 3d of September, 1783* (London, 1783), 7; and Article 2, Treaty of Versailles, September 3, 1783, in *The Definitive Treaty of Peace and Friendship, between His Britannick Majesty, and the King of Spain, Signed at Versailles, the 3d of September, 1783* (London, 1783), 8.

53. Perkins, *Castlereagh and Adams*, 67–68; Protocol of Conference, August 8, 1814, in *ASP: FR*, 3: 708.

54. American commissioners to SS, December 25, 1814, in *ASP: FR*, 3: 732.

55. See Perkins, *Castlereagh and Adams*, 126.

56. See Updyke, *Diplomacy of the War of 1812*, 469–78; and Charles Everett Cayley, "The North Atlantic Fisheries in United States-Canadian Relations: A History of the Fisheries Problems, Their Settlements and Attempted Settlements, with Special Emphasis on the Period since the Establishment of the Dominion of Canada," Ph.D. dissertation (University of Chicago, 1931), esp. chs. 10–11.

57. Washington *National Intelligencer*, November 5, 1814; SS to American commissioners, June 25, 1814, in U.S. Department of State,

*Diplomatic Instructions of the Department of State*, microfilm series M77, National Archives, Washington, DC, reel 2.

58. James F. Zimmerman, *Impressment of American Seamen* (New York, 1925), ch. 9.

59. For the Indian population in this territory, see Carl Benn, *The Iroquois in the War of 1812* (Toronto, 1998), 175.

60. British commissioners to American commissioners, August 19, 1814, in U.S. Department of State, *Records of Negotiations Connected with the Treaty of Ghent, 1813–1815*, microfilm series M36, National Archives, Washington, DC, reel 1.

61. See Hickey, *War of 1812*, 289–90.

62. Article 1, Treaty of Ghent, December 24, 1814, in Heidler and Heidler, *Encyclopedia of the War of 1812*, 583.

63. Article 11 provided that the treaty would "be binding on both parties" when ratifications were exchanged. Ibid., 586.

64. London *Times*, December 28, 1814; London *Morning Chronicle*, December 28, 1814.

65. Jonathan Goodhue to Benjamin Russell, February 11, 1815, in Boston *Columbian Centinel*, February 15, 1815; Washington *National Intelligencer*, February 14 and 15, 1815; U.S. Congress, *Journal of the Senate of the United States of America* (Washington, DC, 1921), 13–3, 618–20.

66. Washington *National Intelligencer*, February 18, 1814; T.C. Hansard, ed., *The Parliamentary Debates from the Year 1803 to the Present Time*, [1st series], 41 vols. (London, 1803–20), 30: 218.

67. Article 2, Treaty of Ghent, December 24, 1814, in Heidler and Heidler, *Encyclopedia of the War of 1812*, 584.

68. Figures are drawn from Robert B. Atkinson to John B. Floyd, February 22, 1858, in B. Franklin Cooling, ed., *The New American State Papers: Military Affairs*, 19 vols. (Wilmington, DE, 1979), 5: 339; U.S Congress, *Report of the Third Auditor Relative to the Officers, Non-Commissioned Officers, and Solders of the Militia, Volunteers, and Rangers of the Late War* [U.S. Serial Set, #302] (Washington, DC, 1836), 78–79.

69. J.C.A. Stagg, "Enlisted Men in the United States Army, 1812–1815: A Preliminary Survey," *William and Mary Quarterly*, 3rd series,

43 (October 1986), 619–23, has shown that the army record keepers did not stay on top of recruitment figures. Hence, the undercount. The militia figures might also be inaccurate, although the states, which picked up the tab for most of the militia serving in the last year of the war, had an interest in establishing a reliable paper trail to secure federal reimbursement.

70. U.S. Department of Defense, *Selected Manpower Statistics* ([Washington, DC], 1974), 19.

71. Maclay, *American Privateers*, 506. Although some privateers never sailed, a larger number probably undertook several voyages with different crews. I am assuming an average crew of 75.

72. U.S. Department of Defense, *Selected Manpower Statistics*, 63.

73. Stagg, "Enlisted Men in the United States Army," 624.

74. This is 5,000 fewer than I estimated in my earlier work. That estimate was based on the flawed assumption that militia in service died at the same rate from disease or accident as regulars. See Hickey, *War of 1812*, 303.

75. Donald E. Graves, "The Redcoats are Coming! British Troop Movements to North America in 1814," *Journal of the War of 1812* 6 (Summer 2001), 17.

76. Hitsman, *Incredible War* (updated ed.), 351n29.

77. For Creek casualties, see Hickey, *War of 1812*, 148–49.

78. This estimate was provided by Carl Benn in a letter to the author, November 25, 2002.

79. Following the lead of Carl Benn and Donald E. Graves, I have estimated that one-fourth of the natives in any tribe were warriors. There were about 15,000 warriors hostile to the U.S. in the North and another 4,000 in the South. The U.S., for its part, could count on 1,800 allied warriors in the North (before the Battle of the Thames brought in more) and 2,000 in the South. Based on a warrior/non-warrior ratio of 1:3, the U.S. had to contend with 45,000 hostile Indians in the North and 16,000 in the South but could count on 7,200 allies in the North and 8,000 in the South. Thus the total number of Indians (warriors

and non-warriors alike) on both sides of the war was around 76,000. Graves's and Benn's figures were supplied in letters to the author dated (respectively) November 25, 2002, and January 17, 2005.

80. Henry Adams, *History of the United States of America [during the Administrations of Jefferson and Madison]*, 9 vols. (New York, 1889–91), 9: 55, 58–59; Wesley B. Turner, *The War of 1812: The War that Both Sides Won* (Toronto, 1990), 13, 129–30. Turner also said that Indians living south and west of Lake Erie lost the war. Ibid.

81. Samuel Perkins, *A History of the Political and Military Events of the Late War between the United States and Great Britain* (New Haven, 1825), 510–12; George Coggeshall, *History of the American Privateers, and Letters-of-Marque, during Our War with England in the Years, 1812, '13 and '14* (New York, 1856), 398; Irving Brant, *James Madison*, 6 vols. (Indianapolis and New York, 1941–61), 6: 371; Marshall Smelser, *The Democratic Republic, 1801–1815* (New York, 1968), 311, 323–24; Owsley, *Struggle for the Gulf Borderlands*, 192–95. See also Reginald Horsman, *The War of 1812* (New York, 1969), 266, which characterizes the war as "a near success" for the United States.

82. James, *Naval Occurrences*, 393–94; H.C. Allen, *Great Britain and the United States: A History of Anglo-American Relations (1783–1952)* (New York, 1955), 336, 345, 347; Hitsman, *Incredible War* (updated ed.), 274; Reilly, *British at the Gates*, 336; Stanley, *War of 1812*, 407.

83. Burt, *United States, Great Britain, and British North America*, 371; Francis F. Beirne, *The War of 1812* (New York, 1949), 391; Glenn Tucker, *Poltroons and Patriots: A Popular Account of the War of 1812*, 2 vols. (Indianapolis, 1954), 2: 670; Harry L. Coles, *The War of 1812* (Chicago, 1965), 255.

84. John R. Elting, *Amateurs to Arms! A Military History of the War of 1812* (Chapel Hill, 1991), 327.

85. The latest contribution to this debate suggests that where you lived determined how you viewed the outcome of the war. See Donald E. Graves, "The Many Wars of 1812," *Journal of the War of 1812* 8 (Spring/Summer 2004), 1–4.

86. Donald E. Graves, "Introduction: 'Mac' Hitsman, Sir George Prevost and the Incredible War of 1812," in Hitsman, *Incredible War* (updated ed.), xxi.
87. See Perkins, *Castlereagh and Adams*, 161–62.
88. See J.C.A. Stagg, *Mr. Madison's War: Politics, Diplomacy, and Warfare in the Early American Republic, 1783–1830* (Princeton, 1983), 510–11; Perkins, *Castlereagh and Adams*, 156–347; Allen, *Great Britain and the United States*, 348–517; and C.P. Stacey, *The Undefended Border: The Myth and the Reality* (Ottawa, 1953).
89. See Ernest R. May, *The World War and American Isolation, 1914–1917* (Cambridge, MA, 1959), chs. 3, 14, and 15. Ch. 3 is entitled "The Shadow of 1812."
90. Madison to Congress, June 1, 1812, in *AC*, 12–1, 628.
91. Article 9, Treaty of Ghent, December 24, 1814, in Heidler and Heidler, *Encyclopedia of the War of 1812*, 586.
92. Quoted in entries of December 11 and 14, 1814, in Charles Francis Adams, ed., *Memoirs of John Quincy Adams*, 12 vols. (Philadelphia, 1874–77), 3: 104, 118.
93. For a lucid analysis of the British capture of Quebec, see C.P. Stacey, *Quebec, 1759: The Siege and the Battle* (1959; updated by Donald E. Graves, Toronto, 2002).
94. See C.P. Stacey, "Brock, Sir Isaac," in *DCB*, 5: 111.
95. CG to Liverpool, May 18, 1812, in Hitsman, *Incredible War* (updated ed.), 286.
96. Ibid., 287–88.

**Epilogue: The Legacy of the War**

1. See James Tertius de Kay, *Chronicles of the Frigate "Macedonian," 1809–1922* (New York, 1995).
2. See Anne McIlroy, "Confederation Wins the Vote for the Greatest Event in Our History," Toronto *Globe and Mail*, September 18, 2000.
3. Gerald M. Craig, *Upper Canada: The Formative Years, 1784–1841* (Toronto, 1963), ch. 7.
4. George Sheppard, *Plunder, Profits, and Paroles: A Social History of the War of 1812 in Upper Canada* (Montreal, 1994), chs. 5, 7–8.
5. See James Eayrs, *In Defence of Canada*, 4 vols. (Toronto, 1972–80), 1: 70–78, and 2: 176.

In 1933 every Canadian military district was ordered to burn all "chapters, instructions, amendments, appendices, etc., in connection with Defence Scheme No. 1." Ibid., 1: 77.
6. For the birth of the Confederation—a story every bit as remarkable as the union of the United States under the Constitution—see W.L. Morton, *The Critical Years: The Union of British North America, 1857–1873* (Toronto, 1964); Ged Martin, *Britain and the Origins of Confederation, 1837–1867* (Vancouver, BC, 1995); and especially P.B. Waite, *The Life and Times of Confederation, 1864–1867: Politics, Newspapers, and the Union of British North America*, 3rd ed. (Toronto, 2001).
7. The most serviceable study of this important treaty, though limited in scope and now dated, is Goldwin Smith, *The Treaty of Washington, 1871: A Study in Imperial History* (Ithaca, NY, 1941).
8. The figures on British deployments were supplied by Donald E. Graves in a letter to the author, August 26, 2000. The pertinent volume in the new *Oxford History of the British Empire* has only a few scattered references to the War of 1812 in 595 pages of text. See P.J. Marshall, ed., *The Eighteenth Century*, vol. 2 of Alaine Low, ed., *The Oxford History of the British Empire* (Oxford, UK, 1998), 195, 369, 382–83, 387–88, 579–80.
9. Brian Jenkins, *Henry Goulburn, 1784–1856: A Political Biography* (Montreal, 1996), 89.
10. Roosevelt, "War with the United States," 7.
11. Eric Jarvis, "Military Land Granting in Upper Canada following the War of 1812," *Ontario History* 67 (September 1975), 121–30.
12. See George F.G. Stanley, *Canada's Soldiers, 1604–1954: The Military History of an Unmilitary People*, 3rd ed. (Toronto, 1974), ch. 11.
13. For more on these important canals, see Gerald M. Craig, *Upper Canada: The Formative Years, 1784–1841* (Toronto, 1963), 149–58; Robert Legget, *Rideau Waterway*, 2nd ed. (Toronto, 1986) and *Ottawa River Canals and the Defence of British North America* (Toronto, 1988); Normand Lafrenière, *The Ottawa River Canal System*, trans. Department of the Secretary of State (Ottawa, 1984); Hugh G.J. Aiken, *The Welland Canal Company: A Study in Canadian Enterprise* (Cambridge,

MA, 1954); and Roberta McAfee Styran, *The "Great Swivel Link": Canada's Welland Canals* (Toronto, 2001).

14. For the development of Penetanguishene, see Barry Gough, *Fighting Sail on Lake Huron and Georgian Bay: The War of 1812 and Its Aftermath* (Annapolis, MD, 2002), ch. 8.

15. For the problem of defending Canada, see J. Mackay Hitsman, *Safeguarding Canada, 1763–1871* (Toronto, 1968), chs. 6–11.

16. See Jackson, "Impressment and Anglo-American Discord," 371–77.

17. For a good discussion of the antagonistic literature, see Perkins, *Castlereagh and Adams*, ch. 10.

18. Hitsman, *Safeguarding Canada*, 231–32.

19. See Smith, *Treaty of Washington*.

20. Bradford Perkins, *The Great Rapprochement: England and the United States, 1895–1914* (New York, 1968).

21. For America's evolving relationship with Great Britain and Canada after the War of 1812, see H.C. Allen, *Great Britain and the United States: A History of Anglo-American Relations (1783–1955)* (New York, 1955); John Bartlet Brebner, *North Atlantic Triangle: The Interplay of Canada, the United States, and Great Britain* (New Haven, 1945); and James Morton Callahan, *American Foreign Policy in Canadian Relations* (New York, 1937).

22. Colin G. Calloway, "The End of an Era: British-Indian Relations in the Great Lakes Region after the War of 1812," *Michigan Historical Review* 12 (Fall 1986), 1.

23. For the fate of the Iroquois, see Carl Benn, *The Iroquois in the War of 1812* (Toronto, 1998), ch. 8.

24. For an analysis of the postwar fate of Canadian Indians, see Robert S. Allen, *His Majesty's Indian Allies: British Indian Policy in the Defence of Canada, 1774–1815* (Toronto, 1992), ch. 8.

25. These treaties can be found in Charles J. Kappler, ed., *Indian Affairs: Laws and Treaties*, 5 vols. (Washington, DC, 1904–41), 2: 105–40.

Chronology

1. The National Park Service compilation appeared under the title of "Revolutionary War and War of 1812 Historic Preservation Study." It went through several drafts. I used the one

that was released in January 2001. The Eshelman-George work, which was completed in December 2000, carries the title "Maryland War of 1812 Battlefields, Selected Skirmishes, Encampments, Earthworks and Riot Sites."

2. Wood, *Select British Documents*; Cruikshank, *Niagara Frontier* and *Surrender of Detroit*; and Dudley and Crawford, *Naval War of 1812*.

### Appendix A: "The Hunters of Kentucky"

1. Nelson F. Adkins, "Woodworth, Samuel," in *DAB*, 19: 512–13; Kendall B. Taft, "Samuel Woodworth," Ph.D. dissertation (University of Chicago, 1936), esp. 93–95, 110, 129–33, 135–36.

2. John William Ward, *Andrew Jackson: Symbol for an Age* (New York, 1955), ch. 2.

3. *Davy Crockett's Almanack, of Wild Sports in the West* 1 (1837), in Franklin J. Meine, ed., *The Crockett Alamanacks: Nashville Series, 1835–1838* (Chicago, 1955), 79.

4. Meine, *Crockett Alamanacks*, xvii.

5. See Donald E. Graves, *Guns across the River: The Battle of the Windmill, 1838*, corrected ed. (Prescott, ON, 2002), esp. Appendix F.

6. This broadside has been reproduced in *Journal of the War of 1812* 2 (Summer 1997), inside back cover.

### Appendix B: "The Bold Canadian"

1. Janet Carnochan, *Sir Isaac Brock [and] The Count de Puisaye* (Niagara, ON, 1907), 16; William Gray, *Soldiers of the King: The Upper Canadian Militia, 1812–1815* (Erin, ON, 1995), 130.

2. Carnochan, *Sir Isaac Brock*, 15–16.

3. James H. Coyne, ed., "The Bold Canadian: A Ballad of the War of 1812," *Papers and Records of the Ontario Historical Society* 23 (1926), 237–42; Morris Zaslow, ed., *The Defended Border: Upper Canada and the War of 1812* (Toronto, 1964), 305.

4. Edith Fowke and Alan Mills, *Canada's Story in Song*, rev. ed. (Toronto, 1965), 64–65. This work was first published in 1960. The revised edition includes the music for guitar accompaniment.

5. Coyne, "The Bold Canadian," 240–42. I have done some light editing of this version.

6. Brock actually departed from York, which was the provincial capital of Upper Canada.
7. By this time, there were very few firelocks in use. Most people had flintlocks.

**Appendix C: Shipwrecks and Rebuilt Ships**

1. Anthony C. Carone, "Preserving the U.S. Brig *Niagara*, 1913–1988," *Journal of Erie Studies* 17 (Fall 1988), 103–05; Charles Alan Watkins and Mark Matusiak, "Is This the Real *Niagara?*" *Naval History* 15 (February 2001), 37–40; Walter Rybka to Kevin Crisman, September 6, 2001 (copy in possession of the author). Rybka's analysis is supported by the ship measurements presented in Robert Malcomson, *Warships of the Great Lakes, 1754–1834* (Annapolis, MD, 2001), 58, 89, 93.
2. James F. Cooper, ed., *Ned Myers; or, A Life before the Mast* (Annapolis, MD, 1989), 56.
3. Daniel A. Nelson, "*Hamilton* and *Scourge*: Ghost Ships of the War of 1812," *National Geographic* 163 (March 1983), 289–313; Kenneth A. Cassavoy, "The *Hamilton* and the *Scourge*: A First Look," in Susan B.M. Langley and Richard W. Unger, eds., *Nautical Archaeology: Progress and Public Responsibility* (Oxford, UK, 1984), 176–98; Emily Cain, *Ghost Ships: "Hamilton" and "Scourge," Historical Treasures from the War of 1812* (New York, 1983).
4. For an overview of this subject, see Kenneth A. Cassavoy and Kevin J. Crisman, "The War of 1812: Battle for the Great Lakes," in George F. Bass, ed., *Ships and Shipwrecks of the Americas: A History Based on Underwater Archaeology* (London, 1988), 169–88; and Art Cohn and Kevin Crisman, "The Archaeological Legacy of the War of 1812," in Norman Ansley, *Vergennes, Vermont and the War of 1812* (Severna Park, MD, 1999), 216–19. See also Christine F. Hughes, "Joshua Barney: Citizen-Sailor," in Charles E. Brodine, Jr., *et al., Against All Odds: U.S. Sailors in the War of 1812* (Washington, DC, 2004), 50–51.
5. Quoted in Tyrone G. Martin, *A Most Fortunate Ship: A Narrative History of Old Ironsides,* rev. ed. (Annapolis, MD, 1997), x.
6. Martin, *Most Fortunate Ship.*
7. Carone, "Preserving the U.S. Brig *Niagara,*" 103–12; Chris J. Magoc, *Erie Maritime Museum and U.S. Brig "Niagara"* (Mechanicsburg, PA, 2001), 25–33; Robert Malcomson,

"*Niagara* Sails Again," *Naval History* 5 (Summer 1991), 37–43.
8. For information on this ship, go to <http://www.michiganmaritimemuseum.org>.
9. Ernest F. Imhoff, "History Resurfaces in Barney's Barges Flotilla," *Baltimore Sun,* September 4, 1996.
10. Greg Pease, Thomas C. Gillmer, and Barbara Bozzuto, *Sailing with Pride* (Baltimore, 1990); and <www.intandem.com/NewPrideSite/Navigate/SiteMap.html>.
11. For more information, go to: <http://www.schoonerfame.com>.
12. See Gilbert Collins, *Guidebook to the Historic Sites of the War of 1812* (Toronto, 1998), 236–37; and <http://www.discoveryharbour.on.ca/>.
13. See Shirley E. Whittington, "British Naval History in Full Sail at Penetanguishene (H.M.S. *Bee* [1817–1831], Her History and Rebirth)," *Fresh Water* 1 (Autumn 1986), 17–20; Steve Killing, "The Designing of H.M.S. *Bee,*" ibid., 21–24; and <http://www.discoveryharbour.on.ca/>.
14. See Robert Malcomson and Thomas Malcomson, *HMS "Detroit": The Battle for Lake Erie* (Annapolis, MD, 1990); Windsor *Star,* February 4, 2006; and <http://www.hmsdetroit.org/>.
15. For details, see A.P. McGowan, *H.M.S "Victory": Her Construction, Career, and Restoration* (London, 1999); and <http://www.hms-victory/com/>.
16. For details, see Andrew Lambert, "*Trincomalee": The Last of Nelson's Frigates* (London, 2002); and <http://www.trincomalee.co.uk/>.

**Appendix D: The Name of the War**

1. Some contemporaries referred to the Civil War as the "War of 1861" and World War I as the "War of 1914," and some scholars still refer to the Spanish-American War as the "War of 1898." But these wars all have more common names. For the "War of 1861," see the document labeled "Widow's Claim for Army Pension," in Kathryn W. Lerch, "The 8th New York Heavy Artillery in Baltimore, 1862–1864," *Maryland Historical Magazine* 92 (Spring 1997), 100. For the other wars, see Desmond Fitzgerald, *The War of 1914: From*

an *American Point of View* (Cambridge, MA, 1914); and Louis A. Perez, *The War of 1898: The United States and Cuba in History and Historiography* (Chapel Hill, NC, 1998).

2. Ralph R. Shaw and Richard H. Shoemaker, comp., *American Bibliography: A Preliminary Checklist [for 1801–19]*, 19 vols. (New York, 1958–63); Richard H. Shoemaker, *et al.*, comp., *A Checklist of American Imprints [for 1820—]*, 27 vols. to date (New York, 1964–97).

3. John C. Fredriksen, *Free Trade and Sailors' Rights: A Bibliography of the War of 1812* (Westport, CT, 1985); Dwight L. Smith, *The War of 1812: An Annotated Bibliography* (New York, 1985).

4. For typical examples, see Elijah Parish, *A Protest against the War: A Discourse Delivered at Byfield, Fast Day, July 23, 1812* (Newburyport, MA, 1812); Alexander McLeod, *A Scriptural View of the Character, Causes, and Ends of the Present War* (New York, 1815); and Timothy Merritt, *A Discourse on the War with England: Delivered in Hallowell, on Public Fast, April 7, 1814* (Hallowell, ME, 1814).

5. [John Lowell, Jr.], *Mr. Madison's War* (Boston, 1812). For similar usage, see the 20-page pamphlet, [De Witt Clinton], *Jefferson against Madison's War* ([Boston?, 1812]).

6. Some modern writers have adopted this label. See Noel B. Gerson, *Mr. Madison's War, 1812: The Second War for Independence* (New York, 1966); and J.C.A. Stagg, *Mr. Madison's War: Politics, Diplomacy, and Warfare in the Early American Republic, 1783–1830* (Princeton, 1983).

7. See, for example, [Robert B. McAfee], *History of the Late War in the Western Country* (Lexington, KY, 1816); [John P. Boyd], *Documents and Facts, Relative to Military Events during the Late War* (Boston, 1816); [Henry M. Brackenridge], *History of the Late War, between the United States and Great-Britain* (Baltimore, 1816); John L. Thomson, *Historical Sketches of the Late War, between the United States and Great Britain* (Philadelphia, 1816); J.C. Gilleland, *History of the Late War between the United States and Great Britain* (Baltimore, 1817).

8. [Alexander J. Dallas], *An Exposition of the Causes and Character of the War* (Washington, DC, 1815).

9. See [Alexander J. Dallas], *An Exposition of the Causes and Character of the Late War* (Boston, 1815), and *An Exposition of the Causes and Character of the Late War with Great Britain* (Philadelphia, 1815).

10. [William McCarty], *History of the American War, of Eighteen Hundred and Twelve, from the Commencement until the Final Termination Thereof, on the Memorable Eighth of January 1815, at New Orleans* (Philadelphia, 1816).

11. [William McCarty], *History of the American War of 1812, from the Commencement, until the Final Termination Thereof, on the Memorable Eighth of January, 1815, at New Orleans*, 2nd ed. (Philadelphia, 1816).

12. [William McCarty], *Geschichte des Americanischen Kriegs, von 1812, vom Anfang bis zum Enlichen Schluss Desselben, an dem Glorreichen Achten Januar, 1815, vor Neu-Orleans* (Philadelphia, 1817).

13. [Richard Emmons], *The Fredoniad, or, Independence Preserved: An Epick Poem on The Late War of 1812*, 4 vols. (Boston, 1827).

14. Theodore Dwight, *History of the Hartford Convention: With a Review of the Policy of the United States Government Which led to the War of 1812* (New York and Boston, 1833).

15. John Armstrong, *Notices of the War of 1812*, 2 vols. (New York, 1836–40).

16. Solomon Van Rensselaer, *A Narrative of the Affair of Queenston: In the War of 1812* (New York and Boston, 1836).

17. Isaac Rand Jackson, *A Sketch of the Life and Public Services of William Henry Harrison, Commander in Chief of the Northwestern Army during the War of 1812* (New York, 1836).

18. Martin Van Buren, *Mr. Van Buren on the War of 1812, '15, and Other Important Subjects* (np, 1839).

19. See James Jarvis, *Reminiscences, 1846 February 22, of the War of the 1812 and the American Revolution* (np, 1846); Joseph. H. Ingraham, *Blanche Talbot; or, The Maiden's Hand: A Romance of the War of 1812* (New York, 1847); R. Thomas, *History of the American Wars: Comprising the War of the Revolution and the War of 1812* (Hartford, 1847); Charles J. Peterson, *The Military Heroes of the War of 1812,*

With a Narrative of the War (Philadelphia, 1848); Thomas Wyatt, *Memoirs of the Generals, Commodores, and Other Commanders Who Distinguished Themselves in the American Army and Navy during the Wars of the Revolution and 1812, and Who Were Presented with Medals by Congress, for Gallant Services* (Philadelphia, 1848); William Jay, *Table of the Killed and Wounded in the War of 1812* (New York, 1849).

20. See, for example, *Norvel Hastings, or The Frigate in the Offing: A Nautical Tale of the War of 1812* (Philadelphia, 1850); *Stories of the War of 1812, and the Mexican War* (Philadelphia, 1851); Nell C. Williams, *Services of Colored Americans, in the Wars of 1776 and 1812* (Boston, 1852); John S. Jenkins, *Jackson and the Generals of the War of 1812* (Philadelphia, 1854); Newton M. Curtis, *The Maid of the Saranac: A Tale of the War of 1812* (New York, 1854); *Narrative of the Life of General Leslie Combs, Embracing Incidents in the History of the War of 1812* ([New York], 1854).

21. See Soldiers of the War of 1812, *Proceedings of the Convention of the Soldiers of the War of 1812, Held at Corinthian Hall, Syracuse, June 20th and 21st, 1843* (Syracuse, NY, 1854); Soldiers of the War of 1812, *Proceedings of the Convention of the Soldiers of the War of 1812, in the State of New York at Schuylerville, Saratoga Co., Oct. 17, 1856* (Schuylerville, NY, 1857); Soldiers of the War of 1812, *Proceedings of the National Convention of the Soldiers of the War of 1812, Held at the Hall of Independence, in the City of Philadelphia, on the Ninth of January, 1854* (Philadelphia, 1854); Soldiers of the War of 1812, *Proceedings of the National Convention of the Soldiers of the War of 1812: Held at the Four-and-a-Half Street Presbyterian Church, in the City of Washington, on the 8th day of January, 1855* (Washington, DC, 1855).

22. New England Association of Soldiers of the War of 1812, *Constitution and By-Laws of the New England Association of Soldiers of the War of 1812* (Boston, 1860); Pennsylvania Association of the Defenders of the Country in the War of 1812, *Constitution of the Pennsylvania Association of the Defenders of the Country, in the War of 1812* (Philadelphia, 1862).

23. Lossing, *Pictorial Field-Book of the War of 1812*, and *The American Revolution and the War of 1812, or, Illustrations, by Pen and Pencil, of the History, Biography, Scenery, Relics, and Traditions of our Wars with Great Britain* (New York, 1874).

24. This organization is still active and is open to descendants of 1812 veterans. For details, go to: <http://www.societyofthewarof1812.org>.

25. Society of the War of 1812, *The Charter, Constitution and Rules of the General Society of the War of 1812* (Philadelphia, 1893); Society of the War of 1812, *The Constitution and Register of Membership of the General Society of the War of 1812, to October 1, 1899* (Philadelphia, 1899).

26. In 1892, a sister organization, the National Society United States Daughters of 1812, was established. This organization is still in existence and is open to females who can trace their lineage to someone who held military or civilian office between 1784 and 1815. For details, go to: <http://usdaughters1812.org>.

27. See Philip Patton, *The Observations of an Admiral on the State of the Navy, and More Particularly as It Is Connected with the American War* (Gosport, UK, 1813); Samuel Graves, *A Letter to the Right Hon. George Canning, M.P., on the Origin and Continuance of the War with America* (London, 1814).

28. See, for example, William Cobbett, *The Pride of Britannia Humbled: or, The Queen of the Ocean Unqueen'd, "by the American Cock Boats"* . . . *Illustrated and Demonstrated by Four Letters Addressed to Lord Liverpool, on the Late American War*, new ed. (Philadelphia and New York, 1815); James, *Naval Occurrences*; Robert Christie, *The Military and Naval Operations in the Canadas, during the Late War with the United States* (Quebec, 1818); David Thompson, *History of the Late War between Great Britain and the United States of America* (Niagara, ON, 1832); Shadrach Byfield, *A Narrative of a Light Company Soldier's Service in the 41st Regiment of Foot, during the Late American War* (Bradford, ON, 1840).

29. The British divided their army in Canada into three divisions: the Right Division in the West, the Center Division in the middle,

and the Left Division farther east. Richardson was attached to the Right Division. For the parameters of this confusing and ever-changing geographical command structure, see John R. Grodzinski, "Command Structure and Appointments in Upper Canada, 1812–1814," *Journal of the War of 1812* 9 (Spring 2005), 20–24.

30. John Richardson, *War of 1812: First Series, Containing a Full and Detailed Narrative of the Operations of the Right Division of the Canadian Army* ([Brockville, ON], 1842). The more common edition of this work is Alexander C. Casselman, ed., *Richardson's War of 1812* (Toronto, 1902).

31. E.A. Cruikshank, *Battlefields of the Niagara Peninsula during the War of 1812–15* (np, 1891); "The Employment of Indians in the War of 1812," *Annual Report of the American Historical Association for 1895* (Washington, DC, 1896), 319–35; *The Origin and Official History of the Thirteenth Battalion of Infantry, and a Description of the Work of the Early Militia of the Niagara Peninsula in the War of 1812 and the Rebellion of 1837* (Hamilton, ON, 1899).

32. See the usage in the essays written between 1908 and 1964 that are reprinted in Morris Zaslow, ed., *The Defended Border: Upper Canada and the War of 1812* (Toronto, 1964). See also James Hannay, *History of the War of 1812, between Great Britain and the United States of America* (St. John, NB, 1901); J. Mackay Hitsman, *The Incredible War of 1812: A Military History* (Toronto, 1965); and Stanley, *War of 1812*.

33. See, for example, Reilly, *British at the Gates;* Alan Lloyd, *The Scorching of Washington: The War of 1812* (Newton Abbott, UK, 1974); H.W. Wilson, "The War of 1812," in *The United States,* vol. 7 of *The Cambridge Modern History* (Cambridge, UK, 1903), 335, 336.

34. See Christopher Duffy, *Borodino and the War of 1812* (New York and London, 1972).

35. Roger Morriss uses three different phrases in his recent biography of George Cockburn. See *Cockburn and the British Navy in Transition: Admiral Sir George Cockburn, 1772–1853* (Columbia, SC, 1997), 2, 12, and title of ch. 3. The contributors to volume 9 of *The New Cambridge Modern History* use four different phrases. See C.W. Crawley, ed., *War and Peace in an Age of Upheaval, 1793–1830* (Cambridge, UK, 1965), 10, 89, 271, 611, 671. And the contribution to vol. 7 of *The Cambridge Modern History* is called "The War of 1812–1815" in the table of contents but "The War of 1812" in the text. See H.W. Wilson, "The War of 1812," in *The United States* (Cambridge, UK, 1903), 335. See also Charles Oman, *Studies in the Napoleonic Wars* (London, 1929), 207; K.S. Dent, "The British Navy in the Anglo-American War of 1812," Master's thesis (University of Leeds, 1949); Michael Lewis, *A Social History of the Navy, 1793–1815* (London, 1960), 128, 377; Philip R.N. Katcher, *The American War, 1812–1814* (Reading, UK, 1974); and Kate Caffrey, *The Twilight's Last Gleaming: Britain vs. America, 1812–1815* (New York, 1977), 11.

36. See Jenkins, *Henry Goulburn,* 111, 439; Bryan Perrett, *The Real Hornblower: The Life of Admiral of the Fleet Sir James Alexander Gordon, GCB* (Annapolis, MD, 1997), 10, 105; P.J. Marshall and Alaine Low, ed., *The Eighteenth Century,* vol. 2 of *The Oxford History of the British Empire* (New York, 1998), 369, 382, 388, 579, 580; and Robert Gardiner, ed., *The Naval War of 1812* (Annapolis, MD, 1999).

37. Carl Benn, *The War of 1812* (Oxford, UK, 2002).

# Index